Blackstone's Guide to the
ENVIRONMENT ACT 1995

Peter Lane,
MA, LLM, Solicitor, Parliamentary Agent

&

Monica Peto,
LLB, LLM, Solicitor, Parliamentary Agent

Partners, Rees & Freres

BLACKSTONE
PRESS LIMITED

First published in Great Britain 1995 by Blackstone Press Limited,
9-15 Aldine Street, London W12 8AW. Telephone 0181-740 1173

ISBN: 1 85431 491 2

Brtish Library Cataloguing in Publication Data
A CIP catalogue record for this book is available from the British Library

Typeset by Style Photosetting Ltd, Mayfield, East Sussex
Printed by Ashford Colour Press, Gosport, Hampshire

Blackstone's Guide to the

ENVIRONMENT ACT 1995

Contents

Abbreviations

APC	air pollution control
AWRA 1906	Alkali, etc., Works Regulation Act 1906
BATNEEC	best available techniques not entailing excessive cost
BPEO	best practicable environmental option
CPA 1974	Control of Pollution Act 1974
CP(A)A 1989	Control of Pollution (Amendment) Act 1989
DoE	Department of the Environment
DWI	Drinking Water Inspectorate
EA	Environment Agency
Edwards Report	*Fit for the Future: Report of the National Parks Review Panel* (CCP334) (Countryside Commission, 1991)
EEA	European Environment Agency
Environment Act	Environment Act 1995
EPA 1990	Environmental Protection Act 1990
HASAWA 1974	Health and Safety at Work etc. Act 1974
HMIP	Her Majesty's Inspectorate of Pollution
HMIPI	Her Majesty's Industrial Pollution Inspectorate
IDO	interim development order
IPC	integrated pollution control
LAAPC	local authority air pollution control
LAWDC	local authority waste disposal company
LDA 1991	Land Drainage Act 1991
LGA 1972	Local Government Act 1972
LG(S)A 1973	Local Government (Scotland) Act 1973
MAFF	Ministry of Agriculture, Fisheries and Food
NH(S)A 1991	National Heritage (Scotland) Act 1991
NPACA 1949	National Parks and Access to the Countryside Act 1949
NPSG	National Parks supplementary grant
NRA	National Rivers Authority
R(PP)(S)A 1951	Rivers (Prevention of Pollution) (Scotland) Act 1951
RSA 1993	Radioactive Substances Act 1993
SEPA	Scottish Environmental Protection Agency
SFC	sea fisheries committee
SFFA 1975	Salmon and Freshwater Fisheries Act 1975
SFRA 1966	Sea Fisheries Regulation Act 1966

SNH	Scottish National Heritage
WA 1989	Water Act 1989
WIA 1991	Water Industry Act 1991
WRA	waste regulation authority
WRA 1991	Water Resources Act 1991

Chapter 1
Introduction

The Environment Act 1995 is a landmark in the development of environmental law in the United Kingdom. The creation of powerful, wide-ranging new environmental agencies is a central feature of the new legislation and is covered in detail in this book. The Act also contains important new law on contaminated land, air quality and waste strategy. Planning law is directly affected by the Act, which provides for the review of mineral planning permissions and reforms the structure and powers of the bodies responsible for the National Parks of England and Wales.

1.1 THE ENVIRONMENT AGENCY
(chapters 2–11)

The Environment Agency (EA) came into being in July 1995, a little over four years after the Prime Minister unveiled the government's intention to create a body which would bring together the functions of Her Majesty's Inspectorate of Pollution (HMIP) and the National Rivers Authority (NRA). The EA will come fully into operation on 1 April 1996 when it will assume responsibility for HMIP's and the NRA's functions, together with the functions of waste regulation authorities and disposal authorities. This book aims to give the reader an overview of all these functions, some of which are themselves modified by the Environment Act. The transferred functions are dealt with under the following headings:

— water resources (chapter 3)
— water pollution control (chapter 4)
— flood defence and land drainage (chapter 5)
— fisheries (chapter 6)
— navigation, harbour and conservancy functions (chapter 7)
— waste regulation and disposal (chapter 8)
— integrated pollution control (chapter 9)
— radioactive substances (chapter 10).

The Environment Act also confers important functions on the EA in respect of contaminated land and abandoned mines (chapters 16, 17).

The structure of the EA (including its advisory committees) is dealt with in chapter 2, together with the background to its establishment, which is important in understanding the way in which the EA will be expected to operate. Besides transferring core functions to the EA, the Environment Act also sets out a specific principal aim and set of objectives for the Agency, which are rooted in the important concept of 'sustainable development'. This aim and objectives are analysed in chapter 11, together with the provisions in the Act which seek to govern the way in which the EA will carry out its duties. Of particular importance is s. 39 which imposes a general duty to have regard to costs and benefits when exercising powers.

1.2   THE SCOTTISH ENVIRONMENTAL PROTECTION AGENCY
(chapters 12 and 13)

The Environment Act establishes the Scottish Environmental Protection Agency (SEPA), which came into being in October 1995 and which, like the EA, will come fully into operation on 1 April 1996, when it assumes the functions of Her Majesty's Industrial Pollution Inspectorate, river purification authorities, waste regulation authorities and air pollution controls under the Environmental Protection Act 1990 (EPA 1990), hitherto the responsibility of local authorities.

Since the functions of river purification authorities are narrower than those of the NRA, SEPA will not have such wide-ranging duties over water pollution and water resources as its counterpart in England and Wales. Its functions, under pre-existing legislation, nevertheless cover the following areas, which are described in chapter 12:

— water resources
— water pollution
— flood warning
— waste regulation
— waste disposal
— integrated pollution control
— air pollution control
— radioactive substances.

As with the EA, the Environment Act also confers important functions on SEPA in respect of contaminated land and abandoned mines (chapters 16, 17).

Unlike the EA, SEPA is given no express statutory principal aim but it is nevertheless to be given guidance by the Secretary of State under s. 31, which must include guidance with respect to the contribution SEPA is expected to make towards advancing the objective of achieving sustainable development. This requirement, together with the other general powers, duties and functions of SEPA, are analysed in chapter 13.

1.3   COMMON FUNCTIONS, CHARGES AND FINANCES
(chapters 14 and 15)

Both the EA and SEPA are given certain common functions by the Environment Act. Of these, the most important is probably the duty in s. 39 to have regard to costs and benefits, described in chapter 11. The remaining common functions cover such matters as delegation, ministerial directions, information and powers of entry, and are described in chapter 14. The structures for charging for environmental licences are standardised in ss. 41 and 42, which enable the EA and SEPA to make charging schemes (see chapter 15).

1.4 CONTAMINATED LAND
(chapter 16)

The Environment Act imposes a new duty on every local authority to identify any contaminated land in its area. Contaminated land is defined in the Act by reference to 'significant harm' or the 'significant possibility' of such harm being caused to human health or property or the health of other living organisms or the pollution of controlled waters. Where the harm or pollution concerned is or is likely to be 'serious' the contaminated land is to be designated as a special site and comes under the jurisdiction of the EA or, in Scotland, SEPA instead of the jurisdiction of the local authority.

The enforcing authority (i.e., the EA or SEPA in the case of special sites or the local authority in the case of other contaminated land) must determine what remediation is to be undertaken in respect of the land and who is 'the appropriate person', i.e., the person who is to be responsible for that remediation.

The appropriate person is any person who caused or knowingly permitted the contaminants in question to be present on the land or, if no such person can be found, the owner or occupier of the land. The person who caused or knowingly permitted the presence of a contaminant on land is also liable for remediation in respect of any other land to which the contaminant escapes.

The enforcing authority must serve a remediation notice on each appropriate person requiring that person to undertake the remedial measures (or the appropriate proportion of the remedial measures) specified in the notice unless that would cause hardship. In default the enforcing authority may undertake the measures itself and has powers to recover its costs including the making of charging orders. In addition, the defaulter is criminally liable. The enforcing authority also has powers to undertake remedial measures itself in an emergency or if no appropriate person can be found who may be required to undertake them. Appeals lie against remediation notices and charging orders.

Each enforcing authority must keep a public register of the contaminated land which has been identified within its jurisdiction. The register must include not only the particulars of the land, its designation as a special site (if applicable) and any remediation notice served in respect of the land but also the remedial measures which have been taken in response to that notice.

Guidance is to be issued by the Secretary of State on how the statutory functions of enforcing authorities are to be exercised.

At the time of writing, the new provisions had not been brought into force except in so far as they confer power on the Secretary of State to make regulations or orders, give directions or issue guidance or make provision with respect to the exercise of any such power.

1.5   CONTAMINATION FROM MINES
(chapter 17)

The owner of an abandoned mine currently enjoys a specific exemption from the offences under s. 85 of the Water Resources Act 1991 which relate to the pollution of controlled waters. This exemption has become controversial as public concern has grown over problems of contamination caused by the leakage of mine water from abandoned mines when pumping stops.

The Environment Act removes the statutory exemption in the case of mines abandoned on or after 1 January 2000. The EA and SEPA will have the same powers in respect of pollution caused by water from mines abandoned after that date as for other discharges into controlled waters. In the meantime a duty is conferred on mine operators to give the EA and SEPA six months' notice of any proposed abandonment so as to provide the Agencies with the opportunity of ensuring that when mines are abandoned this is done in a responsible manner with full regard to the effects on the water environment.

At the time of writing the relevant provisions of the Environment Act had not been brought into force except in so far as they confer power on the Secretary of State to make supplementary provision, such as regulations, relating to them.

1.6   NATIONAL PARKS
(chapter 18)

Part III of the Environment Act concerns National Parks. The fundamental changes made to the system of care and control of the Parks stem from the recommendations of the National Parks Review Panel, chaired by Professor Ron Edwards. The purposes of National Parks which are set out in s. 5 of the National Parks and Access to the Countryside Act 1949 are reformulated by Environment Act, s. 61 in terms which are controversial, owing to their failure to acknowledge expressly the concept of 'quiet enjoyment' recommended by Edwards. Section 62, however, for the first time imposes on government and other public bodies a duty to have regard to the National Park purposes. One of Edwards's major recommendations was the establishment of new National Park authorities, freed from local authority control, and Environment Act s. 63 gives effect to this recommendation. Controversy, however, surrounded the government's late decision to reduce local authority representation in order to accommodate a class of member drawn from parish councils etc. but appointed by the Secretary of State. In certain circumstances, a new Park authority may become the sole planning authority and mineral planning authority for the area of the Park, to the exclusion of any other planning authority (s. 67). Chapter 18 describes these functions, and the other functions of the new authorities.

1.7   AIR QUALITY
(chapter 19)

Part IV of the Environment Act provides for action at both national and local level to improve and safeguard air quality. The Secretary of State is to publish a national strategy to include standards and targets for the main pollutants and a timetable for their achievement. Every local authority is placed under a duty to carry out regular assessments of air quality in its area, to create air quality management areas where levels do not meet targets and to direct action to those areas.

The Environment Act provides the statutory framework for the new system. It is intended that detailed local arrangements will be provided under regulations made by the Secretary of State and in accordance with guidance given by the Secretary of State.

The government has stated that it is establishing with the local authority associations a committee to review what powers may be needed and any resources implications.

1.8 WASTE STRATEGY AND PRODUCER RESPONSIBILITY
(chapter 20)

The EC 'Waste Framework Directive' (75/442/EEC, as amended by 91/156/EEC on waste and the Standardised Reporting Directive 91/692/EEC) requires the drawing up, as soon as possible, of one or more waste management plans to implement the objectives set out in the Directive. The element of the implementation of the Directive which has hitherto been dealt with by local waste management plans under EPA 1990, s. 50 is now to be replaced by national waste strategies to be drawn up for England and Wales by the Secretary of State and for Scotland by SEPA under EPA 1990 ss. 44A and 44B, inserted by Environment Act, s. 92. At the time of writing no order has been made bringing this provision into force.

Sections 93 to 95 of the Environment Act are enabling provisions relating to the new area of producer responsibility for waste. These provisions came into force on 21 September 1995. The Secretary of State is empowered to make regulations imposing producer responsibility obligations on persons to be specified in the regulations in respect of products or materials to be specified in the regulations. The purpose for which the regulations may be made is the promotion or securing of an increase in the re-use, recovery or recycling of products or materials. The regulations will require the relevant persons to take specified steps to secure attainment of specified targets.

The regulations will be subject to affirmative Parliamentary procedure and before making the regulations the Secretary of State must consult with bodies or persons appearing to him to be representative of bodies or persons whose interests are, or are likely to be, substantially affected by the proposed regulations.

The regulations can only be made if, after consultation, the Secretary of State is satisfied amongst other things that the regulations would be likely to result in an increase in the re-use, recovery or recycling of the products or materials in question which would produce environmental or economic benefits which are significant as against the likely costs resulting from the imposition of the proposed producer responsibility obligation.

The regulations may provide for exemption schemes.

1.9 REVIEW OF MINERAL PLANNING PERMISSIONS
(chapter 21)

The Environment Act builds on the process begun by the Town and Country Planning (Minerals) Act 1981 and continued by the Planning and Compensation Act 1991 to update planning controls on mineral workings.

The broad effect of Environment Act, sch. 13 is to provide for an initial review of mineral planning permissions granted after 1948 but before 1982. The identification of all sites to be included in the initial review must take place within three months of the coming into force of sch. 13. Phase I of the initial review must be begun within a further period of three years and the mineral sites to be reviewed in Phase I (active 'Phase I sites') are active sites which are either wholly or mainly controlled by pre-1969 planning permissions or are situated in sensitive areas such as National Parks. Phase II of the initial review — to begin within six years of the identification of the site — will cover the remaining active sites (active 'Phase II sites') i.e., active sites wholly or mainly controlled by planning permissions granted after 1969 but before 1982 which are not situated in sensitive areas. In the case of a dormant site, all relevant planning permissions which relate to the site cease to have effect on the coming into force of sch. 13 unless and until an application for the permissions to be reviewed has been determined.

The first stage in the review process is the preparation by each mineral planning authority of a list of mineral sites in their area indicating whether they are active Phase I sites, active Phase II sites or dormant sites. The authority must also designate — either in that first list or in the second list — the date by which the owner of the site or of mineral rights in the site must apply for the planning conditions relating to that site to be updated. The onus then shifts to the owner to make an application in accordance with the sch. 13 procedures to the mineral planning authority to determine the conditions to which the planning permissions relating to the site are to be subject. Relevant planning permissions relating to Phase I or Phase II sites will cease to have effect (except in so far as they impose restoration or aftercare conditions) unless the site is included in the list and an application is properly made for the planning conditions to be reviewed. Compensation is payable in certain limited circumstances.

The effect of the first review provided for by sch. 13, taken with the provisions of the 1991 Act, is that all pre-1982 planning permissions will have been updated or replaced within the timetable prescribed by that schedule. Thereafter, all mineral planning permissions are to be reviewed at 15-year intervals under Environment Act, sch. 14.

1.10   HEDGEROWS AND THE CONSERVATION OF THE COUNTRYSIDE
(chapter 22)

Section 97 of the Environment Act confers powers to make regulations for the protection of 'important' hedgerows (to be determined in accordance with criteria to be prescribed in the regulations) in England and Wales. The power does not extend to Scotland. It is likely that the regulations will require land managers to give notice of any intention to remove hedgerows to the local planning authority who would have a specified period of time in which to refuse a proposal in accordance with statutory criteria prescribed in regulations. Before making the regulations the Secretary of State must consult with bodies representative of business interests likely to be affected by the regulations, bodies representative of interests of owners or occupiers of land, bodies representing the interests of local authorities and statutory bodies whose functions include the provision to government of advice on matters relating to environmental conservation. The regulations will be subject to affirmative Parliamentary procedure.

Section 98 makes provision for the establishment of schemes for England, Wales and Scotland for the payment of grants to persons who do, or undertake to do, things which are conducive to the conservation or enhancement of the natural beauty or amenity of the countryside (including its flora and fauna and geological and physiographical features) or of any features of archaeological interest there or the promotion of the enjoyment of the countryside by the public.

1.11 SCOTTISH STATUTORY NUISANCES
(chapter 23)

The Environment Act extends to Scotland the provisions for the control of statutory nuisances contained in Part III of the EPA 1990, as amended by the Noise and Statutory Nuisance Act 1993, which have up to now applied only in England and Wales. The Environment Act, sch. 17 makes technical modifications to the statutory nuisance provisions so as to make them consistent with general legislation, and the system for the administration of justice, in Scotland.

At the time of writing no order has been made to bring into force the provisions in the Environment Act which extend the statutory nuisance regime to Scotland.

Chapter 2
The Environment Agency — Background and Structure

2.1 ANNOUNCEMENT OF AN AGENCY

The government's plans to establish the Environment Agency ('EA') were announced by the Prime Minister on 8 July 1991 in a speech delivered at the Sunday Times Environment Exhibition in London. The EA would, he said, 'bring together HMIP [Her Majesty's Inspectorate of Pollution] and related functions of the NRA [National Rivers Authority], to create a new agency for environmental protection and enhancement', adding that 'It is right the integrity and indivisibility of the environment should be reflected in a unified agency'. In October of the same year the then Secretary of State for Environment, Michael Heseltine, launched a consultation paper entitled *The Government's Proposals for a New Independent Environment Agency* (DoE, MAFF, Welsh Office, 1991). This declared that 'the time is right to . . . establish a new and unified body reflecting the cross-media integrity and indivisibility of the environment' and proposed 'to bring together the key regulatory pollution control functions affecting the different media (air, land and water) in a powerful, innovative and independent Environment Agency. The creation of this body would affect the current responsibilities of HMIP, the NRA and local government.'

Precisely how to achieve the creation of a coherent EA, without adversely affecting other important considerations of government policy, was recognised in the consultation paper as a question which would require careful consideration. The government would, in fact, change its mind on certain aspects before the introduction of the Bill into Parliament in December 1994 and the role and functions of the EA were subject to considerable disagreement and debate during the course of the Bill's passage to the statute book.

The main considerations which guided the government were:

(a) the EA must assume responsibility for day-to-day decisions;
(b) the EA is to be responsible for giving advice and making proposals to government on standards in those areas for which it is responsible, and for enforcing them;
(c) overall policy responsibility for environmental issues and the setting of environmental quality standards remains with government, as do negotiations in the EC and other international bodies;

(d) the EA is to have responsibilities for environmental monitoring, both as regards its own functions and generally;

(e) the EA is expected to harness its acquired expertise and knowledge so as to give advice on best practice and support government initiatives on innovation and wealth creation (consultation paper, para. 2).

These aims are substantially reflected in the Environment Act itself.

2.2. AN OVERVIEW OF THE PRE-ACT FRAMEWORK

Before describing the various options for the EA which the government identified in 1991, and the eventual choices made, it is necessary to describe in outline the nature and responsibilities of the various bodies and authorities with responsibility for environmental matters, as they were before the establishment of the EA. It is important to appreciate that, although the EA and the Scottish Environmental Protection Agency ('SEPA') have been established and certain provisions conferring functions on them have been brought into force, it is not intended that the bodies will assume all their statutory functions (including those under pre-existing legislation) until 1 April 1996.

2.2.1 Department of Environment

The Department of Environment has general, overall responsibility for environmental matters, including the formulation of policies for protecting the environment.

Such policies, once formulated, find their expression as legislation, both primary and secondary, imposing requirements which must be met and providing for penalties for failure to do so. Besides acting on the domestic front, DoE is required to participate in EC and other international fora on matters concerned with environmental protection. Enforcement by DoE of standards set by legislation was, before the Environment Act, primarily entrusted to Inspectorates within the Department.

2.2.2 Her Majesty's Inspectorate of Pollution

HMIP was created in 1987 from the Industrial Air Pollution Inspectorate of the Health and Safety Executive and the Radiochemical, Hazardous Waste and Water Inspectorates of the DoE.

HMIP was responsible for regulating those industrial processes or plant with the greatest potential for pollution and, in particular, had the task of commencing the implementation of the system of integrated pollution control (IPC) which was introduced by the Environmental Protection Act 1990 and which will eventually cover approximately 5,000 major industrial installations. Operators of scheduled processes were required to obtain authorisation from HMIP. Such authorisation, if given, would be subject to requirements, including — in all cases — the requirement that the operator must use the best available techniques not entailing excessive cost (BATNEEC) in order to prevent or minimise pollution arising from the process. Through its IPC functions, HMIP thus had a crucial role in controlling major pollution of air, land and water.

Further functions of HMIP included:

(a)   regulating the disposal of radioactive waste and the registration of premises under the Radioactive Substances Act 1993;
(b)   overseeing the performance of local authorities' waste disposal functions.

HMIP's manpower was substantially increased following the introduction of IPC. In October 1994 it had approximately 430 staff and an annual budget of £30 million.

2.2.3   Drinking Water Inspectorate

The Drinking Water Inspectorate was established following the Water Act 1989. Operating as part of the DoE's Water Directorate, its primary function is to monitor the quality of drinking water supplied by water companies, in order to ascertain whether it complies with the requirements of the Water Supply (Water Quality) Regulations 1989 (SI 1989/1147). Besides this monitoring function, the Inspectorate advises Ministers on enforcement and provides them with scientific and technical advice on issues relating to water quality.

2.2.4   National Rivers Authority

Established by the Water Act 1989, the responsibilities of the National Rivers Authority (NRA) covered the protection and improvement of the water environment.

The NRA had the following main functions:

(a)   control of pollution of watercourses;
(b)   regulation of water abstraction;
(c)   flood and coastal defence;
(d)   the maintenance, improvement and development of salmon fisheries, trout fisheries, freshwater fisheries and eel fisheries.

On flood defence and fisheries the Ministry of Agriculture, Fisheries and Food ('MAFF') (or the Welsh Office in Wales) had policy responsibility for the NRA's activities, with DoE having responsibility for the NRA's remaining functions.
    Besides its main functions, the NRA also had certain duties regarding the conservation and recreational use of inland and coastal waters.
    In 1994 the NRA had a staff of 7,500 and an annual budget of £455 million. Only about 20% of its budget was spent on pollution control matters, the remainder being allocated to flood defence (the biggest single item), water resource management, fisheries, recreation and navigation.

2.2.5   Waste regulation authorities

Waste regulation authorities (WRAs) were established by the Environmental Protection Act 1990. Normally the county council (or the district council in Wales and the metropolitan areas), WRAs were responsible for the system of licensing and supervision of waste disposal facilities, the enforcement of that system and the control of hazardous waste movements. The government's policy was to encourage WRAs to establish regional groupings by making joint arrangements for the discharge of their functions.

2.2.6 Other environmental functions of local authorities

In England, district and London borough councils have responsibility for operating the system of air pollution control contained in Part I of the Environmental Protection Act 1990, in the case of the less-polluting 'Part B' prescribed processes. ('Part A' processes were handled by HMIP under the IPC system outlined above.) In Wales, new unitary county or county borough councils assume these functions on 1 April 1996. Further air pollution functions are conferred upon councils by the Clean Air Act 1993 (a consolidation of earlier legislation, including the celebrated Clean Air Act 1956). The 1993 Act specifically excludes prescribed processes from its scope and is primarily concerned with the emission of 'dark smoke' from chimneys and of grit and dust from chimneys other than small domestic furnaces.

Besides these functions, local authorities have a wide range of functions of an environmental nature, including the suppression of statutory nuisances (under Part III of the Environmental Protection Act 1990 and the Noise and Statutory Nuisance Act 1993), litter (under the Litter Act 1983 and Part IV of the Environmental Protection Act 1990), building control (under the Building Act 1984) and food safety (under the Food Safety Act 1990).

2.3 REASONS FOR CHANGE

As concern for the environment has grown, the number of matters which need to be prevented or regulated has increased. Local authorities were, from early times, seen as obvious candidates for such functions and, as we have just seen, they have been given responsibilities for a wide range of environmental problems. More recently, however, the trend has been towards establishing non-elected authorities or units (such as the inspectorates) within central government to undertake important environmental regulatory tasks. Whilst some would see this as an example of the present central government's relative antipathy towards local government, others would view it as an acknowledgment of the growing import-ance of the environment as an issue requiring the working out of national policies — even at the regulatory or operational levels — and the utilisation of both human and financial resources on a scale which local authorities, by their very nature, do not possess. Thus, for example, following the privatisation of the water industry in the late 1980s, the environmental functions of the former water authorities were transferred to a new body, the NRA, covering the whole of England and Wales, rather than to local authorities.

Notwithstanding the establishment of HMIP in 1987 and the NRA in 1989, together with the initial implementation of the IPC system created by the EPA 1990 with its overarching system of IPC, the government's view, expressed as recently as 1990 in the White Paper, *This Common Inheritance* (Cm 1200, 1990), was that it was inappropriate at this stage to create a new body with responsibility for all pollution control matters. Why, then, did the government change its mind, as demonstrated by the Prime Minister's statement, quoted at the beginning of this chapter? The consultation paper, *The Government's Proposals for a New, Independent Environment Agency,* sets out several reasons.

2.3.1 Overlap and potential conflict between agencies

The government acknowledged that there were problems of overlap and potential conflict between HMIP and the NRA. Under the Water Resources Act 1991 the NRA had responsibility for regulating discharges to seas, rivers and other 'controlled waters' within the meaning of that Act. Any person wishing to dispose of effluent must obtain a discharge consent. Such consents contain technical details about the chemicals being discharged, and the permitted maximum quantity and the maximum rate of discharge. However, it was not necessary to obtain a discharge consent if the discharge was authorised by HMIP under the IPC provisions in Part I of the EPA 1990 or (in certain circumstances) if the discharge was covered by a waste management licence or a waste disposal licence from the WRA.

With the gradual extension of the IPC system, persons who might previously have sought a discharge consent from the NRA would apply instead to HMIP for an authorisation which, if granted, would permit discharges to the air, as well as to water, and to generate waste.

The dual responsibilities of the NRA and HMIP required close cooperation between them. In some cases this was written into the legislation. For example, an authorisation under the IPC system could not be given if the NRA certified that the release would result in or contribute to a failure to achieve any water quality objective under Part III of the EPA 1990. The NRA were also able to require HMIP to include in any authorisation such conditions as appeared to the NRA to be appropriate for the purposes of Part I of that Act, as the NRA required by notice in writing to HMIP (EPA 1990, former s. 28(3)).

The government in its consultation paper accepted, however, that these mechanisms 'still fall short of securing a fully integrated, effective and multi-media approach to pollution control', adding that 'it can be confusing to industry and inefficient to deal with different environmental quality regulations, and it therefore makes more difficult the task of delivering a high-quality public service' (para. 13).

2.3.2 Overlap and potential conflict between agencies and local authorities

An instance of the overlap between the NRA and WRAs has already been noted in 2.3.1. Close liaison with the NRA was required from WRAs in settling licence conditions for landfill sites and other waste facilities in order to prevent contamination of water from leachates. Further overlap existed between HMIP authorisations and WRA waste management licences. The government's consultation paper also focused on the difficulties of regulation at local level, discussed earlier:

> As standards and techniques of waste management become increasingly sophisticated, it is becoming more difficult for individual waste regulation authorities either to provide the necessary expertise, or to coordinate policies and standards

over a wide enough area. Although the establishment of voluntary regional groupings of waste regulation authorities would have gone some way towards overcoming these difficulties, it could never provide a truly integrated approach to waste regulation whilst water and air pollution were in the hands of separate regulatory bodies. (*Improving Environment Quality — The Government's Proposals for a New, Independent Environment Agency* (DoE, MAFF, Welsh Office, 1991).)

2.3.3 Other concerns

The consultation paper highlighted other reasons for creating a new agency with wide-ranging functions. The first was 'the need to ensure that decisions about pollution control take full account of the need to select the best practicable environmental option'. Before the Environment Act, each regulatory body had its own set of objectives. The government recognised that 'trade-offs' between these objectives might not always produce a solution which was, overall, the right one for the environment. As an example, the disposal of waste has the potential to pollute air, land and water, depending on the method of disposal chosen. What was required was a body which could look objectively at each potential method — rather than, as in the NRA's case, being constrained to worry about only one medium — and make a judgment on what would be least harmful, having regard to all relevant environmental consequences.

The government also recognised that 'the lack of any central regulatory focus can also lead to gaps and a lack of cohesion', for example, in the case of environmental monitoring which, it was acknowledged, had not been carried out on a coordinated basis. The need for comprehensive environmental data has, in fact, been increased by the recent (1993) establishment (following a period of wrangling over its location) of the European Environment Agency ('EEA'), in consequence of the adoption of Regulation EEC 1210/90. Located in Copenhagen, the EEA is intended to act as coordinator of environmental data, but in doing so it will rely upon national information networks of organisations which regularly collect such data. The EA is, therefore, intended to have a major role in supplying the EEA with data relating to England and Wales.

The final reason cited by the government for the creation of the EA was 'public concern about the different status of the existing agencies and inspectorates'. In this regard, the NRA was acknowledged as the type of institution which the government believed should be used as a model for the EA, since the NRA had 'its independent board' and a 'public standing and voice of its own'. Although the consultation paper did not say so, this comment contained an implicit acknowledgment that HMIP's status as a part of DoE was not such as to endear it in the long term to the public, and that it could only benefit from incorporation into a body which could, if necessary, openly criticise government policy. The NRA's success, during its relatively short life, was in fact widely acknowledged in the Parliamentary debates on the Environment Bill.

2.4 THE GOVERNMENT'S PROPOSALS AND OPTIONS FOR CHANGE

Having identified the problems with the then existing arrangements, the consultation paper sought to identify the benefits which would result from the establishment of an EA, having the major regulatory pollution control responsibilities of HMIP, the NRA and WRAs. The perceived benefits were:

(a)   the ability to develop a consistent and coherent approach to environmental protection and pollution control;
(b)   greater expertise and authority;
(c)   the ability to attract and train high-calibre staff capable of seeing environmental problems in the round;
(d)   the ability to address the problems of overlaps, conflicts and gaps (see above) and the provision of strategic direction;
(e)   the creation of a powerful voice in influencing the adoption of better environmental standards and practices.

2.4.1   Functions of the EA

The government's consultation paper acknowledged that the precise functions of the EA would need detailed consideration and this prediction turned out to be extremely accurate. Much debate was to centre upon the EA's functions both before and during the passage of the Environment Bill. The main responsibilities, identified in 1991, included:

(a)   applying standards by giving authorisations, licences and consents for emissions, discharges and disposals to air, water and land;
(b)   monitoring compliance and enforcement;
(c)   regulating the import, export and movement of waste;
(d)   assessing national waste disposal needs and priorities;
(e)   monitoring environmental conditions, publishing statistics and commissioning research;
(f)   acting as statutory consultee (e.g., in town and country planning matters);
(g)   providing authoritative and independent advice to government and advice and guidance to industry on best environmental practice.

A probable major reason for the government's initial reluctance to contemplate the creation of an EA, and for much of the delay which followed the publication of the consultation paper, was the anxiety which Ministers may have felt as to the likely effects upon business efficiency and competitiveness. Before a decision could be taken to create an EA, the government had to convince itself that these effects would in fact be beneficial, rather than merely restrictive and bureaucratic. Accordingly, para. 20 of the consultation paper, which addresses these issues, is of particular importance and deserves to be quoted in full:

Beyond these core statutory responsibilities, the Agency would be well placed to identify areas where its functions provide opportunities for wealth creation and innovation in the environmental field. The development of IPC will, for example, help to push forward the frontiers of technological development, promoting cleaner industrial operations and creating opportunities for much of British industry to maintain and enhance its competitive edge. Similarly, the growing need for automated pollution control, monitoring and sampling techniques provides substantial scope for new markets. The Government will expect the Environment Agency to harness its expertise, resources and research effort to work with Government, business and commerce to promote the business response to regulation and market opportunities arising from it. It would be able to make an input into the new Advisory Committee on Business and the Environment. And it could contribute to the environmental technology schemes run by the Department of Trade and Industry and DoE by identifying priorities for innovation in technology relevant to regulation and promulgating project results. (*Improving Environmental Quality — The Government's Proposals for a New, Independent Environment Agency* (DoE, MAFF, Welsh Office, 1991).)

Both the content and tone of that passage convey the impression that it was not produced without a considerable amount of effort and it is likely that there were those in government who felt that it contained an element of wishful thinking (see 2.5.2 below).

2.4.2   Possible additional functions

The government's initial ideas included the transfer to the EA of the Drinking Water Inspectorate. The thinking behind this was that, since the EA would control the use by water companies of processes, substances and products which might affect the quality of drinking water, it would be appropriate to confer upon it the Inspectorate's functions of enforcing the legal standards for drinking water and associated monitoring requirements, thereby bringing all regulatory responsibilities for raw drinking water within one body and so enhancing the coordination of action to deal with such common concerns as the monitoring and control of pesticide residue in tap water. The consultation paper did, however, acknowledge that as 'a small unit which operates in a different manner from other components of the proposed Agency, the Drinking Water Inspectorate would need to be integrated into it in an appropriate manner'. In the event, however, the government dropped its proposal, and the inspectorate remains outside the EA, as part of the DoE (see 2.5.1 below).

The government recognised that, even after the creation of the EA, a close eye would need to be kept upon the boundaries between its functions, as initially determined under the Environment Act, and the remaining related functions of other bodies, in particular, local authorities. As has already been seen (2.2.6), local authorities have responsibility for air pollution controls over certain 'less polluting' industrial processes under Part I of the EPA 1990, whilst the EA now steps into the shoes of HMIP as the body responsible for regulating, under the IPC system, the 'more polluting' processes. The consultation paper stated that it will be open to the Secretaries of State to transfer particular processes from local authority to EA control 'or vice versa'.

On the question of waste regulation, the proposed transfer of functions to the EA, together with the transfer of local authorities' own waste disposal operations to private-sector or arm's-length local authority waste disposal companies (LAWDCs), caused the government to re-examine the role of the statutory joint authorities and the voluntary amalgamation arrangements that had been created in London and the metropolitan areas. After the transfers just described, the only functions of those bodies would have been as contract managers or owners of LAWDCs and it was not considered appropriate to retain joint arrangements merely for these. Accordingly, the statutory joint waste disposal authorities and waste regulation authorities would be abolished.

The functions of the NRA, ranging across a wider area than pollution control, raised questions as to the extent to which it should be absorbed into the EA. For example, as at March 1991 only 19% of the NRA's staff were directly engaged in pollution control work, whilst 50% of the staff were employed on flood defence.

2.4.3 Options for change

The consultation paper identified several possible ways of achieving the overall objective of creating 'a strong regulatory pollution control body whilst ensuring that there is no weakening in the protection and effective management of the water environment'.

Option 1 was to combine HMIP and the WRAs, leaving the NRA as a free-standing body, to which HMIP's water responsibilities under IPC would be transferred. There would thus have been one body (the EA) for emissions and disposals to air and land and one body (the NRA) for emissions and disposals to water. The government acknowledged that this would not achieve a fully integrated approach and would leave industry having to deal with different regulators. Option 1 does not appear to have been put forward with much enthusiasm.

Option 2 was to create an 'umbrella body' which would oversee and coordinate the work of the NRA and HMIP. Those bodies would share a common board and headquarters but otherwise be separate. The main advantage of this was that it offered the prospect of an evolutionary approach to integrating pollution control but, given the disparity in the size and responsibilities of the NRA and HMIP, progress would be likely to have been slow and — no doubt a crucial factor for the government — expensive, with little guarantee of eventual success. Again, industry would not benefit from a 'one-stop shop'.

Option 3 was the creation of a fully integrated EA combining HMIP, the WRAs and all the functions of the NRA. Such an EA could, the government thought, be established either as a unitary body or as a 'federal structure' whereby the regulatory and enforcement responsibilities could be managed separately from its operational functions (e.g., flood defence). In either case the advantage would be that the EA would be able to secure an integrated approach to pollution control whilst retaining the framework of integrated river basin management within one organisation. The EA would be able to make efficient use of staff and resources.

Two arguments were, however, advanced in the consultation paper against option 3 (which was the one eventually chosen). The first concerned the wide-ranging nature of the NRA. Since pollution control represented only a part of what the NRA did, combining all its functions in the EA might, the government thought, risk 'blurring the pollution control focus of the new body and creating a large heterogeneous organisation with the major part of its resources dedicated to functions other than pollution control'. Would this more diverse EA be able to police its own operational functions? The problem of locating both regulatory and operational functions within a single body would be raised several times both before and during the passage of the Environment Bill (see 2.8.2 below).

The second possible disadvantage cited by the consultation paper was the potential size of such a fully integrated EA and, in particular, whether 'a body comprising over 9,000 mostly regionally based staff responsible for a budget in excess of £500 million' could be managed 'effectively and efficiently with due regard to the requirements of public and Parliamentary accountability'.

Option 4 was therefore put forward for consultation. This would have placed in the EA only the pollution control responsibilities of the NRA, together with HMIP and the WRAs, thereby leaving the NRA to deal with its remaining functions in a more focused manner and with a more manageable size and structure. Again, the drawbacks to this approach would have been that — despite the statutory and administrative arrangements required to ensure cooperation and liaison — there would still have been two bodies having responsibility for river basin management, with consequent inconvenience to businesses. It was also thought that there would be considerable disruption to the NRA whilst it was being reconstituted.

The consultation paper concluded its analysis of Options 1 to 4 by stating that the government had not reached a firm view as to which would be best and that there might in fact be other options to be considered. Comments were invited on the whole matter.

2.5 CONSULTATION AND THE LONG WAIT

2.5.1 Consultation

The consultation paper, *Improving Environmental Quality — The Government's Proposals for a New, Independent Environment Agency* was published in October 1991. Many of the major responses on the consultation exercise focused on the position of the NRA which, as we have already seen, was the most problematic of the potential candidates for incorporation within the EA, in view of the wide-ranging nature of its functions.

The House of Commons Select Committee on Environment favoured the hiving off of the NRA's pollution control responsibilities to the EA, leaving it with control over abstraction and river flow (Environment Committee, *1st Report, The Government's Proposals for an Environment Agency* (House of Commons Papers, Session 1991–92, 55)). Others, however, were concerned that the removal of the NRA's pollution control functions would seriously weaken the body which remained and even that any change to the NRA could adversely affect the fight to protect the water environment. The NRA itself was concerned at being dismembered, and favoured complete integration into the EA. By the summer of 1992, following consideration of the responses, the government had decided that the NRA would, after all, be completely integrated with the EA. Amongst the concerns of those who had opposed dismemberment of the NRA had been the fear that its remaining functions would be transferred to the Ministry of Agriculture, Fisheries and Food. Indeed, reports of a dispute between MAFF and DoE on this issue had been circulating even before publication of the consultation paper.

The government also decided that:

(a) the EA should take over responsibility for the waste regulation functions of local authorities (i.e., the WRAs);

(b)   the EA would not take over responsibility for the system of air pollution controls vested in local authorities by Part I of the Environmental Protection Act 1990;

(c)   the Drinking Water Inspectorate should not, after all, be transferred to the EA (Hansard, HC, 15 July 1992, written answers, cols 857–8).

The first of these decisions was not unexpected since it was a feature of all but one of the options identified in the consultation paper. The second was also, in retrospect, predictable, although there were those who felt that the central administration's alleged antipathy towards local government was such that even this function was likely to be removed *ab initio* to the EA, instead of merely being on a list of possible future candidates for transfer (see 2.4.2).

The third decision — not to transfer the DWI — was somewhat unexpected and the reasons for it were probed by Joan Ruddock MP during the House of Commons Committee stage of the Bill. According to Ms Ruddock, after the consultation in 1991-2, 'it was simply announced that the Drinking Water Inspectorate would not be transferred. I have tried to discover the outcome of the consultation exercise and any published results, but neither I nor the Library have been able to obtain a copy of the outcome'. (Hansard, HC, Standing Committee B, Environment Bill, Third Sitting, 2 May 1995, col. 90.) The Parliamentary Under-Secretary of State for the Environment (Sir Paul Beresford) responded as follows:

. . . consideration was given to transferring the Drinking Water Inspectorate, which is a Department of the Environment function, to the proposed Environment Agency . . . but, after considerable thought, we concluded that the transfer of function should not take place, because drinking water quality relates to public health rather than to the environment and environmental pollution. The inspectorate is not on a par with HMIP and the National Rivers Authority. Its role as regulator impinges more on public health than on measures to protect the environment. We believe the inspectorate to be effective in ensuring that the drinking water regulations are upheld by considering enforcement action . . . the inspectorate is functioning extremely well as it is and where it is. (cols 91–2.)

When pressed by M.P.s who made the point that it is difficult to separate the process whereby raw water eventually becomes drinking water, the Minister confessed that '. . . the matter comes down to a pure difference of opinion' (col. 94).

2.5.2   The long wait

Government announcements during 1992 and 1993 stated that legislation to establish the EA (and an environmental agency for Scotland) would be introduced at the earliest opportunity, and the Queen's Speech for the 1993–4 session of Parliament actually promised a paving Bill, to be followed by a Bill providing for the agencies' establishment. The concept of a paving Bill was, however, later abandoned, on the ground that work on the main Bill was already well advanced. Instead, an undertaking was given in July 1994 to publish a draft of a Bill, before its introduction into Parliament. The draft Bill appeared on 13 October 1994 and the Environment Bill itself was introduced into the House of Lords on 1 December 1994.

This whole series of delays was graphically illustrated by the Chairman of the National Rivers Authority, Lord Crickhowell, at second reading:

> In June 1941 Germany attacked Russia and by the first week of July in that year the House of Commons had met for the first time in this Chamber. By December 1944 Britain was within five months of the end of the war with Germany. By April 1946 the Labour Government were struggling with the problems of the peace. What has that to do with this Bill? Only this: that in July 1991 the Prime Minister announced his intention to set up an environment agency. Today, in December 1994, we have got to the second reading of the Bill that is to carry out that intention. By April 1996, all being well in an uncertain world, the agency will be taking over its responsibilities. I suppose that among the more charitable conclusions that could be drawn from that comparison of historical events is that it is more difficult to set up an environment agency than to win a war or that this is an unusually well prepared piece of legislation. (Hansard, HL, 15 December 1994, col. 1398.)

What or who was in fact responsible for the delays? The matters involved are, clearly, complex and the Bill as a whole covered considerably more than the establishment of the EA and SEPA. But Lord Crickhowell seems to have been hinting at further reasons, and one of these, at least, was revealed during the second reading debate on the Bill in the House of Commons. Questioned by a Conservative member both as to the cost implications of the EA, as finally proposed, and about the likely effects on industry and consumers of having to comply with environmental standards which could be higher than those of other European countries, the Secretary of State for the Environment (John Gummer) replied that he was a 'late convert to the concept of an agency, on precisely those grounds' (Hansard, HC, 18 April 1995, col. 39). It is therefore likely that some at least of the delay which occurred was due to Michael Howard's replacement of Mr Heseltine as Secretary of State for the Environment in 1992 and John Gummer's assumption of that office in 1993, following which he needed to be convinced that a multipurpose EA would not cause costs to spiral, and then had to convince others in a Cabinet priding itself on its deregulatory credentials.

The Secretary of State said at second reading that he hoped and believed that, by bringing the resources of the various existing bodies together:

> we shall reduce the number of people involved in the agency. Indeed, the agency will have failed if it cannot make its operation as lean as humanly possible. It must get the best value for money, and all those measures can be taken effectively by such an agency. . . . By bringing together those responsibilities it will ensure that its work can be done better and more effectively with fewer people'. (Ibid., col. 39.)

Later in the same debate Mr Gummer said that he was now convinced of the need for the EPA and SEPA 'primarily because of the nature of sustainable development' (ibid., col. 41). This crucial concept, which underlies the principal aim of the EA, as set out in Environment Act, s. 4, originated in the 1987 report of the World Commission on Environment and Development, entitled *Our Common Future,* but generally known as the 'Brundtland Report' (after Mrs Gro Harlem Brundtland, who chaired the Commission). It was taken up at the United Nations Conference on Environment and Development held in Rio de Janeiro in 1992 and is now recognised by the government as an important aim (*Sustainable Development: the UK Strategy* (Cm 2426) (London: HMSO, 1994). The most commonly used 'working' definition of 'sustainable development' is that provided by the Commission itself, namely 'development that meets the needs of the present without compromising the ability of future generations to meet their own needs'. The relevance of sustainable development to the EA is discussed in chapter 11.

2.6   DRAFT ENVIRONMENTAL AGENCIES BILL AND THE ENVIRONMENT COMMITTEE HEARINGS

As already mentioned, the government published in October 1994 a set of draft clauses and schedules entitled 'Environmental Agencies Bill'. Acting with commendable speed (given the tight timescale before introduction of the actual Bill) the House of Commons Environment Committee organised in November 1994 a short series of hearings on the draft Bill at which senior representatives of the NRA, HMIP and local authority bodies were able to give their views on the proposals. Initial reactions to the draft Bill had been critical of certain aspects, in particular clause 7, which dealt with general environmental and recreational duties, and clause 9, which would have imposed a general duty on the EA to have regard to costs and benefits when exercising its powers. As published, clause 7 would have required the EA, in formulating or considering any proposals relating to any of its functions, 'to have regard to the desirability of conserving and enhancing natural beauty and of considering flora, fauna and geological or physiographical features of special interest'. The perceived weakness of the phrase 'have regard to the desirability of', compared with the existing duties of the NRA, was disliked both by environmental groups and by the NRA itself and, even before the Environment Committee had begun its hearings, the government had on 18 November announced a change in the wording of clause 7, whereby the EA's duty would become one of so exercising its functions as to further the conservation and enhancement of natural beauty and the conservation of flora, fauna [etc.]. The Secretary of State said that:

> I have listened carefully to the concerns which have been raised over the wording of the Agency's conservation commitments . . . I wish there to be no doubt about the conservation and the sustainable development role of the agency. I therefore intend to amend the wording so as to provide a clear duty not simply to consider conservation issues in relation to all the Agency's functions but to further conservation as appropriate. (DoE News Release 650, 18 November 1994.)

This revised formulation (which, it is important to note, did not extend to the EA's pollution control functions) managed to allay some, but not all, of the criticism of clause 7, which continued into the Parliamentary stages of the

Environment Bill, as did the debate over the cost/benefit requirements of clause 9 of the draft Bill (which became Environment Act, s. 39 (see chapter 11)).

The other major matters upon which the Environment Committee heard evidence were:

(a) The desirability, or otherwise, of transferring local authorities' waste regulation functions to the EA. Local authority representatives bemoaned what they saw as a further erosion of local accountability, despite the fact that, as the chairman of the Committee pointed out, 'very often waste is disposed of a long way from its source, therefore the local government boundary may not always be appropriate'.

(b) The means for determining the boundaries of the EA's regions. The NRA wished to see them drawn by reference to river catchment areas, whilst HMIP argued for the use of local authority boundaries (see 2.8.1).

(c) The question of whether and, if so, how to separate the EA's regulatory and operational functions. Representatives of the NRA and HMIP disagreed over this issue (see 2.8.2).

2.7 ESTABLISHMENT, MEMBERSHIP AND STATUS OF THE EA

2.7.1 Date of establishment and membership

Environment Act, s. 1(1) establishes the EA as a body corporate 'for the purpose of carrying out the functions transferred or assigned to it by or under this Act' (see especially chapters 3 to 11 and 14 to 17). Section 125 of the Act gives the Secretary of State power to bring the provisions into force by order on a day or days to be specified. Although the EA came into existence in July 1995, the intention is that the EA will begin its day-to-day operations on 1 April 1996 (the 'transfer date' for the purposes of ss. 1 to 19). Section 1(2) provides that the EA itself consists of between eight and 15 members, three of whom are appointed by the Minister of Agriculture, Fisheries and Food and the remainder by the Secretary of State. Of those members, one is designated by the Secretary of State as the chairman and another as deputy chairman.

The Secretary of State and the Minister are required by s. 1(4) in making their appointments to have regard to the desirability of appointing people who have experience of, or who have shown capacity in, some matter relevant to the EA's functions.

On 18 November 1994 the Secretary of State for the Environment announced the membership of the Environment Agency Advisory Committee, which was to assist the government in the establishment of the EA, and most of whose members would form the nucleus of the membership of the EA itself, upon its establishment (DoE News Release 650, 18 November 1994). The chairman of the Advisory Committee (now Chairman of the EA) was Lord De Ramsey who, on the date of his appointment to the Committee stated that as:

a farmer and landowner [in Cambridgeshire] I cannot help but be interested in conservation. Care for the countryside is in my blood, and I want the Agency to be a strong conservation body. At the same time, I recognise the need for the

Agency to play an important part in promoting sustainable development, reconciling the need [for] environmental protection, conservation and development.

Lord De Ramsey has experience as a director of a water company and as President of the Association of Drainage Authorities, besides being a past President of the Country Landowners Association. The other persons appointed to the Committee (and who subsequently became initial members of the EA's Board) were:

Peter Burnham (accountant, member of HMIP Advisory Committee);
Imtiaz Farookhi (Chief Executive, Leicester City Council);
Nigel Haigh OBE (Director, Institute of European Environment Policy, Chairman of Green Alliance);
Christopher Hampson CBE (Chairman, Yorkshire Electricity and HMIP Advisory Committee);
Councillor John Harman (Leader, Kirklees Metropolitan Borough Council);
John Norris (farmer and ex-NRA Board member);
Professor Ron Edwards (Chairman of the 1991 National Parks Review Panel (see chapter 18), board member of NRA).

When the EA was formally established in July 1995, the following persons were also appointed to its board:

Ed Gallagher (Chief Executive, formerly Chief Executive of the NRA);
Sir Richard George (Chairman and Managing Director, Weetabix Ltd);
Karen Morgan (NRA board member);
Dr Anne Powell (Chairman, NRA Thames Region Fisheries Advisory Committee);
Joan Wykes, OBE (Chairman, WRA Thames Region Rivers Advisory Committee).

At the committee stage of the Environment Bill in the House of Lords, Viscount Ullswater explained the government's general approach to appointments to the EA's (and SEPA's) boards:

The Bill requires the Secretary of State and the Minister to have regard to the desirability of appointing a person who has had experience of and shown capacity in some matter relevant to the agencies' functions. It does not require us to assemble boards to be comprised of a panel of technical experts. The boards will have much more of a policy-setting and strategic decision-making role similar to that undertaken by other boards. Where technical expertise is called for, it will be provided primarily by the agencies' officers. Nor should the boards be delegate bodies made up of nominees representing outside interests. The idea . . . of 'a balance of key interests' is alien to the idea of agencies. Rather, each member will be appointed on his or her individual merits and will be expected to act in the interests of the agency as a whole and in accordance with that agency's functions, aims and objectives.

In making appointments in general, we wish to appoint the best available talents for the task, whoever they are. Indeed, we have followed that approach in appointing the Environment Agency Advisory Committee. The committee members are drawn from a wide range of backgrounds and experience, including industry, local authorities, environmental science and finance, each member distinguished in his own right but each equipped to make a distinctive contribution to running a large organisation such as the agency . . .

The agencies will be large organisations with a full range of issues — such as management, personnel and finance — for which the boards must take responsibility. It would be wrong to suppose that all members must necessarily have experience of the agencies' specialist functions if they are to make a useful contribution. (Hansard, HL, 17 January 1995, col. 582.)

The board of the EA (that is to say, its members) is directly responsible to Ministers for all aspects of the EA's organisation and performance, and must ensure both that the EA fulfils its statutory duties, in the light of government guidance, and the proper, effective and efficient running of the organisation.

2.7.2 Further provisions as to membership

Environment Act, sch. 1 contains detailed provisions concerning the appointment and removal of members and its chairman and deputy chairman, the remuneration of members and the handling of members' interests. The provisions of the schedule are in part modelled on the constitution of the NRA in sch. 1 to the Water Resources Act 1991.

Members of the EA (and SEPA) are to hold and vacate office in accordance with the terms of their appointment (subject to resignation or removal by the appropriate Minister (i.e., the Secretary of State or the Minister of Agriculture, Fisheries and Food — see 2.7.1 above)) in certain circumstances, such as prolonged, unauthorised absence from meetings or unfitness to carry out their functions. The EA is empowered to pay its members remuneration and allowances, as may be determined with the appropriate Minister and, if required by the latter, pensions, allowances and gratuities as determined by him. Compensation may be paid by the EA upon a member ceasing to hold office if the appropriate Minister so determines (paras 1, 3).

2.7.3 Staff of the EA

As introduced, the Bill would have required the members of the EA to have obtained the approval of the Secretary of State as to the terms and conditions of service of any of its staff. This requirement was removed from the Bill at committee stage in the House of Lords, when the Minister said that whilst '[i]t will be important for the government to exercise a strategic control over pay, terms and conditions in view of the substantial funding the agencies will receive from charge payers and the public purse . . . the strategic controls required can be exercised under the general power to impose conditions or award of grant to the agencies and would be implemented through their management statements and financial memoranda' (Hansard, HL, 2 March 1995, col. 1602).

The Secretary of State must, however, give his consent before a person can be appointed to act as the EA's chief executive (para. 4(2)). The draft *Environment*

Agency: Management Statement (which was published in October 1994) provides that the chief executive is responsible to the Board for the EA's day-to-day management and is the EA's accounting officer.

2.7.4   Other formal provisions

Schedule 1 also contains certain provisions of a formal nature, such as the EA's ability, in most circumstances, to regulate its own procedure (including quorum) and to delegate its functions to any authorised member, officer or employee or to any committee or subcommittee (paras 5, 6).

Schedule 1, para. 7 contains detailed provisions as to members' interests, designed to ensure that all interests, both direct and indirect, are disclosed, and to enable the Secretary of State, in certain circumstances, to waive members' disabilities caused by their interests.

Further formal provisions are contained in paras 9 (minutes), 10 (application of seal and proof of instruments) and 11 (documents served etc. by or on the EA).

2.7.5   Relationship with Crown

Environment Act, s. 1(5) provides that the EA shall not be regarded as the servant or agent of the Crown or as enjoying any status, immunity or privilege of the Crown, nor as being exempt from any tax, duty, rate, levy or other (local or general) charge by virtue of any connection with the Crown. The EA's property shall not be regarded as property of or held on behalf of the Crown. There is an exception where functions of a Minister are delegated, by agreement, to the EA (see chapter 14).

2.7.6   Relationship with Ministers, departments and Parliament

The draft management statement for the Environment Agency states that the Secretary of State for the Environment is the lead Minister responsible for the EA and, together with other Ministers, sets the environmental policy framework within which the EA operates. This includes setting domestic environmental quality standards or objectives which the EA is to deliver and determining the regulations or instruments which it must enforce or collect. The Secretary of State remains the person who must report to Parliament and the public on the state of the UK environment and participate in EC and other international bodies. The Minister of Agriculture, Fisheries and Food has responsibility in England for the EA's flood defence and fisheries functions, as well as specific duties relating to radioactive waste, and for terrestrial and aquatic monitoring. The Secretary of State for Wales sets the policy framework within which the EA carries out its flood defence, fisheries and waste (including nuclear waste) regulation activities within Wales and discharges its functions in Wales.

Each of the Ministers can give the EA directions (with which it must comply) relating to its activities in that Minister's areas of responsibility. Except in emergency, Ministers will consult the EA before making directions.

As has been mentioned, the EA's board is directly responsible to Ministers for all aspects of the EA's organisation and performance, with the chairman having a particular responsibility for the proper discharge by the board of its collective role. The EA's chief executive has particular responsibilities to the Department of the Environment for meeting various financial management standards, including any recommendations of the Public Accounts Committee, and for putting into effect any other recommendations of Parliamentary bodies which have been accepted by the government.

The Secretary of State for the Environment is accountable to Parliament for the policy framework within which the EA operates, for its overall performance, for specific aspects relating to his responsibilities and for appointments to the EA. The other Ministers are similarly accountable to Parliament for policy and performance relating to their responsibilities and appointments.

The EA must submit its annual report and audited accounts to the Ministers, and the Secretary of State must lay these documents before Parliament. The Comptroller and Auditor General may inspect the EA's accounts etc. and report any findings to the House of Commons, and may also investigate the EA's value for money.

The Parliamentary Commissioner for Administration (or 'Ombudsman') may investigate all the EA's functions, other than land drainage and flood defence, which are within the remit of the Local Government Ombudsman (being largely funded by levies on local authorities).

2.8 STRUCTURE OF THE EA

2.8.1 Regions

From the outset it was intended that the EA would have a regional structure. Environment Act, s. 11 requires there to be an advisory committee for Wales, whilst s. 12 requires the EA to establish and maintain advisory committees 'for the different regions of England and Wales' (see 2.9 below). The draft *Environment Agency: Management Statement* considered that regional boundaries would be for the EA to determine, subject to certain exceptions including the assurance that (in line with Environment Act, s. 12) the EA's Welsh region will consist wholly or mainly of the geographical area of Wales, the precise boundaries being determined by the Secretary of State for Wales, consulting the other relevant Ministers, on the basis of proposals from the EA.

As has been mentioned in 2.6, the NRA and HMIP disagreed when they appeared before the Environment Committee in late 1994 over whether to use river catchment areas or some other criteria (such as local authority boundaries) for the EA's regions. The chief executive of the NRA told the Select Committee that the NRA had thought:

very, very seriously about our response because we would obviously be thought guilty of not really seeing beyond the end of our noses simply to say we want river catchments because we already have them. In our view to manage rivers other than on river catchments introduces a degree of complexity into the organisation which would make it very, very much more costly and ineffective. We believe that issues of land management and air management can be handled much more easily with river catchments than rivers can be handled by different boundaries. (Environment Committee, *Environment Bill: Hearings on the Draft*

Environment Agencies Bill (House of Commons Papers, Session 1994–95, 40—i, ii and iii, p. 6.)

The functions of the WRAs, also transferred to the EA, were previously exercised by reference to local authority boundaries. The Chief Inspector and Director of HMIP preferred to see the EA's regional structure based on local authority areas. 'A local authority boundary, I think, is required for local accountability, local liaison, communication and in the way that HMIP runs, ownership of the patch, if you like, and that from the regulators is very important' (ibid., p. 9).

The NRA felt that the importance of local authority boundaries in achieving local accountability was overstated, and that the NRA had 'been able to work very satisfactorily with local authorities using river catchments' (ibid., p. 6).

The Environment Agency Advisory Committee subsequently made various recommendations to the Secretary of State regarding regional boundaries which in July 1995 were almost entirely accepted by him. Under the agreed recommendations, separate boundaries will apply in the case respectively of water management and pollution control. For water management, the regional boundaries will follow exactly the eight NRA regions, which are based on river catchments. For pollution control, the boundaries will be those eight regions modified to fit the county or district council boundary which is closest to the water management boundary. These 'pollution control' boundaries will, in practice, be the ones of which the public will be aware. The 'water management' boundaries are intended to be for internal management purposes.

The Advisory Committee recommended that the 'pollution control' boundary for Wales should extend to encompass the area of the proposed new Herefordshire unitary authority. The government did not accept this recommendation, preferring a boundary which exactly follows the boundary of the Principality.

2.8.2 Operational and regulatory functions

The question of how the EA should organise its regions is closely tied to the question of whether its operational functions should be carried out separately from its regulatory functions. The EA's regulatory functions of pollution control are thought by some to require separation from its operational activities (inherited from the NRA), such as in connection with water resources and flood defence, in order to avoid conflicts of interest. In the view of HMIP's Chief Inspector and Director:

> . . . it has long been recognised that there may be potential conflicts of interest in any large body which has to carry out activities and then has to regulate people for pollution caused by such activities. I think it is vital that the Agency's credibility is not undermined by allegations of self-policing. (Ibid., p. 8.)

The NRA wished to have operational and regulatory functions kept together, maintaining that the regulatory/operational dichotomy is not clear-cut. Again, to quote its Chief Executive:

> The functions which the NRA does in water resources and flood defence are operational. We do operate weirs and we do maintain flood defences but we also

regulate in those areas. In water resources we grant abstraction licences which is a regulatory activity, in flood defence we work with local councils on flood plain development planning controls and we also issue land drainage consents. On our operational side there is a regulatory aspect. There is also a regulatory aspect and an operational aspect on our pollution control activities. The pollution control officer who issues the licence for discharges also gives precautionary advice to the person who has the licence. He also does the enforcement and the prosecutions but when a pollution incident occurs he will also be out there oxygenating the water with specialist equipment and he will be controlling the flows and levels of the river. He does it because he can understand the physical situation on the ground. (Ibid., p. 3.)

The NRA also played the important 'costs' card.

We have done an investigation in our Welsh region which indicates that if we were to keep those two functions separate — a regulator who did not get too much on the ground and all these activities were contracted out to other organisations — we could add as much as 20 per cent to the operating costs of our organisation and that would be an extra £2 million a week if applied universally across the NRA's activities. (Ibid., loc. cit.)

2.8.3 Management structures

The DoE commissioned Touche Ross to identify and evaluate the various options for geographical and management structures of the EA and to assess the advantages and disadvantages of each. Their report was produced in June 1994 (Department of the Environment, *Options for the Geographical and Managerial Structure of the Proposed Environment Agency,* Touche Ross & Co., June 1994, deposited paper ns 348). The following options were identified:

Model A
— NRA, HMIP and WRAs continue to run in parallel;
— a new regional and national structure for waste;
— integration brought about by joint input in planning and policy at national level and regional (and sub-regional) co-operation;
Model B
— separation of operations and regulation;
— three 'field' directorates (Regulation, Flood Defence and River Basin Management);
— Environmental Quality Directorate for policy and planning;
— multimedia regulatory teams working to regional managers;
— common (local authority) boundaries.
Model C
— small head office with one policy-making directorate;
— single field or operations directorate;
— common (river catchment) boundaries;
— multi-disciplinary managers with multimedia teams;
— co-located staff with shared support resources.

Model D
— regulation and operations separate;
— two field directorates (Regulation and the rest);
— co-located regional offices
— representation at sub-regional level dependent on local need;
— single policy-making directorate;
— separate boundaries for regulation (local authority) and operations (river catchments);
— two stages of evolution for regulation: separate national teams for waste, water and IPC moving to multimedia teams.

Model E
— separate regulation and operations but brought together at head office level;
— multi-skilled industry-facing regulators;
— common boundaries: river catchments;
— co-located regulatory and operations staff;
— single policy-making directorate;
— facilities testing and market-testing of all operational functions.

Model A was never a likely candidate for adoption. Model B would have involved complete rejection of the NRA's arguments to the Environment Committee described above, including the (no doubt, to the government, telling) argument as to costs. Conversely, Model C would have involved rejection of the HMIP's arguments and would also have been unpopular with environmental lobby groups. Model D was always the most likely choice, particularly on grounds of cost and ease of implementation, although it risked jeopardising the 'one-stop shop' which was the major selling point for industry. As at the time of writing, the main management reporting lines have been decided in principle down to area manager level. Head office will be responsible for overall policy, with operational work being carried out almost entirely at area level, except where the operational unit is too small to be divided between areas. Regional general managers are to be responsible for delivering operational activities and for forming structural links between specialists at area and head office levels. The perceived advantages of this are the provision of policy coordination and quality assurance, as well as giving specialist staff a career structure, through area and region, to head office (Environment Agency Update, No. 5, August 1995).

2.9   THE EA'S ADVISORY COMMITTEES

2.9.1   Advisory Committee for Wales

Environment Act, s. 11 imposes upon the Secretary of State a duty to establish and maintain a committee for advising him with respect to matters affecting, or otherwise connected with, the carrying out in Wales of the EA's functions. The committee is to consist of such persons as may from time to time be appointed by the Secretary of State and must meet at least once a year (s. 11(2), (3)). In the House of Lords the Minister (Viscount Ullswater) acknowledged that:

the committee is likely to need to meet more than the minimum of once [a year] but of course the provisions do not preclude that. This requirement is based on the legislation under the Water Resources Act which the existing National Rivers Authority Advisory Committee for Wales operates. In practice, that committee usually meets around three or four times a year, as necessary. I think a similar flexibility would be most useful for the Advisory Committee for Wales. (Hansard, HL, 19 January 1995, col. 844.)

As to the composition of the committee, the Minister agreed:

> that the advisory committee for Wales will need to comprise a wide range of representative views, knowledge and experience relevant to the discharge of the agency's functions in Wales. Indeed, that will be vital for the committee to provide effective advice. Nature conservation and pollution control experience will be useful to the advisory committee, but they are only two of the numerous areas of expertise which it may need. My right honourable friend the Secretary of State for Wales has already committed himself to include locally elected members on the committee, as that is important to facilitate responsiveness to local needs. (Ibid., loc. cit.)

The government rejected calls during the passage of the Environment Bill for a separate agency for Wales. Although the option of separate English and Welsh agencies was considered in 1991 when the initial proposals to establish an environment agency were made, the government decided, after a wide-ranging consultation exercise, that a joint agency would be the most effective way to improve environmental protection across England and Wales. A joint agency has the benefit of cost-effectiveness, but the main reason given for the government's decision was that:

> the problems that the environment agency will need to address are common to both England and Wales and the agency will need to apply common solutions. A joint agency for England and Wales will operate to consistent standards of regulation throughout England and Wales, which has not been the case in the past under separate systems; for example, in the regulation of waste management by local authorities across England and Wales. (Hansard, HL, 17 January 1995, cols 602–3.)

2.9.2 Environment protection advisory committees

Environment Act, s. 12 (which came into force on 28 July 1995) requires the EA to establish and maintain environment protection advisory committees for the different regions of England and Wales. The EA must consult the advisory committee for any region on proposals relating generally to the manner in which the EA carries out its functions in that region, and consider any representations made to it by the committee (whether or not in response to such consultation) as to the manner in which the EA carries out its functions in that region.

The advisory committee for any region consists of a chairman appointed by the Secretary of State and such other members as the EA may appoint in accordance with the approved membership scheme for the region.

2.9.2.1   Approved membership schemes   Environment Act, sch. 3 sets out the requirements for approved membership schemes. The EA is required to prepare for each of its regions a scheme for the appointment of members of the advisory committee for that region. The EA submits the scheme to the Secretary of State for his approval before such date as may be specified in guidance issued by the Secretary of State. Each scheme must specify descriptions of bodies which, or persons who, appear to the EA likely to have a significant interest in matters likely to be affected by the way it carries out its functions in that region. It must also indicate how membership of the committee is to reflect the different descriptions of bodies or persons so specified, as well as specifying or describing the bodies or persons the EA proposes to consult on appointments to the committee. A scheme is not to come into force until it has been approved by the Secretary of State. On submitting a scheme, the EA must publish it in such a manner as it considers appropriate for the purpose of bringing it to the attention of people likely to be interested in it. The procedure contains opportunity for representations or objections to be made, and considered by the Secretary of State. The scheme, as approved, with or without modifications, must then be published in the manner just described.

2.9.2.2   Members of advisory committees   Environment Act, s. 12(4) provides that the members of the advisory committees must not be members of the EA, but must be persons who appear to the EA to have significant interests in matters likely to be affected by the manner in which the EA carries out any of its functions in the region of the advisory committee in question.

2.9.2.3   Requirements as to regions   Environment Act, s. 12(5) requires the EA to establish and maintain an advisory committee for each area which the EA considers it appropriate for the time being to regard as a region of England and Wales for the purposes of s. 12. The question of regions is discussed at 2.8.1 above. Section 12(6) ensures that one of these regions is to consist wholly or mainly of, or of most of, Wales.

2.9.3   Fisheries advisory committees

Environment Act, s. 13 requires the EA to establish and maintain regional and local fisheries advisory committees. These committees are described in chapter 6.

2.10   TRANSFER OF PROPERTY, RIGHTS AND LIABILITIES TO THE EA

On the transfer date, to be appointed by the Secretary of State for or in connection with Environment Act, ss. 1 to 19 (and which is expected to be 1 April 1996), all functions of the NRA and the London Waste Regulation Authority are transferred to the EA and those bodies are abolished. Accordingly, Environment Act, s. 3(1) provides that, on that date, the property, rights and liabilities of those bodies are to be vested in the EA.

Section 3(2) also confers power on the Secretary of State to make a scheme for the transfer to the EA of such of his property, rights or liabilities or those of HMIP as appear to him to be appropriate consequent on the transfer of functions under s. 2. Section 3(3) requires each WRA, other than the London Waste Regulation Authority, to make a scheme for such a transfer after consultation with the EA, and to submit it to the Secretary of State for approval. The Secretary of State may approve, modify or reject such a scheme and has default powers to make a scheme himself (s. 3(5), (6)). On 29 August 1995 the Secretary of State issued guidance to WRAs on the transfer of their functions, in the form of Circular 15/95, which includes a model transfer scheme at annex B.

Environment Act, sch. 2 contains supplementary provisions as to transfers of property etc. both under s. 3 and under s. 22, which contains provisions relating to the transfer of property, rights and liabilities to SEPA (see chapter 12).

Paragraph 2 of sch. 2 deals with the property, rights and liabilities which may be transferred by a transfer scheme. They include:

(a)   property, rights and liabilities that would not otherwise (that is to say, under private law principles) be capable of being transferred or assigned by the transferor;

(b)   property, rights and liabilities arising etc. between the making of the scheme and the transfer date;

(c)   property, wherever situated;

(d)   rights and liabilities under enactments (i.e., primary and subordinate legislation);

(e)   rights and liabilities under the law of any part of the UK or any foreign country or territory.

Paragraph 3 of sch. 2 provides for a transfer scheme to be able to transfer any rights or liabilities of the employer relating to contracts of employment of persons employed in the civil service, by a WRA in England and Wales or by a local authority in Scotland, whom it is necessary or expedient to transfer to the EA (or SEPA). Protection is provided for terms and conditions of employment, equivalent to that provided by transfers under the Transfer of Undertakings (Protection of Employment) Regulations 1981 (SI 1981/1794).

Paragraph 5 provides that a transfer scheme may create new rights, interests or liabilities relating to the transferor or the EA (or SEPA). Transfer schemes may be modified retrospectively by the Secretary of State (after due consultation) (para. 7), whilst para. 8 requires a chief inspector (i.e., of HMIP), WRAs, local authorities and their officers to provide the Secretary of State or the EA with such information as may be reasonably required in respect of transfer schemes. Paragraph 8(2) makes similar provision in the case of SEPA, in the case of the chief inspector for Scotland, any local authority or any officer of a local authority.

Supplementary provisions (in paras 10, 11 and 12) ensure the continuity of agreements etc., the translation of references to the transferor in deeds etc., as references to the EA (or SEPA), the continuation of legal proceedings (and generally as to the preservation of remedies) and the perfection of vesting of foreign property, rights and liabilities.

2.11   CONTINUITY OF EXERCISE OF FUNCTIONS

Environment Act, s. 55 ensures the necessary continuity of functions between the predecessor bodies of the EA and SEPA and those agencies. In particular, the abolition of the NRA, the London Waste Regulation Authority or a river purification board shall not affect the validity of anything done by that body before the date when it is abolished (s. 55(1)). Section 55 is not intended to deal with matters in respect of which transfer schemes have been made (see 2.10) but, rather, operates so as to ensure a smooth transition in the case of regulatory etc. matters. The Secretary of State has wide order-making powers to modify s. 55(1) to (6) in order to achieve this result (s. 55(7)). Reference should also be made to the transitional and transitory provisions contained in Environment Act, sch. 23.

Chapter 3
Water Resources

The water resources management functions of the NRA under Part II of the Water Resources Act 1991 (WRA 1991) are transferred to the EA by s. 2(1)(a)(i) of the Environment Act.

3.1 GENERAL DUTIES

As with the other functions of the EA, those functions relating to water resources are subject to the principal aim and objectives of the EA laid down under Environment Act, s. 4 including the objective of sustainable development. The EA must also pursue conservation and recreational aims under Environment Act, s. 6(1) besides being subject to general environmental and recreational duties under s. 7. The relevant provisions of ss. 4, 6 and 7 are described in chapter 11. The draft guidance issued in April 1995 (which, in its final form, will be issued under Environment Act, s. 4) sets out how the EA is expected by the government to exercise its water management and water resources functions. This Guidance is described in chapter 11.1.4.8 and 9.

Environment Act, s. 6(2) imposes a general duty on the EA specifically in relation to water resources. The EA must take all such action as it may from time to time consider (in accordance with any s. 40 directions) to be necessary or expedient for the purpose of conserving, redistributing or otherwise augmenting water resources in England and Wales, and of securing the proper use of water resources in England and Wales. This duty is not to be construed as relieving any water undertaker of the obligation to develop water resources under s. 37 of the Water Industry Act 1991, (WIA 1991) which imposes on those undertakers a general duty to maintain the water supply system.

Environment Act, s. 10 confers various incidental functions on the EA, including the supply of water in bulk (whether or not such supplies are provided for the purposes of, or in connection with, the carrying out of any other functions of the EA), the provision of houses and other buildings for the use of the EA's employees, and the provision of recreation grounds for such persons.

3.2 GENERAL MANAGEMENT FUNCTIONS

Under WRA 1991, Part II the EA has general management functions in respect of water resources, including the power to impose restrictions on abstraction and impounding of certain waters, through a licensing system which it administers.

Under WRA 1991, s. 20, the EA must, so far as reasonably practicable, enter into and maintain arrangements with water undertakers for securing the proper management or operation of waters available to those undertakers for the purposes of or the carrying out of their functions and any reservoirs, apparatus or other works belonging to, operated by or otherwise under the control of water undertakers for the purposes of etc. their functions. This duty applies to the extent that the EA regards such arrangements as appropriate for the purpose of its general functions under Environment Act, s. 6(2).

The EA has power under WRA 1991, ss. 21 and 22 in relation to minimum acceptable flows of inland waters (excluding certain types of lakes, ponds etc. which are within the definition of 'discrete waters' in s. 221(1)). The EA submits a draft statement to the Secretary of State containing provision for determining the minimum acceptable flow of the relevant waters (or provision for amending a previous statement). The EA must have regard to certain matters, including, in the light of its duties under Environment Act, ss. 6(1), 7 and 8, the character of the inland waters and their surroundings. It must also consult with particular bodies (such as any water undertaker having the right to abstract water from those waters), and must specify a flow which is not less than the minimum which it considers is needed for safeguarding public health and meeting the requirements of existing lawful uses such as agriculture, industry and water supply. WRA 1991, sch. 5 contains procedural provisions regarding statements on minimum acceptable flows, including the procedure whereby the Secretary of State may approve a draft statement (with or without modifications). WRA 1991, s. 22 empowers the Secretary of State to direct the EA to consider the minimum acceptable flow of particular inland waters and submit either a draft statement as described above, or a draft statement that no minimum acceptable flow ought to be determined or that no change in that flow is needed. Section 23 enables the EA to look at volume or levels instead of, or in addition to, flows.

The provisions of ss. 21 to 23 have never been used and at one stage the government were minded to repeal them on the basis that there were no reliable long-term river flow data to determine flows with the necessary accuracy, and that there was no consensus on what constitutes a minimum acceptable flow. The NRA in practice operated a non-statutory system of assessing minimum residual flow.

3.3   ABSTRACTION AND IMPOUNDING

Chapter II of Part II of the WRA 1991 concerns abstraction and impounding. The controls, exercisable now by the EA, extend to all inland waters, other than the River Tweed and certain parts of the River Esk and River Sark and of their tributaries (Environment Act, s. 6(3)), and make it an offence to abstract or impound without a licence from the EA.

WRA 1991, s. 24 creates the offence of unauthorised abstraction, whilst s. 25 makes similar provision with respect to the construction or alteration of impounding works (other than in discrete waters, as defined in s. 221(1)). Both sections make it an offence to fail to comply with the conditions or requirements of any licence to abstract or impound which may have been issued. The EA may give directions requiring any person who is abstracting water to give it such information regarding that abstraction as is specified in the directions (s. 201).

Certain exceptions exist to the system of control of abstraction just described:

(a)   Transfers of waters by navigation, harbour or conservancy authorities in the carrying out of their functions (s. 26).

(b)   Abstraction of small quantities of water (specified in s. 27 and qualified in s. 28).

(c)   Abstraction in the course of, or resulting from, land drainage operations or to prevent interference with any mining, quarrying, engineering, building or other operations or to prevent discharge to works resulting from such operations (s. 29). In certain circumstances the EA must be notified before the work begins, enabling the EA to serve a conservation notice requiring reasonable measures to be taken for conserving water (s. 30).

(d)   Abstraction by a vessel for use on it (s. 32(1)).

(e)   Abstraction for fire-fighting, testing and training (s. 32(2)).

(f)   Abstraction in the course of testing for and evaluating ground water with the consent of the EA and in accordance with its conditions (s. 32(3), (4)).

(g)   Abstraction authorised by an exemption order of the Secretary of State under s. 33 in respect of a specified source of supply on the application of the EA, or a navigation, harbour or conservancy authority.

3.4   LICENCES

Sections 34 to 69 of WRA 1991 contain the system of licences for abstraction or impounding (or a combined abstraction and impounding licence under s. 36).

Applications for licences must be made in the prescribed form (currently set out in the Water Resources (Licences) Regulations 1965 (SI 1965/534)) and, in the case of an abstraction licence, may be made only by a person who occupies land contiguous to the waters concerned or who will, when the licence is granted, have access to that land. In the case of abstraction from underground strata, the test is, broadly, whether the person occupies land consisting of those strata or will when the licence is granted (s. 35). Only the British Waterways Board may be licensed to abstract or impound inland waters which it owns or manages, except where the Secretary of State directs otherwise (s. 66). The EA itself may apply for a licence to the Secretary of State under regulations made under s. 64. Section 189 requires the EA to keep a register of abstraction and impounding licences.

3.4.1   Consideration of licence applications

Sections 38 to 40 of WRA 1991 govern the criteria for consideration by the EA of applications to it for licences. The EA may grant a licence containing such provisions as it considers appropriate or may refuse a licence (s. 38(2)). Before reaching a decision the EA must have regard to any written representations received before the end of the period specified in the newspaper and *London Gazette* notices which must be published in accordance with the requirements set out in s. 37. The EA must also have regard to the requirements of the applicant, so far as it considers these to be reasonable. Section 39 requires the EA to have regard to rights and privileges which are protected rights for the purposes of Chapter II of Part II. The EA cannot issue a licence which will derogate from protected rights, except with the consent of the person entitled to the right. Protected rights are:

(a)   Abstraction from any inland waters by or on behalf of an occupier of contiguous land where the abstraction is for use on a holding consisting of the contiguous land (with or without other land held with it) or for use on that holding for domestic purposes of the occupier's household and/or agricultural purposes other than spray irrigation. The abstraction is not protected if it exceeds 20 cubic metres in any 24-hour period (s. 27(3), (4), (6)).

(b)   Abstraction from underground strata by or on behalf of an individual as a supply for his or her household domestic purposes, again, unless it exceeds 20 cubic metres in any 24-hour period (s. 27(5), (6)).

(c)   Abstraction in accordance with an abstraction licence (s. 48(1)).

The grant of a licence which does adversely affect protected rights will not be invalid but the EA will be liable in damages for breach of statutory duty (s. 60).

WRA 1991, s. 39(2) requires the EA, in considering an application for abstraction from underground strata, to have regard to the requirements of existing lawful uses of water abstracted from those strata, whilst s. 40 requires it, in all cases, to take account of considerations of minimum acceptable flow (see s. 21).

3.4.2   Call-in of applications and appeals

Sections 41 and 42 of the WRA 1991 contain a mechanism whereby the Secretary of State can call in applications for licences to be dealt with by him, rather than the EA. Section 43 entitles an applicant who has been refused a licence by the EA (or where the EA has failed to determine the application), or who is dissatisfied with any conditions etc. attached to the licence, to appeal to the Secretary of State.

As a result of s. 114 of the Environment Act, the Secretary of State can delegate his functions of determining appeals under WRA 1991, s. 43 to an appointed person.

WRA 1991, s. 44 enables the Secretary of State to hold an inquiry or hearing before determining the appeal. The Secretary of State may order the EA to grant a licence which would derogate from protected rights without the owners' consent. In such a case the owner may proceed against the EA for damages under s. 60. The Secretary of State must, however, have regard to whether the licence would derogate from such rights, in reaching his decision, and he must also have regard to the reasonable requirements of the applicant and river flow.

3.4.3   Form, contents and effect of licences

WRA 1991, s. 46 makes provision for the form and content of licences. Abstraction licences must:

(a)   make provision as to the quantity of water authorised to be abstracted during the period or periods specified in the licence;

(b)   make provision as to the way in which that quantity is to be measured;

(c)   provide for determining what quantity is to be taken to have been abstracted during any such period;

(d)   indicate the means by which water is authorised to be abstracted;

(e)   (except where the licence is to the EA, a water or sewerage undertaker or other water supplier), specify the land on which, and purposes for which, the water is to be used;

(f)   state whether the licence is to remain in force until revoked or is to expire at a time specified in the licence.

The Secretary of State may specify in regulations further requirements as to the form of licences.

WRA 1991, s. 47(1) also requires a licence to abstract or impound to specify the person to whom it is granted.

An impounding licence is entirely personal to the holder, whereas an abstraction licence may run with the land in question in certain circumstances (ss. 49, 50). Environment Act, sch. 22, para. 35 corrects an error in WRA 1991, s. 50, which had the unintended effect of restricting the 'succession' provisions where a licence holder occupied only part of the land specified in the licence.

A licence holder is entitled, under s. 48, to abstract or impound water in accordance with the licence and has a defence in an action brought against him (otherwise than for negligence or breach of contract) by a third party in respect of that abstraction or the consequent abstraction etc. caused by the impounding.

3.4.4   Modification etc. of licences

Licences may be modified or revoked, at the request of the licence holder (s. 51) or at the initiative of the EA or at the direction of the Secretary of State (s. 52). If the EA proposes to revoke or vary the licence, and the licence holder objects within the period for consultation, the EA must refer the matter to the Secretary of State for determination (s. 53) in accordance with the procedure set out in s. 54.

WRA 1991, s. 55 authorises a person who owns fishing rights to apply in certain circumstances to the Secretary of State to revoke or vary an abstraction licence, on the grounds that the owner of fishing rights has sustained loss or damage directly attributable to abstraction in pursuance of the licence and either:

(a)   the owner is not entitled to a protected right (see above),

(b)   though entitled to a protected right, he has sustained loss or damage which is not attributable to the EA's breach of statutory duty under s. 60 in granting the licence or is in addition to any loss or damage which is so attributable.

The owner must notify both the licence holder and the EA, who can make representations to the Secretary of State. The Secretary of State may hold an inquiry or hearing as he thinks fit and, in any event, shall not revoke or vary the licence unless he finds the grounds of the application have been substantiated and he is satisfied that the extent of the loss or damage which the fishing right holder has sustained is such as to justify revocation or variation. The Secretary of State is also required not to revoke or vary if the loss or damage was wholly or mainly attributable to exceptional shortage of rain, accident or other unforeseen act or event not caused by, and outside the control of, the EA (s. 56).

Licences may be varied so as to impose a temporary restriction on licence holders for abstraction for use in spray irrigation, in the case of exceptional shortage of rain (s. 57).

Section 58 (which empowered the NRA to revoke licences for non-payment of charges) is repealed by para. 136 of sch. 22 to the Environment Act. The EA is given a general power by Environment Act, s. 41(6) to suspend or revoke an environmental licence (which includes licences under WRA 1991, Part II) in accordance with the appropriate procedure, if the charges due and payable in respect of that licence have not been paid.

Where a licence is revoked or varied in pursuance of WRA 1991, s. 54 or s. 55, compensation is payable for abortive expenditure or other loss or damage directly attributable to the revocation or variation under s. 61.

The right to compensation arises where the modification is in pursuance of a direction by the Secretary of State. The owner of fishing rights is entitled to similar compensation under s. 62 if the Secretary of State decides under the s. 55 procedure not to revoke or vary the abstraction licence which the fishing rights owner has challenged. Section 63 empowers the Secretary of State to indemnify the EA where the latter has paid damages under s. 60 to any person in consequence of its compliance with a direction given by the Secretary of State (see 3.4.2).

WRA 1991, s. 64 deals with the situation where the EA itself wishes to abstract or impound water. Regulations provide for the provisions of Chapter II of Part II to have effect with modifications, whereby (inter alia) licences are granted by the Secretary of State.

For the system of charges for licences see 3.7 below.

3.5 DROUGHT ORDERS AND PERMITS

3.5.1 Drought orders

Chapter III of Part II of WRA 1991 relates to drought orders.

Schedule 22 to the Environment Act makes certain substantive changes to the drought order process. As amended by para. 139 of that schedule, WRA 1991, s. 73 empowers the Secretary of State to make a drought order if he is satisfied that, by reason of exceptional shortage of rain, there exists or is threatened:

(a)   a serious deficiency of supplies of water in any area, or

(b)   such a deficiency in the flow or level of water in any inland waters as to pose a serious threat to any of the flora or fauna which are dependent on those waters (s. 73(1)(a) and (b)).

A drought order shall not be made except on an application by the EA or, except in a s. 73(1)(b) case, by a water undertaker.

An 'ordinary' drought order made on the application of the EA may authorise the EA to take water from any specified source, discharge water to any specified place, or prohibit the taking of water from a specified source if it is satisfied that the taking of water from that source seriously affects the EA's supplies, or those of any other supplier, besides suspending or modifying consents for the discharge of effluent.

An 'emergency' drought order made on the application of the EA may contain any of the provisions that can be contained in an ordinary order but, if applied for by a water undertaker, an emergency order can also authorise that undertaker to

prohibit or limit the use of water for such purposes as the water undertaker thinks
fit and to supply water by means of standpipes and water tanks (s. 75).

WRA 1991, s. 77(3) provides that where a drought order is made on the
application of a water undertaker which confers power on the EA to prohibit or
limit the taking of water from any source or to suspend or vary, or attach conditions
to, any consent for the discharge of any effluent, the EA shall exercise this power
in such manner as will ensure that, so far as reasonably practicable, the supplies
of water available to the undertaker are not seriously affected. A drought order may
authorise the EA to carry out works required for the performance of any duty it
has under the order and to enter and occupy land for that purpose (s. 78).
Compensation is payable in accordance with sch. 9 where a drought order has been
made.

3.5.2 Drought permits

WRA 1991, s. 79A (inserted by para. 140 of sch. 22 to the Environment Act)
contains a new system of drought permits, whereby if the EA is satisfied that, by
reason of an exceptional shortage of rain, a serious deficiency of water supplies in
any area exists or is threatened, the EA may (on application by a water undertaker
in that area) issue to that undertaker a drought permit making such provision as
appears to the EA to be expedient for meeting the deficiency.

A drought permit may authorise the water undertaker to take water from a source
specified in the permit and suspend or modify any restriction or obligation to which
the undertaker is subject as respects the taking of water from any source. A drought
permit is limited to a maximum duration of six months which may be extended so
as finally to expire not later than one year from the date on which it came into
force. Where a drought permit affects a source from which water is supplied to an
inland navigation, the consent of every navigation authority for the canal or inland
navigation is required before the permit may be issued. The procedure for using
drought permits follows that in WRA 1991, sch. 8 for drought orders and the
compensation provisions in WRA 1991, s. 79 and sch. 9 also apply to drought
permits.

For the purposes of WRA 1991, ss. 125 to 129 (which make provision as to
charges) water abstracted under a drought permit is treated as if it had been
abstracted under an abstraction licence, whether the undertaker has such a licence
or not.

3.5.3 Offences

It is an offence to fail to comply with a prohibition or limitation imposed by or
under a drought order or a drought permit or otherwise to fail to comply with such
an order or permit (WRA 1991, s. 80, as amended by para. 141 of sch. 22 to the
Environment Act).

3.6   LAND AND WORKS POWERS

The EA has power under Environment Act, s. 37 to do anything which is calculated
to facilitate, or is conducive or incidental to, the carrying out of its functions. By

virtue of WRA 1991, s. 158 those powers include power to enter into an agreement with any water or sewerage undertaker, local authority or joint planning board, or the owner or occupier of land, with respect to works, whereby the other party carries out and maintains works which the EA considers necessary for its water resource management functions. The Secretary of State may require certain agreements to have his consent before they are entered into by the EA. Powers to acquire land by agreement or compulsorily are conferred by WRA 1991, s. 154, and the EA also enjoys powers to lay pipes (ss. 159 and 160) and to enter land for the purposes of enforcement and of certain works (ss. 169 and 170)

3.7   BYELAWS

The EA has power (subject to Ministerial confirmation) to make byelaws for regulating the use of certain inland waters under WRA 1991, sch. 25, para. 1. Byelaws may prohibit the use of such waters for boating, swimming or other recreational purposes (para. 1(1)(a)). This power is subject to the EA's general recreational duties described in 3.9 below.

3.8   FINANCIAL PROVISIONS

3.8.1   Water resource charges

Environment Act, s. 41(1)(a) enables the EA to require payment to it of such charges as may from time to time be prescribed by a scheme in respect of abstraction and impounding licences under Part II of the WRA 1991. The provisions (ss. 123 and 124) of the WRA 1991 which provided for charging schemes are repealed and replaced by Environment Act, ss. 41 and 42. These provisions (which also apply to other environmental licences) are described in chapter 15.

WRA 1991, s. 125 exempts water abstracted for producing electricity from water resource charges (other than for the EA's administrative expenses in relation to the licence application). Water authorised by licence to be abstracted from underground strata is also exempt, provided it is not for spray irrigation nor exceeds 20 cubic metres in any 24 hours. Section 126 empowers the EA to agree exemptions from water resources charges, subject to the supervision of the Secretary of State.

Special charges may be levied under WRA 1991, s. 127 in respect of spray irrigation, following an application by a licence holder. Such agreements allow for charges to be payable partly in respect of basic charges calculated by reference to the quantity of water authorised to be abstracted, and partly on the quantity measured or assessed as being abstracted. Either party may refer disputes to the Secretary of State (s. 129). Special provisions may also be agreed (or imposed by the Secretary of State) in the case of abstractions by the British Waterways Board (s. 130).

3.8.2   Contributions between EA and other authorities

WRA 1991, s. 120 requires the EA to contribute towards expenditure incurred or to be incurred by a navigation, harbour or conservancy authority, where it appears to the EA that works constructed or to be constructed by that authority have made, or will make, a beneficial contribution towards the EA's water resources functions.

Section 120 also makes corresponding provision for the opposite situation, i.e., where the EA's works have contributed or will contribute to another authority's functions. The Secretary of State has powers to settle certain disputes.

3.9   ENVIRONMENTAL AND RECREATIONAL DUTIES

The provisions, formerly contained in WRA 1991, ss. 16 to 18, which imposed various environmental and recreational duties on the NRA, are repealed by the Environment Act, since that Act itself imposes very similar general duties on the EA, besides some important additional duties. Environment Act, s. 4 establishes as the principal aim of the EA, in discharging its functions, so to protect the environment, taken as a whole, as to make a contribution towards attaining the objective of achieving sustainable development. Environment Act, s. 6 contains general duties with respect to water, including the conservation and enhancement of the natural beauty of inland waters and land associated with such waters, the conservation of flora and fauna which are dependent on an aquatic environment and the use of inland waters for recreational purposes. Environment Act, s. 7 imposes general environmental and recreational duties on the EA in very similar terms to former WRA 1991, s. 16. Environment Act, s. 8 imposes special duties in the case of sites of special scientific interest notified by England Nature or the Countryside Council for Wales (based on former WRA 1991, s. 17). Environment Act, s. 9, like former WRA 1991, s. 18, deals with environmental codes of practice. These general aims and duties are described in more detail in chapter 11.

3.10   PROMOTION OF EFFICIENT USE OF WATER

Environment Act, sch. 22, para. 102, amends the Water Industry Act 1991 by inserting an entirely new Part IIIA, consisting of four sections (93A to 93D) for the purpose of ensuring that water undertakers promote the efficient use of water by their customers. Section 93A imposes such a duty on every water undertaker, to be enforced by the Secretary of State or the Director General of Water Services (with the Secretary of State's consent). Section 93B enables the Director to set standards of performance, where necessary, after taking account of the water resource situation in the undertaker's area and after consultation with the under-taker. The Director may arrange for the requirements he sets under s. 90B to be publicised (s. 93C) whilst s. 93D enables the Director to require the undertaker to inform the public of the undertaker's level of performance.

The minister said in the House of Lords on 11 July 1995 that the government expects the standards of performance:

to include the offering to customers of facilities, such as a low-cost voluntary metering scheme, and information on water use, which will enable them to make informed choices about how to use water efficiently. But there will be no compulsion on customers. The tone is one of encouragement. There is a dearth of information about the efficient use of water available to customers. Inefficient use of water will lead to requirements for new resources to be developed, the construction of new or expanded water treatment and waste water treatment plant and a consequent increase in customers' bills to pay for all that capital expenditure. I believe that the proposals here will help to inform customers and lead to a reduction in water use. Hansard, HL, 11 July 1995, col. 1651.)

Chapter 4
Water Pollution Control

Section 2(1)(a)(ii) of the Environment Act transfers to the EA the NRA's pollution control functions under Part III of the Water Resources Act 1991 (WRA 191). Subsections 2(1)(h) and (2)(b) of s. 2 transfer to the EA the Secretary of State's functions under Chapter III of Part IV of the Water Industry Act 1991 (WIA 1991) in relation to special category effluent (other than any function of making regulations or orders under WIA 1991, s. 139).

In addition to these specific water pollution functions, the EA has important functions under the integrated pollution control (IPC) system of Part I of the Environmental Protection Act 1990 (EPA 1990), which covers land, air and water. The IPC system is described in Chapter 9. The draft Guidance issued in April 1995 (which, in its final form, will be issued under Environment Act s. 4) sets out how the EA is expected by the government to exercise its water protection and related functions. This Guidance is described in chapter 11.1.4.6.

Section 2(1)(h) and (2)(e) of the Environment Act, transfer to the EA the Secretary of State's functions under certain provisions of the Sludge (Use in Agriculture) Regulations 1989 (SI 1989/1263).

4.1 POLLUTION OF WATER RESOURCES

WRA 1991, Part III confers on the EA important responsibilities in relation to the pollution of water resources. Chapters I to IV of Part III deal respectively with water quality objectives, pollution offences, the prevention and control of pollution and various supplemental provisions with respect to water pollution.

4.1.1 Water quality objectives

Under WRA 1991, s. 82 the Secretary of State has power, in relation to various descriptions of controlled waters, to prescribe a system of classifying the quality of those waters according to specified criteria. Five sets of classifications have been made under this section in relation to England and Wales:—

(a)   Surface Waters (Classification) Regulations 1989 (SI 1989/1148);

(b)   Surface Waters (Dangerous Substances) (Classification) Regulations 1989 (SI 1989/2286);

(c) Surface Waters (Dangerous Substances) (Classification) Regulations 1992 (SI 1992/337);

(d) Bathing Waters (Classification) Regulations 1991 (SI 1991/1597);

(e) Surface Waters (River Ecosystem) (Classification) Regulations 1994 (SI 1994/1057).

For the purpose of maintaining and improving the quality of controlled waters, the Secretary of State may, under WRA 1991, s. 83, establish the water quality objectives for any waters which are, or are included in, waters for which classifications have been prescribed in the regulations. The objectives must be stated in a notice served on the EA which specifies the classifications to which the objectives apply and, for each classification, a date. It then becomes the duty of the Secretary of State and the EA to exercise their powers under the water pollution provisions of WRA 1991 in such a manner as to ensure that, so far as is practicable, the water quality objectives are achieved at all times (s. 84(1)). It is also the duty of the EA to monitor the extent of pollution in controlled waters for the purpose of carrying out its functions under WRA 1991 and to consult as appropriate with SEPA in Scotland.

4.1.2 Pollution offences

Chapter II of Part III of WRA 1991 creates offences relating to the pollution of controlled waters. WRA 1991, s. 85 creates six main offences:

(a) causing or knowingly permitting any poisonous, noxious or polluting matter or any solid waste matter to enter any controlled waters (s. 85(1));

(b) causing or knowingly permitting any matter, other than trade effluent or sewage effluent, to enter controlled waters by being discharged from a drain or sewer in contravention of a s. 86 prohibition (s. 85(2));

(c) causing or knowingly permitting the discharge of trade effluent or sewage effluent into controlled waters or by means of a pipe from land in England and Wales into the sea outside the limit of controlled waters (s. 85(3));

(d) causing or knowingly permitting any trade effluent to be discharged (in contravention of a s. 86 prohibition) from a building or any fixed plant on to or into any land or into any waters of a lake or pond which are not inland freshwaters (s. 85(4));

(e) causing or knowingly permitting any matter whatever to enter any inland freshwaters so as to tend to impede the proper flow of the waters in a manner leading, or likely to lead, to a substantial aggravation of pollution due to other causes or the consequences of such pollution (s. 85(5));

(f) contravening the conditions of any consent given under Chapter II (a 'discharge' consent) (s. 85(6)).

WRA 1991, s. 86 provides for the EA to issue prohibition notices for the purposes of s. 85. A person contravenes a prohibition notice by causing or knowingly permitting effluent to be discharged if the EA has given him notice prohibiting him from making or, as the case may be, continuing the discharge or the EA has given that person a notice prohibiting him from making or, as the case may be, continuing the discharge unless specified conditions are observed, and those conditions are not observed (s. 86(1)).

A discharge is also a contravention of a prohibition notice if it contains a prescribed substance or a prescribed concentration of such a substance or derives from a prescribed process or from a process involving the use of prescribed substances or the use of such substances in quantities which exceed the prescribed amounts (s. 86(2)). As at the date of writing, no substances, concentrations, amounts or processes have been prescribed for the purposes of s. 86(2).

WRA 1991, s. 87 provides that even if a discharging undertaker did not cause or knowingly permit a s. 85(3) or (4) discharge, he is deemed to have caused it in certain circumstances. WRA 1991, s. 88 is an important provision providing defences to the s. 85 offences. A person is not to be guilty of an offence under s. 85 if the entry or discharge occurs or is made under and in accordance with, or as a result of, any act or omission under and in accordance with certain specified consents, authorisations or licences. These are as follows:

(a)   a discharge consent under Chapter II or under Part II of the Control of Pollution Act 1974 (CPA 1974) (which makes corresponding provision for Scotland);

(b)   an authorisation for a prescribed process designated for central control under Part I of the Environmental Protection Act 1990, now given by the EA (see Chapter 9);

(c)   a waste disposal licence issued under s. 5 of the CPA 1974 or a waste management licence granted under Part II of the EPA 1990 (again, both types of licence are now to be granted by the EA — see Chapter 8);

(d)   a licence to 'dump' at sea issued by the Minister of Agriculture, Fisheries and Food (in England and Wales) under Part II of the Food and Environment Protection Act 1985;

(e)   discharges made under and in accordance with s. 163 of the WRA 1991 or s. 165 of the WIA 1991 (discharges for works purposes made respectively by (now) the EA and by a water undertaker);

(f)   discharges made under any local statutory provision or statutory order which expressly confers power to discharge effluent into water; or

(g)   any prescribed enactment (s. 88(1)).

4.1.3   Discharge consents

WRA 1991, s. 88(2) introduces sch. 10, which contains the procedure for making applications for discharge consents (see s. 88(1)(a)) and provisions for the giving, revocation and modification of consents.

An entirely new sch. 10 is substituted into WRA 1991 by para. 183 of sch. 22 to the Environment Act, to come into force when the EA takes over the NRA's functions. However, sch. 22, para. 182 amends the existing WRA 1991, sch. 10 (with effect from 21 September 1995) so as to enable the Secretary of State, in the intervening period, to direct the NRA to review all discharge consents or any description of such consents. Proposals are to be made to the Secretary of State by the NRA as to the modification of consents or the imposition of conditions on hitherto unconditional consents. The Secretary of State may give effect to the proposals (with or without his own modifications). These changes give effect to proposals for deregulation put forward for consultation in October 1993. They are also intended to increase consistency between the various legislative provisions across the range of the EA's functions.

The new WRA 1991, sch. 10 provisions are in many respects modelled on the corresponding provisions for authorisations in sch. 1 to the EPA 1990 and provide for a greater degree of delegation of the detailed requirements to regulations and directions (to be made by the Secretary of State) than was the case under the old sch. 10.

In essence, WRA 1991, sch. 10 now provides as follows:

(a)   Applications for discharge consents are made to the EA on a form provided by it and must be advertised by or on behalf of the applicant in such manner as may be required by regulations (para. 1(1)).

(b)   The applicant must provide such information as the EA may reasonably require and as may be prescribed by the Secretary of State, but, although a failure to provide information will entitle the EA not to proceed with the application, it will not invalidate the application and (hence) any licence granted in respect of it (paras 1(2) and 3(3)).

(c)   The EA must give notice of any application (and a copy of it) to the persons who are prescribed or directed to be consulted, but the Secretary of State may, by regulations, exempt any class of application from these requirements or exclude any class of information from these requirements (para. 2(1) and (2)).

(d)   Representations made within the period allowed must be considered by the EA (para. 2(3) to (5)).

(e)   The period allowed for making representations is six weeks from the giving of notice (for those prescribed or directed to be consulted) or from the advertisement of the application, in other cases, but the Secretary of State has power to alter these periods by regulations (para. 2(6) and (7)).

(f)   In the case of a properly made application the EA must decide whether to give consent, either unconditionally or subject to conditions, or to refuse it (para. 3(1)).

(g)   Conditions may be imposed in respect of a wide variety of matters, including the places for discharge, design and construction of outlets, nature, origin, composition, temperature, volume and rate of discharges, steps to be taken to minimise pollution, facilities for sampling and testing and keeping of records (para. 3(4)).

(h)   The failure of the EA to reach a decision within four months from receipt of the application or such other period as may be agreed may be treated as a refusal (thereby triggering the appeal machinery — see below). The Secretary of State may alter the four-month period by regulations (para. 3(2) and (5)).

(i)   The Secretary of State may direct the EA not to determine, or not to proceed to determine, an application or class of applications until the end of a specified period or until directed by the Secretary of State and he may direct the EA to transmit an application or applications to him, for his determination (paras 4 and 5(1)).

(j)   The Secretary of State has the power to hold an inquiry or hearing before determining the application and must do so if so requested by the applicant or the EA (para. 5(4) and (5)).

(k)   The Secretary of State, having determined the application (if properly made), must direct the EA to give or refuse consent or give it subject to specified conditions (para. 5(6)).

(l)   In certain circumstances, the EA may give consents without applications having first been made, in cases where unauthorised discharges have occurred, and may occur again (para. 6).

(m)   The EA may review consents and, by notice, revoke a consent, impose conditions or make modifications to it and may in particular revoke a consent where no discharge has taken place during the last 12 months (para. 7(1) to (3)).

(n)   The Secretary of State may direct the EA to revoke a consent, impose conditions or make modifications to it where it is appropriate to do so to enable the government to give effect to EC obligations or international agreements, for the protection of public health or of flora or fauna dependent on an aquatic environment or in consequence of any representations or objections made to him or otherwise. Compensation is payable by the EA if a person suffers loss or damage in certain cases where a direction is given in order to protect public health or aquatically dependent flora and fauna (para. 7(4) and (5)).

(o)   Consents of the EA under paras 3 or 6 must specify a period during which no notice may be served by the EA revoking or modifying consent (except if directed by the government in the case of EC or international obligations or to protect public health or flora and fauna, or if the holder of consent agrees to modifications). Except by agreement, the period is to be not less than four years. In certain cases, the EA may revoke or modify consent by notice served within three months of the period for making representations and objections with respect to the consent if the EA or the Secretary of State considers that notice should be served, as a result of any representations or objections received during that period (para. 8).

(p)   Paragraph 9 enables the Secretary of State to direct the EA to review all discharge consents or any description of such consents. Proposals are to be made by the EA to the Secretary of State as to modifications or other impositions of new conditions. These proposals may be given effect by the Secretary of State (with or without modifications).

(q)   The holder of a consent may apply, on a form provided by the EA, for a variation of consent.

(r)   A consent may be transferred:

(i)   to a person who proposes to carry on the discharges in place of the holder,

(ii)   as part of the personal estate of a deceased consent holder, or

(iii)   on the bankruptcy of a consent holder.

There are requirements as to the giving of notice to the EA, with penalties for failure to comply (paras 10, 11).

4.1.4   Further defences and offences

WRA 1991, s. 89 provides for other defences to the principal (i.e., s. 85) offence:

(a) *Emergency actions.* If the entry or discharge occurred in emergency in order to avoid danger to life and health, all reasonably practicable steps were taken to minimise the discharge, entry or pollution and the EA was notified as soon as reasonably practicable (s. 89(1)).

(b) *Vessels.* The discharge of trade or sewage effluent from a vessel is not an offence under s. 85 (s. 89(2)).

(c) *Water from abandoned mines.* A person is not guilty of an offence under s. 85 by reason only of his permitting water from an abandoned mine or an abandoned part of a mine to enter controlled waters, but by WRA 1991, s. 89(3A) (inserted by Environment Act, s. 60) this defence shall not apply to the owner or operator of any mine or part of a mine if the mine or part in question became abandoned after 31 December 1999. Environment Act, s. 58 also inserts a wholly new Chapter IIA (ss. 91A and 91B) into WRA 1991. These provisions, which include certain functions for the EA to perform, are described in chapter 17.

(d) *Solid refuse of mines and quarries.* A person is not guilty of an offence under WRA 1991, s. 85 by reason of depositing solid refuse of a mine or quarry on any land so that it falls or is carried into inland freshwaters if he deposits it with the consent of the EA, no other site is reasonably practicable and he takes all reasonably practicable steps to prevent the refuse from entering the inland freshwaters. This defence does not apply where the matter in question is poisonous, noxious or polluting (s. 89(4)).

(e) *Highway authorities.* A highway authority or other person entitled to keep open a drain under s. 110 of the Highways Act 1980 has a defence to a charge of causing or permitting a discharge to be made from the drain unless the discharge is made in contravention of a WRA 1991, s. 86 prohibition notice (s. 89(5)).

With WRA 1991, s. 90, we return from defences to offences. A s. 90 offence is committed by a person who removes from any part of the bottom, channel or bed of any inland freshwaters a deposit which has accumulated by reason of any dam, weir or sluice which holds back the waters, and causes the deposit to be carried away in suspension in the waters. Section 90 also makes it an offence (without the consent of the EA) to cause or permit a substantial amount of vegetation to be cut or uprooted in any inland freshwater or to be cut or uprooted so near to the waters that it falls into them, and in either case to fail to take all reasonable steps to remove the vegetation from those waters (s. 90(1) and (2)).

4.1.5 Consents under ss. 89 and 90

New ss. 90A and 90B are inserted into WRA 1991 by para. 142 of sch. 22 to the Environment Act. Section 90A (applications for consent under s. 89 or s. 90) concerns the procedure for making applications for consent for the purposes of s. 89(4)(a) (consent to deposit solid refuse of a mine or quarry — see above) and s. 90(1) and (2) (consent for removal of bottom etc. of freshwaters and deposit of vegetation — see above). Before the Environment Act no procedures had been laid down for making applications for such consents. The provisions of s. 90A are modelled on the new sch. 10 to WRA 1991 (discussed above). Any application for consent must be made on a form provided for the purpose by the EA and advertised in such manner as may be required by regulations made by the Secretary of State (subject to any exemptions specified in the regulations). Information must be provided, as reasonably required by the EA, and a failure to do so entitles the EA to refuse to proceed with the application.

4.1.6 Enforcement notices

WRA 1991, s. 90B confers on the EA a power to serve an enforcement notice on the holder of a 'relevant consent' (that is, a s. 89(4)(a) or s. 90(1) or (2) consent, or a discharge consent), if the EA considers the holder is contravening any condition of the consent, or is likely to contravene it.

Section 90B(2) provides that an enforcement notice shall specify the contravention or likely contravention and the steps to be taken to remedy the situation.

Penalties are specified for contravention of an enforcement notice (and these correspond to those in s. 85(6)). Section 90B(4) enables the Secretary of State to give the EA directions as to whether it should exercise its powers, and as to the steps that must be taken. Overall, s. 90B is modelled on s. 13 of the EPA 1990, which contains enforcement notice powers as part of the IPC system.

4.1.7 Appeals

Appeals in respect of consents under WRA 1991, Part III, Chapter II (that is to say discharge consents and consents under s. 89(4)(a) and s. 90) are dealt with in WRA 1991, s. 91, which is heavily amended by para. 143 of sch. 22 to the Environment Act. Appeals may be made against adverse decisions of the EA, except decisions made in pursuance of a direction of the Secretary of State. The changes made by the Environment Act include the introduction of a right to appeal against a refusal to vary a consent or, in allowing any such variation, making the consent subject to conditions (s. 91(1)(g)), and a right of appeal against an enforcement notice under s. 90B (s. 91(1)(h)). New subsections (2A) to (2K) of s. 91 are new procedural provisions. Subsection (2A) provides that s. 91 is subject to s. 114 of the Environment Act, which empowers the Secretary of State to delegate the determination of appeals to appointed persons. Subsection (2B) provides for appeals to be advertised as prescribed by regulations under subsection (2H). Subsection (2C) provides that if either party so requests, or the Secretary of State so decides, an appeal shall be or, if started, shall continue in the form of a hearing (which may be either wholly or partly in private).

New subsections (2D) and (2E) specify the powers of the Secretary of State in respect of the determination of appeals. If an appeal is against (a) the revocation of a discharge consent, (b) a decision to modify the conditions of a discharge consent or (c) a decision to provide that any such consent which was unconditional shall be subject to conditions, then the revocation etc. shall not take effect pending the final determination or withdrawal of the appeal (new s. 91(2F)). But subsection (2G) provides that this does not apply where the EA states in the notice that the revocation etc. is necessary for the purpose of preventing or minimising the entry into controlled waters of any poisonous, noxious or polluting matter or any solid waste matter, or preventing or minimising harm to human health. Compensation may be recovered, in certain circumstances, under subsection (2H) where the person determining the appeal determines that the EA acted unreasonably in making such a statement in the revocation etc. notice. Subsection (2J) provides that the bringing of an appeal against an enforcement notice shall not have the effect of suspending the operation of the notice. Subsection (2K) enables the Secretary of State to make regulations covering such matters as appeal periods and how appeals are to be considered.

4.1.8 Prevention and control of pollution

WRA 1991, s. 92 enables the Secretary of State to make regulations prohibiting the custody or control of poisonous, noxious or polluting matter unless prescribed works and precautions etc. have been carried out or taken to prevent or control the entry of the matter into controlled waters. The regulations may also require a person who already has custody etc. of such matter to carry out such works and take such precautions as may be prescribed (s. 92(1)).

Regulations may furthermore empower the EA to take precautionary action to prevent pollution (s. 92(2)) and may provide for appeals to the Secretary of State (subject to his power to delegate under s. 114 of the Environment Act — see above). The Control of Pollution (Silage, Slurry and Agricultural Fuel Oil) Regulations 1991 (SI 1991/324) have been made under this section.

WRA 1991, s. 93 also aims at anticipating and preventing water pollution. It enables the Secretary of State to designate areas as water protection zones and to prohibit or restrict the carrying on in that area of such activities as may be specified or described in the order. Where an order is made, wide powers may be conferred on the EA under s. 93(4), e.g., to determine in what circumstances activities may be carried on and to give consents.

WRA 1991, s. 96 enables the Secretary of State to make regulations for the purposes of orders under s. 93 which require the consent of the EA so as to make provision for applications for such consent, conditions, revocation or variation and appeals (subject to s. 114 of the Environment Act). Section 97 enables Ministers to approve codes of good agricultural practice, the actual or likely contravention of which the EA must take into account in deciding whether to impose a prohibition notice or when exercising any powers given them by regulations under s. 92.

4.1.9 Registers

WRA 1991, s. 189 and s. 190 require the EA to keep a register of abstraction and impounding licences, and a register of pollution control matters. Section 190 is expanded by Environment Act, sch. 22, para. 169 to include additional matters such as enforcement notices, revocations, appeals, works notices (see below) and certain pollution convictions. New ss. 191A and 191B (added by Environment Act, sch. 22, para. 170) provide for the exclusion from registers of information affecting national security and certain commercially confidential information.

4.1.10 Supplementary

WRA 1991, s. 99 enables the Secretary of State to modify the water pollution provisions of Chapter II in the case of consents required by the EA and discharges by the EA. The Control of Pollution (Discharges by the National Rivers Authority)

Regulations 1989 (SI 1989/1157) provided that consents required by the NRA shall be given by the Secretary of State instead of the NRA. As a result of the Environment Act these regulations now apply to the EA.

4.2 ANTI-POLLUTION WORKS AND OPERATIONS

The Environment Act amends the provisions relating to anti-pollution works and operations in WRA 1991 and introduces a system of notices whereby third parties can be required to carry out such works.

WRA 1991, s. 161 enables the EA itself to carry out anti-pollution works and operations. Under s. 161(1) where it appears to the EA that any poisonous, noxious or polluting matter or any solid waste matter is likely to be or to have been in, controlled waters the EA may carry out preventative or, as the case may be, removal or remedial etc. works, or works of restoration (including of flora and fauna). Environment Act, sch. 22, para. 161, amends WRA 1991, s. 161 so that the above powers will henceforth be exercisable only when the EA considers that works or operations are required forthwith, or no person can be found on whom a notice under WRA 1991, new s. 161A can be served. It should, however, be noted that under WRA 1991, new s. 161D, the EA may carry out the works which a person on whom a notice has been served fails to carry out, and may recover the costs of so doing from that person.

Environment Act, sch. 22, para. 162 inserts new ss. 161A to 161D into WRA 1991. Under s. 161A the EA may serve a 'works notice' in the same circumstances as those described in s. 161(1). The notice is to be served on the person who caused or knowingly permitted the poisonous etc. matter to be present in the controlled waters or in a place from which such entry is likely. Regulations may prescribe the form or content of notices and other details, and notices are not to be served where the required works would prevent or impede a discharge under a discharge consent, nor in the case of water from certain abandoned mines.

WRA 1991, new s. 161B enables a works notice to require a person to carry out works etc., notwithstanding that he is not entitled to carry them out, and a third party to give that person the necessary rights to carry out those works. In those circumstances, compensation to the third party is payable by the person carrying out the works.

WRA 1991, new s. 161C enables appeals to be made to the Secretary of State against works notices within 21 days of such notices being served. Again, the details of the system are left to regulations. New s. 161D provides that it is an offence to fail to comply with a works notice. The offence is triable either way, with a maximum of three months' imprisonment and/or a £20,000 fine in the case of summary conviction.

Under WRA 1991, s. 162 the EA has additional powers on its own land (or over which it has the necessary rights) to construct and maintain drains, sewers etc. for intercepting, treating or disposing of foul water arising or flowing on that land or otherwise preventing pollution.

4.3 SPECIAL CATEGORY EFFLUENT

Under WRA 1991, s. 87(3) a person is not guilty of an offence under s. 85 (see above) in respect of a discharge into a sewer if the sewerage undertaker was bound to receive the discharge there either unconditionally or subject to conditions which were observed. Chapter III of Part IV of the WIA 1991 contains the mechanism whereby a person may obtain consent to discharge trade effluent into a sewer. Under WIA 1991, s. 118 the occupier of trade premises may discharge trade effluent from those premises into the undertaker's public sewers if he has the undertaker's consent. To do so without consent is an offence. Applications for consent must be made under WIA 1991, s. 119 by notice to the undertaker concerned.

A special set of requirements apply where the application relates to 'special category effluent'. This expression is defined in WIA 1991, s. 138, basically as effluent which contains prescribed substances or such substances in prescribed concentrations, or which is effluent from prescribed processes or from processes that use prescribed substances or such substances in excess of prescribed amounts. See the Trade Effluents (Prescribed Processes and Substances) Regulations 1989 (SI 1989/1156, as amended by SI 1990/1629) and the Trade Effluent (Prescribed Processes and Substances) Regulations 1992 (SI 1992/339).

In the case of applications involving special category effluent, the undertaker must now refer to the EA the questions whether the discharges to which the notice relates should be prohibited and, if not, whether any requirements should be imposed as to the conditions on which they are made (WIA 1991, s. 120(1)).

Under WIA 1991, new s. 120(9) it is an offence for an undertaker to fail to comply with its duty to refer any question to the EA. Under new s. 120(10), if the EA becomes aware of such a failure, it may review (under ss. 127 or 131) any consent which has been given or, in any other case, proceed as if the undertaker had in fact referred the matter as he is supposed to do. These new subsections are inserted by the Environment Act, sch. 22, para. 105.

A wide range of conditions may, under WIA 1991, s. 121, be attached to consents, but a person aggrieved may appeal against a condition (or a refusal) to the Director General of Water Services under s. 122. Appeals in respect of special category effluent are, however, subject to special provisions contained under s. 123, which restrict the Director's powers so that he cannot overturn the decision unless and until reference has been made to the EA. Under s. 127 the EA has powers to review consents relating to special category effluent in order to determine whether the discharges should in fact be prohibited and, if not, whether any requirements should be imposed as to the conditions on which they are made.

WIA 1991, section 129 enables an undertaker to enter into agreements with the owner or occupier of trade premises for the reception and disposal by the undertaker of trade effluent or for the removal of substances produced in the course of treating trade effluent. Where the proposed agreement relates to special category effluent, the undertaker must refer to the EA questions of the kind described above. WIA 1991, new s. 130(7) makes it an offence for a sewerage undertaker to fail to comply with this duty. If the EA becomes aware of such a failure, it may exercise its powers to consider or review questions relating to the discharge (Environment Act, sch. 22, para. 108).

WIA 1991, s. 131 enables the EA to review the questions described above where an agreement is in force in respect of special category effluent. The EA's powers on references and reviews under WIA 1991, ss. 120, 123, 127, 130 or 131 are set out in s. 132. The EA is required to afford the undertaker, discharger or intended discharger an opportunity to make representations or objections and to consider these, before making a formal determination. The power of entry under s. 132(7) is repealed, since the EA's general powers of entry are now contained in ss. 108 to 110 of the Environment Act (see chapter 14).

Where a sewerage undertaker is served by the EA with notice under WIA 1991, s. 132, it is the duty of the undertaker and, in certain cases, the Director, to secure compliance with the notice (s. 133). An undertaker who fails to do so is guilty of an offence (new s. 133(5) and, in such circumstances, the EA may itself vary or revoke the consent or agreement (new s. 133(6)).

Compensation is payable by the EA under WIA 1991, s. 134 in respect of loss or damage sustained as a result of notices under s. 132 served in certain circumstances.

WIA 1991, s. 135A enables the EA, for the purpose of discharging its functions under WIA 1991, Chapter III, to serve a written notice requiring a person to supply any information it reasonably considers necessary. It is an offence to fail to comply, or to make false or misleading statements (Environment Act, sch. 22, para. 113).

4.4 OTHER FUNCTIONS UNDER THE WATER INDUSTRY ACT 1991

Schedule 22 to the Environment Act also confers upon the EA the NRA's functions under WIA 1991. These functions (which primarily involve being consulted) occur in ss. 3, 5, 40, 40A, 71 and 110A.

4.5 PROVISION OF SEWERS BY SEWERAGE UNDERTAKERS

Environment Act, sch. 22, para. 103 inserts new s. 101A into WIA 1991 so as to impose upon sewerage undertakers a further duty (in addition to that under WIA 1991, s. 98) to provide a public sewer to be used for domestic sewerage purposes of premises in a particular locality that are not connected with a public sewer where there are adverse effects (e.g., smells and nuisance) to the environment or amenity from the existing system and where the provision of the first-time connection of the premises to mains sewerage is the most cost-effective solution. In the event of any dispute, there is a right to apply to the EA to rule on whether there is a case for extending the mains sewerage network. The new duty only relates to existing properties (as at 20 June 1995).

4.6 SEWAGE SLUDGE

The Sludge (Use in Agriculture) Regulations 1989 (SI 1989/1263) implement Directive 86/278/EEC on the protection of the environment where sewage sludge is used in agriculture. A sewage sludge producer is required by reg. 6 to keep a register containing various specified particulars relating to sewage sludge, including details of the persons to whom it was supplied. The producer must keep the register available for inspection by the EA at all reasonable times and must furnish the EA with such information and facilities as it may reasonably require, including facilities for analysis (reg. 7(1)). The sludge producer must notify the EA in writing of the address and area of every dedicated site (see reg. 2(1)) to which he supplies sludge. The EA may in certain circumstances request the testing of soil under sch. 2.

Chapter 5
Flood Defence and Land Drainage

The flood defence and land drainage functions of the NRA under Part IV of the Water Resources Act 1991 (WRA 1991) and the Land Drainage Act 1991 (LDA 1991) are transferred to the EA by Environment Act, s. 2(1)(a)(iii), as are the functions that were transferred to the NRA by virtue of s. 136(8) of, and para. 1(3) of sch. 15 to, the Water Act 1989 (WA 1989) (transfer of land drainage functions under local legislation). Environment Act, s. 6(4) imposes on the EA a duty to exercise a general supervision over all matters relating to flood defence in England and Wales.

5.1 MEANING OF 'DRAINAGE'

'Drainage' in WRA 1991 is defined (in s. 113(1)) as including defence against water, including sea water, irrigation other than spray irrigation and warping. The expression thus encompasses both coastal and inland flood defence. The same definition of 'drainage' is found in LDA 1991, s. 72(1).

Environment Act, s. 100 (which came into force on 21 September 1995) amends both definitions in order to make it clear that the flood defence powers of the EA and the land drainage powers of internal drainage boards and local authorities (see below) include the management of water levels. In each case a new para. (d) is inserted, covering 'the carrying on, for any purpose, of any other practice which involves management of the level of water in a watercourse'.

5.2 FLOOD DEFENCE COMMITTEES

The EA's flood defence and land drainage functions are (as was the case with the NRA) to be carried out by regional flood defence committees. So the EA's functions are performed, in relation to the area of each regional flood defence committee, by the committee for that area, and, in cases involving the areas of more than one regional flood defence committee, by such committee, or jointly by such committees, as may be determined in accordance with arrangements made by the EA (WRA 1991, s. 106(1)). These committees do not, however, handle the EA's functions of issuing levies or drainage charges (s. 106(2)). The EA may give regional flood defence committees directions of a general or specific character

(s. 106(3)). The EA's flood defence functions extend to the territorial sea adjacent to England and Wales in so far as the area of any regional flood defence committee includes any area of the territorial sea, or in so far as WRA 1991, s. 165(2) or (3) provides for the exercise of works powers for flood defence and drainage in the territorial sea (Environment Act, s. 6(5)).

5.2.1 Regional flood defence committees

The regional flood defence committees are established by Environment Act, s. 14. Section 14(2) provides that (subject to sch. 4) there shall be a regional flood defence committee for each of the areas for which there was an old committee (under the WRA 1991) immediately before the transfer of functions under Environment Act, s. 2 to the EA, but where any function of the EA falls to be carried out at a place beyond the seaward boundaries of the committee's area, that place shall be assumed to be within the area of the committee whose area is adjacent to the area where that place is situated. The EA is required to maintain a principal office for each regional flood defence committee's area (s. 14(3)). Environment Act, sch. 4 makes provision for regional flood defence committee areas as were contained in sch. 3 to the WRA 1991 to be altered or amalgamated by ministerial order. Where orders are proposed, provision is made by sch. 4 for advertisement, objections, consideration of objections by the relevant Minister and, in certain cases, the application of special Parliamentary procedure (para. 4).

Environment Act, s. 15 deals with the composition of regional flood defence committees. Each committee is to comprise a chairman, a number of members appointed by the relevant Minister (Secretary of State for Wales or the Minister of Agriculture, Fisheries and Food in England), and a number of members appointed by or on behalf of the 'constituent councils' (i.e., the local authorities for any part of a committee's area). None of the committee's members may be members of the EA. By s. 15(2) any person who, immediately before the transfer date was the chairman or a member of a regional flood defence committee is to continue in office for the rest of the period for which he was appointed as if he had been duly appointed a chairman or member of the new committee. Unless any changes have been made under sch. 4, the total number of members of each new committee is to be the same as the total of the corresponding old committee (s. 15(3)).

Where constituent councils are to make joint appointments (following the previous arrangements or because of changes under s. 16) but they cannot agree, the relevant Minister shall appoint the member or members concerned (s. 15(4)).

The relevant Minister or constituent council (but not the EA) must, in making appointments, have regard to the desirability of appointing a person who has experience of, and has shown capacity in, some matter relevant to the functions of the committee. This may not necessarily be flood defence itself but could, for example, include agriculture or nature conservation.

Environment Act, s. 16 deals with changes of composition of regional flood defence committees. It enables the EA to make a determination varying the number of members of a regional flood defence committee (subs. (1)). There must not be fewer than 11 members of a committee (subs. (2)(a)) and if the EA determines that a committee should consist of more than 17 members, the determination will take effect only if the relevant Minister makes an order to that effect (subss. (3)(b), (4)).

The relevant Minister may also, by order, vary the number of members appointed by constituent councils where changes in circumstances so require, provided that the total of Ministerial appointees and EA appointees (combined) is one less than the total number appointed by constituent councils (subss. (5) to (7)). Environment Act, s. 16 is based on WRA 1991, s. 11, which is repealed.

5.2.2 Local flood defence committees

Environment Act, s. 17 provides for the creation, by schemes, of local flood defence districts within the area of a regional flood defence committee. The scheme may provide for the constitution, membership, functions and procedure of a committee for each such district (a 'local flood defence committee') (subs. (1)). Existing local flood defence schemes, whether made under WRA 1991, s. 12 (which is repealed) or under previous legislation, continue in force as if created under Environment Act, s. 17, as do existing local flood defence committees (s. 17(2)). A regional flood defence committee may submit to the EA a local flood defence scheme for any part of its area, where a scheme is not already in force, or it may submit a scheme to vary or revoke an existing scheme or replace it with another scheme (subs. (3)).

There is an obligation for the regional flood defence committee to consult local authorities for the area of the proposed scheme, as well as organisations representative of persons interested in flood defence, before submitting a scheme to the EA (subs. (4)). The EA must send any submitted scheme to one of the Ministers, who may approve it with or without modifications and, if so, shall specify a date for its carrying into force (subss. (5), (8)). Subsection (6) provides for a scheme to define the district by reference to districts that were local land drainage districts immediately before 1 September 1989 (the date of the establishment of the NRA), or by reference to the area of the regional flood defence committee in question, by reference to a map, or by any combination of these means. Environment Act, s. 17 is based upon former WRA 1991, s. 12.

Environment Act, s. 18 provides for the composition of local flood defence committees as established in local flood defence schemes under s. 17. A local flood defence scheme must specify that each local flood defence committee shall consist of not less than 11 nor more than 15 members, but a regional flood defence committee can recommend to the EA (in its submitted scheme) that a local flood defence committee should comprise more than 15 members (s. 18(1), (2)). Section 18(3) provides that the power confirmed on Ministers by s. 17(8) includes a power to direct that the size of a local flood defence committee in a scheme submitted with such a recommendation should be the recommended number or some other number greater than 15.

The chairman of a local flood defence committee shall be one of the members of the regional committee, appointed by them, and the local committee shall also comprise other members appointed by the regional committee, as well as members appointed by or on behalf of constituent councils (in accordance with the scheme) (s. 18(4)). The number of members appointed by or on behalf of constituent councils must be one more than the total appointed by the regional committee (s. 18(5)). The regional committee must have regard to the desirability of appointing those with relevant experience and who have shown some capacity in some relevant matter (s. 18(6)). Section 18(7) provides for existing chairmen and members of local flood defence committees to be treated as if they had been duly appointed by a s. 17 scheme.

Environment Act, s. 18 is based on former WRA 1991, s. 13.

5.2.3   Membership and proceedings of flood defence committees

Environment Act, s. 19 introduces sch. 5 which provides for the terms of membership and proceedings of regional and local flood defence committees, and other formal matters, some of which are similar to those contained in sch. 1 in the case of the EA. Schedule 5 is based upon WRA 1991, sch. 4 (which is repealed).

5.3   LAND DRAINAGE ACT 1991

Responsibility for land drainage under the LDA 1991 is given to internal drainage boards, under the general supervision of the EA (LDA 1991 ss. 1, 7), although local authorities also have certain functions (see e.g., LDA 1991, s. 14). The EA may also itself become an internal drainage board (see 5.3.2 below). It is important to mention at this stage that, in relation to 'main rivers', the functions exercised by internal drainage boards under the LDA 1991 in respect of watercourses which are not 'main rivers' are directly conferred upon the EA (WRA 1991, s. 107). These 'main rivers' functions of the EA are described in 5.4 below.

5.3.1   Internal drainage boards and their supervision by the EA

Powers of general supervision of internal drainage boards are contained in LDA 1991, s. 7 which entitles the EA to give a board general or special directions to guide it in the exercise and performance of its powers and duties. The EA has powers to redraw the boundaries of an internal drainage district (subject to Ministerial approval in certain cases) (LDA 1991, s. 2) and to reorganise districts and boards (subject to Ministerial approval) (LDA 1991, s. 3). The EA can exercise the powers of an internal drainage board where land is endangered by flooding or poor drainage and the board is not exercising its powers at all or to the necessary extent (LDA 1991, s. 9). The EA can also (under LDA 1991, s. 11) enter into agreements with internal drainage boards whereby those boards will carry out powers of the EA over a 'main river' (basically, a watercourse shown as such on a main river map — see WRA 1991, ss. 113(1), 137(4)).

5.3.2   Power to make EA an internal drainage board

The relevant Minister (primarily the Minister of Agriculture in England and Wales and the Secretary of State for Wales in Wales) may, on a petition by the EA, establish the EA as an internal drainage board, either in place of an existing board, or in respect of a newly constituted district (LDA 1991, s. 4). Conversely, the relevant Minister has power under LDA 1991, s. 5 to transfer the EA's functions back to an internal drainage board constituted for the purpose.

5.3.3   Supervision of drainage boards by EA

The EA may give guidance in the form of general or special directions to internal drainage boards for the purpose of securing both the efficient working and maintenance of existing drainage works and the construction of necessary new works (LDA 1991, s. 7). A board must in any event obtain the consent of the EA to works which affect another board. Works that affect a main river require the agreement of the EA and the relevant Minister. Where in the opinion of the EA land is injured or likely to be injured by flooding or inadequate drainage which might be remedied wholly or partly by the exercise of drainage powers vested in an internal drainage board which are either not being exercised at all or, in the EA's opinion, not to the necessary extent, the EA may exercise all or any of the board's powers. If the board objects, the Minister decides whether the EA should exercise the powers concerned. LDA 1991, s. 10 enables the EA, on the application of a local authority, to direct that LDA 1991, s. 9 powers be conferred on that local authority in its area. If the EA refuses, there is, again, an appeal to the relevant Minister.

LDA 1991, s. 11 enables the EA to enter into arrangements with a board, whereby the board will carry out works in connection with a main river which the EA is empowered to carry out. Conversely, the EA and the board may arrange for the EA to carry out and maintain works which the board is empowered to do in respect of watercourses that are not main rivers and a board may arrange to carry out and maintain works in another board's district.

5.3.4 General drainage powers

Part II of the LDA 1991 sets out the general powers of the EA, internal drainage boards and local authorities.

LDA 1991, s. 14 confers powers to maintain, improve or construct drainage works, whilst LDA 1991, s. 21 enables boards to enforce obligations (e.g., arising by custom or prescription) to repair watercourses, bridges etc. Sections 23 and 24 of LDA 1991 give boards powers to deal with obstructions of watercourses. The powers of ss. 21 and 23 are, however, exercisable concurrently by the board and the EA (LDA 1991, s. 8). LDA 1991, s. 25 gives the boards, or the EA where there is no board, powers to require works to be carried out for maintaining the flow of watercourses. LDA 1991, s. 18 enables the EA, where land requires drainage works but the creation of an internal drainage district would not be practicable, to make a scheme for entering the land and carrying out the works. Schedule 4 sets out the procedural requirements for a scheme which, when made, takes effect as a local land charge.

The EA has powers under Part III of the LDA 1991 to submit schemes to the appropriate Minister for the variation or revocation of any award made under a public or local Act which in any manner affects or relates to the drainage of land (s. 32), to commute (with Ministerial consent) obligations imposed on any person by reason of tenure, custom, prescription etc. to carry out drainage works (ss. 33, 34) and to apply to the Minister for the variation of local enactments conferring functions on navigation authorities where the latter are not properly exercising their powers, and it is desirable to vary these enactments to secure better land drainage (s. 35).

Part IV of the LDA 1991 concerns financial provisions and is dealt with separately below in 5.8.1.

5.3.5 Supplementary powers of boards

Part V of the LDA 1991 confers supplementary powers on internal drainage boards, including powers to acquire land (by agreement or compulsorily) (s. 62), to dispose of land (s. 63), and to make byelaws (s. 66). The EA enjoys, by virtue of sch. 6, certain protection against, *inter alia,* works carried out by boards under the LDA 1991 but such protection is not enjoyed by other undertakings (e.g., those of public utilities and harbour authorities) if the works in question are carried out by the EA. In such cases, however, the very similar protection afforded by sch. 22 to the WRA 1991 is to apply (LDA 1991, s. 67).

The Environment Act introduces a new s. 61F into Part V of the LDA 1991 (Environment Act, sch. 22, para. 193) giving internal drainage boards and local authorities powers to facilitate spray irrigation. Under LDA 1991, s. 61F any internal drainage board or local authority may, with the consent of the EA, operate any drainage works under the board's control or authority so as to manage the level of water in a watercourse for the purpose of facilitating spray irrigation. The power is, however, without prejudice to the board's or authority's drainage powers, and to any requirement for any licence etc. whether from the EA or another person.

5.4   WATER RESOURCES ACT 1991

Part IV of the WRA 1991 also confers various flood protection and local drainage functions on the EA. In relation to main rivers, WRA 1991, s. 107 confers on the EA the functions of drainage boards under the LDA 1991 in relation to other watercourses. A 'main river' is defined in WRA 1991, s. 113(1), basically as a watercourse shown as such on a main river map. These maps are required by WRA 1991, s. 193 to be kept by the EA for the area of each regional flood defence committee at the principal office of the EA for that area. The map shows by a distinctive colour the extent to which any watercourse in that area is to be treated as a main river and must also show which watercourses are designated in a special drainage scheme under WRA 1991, s. 137. Disputes as to whether works are, or would be, drainage works in connection with a main river are settled by a Minister under LDA 1991, s. 73. In respect of main rivers, subss. (2) and (3) of WRA 1991, s. 107 extend to the EA the powers under LDA 1991, ss. 21 and 25 (see above). Where a person is under a duty because of tenure, prescription etc. to carry out drainage works connected with a main river, the EA has a duty under LDA 1991, s. 33 to commute that obligation (WRA 1991, s. 107(4)).

The EA may submit to either of the Ministers schemes for transferring to the EA from any drainage body (including internal drainage boards) all the functions and property of that body connected with a main river and the Minister may confirm it by order (WRA 1991, s. 108). WRA 1991, s. 109 prohibits a person from erecting any structure in, over or under a watercourse which is a main river (or part) without the consent of the EA and in accordance with plans and sections approved by it. Similar restrictions apply to certain works of alteration, repair and diversion.

The EA may, under WRA 1991, s. 111, enter into arrangements with navigation and conservancy authorities, with a view to improving the drainage of land.

5.5 LAND DRAINAGE FUNCTIONS UNDER LOCAL STATUTORY PROVISIONS AND SUBORDINATE LEGISLATION

Section 2(1)(a)(iii) of the Environment Act transfers to the EA functions which were transferred to the NRA by virtue of s. 136(8) of the WA 1989 and para. 1(3) of sch. 15 to that Act. WA 1989, s. 136(8) transferred to the NRA the flood defence functions of the former water authorities which those authorities had by virtue of any local statutory provision (e.g., under a local Act of Parliament). Paragraph 1(3) of sch. 15 to the WA 1989 achieved the same result in the case of certain schemes and orders.

5.6 LAND AND WORKS POWERS

The EA has a range of powers under Part VII of the WRA 1991 which it may exercise in connection with works for flood defence and land drainage. WRA 1991, s. 165 confers on the EA general powers, in connection with a main river, to maintain, improve and construct works whilst s. 167 enables the EA to dispose of spoil in connection with flood defence works. WRA 1991, s. 166 provides that, without prejudice to its general powers under Environment Act, s. 37 (which gives the EA general powers to do things conducive or incidental to its functions), the EA may provide and operate flood warning systems and apparatus. In certain circumstances s. 166 powers may be exercised in Scotland. In addition the EA is given powers for the compulsory purchase of land as well as powers of entry (WRA 1991, ss. 169, 170), which extend to all functions of the EA (other than pollution control functions) under any enactment besides the WRA 1991.

It should also be recalled that the EA, in its capacity as an internal drainage board, has powers to carry out works and powers of compulsory purchase etc. under the LDA 1991 (see 5.3.4 and 5.3.5 above).

5.7 BYELAWS

LDA 1991, s. 66 enables an internal drainage board to make byelaws, to be confirmed by the relevant Minister. WRA 1991, sch. 25, para. 5 confers byelaw-making powers on the EA for securing the efficient working of any drainage system including the proper defence of any land against the sea or tidal water. These byelaws also must be confirmed by the relevant Minister (WRA 1991, sch. 26).

5.8 FINANCIAL PROVISIONS

5.8.1 Financing of internal drainage boards

Part IV of the LDA 1991 provides for the financing of internal drainage boards. The expenses of the boards (including any contributions to the expenses of the EA) are, by LDA 1991, s. 36, in so far as not met by the EA, to be raised by means of drainage rates under Chapter II of Part IV and special levies by virtue of the Local Government Finance Act 1988. Part IV of the LDA 1991 makes provision for the apportionment of rates (s. 37) and for the levying of differential rates by subdividing districts for that purpose (s. 38). The EA plays a central role in determining whether a district should be subdivided, where the EA is not the board. Where it is, the decision is automatically one for the relevant Minister (s. 39). Chapter II of Part IV of the LDA 1991 concerns the levying of drainage rates in respect of agricultural land and buildings including the determination of annual values (ss. 40 to 46), exemptions from rating (in respect of which the EA acts as an appellate body in cases where it is not the board) (s. 47), the procedure for rating (s. 48) and assessment (s. 49). Chapter III of Part IV of the LDA 1991 contains further financial provisions involving the EA. Under s. 57 the EA has power in certain circumstances, on an application from a board, to pay contributions to that board. If the board is dissatisfied by the EA's response, it may appeal to the relevant Minister. LDA 1991, s. 58 enables the EA, where it is itself the internal drainage board for a district, to allocate from its revenues received otherwise than as a board, a sum corresponding to that which it would have made to the board under s. 57, if it were not itself the board. Conversely, since under WRA 1991, s. 139 (see 5.8.4 below) the EA may, in certain circumstances, require a board to give it contributions to the EA's expenses. LDA 1991, s. 58 also enables the EA to defray, out of the sums received by it as the board, an amount equal to the contribution it could have required the board to pay to it under s. 139, were it not the board. A sufficient number of qualified persons (see s. 72 and above) may appeal to the relevant Minister against a decision of the EA under this section. LDA 1991, s. 59 enables Ministers to make grants towards expenditure incurred by internal drainage boards or by other bodies (except the EA) in the exercise of their functions in carrying out drainage schemes. Environment Act, s. 101 amends LDA 1991, s. 59 to enable grants to be made towards strategic study and post-project construction and performance evaluations. These amendments correspond to those made to WRA 1991, s. 147 (see 5.8.7 below) and came into force on 21 September 1995 (Environment Act 1995 (Commencement No. 1) Order 1995 (SI 1995/1983)).

5.8.2 Financing of the EA

For the purposes of its flood defence functions (of which a new definition is substituted in WRA 1991, s. 221, by para. 177(7) of sch. 22 to the Environment Act), the EA is a levying body within the meaning of s. 74 of the Local Government Finance Act 1988, which provides for the making of regulations authorising a levying body to issue a levy on local authorities. See also 5.8.7 below.

5.8.3 General and special drainage charges

Sections 134 to 136 of WRA 1991 provide for the EA to levy general charges at a uniform amount per hectare of chargeable land in a local flood defence district, to be determined in accordance with ss. 135 and 136. Where it appears to the EA that the interests of agriculture require the carrying out, improvement or maintenance of drainage works in connection with any watercourses, in the area of any regional flood defence committee, it may submit (for Ministerial confirmation) a scheme for making a special drainage charge on the lands to be benefited. A special drainage charge is to be at a uniform amount per hectare of the relevant chargeable land (WRA 1991, s. 138).

5.8.4 Contributions from internal drainage boards

The EA is under a duty imposed by WRA 1991, s. 139 to require every internal drainage board to make such contribution towards the expenses of the EA as the EA considers to be fair. There are exceptions in the case of main internal drainage districts and provisions for appeals (WRA 1991, s. 140). For the position where the EA is the board, see 5.8.1 above.

5.8.5 Special duties with respect to flood defence revenue

WRA 1991, s. 118 provides that, subject to certain exceptions, revenue raised by the EA in relation to flood defence and land drainage, shall be spent only in the carrying out of the EA's flood defence functions (which include land drainage) in or for the benefit of the local flood defence district in which it was raised and shall be disregarded in determining the amount of any surplus for the purposes of Environment Act, s. 44(4), which enables the appropriate Minister to direct the EA to pay to him the whole or part of any surplus on capital or revenue account (Environment Act, sch. 22, para. 150).

5.8.6 Navigation tolls

WRA 1991, s. 143 enables the EA (with the consent of the Secretary of State) to levy navigation tolls in respect of navigable waters in England and Wales and so much of the territorial sea adjacent to England and Wales as is included in the area of a regional flood defence committee, where those waters are not under the control of any navigation authority, harbour authority or conservancy authority. The Secretary of State must be satisfied that the cost of the maintenance or works in connection with the waters has been or will be increased as a result of the use of those waters for the purposes of navigation.

5.8.7 Grants

The relevant Minister may make grants towards expenditure incurred by the EA in the improvement of existing drainage works and the construction of new drainage (s. 147). Environment Act, s. 101 extends these grant provisions to enable Ministers to make grants towards strategic studies, to assess whether drainage works should be carried out and to obtain and organise information, including information about natural processes affecting the coastline, so that coastal defence plans can be formulated. Section 101 also amends WRA 1991, s. 147 to enable grants to be made towards post-project construction and performance evaluations. These changes came into force on 21 September 1995 (Environment Act 1995 (Commencement No. 1) Order 1995 (SI 1995/1983)). WRA 1991, s. 148 enables Ministers to make grants towards expenditure incurred by the EA in providing or installing apparatus, or carrying out other engineering or building operations, for the purposes of flood warning systems. Further grant powers are contained in WRA 1991, s. 149 in respect of the exercise by the EA of its land drainage powers under Part VII, including the cost of acquiring land.

5.9 ENVIRONMENTAL AND RECREATIONAL DUTIES

5.9.1 Duties under Land Drainage Act 1991

Environmental and recreational duties are imposed upon internal drainage boards, Ministers and the EA by Part IVA of the LDA 1991, which was inserted by the Land Drainage Act 1994. LDA 1991, s. 61A places a duty on the board and the EA in formulating or considering any proposals relating to any functions of a board — so far as may be consistent with the purposes of the enactment in question — so to exercise any power conferred on the board or the EA as to further the conservation and enhancement of natural beauty and the conservation of flora, fauna and geological or physiographical features of special interest. They must also have regard to the desirability of conserving buildings, sites etc. of archaeological, architectural or historic interest and must take account of any effect which the proposals would have on the beauty or amenity of any rural or urban area or on any such flora, fauna, features, buildings, sites or objects. LDA 1991, s. 61A also imposes duties of a similar nature in respect of preserving public access to places of natural beauty such as woodland, cliffs, foreshore etc. and archaeological etc. sites. These duties also apply to a board in relation to proposals from the EA, water undertakers or sewerage undertakers, including such undertakers' proposals for the management of their land (subs. (3)). Boards must also seek, so far as reasonably practicable, to secure that their rights over water or land are exercised so as to ensure that the water or land is made available for recreational purposes, and in the best manner.

5.9.2 Duties under Environment Act

The duties just described, which replace similar provisions formerly contained in LDA 1991, ss. 12 and 13, should be read in conjunction with ss. 4 and 6 to 8 of the Environment Act. Environment Act, s. 4 establishes as the principal aim of the EA, in discharging its functions, so to protect the environment, taken as a whole, as to make such contribution towards attaining the objective of achieving sustainable development as the Ministers consider appropriate.

Environment Act, s. 6 contains general duties with respect to water, including the conservation and enhancement of the natural beauty of inland waters and land associated with such waters, the conservation of flora and fauna which are dependent on an aquatic environment and the use of inland waters for recreational purposes. Environment Act, s. 7 imposes general environmental and recreational duties on the EA in very similar terms to former WRA 1991, s. 16 which is repealed. Section 8 imposes special duties in the case of sites of special interest notified by English Nature on the Countryside Council for Wales (based on former WRA 1991, s. 17, which is also repealed). Environment Act, s. 9, like the repealed WRA 1991, s. 18, deals with environmental codes of practice. These general aims and duties are described in more detail in chapter 11. The draft Guidance issued in April 1995 (which, in its final form, will be issued under Environment Act, s. 4) sets out how the EA is expected by the government to exercise its flood defence functions. This Guidance is described in 11.1.4.10.

Chapter 6
Fisheries

This chapter deals with the fisheries functions of the EA and with the various general changes made by the Environment Act in fisheries legislation.

6.1 FISHERIES FUNCTIONS OF THE NRA TRANSFERRED TO THE EA

Section 2(1)(a)(v) of the Environment Act transfers to the EA the functions of the NRA under or by virtue of the Diseases of Fish Act 1937, the Sea Fisheries Regulation Act 1966 (SFRA 1966), the Salmon and Freshwater Fisheries Act 1975 (SFFA 1975), Part V of the Water Resources Act 1991 (WRA 1991) or any other enactment relating to fisheries. The precise mechanism whereby references to the NRA are replaced by references to the EA is contained in sch. 15 to the Environment Act.

6.2 GENERAL FISHERIES DUTY OF THE EA

The EA's general obligation with respect to fisheries is imposed by Environment Act s. 6(6) which provides that it shall be the duty of the EA to maintain, improve and develop salmon fisheries, trout fisheries, freshwater fisheries and eel fisheries. The NRA had a corresponding duty under the now repealed WRA 1991, s. 114. The area in respect of which the EA is to carry out its fisheries functions is the whole of England and Wales, together with so much of the territorial sea adjacent to England and Wales as extends for six miles from the baselines from which the breadth of that sea is measured (Environment Act, s. 6(7)(a)). In the case of the Diseases of Fish Act 1937, the SFFA 1975, Part V of the WRA 1991 and its general duty under Environment Act s. 6(6), the EA's jurisdiction also covers so much of the River Esk, with its banks and tributary streams up to their source, as is situated in Scotland, but excluding the River Tweed.

6.3 REGIONAL AND LOCAL FISHERIES ADVISORY COMMITTEES

Environment Act, s. 13 requires the EA to establish and maintain regional and, where deemed necessary, local fisheries advisory committees and to consult those committees as to the manner in which the EA is to perform its general s. 6(6) duty. These advisory committees are to consist of persons who are not members of the EA but who appear to it to be interested in salmon fisheries, trout fisheries, freshwater fisheries or eel fisheries for different parts of the 'controlled area' (defined by s. 13(8) as the area specified in Environment Act, s. 6(7) (see above) in respect of which the EA carries out functions under s. 6(6) and Part V of the WRA 1991 (see below)). One of the regions for which regional advisory committees are established and maintained is to consist wholly or mainly of, or of most of, Wales (Environment Act, s. 13(5)).

These regional and local committees are similar to the ones which the NRA were required to establish and maintain under the now repealed WRA 1991, s. 8. However, Environment Act, s. 13 goes further in two respects.

First, under subs. (2), if the EA (with the consent of the Secretary of State and the Minister of Agriculture, Fisheries and Food) so determines, the EA is also under a duty to consult the committees (or such of them as may be specified or described in the determination) as to the way the EA performs its duties in relation to recreation, conservation or navigation. The EA may, for this purpose, and subject to the same consent, expand the membership of the committees to include persons interested in such matters (subs. (3)). The EA is required by Environment Act, s. 12 to establish and maintain environment protection advisory committees but, as Viscount Ullswater acknowledged on behalf of the government during report stage in the House of Lords:

> . . . we recognise that because the responsibilities of the agency will be wider than those of the NRA it is possible that the environment protection advisory committees would not be able to do full justice to recreation and navigation issues. It is for that reason we have provided that the agency may, with the consent of Ministers, consult additionally the fisheries committees as to the way in which it performs its duties in respect of recreation, navigation, or indeed conservation, and may expand their membership accordingly (Hansard, HL, 2 March 1995, col. 1686.)

The second difference from the previous system is that the chairmen of the regional (but not local) committees are appointed by the Secretary of State in the case of the Welsh region, and by the Minister of Agriculture, Fisheries and Food in all other cases. This change is intended to put the chairmen on a par with the chairmen of the environment protection advisory committees established under Environment Act, s. 12.

6.4 DISEASES OF FISH ACT 1937

The EA has a duty under s. 3 of the Diseases of Fish Act 1937 to report to the Minister where it has reasonable ground for suspecting that any inland waters, not being a fish farm, are infected waters. In such circumstances the EA may take any practicable steps to secure the removal of dead or dying fish from the waters. Where an order is in force in respect of an area under s. 2 of the 1937 Act (on the ground that the waters in question are, or may become, infected waters) the Minister may authorise the EA to remove fish from waters in that area (not being a fish farm), including by methods which would otherwise be illegal. All fish so removed must be destroyed or otherwise properly disposed of. If anyone entitled to take fish from inland waters reasonably suspects they are infected waters, that person must inform the EA (if the waters are not a fish farm (s. 4)). The EA may demand that the Minister cause an inspector to examine waters in order to discover whether they are infected waters (s. 5).

6.5   SEA FISHERIES REGULATION ACT 1966

The SFRA 1966 enables Ministers (which expression includes the Secretary of State) to create a sea fisheries district within the territorial waters adjacent to England or Wales and constitute for that district a local fisheries committee (normally known as a 'sea fisheries committee' (SFC)) in order to regulate sea fisheries carried on within the district. The Minister's power is triggered by an application by a county or metropolitan council, or by 20 or more inhabitants, if the council refuses to apply (SFRA 1966, ss. 2, 3). Half of the committee is appointed by the constituent council (which also funds it). One member is appointed by the EA, and the remainder are appointed by the Minister 'as being persons acquainted with the needs and opinions of the fishing interests' of the district. Prior to the Environment Act there had, however, been concern that SFCs had powers of regulation only for fisheries purposes, and did not concern themselves with wider environmental purposes. The government issued a consultation paper in August 1994 advocating the widening of the role of SFCs. As a result Environment Act, s. 102 amends SFRA 1966, s. 2 so that Ministers may now also appoint to SFCs persons 'having knowledge of, or expertise in, marine environmental matters'. SFCs are also now given the power themselves to appoint additional members with such knowledge or expertise for those occasions when the SFC is considering actual or proposed byelaws under SFRA 1966, s. 5 or s. 5A (see below). Marine environmental matters are defined by new SFRA 1966, s. 2(7) as the conservation or enhancement of the natural beauty or amenity of marine or coastal areas (including their geological or physiographical features) or of any features of archaeological or historic interest in such areas, or the conservation of flora or fauna which are dependent on, or associated with, a marine or coastal environment (Environment Act, s. 102(4)). These changes came into force on 21 September 1995 (Environment Act 1995 (Commencement No. 1) Order 1995 (SI 1995/1983)).

SFCs have power under SFRA 1966, s. 5 to make byelaws for (inter alia) prohibiting or restricting fishing for all or specified kinds of sea fish, prohibiting or restricting specified methods of sea fishing and regulating etc. shellfish fisheries. Environment Act, s. 102(5) (which also came into force on 21 September 1995) inserts new s. 5A which expands the SFCs' byelaw-making powers to encompass marine environmental purposes thus enabling SFCs to regulate sea fishing etc. on environmental grounds. Before submitting any byelaws for Ministerial confirmation under SFRA 1966, s. 6, the SFC is required by SFRA 1966, s. 5 to consult English Nature or the Countryside Council for Wales, as appropriate.

Byelaws made by SFCs must not affect any river byelaws of the EA (SFRA 1966, s. 6).

A SFC may appoint fishery officers under SFRA 1966, s. 10 for enforcing its byelaws within its district.

A local fisheries committee may, with the EA's consent, appoint an officer of the EA as an officer of the committee and the EA may appoint as an officer of the EA any officer of the committee (SFRA 1966, s. 10(4)). The Minister is required to draw the limits of a sea fisheries district at or near the mouth of every river or stream flowing into the sea or any estuary, or near the mouth of any estuary, so that the district shall not extend into the river etc. above that line (SFRA 1966, s. 18(1)). The Minister may, however, by order, provide that the EA shall, with respect to that river etc., have the powers of a local fisheries committee (which include powers to make byelaws regulating sea fisheries). The Minister also has power to give the EA such powers where an application to create a sea fisheries district has not been made or has been refused (SFRA 1966, s. 18(2)).

6.6   SEA FISH (CONSERVATION ACT) 1967 AND INSHORE FISHING (SCOTLAND) ACT 1984

Environment Act, s. 103 amends the Sea Fish (Conservation) Act 1967 and the Inshore Fishing (Scotland) Act 1984 to provide that Ministers' powers to make orders under those Acts may encompass environmental purposes. Section 103(1) inserts new s. 5A in the Sea Fish (Conservation) Act 1967 which enables the Ministers' power to restrict fishing for sea fish to be exercised for marine environmental purposes, in addition to any existing purposes. The definition of 'marine environmental purposes' follows the definition in s. 102(4) (see above). Section 103(2) inserts s. 2A in the Inshore Fishing (Scotland) Act 1984 authorising the Secretary of State to make orders under ss. 1 or 2 of that Act for marine environmental purposes (again, defined as above). These changes came into force on 21 September 1995 (Environment Act 1995 (Commencement No. 1) Order 1995 (SI 1995/1983)).

6.7   SALMON AND FRESHWATER FISHERIES ACT 1975

The SFFA 1975 confers important functions upon the EA. As well as transferring to the EA the responsibilities of the NRA under the SFFA 1975, the Environment Act also confers upon the EA certain functions previously exercisable by Ministers and amends the SFFA 1975 in other significant respects (Environment Act, ss. 104, 105, sch. 15).

Part I of the SFFA 1975 contains prohibitions on certain methods of taking or destroying fish. In addition to its approval function under SFFA 1975, s. 2, in the case of the use of fish roe etc. for fishing purposes, the EA may permit the use of explosives, poison etc. to take or destroy fish, and the requirement for Ministers to approve the giving of such permission for the use of noxious substances is removed (Environment Act, sch. 15, para. 7).

Part II of the SFFA 1975 concerns obstructions to the passage of fish. The function under SFFA 1975, s. 8 of approving fish passes attached to fishing mill dams is transferred from Ministers to the EA, as is the approval of the form and dimensions of fish passes under s. 9 (Environment Act, sch. 15, paras 9, 10). The EA may itself determine the form and dimensions of fish passes which it constructs under SFFA 1975, s. 10, without the need for Ministerial approval, which is likewise no longer required in the case of alterations, etc. to existing fish passes

(Environment Act, sch. 15, para. 11). The EA, rather than Ministers, may give provisional approval under SFFA 1975, s. 11 to fish passes, and that section is further amended so as to make the applicant for approval of a fish pass responsible for meeting the costs involved in determining whether a fish pass which has been provisionally approved is functioning to the EA's satisfaction. The Ministerial functions of approval and certification of fish passes under SFFA 1975, s. 11 are transferred to the EA (Environment Act, sch. 15, para. 12).

Environment Act, sch. 15, para. 13 replaces SFFA, s. 14 (gratings) with an entirely new section, entitled 'Screens'. 'Screen' is now defined in SFFA 1975, s. 41 as a grating or other device which, or any apparatus the operation of which, prevents the passage of salmon or migratory trout and, if the screen is required in connection with a fish farm, the passage of any fish farmed at that fish farm, or any combination of devices or apparatus which, taken together, achieve that result (Environment Act, sch. 15, para. 20). The previous requirement to set gratings applied only to water or canal undertakers, but new s. 14 is expressed to apply also to fish farms (the term 'fish farm' being defined in s. 41(1) as having the same meaning as in the Diseases of Fish Act 1937). Such screens must be capable of preventing the entry of wild fish and the escape of farmed fish. The EA has power under SFFA 1975, s. 15 to use screens or other means to limit the movements of salmon and trout, without Ministerial approval (Environment Act, sch. 15, para. 14). The provisions relating to screens come into force on 1 January 1999 (Environment Act 1995 (Commencement No. 1) Order 1995 (SI 1995/1983)).

Where the EA proposes to carry out specified works under SFFA 1975, s. 10 or works under s. 15 it must first give reasonable notice to owners and occupiers and consider any objections from them (SFFA 1975, s. 18(2); Environment Act, sch. 15, para. 16).

Part III of the SFFA 1975 contains various restrictions on fishing and selling fish, including provisions (in sch. 1) relating to close seasons and close times for particular descriptions of fish. Part IV of the SFFA 1975 contains provisions whereby the EA is able, by means of a licensing system, to regulate fishing for salmon, trout, freshwater fish and eels. Part V of the SFFA 1975 enables the EA to enforce the controls, offences etc. in the Act, giving the EA's water bailiffs and other officers powers of search and entry. SFFA 1975, s. 35, as amended by Environment Act, sch. 15, para. 18, empowers a water bailiff or other officer of the EA or any constable to require a person to produce a fishing licence and state his name and address. Production of the licence may be made within seven days to the appropriate office of the EA, which is the office specified by the water bailiff etc. or, in any other case, any office of the EA.

Environment Act, s. 104 introduces (by new SFFA 1975, s. 37A) a fixed penalty system for offences under salmon and freshwater fisheries legislation. SFFA 1975, s. 37A enables certain offences to be dealt with under a fixed penalty system operated by the EA, under which the accused will be able to discharge his liability to conviction by paying a fixed penalty during a specified period. Section 37A essentially provides a framework for the system; the details are to be prescribed by regulations, which will specify which offences are to be covered and the amount of the fixed penalties. Potentially, all offences under the SFFA 1975 or the Salmon Act 1986, together with certain fisheries offences under regulations made under the WRA 1991, can be the subject of such regulations.

Approximately 5,000 prosecutions were brought each year by the NRA, of which the majority were for minor offences such as unlicensed fishing with rod and line. It is estimated that dealing with these by fixed penalties will save the EA considerable costs, besides easing the burden on the courts. Water bailiffs will also be able to spend more time on enforcing more serious offences.

SFFA 1975, s. 39 deals with the jurisdictional problem of enforcement on the Scottish border. Section 39(1B) enables water bailiffs to pursue poachers suspected of fishery offences committed within the River Esk system throughout the Scottish part of the River Esk catchment (Environment Act, sch. 15, para. 19).

6.8 WATER RESOURCES ACT 1991

Part V of the WRA 1991 enables Ministers, on the application of the EA, to make provision by order in respect of an area defined by the order, modifying any of the provisions of the SFFA 1975 relating to the regulation of fisheries, the power in WRA 1991, s. 156 to acquire land (whether compulsorily or by agreement) for the purpose of fisheries, or any local Act relating to fisheries in that area. Compensation may be payable under the order to those injuriously affected by the modifications. WRA 1991, s. 116 enables Ministers to modify the EA's statutory functions relating to fisheries to enable the government to give effect to EC obligations or international agreements.

6.8.1 Byelaws

WRA 1991, sch. 25, para. 6 enables the EA to make byelaws for the better execution of the SFFA 1975 and the better protection, preservation and improvement of any salmon fisheries, trout fisheries, freshwater fisheries and eel fisheries. The powers are widely framed, covering such matters as the taking or removal of fish, the use of nets and fixed engines and the fixing or altering of close seasons.

Environment Act, s. 103(3) inserts new para. 6A in WRA 1991, sch. 25 so as to enable the EA additionally to make fisheries byelaws for marine or aquatic environmental purposes. This power is intended to complement the new power inserted by Environment Act, s. 102(1) in the SFRA 1966 (see 6.5 above). The change came into force on 21 September 1995 (Environment Act 1995 (Commencement No. 1) Order 1995 (SI 1995/1983)).

6.9 ENVIRONMENTAL AND RECREATIONAL DUTIES

In carrying out its fisheries functions, the EA must act in accordance with Environment Act, ss. 4 and 6 to 8. See chapter 5.9.2 and more generally chapter 11. The draft Guidance issued in April 1995 (which, in its final form, will be issued under Environment Act, s. 4) sets out how the EA is expected to exercise its fisheries functions. This Guidance is described in 11.1.4.11.

Chapter 7
Navigation, Harbour and
Conservancy Authority Functions

Section 2(1)(a)(vi) of the Environment Act transfers to the EA the NRA's functions as a navigation authority, harbour authority or conservancy authority which were transferred to the NRA by virtue of Chapter V of Part III of the Water Act 1989 or para. 23(3) of sch. 13 to that Act, or which have been transferred to the NRA by any order or agreement under sch. 2 to the WRA 1991.

A navigation authority is a person who has a duty or power under any enactment to work, maintain, conserve, improve or control any canal or other inland navigation, navigable river, estuary, harbour or dock. A harbour authority is a person or body of persons who (not being a navigation authority) is empowered by any enactment to make charges in respect of vessels entering a harbour in the UK or using facilities therein. A conservancy authority is any person who has a duty or power under any enactment to conserve, maintain and improve the navigation of a tidal water and is not a navigation authority or a harbour authority (WRA 1991, s. 221(1); Prevention of Oil Pollution Act 1971, s. 8(2)).

Chapter V of Part III of the WA 1989 consists of s. 142. Section 142(1), which was repealed by the Water Consolidation (Consequential Provisions) Act 1991, provided that where the functions of a water authority immediately before 1 September 1989 included (by virtue of any local statutory provision) any functions of a navigation authority, conservancy authority or harbour authority and those functions were not otherwise transferred by the Act, those functions became the functions of the NRA on that date.

Paragraph 23(3) of sch. 13 to the WRA 1991 transferred to the NRA on 1 September 1989 those navigation, conservancy and harbour authority functions of a water authority which were such functions by virtue of an order or agreement made under s. 82 of the Water Resources Act 1963 (which had enabled a water authority to apply for an order transferring to it the functions of such authorities). Under sch. 2 to the WRA 1991 the NRA itself had power to apply to Ministers for an order transferring to it the functions of a navigation, harbour or conservancy authority. Environment Act, s. 2(1)(a)(vi) accordingly transfers all the NRA's navigation, harbour and conservancy authority functions, however acquired.

Environment Act s. 2(1)(a)(vii) enables the EA to apply for orders under WRA 1991, sch. 2.

The EA has power under WRA 1991, sch. 25, paras 1 to 3 to make byelaws regulating the use of inland waters, navigable waters and any waterway owned or managed by it.

Environment Act, s. 6(1) requires the EA to promote both the conservation of inland and coastal waters and the use of such waters for recreational purposes. The draft Guidance issued in April 1995 (which in its final form will be issued under Environment Act, s. 4) sets out how the EA is expected by the government to exercise its navigation functions. This Guidance is described in 11.1.4.13.

It is perhaps questionable whether the EA, given its primary functions of pollution control, water resources regulation and land drainage, is the most appropriate body to have extensive navigation functions (including, at present, lengths of such rivers as the Thames, Medway and the Dee). The Department of the Environment consulted on this question in 1991–92 (as part of an exercise which also covered the functions of the British Waterways Board). In early 1995, a further consultation exercise was undertaken, seeking views on six different options. Under several of these the EA would lose some or all of its navigation functions. The government's forthcoming decisions on this subject may, therefore, result in early changes to the relevant provisions of the Environment Act.

Chapter 8
Waste Regulation and Disposal

Section 2(1)(b) of the Environment Act transfers to the EA the functions of waste regulation authorities conferred or imposed by or under the Control of Pollution (Amendment) Act 1989 (CP(A)A 1989) or Part II of the Environmental Protection Act 1990 (EPA 1990), or which are assigned to those authorities by or under any other enactment, apart from the Environment Act itself.

Section 2(1)(c) of the Environment Act transfers to the EA the functions of disposal authorities under or by virtue of the waste regulation provisions of the Control of Pollution Act 1974 (CPA 1974).

8.1 WASTE REGULATION UNDER PART II
OF THE ENVIRONMENTAL PROTECTION ACT 1990

8.1.1 Introduction

Part II of the EPA 1990 deals with waste on land. It is intended that Part II will eventually replace the provisions dealing with this subject which are contained in Part I of the CPA 1974. However, CPA 1974, Part I has not been wholly repealed as at the date of writing and, accordingly, the Environment Act transfers to the EA the remaining waste functions of disposal authorities under Part I (see 8.3 below).

Part II of the EPA 1990, as originally enacted, established county councils, metropolitan councils and Welsh district authorities as waste regulation authorities (WRAs). In London a joint authority, known as the London Waste Regulation Authority, was formed. The Environment Act transfers the functions of waste regulation authorities in England and Wales to the EA, and the London Waste Regulation Authority is abolished (Environment Act, s. 2(3)). EPA 1990, s. 30(1) is amended by para. 62 of sch. 22 to the Environment Act so that references throughout Part II of the EPA 1990 to a WRA are now to be read, in relation to England and Wales, as references to the EA. Part II is further amended by Environment Act, sch. 22 both to make provision consequential upon the transfer of functions to the EA and in a number of substantive respects.

8.1.2 Meaning of 'waste' etc.

A WRA's functions are exercisable in respect of 'waste', as defined in EPA 1990, s. 75. This definition is replaced by a new s. 75(2), (10) to (12) and sch. 2B (inserted by paras 88 and 95 of Environment Act, sch. 22). These amendments are made for the purpose of assigning to 'waste' in EPA, Part II the meaning which it has in the EC 'Waste Framework Directive' (75/442/EEC), as amended by 91/156/EEC and by the Standardised Reporting Directive 91/692/EEC. New EPA 1990, s. 75(11) expressly states that the amendments have been made for this purpose and requires the new definition to be construed accordingly, so that if uncertainty should arise as to its meaning, a court will presumably be required to look to the Directive itself (and its purpose).

Under the new definition 'waste' means any of the substances or objects in the categories set out in EPA 1990, sch. 2B which the holder discards, or intends, or is required to discard. A 'holder' means the producer of the waste or the person who is in possession of it, and 'producer' means any person whose activities produce waste, or any person who carries out pre-processing, mixing or other operations resulting in a change in the nature or composition of this waste. Sch. 2B is derived from Annex I to the Waste Framework Directive. It lists the categories of waste to which the new definition of 'waste' is to apply. These are:

1. Production or consumption residues not otherwise specified below.
2. Off-specification products.
3. Products whose date for appropriate use has expired.
4. Materials spilled, lost or having undergone other mishap, including any materials, equipment, etc. contaminated as a result of the mishap.
5. Materials contaminated or soiled as a result of planned actions (e.g., residues from cleaning operations, packing materials, containers, etc.).
6. Unusable parts (e.g., reject batteries, exhausted catalysts, etc.).
7. Substances which no longer perform satisfactorily (e.g., contaminated acids, contaminated solvents, exhausted tempering salts, etc.).
8. Residues of industrial processes (e.g., slags, still bottoms, etc.).
9. Residues from pollution abatement processes (e.g., scrubber sludges, baghouse dusts, spent filters, etc.).
10. Machining or finishing residues (e.g., lathe turnings, mill scales, etc.).
11. Residues from raw materials extraction and processing (e.g., mining residues, oil field slops, etc.).
12. Adulterated materials (e.g., oils contaminated with PCBs, etc.).
13. Any materials, substances or products whose use has been banned by law.
14. Products for which the holder has no further use (e.g., agricultural, household, office, commercial and shop discards, etc.).
15. Contaminated materials, substances or products resulting from remedial action with respect to land.
16. Any materials, substances or products which are not contained in the above categories.

8.1.3 Functions of WRA

The main functions of a WRA under Part II of the EPA 1990 are the operation of the waste management licensing system, the regulation of special waste, the supervision of the statutory duty of care as to waste and general enforcement.

8.1.4 Waste management licensing

The system of waste management licensing came into force on 1 May 1994.

EPA 1990, s. 33 prohibits the deposit etc. of controlled waste on land without a waste management licence, or so as to cause pollution or harm to health, subject to exceptions in subss. (2) and (3) which respectively relate to household waste disposed of within the curtilage of a dwelling and cases prescribed in regulations made by the Secretary of State. The current prescribed exemptions are set out in regs 16 and 17 of, and sch. 3 to, the Waste Management Licensing Regulations 1994 (SI 1994/1056). They include certain disposals of waste under authorisations granted under the integrated pollution control system established by Part I of the EPA 1990 and under consents under Chapter II of Part III of the WRA 1991 (for both of which the EA is now also responsible). 'Controlled waste' is defined by EPA 1990, s. 75(4) as household, industrial and commercial waste or any such waste. EPA 1990, s. 33(7) provides a defence in certain circumstances to the offence created by s. 33, one of which was formerly that the action was taken in an emergency to avoid danger to the public and details were given to the WRA as soon as reasonably practicable thereafter. Paragraph 64 of sch. 22 to the Environment Act substitutes a new s. 33(7)(c), as a result of which the defence will only operate where the emergency acts were done to avoid danger to human health and all reasonably practicable steps were taken to minimise pollution of the environment and harm to human health. The requirement to give details still applies.

The EA's powers as a WRA to grant waste management licences, and the procedure for applications, are set out in EPA 1990, ss. 35 and 36, which must be read together with the Waste Management Licensing Regulations 1994 and the definition, in EPA 1990, s. 74, of who is a 'fit and proper person' to hold a licence. An advantage of bringing together the NRA's functions and those of WRAs can be seen from the repeal in EPA 1990, s. 36 of the provisions which formerly required a WRA to consult the NRA before granting a licence, on the ground that water pollution could be caused by leachate escape from the disposal site. The EA is able to consider such matters in the light of its water pollution control functions (see chapter 4).

The licensing system is tightened by new subss. (7A) to (7C) of EPA 1990, s. 35, which provide that where a waste management licence requires an entry to be made in a record as to the observance of a licence condition, a failure to make such an entry is admissible as evidence that the condition has not been observed. It is an offence to make a false entry in a record required to be kept under a licence condition. Where there is an intention to deceive it is also an offence to forge or use a licence or make a document so closely resembling a licence as to be likely to deceive, or have such a document in one's possession (Environment Act, sch. 22, para. 66). Under s. 36 as amended by Environment Act, sch. 22, para. 68, applications for licences must be on a form provided by the EA and be accompanied by such information as the EA reasonably requires and by the charge prescribed under Environment Act, s. 39. The EA is empowered by EPA 1990, s. 36(1A) not to proceed with an application where the required information is not provided. In place of the previous requirement to consult the WRA (see above) the EA is required by s. 36(4) to consult the appropriate planning authority before issuing a licence. The appropriate planning authority is the planning authority with responsibility for waste planning in the area in question (s. 36(11)), but the

Secretary of State has power to amend this definition (s. 36(13)). Under s. 36(10) the appropriate planning authority, the Health and Safety Executive and the appropriate nature conservation body (e.g., English Nature) now have 28 (instead of 21) days to make representations to the EA on a proposed licence.

EPA 1990, s. 35(3) enables the EA to impose conditions on the grant of a licence and s. 35(4) provides that conditions may require the holder of a licence to carry out works or do other things notwithstanding that the licence holder is not entitled to carry out the works or do the thing. Any person whose consent would be required must grant, or join in granting, the holder the rights which will enable the latter to comply with the licence. EPA 1990, new s. 35A (inserted by Environment Act, sch. 22, para. 67) now enables those who have granted such rights to be paid compensation by the licence holder. The details of the compensation scheme (including the descriptions of the loss and damage for which compensation is payable) are to be specified by the Secretary of State in regulations.

EPA 1990, new s. 36A (inserted by Environment Act, sch. 22, para. 69) requires the EA, before issuing a licence, to consult with those who, if the licence is granted, are likely to be required to grant rights to the licence holder in accordance with s. 35(4).

The EA can vary a licence under EPA 1990, s. 37, either on request, or of its own volition where it considers it desirable and unlikely to require unreasonable expenditure on the part of the holder. EPA 1990, new s. 37A makes corresponding provision to that contained in s. 36A where the proposed variation would require the grant of rights by a third party, except that consultation may be postponed in any emergency (Environment Act, sch. 22, para. 71).

EPA 1990, s. 38 deals with the revocation or suspension of licences. New subss. (9A) and (9B) (inserted by Environment Act, sch. 22, para. 72) enable the EA to require a licence holder whose licence is suspended to carry out works etc. and to require a third party to grant or join in granting rights, as is the case with s. 35(4) (see above). EPA 1990, new s. 35A (inserted by Environment Act, sch. 22, para. 67) provides for compensation to be payable in this case, as with the case where a licence is proposed to be granted. The consultation provisions of s. 36A also apply, subject to postponement in emergencies (EPA 1990, new s. 38(9C)).

The EA's enforcement powers in s. 38 cases are strengthened by new s. 38(13) under which the EA is given power to take enforcement proceedings in the High Court to compel the holder of a suspended licence to take measures to deal with pollution or harm (Environment Act, sch. 22, para. 72). Surrender of a licence under s. 39 cannot be accepted by the EA unless it refers the proposal to the appropriate planning authority (see above) and considers its representations (EPA 1990, s. 39(7)). The previous power of the NRA to block acceptance of surrenders pending resolution by the Secretary of State of a dispute between the WRA and the NRA is repealed — another benefit of transferring both authorities' functions to the EA (Environment Act, sch. 22, para. 73). Licences may be transferred under EPA 1990, s. 40 on application to the EA. As with surrender applications, these must be made in accordance with a form provided by the EA and accompanied by such information as it reasonably requires, together with the charge prescribed under Environment Act, s. 41 (Environment Act, sch. 22, para. 74). The unified regime for all EA charges contained in Environment Act, s. 41 enables EPA 1990, s. 41 to be repealed (Environment Act, sch. 22, para. 75).

A WRA has important duties under EPA 1990, s. 42 to supervise licensed activities, so as to ensure that they do not cause pollution or harm to health or become seriously detrimental to local amenities, as well as to ensure that the conditions of the licence are complied with. Again, provisions requiring consultation with the NRA are repealed by Environment Act, sch. 22, para. 76 and the section is further amended to ensure that the liability of a former holder of a licence to meet the cost of expenditure by the EA on emergency work is not limited to cases where the licence was terminated as a result of surrender. The former holder is therefore now also liable where the licence was revoked. Section 42(5) allows the EA to take action to require the holder of a licence to comply with a condition of it, both where the EA considers that the condition is not being complied with and where it believes the condition is likely not to be complied with.

EPA 1990, new s. 44 provides for offences of making false or misleading statements in connection with such matters as obtaining a licence (Environment Act, sch. 19, para. 4).

EPA 1990, s. 45(2)(a) now requires the EA to serve notice of the breach of condition on the licence holder detailing the breach and the remedial steps and specifying the period within which those steps must be taken. EPA 1990, s. 42(6A) allows the EA to take High Court proceedings if it considers that the revocation or suspension of a licence would be an ineffectual remedy against a person who has failed to comply with any requirement imposed under s. 42(5)(a) (Environment Act, sch. 22, para. 76).

EPA 1990, s. 43 provides for appeals to the Secretary of State against decisions of the EA concerning licences. Environment Act, s. 114 enables the Secretary of State to delegate the determination of such appeals to an appointed person (Environment Act, sch. 22, para. 77).

8.1.5 Waste disposal plans

WRAs were formerly under a duty imposed by EPA 1990 s. 50 to produce local waste disposal plans. These are now replaced by the Secretary of State's national waste strategy — to be drawn up under EPA 1990, s. 44A (inserted by Environment Act, s. 92). The national waste strategy is dealt with in chapter 20. EPA 1990, s. 50 is therefore repealed (Environment Act, sch. 22, para. 78).

8.1.6 Closed landfills

Environment Act, sch. 22, para. 79 repeals EPA 1990, s. 61. This section, which had in fact never been brought into force, imposed a duty on WRAs as respects closed landfills. Under it, a WRA had to inspect its area in order to determine if there was anything affecting land so as to cause pollution or harm to health, where controlled waste had been deposited on land or where the WRA believed there were concentrations or accumulations of landfill gases or noxious liquids. Where such sites were likely to cause pollution or harm, WRAs were required to carry out work, and empowered to recover reasonable costs from the owner.

Strong criticisms were made of s. 61 by the property industry, and its repeal by the Environment Act is not unexpected. The government intends the provisions of the Environment Act relating to contaminated land to be a substitute for s. 61, with responsibilities for dealing with such land being shared between the EA and local authorities (see chapter 16).

8.1.7 Special waste and non-controlled waste

It is intended that, under EPA 1990, s. 62 the EA will be given functions by the Secretary of State with respect to the treatment, keeping or disposal of 'special waste' (namely, waste which is so dangerous or difficult to treat, keep or dispose of that special provision is required for dealing with it). Section 62(3)(a) enables new Special Waste Regulations to provide for the EA (as a WRA) to supervise special waste activities authorised by virtue of the Regulations and of persons who carry on activities by virtue of which they are subject to the Regulations. Persons who carry on activities authorised by virtue of the regulations may, as before, also be supervised under the Regulations, and the costs of the EA recovered from them (Environment Act, sch. 22, para. 80).

EPA 1990, s. 63(1) (not yet in force) enables the Secretary of State to make Regulations providing for prescribed provisions of Part II to have effect in a prescribed area as if references to controlled waste etc. included references to specified kinds of mining, quarrying and agricultural waste (EPA 1990, s. 75(7)(c)).

EPA 1990, new s. 63(2) provides that a person who deposits, or knowingly causes or knowingly permits the deposit of, any waste, which is not controlled waste but which, if it were controlled waste, would be special waste, shall be guilty of an offence under s. 33 (see above) if he would have been so guilty if the waste were in fact special waste and he did not have a waste management licence for it (Environment Act, sch. 22, para. 81).

8.1.8 Publicity

EPA 1990, s. 64 requires a WRA to maintain a register of licences, applications, modifications, notices, appeals, convictions etc. New s. 64(2A) enables the Secretary of State to direct the EA to remove from a register any information which is not required to be kept on the register or which is required to be excluded from it under EPA 1990, ss. 65 and 66 (which relate to national security and commercial confidentiality). Section 64(4) requires all waste collection authorities (which are district councils or London borough councils) to keep a local register containing prescribed particulars of entries in the waste regulation register relating to the area of the collection authority. Since this duty previously only extended to those collection authorities which were not also WRAs, it was necessary for the duty to be redrawn in consequence of the EA taking over the local authorities' waste regulation functions. Section 64(5) requires the EA to provide collection authorities with information necessary for them to carry out their record-keeping duties. Section 64(6) enables the Secretary of State to prescribe places where the EA and waste collection authorities are to make their registers available for inspection or at which they are to afford copying facilities (Environment Act, sch. 22, para. 82). Commercially confidential information can be kept off public registers under EPA 1990, s. 66 if the WRA accepts its confidentiality, or the Secretary of State does so on appeal. Where an appeal is made, s. 66(5) requires the information to be kept off the register until seven days after final determination or withdrawal of the appeal. Any appeal must now be heard in private, and may also be delegated to an appointed person under Environment Act, s. 114 (Environment Act, sch. 22, para. 83). The requirement, under former EPA 1990, s. 67 for a WRA to produce annual reports is removed, in view of the EA's general duty under Environment Act, s. 52 to produce annual reports (Environment Act, sch. 22, para. 84).

8.1.9   Supervision and enforcement

EPA 1990, ss. 68 to 70 are repealed. These provided for the overseeing of WRAs, the appointment of inspectors, their powers of entry and other powers — all matters now covered by Environment Act, ss. 108 and 109 in relation to the entire range of the EA's functions — and by that Act's general provision for government supervision of the EA. EPA 1990, ss. 71(1) and 72 are repealed for similar reasons.

8.1.10   Duty of care etc. as respects waste

An important feature of Part II of the EPA 1990 is the creation in s. 34 of a statutory duty of care with regard to waste, breach of which is a criminal offence. In essence a person who deals with controlled waste is required to take reasonable and proper steps to avoid a s. 33 contravention by any other person, to prevent the escape of waste and, on transfer, to secure that it goes only to authorised persons and with a proper written description of the waste. Section 34(3) specifies the 'authorised persons' to whom waste may be transferred. New s. 34(3A) enables the Secretary of State by regulations to add to the list persons who may be authorised to receive waste generally or only in prescribed circumstances (Environment Act, sch. 22, para. 65).

8.2   WASTE REGULATION UNDER THE CONTROL OF POLLUTION (AMENDMENT) ACT 1989

The CP(A)A 1989 introduced a system of registration for carriers of waste. Such carriers were required to register with a WRA. This function is, in the case of England and Wales, transferred to the EA and the definition of 'regulation authority' in CP(A)A 1989, s. 9(1) amended accordingly (Environment Act, sch. 22, para. 37).

CP(A)A 1989, s. 1(1) makes it an offence for an unregistered person to transport controlled waste. There are specific exemptions in s. 1(2) (e.g., transportation within the same premises) and further exemptions are contained in the Controlled Waste (Registration of Carriers and Seizure of Vehicles) Regulations 1991 (SI 1991/1624), which generally supplement the Act.

Applications for registration must be made to the EA (CP(A)A 1989, s. 2). Amendments are made by the Environment Act, sch. 22, para. 37 in respect of charges and the need to supply information with an application, which correspond to those made in the case of the waste management licences (see above). The only substantive ground under the Regulations for refusal of registration is that the applicant is not a desirable carrier (cf. the 'fit and proper person' test under the waste management licensing system). Appeals against refusal (or deemed refusal) to register lie under CP(A)A 1989, s. 4 to the Secretary of State who may delegate his function to an appointed person under Environment Act, s. 114.

The EA has power to enforce the CP(A)A 1989 by stopping and searching vehicles (s. 5) and requiring production of registration certificates. The power under s. 6 to seize and dispose of vehicles used for illegal waste disposal is extended by new s. 6(6) which allows regulations to sanction the immediate sale or destruction of seized property where the condition of the property requires it to be disposed of without delay (Environment Act, sch. 22, para. 37).

CP(A)A 1989, s. 7(2) (which facilitated the exchange of information between authorities and the Secretary of State etc.) is repealed so as to ensure that CP(A)A 1989 is consistent with the provisions as to disclosure of information in Environment Act, s. 113.

8.3 WASTE DISPOSAL

Notwithstanding the introduction on 1 May 1994 of the waste management licensing system under Part II of the EPA 1990, ss. 1 to 21 of the CPA 1974 (including the waste licensing system in ss. 3 to 11) have not yet been completely repealed. The 'old' system still at present covers activities subject to pending applications for disposal licences, or to appeals, as well as activities which are covered by disposal licences but which would be excluded or exempted from waste management licensing (see above) if authorised by the IPC system in Part I of the EPA 1990 (see Environmental Protection Act 1990 (Commencement No. 15) Order 1994 (SI 1994/1096)).

Accordingly, Environment Act, s. 2(1)(c) provides for the transfer to the EA of the remaining waste functions of 'disposal authorities'.

8.3.1 Disposal licences

The unlicensed disposal of waste is prohibited by CPA 1974, s. 3. Under CPA 1974, s. 5(3) the EA is under a duty not to grant a disposal licence unless a planning permission is in force but it must not reject an application where such a permission is in force unless it is necessary to prevent pollution of water or danger to health. Instead of referring applications to the NRA (whose functions are subsumed within the EA), s. 5(4) now requires the EA to refer the proposal to the relevant collection authority (i.e., district council or London borough). The EA must keep a register of licences (CPA 1974, s. 6). Variations of conditions and revocation of licences are governed by s. 7, and transfer and relinquishment of licences by s. 8. The EA has a duty under s. 9 to supervise licensed activities and appeals against its decisions with respect to licences lie to the Secretary of State under s. 10. The EA may, under s. 16, remove waste deposited in breach of the licensing system.

CPA 1974, s. 11 dealt with cases where land was occupied by disposal authorities, and was intended to be used for the deposit of waste. Subsections (1) to (11) are repealed by Environment Act, sch. 22, para. 25 since they are redundant following the transfer to the EA of the remaining waste regulation functions of disposal authorities. Resolutions passed under s. 11 by disposal authorities before the repeal take effect as if they were waste management licences under EPA 1990, Part II (Environment Act, sch. 23, para. 13). The number of sites operated under s. 11 resolutions has in fact been reduced as a result of EPA 1990, s. 32 which requires disposal authorities to direct their waste disposal operations by contracting them out to the private sector or to arm's length companies.

WASTE STRATEGY

By EPA 1990, new s. 44A (inserted by Environment Act, s. 92) the EA is given important duties in connection with the production by the Secretary of State of a national waste strategy. The strategy is described in chapter 20. The draft Guidance issued in April 1995 (which, in its final form, will be issued under Environment Act, s. 4) describes the role which the EA is to have in delivering the strategy (see 11.1.4.5).

Chapter 9
Integrated Pollution Control

Section 2(1)(d) of the Environment Act transfers to the EA the functions of HMIP under Part I of the Environmental Protection Act 1990 (EPA 1990) or assigned to it by or under any other enactment apart from the Environment Act itself. Accordingly, the EA becomes responsible for operating the system of integrated pollution control (IPC) created by EPA 1990, Part I.

9.1 INTRODUCTION

Part I of the EPA 1990 establishes both the IPC system and the system of local authority air pollution control (LAAPC). IPC covers the more polluting processes, of any environmental medium, whilst LAAPC is confined to atmospheric releases from less polluting processes. Both central (IPC) and local (LAAPC) controls are exercisable over processes or substances which have been prescribed by regulations made by the Secretary of State under EPA 1990, s. 2. The current regulations are the Environmental Protection (Prescribed Processes and Substances) Regulations 1991 (SI 1991/472, as amended by SI 1992/614). The regulations prescribe processes by reference to the following main industry sectors: fuel and power, metal production and processing, minerals, chemicals, waste disposal and recycling, and miscellaneous. Each sector is subdivided into main categories of process which in turn are divided into detailed descriptions of actual processes or operations, falling within Part A or Part B. Part A processes are within the IPC system, whilst Part B are within LAAPC. EPA 1990, s. 3 enables the Secretary of State to make regulations establishing standards, objectives or requirements in relation to particular prescribed processes or particular substances.

It is an offence to carry out a prescribed process without the appropriate authorisation. All authorisations are subject to a general condition requiring the use of best available techniques not entailing excessive cost (BATNEEC) (EPA 1990, s. 7). DoE guidance (news release No. 271, 26 April 1990) on the interpretation of BATNEEC should be read together with s. 7 (see below).

The Environment Act leaves responsibility for LAAPC with local authorities in England and Wales, but in Scotland SEPA takes over the operation of both the IPC and LAAPC systems (see chapter 12).

9.2   THE EA AND IPC

9.2.1   Functions of EA

The EA is given functions under EPA 1990, s. 4 in respect of IPC for the purpose of preventing or minimising pollution of the environment due to the release of substances into any environmental medium. Under subs. (4) the Secretary of State has power to direct that LAAPC functions shall be exercised instead by the EA while the direction is in force, or during a period specified in the direction, but where such a direction is made the EA cannot exercise the LAAPC functions otherwise than in relation to the air (i.e., it cannot exercise those functions across all media, as it can with IPC).

9.2.2   Authorisation

EPA 1990, s. 6 contains the key provision that no person shall carry on a prescribed process after the date prescribed or determined for that description of process by or under s. 2 regulations except under an authorisation granted by the 'enforcing authority' (now defined, in EPA 1990, s. 1, as the EA, in the case of IPC in England and Wales). Exceptions exist for transitional arrangements provided by the regulations — see sch. 6 to the Environmental Protection (Prescribed Processes and Substances) Regulations 1991.

The EA shall, on application for IPC authorisation, either grant the authorisation, subject to s. 7 conditions, or refuse it. An application shall not be granted unless the EA considers that the applicant will be able to carry on the process so as to comply with the conditions which would be included in the authorisation. The EA must review authorisations at least every four years (EPA 1990, s. 6(3), (4), (6)). The detailed procedure for the determination of applications is contained in Part I of sch. 1 to the EPA 1990, which provides for consultation and power for the Secretary of State to call in applications for determination by himself.

Although the release of prescribed substances will usually be part of the carrying out of a prescribed process, regulation 6 of the 1991 Regulations prescribes various substances, the release of which into specified environmental media is to be controlled under EPA 1990, ss. 6 and 7.

9.2.3   BATNEEC and BPEO

EPA 1990, s. 7(1) requires an authorisation to contain such specific conditions as the EA considers appropriate for achieving certain objectives, together with any conditions specified by the Secretary of State's direction and such other conditions, if any, as appear to the EA to be necessary.

The objectives just referred to are specified in s. 7(2). They include that, in carrying on a prescribed process, the best available techniques not entailing excessive cost (BATNEEC) will be used for preventing release of substances and rendering harmless other substances which might cause harm, if released, and ensuring compliance with EC obligations and international treaties.

Section 7(4) provides that except as regards an aspect of the process which is covered by a condition under s. 7(1), there is implied in every authorisation a general condition that the person carrying on the authorised process must use BATNEEC for preventing the release of prescribed substances and rendering harmless any other substances which might cause harm, if released. Section 7(7) provides that in IPC cases including release into more than one medium, the s. 7(2) objectives include ensuring BATNEEC will be used to minimise pollution to the environment as a whole having regard to the best practicable environmental option available (BPEO). A reference to BATNEEC includes (in addition to references to any technical means and technology) references to the number, qualifications, training and supervision of persons employed in the process and the design, construction, layout and maintenance of the buildings in which it is carried on. The EA must have regard to guidance issued by the Secretary of State in operating s. 7(2) and (7). Reference should be made to the 1990 DoE guidance (see 9.1 above) which, amongst other things, indicates that a different view will be taken of excessive cost depending upon whether the process is an existing or new one. The guidance also makes it clear that BATNEEC is only 'one feature of a complex of objectives'.

The draft Guidance issued in April 1995 (which, in its final form, will be issued under Environment Act, s. 4) refers to specific guidance on both BATNEEC and BPEO which is to be given to the EA later in 1995 and describes BPEO as 'central to IPC. The most sustainable form of development is that which achieves the optimum distribution of any pollutants to the three media of air, water and land, according to the ability of those media to accept such pollutants without, for example, exceeding critical loads. By requiring an assessment of the BPEO where emissions from an IPC process are likely to affect more than one medium, IPC seeks to ensure that a sustainable outcome for the environment as a whole will be achieved'. (Draft Guidance to the Environment Agency under the Environment Bill on its Objectives, DoE, MAFF, Welsh Office, April 1995, para. 7.6. See also 11.1.4.3).

9.2.4 Fees and charges

EPA 1990, s. 8 now deals only with fees and charges for LAAPC authorisations in England and Wales since the EA's charging powers are in Environment Act, s. 41 (see chapter 15).

9.2.5 Transfers, variations, revocations and prohibitions

EPA 1990, s. 9 enables authorisations to be transferred, on notice to the EA. EPA 1990, s. 10 enables the EA to vary an IPC authorisation, and requires it to do so if it appears at any time that s. 7 requires conditions to be included which are different from the subsisting ones. The mechanism for doing this involves the service by the EA of a 'variation notice'. Under EPA 1990, s. 10(3A) (inserted by Environment Act, sch. 22, para. 51) the EA (and local authorities in the case of LAAPC) may serve a further notice which varies a variation notice. A person carrying on the prescribed process under an authorisation who wishes to make a relevant change in the process may apply to the EA under EPA 1990, s. 11. The procedure under s. 11 is complex, but is intended to enable the EA to consider whether a change in the authorisation conditions would be required, in which case the person concerned must formally apply for such a variation. Alternatively, if the person is clear from the outset that such a variation would be required, as a result of his proposed change in the process, he may proceed to apply for this without going through the initial notification procedure. The procedure for variation of authorisations is contained in Part II of sch. 1 to the EPA 1990 which is amended by the Environment Act to enable the Secretary of State to call in applications for variations, as he can in the case of applications for authorisations (Environment Act, sch. 22, para. 93).

The EA may at any time revoke an authorisation by notice in writing to the holder (EPA 1990, s. 12). If the EA is of the opinion that the holder is contravening a condition of his authorisation, or is likely to do so, it may serve on him an 'enforcement notice', specifying the contravention or likely contravention, the remedial steps to be taken and the timescale for these. EPA 1990, new s. 13(4) enables the EA to withdraw an enforcement notice (Environment Act, sch. 22, para. 53).

Under EPA 1990, s. 14, if the EA is of the opinion that the carrying on of a prescribed process under an authorisation involves an imminent risk of serious pollution of the environment, it must serve a prohibition notice on the person carrying on the process. This duty applies whether or not a condition is being breached and extends to any aspect of the process, whether or not regulated by the conditions. A prohibition notice is to be withdrawn by further notice when the EA is satisfied that the steps required by the notice have been taken.

9.2.6 Appeals

EPA 1990, s. 15 enables appeals to be brought against refusals of authorisations, unwelcome conditions, refusals of variations and revocations of authorisations. In addition, appeals may be brought by those on whom variation, enforcement or prohibition notices are served.

Appeals lie to the Secretary of State but no appeal may be brought where the decision in question implements a direction of his. The Secretary of State may delegate the hearing of appeals, under Environment Act, s. 114, or he may cause the appeal to take the form of a hearing (which may be in private), or else cause a local inquiry to be held (EPA 1990, s. 15(3), (5); Environment Act, sch. 22, para. 54). The details of appeal procedures are prescribed by the Environmental Protection (Applications, Appeals and Registers) Regulations 1991 (SI 1991/507).

9.2.7 Information and publicity

EPA 1990, s. 19 enables the Secretary of State to require the EA to furnish him with information about the discharge of its functions under Part I. Likewise, the EA may require a person to furnish it by a specified time with information which it reasonably considers it needs for the purpose of the discharge of its functions.

EPA 1990, s. 20 requires the EA to maintain registers of applications, authorisations, variations, revocations, appeals, convictions etc. Under subs. (7) the Secretary of State may specify places where registers are to be kept or inspection and copying facilities are to be available.

EPA 1990, s. 21 enables the Secretary of State to secure the exclusion from registers of information whose inclusion would, in his opinion, be contrary to the interests of national security, whilst s. 22 prohibits the inclusion in a register of certain commercially confidential information. The determination of whether s. 22 applies to particular information is for the EA, but its decision may be appealed to the Secretary of State, in which case the information is to be excluded until seven days after the final decision (or withdrawal of the appeal) (Environment Act, sch. 22, para. 58).

9.2.8 Offences

Under EPA 1990, s. 23(1) it is, *inter alia,* an offence for a person to contravene s. 6(1) (s. 23(1)(a)), fail to give a notice of transfer as required by s. 9(2) (s. 23(1)(b)), fail to comply with or contravene an enforcement notice or prohibition notice (s. 23(1)(c)) or fail to comply with a court order under s. 26 (s. 23(1)(l)). The maximum punishment on summary conviction for offences under s. 23(1)(a), (c) or (l) is £20,000 or (now) 3 months' imprisonment or both (EPA 1990, s. 23(2)(a); Environment Act, sch. 22, para. 59). Other offences under s. 23 include failure to comply with a s. 19 notice, making a false statement, and forging s. 7 authorisations. Under EPA 1990, s. 24 if the EA is of the opinion that proceedings for the offence of failing to comply with or contravening an enforcement notice or prohibition notice would be an ineffectual remedy it may take High Court proceedings for securing compliance with the notice.

Where a person is convicted of a s. 23(1)(a) or (c) offence the court may order him to remedy the matters in question (EPA 1990, s. 26). In the case of such offences which cause remediable harm, the EA can, under EPA 1990, s. 27, with the written approval of the Secretary of State, arrange for any reasonable steps to be taken towards remedying the harm and recover the cost from the convicted person.

9.2.9 Authorisations and other statutory controls

One of the major reasons for creating the EA was to reduce the instances of overlap between the functions of separate environmental authorities. By combining the functions of HMIP, the NRA and WRAs, the Environment Act removes the need for notification of and consultation with another such authority before the EA grants the authorisation in question. The various separate statutory consent and authorisation systems are, however, preserved intact, although the EA will no doubt be expected in time to bring forward recommendations for further streamlining, perhaps involving the integration of certain of these statutory systems.

The immediate results of the creation of the EA can be seen in the amendments to EPA 1990, s. 28, which deals with the relationship between Part I authorisations and other statutory controls. Subsections (3) and (4), which involved liaison between HMIP and the NRA in the case of the release of substances into controlled waters, are repealed. So too is the requirement in subs. (1) to notify a WRA under Part II where the authorised process involves the final disposal of controlled waste by deposit in or on land. However, s. 28(1) still prohibits a condition being attached to an IPC authorisation so as to regulate the final disposal in or on land of such waste (Environment Act, sch. 22, para. 61).

In the case of discharges into water, WRA 1991, s. 88 provides that these are not to constitute an offence under s. 85 of that Act if they are authorised under

EPA 1990, Part I. The EA, which now has the NRA's functions, will be expected to ensure that appropriate conditions are attached to such an authorisation, in order to protect the water environment, or (in certain cases) to refuse authorisation altogether.

Overlap also exists in the case of the discharge of trade effluent which may be subject to IPC control, as well as requiring consent from the sewerage undertaker under s. 118 of the WIA 1991.

If a local authority wish to initiate proceedings for statutory nuisance under EPA 1990, Part III, they must first obtain the consent of the Secretary of State if proceedings in respect of it could be brought under EPA 1990, Part I (s. 79(10)).

If activities covered by a prescribed process are regulated by an IPC authorisation and are also registered or authorised under the Radioactive Substances Act 1993, any conditions imposed by the IPC authorisation are not binding if they conflict with obligations imposed under the 1993 Act system (EPA 1990, s. 28(2)). The EA has now taken over HMIP's functions under the RSA 1993 (see chapter 10). An IPC condition may not be imposed for the purpose only of securing the health of persons at work (EPA 1990, s. 7(1)).

9.3   FUNCTIONS UNDER LEGISLATION TO BE REPLACED BY IPC

The progressive introduction of IPC under EPA 1990, Part I means that, ultimately, certain pollution control systems under earlier enactments will be wholly super-seded and those enactments repealed, by commencement orders triggering pros-pective repeals in EPA 1990, sch. 16. Until that time, however, subss. (1)(f) and (g) and (2)(c) and (d) of Environment Act, s. 2 ensure that what were the functions of HMIP under those enactments (together with certain functions of the Secretary of State) will be carried out by the EA.

The enactments in question are the Alkali, etc., Works Regulation Act 1906 (AWRA 1906) and certain provisions of the Health and Safety at Work etc. Act 1974 (HASAWA 1974).

9.3.1   Alkali etc., Works Regulation Act 1906

Sections 1 and 2 of AWRA 1906 require alkali works to be carried on in such manner as to secure the condensation, to the EA's satisfaction, of hydrochloric acid gas to specified extents, and require the use of best practicable means for preventing the escape of noxious or offensive gases, for preventing the discharge of such gases into the atmosphere and for rendering such gases harmless and inoffensive. Sections 1 and 2 do not apply to any process which is a prescribed process under EPA 1990, Part I as from the date which is the determination date for that process, that is to say, the date of authorisation, or refusal of authorisation, for the process (AWRA 1906, s. 2A). Under AWRA 1906, s. 9 alkali works or any works specified in sch. 1 to the Health and Safety (Emissions into the Atmosphere) Regulations 1983 (SI 1983/943) (see below) must not be carried on unless registered by the EA. Again, this requirement does not apply to any process which is a prescribed process as from the date which is the determination date for that process (AWRA 1906, s. 24A).

9.3.2   Health and Safety at Work etc. Act 1974

Sections 1(1)(d) and 5 of HASAWA 1974 provide for controls over the emission into the atmosphere of noxious or offensive substances from prescribed premises. Besides the 1983 regulations referred to in 9.3.1 above, the Control of Industrial Air Pollution (Registration of Works) Regulations 1989 (SI 1989/318) and the Control of Asbestos in the Air Regulations 1990 (SI 1990/556) have been made in part under HASAWA 1974, s. 1(1)(d).

Under HASAWA 1974, s. 5 it is the duty of any person having control of any premises of a class prescribed for the purposes of s. 1(1)(d) to use best practicable means for preventing the emission into the atmosphere from the premises of noxious or offensive substances or for rendering harmless and inoffensive such substances as may be emitted. As with the AWRA 1906, this requirement does not apply in relation to any process which is a prescribed process under EPA 1990, Part I as from the determination date for that process (HASAWA 1974, s. 5(5)). The EA now has the function of enforcing HASAWA 1974, s. 5.

Chapter 10
Radioactive Substances

Environment Act, s. 2(1)(e) transfers to the EA HMIP's functions under the Radioactive Substances Act 1993, or assigned to HMIP by or under any other enactment, apart from the Environment Act.

Environment Act, s. 2(2)(a) transfers to the EA the Secretary of State's functions under RSA 1993, s. 30(1) (which consist of power to dispose of radioactive waste). Guidance issued in April 1995 (which, in its final form, will be issued under Environment Act, s. 4) sets out how the EA is expected by the government to exercise its functions with respect to radioactive substances. The Guidance is described in 11.1.4.4.

10.1 REGISTRATION

RSA 1993, s. 6 prohibits a person from keeping or using radioactive material on premises used for the purpose of an undertaking carried on by him, unless he is registered under RSA 1993, s. 7, or exempted from registration, or unless the material is mobile radioactive apparatus in respect of which a person is registered (or exempt from registration). Breach of s. 6 is a criminal offence under RSA 1993, s. 32. 'Radioactive material' is defined in s. 1 as anything which, not being waste, is either a substance to which subs. (1) applies (by virtue of subs. (2)) or an article made wholly or partly from, or incorporating, such a substance. Subsection (2) applies subs. (1) to particular substances by reference to a list in RSA 1993, sch. 1.

Applications for registration are made to the EA under s. 7, which requires information to be supplied as to the premises and substances etc., together with the charge prescribed for the purpose of a charging scheme under Environment Act, s. 41. The EA may grant or refuse the application, and may impose conditions relating to the premises, apparatus etc., the furnishing of information or the sale or supply of the radioactive material. Except in the case of conditions relating to the furnishing of information or sale or supply, the EA, in exercising its powers, shall have regard exclusively to the amount and character of the radioactive waste likely to arise from the keeping or use of radioactive material on the premises. 'Radioactive waste' is defined by RSA 1993, s. 2 as a substance or article which, if it were not waste, would be radioactive material or which has been contaminated in the course of the production, keeping or use of radioactive material or by contact etc. with other radioactive waste.

RSA 1993, s. 8 provides an exemption from the requirements of registration, primarily for premises in respect of which a nuclear site licence under the Nuclear Installations Act 1965 is in force. The Secretary of State also has power under subs. (6) to specify by order further exemptions from registration. Some 16 such orders relating to such matters as luminous articles, smoke detectors and low activity substances, and to such premises as schools and hospitals, have been made.

RSA 1993, s. 10 provides for the registration of mobile radioactive apparatus, but the Secretary of State may under RSA 1993, s. 11 by order grant exemptions from registration under s. 10.

The EA may at any time cancel or vary a registration under ss. 7 or 10, or the conditions relating to registration, or may impose conditions in the case of a previously unconditional registration (s. 12).

10.2 AUTHORISATION OF DISPOSAL AND ACCUMULATION OF RADIOACTIVE WASTE

RSA 1993, s. 13 prohibits the unauthorised disposal of radioactive waste from premises or from mobile radioactive apparatus. Section 14 prohibits accumulation of radioactive waste otherwise than in accordance with an authorisation granted under s. 14 or an authorisation to dispose granted under s. 13. Section 15 provides exemptions from the ss. 13 and 14 requirements in the case of radioactive waste arising from clocks or watches, in certain circumstances.

Authorisations under ss. 13 and 14 are granted by the EA, on application under s. 16, including in cases of disposals on or from nuclear sites, but in such cases the EA must consult with the Minister of Agriculture, Fisheries and Food and the Health and Safety Executive, as well as relevant local authorities, water bodies and other public authorities (RSA 1993, s. 16(4A), (5), (11); Environment Act, sch. 22, para. 205). Applications under s. 16 may be granted or refused and conditions may be imposed upon authorisations. RSA 1993, s. 17 enables authorisations under ss. 13 and 14 to be revoked or varied, including those relating to nuclear sites (again, following consultation with the Minister of Agriculture, Fisheries and Food).

Where the disposal of radioactive waste is likely to require special precautions to be taken by a local authority, relevant water body (i.e., water or sewerage undertaker or local fisheries committee) or other public or local authority, the EA must consult with that public or local authority before granting the s. 13 authorisation, and that authority may make a charge for taking precautions (RSA 1993, s. 18).

10.3 ENFORCEMENT AND PROHIBITION NOTICES

The EA may serve an enforcement notice under RSA 1993, s. 21 if of the opinion that a person to whom a s. 7 and 10 registration relates is failing to comply with any limitation on or condition of registration or is likely to do so. A prohibition notice may be served by the EA under RSA 1993, s. 22 if of the opinion that the continuation of a registered or authorised activity involves an imminent risk of pollution of the environment or of harm to human health. A prohibition notice may suspend the registration authorisation, to the extent directed in the notice.

10.4 POWERS OF SECRETARY OF STATE IN RELATION
TO APPLICATIONS ETC.

The Secretary of State may give directions to the EA under RSA 1993, s. 23 as to applications for registration or authorisation whereby the EA is required to refuse the application, attach specified limitations or conditions or cancel or revoke a registration or authorisation (or not to do so). The Secretary of State may also require the EA to serve an enforcement notice or prohibition notice. In the case of s. 13 applications or authorisations, the power to give directions lies with both the Secretary of State and the Minister of Agriculture, Fisheries and Food (RSA 1993, s. 23(4A); Environment Act, sch. 22, para. 211).

RSA 1993, s. 24 enables the Secretary of State (with the Minister of Agriculture, Fisheries and Food in the case of nuclear sites — see above) to call in certain applications for his determination, and to hold a local inquiry before making his decision.

RSA 1993, s. 25 enables the Secretary of State to direct the EA that knowledge of specified information should be restricted in the case of a particular application etc. on the grounds of national security, but this requirement is not to affect the EA's power or duty to consult the Minister of Agriculture, Fisheries and Food or the information to be sent by the EA to him (RSA 1993, s. 25(3A); Environment Act, sch. 22, para. 213).

10.5 APPEALS

Appeals against decisions of the EA under the registration provisions of the Act lie to the Secretary of State (and the Minister of Agriculture, Fisheries and Food in the case of a nuclear site), except where the decision is taken following his direction under RSA 1993, s. 23 or s. 24 (s. 26). Appeals may be delegated to appointed persons under Environment Act, s. 114. The procedure for appeals is contained in the Radioactive Substances (Appeals) Regulations 1990 (SI 1990/2504).

10.6 FURTHER POWERS IN RELATION
TO RADIOACTIVE WASTE

Under RSA 1993, s. 29 the Secretary of State may arrange for the provision of facilities for the safe disposal or accumulation of radioactive waste, where it appears to him that these are not otherwise available.

If there is radioactive waste on any premises and the EA is satisfied that the waste ought to be disposed of but, because the premises are unoccupied, the occupier is absent or insolvent or for some other reason, it is unlikely the waste will otherwise be lawfully disposed of, the EA has power to dispose of that waste as it thinks fit, and recover its reasonable expenses of so doing (RSA 1993, s. 30).

10.7 OFFENCES, ENFORCEMENT AND RECORDS

The main offences under the Act are contained in RSA 1993, s. 32. The maximum fine on summary conviction is £20,000 and the maximum prison sentence is six months. On indictment, an unlimited fine and/or five years' imprisonment are the maximum penalties that may be imposed. Under s. 32(3) if the EA is of the opinion that proceedings for an offence relating to an enforcement notice or prohibition notice would be an ineffectual remedy, it may take proceedings in the High Court, for the purpose of securing compliance (Environment Act, sch. 22, para. 219).

Powers of entry and inspection (in former RSA 1993, s. 31) and the offence of obstruction (in former RSA 1993, s. 35) are now covered by Environment Act, ss. 108 to 110 (see 14.5).

RSA 1993, s. 34A (inserted by Environment Act, sch. 19, para. 6) introduces an offence of making false or misleading statements, for the purpose of obtaining registration or authorisation, etc, and making false entries in records required to be kept under or by virtue of the Act.

RSA 1993, s. 39 requires the EA to keep records of applications made to it, documents issued by it, and of convictions under the Act. Copies of these are to be made available to the public except where a trade secret is involved (see s. 34) or the Secretary of State has directed that knowledge of information should be restricted on grounds of national security (see above — s. 25).

Chapter 11
Aims, Objectives and General Functions
of the Environment Agency

This chapter deals with the following sections of the Environment Act:

section 4 — Principal aim and objectives of the EA
sections 5 and 6 — General functions with respect to pollution control and water
section 7 — General environmental and recreational duties
section 8 — Environmental duties with respect to sites of special interest
section 9 — Codes of practice with respect to environmental and recreational duties
section 39 — General duty of the new agencies to have regard to costs and benefits in exercising powers.

Sections 4, 7, 9 and 39 came into force upon the establishment of the EA on 28 July 1995 (Environment Act 1995 (Commencement No. 1) Order 1995 (SI 1995/1983). Sections 5, 6 and 8 are expected to come into force on the 'transfer date' (which is proposed to be 1 April 1996).

11.1 PRINCIPAL AIM AND OBJECTIVES

Environment Act, s. 4 is a key provision which sets out the principal aim and objectives of the EA. Subsection (1) provides that it shall be the principal aim of the EA, in discharging its functions, so to protect or enhance the environment, taken as a whole, as to make the contribution towards attaining the objective of achieving sustainable development mentioned in subs. (3). Subsection (2) requires 'Ministers' (i.e., the Secretary of State and the Minister of Agriculture, Fisheries and Food) from time to time to give guidance to the EA with respect to objectives which they consider it appropriate for the EA to pursue in the discharge of its functions but subs. (3) provides that any such guidance must include guidance with respect to the contribution which, having regard to the EA's responsibilities and resources, the Ministers consider it appropriate to the EA to make, by the discharge of its functions, towards attaining the objective of achieving sustainable development. There are, however, two important qualifications to the principal aim set out in subs. (1). The words in parentheses in that subsection make the principal aim 'subject to and in accordance with' the provisions of the Environment Act itself 'or any other enactment'. Accordingly, where an enactment expressly or impliedly requires the EA to adopt a particular course, or to have regard to particular matters, in exercising a function, that will have precedence over the EA's principal aim. Secondly, the words in parentheses in subs. (1) provide that, in following the principal aim, the EA must 'take into account any likely costs'. This requirement must be read together with s. 39 which requires the EA (and SEPA) to have regard to costs and benefits, in exercising its powers. These provisions are discussed at 11.1.2.

11.1.1 Sustainable development

As mentioned in chapter 2.5, the concept of sustainable development originated in the 1987 Report of the World Commission on Environment and Development (or 'Brundtland Report') (see *Sustainable Development: the UK Strategy* (Cm. 2426) (London: HMSO, 1994).

'Sustainable development' has been defined as 'development that meets the needs of the present without compromising the ability of future generations to meet their own needs'. (ibid., p. 27). During the passage of the Environment Bill, Ministers were, however, reluctant to give an actual definition of the expression. Thus, for example, Viscount Ullswater said at report stage in the House of Lords that:

> the concept of sustainable development should be left to the guidance produced by Ministers which will be subject to review. I do not believe that it would be right for me to indicate what I believe sustainable development to be. Especially after *Pepper* v *Hart,* it would be better left to the guidance which will be issued by Ministers. (Hansard, HL, 2 March 1995, col. 1631.)

The question of guidance is dealt with at 11.1.3 below. Nevertheless, during the second reading of the Bill in the House of Commons on 18 April 1995, the Secretary of State for the Environment (John Gummer MP) commented extensively on the expression:

> Balance is at the heart of sustainable development. The two words, sustainability and development, need to be held together if we are to get a sensible answer. We need to grow, if we are to provide the resources our people need, but at the same time we need to grow in a sustainable way. It is not easy to keep those two words together. When people talk about sustainability but fail to talk about growth, they are talking about the destruction of society, for a society without the resources for improvement, change and betterment is not one in which we would wish to live.
>
> Those who talk about growth without giving any indication of how to make it sustainable are betraying the next generation. The two words must be kept permanently together. That means reconciling the needs of the environment and of economic development, rather than pursuing one at the cost of the other. It means placing the concept of the environment at the centre of decision making, rather than as an add-on extra. (Hansard, HC, 18 April 1995, cols. 37–8.)

11.1.2 Costs and benefits

The requirement in Environment Act, s. 4 for the EA to take into account likely costs has been criticised by environmental groups, as has s. 39, which provides that the EA (or SEPA), in considering whether or not to exercise any power conferred on it by or under any enactment, or in deciding the manner in which to exercise any such power, shall take into account the likely costs and benefits of the exercise or non-exercise of the power or its exercise in the manner in question. That duty does not, however, apply if or to the extent that it is unreasonable for the EA to take account of likely costs and benefits (a) in view of the nature or purpose of the power or (b) in the circumstances of the particular case. Subsection (2) provides that the duty does not affect the EA's (or SEPA's) obligation to discharge any duties, comply with any requirements, or pursue any objectives, imposed upon or given to it otherwise than under s. 39.

During the passage of the Bill through the House of Lords, concern was expressed that clause 37 (as it then was) would invite applications by, for example, industry or landowners for judicial review of almost anything that the EA did, on the grounds that it had paid insufficient regard to the costs of having to comply with environmental requirements. The government did not share these concerns but it undertook to look at the question of whether the references to 'costs and benefits' in clause 37 were expressed in sufficiently wide terms to enable them to cover *environmental* benefits and *environmental* costs, as well as financial ones (see Hansard, HL, 31 January 1995, col. 1376). The wording of the clause was subsequently amended at report stage to produce what is now s. 39, in consequence of the introduction of what is now s. 4. At the same time, the interpretation provision for Part I (now s. 56(1)) was amended to provide expressly that references to 'costs' in that Part include costs to any person and costs to the environment (Hansard, HL, 2 March 1995, col. 1621).

The Secretary of State explained the government's thinking with regard to costs and benefits at second reading in the House of Commons:

> . . . we must take proper account of costs and benefits. Only in that way can we ensure that environmental priorities are central to the way in which we make up our minds about what we do, and are not something that one bothers about only when one can afford it.
>
> Costs are important. We cannot deliver on environmental demands unless we take into account the costs and ensure that they are proportionate to the benefits that we gain. We can all give a list of desiderata, but we also need a list of priorities for we must ensure that we do not do the least important things first, or we will find that there are no resources left for doing the things that really matter. . . .
>
> If one does not undertake cost-benefit analysis — if one does not make it necessary to express the importance of the environment in the imperative language that will appeal to bankers, as well as those who are naturally enthusiastic about flora and fauna — one will not give the environment the importance that it should have. Cost-benefit analysis is a crucial way of raising the profile of the environment, not only through the agency but elsewhere. (Hansard, HC, 18 April 1995, cols. 38, 43.)

11.1.3   Guidance to the EA on its objectives

As has already been mentioned, Environment Act, s. 4 requires the Ministers to give guidance to the EA on its objectives, including guidance on the contribution which the EA should make towards attaining the objective of achieving sustainable development. Subsection (4) requires the EA, in discharging its functions, to have regard to such guidance.

The power of the Ministers to give guidance to the EA is exercisable only after consultation with the EA and such other bodies or persons as the Ministers consider it appropriate to consult in relation to the guidance in question. Although the guidance is not required to be contained in a statutory instrument, subss. (6) to (8), somewhat unusually, provide for it to have certain of the characteristics of a statutory instrument which is subject to what is known as 'negative resolution' procedure. Under the provisions, the draft guidance is to be laid before each House of Parliament and may not be given until after 40 days from the date of laying (or, if the draft is laid on different days, the later of the two days). If either House of Parliament resolves within the 40 day period, that the guidance should not be given, the Ministers shall not give it. Subsection (9) requires the Ministers to arrange for any guidance given under s. 4 to be published in such manner as they consider to be appropriate.

11.1.4   Draft guidance of April 1995

In order to be ready with draft guidance to be laid before Parliament after the establishment of the EA the government published on 20 April 1995 draft guidance, for consultation, under the title 'Guidance to the Environment Agency under the Environment Bill on its objectives, including the contribution it is to make towards the achievement of sustainable development'.

11.1.4.1   Principles of sustainable development   The draft guidance contains a long section on the principles of sustainable development, drawing upon the Rio Declaration and the UK's own Sustainable Development Strategy (see 11.1.1). Although many forms of economic development are acknowledged to make demands upon the environment, the draft states that:

> there are also many ways in which the right kind of economic activity can protect or enhance the environment. Sustainable development does not mean having less economic development; on the contrary, a healthy economy is better able to generate the resources to meet people's needs, and new investment and environmental improvement often go hand in hand. Nor does it mean that every aspect of the present environment should be preserved at all costs. What it requires is that decisions throughout society are taken with proper regard to their environmental impact. (4.2.)

The draft refers to the complementary or supporting principles which have recently been developed. Although the government 'remains committed to basing action on fact, using the best scientific information available', the draft reaffirms the UKs acceptance of the 'precautionary principle', under which, 'where there are significant risks of damage to the environment, the government will be prepared to take precautionary action to limit the use of potentially dangerous materials or the spread of potentially dangerous pollutants, even where scientific knowledge is not conclusive, if the balance of likely costs and benefits justifies it' (4.6).

The draft also refers to cost-benefit considerations:

> Sometimes environmental costs have to be accepted as the price of economic development, but on other occasions a site, or an ecosystem, or some other aspect of the environment, has to be regarded as so valuable that it should be protected from exploitation. Such judgments should make a proper allowance for the interests of future generations and for the pressures that society places upon the global environment. (4.9.)

The 'polluter pays' principle, adopted by the OECD in 1972, is affirmed so that 'if the polluter, or ultimately the consumer, is made to pay, then the costs of pollution, waste and the consumption of natural resources are brought into the calculations of the enterprise' (4.10).

The draft acknowledges that 'translating principles into practice is not easy', since whilst 'in principle, it should be possible through cost-benefit analysis to place values upon any of the impacts made on the environment by economic development, in practice it is not always possible to quantify the value of improvements or losses to the environment' (4.11).

11.1.4.2 Contribution EA is to make towards achieving sustainable develop-ment Having dealt with the principles of sustainable development, the draft guidance sets out, in sect. 5, the contribution which the EA is to make towards achieving that goal. Paragraph 5.1 states that Ministers, having reflected on the principles outlined in s. 4 of the draft guidance, have concluded that the EA will make the appropriate contribution towards achieving sustainable development in discharging its functions if it acts in accordance with the guidance in paras 5.2 to 5.7 and, in relation to costs and benefits, at paras 6.2 to 6.7. The EA must also have regard to the guidance referred to in section 7 of the document.

Paras 5.2 to 5.7 require the EA, *inter alia*:

(a)   to strive to optimise benefit to the environment as a whole;

(b)   to exercise its functions in a manner which takes account of cross-media impacts;

(c)   to take account of longer-term implications and effects, especially those that may be irreversible or reversible only at high cost over a long timescale;

(d)   to pay particular attention to conservation issues and the carrying capacity of relevant habitats or ecosystems, when considering proposals affecting important sites such as Sites of Special Scientific Interest and Special Areas of Conservation;

(e)   to recognise that the greatest scope for reconciling the needs of the environment and development is likely to lie in the adoption of improved technologies and management techniques and, accordingly, to discharge its functions where possible in partnership with business;

(f)   to develop close and responsive relationships with the public, local communities and regulatory organisations and to work in partnership with relevant non-governmental organisations, local government and other parts of central government;

(g)   to strive to become a recognised centre of knowledge and expertise.

Paragraph 6.2 explains the requirement in Environment Act, s. 4 for the EA to take into account any likely costs. This duty is intended to ensure proper consideration by the EA of the implications for sustainable development of the options open to it, both in its strategic planning and in individual cases, such as to ensure that measures which have environmental benefits, or the avoidance of environmental costs, do not impose disproportionately large economic costs. The duty will, it is considered, generally involve assessments about whether or not to take action, the appropriate levels of any controls and the various options for achieving a given environmental objective. Risk analysis techniques and cost-benefit analyses will be useful in this regard, but costs and benefits which are unquantifiable or which cannot be given monetary valuations should also be considered. Overall, 'the duty is one which ultimately requires the exercise of judgment by the Agency'.

On the question of costs and benefits, reference should also be made to Environment Act, s. 39 (see 11.1.2).

Paragraphs 6.2 to 6.7 require the EA, *inter alia*:

(a)   to concentrate on the costs and benefits of its actions for society as a whole, the effects on the welfare of people and business, changes in the use of resources and impacts on the environment;

(b)   to take account of longer-term implications and effects;

(c)   to develop practical procedures to ensure that it meets the requirements of the duty to take account of any likely costs, including relevant advice to staff.

Paragraph 7 concerns guidance material. The EA is required to comply with and enforce 'all relevant legislation and directions'. There follows a set of guidance provisions structured by reference to the EA's main functions, although para. 7.2 states that the EA 'must have due regard to the interplay within and between the pollution control and water management functions and seek to identify the best practicable environmental option, taking a holistic approach to the environment'.

11.1.4.3   Integrated pollution control (IPC)   The draft guidance states that the government's policy aims for IPC explicitly recognise the principles of sustainable development through the use of the concepts of BATNEEC (best available techniques not entailing excessive cost) and BPEO (best practicable environmental option). These two concepts 'are designed to achieve levels of pollution control from installations covered by IPC which achieve a sustainable balance between society's interests in the environment and in industry, in both the short and the long term'. More detailed specific guidance on BATNEEC and BPEO is intended to be issued later in 1995. Ministers expect the EA to continue to apply the concepts of BATNEEC and BPEO through IPC authorisations in such a way as to ensure that its IPC functions respect the principles of sustainable development. However, the EA is also expected to consider whether either or both of these concepts could be of wider relevance in its work.

11.1.4.4 Radioactive substances The government's consultation document of August 1994 sets out its policy aims on radioactive waste management, which recognise the principles of sustainable development by seeking to minimise the creation of nuclear wastes, to ensure that the treatment and handling of wastes are carried out with due regard to environmental considerations (without unacceptable exposure of the workforce) and to ensure that wastes are disposed of in appropriate ways, at appropriate times and in appropriate places. Within this framework, waste producers should be responsible for developing their own waste management strategies, in accordance with the 'polluter pays' principle. The guidance on radioactive substances will, however, be recast following publication of the government's forthcoming White Paper.

11.1.4.5 Waste regulation The production of a national waste strategy under EPA 1990, s. 44A, is dealt with in chapter 20. At the time of writing a revised version of the government's draft waste strategy, which was first published in January 1995, is awaited. The existing draft strategy was based on three key objectives:

(a)   to reduce the amount of waste that society produces;
(b)   to make best use of the waste that is produced;
(c)   to choose waste management practices which minimise the risk of immediate and future environmental pollution and harm to human health.

These objectives are intended to be achieved by a 'waste hierarchy' based upon reduction, reuse, recovery and disposal, with an increase in the proportion of waste managed by the options towards the top of the waste hierarchy. The EA's role in the delivery of the national waste strategy is through its regulatory functions in relation to wastes (to be augmented by new responsibilities in relation to producer responsibility — see Environment Act, ss. 93 and 94 and chapter 20, through advice and guidance, by sponsoring research, and through the improved collection of data. The EA is expected to exercise its functions so as to help achieve the aims and objectives of the national waste strategy and thereby to contribute to sustainable development (draft guidance to the EA, 7.17).

11.1.4.6 Water protection The draft guidance states that the general aim of the exercise of the EA's water protection powers and duties should be to prevent deterioration of the quality of the water environment, except where unavoidable, and to seek its improvement according to agreed priorities. The EA must give effect to all legal (including EC) obligations in this area, taking into account the costs and benefits of the specific measures proposed, when it is free to do so.

11.1.4.7 Contaminated land and abandoned mines The government's policies in respect of this subject are set out in the context of sustainable development in the document, *A Framework for Contaminated Land,* published in November 1994 (see chapter 16). The government is committed to the 'suitable for use' approach to the control and treatment of contamination, which reduces damage from past activities and permits contaminated land to be kept in, or returned to, beneficial use wherever practicable thereby minimising pressure for development of greenfield sites. Since the wealth-creating sections of the economy could not afford to deal with all land contaminated by past activities at once, urgent and real problems should be dealt with in 'an orderly and controlled fashion with which the economy at large and individual businesses and landowners can cope' (draft guidance to the EA, 7.23). Forthcoming government guidance on the extent to which contamination causes or is likely to cause 'significant harm', and thus requires remedial action, will play an important part in delivering the 'suitable for use' approach. The EA will be expected to contribute towards sustainable development by exercising its functions in relation to contaminated land and abandoned mines.

11.1.4.8   Water management   The draft guidance stresses that, in order to protect and enhance the water environment, the EA must (subject to any remaining legal constraints) exercise its various functions in an integrated manner (7.26), such integration to cover not only the EA's activities which are primarily concerned with water, but also its other activities that can have a direct or indirect effect on water, such as IPC, waste regulation and contaminated land regulation. Since the sea is the natural final recipient in the hydrological cycle, the EA must additionally take into account the sustainability of relevant marine environments and the UK's international obligations. The key elements which the government considers should govern the EA's activities are:

(a)   a strategic approach to river management,
(b)   proper recognition of the need to work with natural river and coastal processes, rather than against them, wherever possible,
(c)   an integration of technical, economic and environmental factors in decision-making,
(d)   assessment of costs and benefits, including those to people and the environment, and
(e)   proper consultation with landowning, commercial and environmental interests affected by the EA's water management activities.

11.1.4.9   Water resource control   Paragraph 7.27 states that the EA, in regulating river flow and access to water resources, must balance the frequently competing requirements of human beings, enterprises of various kinds, natural habitats, fisheries and (in some cases) recreation and navigation. The EA has a duty to conserve, redistribute and augment water resources. The government considers that, in the longer term, pressures on water resources will be a significant issue in sustainable development (particularly in the South and East of England) and the EA's use of its regulatory and other powers will be crucial in securing adequate supplies for domestic, agricultural, commercial and industrial purposes, while maintaining and improving the natural environment. The EA will be expected to use its powers and to encourage water conservation in areas of potential shortage, where it is economic to do so. The EA should also pursue and develop the NRA's 1994 National Water Resource Strategy.

11.1.4.10   Flood defence   The government's aim is 'to reduce the risks to people and to the developed and natural environment from flooding and coastal erosion' (7.28). Except where life (the highest priority) or important natural or man-made assets are at risk, natural river or coastal processes should not be disrupted. The effects on wildlife habitats are, however, 'a key consideration'. 'Sustainable flood and coastal defence schemes are those which take account of natural processes and other defences and developments within a river catchment or coastal sediment cell and which avoid as far as possible committing future generations to inflexible and expensive options for defence' (7.29).

11.1.4.11 Fisheries According to the government, the health and abundance of freshwater fish stocks in England and Wales will demonstrate the EA's success in meeting water protection and management objectives. In exercising its duty under Environment Act, s. 6(6) to maintain, improve and develop salmon, trout, freshwater and eel fisheries the EA is required to seek to develop sustainable fisheries, having particular regard to the need to maintain and (where appropriate) enhance the natural diversity of fish species and to maintain the genetic integrity of individual stocks (7.30–1).

11.1.4.12 Recreation The EA inherits the NRA's duty to promote the use of inland and coastal waters and land associated with such waters for recreational purposes (without prejudice to the conservation and enhancement of natural beauty and the conservation of flora, fauna and geological or physiographical features of special interest). Paragraph 7.32 provides that the government's code of practice on 'Conservation, Access and Recreation', issued under s. 10 of the Water Act 1989, still applies to this duty. Under the code the EA must secure the best recreational use of suitable existing and new resources, catering fairly for as broad a range of interest groups as practicable, and ensure that the recreational needs of the surrounding area are taken fully into account. Public use of recreational facilities should be subject to suitable terms and conditions.

11.1.4.13 Navigation Following the code of practice just referred to, the EA should have regard, in its navigation duties, to landscape, nature and archaeological conservation and environmental protection and enhancement. Necessary steps should be taken to protect wildlife and landscape from the harmful effects of navigation (in particular, controlling the speed and level of boat traffic) (7.33).

11.2 GENERAL FUNCTIONS WITH RESPECT TO POLLUTION CONTROL

Environment Act, s. 5(1) provides that the EA's pollution control powers shall be exercisable for the purpose of preventing or minimising, or remedying or mitigating the effects of, pollution of the environment.

The EA is required, by Environment Act, s. 5(2), to compile information relating to the pollution of the environment, for the purpose of facilitating the carrying out of its pollution control functions or of enabling the EA to form an opinion of the general state of pollution of the environment. Such information may be compiled by the EA carrying out its own observations or be obtained in any other way.

Environment Act, s. 5(3) places the EA under a duty to provide Ministers with information about environmental pollution which they specifically request from it. The EA may be required to carry out general or specific assessments of the effect, or likely effect, on the environment of existing or potential levels of pollution, and report its findings. It may also be required to report to Ministers on the options available for preventing or minimising, or remedying or mitigating the effects of, pollution of the environment (together with the costs and benefits of such options, as identified by the EA).

The EA is required by Environment Act, s. 5(4) to follow developments in technology, and techniques for preventing or minimising, or remedying or mitigating the effects of, pollution of the environment.

Environment Act, s. 5(5) defines the EA's 'pollution control powers' and 'pollution control functions', for the purposes of s. 5, by reference to a list of enactments, which are covered in chapters 4, 8, 9, 10, 16 and 17, together with 'regulations made by virtue of section 2(2) of the European Communities Act 1972, to the extent that the regulations relate to pollution' (s. 5(5)(j)).

11.3 GENERAL PROVISIONS WITH RESPECT TO WATER

Environment Act, s. 6 requires the EA, to such extent as it considers desirable, to promote the conservation and enhancement of the natural beauty and amenity of inland and coastal waters and of land associated with such waters, the conservation of flora and fauna which are dependent on an aquatic environment and the use of such waters and land for recreational purposes. The EA is required, in determining what steps to take in the performance of its duty to promote the recreational use of water, to take account of the needs of persons who are chronically sick or disabled.

The duties just described are expressed to be without prejudice to the EA's duties under Environment Act, s. 7 (see below). When an amendment was moved in Committee in the House of Lords to leave out this last provision, the Minister (Viscount Ullswater) explained the government's view of the relationship between clauses 6 and 7 (as they then were):

Clause 7 requires the agency to further conservation (or to have regard to it) generally, not just in relation to inland and coastal waters and land associated with those waters. That duty applies whenever the agency is formulating or considering proposals relating to its functions. Clause 6 gives the agency an independent role in relation to conservation and recreation in relation to the 'watery' environment. Clause 7 ensures that the agency does what it can in relation to conservation in performing its other functions. . . . the clause 6 duty does not detract from the duty imposed by clause 7; in other words, the duties are independent of each other and are accumulative. The noble Lord [Moran] seeks to remove the 'without prejudice' provision. As I understand it, that would leave the relationship between the two clauses unclear. For that reason, the amendment should not be accepted by the committee. (Hansard, HL, 19 January 1995, col. 806.)

Environment Act, s. 6(2) provides that it shall be the duty of the EA to take all such action as it may from time to time consider, in accordance with directions given under Environment Act, s. 40 (which provides for Ministerial directions to the EA and SEPA — see chapter 14), to be necessary or expedient for the purpose of conserving, redistributing or otherwise augmenting water resources in England and Wales and of securing the proper use of water resources in England and Wales. However, nothing in s. 6(2) is to be construed as relieving any water undertaker of the obligation to develop water resources for the purpose of performing any duty imposed on that undertaker by virtue of WIA 1991, s. 37 (which provides for the general duty to maintain the water supply system).

Environment Act, s. 6(3) restricts the operation of certain water resources provisions in the WRA 1991 (namely, abstraction and impounding) in the case of certain rivers on the borders of England and Scotland (see 3.3), whilst s. 6(4) imposes on the EA a general supervisory duty over all matters relating to flood defence (see chapter 5). The EA's flood defence functions extend to certain parts of the territorial sea (Environment Act, s. 6(5) — see 5.2).

Environment Act, s. 6(6) imposes on the EA a general duty to maintain, improve and develop salmon fisheries, trout fisheries, freshwater fisheries and eel fisheries, in respect of the whole of England and Wales, and certain sea and river areas described in s. 6(7) (see 6.2).

11.4   GENERAL ENVIRONMENTAL AND RECREATIONAL DUTIES

The background to what became clause 7 of the Environment Bill (now section 7 of the Act) has been described in 2.6.

11.4.1   Duty to further conservation etc.

Environment Act, s. 7(1)(a) imposes a duty on Ministers and the EA, in formulating or considering any proposals relating to any functions of the EA, other than its pollution control functions (see 11.2 above), so to exercise any powers conferred on them or it as to further the conservation and enhancement of natural beauty and the conservation of flora, fauna and geographical or physiographical features of special interest. The duty applies to such proposals so far as may be consistent:

(a)   with the purposes of any enactment relating to the functions of the EA;
(b)   in the case of Ministers, with the objective of achieving sustainable development;
(c)   in the case of the EA, with any guidance given under s. 4 (see above); and
(d)   in the case of the Secretary of State, with his general duties with respect to the water industry under WIA 1991, s. 2.

11.4.2   Duty to have regard to desirability of conservation etc. in case of pollution control functions

Environment Act, s. 7(1)(b) provides that, when formulating or considering any proposals relating to the EA's pollution control functions, Ministers and the EA have a duty to have regard to the desirability of conserving and enhancing natural beauty and of conserving flora, fauna and geological or physiographical features of special interest.

11.4.3   The exception to the s. 7(1) duty

The exception, in Environment Act, s. 7(1), of the EA's pollution control functions from the stricter duty imposed by that subsection, was heavily criticised both inside and outside Parliament, and several attempts were made during the passage of the Environment Bill to have the exception removed. The NRA, whose own statutory duty was unqualified, told the House of Commons Environment Committee that it wanted to see the proposed new duty 'to further conservation', extended to the EA's pollution control functions. HMIP, however, did not see the necessity for such a duty, nor did the government. During report stage in the House of Lords, an amendment was moved to delete the exception. For the government, Viscount Ullswater explained that they had:

considered carefully the conservation role of the agency. We are sure that it is right that it should have proper regard for the needs of conservation in discharging all its functions, and the Bill seeks to ensure that. We have already rehearsed the arguments on this duty on a number of occasions. As I have said before, the NRA's existing duty is not unqualified and must be adapted to the broader functions of the agency. To further conservation in every case would be inconsistent with the agency's role in issuing environmental licences. And I do not believe that the changes to the duty in relation to water discharge consents [see chapter 4.1.3] will in practice damage the interests of conservation. (Hansard, HL, 2 March 1995, cols. 1659–60).

The legal arguments for and against the exception were described by Sir Kenneth Carlisle MP in committee in the House of Commons:

The duty 'to further conservation' was consolidated in the Water Resources Act 1991, but it was always qualified and weakened by the stated need to be consistent with the purposes of other Acts. The other most relevant Act in that respect is the Environmental Protection Act 1990, which sets the rules for Her Majesty's Inspectorate of Pollution to license emissions within the framework of best available technique, not entailing excessive cost and best practicable environmental option. Therefore, the higher duty of the Water Resources Act — that is, to further conservation — always had to give way to the lower duties enacted in the Environmental Protection Act 1990. That is a confused issue, which was never tested in the courts. If that duty for further [sic] conservation is carried forward strictly into the Environment Bill, the government are worried that a clash with the Environmental Protection Act might lead to problems. For example, the Environment Agency might license a new process, which still pollutes, but which pollutes less than the existing technology that it will replace. As pollution of any sort cannot further nature conservation, the agency might have to turn the application down even though the new process would lead to less pollution.
    All that is a little convoluted and there are conflicting views on the right interpretation. I believe, first, that the duty in the Water Resources Act 1991 to further conservation was heavily qualified. Secondly, there is a fear that imposing a strict duty on the Environment Agency would, in rare cases, lead to

more pollution. Thirdly, and more broadly, the government believe that, under the Bill, the new agency will be able fairly to take into account all the many conflicting demands placed before it by all those who will look to it for a solution. That, as I understand it, is the government's argument for the clause. (Hansard, HC, Standing Committee B, Environment Bill, Sixth Sitting, 11 May 1995, cols 192–3.)

The Minister (Robert Atkins MP) replied that:

we considered very carefully similar amendments when they were debated in the other place. But we remain convinced that it [the EA] should have proper regard to the needs of conservation in discharging all its functions, and the Bill seeks to ensure that. It must do so in ways which are consistent with the agency's key role in issuing environmental licences. An overriding duty to further conservation in every case would be inconsistent with the effective discharge of these functions. (Ibid., col. 196.)

11.4.4   Duty to have regard to buildings, sites, natural beauty etc.

Environment Act, s. 7(1)(c) requires Ministers and the EA, in formulating or considering any proposals relating to any functions of the EA:

(i)   to have regard to the desirability of protecting and conserving buildings, sites and objects of archaeological, architectural, engineering or historic interest;
(ii)   to take into account any effect which the proposals would have on the beauty or amenity of any rural or urban area or on any such flora, fauna, features, buildings, sites or objects and;
(iii)   to have regard to any effect which the proposals would have on the economic and social well-being of local communities in rural areas.

The requirement in s. 7(1)(c)(iii) was not present in former WRA 1991, s. 16(1), upon which Environment Act, s. 7(1)(c) is based. It was added at report stage in the House of Lords, as an amendment of Lord Wade of Chorlton who stated that:

The environment of our rural areas is a managed one. It depends on the people who live there, who create it and those who have businesses there. In an earlier part of the discussion on the new clause my noble friend mentioned the fact that sustainable development is a balance between ensuring the environmental advantage on the one side and how to achieve development within it on the other. . . . I believe that we also need to have a balance on the face of the Bill.
. . .

I am sure that all noble Lords will agree with me that it is very important that this Bill pays due recognition to the importance of the people who work and have their well-being within our rural areas. (Hansard, HL, 2 March 1995, col. 1664.)

11.4.5   Duty to have regard to desirability of preserving public access etc.

Environment Act, s. 7(2) is based upon former WRA 1991, s. 16(2). Section 7(2) requires Ministers and the EA, in formulating or considering proposals relating to any functions of the EA:

(a)   to have regard to the desirability of preserving for the public any freedom of access to areas of woodland, mountains, moor, heath, down, cliff or foreshore and other places of natural beauty;

(b)   to have regard to the desirability of maintaining the availability to the public of any facility for visiting or inspecting any building, site or object of archaeological, architectural, engineering or historic interest; and

(c)   to take into account any effect which the proposals would have on any such freedom of access or on the availability of any such facility.

11.4.6   Application of s. 7(1) and (2) duties in relation to certain proposals

Environment Act, s. 7(3) applies s. 7(1) and (2) so as to impose duties on the EA in relation to any proposals relating to the functions of a water or sewerage undertaker, the management of any land held by a company appointed as such an undertaker and certain disposals of protected land covered by WIA 1991, s. 156(7). These cases fall to be treated as if the proposals related to the EA's own functions, and Environment Act, s. 7(1)(a) and (2) accordingly apply.

11.4.7   Exercise of rights to use water etc.

Where the EA has rights to use water, or land associated with water, Environment Act, s. 7(4) requires the EA to take such steps as are reasonably practicable, and consistent with the purposes of the various enactments relating to the EA's functions, to use the rights to ensure that the water or land is made available in the best manner for recreational purposes. The duty is subject to the EA obtaining consents from any navigation authority, harbour authority or conservancy authority before doing anything which causes obstruction of, or other interference with, navigation which is within the control of that authority. For an explanation of the nature of navigation, harbour and conservancy authorities, see chapter 7.

It is important to note that Environment Act, s. 7(6) expressly provides that nothing in s. 7, the following provisions of the Environment Act or the WRA 1991 shall require recreational facilities provided by the EA to be made available free of charge.

11.5   ENVIRONMENTAL DUTIES WITH RESPECT TO SITES OF SPECIAL INTEREST

Environment Act, s. 8 is based on former WRA 1991, s. 17. It enables the Nature Conservancy Council for England, the Countryside Commission for Wales, a National Park authority or the Broads Authority to notify the EA that land is of special interest, whereupon the EA is required to consult the notifying body before carrying out or authorising certain works, operations or activities which are likely to affect that land.

Under s. 8(1) the bodies referred to above may notify the EA if of the opinion that land is of special interest by reason of its flora, fauna or geological or physiographical features and that the land may at any time be affected by schemes, works, operations or activities of the EA or by an authorisation given by the EA. In addition, where a National Park authority (see chapter 18) or the Broads Authority (see the Norfolk and Suffolk Broads Act 1988) is of the opinion that any area in a National Park or the Broads is land in respect of which Environment Act, ss. 6(1) and 7 have particular relevance and is land which may at any time be affected by schemes etc. as just described, the authority shall notify the EA of that fact, and of the reasons therefor. There is an exception where the relevant matter relates to the economic and social well-being of communities in rural areas (see s. 7(1)(c)(iii) and 11.4.5 above). Section 8(3) requires the EA, where it has received a s. 8(1) or (2) notification, to consult the notifying body before carrying out or authorising any works, operations or activities which appear to the EA to be likely to destroy or damage flora, fauna etc. or significantly prejudice anything of importance which was, in effect, one of the reasons for the s. 8(2) notification.

Section 8(4) qualifies the s. 8(3) duty in cases of emergency where particulars of what is done and of the emergency are notified to the body in question as soon as practicable thereafter.

11.6   CODES OF PRACTICE WITH RESPECT TO ENVIRONMENTAL AND RECREATIONAL DUTIES

Environment Act, s. 9 is based on former WRA 1991, s. 18. It enables Ministers to approve codes of practice to be issued for the purpose of giving practical guidance to the EA on the purposes behind Environment Act, ss. 6(1), 7 and 8, and promoting desirable practices by the EA on those matters. The approval power is exercisable by order, and Ministers may at any time by such an order approve a modification of a code or withdraw approval of a code or modification.

The order-making power is exercisable only after consultation with the EA itself, the Countryside Commission, the Nature Conservancy Council for England, the Countryside Council for Wales, the Historic Buildings and Monuments Commission for England ('English Heritage'), the Sports Council for Wales and such other persons as the Minister in question considers it appropriate to consult.

Environment Act, s. 9(2) requires the EA, in discharging its duties under s. 6(1), 7 or 8, to have regard to any code of practice, and any modification of a code of practice, for the time being approved under s. 9.

Chapter 12
The Scottish Environmental Protection Agency

12.1 INTRODUCTION

The intention to create a separate environment agency for Scotland was announced by the government at the same time as it unveiled its plans to establish the EA for England and Wales. The Scottish agency, now called the Scottish Environmental Protection Agency (SEPA), is established by the Environment Act in a similar way to the EA (see below). Its role is, however, somewhat different to that of its counterpart in England and Wales, largely because there was in Scotland no equivalent of the National Rivers Authority, with its wide-ranging functions, including important pollution control and water resources duties.

In Scotland, the nearest equivalents to the NRA were the river purification authorities, but they did not have the wider environmental responsibilities of the NRA. By assuming the functions of river purification authorities, SEPA therefore has a narrower remit in water matters than does the EA.

By contrast, SEPA assumes pollution control functions which are not transferred to the EA. Owing to the relatively small number of air-polluting processes in Scotland under Part I of the EPA 1990, once the decision had been taken to establish SEPA as a separate organisation, the government concluded that it should also absorb the '25 or so' staff in Scotland working on local authority air pollution control. Accordingly, SEPA assumes local authorities' responsibilities as enforcing authorities for air pollution control under Part I, thereby achieving a more fully integrated approach than was considered to be appropriate in the case of England and Wales, where some 14,000 air emission processes fall within the scope of Part I.

This chapter describes the establishment and structure of SEPA, and the various functions transferred to it by Environment Act, s. 21. SEPA was formally established on 12 October 1995 (Environment Act 1995 (Commencement No. 2) Order 1995). As with the EA, the text is written on the basis that SEPA has come fully into operation, although this does not happen until the 'transfer date' which is proposed to be 1 April 1996.

12.2   ESTABLISHMENT, MEMBERSHIP AND STRUCTURE OF SEPA

12.2.1   Establishment and membership

Environment Act, s. 20(1) establishes SEPA as a body for the purpose of carrying out the functions transferred or assigned to it by or under the Act. Environment Act, sch. 6 confirms that SEPA is a body corporate with a common seal. SEPA is to consist of not less than eight, nor more than 12, members, all of whom are appointees of the Secretary of State. In making appointments, the Secretary of State must have regard to the desirability of appointing persons who have knowledge or experience in some matter relevant to the functions of SEPA. The Secretary of State has power by order made by statutory instrument to alter the minimum and maximum membership of SEPA.

The Secretary of State is required to appoint one of the members of SEPA to be chairman and another to be deputy chairman.

Like Environment Act, sch. 1 in the case of the EA, sch. 6 contains detailed provisions concerning the appointment and removal of members and the chairman and deputy chairman, the remuneration of members and staff, rules of procedure and the handling of members' interests.

Unlike sch. 1, however, para. 10 of sch. 6 requires the Secretary of State to make the first appointment of chief officer of SEPA, after consultation with the chairman or chairman designate (if there is such a person). Thereafter SEPA may make subsequent appointments to the office of chief officer, with the approval of the Secretary of State.

On 19 July 1995, it was announced that the Secretary of State for Scotland had identified Professor William Trumeau as chairman designate of SEPA.

12.2.2   Committees etc.

Environment Act, sch. 6 enables SEPA to appoint persons who are not members of it to be members of any committee established by SEPA, provided that at least one member of the committee is a SEPA member. Anything authorised or required by or under any enactment to be done by SEPA may be done by any of its committees or employees, provided that the committee or employee concerned is authorised to do so by SEPA (whether generally or specifically).

12.2.3   Regional Boards.

Unlike the EA, SEPA is given an express statutory duty in Environment Act, sch. 6, para. 16, to establish committees to be known as 'Regional Boards', for the purposes of discharging, in relation to such areas as it may (with the Secretary of State's approval) determine, such of its functions as it may determine (again with the Secretary of State's approval).

A Regional Board shall have its own chairman (who must be a SEPA member).

SEPA is required to comply with any guidance given by the Secretary of State regarding Regional Boards, including the size of the Boards and their composition.

12.3 TRANSFER OF PROPERTY, RIGHTS AND LIABILITIES TO SEPA

Environment Act, s. 22(1)(a) provides that on the transfer date (see above), the property, rights and liabilities of every river purification board are transferred to, and vested in, SEPA. As described later in this chapter, the entire functions of river purification authorities are transferred to SEPA under s. 21(1), with the result that all river purification boards are dissolved on the transfer date (s. 21(3)).

12.3.1 Transfer schemes

Environment Act, s. 22(1)(b) also transfers to SEPA all property, rights and liabilities which are subject to a scheme made by the Secretary of State or made by a local authority (and approved by the Secretary of State). The Secretary of State has power under s. 22(2) to make a scheme for the transfer of his property, rights and liabilities and the property, rights and liabilities of inspectors under EPA 1990, RSA 1993, AWRA 1906 and HASAWA 1974, whose functions are transferred to SEPA by Environment Act, s. 21(1) (see below). The property, rights and liabilities to be covered by the scheme are those which the Secretary of State considers it appropriate to be transferred in consequence of the transfers to SEPA of inspectors' and the Secretary of State's functions under s. 21. Every district or islands council in Scotland is required by s. 22(3) to make schemes for the transfer of such property and rights as are held by the local authority in question for the purposes of its functions as a waste regulation authority, disposal authority, air pollution enforcing authority (under Part I of the EPA 1990) and, in the case of an islands council, a river purification authority, together with related liabilities.

A local authority scheme must be submitted to the Secretary of State for approval and, in preparing its scheme, a local authority must take into account any guidance given by the Secretary of State.

The Secretary of State has power to approve or reject the scheme, or approve it subject to modifications (after consultation with SEPA and the local authority concerned). The Secretary of State is also given certain default powers to make schemes relating to local authority transfers.

Environment Act, sch. 2 contains supplementary provisions as to transfers of property etc. under Environment Act, s. 3 (in the case of the EA) and s. 22 (in the case of SEPA). These provisions are described in 2.10.

12.3.2 Functions of staff commission in respect of transfers to SEPA

Environment Act, s. 23 (which came into force on 12 October 1995) extends the remit of the staff commission established under s. 12 of the Local Government etc. (Scotland) Act 1994 so as to require the commission to consider and keep under review the arrangements for the transfer to SEPA of local authority staff, consider any staffing problems arising out of the transfer of staff that may be referred to the commission by the Secretary of State or a local authority and advise the Secretary of State on the steps necessary to safeguard the interests of local authority staff who are transferred to SEPA.

12.4   TRANSFER OF FUNCTIONS

Environment Act, s. 21 transfers to SEPA on the transfer date the functions of river purification authorities, local authorities' functions in respect of waste regulation and local air pollution control, the functions of Her Majesty's Industrial Pollution Inspectorate (HMIPI), and certain functions to direct local authorities to create smoke control areas in Scotland and to dispose of radioactive waste. The various functions transferred to SEPA are described in the following parts of this chapter.

12.5   TRANSFER OF FUNCTIONS OF RIVER PURIFICATION AUTHORITIES

Environment Act, s. 21(1)(a) transfers to SEPA on the transfer date the functions of river purification authorities with respect to water resources, water pollution, enforcement under Part I of the EPA 1990 and flood warning systems, as well as 'the functions assigned to them by or under any other enactment apart from this Act' (s. 21(1)(a)(v)). River purification authorities were river purification boards established under s. 135 of the Local Government (Scotland) Act 1973 and islands councils.

12.5.1   Water resources

Environment Act, s. 21(1)(a)(i) transfers to SEPA the functions of river purification authorities under or by virtue of Part III of the Rivers (Prevention of Pollution) (Scotland) Act 1951 (R(PP)(S)A 1951), and Part II of the Natural Heritage (Scotland) Act 1991 (NH(S)A 1991).

12.5.1.1   Information etc.   R(PP)(S)A 1951, s. 17 which, *inter alia,* imposed upon river purification authorities a duty 'to conserve so far as practicable the water resources of their areas' is repealed by Environment Act, sch. 22, para. 3(2). However, Environment Act, s. 34(1)(b) imposes upon SEPA a duty 'to conserve so far as practicable the water resources of Scotland' (see 13.4).

R(PP)(S)A 1951, s. 18 is amended by Environmental Act, sch. 22, para. 3(3). It relates to the provision and obtaining of information about SEPA's water resources and water pollution functions (see below). SEPA is empowered to make surveys and gauge and keep records of the flow or volume and other characteristics of any stream (which includes a river, watercourse or inland water and certain tidal waters, but not a local authority sewer).

SEPA may also take steps for the measurement and reading of rainfall and for the installation and maintenance of gauges etc. and may take any other necessary steps to obtain any information so required.

The Secretary of State may give SEPA directions requiring it to exercise all or any of the powers just described and to supply him with information.

SEPA must provide reasonable facilities for the inspection of rainfall records or records of the flow or volume of any stream etc. and for the taking of copies etc. Such facilities are free of charge to all local authorities.

12.5.1.2 Control of abstraction Under NH(S)A 1991, s. 15 as amended by Environment Act, sch. 22, para. 96(2), the Secretary of State may, on the application of SEPA acting in pursuance of its duties under Environment Act, s. 34(1), make a 'control order' in respect of abstraction for the purposes of irrigation. The Secretary of State may require SEPA to apply for a control order if he considers there is a prima facie case for making such an order in pursuance of his water conservation or water cleanliness responsibilities. Control orders apply to all inland or ground waters within the area specified in the order (the 'control area') and shown in a map or plan contained in the order. A control order relates to the abstraction of water for irrigation in any form and for the benefit of any agricultural or horticultural activity which, in itself, is carried out on a commercial basis.

NH(S)A 1991, sch. 5 as amended by Environment Act, sch. 22, para. 96(7) contains detailed provisions as to control orders, and applications for control orders. SEPA must, in its application for a control order, specify the area to which the order is to apply and shall so far as practicable include a statement of what SEPA considers to be the minimum acceptable flow for each water, as measured at control points described in the statement. Notice of the application must be published locally and in the *Edinburgh Gazette,* specifying the place where the application and the map or plan may be inspected within the period of 28 days beginning with the date of first publication and stating that a person may object to the application to the Secretary of State within that period. Copies of the notice of application must also be served by SEPA on every local authority whose area is comprised wholly or partly within the proposed control area, and on affected statutory bodies and other bodies representative of persons who may be so affected. The making of an objection from any such body will require a public local inquiry to be held before the order can be made, unless the objection is subsequently withdrawn. The Secretary of State has power to make the order as applied for or, in certain circumstances, subject to modifications. Any legal challenge to an order must be brought within six weeks but otherwise an order may not be questioned in any legal proceedings.

A person who abstracts water for the purpose of irrigation in an area to which a control order applies, or causes or permits any other person to abstract water for that purpose, shall be guilty of an offence, which carries a maximum penalty on summary conviction of three months' imprisonment or a fine not exceeding the statutory maximum, or two years' imprisonment or an unlimited fine on conviction on indictment (NH(S)A 1991, s. 16(1), (3)).

NH(S)A 1991, s. 16(4) creates a defence to the s. 16(1) offence where the abstraction is under and in accordance with a valid licence under Part II, during a period when restrictions have been lifted by virtue of a s. 18(3) declaration or where these restrictions have been temporarily relaxed by virtue of such a declaration, to the extent that the abstraction is covered by that relaxation (see below).

NH(S)A 1991, s. 17 enables SEPA to grant abstraction licences in respect of inland or ground waters in an area to which a control order applies, in favour of (and on an application by) a person who is, or will be when the licence comes into force, the occupier of land within a control area. Licences remain in force during the calendar year following the year in which they are granted. The control order itself must specify the 'closing date' by which applications have to be made.

The procedure for applications etc. for licences is governed by NH(S)A 1991, sch. 6, which is amended by Environment Act, sch. 22, para. 96(8). An applicant must give certain information about the waters, point of abstraction, and land to be irrigated etc. SEPA must, each year within 14 days of the closing date, publish in a local newspaper the nature of any application made for a licence in the control area, together with details about inspection and the making of objections. SEPA must keep a register of applications, which must be available for free public inspection. Objections to applications must be made in writing within 28 days of the closing date.

Under NH(S)A 1991, s. 17(3), which is amended by Environment Act, sch. 22, para. 96(3), SEPA, having regard to its duties under the NH(S)A 1991 or any other enactment, and after considering the application and any duly made objection to it, may grant the licence, with or without reasonable conditions, or may refuse it. A licence granted under s. 17 must specify the person to whom it is granted, the waters to which it relates, the year in respect of which it is to be in force, the land to be irrigated and the purpose of that irrigation, and any conditions to which it is subject.

An applicant aggrieved by a decision of SEPA in respect of an abstraction licence may appeal to the Secretary of State, in accordance with sch. 6. If objections have been made to the application, the Secretary of State must require SEPA to serve copies of the notice of appeal on the objectors and he must take into account any further written objections from those objectors. The appellant, SEPA and an objector all have a right to request the Secretary of State to afford them an opportunity of appearing before and being heard by a person appointed for the purpose by the Secretary of State. The Secretary of State's decision is final.

Schedule 6 also contains provisions as to the variation of a licence by SEPA, an application by the licence holder, and applications made after the closing date.

If the holder of a licence is convicted of a s. 16 offence, SEPA may revoke the licence. The validity of licences depends upon occupation of the land in question by the licence holder but may in certain circumstances be transferred to a succeeding occupier.

SEPA has power under NH(S)A 1991, s. 18(1) as amended by Environment Act, sch. 22, para. 96(4) to limit or suspend the operation of a licence, in the event of exceptional shortage of rain or any unforeseen event having a substantial effect on the availability of water. Any such limitation or suspension must apply equitably to all licences relating to the affected waters and has effect until SEPA decides that it is no longer necessary.

Conversely, where because of an abundance of water it appears to SEPA that restrictions on abstraction in a control area may be temporarily relaxed or lifted, SEPA may so declare and shall relax the operation of licences to the extent authorised by the declaration (which, again, must apply equitably). Any such relaxation shall have effect until SEPA declares that the restrictions are once more to apply.

SEPA has a duty to communicate any decision taken under s. 18 to the holder of any affected licence.

Fees for abstraction licences are determined in accordance with charging schemes under Environment Act, s. 41 (see chapter 15).

12.5.2 Water pollution

Environment Act, s. 21(1)(a)(ii) transfers to SEPA the functions of river purification authorities with respect to water pollution under or by virtue of Part III of the R(PP)(S)A 1951, the Rivers (Prevention of Pollution) (Scotland) Act 1965 and Part II of the CPA 1974.

12.5.3 Samples

The two earlier Acts are now of limited relevance, compared with CPA 1974, Part II which is considerably amended and strengthened by the Environment Act (see below). Besides the provisions in R(PP)(S)A 1951, s. 18 relating to the provision and obtaining of information, already described, s. 19 gives SEPA the right to obtain and take away samples of water from any stream etc. or of any effluent which is passing from any land or vessel into any stream etc. Environment Act, s. 111 repeals s. 19(2) to (2B) which contained formal procedures that had to be complied with if the result of any analysis of a sample so taken were to be admissible as evidence in legal proceedings.

Section 10(1) of the Rivers (Prevention of Pollution) (Scotland) Act 1965, as amended by the Environment Act, sch. 22, para. 6, provides that in any legal proceedings it shall be presumed, until the contrary is shown, that any sample of effluent taken from an inspection chamber, manhole or other place provided in compliance with a condition under ss. 34 to 40 of the CPA 1974 in relation to any waters is a sample of what was passing from the land or premises to those waters. Section 10(2) enables SEPA to agree with the occupier of the land or premises from which effluent is discharged on the point or points at which, in the exercise of SEPA's rights under R(PP)(S)A 1951, s. 19, samples are to be taken of the effluent passing into any waters, and in any legal proceedings it shall be presumed (until the contrary is shown) that any sample of effluent taken at a point fixed under s. 10 is a sample of what was passing from the land or premises to those waters. Either SEPA or the occupier may at any time terminate the agreement. In default of a s. 10(2) agreement SEPA may apply to the Secretary of State who, after considering representations, may fix the point at which samples are to be taken. That decision may be reviewed or varied by the Secretary of State on the application of SEPA or the occupier. SEPA must keep a register of sampling points, as directed by the Secretary of State, and that register is open to inspection.

12.5.4 Control of Pollution Act 1974

SEPA has important water pollution control functions under Part II of the CPA 1974, which is significantly amended by the Environment Act. These functions extend over 'controlled waters', as defined in CPA 1974, s. 30A, which encompass inland waters and ground waters as well as certain coastal and territorial waters.

The Secretary of State has power under CPA 1974, s. 30B, in relation to various descriptions of controlled waters, to prescribe a system of classifying the quality of those waters according to specified criteria. Under CPA 1974, s. 30C, the Secretary of State, for the purpose of maintaining and improving the quality of controlled waters, may serve notice on SEPA specifying one or more of the classifications prescribed in the regulations. Section 30C corresponds with WRA 1991, s. 83, in the case of the EA (see 4.1.1). SEPA's general duties under CPA 1974, s. 30D to achieve and maintain the objectives corresponds with WRA 1991, s. 84. In the performance of its functions in relation to waters partly in Scotland and partly in England, SEPA is required, in matters of common interest, to 'consult and collaborate' with the EA (CPA 1974, s. 30E).

12.5.4.1 Pollution offences   Environment Act, sch. 16 amalgamates the previous Scottish water pollution offence provisions in CPA 1974, ss. 31 and 32, so as to bring all the relevant criminal offences into a single section, which is a new s. 30F of the CPA 1974. The Scottish offence provisions are also broadly brought into line with the corresponding provisions for England and Wales, found in WRA 1991.

Environment Act, sch. 16 introduces into CPA 1974 new ss. 30F (pollution offences), 30G (prohibition of certain discharges by notice or regulations), 30I (defence to principal offences in respect of authorised discharges) and 30J (other defences to principal offences), which correspond in all material respects to (respectively) WRA 1991, ss. 85, 86, 88 and 89 (which are described in 4.1.2 and 4.1.4). CPA 1974, s. 30H concerns discharges into and from sewers etc. It broadly corresponds to WRA 1991, s. 87 (see 4.1.2).

As a result, the offence provisions in CPA 1974, s. 31 and the whole of s. 32, are repealed (Environment Act, sch. 16, para. 3). Section 31(4) enables the Secretary of State to make regulations prohibiting or restricting the carrying on in a particular area of activities which are likely to result in pollution of controlled waters. Under s. 31(6) SEPA may make byelaws prohibiting or regulating the washing or cleaning of specified things in controlled waters.

CPA 1974, s. 31A (requirements to take precautions against pollution) follows WRA 1991, s. 92 (see 4.1.8).

12.5.4.2 Discharge consents   CPA 1974, s. 34 enables SEPA, on application, to grant discharge consents in respect of effluent or other matter. Consent may be given subject to reasonable conditions, including conditions relating to the places at which discharges may be made and the nature, origin etc. of those discharges. Under s. 35 the Secretary of State has power to direct SEPA to transmit to him certain applications for consent, following a local inquiry or hearing. The receipt by SEPA of an application for consent triggers the requirement in s. 36 for SEPA to advertise the fact and notify relevant local and water authorities, and consider any representations received (which may lead to a s. 35 direction). However, new subss. (2A) and (2B) of s. 36 (inserted by Environment Act, sch. 22, para. 29(11)) enable a person to apply to the Secretary of State for a certificate of exemption from the advertisement requirements on the grounds of national security or because it would unreasonably prejudice that person's commercial interests.

Under CPA 1974, s. 37 (as amended by Environment Act, sch. 22, para. 29(12)) SEPA may from time to time review any consent given in pursuance of s. 34, and the conditions, if any, to which the consent is subject. Consents may, accordingly, be revoked or modified, by notice, if it is reasonable to do so. In certain circumstances, the Secretary of State may direct SEPA to serve a notice under s. 34(1) (e.g., to comply with international obligations).

CPA 1974, s. 38A (added by Environment Act, sch. 22, para. 29(14)) enables the Secretary of State to direct SEPA to undertake a general review of all consents, or of specified descriptions of consents, together with the conditions, if any, to which those consents are subject. SEPA reports its proposals to the Secretary of State, who may then give the agency appropriate directions.

CPA 1974, s. 39 provides an appeal mechanism against various decisions of SEPA. Appeals lie to the Secretary of State.

12.5.4.3 Registers Under CPA 1974, s. 41, registers of applications and consents (as well as such things as samples taken under R(PP)(S)A 1951, s. 19 — see 12.5.3) are required to be kept by SEPA. The list of matters to be registered is extended by Environment Act, sch. 22, para. 29(17) to include such things as enforcement notices, Secretary of State directions, water pollution, convictions of consent holders and works notices (see 12.5.4.4).

New ss. 42A and 42B of CPA 1974 provide for the exclusion from the registers of information affecting national security and certain commercially confidential information. Previous s. 42 is repealed (Environment Act, sch. 22, para. 29(20)).

12.5.4.4 Anti-pollution operations CPA 1974, s. 46 enables SEPA to carry out anti-pollution works and operations. Section 46 follows WRA 1991, s. 161 and is amended by Environment Act, sch. 22 in the same way as is that section, so that SEPA's works etc. powers will be exercisable only when it considers that works or operations are required forthwith or where no person can be found on whom a new works notice can be served. The works notice system is introduced by new ss. 46A to 46D, which correspond with WRA 1991, ss. 161A to 161D (see 4.2). The definition of 'operations' in CPA 1974, s. 56(1) is amended to include 'works' (Environment Act, sch. 22, para. 29(29)).

12.5.4.5 Pollution from vessels Under CPA 1974, s. 33 as amended by Environment Act, sch. 22, para. 29(8) SEPA may make byelaws for prohibiting the keeping or use, on controlled waters, of vessels of a kind specified in the byelaws which are provided with sanitary appliances. CPA 1974, s. 47 requires SEPA to arrange for the collection and disposal of waste from vessels which needs collection in consequence of s. 33, and to arrange for the provision of facilities for washing out prescribed appliances from vessels, and it may arrange for the provision of facilities such as WCs for the use of persons from vessels. Where it appears to SEPA appropriate to do so for the purpose of preventing the pollution of inland waters, it may, under CPA 1974, s. 48, make byelaws prohibiting the presence in those waters of vessels which have not been registered by SEPA. A reasonable charge may be made for registration.

12.5.4.6 Vegetation in rivers, etc. Under CPA 1974, s. 49 if, without the consent of SEPA (which shall not be unreasonably withheld), a person removes a deposit accumulated by a dam, weir or sluice holding back inland waters so as to cause that deposit to be carried away in suspension in the waters, or any substantial vegetation is allowed to fall etc. into inland waters and a person allows it to remain by wilful default, the person in question is guilty of an offence, except where the thing in question was done in the exercise of statutory land drainage, flood prevention or navigation powers. The Secretary of State decides whether SEPA's consent under s. 49 has been unreasonably withheld, but, by new s. 49(5) inserted by Environment Act, sch. 22, para. 29(25), he may delegate his functions to an appointed person under Environment Act, s. 114.

12.5.4.7 Enforcement notices   New ss. 49A and 49B of CPA 1974 (inserted by Environment Act, sch. 22, para. 29(26)) introduce the system of enforcement notices in respect of discharge consents. Section 49A corresponds with WRA 1991, s. 90B. The appeals provisions in CPA 1974, s. 49B follow amended WRA 1991, s. 91 (see 4.1.6 and 4.1.7).

12.5.4.8 Abandoned mines   CPA 1974, s. 50 as amended by Environment Act, sch. 22, para. 29(27), empowers SEPA to carry out studies in order to ascertain what water pollution problems may arise or have arisen from the abandonment of a mine, or might arise if the mine were abandoned, and what steps are likely to be appropriate in order to deal with the problems (and what the costs would be). See also 12.10.

12.5.4.9 Repeals   Sections 53 (charges for consents), 54 (directions to river purification authorities) and 55 (discharges by islands councils) of CPA 1974 are repealed by Environment Act, sch. 22, para. 29(28) since they are rendered obsolete by the creation of SEPA or the enactment of general provisions as to charges and directions in the Environment Act itself (see Environment Act, ss. 31 and 40 to 43 and chapters 13–15).

12.5.5   Functions of river purification authorities under Part I of the Environmental Protection Act 1990

Part I of the Environmental Protection Act 1990 establishes the system of integrated pollution control (IPC) for the more polluting processes. Before the creation of SEPA, responsibility for administering that system in Scotland was divided between HMIPI and river purification authorities. This position contrasted with that in England and Wales, where HMIP was the sole enforcing authority in respect of releases of substances into the environment (as opposed to the air).

The IPC system is exercisable in respect of processes which have been prescribed by the Secretary of State under EPA 1990, s. 2. Under the pre-SEPA regime responsibility for enforcing the IPC system in the case of prescribed processes in Scotland depended upon the nature of the process in question, the precise determination being left to the Environmental Protection (Determination of Enforcing Authority etc.) (Scotland) Regulations 1992 (SI 1992/530) which in turn referred back to the various schedules of prescribed substances in the Environmental Protection (Prescribed Processes and Substances) Regulations 1991 (SI 1991/472). This division of responsibilities within the same system was not satisfactory and the creation of SEPA enables it to be swept away, with the functions of both river purification authorities and HMIPI being transferred to the new Agency (see 12.8).

12.5.6   Flood warning systems and assessments of flood risks

12.5.6.1   Flood warning systems   Under Agriculture Act 1970, s. 92 as amended by Environment Act, sch. 22, para 14, SEPA may provide and operate flood warning systems and install and maintain apparatus and carry out engineering or building operations required for the purposes of any such systems. Before exercising these powers (other than to maintain apparatus) SEPA must consult the local authorities for the area in question and (in certain cases) the chief constable of the region etc. in question. SEPA may enter into arrangements with other persons under Agriculture Act 1970, s. 94 to the effect that apparatus belonging to any such person may be incorporated with apparatus belonging to SEPA for the purposes of a flood warning system. SEPA may contribute towards the expenses reasonably incurred by any person in connection with the incorporation of apparatus with that of SEPA.

12.5.6.2   Assessments of flood risks   Although not a function transferred from river purification authorities, this is the appropriate place to mention Environment Act, s. 25 which confers upon SEPA (without prejudice to its functions under Agriculture Act 1970, s. 92), the function of assessing, as far as it considers it appropriate, the risk of flooding in any area of Scotland. If requested by a local planning authority, SEPA must provide the authority with advice on the risk of flooding in any part of the authority's area on the basis of the information SEPA holds.

12.6   WASTE REGULATION

12.6.1   Functions under Part II of the Environmental Protection Act 1990.

SEPA is, in relation to Scotland, the waste regulation authority under Part II of the EPA 1990 (s. 30(1), as amended by Environment Act, sch. 22, para. 62). SEPA's functions correspond with those of the EA in the case of England and Wales, and are described in 8.1. It should, however, be noted that in the case of granting licences under EPA 1990, s. 36, and surrenders under s. 39, the appropriate planning authority, to which SEPA must make reference, is the council constituted under s. 2 of the Local Government etc. (Scotland) Act 1994 for the area in which the land to which the licence relates is located (Environment Act, sch. 22, paras 68, 73).

12.6.2   Functions under the Control of Pollution (Amendment) Act 1989

SEPA becomes, for Scotland, the regulation authority for the purposes of the CP(A)A 1989, which introduced a system of registration for carriers of waste (see Environment Act, sch. 22, para. 37). The regulation authority for England and Wales is the EA. The functions of each Agency under the CP(A)A 1989 are the same and are described in 8.2.

12.7   WASTE DISPOSAL

Environment Act, s. 21(1)(c) transfers to SEPA the functions of disposal authorities under or by virtue of ss. 3 to 10, 16, 17(1)(a) and 17(2)(b) to (d) of the CPA 1974. SEPA's powers as disposal authority correspond to those of the EA described in 8.3.

Before leaving the subject of waste, it should be mentioned that SEPA has a duty to prepare a national waste strategy for Scotland under EPA 1990, new s. 44B. This duty is described in chapter 20.

12.8   INTEGRATED POLLUTION CONTROL

Environment Act, s. 21(1)(d) transfers to SEPA the functions of HMIPI under Part I of the EPA 1990. As has been mentioned in 12.5.5 above, the previous position in Scotland involved a division of responsibility for IPC control between HMIPI and river purification authorities. That division disappears, with SEPA taking over both sets of functions. As a result, SEPA's functions in relation to IPC mirror those of the EA in England and Wales (see 9.1 and 9.2).

SEPA also assumes the functions of HMIPI (and the Secretary of State) under certain enactments which are eventually to be repealed by the EPA 1990, as the IPC system is progressively introduced. The legislation in question is the AWRA 1906 and certain provisions of the HASAWA 1974, (Environment Act, s. 21(1)(f) and (g) and (2)(a) and (b)) (see 9.3).

12.9   AIR POLLUTION CONTROL

12.9.1   Part I of the Environmental Protection Act 1990

Unlike the EA, SEPA assumes responsibility from Scottish local authorities for air pollution control (APC) under Part I of the EPA 1990. The APC system is similar to that which applies in the case of IPC but the processes which APC covers are less polluting than those covered by IPC. The Environmental Protection (Prescribed Processes and Substances) Regulations 1991 (SI 1991/472) prescribe in Part A the processes to be covered by IPC, whilst those to be dealt with by APC are prescribed in Part B. In many cases the overall description of the process is the same for Parts A and B. For example, under the heading 'Combustion processes' Part A covers (*inter alia*) burning fuel, in certain circumstances, in a boiler or furnace with a net rated thermal input of 50 megawatts or more, whilst Part B covers burning fuel in a boiler or furnace with a net rated thermal output of not less than 20 megawatts, but less than 50 megawatts. Under 'Iron and steel', Part B covers (*inter alia*) making, melting or refining iron, steel or any ferrous alloy in an electric arc furnace with a designed capacity of less than 7 tonnes, whilst Part A covers (*inter alia*) making, melting or refining iron, steel or any ferrous alloy in any furnace other than a furnace described in Part B.

Regulation 6 of the 1991 Regulations also prescribes various substances the release of which into specified environmental media is to be controlled under EPA 1990, ss. 6 and 7.

The substances listed in sch. 4 to the 1991 Regulations are subject to control under IPC and APC. These are:

Oxides of sulphur and other sulphur compounds
Oxides of nitrogen and other nitrogen compounds
Oxides of carbon
Organic compounds and partial oxidation products
Metals, metalloids and their compounds
Asbestos (suspended particulate matter and fibres), glass fibres and mineral fibres
Halogens and their compounds
Phosphorus and its compounds
Particulate matter.

As has been mentioned, the system of APC is similar to that of IPC and reference should therefore be made to the overview of that system contained in chapter 8. It should, however, be noted that the fees and charges provisions in EPA 1990, s. 8, now apply only in the case of APC by local authorities in England and Wales. SEPA's charging powers in respect of both IPC and APC are covered in Environment Act, ss. 41 and 42, with the result that EPA 1990, s. 8 no longer applies to Scotland (Environment Act, sch. 22, para. 50).

12.9.2   Section 19 of the Clean Air Act 1993

Environment Act, s. 21(2)(c) transfers to SEPA the Secretary of State's functions under s. 19 of the Clean Air Act 1993 with respect to the creation of smoke control areas by local authorities. Accordingly, SEPA may, after consultation with a local authority, direct that authority to prepare and submit to SEPA for its approval proposals for making and bringing into operation smoke control orders within such period as the local authority think fit. SEPA's powers of direction arise where it is satisfied that it is expedient to abate air pollution by smoke in the district or part of the district of the local authority concerned and that the authority have not exercised, or have not sufficiently exercised, their powers under s. 18 of the Act to declare a smoke control area in the whole or part of their district. SEPA may reject the proposals or approve them in whole or part, with or without modifications. Default powers may be exercised by SEPA (with the consent of the Secretary of State) where a local authority fail to submit proposals or submit proposals which are wholly or partly rejected. (Environment Act, sch. 22, para. 196).

12.10   RADIOACTIVE SUBSTANCES

Environment Act, s. 21(1)(e) transfers to SEPA the functions of HMIPI under the RSA 1993, or assigned to HMIPI by or under any other enactment, apart from the Environment Act. Environment Act, s. 21(2)(d) transfers to the EA the Secretary of State's functions under RSA 1993, s. 30(1) (which consist of power to dispose of radioactive waste). SEPA's functions correspond to those of the EA, which are described in chapter 10.

12.11   CONTAMINATED LAND AND ABANDONED MINES

SEPA's functions in respect of contaminated land (under Part IIA of the EPA 1990) and abandoned mines (under Part IA of the CPA 1974) are described in chapters 16 and 17.

12.12   GUIDANCE TO SEPA

In carrying out its functions, SEPA must have regard to guidance issued by the Secretary of State under Environment Act, s. 31. Draft guidance has been issued by the Secretary of State for Scotland and this is described in chapter 13.

Chapter 13
General Powers, Duties and Functions of SEPA

13.1 GUIDANCE ON SUSTAINABLE DEVELOPMENT AND OTHER AIMS AND OBJECTIVES

Environment Act, s. 31 (which came into force upon the formal establishment of SEPA on 12 October 1995) requires the Secretary of State to give guidance to SEPA from time to time with respect to aims and objectives which the Secretary of State considers it appropriate for SEPA to pursue in the performance of its functions. Unlike Environment Act, s. 4, which makes provision for the EA's principal aim (in terms of its contribution to sustainable development), SEPA is given no express principal aim by the Environment Act. The reason for this difference lies in the comparative narrowness of SEPA's statutory functions. As the Parliamentary Under-Secretary of State for Scotland (Sir Hector Monro) explained in standing committee in the House of Commons:

> The river purification boards in Scotland, whose responsibilities are to go to SEPA, never had the much wider responsibilities of the National Rivers Authority for a whole host of environmental concerns in England. Clause 31 [now s. 31] spells out SEPA's responsibilities. That is much clearer and gives a much narrower focus to the agency in Scotland which will deal particularly with pollution prevention and control, as opposed to the wider aspects of environmental protection covered by the agencies in England and Wales. It is important to realise that difference. (Hansard, HC, Standing Committee B, Environment Bill, Seventh Sitting, 16 May 1995, col. 231.)

Nevertheless, s. 31(3) requires SEPA, in performing its functions, to have regard to guidance given under s. 31(1) and that guidance must include 'guidance with respect to the contribution which, having regard to SEPA's responsibilities and resources, the Secretary of State considers it appropriate to make, by the performance of its functions, towards attaining the objective of achieving sustainable development' (s. 31(2)).

Guidance under s. 31(1) is exercisable only after consultation with SEPA and other bodies which the Secretary of State considers it appropriate to consult. The procedure for laying draft guidance before Parliament follows that in s. 4 (see chapter 11).

13.1.1 Draft guidance on sustainable development

In May 1995, the Scottish Office issued for consultation a document entitled *Draft Guidance to SEPA under clause 29 of the Environment Bill.* The document will be refined before the final text is published in early 1996.

The draft guidance explains that its purpose is 'to provide a steer to SEPA on the way in which it is to approach the discharge of its functions generally, for example, when establishing its policies, plans and targets'. Broadly similar draft guidance has been published separately for the EA, although that guidance reflects the wider functions of the EA (see chapter 11).

13.1.1.1 Main objectives of SEPA   The draft management statement for SEPA, published in October 1994, set out the following main objectives for the Agency:

(a)   to provide effective environmental protection, in a way that takes account of impacts on all aspects of the environment;

(b)   to impose the minimum burden on industry and others consistent with that first objective;

(c)   to develop single points of contact through which operators can deal with SEPA;

(d)   to operate to high professional standards, based on the best possible information and analysis of the environment and of processes which affect it;

(e)   to organise its activities in ways which reflect good environmental practice and provide value for money for those who pay its charges and taxpayers as a whole;

(f)   to provide clear and readily available advice and information on its work;

(g)   to develop a close and responsive relationship with the public, local communities and regulated organisations.

13.1.1.2 Principles of sustainable development   Unlike its counterpart in England and Wales, which deliberately avoids any express definition of sustainable development, the Scottish draft guidance refers directly to 'the most commonly used working definition of sustainable development, namely that provided in the Brundtland Report of 1987, which is "Development that meets the needs of the present without compromising the ability of future generations to meet their own needs"' (draft guidance, 4.2). The draft guidance also identifies in the UK's own Strategy on Sustainable Development (see chapters 2 and 11) the following five principles which are considered to be especially relevant to SEPA:

(a)   the precautionary principle;
(b)   the 'polluter pays' principle;
(c)   the wise use of natural environmental capital;
(d)   the carrying capacity of habitats and ecosystems;
(e)   the interests of future generations.

The precautionary principle means that where, despite the deployment of the best scientific techniques, potential environmental damage is both uncertain and significant, the lack of scientific certainty must not be used as a reason for postponing cost-effective measures to prevent environmental degradation. 'Polluter pays' requires the cost of necessary environmental measures to be borne by the producer of the pollution, not by society at large. Natural environmental capital consists of both renewable and non-renewable resources; sustainable development requires ways to be found of enhancing total wealth whilst using natural resources prudently, so that resources can be conserved or used at a rate which considers the needs of future generations. The carrying capacity of habitats and ecosystems is the population of a species which that ecosystem can sustain, but the term is sometimes used to refer to the capacity of the environment to absorb pollution or waste. SEPA will need, from time to time, to assess carrying capacities and critical loadings of ecosystems.

The draft guidance acknowledges that judgments will have to be made about the weight to be put on these factors in particular cases.

13.1.1.3 SEPA's contribution to sustainable development The draft guidance identifies SEPA's role as ensuring environmental protection within its areas of responsibility and managing its own resources in a sustainable manner. 'It cannot by itself achieve sustainable development but it is expected to make a significant contribution to it in relation to its functions' (5.1). Importantly, the draft guidance observes that SEPA will need to consider the distinctive characteristics of Scotland's environment and economy in executing its functions. 'Scotland's diverse natural environment, its remote rural communities and extremes of population density may, for example, mean that national standards need to be tempered by sensitivity to local circumstances, except where significant global effects would suggest otherwise' (5.2).

SEPA's contribution to sustainable development is considered by the draft guidance to be the discharge of its functions, wherever possible in partnership with business, having regard to the following aims:

(a)   to establish clear, long-term goals;
(b)   to encourage organisations to respond in ways that minimise costs and where possible assist the competitive position of the UK;
(c)   to encourage best available techniques for preventing or minimising pollution;
(d)   to base its decisions on sound science;
(e)   to operate to high professional standards;
(f)   to ensure actions to ensure compliance are proportionate to the objectives concerned (5.4).

13.1.2 Costs and benefits

Environment Act, s. 39 requires SEPA, in considering whether or not to exercise any power conferred upon it by or under any enactment, or in deciding the manner in which to exercise any such power, to take into account the likely costs and benefits of the exercise or non-exercise of the power or its exercise in the manner in question. The duty does not apply if or to the extent that it is unreasonable for

SEPA to have such regard, in view of the nature or purpose of the power or in the circumstances of the particular case. The duty on SEPA does not affect SEPA's obligation to discharge any duties, comply with any requirements, or pursue any objectives, imposed upon or given to it otherwise than under s. 39.

This controversial duty also applies to the EA and is discussed in 11.1.2. The draft guidance seeks to explain how the Secretary of State intends the s. 39 duty to apply to SEPA in practice. It 'is intended to ensure proper consideration by SEPA of the implications for sustainable development of the options open to it, both in its strategic planning and for individual cases, such as to ensure that measures which secure environmental benefits, or the avoidance of environmental costs, do not impose disproportionately large economic costs' (7.2). Risk analysis techniques and formal cost-benefit analyses are identified as useful aids, although the duty is recognised to be one which ultimately requires the exercise of judgment by SEPA.

SEPA's primary concern should be the costs and benefits of its actions for society as a whole, the effects on the welfare of people and business, changes in the use of resources and impacts on the environment. The draft guidance acknowledges that SEPA may need to take into account:

(a)	the views of the Chief Medical Officer on the effects on human health;
(b)	the impacts on individual companies and industry sectors;
(c)	the distribution of costs and benefits across the economy (7.3).

SEPA must develop practical procedures to ensure it meets the s. 39 duty, having regard to the guidance.

## 13.2	GENERAL ENVIRONMENTAL AND RECREATIONAL DUTIES

The narrowness of SEPA's functions, compared with those of the EA, meant that the government was not faced with a campaign to widen the ambit of Environment Act, s. 32 on the same scale as that which resulted in the recasting of what is now Environment Act, s. 7, which imposes on the EA a duty to further conservation, etc. (see chapters 2 and 11). Accordingly, s. 32 (which came into force on 12 October 1995) is of a more limited nature. It requires the Secretary of State and SEPA, in formulating or considering any proposals relating to any of SEPA's functions, to have regard to the desirability of conserving and enhancing Scotland's natural heritage and the desirability of protecting and conserving buildings, sites and objects of archaeological, architectural, engineering or historic interest, to take into account any effect which the proposals would have on Scotland's natural heritage or on any such buildings etc. and to have regard to the social and economic needs of any area or description of area of Scotland and, in particular, to such needs of rural areas.

In s. 32 'building' includes structure and 'the natural heritage of Scotland' means the same as in the NH(S)A 1991, s. 1(3) of which provides that the expression includes the flora and fauna of Scotland, its geological and physiographical features, its natural beauty and amenity.

Environment Act, s. 32(2) imposes upon the Secretary of State and SEPA certain duties to have regard to the desirability of preserving public access etc. to various natural and built features of beauty or interest, and to take into account any effect which SEPA's proposals might have on such freedom of access etc. Section 32(2) corresponds to s. 7(2) which is described in 11.4.5.

13.3 GENERAL POLLUTION CONTROL DUTIES

Environment Act, s. 33(1) provides that SEPA's pollution control powers shall be exercisable for the purpose of preventing or minimising, or remedying or mitigating the effects of, pollution of the environment. This duty mirrors that of the EA in s. 5(1), and s. 33(2) to (4) also correspond to s. 5(2) to (4) (see 11.2). SEPA's pollution control functions are those described in chapter 12 in relation to IPC, APC (including s. 19 of the Clean Air Act 1993), the water pollution functions formerly exercisable by river purification authorities, waste regulation, waste disposal, radioactive substances, contaminated land and abandoned mines, together with any functions arising under or by virtue of regulations made by virtue of s. 2(2) of the European Communities Act 1972, to the extent that the regulations relate to pollution (Environment Act, s. 33(5)).

13.4 GENERAL WATER DUTIES

Environment Act, s. 34 contains a set of duties with respect to water which are less comprehensive than those imposed on the EA by Environment Act, s. 6. As before, the reason for the difference lies in the narrower range of functions carried out by river purification authorities, as opposed to those of the NRA in England and Wales. Environment Act, s. 34(1) requires SEPA to promote the cleanliness of rivers, other inland waters and ground waters in Scotland, and the tidal waters of Scotland, and to conserve as far as practicable the water resources of Scotland. This last duty does not affect the duties of the Secretary of State and water authorities with respect to water resources etc. under the Water (Scotland) Act 1980. SEPA must also promote the conservation and enhancement of the natural beauty and amenity of inland and coastal waters and of land associated with such waters, and the conservation of flora and fauna which are dependent on an aquatic environment.

13.5 DUTIES AS RESPECTS NATURAL HERITAGE AREAS AND SITES OF SPECIAL INTEREST

The NH(S)A 1991 established Scottish National Heritage and (amongst other things) gave it the task of recommending to the Secretary of State that certain areas should be designated as Natural Heritage Areas because their outstanding value to the natural heritage of Scotland necessitates the taking of special protection measures (NH(S)A 1991, s. 6).

Under Environment Act, s. 35, where an area has been designated as a Natural Heritage Area or is in SNH's opinion of special interest by reason of its flora, fauna or geological or physiographical features, and SNH consider it may be affected by schemes, works etc. of SEPA, or by an authorisation, consent, licence or permission given by SEPA, then SNH are required to give SEPA notice specifying, in the case of a Natural Heritage Area, SNH's reasons for considering the area to be of outstanding value and in the case of 'special interest' land, SNH's reasons for holding the opinion that it is of such interest. Unless the area ceases to be a Natural Heritage Area or of 'special interest' to SNH, SEPA must consult SNH before carrying out potentially harmful or damaging schemes, works, operations or activities. There is an exception to this duty in cases of emergency if particulars are subsequently given to SNH as soon as practicable.

13.6   CODES OF PRACTICE

Environment Act, s. 36 enables the Secretary of State to approve by order codes of practice giving practical guidance to SEPA with respect to ss. 32, 34(2) and 35 matters and promoting desirable practices by SEPA with respect to those matters. In discharging its duties under those provisions SEPA must have regard to the code of practice. Environment Act, s. 36 came into force on 12 October 1995.

Before approving a code, the Secretary of State must consult with SEPA, SNH, Scottish Enterprise, Highlands and Islands Enterprise, the East, North and West of Scotland Water Authorities and such other persons as he considers it appropriate to consult (s. 36(3)).

13.7   CONSULTATION WITH RESPECT TO DRAINAGE WORKS

SEPA must be consulted by any person proposing to carry out drainage works, as to precautions to be taken to prevent pollution to controlled waters as a result of the works. In carrying out the works, the person concerned must take account of SEPA's views (Environment Act, s. 24(1)). This requirement does not apply to works of a type prescribed by regulations made by the Secretary of State under s. 24(2).

13.8   MISCELLANEOUS FUNCTIONS

Environment Act, s. 26 enables the Secretary of State to authorise SEPA to purchase land compulsorily for the purpose of any of its functions. The standard provisions of the Acquisition of Land (Authorisation Procedure) (Scotland) Act 1947 apply, as if SEPA were a local authority.

Environment Act, s. 27 enables SEPA to obtain information relating to land, with a view to performing a function conferred on it by any enactment (and not merely its powers of compulsory acquisition). Failure by the occupier, or any person with an interest in the land, who is served with the requisite notice by SEPA to comply with its requirements is a criminal offence, as is the intentional or reckless making of a false statement (s. 27(3)).

Environment Act, s. 28 confers express powers on SEPA (with the Secretary of State's consent) to promote private legislation in Parliament under the Private Legislation Procedure (Scotland) Act 1936 or to oppose private legislation promoted by others.

Environment Act, s. 29 applies to SEPA the powers of local authorities to make etc. byelaws under the Local Government (Scotland) Act 1973. A copy of any byelaws so made must be sent by SEPA to any local authority in whose area the byelaws will apply.

Environment Act, s. 30 (which came into force on 12 October 1995) requires SEPA to ensure that its records (including those it inherits under s. 22 but excluding those it adjudges to be not worthy of preservation) are preserved and managed in accordance with such arrangements as it shall put into effect after consultation with the Keeper of Records of Scotland, who is to have unrestricted access (at all reasonable hours) to those records. In addition, SEPA may afford members of the public facilities for inspecting and copying records, either free of charge or on payment of a reasonable charge. Section 30 gives way to any enactment which contains inconsistent provision as to records of a specific kind.

Chapter 14

Further Functions of the Environment Agency and SEPA

14.1 INCIDENTAL GENERAL FUNCTIONS

Environment Act, s. 37 confers incidental powers and duties on the EA and SEPA. The Agencies are empowered to do anything which in their opinion is calculated to facilitate or is conducive or incidental to, the carrying out of their functions. Environment Act, s. 37(1)(b) specifies, in particular, the power to acquire and dispose of land and other property and the carrying out of engineering or building operations. In addition the EA is given power to institute criminal proceedings.

Certain provisions of s. 37 came into force on 28 July 1995 (Environment Act 1995 (Commencement No. 1) Order 1995 (SI 1995/1983)).

14.1.1 Advice and assistance

We have seen in chapter 2 how the government had recognised at an early stage that the proposed new Agencies would be important in supplying comprehensive environmental data and authoritative advice to government and that a major 'selling point' for the Agencies was their perceived ability to provide 'advice and guidance to industry on best environmental practice', as well as contributing to environmental technology schemes (see 2.3.3–2.4).

Subsections (2) to (7) of Environment Act, s. 37 accordingly make specific provision for these matters.

(a)   The EA and SEPA have duties to provide Ministers with such advice and guidance as they may request.

(b)   The EA and SEPA have power to provide any person with advice or assistance, including training facilities, on any matter in respect of which they have skill or experience. The power extends to the provision of advice etc. to persons outside the United Kingdom, with the written consent of the appropriate Minister.

(c)   They have duties to carry out research and related activities and power to make the results available for payment of a fee, or free of charge. They will, in particular, be expected in practice to supply environmental data to the newly established European Environment Agency.

(d)   They have power by agreement to charge for advice and assistance in connection with any matter concerning environmental licences.

14.2 DELEGATION

Another advantage of the EA and SEPA, from the government's perspective, is that the creation of the Agencies enables it to delegate to them certain of its functions, in accordance with 'Next Steps' principles.

Environment Act, s. 38(1) allows a Minister of the Crown and a new Agency to agree to authorise the Agency or any of its employees to exercise on the Minister's behalf an 'eligible function', that is to say, a function which the Secretary of State considers can appropriately be exercised by the Agency, having regard to the functions conferred on it by the Environment Act or any other enactment. A delegation agreement may not extend to powers to make regulations or other instruments of a legislative character, nor to a power to fix fees or charges (s. 38(2)).

Subsections (4) to (6) of Environment Act, s. 38 provide for anything done or omitted to be done by the Agency or its employees in connection with the exercise or purported exercise of the function to be treated as done or omitted to be done by the Minister concerned in his capacity as such, except (a) for the purposes of the delegation agreement itself so far as it relates to the exercise of the function or (b) for the purposes of criminal proceedings.

Notwithstanding a delegation agreement, the Minister may still himself exercise the function to which the agreement relates (s. 38(7)) and the Minister's power to make a delegation agreement is additional to any other power for others to exercise his functions (s. 38(9)). In certain cases, the Minister may arrange for payments from third parties to be made to him or the Agency where the latter acts under a delegation agreement.

Environment Act, s. 38 came into force upon the establishment of the EA on 28 July 1995.

14.3 MINISTERIAL DIRECTIONS

Environment Act, s. 40 (which also came into force on 28 July 1995) enables Ministers to give the EA or SEPA directions of a general or specific character with respect to the carrying out of any of its functions. General and specific directions may also be given to an Agency in order to implement UK obligations under EC Treaties or any international agreement to which the UK is a party. Directions of the latter kind must be published in such a way as to bring them to the attention of people likely to be affected by them. The Agency in question must comply with any direction.

In determining any appeal against or reference or review of a decision of the EA or SEPA, or any application transmitted from it, the person or body making the determination shall be bound by any direction given by Ministers under s. 40 or any other enactment to the same extent as the Agency is bound (s. 40(5)).

14.4 INFORMATION, ANNUAL REPORTS AND INQUIRIES

Environment Act, s. 51 imposes on the EA and SEPA a duty to supply the appropriate Minister with such information as he reasonably requires regarding its property, functions and responsibilities. The information which the Agency may be required to furnish includes information which the Agency may not have, but which it is reasonable for it to obtain.

As soon as practicable after the end of each financial year the EA and SEPA must prepare reports on their activities during that year and supply copies to Ministers (s. 52(1)). These annual reports must set out any s. 40 directions given to the Agency during the year, except s. 40(1) directions whose disclosure would be contrary to the interests of national security (s. 52(2)). The annual reports are to be laid by the Secretary of State before Parliament and must be published (s. 52(3)). The form of the reports and the information to be supplied in them are to be as directed by Ministers (s. 52(4)).

Environment Act, ss. 51 and 52 came into force on 28 July 1995.

Environment Act, s. 53 enables Ministers to hold an inquiry or other hearing in connection with any of the functions of the EA or SEPA or in connection with any of the Ministers' functions in relation to the Agencies. The procedural rules are those contained in the Local Government Act 1972, s. 250(2) to (5) (in the case of the EA) and the Local Government (Scotland) Act 1973, s. 210(2) to (8) (in the case of SEPA).

14.5 POWERS OF ENTRY

Persons authorised by the EA and SEPA are given certain powers of entry by Environment Act, s. 108 in connection with their pollution control functions. These powers are also conferred upon local authorities exercising APC functions under Part I of the EPA 1990, air quality functions under Part IV of the Environment Act, (see chapter 19) and functions in respect of contaminated land under Part IIA of the EPA 1990 (see chapter 16).

Environment Act, s. 108 brings together and standardises powers of entry relating to pollution control functions in other legislation which become functions of the EA and SEPA. The various separate powers contained in that legislation are accordingly repealed.

Section 108 is based on the powers of HMIP in Part I of the EPA 1990 and of WRAs in Part II of that Act, with additional provisions being based on the NRA's powers under the WRA 1991 and inspectors' powers under the RSA 1993.

The powers in Environment Act, s. 108 may be exercised for one or more of the following purposes:

(a)   determining whether any pollution control legislation is being or has been complied with,

(b)   exercising or performing pollution control functions,

(c)   determining whether and, if so, how such a function should be exercised or performed (s. 108(1)).

In addition the EA and SEPA may authorise persons to exercise powers of entry for the purpose of carrying out assessments or preparing reports under Environment Act, s. 5(3) or s. 33(3), in cases where the Minister who required the assessment or report has notified the EA or SEPA that it appears to relate to an incident or possible incident involving or potentially involving serious pollution or harm to human health or danger to life or health (s. 108(2), (3)).

The powers of entry include making examinations and investigations, taking measurements, photographs and samples and seizing polluting articles for examination etc. Persons may be required to answer questions relating to any examination or investigation, and records (including those in computerised form) may be inspected.

Environment Act, sch. 18 contains supplementary provisions relating to the s. 108 powers, including the issue of warrants for entry. Full compensation is payable to anyone who sustains loss or damage by reason of the exercise of a s. 108 power or the failure of the authorised person on leaving to secure unoccupied premises as effectively as when he found them. Compensation is not payable if the loss or damage is attributable to the default of the person who sustained it or is compensatable by virtue of other pollution control legislation (sch. 18, paras 5, 6).

Environment Act, s. 109 enables a person authorised for the purposes of s. 108 to enter premises to seize and render harmless (whether by destruction or otherwise) any article found on the premises which he has reasonable cause to believe is a cause of imminent danger of serious pollution of the environment or serious harm to human health.

Chapter 15
Charging and Finances

The 'financial' provisions of the Environment Act which relate to the EA and SEPA are to be found in ss. 41 to 50. Of these, the most significant so far as the public is concerned are ss. 41 and 42 which enable the Agencies to make charging schemes in order to recover costs incurred in connection with environmental licences.

The power in s. 41 to make schemes (together with s. 42) came into force on 21 September 1995. Sections 43 to 50 came into force on 28 July 1995 (Environment Act 1995 (Commencement No. 1) Order 1995 (SI 1995/1983)).

15.1 CHARGING SCHEMES

Environment Act, s. 41 concerns the power of the EA and SEPA to charge in respect of an environmental licence, which, in relation to the EA, is defined in s. 56 as any one of the following:

(a) registration as a controlled waste carrier (CP(A)A 1989, s. 2)

(b) authorisation under EPA 1990, Part I (other than an APC authorisation granted by a local authority)

(c) waste management licence (EPA 1990, Part II)

(d) abstraction and impounding licence (WRA 1991, Part II)

(e) discharge consent (WRA 1991, s. 88(1)(a))

(f) consent to deposit certain refuse etc. (WRA 1991, s. 89(4)(a), 90)

(g) registration under RSA 1993

(h) authorisation under RSA 1993

(j) registration as a controlled waste broker etc. (Waste Management Licensing Regulations 1994 (SI 1994/1056)).

In relation to SEPA, paras (a), (c), (f), (g), (h) and (j) apply. In addition, SEPA's environmental licences include:

(a) all authorisations under EPA 1990, Part I (including APC authorisations)

(b) discharge and other consents under CPA 1974, Part II

(c)   abstraction licences (NH(S)A 1991, s. 17).

Environment Act, s. 41 empowers the EA to require payment in the case of an abstraction or impounding licence. The EA and SEPA may charge in order to recover costs incurred in carrying out functions by virtue of EPA 1990, s. 62 (dangerous or intractable waste — see 8.1.7). Otherwise, Environment Act, s. 41(1) imposes a duty on the EA and SEPA to make charges in respect of environmental licences. In all cases the charges are to be specified in or determined under a charging scheme made by the Agency in question. Charges may be prescribed in respect of the following, so far as they relate to environmental licences, namely, applications, grants, variations, subsistence, transfers (where permitted), renewals (where permitted), applications for transfers and renewals, surrenders (where permitted), applications for surrenders and applications for revocation (s. 41(2)).

Charging schemes are able to provide considerable flexibility as to the imposition etc. of charges. Single charges may be prescribed covering the whole period in which the licence is in force or else separate charges for different parts of that period. Alternatively, a combination of single charges and separate charges may be imposed (s. 41(3)). Different charges may be set according to the type of licence or activity covered by the licence, the scale of the activity, the type or amount of substance to which the activity relates and the number of different authorised activities carried on by the same person (s. 41(4)). Schemes may also make different provision for different cases (s. 41(7)).

Charging schemes must specify who is liable to pay the charge and may provide that it is a condition of the licence that the charge relating to it shall be paid (s. 41(5)). In addition, if an Agency finds that charges have not been paid, it may suspend or revoke the licence to the extent that it authorises the carrying on of the activity. In doing so, the Agency must follow the procedure specified in regulations made for the purpose by the Secretary of State (s. 42(6), (10)).

In the case of abstraction and impounding licences under WRA 1991, charging schemes are subject to any exemptions or special charges covered by ss. 125 to 130 of that Act (Environment Act s. 41(8)).

15.2   APPROVAL AND MAKING OF CHARGING SCHEMES

Neither the EA nor SEPA can make a charging scheme unless it has been approved by the Secretary of State. The procedure for approval is contained in Environment Act, s. 42.

The first step is for the Agency to publish its proposals for a scheme, specifying the period within which representations or objections should be made to the Secretary of State. The Agency then submits the proposed scheme to the Secretary of State who must consider outstanding representations and objections and also the desirability of ensuring that the amounts recovered by the Agency concerned meet the costs and expenses of carrying out its functions to which the proposed charging scheme relates. In the case of a scheme covering authorisations under RSA 1993, s. 13(1), the amounts recovered must also cover certain costs incurred by Ministers in carrying out functions under that Act (Environment Act, s. 42(1) to (3)). In determining what are appropriate 'costs and expenses' to attribute to the carrying out of the Agency's (and Ministers') functions, account must be taken of any determination of the Agency's financial duties under Environment Act, s. 44 (see 15.4.1). Account may also be taken of depreciation of, and the provision of a return on, assets (s. 42(4)).

Environment Act, s. 42(5) ensures that charges relating to abstracting and impounding licences under WRA 1991 can cover expenses incurred by the EA in carrying out its functions under Part II of that Act, or under its general 'water resources' duties contained in Environment Act, s. 6(1).

The Secretary of State himself requires Treasury consent before he can approve a charging scheme. In the case of radioactive substances authorisations in England and Wales, the Minister's approval is also needed (s. 42(7)).

Once a charging scheme has been approved and made, the Agency making it must take steps to bring the scheme (as in force) to the attention of persons likely to be affected by it (s. 42(8)).

15.3 INCIDENTAL POWER TO IMPOSE CHARGES

Environment Act, s. 43 provides that, without prejudice to s. 37(1)(a) and subject to any express charging provision in ss. 37 to 42 or any other enactment, the EA and SEPA shall have power to fix and recover charges for services and facilities provided in the course of carrying out their functions. Section 43 in effect re-enacts WRA 1991, s. 144 which conferred such powers on the NRA, but extended so as to cover all the EA's functions, as well as those of SEPA, which inherits none of the NRA's functions. As statutory bodies may only do what Parliament expressly or impliedly authorises them to do, a provision ensuring that charges can be made by such a body for services and facilities is often included in the relevant legislation.

15.4 OTHER FINANCIAL PROVISIONS

15.4.1 Duties and directions

Environment Act, s. 44 enables Ministers (with Treasury approval) to determine the financial duties of the EA and SEPA, after consultation with the Agencies themselves. Different determinations may be made for different functions and activities of the Agency concerned. The EA and SEPA may be directed to pay to the appropriate Minister all or part of any surplus on its capital or revenue account. Special requirements apply, however, in the case of the EA's flood defence revenue.

15.4.2 Accounts, records and audit

The EA and SEPA are required by Environment Act, s. 45 to keep proper accounts and proper accounting records and to prepare an annual statement of accounts, containing information etc. required by Ministers (with Treasury consent).

The accounts of the EA and SEPA are to be audited by an auditor appointed for each accounting year by the Secretary of State, and copies of the accounts and auditor's report are to be sent to Ministers. The Comptroller and Auditor General is entitled to inspect the accounts and records and report thereon to the House of Commons (Environment Act, s. 46).

15.5   GRANTS, BORROWING AND LOANS

The appropriate Minister may make grants to the EA or SEPA, subject to Treasury approval (Environment Act, s. 47). Borrowing by the Agencies is governed by Environment Act, s. 48 under which the consent of the appropriate Minister and the approval of the Treasury are, again, required. Conditions may be attached to any consent. Aggregate borrowing may not exceed £100 million (in the case of the EA) or £5 million (in the case of SEPA) but the Minister may extend this by order to £160 million and £10 million respectively. In the Bill as introduced, SEPA's borrowing limits were £2 million (extendable to £5 million). These limits were criticised as being too low (and as giving the impression that SEPA was regarded as of little importance). The government amended the Bill in the House of Commons in the light of these criticisms.

The appropriate Minister may (subject to Treasury approval) lend sums to the EA or SEPA which it has power to borrow. The Comptroller and Auditor General must examine, certify and report to Parliament on annual accounts of loans, prepared by Ministers (Environment Act, s. 49).

The appropriate Minister may (with Treasury consent) guarantee borrowing by the EA and SEPA (Environment Act, s. 50).

Chapter 16
Contaminated Land

16.1 INTRODUCTION

16.1.1 Background to the new provisions

Section 57 of the Environment Act makes provision as regards contaminated land by inserting a new Part IIA into the Environmental Protection Act 1990 (EPA 1990), which replaces, as regards contaminated land, the statutory nuisance provisions in ss. 79 to 82 of the EPA 1990. The new provisions of the EPA 1990 (ss. 78A to 78YC) referred to in this chapter are set out in s. 57 of the Environment Act.

The new contaminated land provisions follow extensive consultation over a two-year period. The policy on which they are based is contained in *Framework for Contaminated Land* (DoE, November 1994) which sets out the government's conclusions and general proposals following a consultative exercise initiated by the consultation document, *Paying for our Past* (DoE, March 1994).

The key to the new provisions lies in defining 'contaminated land' as land the condition of which will cause significant harm (see 16.2 below). Previously, EPA 1990, s. 143 had sought to tackle the problem of contaminated land by providing for the registration of land subject to contamination. This was defined as 'land which is being or has been put to a contaminative use', i.e., 'any use of land which may cause it to be contaminated with noxious substances'.

The shift of emphasis in the new statutory regime from the previous use of land to the presence of substances which may cause significant harm, marks an important change of policy. The previous approach required only an investigation into the actual *use* to which the land had been put regardless of whether or not the use had actually caused the land to be contaminated with noxious substances or whether those noxious substances would cause harm in the context of any specified proposed use. The intention behind EPA 1990, s. 143 had been that a register would be kept of all contaminated land. In its first consultative paper on that provision (*Public Registers of Land which May Be Contaminated* (DoE, May 1991)), the Government specified some 40 uses of land which might cause it to be contaminated with noxious substances. By the time a further consultation paper (*Environmental Protection Act: Section 143 Registers*) was issued in July 1992, this list had been reduced to eight uses considered to be the most contaminative uses of land.

The Department of the Environment announced on 24 March 1993 that the proposed registration of contaminated land under EPA 1990, s. 143 would not proceed but would be replaced by a review of responsibility for contaminated land. The Government had been persuaded, in the light of the comments received on consultation, that the registration of land which had been used for certain contaminative purposes might discourage the development of brownfield sites, causing land values to fall and increasing the pressure on the development of greenfield sites. The reasons given for the abandonment of registers under s. 143 was that registers based on potential contamination would not discriminate sufficiently between clean land and contaminated land, that there was no machinery for deregistering land once it had been cleaned up and that, most importantly, registration did not tackle the remediation of the land or the identification of persons who would be liable for that remediation.

The Government's new policy as set out in *Framework for Contaminated Land* is to identify contaminated land by reference to the risk posed by the contaminates on a particular site in the context of its intended use (as opposed to the classification of land by the mere presence of contaminates), to balance the cost of cleaning up against the risk of the type of harm involved and to identify the persons liable for the cost of cleaning up preserving the *caveat emptor* ('buyer beware') principle.

16.1.2   Outline of new provisions

The new EPA 1990, Pt. IIA imposes on local authorities a duty to identify any contaminated land in their area. Contaminated land is defined in the Act by reference to 'significant harm' or the 'significant possibility' of such harm being caused to human health or property or the health of other living organisms or the pollution of controlled waters. Where the harm or pollution concerned is or is likely to be 'serious' the contaminated land is to be designated as a special site and comes under the jurisdiction of the EA or, in Scotland, SEPA instead of the jurisdiction of the local authority.

The enforcing authority (i.e., the EA or SEPA in the case of special sites or the local authority in the case of other contaminated land) must determine what remediation is to be undertaken in respect of the land and who is 'the appropriate person', i.e., the person who is to be responsible for that remediation. Remediation includes the whole process of cleaning up including assessing the condition of the land, the actual clean up or containment operations and subsequent monitoring.

The appropriate person is any person who caused or knowingly permitted the contaminants in question to be present on the land in question or, if no such person can be found, the owner or occupier of the land. The person who caused or knowingly permitted the presence of a contaminant on land is also liable for remediation in respect of any other land to which the contaminant escapes. Where there are two or more appropriate persons, the enforcing authority must determine which of them is or are to be liable and, in the case of those that are to be liable, the proportion in which they will bear the cost of remediation.

The enforcing authority must serve a remediation notice on each appropriate person requiring that person to undertake the remedial measures (or the appropriate proportion of the remedial measures) specified in the notice unless that would cause hardship. In default the enforcing authority may undertake the measures itself and has powers to recover its costs including the making of charging orders. In addition, the defaulter is criminally liable. The enforcing authority also has powers to undertake remedial measures itself in an emergency or if no appropriate person can be found to be required to undertake them.

Appeals lie against remediation notices and charging orders.

Each enforcing authority must keep a public register of the contaminated land which has been identified within its jurisdiction. The register must include not only the particulars of the land, its designation as a special site (if applicable) and any remediation notice served in respect of the land but also the remedial measures which have been taken in response to that notice. Information may be excluded from the register if it is commercially confidential but not merely because it relates to the ownership or occupation of the land or its value. Information affecting national security is also excluded.

Guidance is to be issued by the Secretary of State on how the statutory functions of enforcing authorities are to be exercised.

At the time of writing, the new provisions had not been brought into force except in so far as they confer power on the Secretary of State to make regulations or orders, give directions or issue guidance or make provision with respect to the exercise of any such power.

16.1.3   Civil liability

Polluters or owners of contaminated land may be civilly liable for environmental damage to others, at common law, in negligence, in nuisance or under the rule in *Rylands* v *Fletcher* (1868) LR 3 HL 330 or for breach of statutory duty.

Civil liability at common law was recently reviewed by the House of Lords in *Cambridge Water Co.* v *Eastern Counties Leather plc* [1994] 2 AC 264. That case has established that, so far as nuisance or the rule in *Rylands* v *Fletcher* is concerned, a plaintiff must establish that the damage caused was reasonably foreseeable at the time of the polluting act or omission.

The *Cambridge Water* case stimulated some calls for changes in the law such as reversing the burden of proof at common law on causation or fault in environmental cases. The Government, however, considers that the position at common law strikes the right balance between the parties (see para. 6.1 of *Framework for Contaminated Land*) and, accordingly, the new provisions on contaminated land do not make any changes to the civil law. Neither does it appear that the provisions confer any right on third parties to sue for damage caused by failure to comply with a remediation notice. This contrasts with the provisions in EPA 1990, s. 73(6) to (9) that damage caused by illegal deposits of waste in or on land contrary to EPA 1990, s. 33(1) or s. 63(2) may be actionable in civil law.

The Government considers that different considerations apply to the new statutory liability for remediation of land which has been contaminated by substances which have escaped from other land. Attempts made during the passage of the Environment Bill to introduce a 'state of the art' defence by analogy with the *Cambridge Water* case were resisted. See 16.6.5 below.

The statutory nuisance provisions in ss. 79 to 82 of EPA 1990 (briefly described in chapter 23 below) are disapplied to the extent that the statutory nuisance consists of, or is caused by, any land being in a contaminated state (EPA 1990, s. 79(1A) and (1B), inserted by the Environment Act sch. 22, para. 89). It follows that persons aggrieved are no longer able to take summary proceedings under EPA 1990, s. 82 on the grounds that contaminative substances on land constitute a statutory nuisance for the purposes of that provision.

16.1.4 Town and country planning and contaminated land

The role of local planning authorities in respect of land which is or may be contaminated is intended to complement rather than duplicate the statutory functions of enforcement authorities under the new EPA 1990, Pt. IIA. A framework of guidance for local planning authorities in England is set out in Planning Policy Guidance (PPG) No. 23, *Planning and Pollution Control* (DoE, July 1994) which updated and replaced the earlier advice to authorities contained in DoE Circular 21/87 (WO 22/87). PPG23 sets its guidance in the context of the 'suitable for use' approach, the Government's policy being to establish the balance between greenfield and brownfield development and to take the opportunities offered by redevelopment to remediate contaminated land in a cost-effective way. (See para. 3.3 of *Framework for Contaminated Land* (DoE, November 1994).) At the time of writing, Circular WO 22/87 remains in force for Wales.

16.2 MEANING OF 'CONTAMINATED LAND'

16.2.1 Definition of 'contaminated land'

The all-important definition of 'contaminated land' is contained in the new EPA 1990, s. 78A(2):

'Contaminated land' is any land which appears to the local authority in whose area it is situated to be in such a condition, by reason of substances in, on or under the land, that—
(a) *significant harm* is being caused or *there is a significant possibility of such harm being caused* or
(b) pollution of controlled waters is being, or is likely to be, caused
(emphasis added).

For this purpose 'harm' means 'harm to the health of living organisms or other interference with the ecological systems of which they form part and, in the case of man, includes harm to his property' (s. 78A(4)). 'Substance' means 'any natural or artificial substance, whether in solid or liquid form or in the form of a gas or vapour' (s. 78A(9)).

The definition of contaminated land was originally drafted in terms simply of 'harm'. The qualifications that the harm had to be 'significant' or that there must be a 'significant possibility of such harm being caused' were added to the provision by amendments made at the Report stage in the House of Lords. On moving the amendments, Viscount Ullswater explained their intended effect:

[The qualification] reflects the Government's original intentions, and our overall 'suitable for use' approach. It will also, I believe, meet many of the concerns as to the scope of these provisions raised by noble Lords in our debate on this clause in committee.

That notion of 'significant' harm includes the consideration together of the extent of any harm and of the nature of what might be affected — what is called in the technical jargon, the 'target'. For some potential targets — human health, for example, — quite small amounts of harm might be unacceptable. But when considering damage to property, as another example, the test might be less stringent.

Moving beyond that, some targets will be disregarded altogether. It is not the Government's intention, for example, to introduce through these provisions new requirements for the protection of habitats and ecological systems over and above those already in place under existing wildlife and habitat legislation.

The second major element of [the amendment] is the new test relating to the 'significant possibility' of harm being caused. In deciding whether remediation might be required on any site, a balance needs to be struck between the probability of any harm arising, and the consequences if it does. For example, the chances of methane gas on a site actually resulting in an explosion at any given time may not be all that high, but the consequences of an explosion to people living nearby would be so great as to require action to be taken to reduce even that slight possibility. (Hansard, HL, 7 March 1995, cols 137–8.)

The harm-based definition of contaminated land is new and is intended to reflect the 'suitable for use' approach adopted by the Government as described in 16.1.1 above. This approach was foreshadowed by the Department of the Environment when the Department, in evidence to the Environment Committee in 1989, defined contaminated land as 'land which represents an actual or potential hazard to health or the environment as a result of current or previous use' (Environment Committee, *1st Report. Contaminated Land*, vol. 1, House of Commons Papers, Session 1989–90, 170–I, para. 14). It follows, as the Department of the Environment stated on that occasion, that the question of whether land can be considered contaminated depends crucially on the actual or potential use of the land. What would be a hazard in relation to subsequent agricultural use might be of no account in the construction of an office block. It also follows that land which has been determined not to be contaminated land in the context of one use (such as a car park) might be considered contaminated if the use is changed to one which is more sensitive (such as a school). For the interface between the new regime and town and country planning see 16.1.4 above.

'Harm', defined as set out above, does not, as in EPA 1990, s. 29, include offence to the senses. This omission was deliberate because the Government did not consider that land should be taken to be contaminated on the basis of any smells which are not of themselves harmful to health or to the wider environment. Smells will continue to be dealt with under the statutory nuisance provisions in Part III of the EPA 1990 (Viscount Ullswater, Hansard, HL, 31 January 1995 col. 1440).

The second test of whether land is contaminated, that 'pollution of controlled waters is being, or is likely to be, caused' reflects s. 161 of the WRA 1991 which can also be used to deal with land which is likely to pollute water. Pollution of controlled waters is, following the terminology in WRA 1991, s. 161, defined as meaning 'the entry into controlled waters of any poisonous, noxious or polluting matter or any solid waste matter' (EPA 1990, s. 78A(9)). The Government's purpose in including water pollution within the definition of 'contaminated land' was not to create any additional liability with respect to the pollution of controlled water but to try to ensure that individual sites do not face dual regulation and that a single process can address all of the problems associated with contaminants in the land (Viscount Ullswater, Hansard, HL, 7 March 1995, col. 138).

It should be noted that the definition of contaminated land is in terms of land 'appearing' to the local authority concerned to be such. In many cases it will not be possible to ascertain whether the contaminants in question are present on the land in sufficient concentration to cause significant harm etc. without carrying out proper assessments. Remediation notices may require such assessments to be carried out. See 16.5 below. The issue is whether it appears to the local authority that the land in question *is* (not may be) in a condition such that significant harm etc. may be caused. It would seem that the authority must justify why land 'appeared' to it 'to be' in such a condition by reference to some evidence — mere speculation would not be sufficient.

16.2.2   Guidance by the Secretary of State

In determining whether land appears to be contaminated land a local authority must act in accordance with guidance issued by the Secretary of State (EPA 1990, s. 78A(2)). Guidance by the Secretary of State will also be given for determining:

(a)   what harm is to be regarded as 'significant';
(b)   whether the possibility of significant harm being caused is 'significant'; and
(c)   whether pollution of controlled waters is being, or is likely to be, caused.

The guidance may assign different degrees of importance to different types of target and different categories of harm (EPA 1990, s. 78A(6)). For guidance given by the Secretary of State see further 16.12 below.

On 5 May 1995 the Department of the Environment issued for consultation draft guidance on determination of whether land is contaminated land under the provisions of Part IIA of the EPA 1990. This draft guidance builds on the 'suitable for use' approach outlined in *Framework for Contaminated Land* and discussed in 16.1.1 above.

Paragraphs 24 to 26 of the draft guidance set out the guidance on the meaning of significant harm. Because these are key provisions they are set out below:

24.   For the purposes of defining contaminated land, the authority should disregard any harm or interference other than:
• harm to health of human users or occupiers of the land in its current use or to health of current human users or occupiers of other land;
• harm to or interference with the ecosystems protected under the Wildlife and Countryside Act 1981, EC Directive 79/409/EEC on the Conservation of Wild Birds, or the EC Habitats Directive 92/43/EEC, particularly in the light of

authorities' statutory duties under reg. 3(4) of the Conservation (Natural Habitats etc.) Regulations 1994;
• harm to property, [including livestock, crops], in relation to the present use of the land or other land.
25.   Further, for the purpose of determining whether land is contaminated land, the authorities should disregard any harm or interference other than:
• in the case of harm to human health: death, serious injury or clinical toxicity;
• in the case of harm to or interference with ecosystems: a significant change in the functioning of the ecosystems in protected areas, such as Sites of Special Scientific Interest, Ramsar sites, or European sites under the Conservation (Natural Habitats etc.) Regulations 1994;
• in the case of harm to property: physical damage which is continuing and which cannot be put right without substantial works and, in the case of animals and crops, disease or other physical damage causing loss in value.
26.   Any harm to living organisms or to property or interference with an ecosystem should be disregarded where the harm or interference is an intended and legal result of the addition of substances to that land, for example where harm is caused to a pest by the controlled use of pesticides.

The draft guidance goes on to state that the approach to the determination of the health and environmental effects arising from the contamination of land should follow the principle of risk assessment. In assessing risk, for this purpose, local authorities are directed:

(a)   to identify the targets to be protected;
(b)   to identify and make a preliminary assessment of possible sources: the possible presence of substances in, on or under the land which have the potential to cause the types of harm set out in para. 25 or to cause pollution of controlled waters;
(c)   to establish a plausible source–pathway–target relationship (as explained later in the guidance);
(d)   to confirm and make a further assessment of the actual presence of substances and their potential to cause the relevant harm; and
(e)   to estimate the risk: the probability and degree of harm.

16.2.3   Power to consider sites together

If it appears to a local authority that two or more sites, when considered together, would fall within the definition of contaminated land even if each of them taken individually would not, each of the sites will be treated as contaminated land (EPA 1990, s. 78X(1)).

16.3   IDENTIFICATION OF CONTAMINATED LAND

Local authorities are placed under a duty by the new EPA 1990, s. 78B to cause their areas to be inspected to identify contaminated land and to enable them to decide whether any of that land is required to be designated as a special site (see 16.4 below). In carrying out the inspection and making those determinations, the authority must act in accordance with guidance issued by the Secretary of State (see further 16.12 below). Draft guidance was issued on 5 May 1995 (see 16.2.2 above).

Notice of the identification of contaminated land must be given by the local authority to the EA (or, in Scotland SEPA), to the owner of the land (as defined in EPA 1990, s. 78A(9)), to any person who appears to be in occupation of the whole or any part of the land and to each person who appears to the local authority to be liable to have a remediation notice served on him with respect to the land (see 16.6.1 and 16.7.2 below). If at any later time it appears to the local authority that there is any other person who is liable to have a remediation notice served on him in respect of the land, notice must also be served on that person informing him that the land is contaminated land and that it appears that he is liable to have a remediation notice served on him. Notices may be served by post in accordance with EPA 1990, s. 160.

For the purposes of the provisions relating to contaminated land, a local authority is (by s. 78A(9)), in England and Wales, any unitary authority (i.e., a county council, so far as it is the council of an area for which there are no district councils, the council of any district comprised in an area for which there is no county council, a London borough council and, in Wales, a county borough council), any district council so far as it is not a unitary authority, the Common Council of the City of London and, as respects the Temples, the Sub-Treasurer of the Inner Temple and the Under-Treasurer of the Middle Temple. In Scotland, 'local authority' means a council for an area constituted under s. 2 of the Local Government etc. (Scotland) Act 1994.

16.4   SPECIAL SITES

In general the primary functions conferred by the new Part IIA of EPA 1990 relating to the remediation of contaminated land and the keeping of registers are conferred on local authorities. For the meaning of 'local authority' see 16.3 above. However, in the case of a particular category of contaminated land — 'special sites' — those functions are instead exercisable by the EA or, in Scotland, by SEPA.

Contaminated land is required to be designated as a special site by the local authority in whose area it is situated if it is of a description prescribed by regulations made by the Secretary of State (EPA 1990, s. 78C(8)). The regulations may, in particular, have regard to whether the harm or pollution of controlled waters which would or might be caused by the contaminated land is *serious* or whether the EA or SEPA is likely to have expertise in dealing with the kind of significant harm, or pollution of controlled water, concerned (EPA 1990, s. 78C(10)). At the time of writing no such regulations have yet been made.

It should be noted that, although many closed landfill sites are likely to be required to be designated as special sites, the legislation does not treat such sites as a special category. When the Environment Bill was introduced the new EPA 1990, Part IIA imposed a requirement for the separate identification of closed landfill sites and applied extra procedural stages to them. In doing so it followed EPA 1990, s. 61 (now superseded by the new Pt. IIA and repealed) which would have imposed special duties on waste regulation authorities in respect of closed landfill sites but which was never brought into force. However, during the passage of the Environment Bill through Parliament the Government was persuaded that it would be more flexible for special treatment to be afforded to categories of land to be prescribed by regulations. The requisite amendments were made in standing committee in the House of Commons.

If it appears to a local authority that any contaminated land within its area may be required to be designated as a special site, it must request the advice of the EA or, in Scotland, SEPA. If, having had regard to that advice, it decides that the land is indeed required to be designated as a special site because it falls within the prescribed description of such sites, the authority must give notice of that decision to the EA or SEPA, the owner of the land (as defined in EPA 1990, s. 78A(9)), any person appearing to the authority to be in occupation of the whole or any part of the land and to each person who appears to the local authority to be liable to have a remediation notice served on him in respect of the land (EPA 1990, s. 78C(2), (5)).

Unless the EA or SEPA serves a notice on the local authority disagreeing with its decision, the designation will take effect within 21 days or, if earlier, on the EA or SEPA notifying the local authority that it agrees that the land should be designated.

If the EA or SEPA disagree with the proposed designation of the land, the Agency may, within 21 days, serve a notice and statement of its reasons for disagreement on the authority and on the Secretary of State. The authority must then refer the decision to the Secretary of State (EPA 1990, s. 78D(1)). Notice of the referral must be given to the same persons who were required to be served with notice of the local authority's original decision. On a referral, the Secretary of State may confirm the decision to designate the whole of the land, confirm the decision with respect to only part of the land or reverse the decision (s. 78D(4)). Notice of the Secretary of State's decision must be given to the local authority and to the same persons who were required to be served with notice of the original decision of the local authority. Where the Secretary of State decides that some or all of the land should be designated as a special site, the designation will take effect on the day after the notice has been served (s. 78D(6)).

Alternatively, the EA or SEPA may at any time itself serve notice on the local authority that it considers that any contaminated land within the authority's area is land which is required to be designated as a special site (s. 78C(4)). The local authority must then decide whether or not it agrees with the Agency concerned and notify its decision to the Agency. If the Agency disagrees, the Agency has 21 days in which to notify the local authority and the Secretary of State of its disagreement with a statement of reasons whereupon the local authority must refer the matter to the Secretary of State. On such a referral, the powers of the Secretary of State, and the procedure, are the same as set out above.

Once land is designated as a special site, the functions relating to remediation and registers are exercisable by EA or, in Scotland, SEPA ('the appropriate Agency'). The appropriate Agency may inspect the land to keep its condition under review (s. 78Q(3)). If it appears to the appropriate Agency that the land comprising the special site no longer requires to be designated as such, it may terminate the designation by giving notice to the Secretary of State and the local authority in whose area the site is situated without prejudice to the land being designated as a special site on a subsequent occasion (s. 78Q(4) and (5)). Guidance will be given by the Secretary of State on how those functions are to be exercised (s. 78Q(6) and see also para. 16.12 below).

16.5 REMEDIATION IN OUTLINE

16.5.1 Meaning of 'remediation'

Remediation is widely defined in the new EPA 1990, s. 78A(7) as constituting the whole process of cleaning up, including assessing the condition of the land in question, the actual cleaning up or containment operation and subsequent monitoring to check that the cleaning up operations have been effective. Remediation requirements may extend not only to the contaminated land in question but to controlled waters affected by the land and any adjoining or adjacent land.

16.5.2 Obligation to undertake remediation

In contrast to the registration requirement under EPA 1990, s. 143 which it replaces, it is the remediation of contaminated land which lies at the heart of the new contaminated land regime. Broadly speaking, remediation is secured in two ways. First, for each piece of contaminated land or water, a person is identified who is to bear the responsibility for undertaking remediation. That person is referred to in the Act and below as 'the appropriate person'. Secondly, for each piece of contaminated land or water, there is an enforcing authority who has the duty to enforce the appropriate person's obligation by serving him with a remediation notice. In the case of a special site (see 16.4 above), the enforcing authority is the EA or, in Scotland, SEPA. In the case of other contaminated land, the enforcing authority is the local authority in whose area the land is situated. (See EPA 1990, s. 78A(9).)

A remediation notice must specify what the person on which it is served must do by way of remediation and the time within which each specified step must be carried out.

16.5.3 What remediation may be required

Although it is left to the enforcing authority to specify what is to be done by way of remediation, the authority is required to balance the interest of the environment against the cost of undertaking the remediation. The authority may only require things to be done if it considers them to be reasonable having regard both to the costs likely to be involved of taking the action concerned and to the seriousness of the harm and pollution in question (EPA 1990, s. 78E(4)). In determining what is to be done by way of remediation, the standard to which it should be done and what is or is not to be regarded as 'reasonable', the enforcing authority must have regard to guidance issued by the Secretary of State (see 16.12 below). Where the enforcing authority determines that remedial measures cannot be required because the cost of the measures would outweigh the seriousness of the harm or pollution in question, it must prepare, publish and register a remediation declaration recording its decision. See 16.7.4 and 16.10.1 below.

A remediation notice may require things to be done by way of remediation even if third party consents are required to carry out the necessary works, e.g., if it is necessary to enter neighbouring land. See 16.9 below.

16.6 LIABILITY FOR REMEDIATION

16.6.1 Who is liable?

It has already been mentioned (16.5.2) that the new statutory regime identifies in each case the person or persons — 'the appropriate person' — who will bear the responsibility for undertaking the things that the enforcing authority determines should be done by way of remediation in any particular case. The rules for determining the appropriate person are set out in EPA 1990, s. 78F. The person primarily responsible is the polluter and it is only if there is no polluter or the polluter cannot be identified that responsibility falls on the current owner or occupier of the contaminated land in question.

In order to be treated as a polluter (a term which, however, is not used in the new provisions) a person must have 'caused or knowingly permitted' all or some of the contaminated substances in question to be on the land (s. 78F(2)). A polluter is only responsible to undertake so much of the remediation as is referable to the actual contaminative substances he caused or knowingly permitted to be on the land s. 78F(3)). But he is responsible for all remediation in respect of the substance in question even if he only caused a small part of the total amount of the substance on the land to be there or if the remediation is needed because of the interaction between that substance and another substance which he did not cause to be there (s. 78F(10)). So, for instance, where an industrial process entailing the keeping of contaminating substances on land has been carried on by successive persons, each of them will, subject to what is said in 16.6.2 below, be responsible for remediation in respect of those substances.

If more than one person caused or knowingly permitted the contaminated substances to be on the land, each of them may be made responsible for remediation. See 16.6.2 below.

It can be seen that the key question is what is meant by 'causing or knowingly permitting'. This expression appears in many other enactments, notably s. 85(1) to (5) of the WRA 1991 and has been the subject of several decided cases. In the case of contamination caused by the storage or use of contaminating materials by a body which, or a statutory successor of which, is still in existence, there will be no difficulty in establishing causation. 'Causing' does not here import any negligence or any knowledge that contamination of land would result (see *Alphacell Ltd* v *Woodward* [1972] AC 824 (HL) and *NRA* v *Yorkshire Water Services Ltd* [1995] 1 AC 444 (HL). However, the mere failure to take preventative action is probably not to be taken as 'causing contamination'. (*Price* v *Cromack* [1975] 1 WLR 988). See also 17.2.2 below.

Difficult questions arise as regards what is meant by 'knowingly permitting' a detailed consideration of which would be outside the scope of this work. The key issue is to what extent the person concerned must have been aware not only of the existence of the substance in question but also of its harmful properties and that the substance would contaminate the land concerned. Once it is established that the person in question has sufficient knowledge, the next question is what is meant by 'permitting'. The term implies that the person in question has the legal power and, possibly, the financial means to remove the substance in question. (*Tophams Ltd v Earl of Sefton* [1967] AC 1 50). It can be argued (though it is not clear) that if a person responsible for land knows that a contaminating substance is present on the land and does not do what is reasonable to prevent it from contaminating that or other land he has knowingly permitted the contamination. If that is the case the owner of the land will be taken to have 'knowingly permitted' the contaminant to be present on the land once he becomes aware of it and fails to take remedial action. An occupier would only be so liable if the terms of his occupation enable him to take remedial action.

Once it is established that a person caused or knowingly permitted a particular substance to be on the land, he will also be responsible for remediation in respect of other substances which are present on the land as a result of chemical reactions or biological processes affecting the first substance (EPA 1990, s. 78F(9)).

If after reasonable enquiry by the enforcing authority, no polluter is found, the owner or occupier of the land must bear the responsibility for remediation (s. 78F(4)). As mentioned above, the polluter is only liable to the extent that the contamination is attributable to the contaminating substance he has caused to be on the land. If the contamination is attributable also to another substance, the owner or occupier must bear responsibility for remediation in respect of that other substance unless the polluter in relation to that substance can be found (s. 78F(5)). In other words, the buck stops at the owner or occupier — he must bear the cost of any remediation for which no polluter can be made responsible, subject to special protection in hardship cases (see 16.7.3 below).

The definition of 'owner' in s. 78A(9) includes a trustee but excludes a mortgagee who is not in possession. The Government's policy with regard to financial institutions was explained by Viscount Ullswater at the committee and report stages of the Environment Bill in the House of Lords. He said that the government does not consider that the simple act of lending money should of itself render the lender liable for remediation. The lender should retain the right to walk away from his security in a case where he considers that taking possession of contaminated land held as a security would mean acquiring a net liability. Although concerns had been expressed by banking interests that in some cases a mortgagee might take possession involuntarily at the instigation of the mortgagor and so acquire liability for contaminated land without having the option of walking away, the Government considered that the procedures already developed by banks to ensure that possession is not normally taken of mortgaged land would be adequate protection for them (Hansard, HL, 31 January 1995, col. 1448–9; 7 March 1995, col. 165).

As introduced, the Environment Bill contained a provision exempting from liability a person who had caused or knowingly permitted contaminants to be on the land if he had directly or indirectly transferred that liability to the owner or occupier for the time being. This exemption was, however, removed at the report stage in the House of Commons so that it is no longer possible to transfer primary liability under the new provisions. But, of course, it remains open to persons selling contaminated land to negotiate indemnities in respect of their statutory liabilities which will be enforceable in contract.

16.6.2   Liability where more than one person is responsible

There will be many cases of contaminated land where there are several persons who are, on the face of it, liable to carry out the same action by way of remediation. For instance, several persons, acting in partnership, may have carried on the industrial process which occasioned the contaminating substance to be brought on the land. They may, in turn, have been succeeded by others who may either have brought further contaminating substances on the land or may be said to have knowingly permitted the original substance to remain there. Or the contaminated land may be owned by one person and occupied by his lessees.

Where more than one person is, on the face of it, responsible, the enforcing authority must first determine, in accordance with guidance issued by the Secretary of State, whether any of those persons is to be treated as not being responsible for the remediation (EPA 1990, s. 78F(6)). If after that has been done, there still remains more than one person liable for the same remediation action, the enforcing authority must apportion the cost of remediation between them (s. 78F(7)). Again this apportionment must be done in accordance with guidance issued by the Secretary of State. As to guidance, see 16.12 below.

It is expected that the most complex, controversial and potentially litigious issues which will arise under the new regime will be the apportionment of liability between persons who are each of them on the face of it responsible for cleaning up. It is not necessarily the case that justice requires the original polluter to pay for the costs of cleaning up. It would, for example, be unfair for him to pay for remediation if he had sold his land at a price which reflected the contamination problems but without taking an express indemnity for the costs of remediation.

16.6.3   Persons acting in insolvencies

As a general principle, a person acting in an insolvency is not personally liable to bear the whole or any part of the costs of doing anything by way of remediation nor will he be guilty of an offence under the new EPA 1990, Pt. IIA (EPA 1990, s. 78X(3)). However, this exemption does not apply if and to the extent that the contamination is referable to substances which are on the land as a result of any act or omission of his which it was unreasonable for a person in his position to do or make. If, in consequence of such an unreasonable act or omission, he is made personally liable to bear the whole or part of the cost of remediation, he will be guilty of an offence for any non-compliance with the requirement to do the thing in question.

For this purpose, the protected persons are those listed in s. 78X(4), i.e., insolvency practitioners, the official receiver acting as an insolvency practitioner or as receiver or manager, a special manager, the Accountant in Bankruptcy acting as permanent or interim trustee in a sequestration and a person acting as a receiver or receiver and manager.

16.6.4   Liability for water pollution

It has already been seen (in 16.2.1 above) that one of the tests of whether the land is contaminated is whether 'pollution of controlled waters is being, or is likely to be, caused' and that this follows the similar terminology in s. 161 of the WRA 1991. EPA 1990, s. 78J is intended to secure that the overlapping obligations imposed by the new regime and those imposed under WRA 1991 are consistent. So s. 78J(2) expressly ensures that an enforcing authority cannot by serving a remediation notice impose on a person any liability over and above his liabilities under WRA 1991. Section 78J(3) preserves the defence currently afforded by WRA, 1991 s. 89(3) as respects contamination caused by abandoned mines (see 17.2.2 below) while subss. (4) to (6) of EPA 1990, s. 78J disapply that defence in the case of mines abandoned after 31 December 1999. Those provisions mirror the modifications made to WRA 1991, s. 89(3) by s. 60 of the Environment Act (see 17.2.3 below).

Although the enforcing authority is precluded from imposing any additional liability on another person as respects remediation of controlled waters, the authority may undertake the remediation at its own expense (s. 78J(7)). See further 16.8 below.

EPA 1990, s. 78YB(4) ensures that a remediation notice may not require anything to be done which would override a consent for a discharge into controlled waters under WRA 1991, Pt. III, Chapter II or, in Scotland, the Control of Pollution Act 1974, Pt. II. See 16.14.5 below.

16.6.5 Liability in respect of contaminating substances which escape to other land

EPA 1990, s. 78K makes provision regarding liability for substances which escape to other land.

16.6.5.1 The case postulated by EPA 1990, s. 78K

(a)   X has 'caused or knowingly permitted' a contaminated substance to be in, on or under land Y.

(b)   The substance 'appears' to the enforcing authority to have escaped to land A.

16.6.5.2 Liability of X   X is taken to have 'caused or knowingly permitted' the contaminating substance to be in, on or under land A and is therefore liable not only for remediation in respect of land Y (see 16.6.1 above) but also for remediation in respect of land A (s. 78K(1)).

It is not necessary for the escape to be proved but only for it to 'appear' to the enforcing authority that the contaminating substance on land A has emanated from land Y (s. 78K(7)). An earlier version of this provision which provided that the substance must have appeared to the enforcing authority, the appropriate Agency or the Secretary of State to have escaped from land Y was amended in the House of Commons. In the provision as enacted it is only the view of the enforcing authority which is relevant.

It is also significant that, unlike the position at common law as established by *Cambridge Water Co.* v *Eastern Counties Leather plc* [1994] 2 AC 264 (see 16.1.3 above), it is no defence for X to show that the contamination of land A could not, in the then state of scientific and technical knowledge, have been reasonably foreseen at the time when the substances in question were caused or permitted to be present on land Y. During the passage through Parliament of the Environment Bill attempts were made to introduce a 'state of the art' exemption from statutory liability for contaminated land by analogy with the *Cambridge Water* case. But this was rejected by the Government in the following terms:

> While this might appear to reflect the same test of 'reasonable foreseeability', which was recently established in the common law through the decision in the *Cambridge Water* case, the Government do not believe that the comparison is justified. Common law and statute law in this area do not have the same purposes. Actions at common law seek to provide remedies for private persons in respect of a variety of tortious acts; this proposed statute seeks to establish a regulatory framework to remove risks to health and the environment without introducing any notion of compensation. Given those essential differences, it is reasonable for the two systems to diverge.
>
> In practical terms, the availability of this exemption would leave almost any attempt by the enforcing authorities to deal with any contamination open to litigation attempting to prove the state of knowledge in the past. Another perverse effect could be to provide an incentive to hold back developments in the state of science, as greater understanding could result in greater future liabilities. (Viscount Ullswater, Hansard, HL, 31 January 1995, col. 1457.)

16.6.5.3   Liability of owner or occupier of land A   The owner or occupier of land A (assuming that he has not caused or knowingly permitted the substance in question to be on land A) is liable only for remediation in respect of the land or waters of which he is the owner or occupier. He cannot be required to do anything by way of remediation of any other land or controlled waters not owned or occupied by him which is adversely affected by the condition of land A or to which the contaminating substance in question has escaped from land Y via land A (s. 78K(3), (4)).

16.6.5.4   Liability of X's successor in title   X's successor (i.e., any subsequent owner or occupier of land Y) cannot be required to do anything by way of remediation of land A in consequence of X's apparent acts or omissions except to the extent that the successor himself has caused or knowingly permitted the escape (s. 78K(5)).

16.6.5.5   Remediation by enforcing authority   In the above cases, the enforcing authority may itself undertake remediation measures if X cannot be found (see 16.8.1 below) but cannot recover from the owner or occupier of land A or from X's successor the cost of doing anything which the authority is precluded from requiring that person to do (s. 78K(6)).

16.7   REMEDIATION NOTICES

16.7.1   Service of notice

It has already been mentioned (in 16.5.2 above) that the purpose underlying the new regime is to secure the remediation of contaminated land by fixing the appropriate person or persons with the responsibility for undertaking remediation. This purpose is achieved by the service of a remediation notice on the appropriate person or persons (determined under EPA 1990, s. 78F: see 16.6.1 above).

Once a special site has been designated or any other contaminated land has been identified, the enforcing authority (see 16.5.2 above) has a duty under EPA 1990, s. 78E to serve a remediation notice, in accordance with regulations, on each appropriate person specifying what that person is to do by way of remediation and the periods within which he is required to do each specified thing. The notices may require different things to be done if there are two or more contaminating substances.

There may be two or more appropriate persons in relation to any particular thing which is to be done by way of remediation. In that case, the remediation notice served on each of them must state the proportion of the cost which the enforcing authority has determined that that person must bear (s. 78E(3)). See further 16.6.2 above.

Before serving a remediation notice the enforcing authority must, in accordance with regulations, make reasonable endeavours to consult the person on whom the notice is to be served and the owners and occupiers of the land concerned as to what should be done by way of remediation and whether any consent is needed from a third party to carry out the remediation (ss. 78G(3) and 78H(1)). However, no consultation is required where there is an imminent danger of serious harm, or serious pollution of controlled waters, being caused (s. 78H(4)).

Section 78H(3) provides for time restrictions on the service of remediation notices, the effect of which is, broadly speaking, that a remediation notice cannot be served until three months has expired from the time that the owners and occupiers and other relevant persons were notified that the land concerned had been identified as contaminated land or, as the case may be, designated as a special site. Again, these restrictions do not operate where there is urgency because there is imminent danger of serious harm, or serious pollution of controlled waters (s. 78H(4)).

If a remediation notice is not complied with, the appropriate authority may itself carry out anything specified in the notice which has not been carried out and recover the costs of doing so from the person on whom the notice was served (ss. 78N(3)(c), (4)(c) and 78P). See 16.8.2 below. Failure to comply with the remediation notice is also an offence. See 17.7.6 below.

16.7.2   On whom should the notice be served?

Each remediation notice must be served on the 'appropriate person or persons' as determined by the enforcing authority under EPA 1990, s. 78F. See 16.6.1 above.

16.7.3   Hardship cases

As originally presented to Parliament, the Environment Bill would have required a remediation notice to be served on 'the appropriate person' regardless of his means. So a householder who had had the misfortune to purchase a house built on a former industrial site subsequently identified as contaminated land would have been served with a remediation notice requiring him to undertake remediation.

Although provision was made in the Bill for the enforcing authority to undertake the work required to be done in the remediation notice and not to recover its costs where this would cause hardship, the point was made forcibly during the Bill's passage through the House of Lords that this was not satisfactory since hardship could be considered only after a remediation notice had been served and the householder had committed the offence of not complying with its terms. To meet this concern amendments were brought forward by the Government in standing committee in the House of Commons to require enforcing authorities to consider and take account of any hardship in deciding whether to serve a remediation notice.

Under EPA 1990, s. 78H(5)(d) (read with ss. 78N(3)(e) and 78P(2)), the enforcing authority is precluded from serving a remediation notice on a person if it would cause hardship to that person to bear the cost of carrying out the remedial measures specified in the notice. In deciding whether hardship may be caused the enforcing authority must have regard to any guidance issued by the Secretary of State (s. 78P(2)(b)). See 16.12 below. This provision was intended to protect householders and small and medium-sized businesses.

Where the enforcing authority is precluded from serving a remediation notice by reason of hardship, it must prepare and publish a remediation statement (which must be registered in the statutory register – see 16.10.1 below) recording the things which are to be done by way of remediation, the name and address of the person who will do those things and the period within which each of those things is to be done (s. 78H(7)). The enforcing authority is only precluded from serving a remediation notice on a person if and so long as the service of the notice would cause hardship. If circumstances change so that the service of a notice would no longer cause hardship — perhaps if the ownership of the land has changed or the original owner has won the national lottery — the notice must be served immediately without any need for further consultation if consultation has already taken place (s. 78H(10)).

16.7.4   Other cases where a notice must not be served

Section 78H(5) of the EPA 1990 provides for further cases in which a remediation notice must not be served:

(a)   The enforcing authority cannot serve a remediation notice if it is satisfied that, although the land is contaminated, no remedial measures can reasonably be carried out because the cost of the measures would outweigh the seriousness of the harm or pollution of controlled waters in question. See 16.5.3 above. However, in any such case the enforcing authority must prepare and publish a remediation declaration recording the reasons why the authority would have specified the remedial measures in question (but for the question of costs) and the grounds on which the authority is satisfied that it would not be reasonable to require those measures to be undertaken (s. 78H(6)). The requirement to publish a remediation declaration applies also if the authority does serve a remediation notice but omits a particular measure from it on the grounds of reasonableness.

(b)   A notice cannot be served where the enforcing authority is satisfied that appropriate remediation will be carried out on a voluntary basis and there is therefore no need to serve a notice. In such a case the person carrying out the remedial measures must prepare and publish a remediation statement recording what is to be done by way of remediation, the name and address of the person who is to do each thing specified and the period within which each thing will be done (s. 78H(7)). In default, the enforcing authority may itself prepare and publish the remediation statement and recover the reasonable costs of doing so from the person carrying out the works.

(c)   No notice is to be served where the person on whom the notice would be served is the enforcing authority itself. In such a case, however, the authority must prepare and publish a remediation statement containing the particulars set out above (s. 78H(7)).

(d)   No notice can be served if the authority is satisfied that the powers conferred on it by s. 78N to do what is appropriate by way of remediation are exercisable. This applies not only where the powers are exercisable because it is a hardship case (see 16.7.3 above) but also in an emergency case where the enforcing authority decides to undertake the remediation measures itself because there is an imminent danger of serious harm or serious pollution of controlled waters. Here again a remediation statement must be prepared and published by the enforcing authority as mentioned above.

Particulars of remediation declarations and statements are required to be registered in the statutory register kept by the enforcing authority. See 16.10.1 below.

In all the above cases, the enforcing authority is only prevented from serving a remediation notice for so long as the precluding conditions apply. If circumstances change, a remediation notice must be served without any need for further consultation if consultation has already taken place (s. 78H(10)).

16.7.5   Appeals against remediation notices

A person served with a remediation notice may appeal under EPA 1990, s. 78L. The appeal must be brought within 21 days of the service of the notice and lies to the magistrates' court (or, in Scotland, to the sheriff) if it was served by a local authority or to the Secretary of State if it was served by the EA or SEPA. Appeals to the Secretary of State may be heard by a delegate under s. 114 of the Environment Act. The hearing of appeals by magistrates' courts is in keeping with other environmental legislation giving similar jurisdiction to magistrates (e.g., EPA 1990, Pt. III (statutory nuisance)). Critics have argued that a magistrates' court is not a proper forum in which to decide the technical issues of fact and complex issues of law which are likely to arise in contested cases. Nor will dealing with such cases on a local basis facilitate uniformity of decision making. But these concerns may be met, in part, if further appeals are to be heard by specialist tribunals. See below.

On an appeal, the remediation notice may be confirmed with or without modifications or quashed. It must be quashed if there is a material defect in it. If the notice is confirmed the period specified in the notice for taking any remedial measure may be extended.

Further provision relating to appeals is to be made by regulations. There is power for the regulations to prescribe the grounds on which an appeal may be brought and to provide for further appeals against decisions of the appellate authority. It is notable that the regulations may provide for the further appeals to be heard by 'a tribunal'. This seems to suggest that consideration is being given to the setting up of specialist tribunals to deal with environmental issues.

16.7.6 Offences

Under EPA 1990, s. 78M it is a summary offence for a person to fail, without reasonable excuse, to comply with any of the requirements of a remediation notice. In a case where the cost of undertaking remediation measures has been apportioned between two or more persons (see 16.6.2 and 16.7.1 above), it is an additional defence for one of them to prove that the only reason why he has not complied with the requirement is because of a failure on the part of one or more of the others to bear his or their required proportion of the cost (s. 78M(2)).

The usual penalty for the offence is a maximum fine of level 5 on the standard scale and a daily fine equal to one tenth of level 5 for each day on which the failure to comply with the requirement in the notice continues after conviction and before the enforcing authority has begun to carry out remedial measures itself. However, the fine is greater where the contaminated land in question consists of premises used for industrial, trade or business purposes (including any treatment or process) or for the burning of matter in connection with those purposes. In such a case the fine is £20,000 and the daily rate one tenth of that sum. The sum of £20,000 may be increased by order made by the Secretary of State.

Under s. 78M(5), the enforcing authority may take proceedings in the High Court (or, in Scotland, in any court of competent jurisdiction) to secure compliance with the remediation notice if it considers that criminal proceedings would not provide an effectual remedy.

16.7.7 Adoption of notice where land becomes a special site

If a remediation notice has been served by a local authority and the contaminated land in question is subsequently designated as a special site, the notice will continue to have effect as if it had been given by the EA or, in Scotland, SEPA provided that it is adopted by that Agency. Notice of adoption must be given by the Agency concerned to the person on whom the remediation notice was served and to the local authority (EPA 1990, s. 78Q(1)). No time limit is given for the making of the decision to adopt the remediation notice but it is assumed that the decision must be made within a reasonable time of the designation of the site and that unless and until the remediation notice is adopted it cannot be enforced either by the local authority or by the Agency concerned.

16.8 REMEDIATION BY ENFORCING AUTHORITIES

16.8.1 Power to effect remediation

In several circumstances the enforcing authority may itself undertake remediation measures relating to contaminated land within its jurisdiction. These measures can only be taken if the authority considers them to be reasonable having regard to their cost and the seriousness of the harm or pollution of waters in question. This is the same test as the authority must apply when determining whether to specify measures in a remediation notice, and the guidance given by the Secretary of State for that purpose also applies here. See 16.5.3 above.

The cases where the enforcing authority may undertake remediation measures fall into three categories:

(a)   The enforcing authority may undertake remediation measures in a case of an emergency where it is not practicable to wait for a remediation notice to be served. In such a case the authority may undertake any measures which it considers necessary to avert any imminent danger of serious harm or serious pollution of controlled waters (EPA 1990, s. 78N(3)(a), (4)(a)).

(b)   The authority may undertake remediation measures where a remediation notice has been served if the person on whom it is served fails to comply with the notice or, alternatively, agrees with the authority that the authority shall at that person's expense do anything required to be done by the notice (s. 78N(3)(b) and (c)).

(c)   The authority may carry out remediation measures where it is appropriate to carry them out and no remediation notice requiring another person to carry them out can be served. This may arise where the authority is precluded from serving a notice because it would cause hardship to the appropriate person to bear the costs of the works (see 16.7.3 above), if it would place the appropriate person under a liability additional to that under the WRA 1991 (see 16.6.4 above), if it is an escape case for which the appropriate person is not liable (see 16.6.5 above) or if it has not been possible, after a reasonable inquiry, to find the person who is the appropriate person to undertake the measure in question (s. 78N(3)(d), (e) and (f)).

16.8.2   Recovery of costs by enforcing authority

In most cases the enforcing authority may recover the reasonable cost of undertaking any remediation measures from the appropriate person, i.e., the person who would have been liable to undertake the measures if the local authority had not done so (EPA 1990, s. 78P). If there are two or more appropriate persons in relation to a measure, the cost may be recovered from them in proportions determined by the authority as mentioned in 16.6.2 above. However, the cost of undertaking a measure can only be recovered if or to the extent that this would not cause hardship to the person from whom the cost is recoverable. In determining whether to recover costs, the enforcing authority is directed by s. 78P(2) to have regard to any hardship that this would cause and to guidance issued by the Secretary of State.

In a case where the local authority is undertaking the remediation measures concerned by agreement with the appropriate person, the amount of costs to be recovered will be determined in accordance with the agreement rather than by applying the objective reasonableness test.

The cost of undertaking a measure cannot be recovered from a person who could not have been required to undertake that measure by the appropriate authority by virtue of s. 78J(7) or s. 78K(6) (see 16.6.4 and 16.6.5 above).

The recovery of the cost of remediation by the enforcing authority can be enforced by a charging notice in accordance with the provisions of s. 78P(3) to (13) which are similar to the equivalent provisions relating to statutory nuisance in EPA 1990, ss. 81A and 81B. A charging notice can only be served on a person who both owns the contaminated land in question and who polluted it, i.e., who caused or knowingly permitted the contaminating substances to be on the land. Where a charging notice is served, the enforcing authority may specify in the notice that the amount of cost claimed shall carry interest at a reasonable rate determined by the enforcing authority from the date of service of the notice until the whole amount of the cost is paid.

The effect of serving a charging notice is to make the cost and accrued interest a charge on any premises of the owner consisting of or including the contaminated land in question. The charge takes effect 21 days after the service of the notice or the determination or withdrawal of any appeal and continues until the cost and interest have been fully recovered. The enforcing authority may by order declare the cost to be payable with interest by instalments within a period not exceeding 30 years from the date of service of the notice. The charge is enforceable as if it were a mortgage by deed having powers of sale and lease, of accepting surrenders of leases and of appointing a receiver.

An appeal against the service of a charging notice lies to the county court within 21 days of the service of the notice (s. 78P(8)). On an appeal the court may confirm the notice without modification, increase or decrease the amount charged or order that the notice is to be of no effect. The appeal procedure is to be prescribed by regulations which may also prescribe the grounds on which appeals may be made.

The provisions relating to charging notices do not apply in Scotland (s. 78P(14)).

Where a local authority have begun to undertake remediation measures under s. 78N and the contaminated land in question becomes a special site, the authority may continue to undertake the measures and may recover the cost incurred in doing so as if they had continued to be the enforcing authority (s. 78Q(2)).

16.9 THIRD PARTY CONSENTS

In some cases it may not be possible for the appropriate person to undertake remedial measures without obtaining the consent of a third party. This will apply, for instance, where it is necessary to enter neighbouring land to undertake works or carry out inspections or monitoring. If the measures required to be carried out by a remediation notice cannot be carried out by the appropriate person without the consent of a third party, the third party is obliged by EPA 1990, s. 78G(2) to grant the necessary rights.

In such a case, the enforcing authority must, before serving the remediation notice, consult the owners and occupiers of the contaminated land in question, the controlled waters affected by the land or the adjoining or adjacent land concerned and any person whose consent may be required to enable compliance with the remediation notice (s. 78G(3), (7)). Prior consultation is not, however, required in the case of an emergency (s. 78G(4) and see 16.7.1 above).

The third party is entitled to claim compensation from the appropriate person in accordance with procedures to be prescribed by regulations (s. 78G(5)).

16.10   REGISTERS OF CONTAMINATED LAND

16.10.1   Duty to keep registers

Each enforcing authority is required under EPA 1990, s. 78R to maintain a register of the contaminated land for which it is responsible. EPA 1990, s. 143, which placed on local authorities a duty to maintain a public register of contaminated land and which was never brought into force, is superseded by s. 78R and therefore repealed. See 16.1.1 above.

The new register must be available for inspection by the public free of cost at all reasonable times and members of the public must be given public photocopying facilities on payment of reasonable charges.

The register will contain information not only in cases where remediation notices have been served but also in cases where although there is no remediation notice, a remediation statement or remediation declaration has been prepared and published (see 16.7.3 and 16.7.4 above). It is intended that regulations will be made requiring the appropriate person or the owner or occupier of land which is included in the register to notify the enforcing authority of what has been done by way of remediation and for that information to be registered so that any person enquiring can ascertain the current state of the land. However, the entry in the register of such information does not constitute any representation by the authority that the remedial measures concerned have been carried out satisfactorily or at all (s. 78R(3)). Appeals against remediation notices or charging notices and convictions for non-compliance of remediation notices are also required to be registered.

There is no provision for the removal of land from the register once remediation has been carried out. This is because the measures required by a remediation notice, even if properly carried out, do not constitute any guarantee that the land has been completely restored to its original condition. It is a necessary concomitant of the 'suitable for use' approach that remediation is a relative concept and must be viewed in the context of existing use. Further remediation may be required if the use of the land changes or if there is new scientific evidence to show that further measures are needed.

Where land is or has been designated as a special site, the register kept by the enforcing authority must contain the notice of designation and any notice terminating that designation.

Where the register is kept other than by the local authority in whose area the land is situated (e.g., the EA or SEPA), the enforcing authority must send copies of all particulars entered in the register to the local authority in whose area the land in question is situated which must then enter those particulars on its register of contaminated land (s. 78R(4) to (6)). This is intended to ensure that the register kept by a local authority of contaminated land in its area is comprehensive.

16.10.2   Exclusion of information relating to national security

Registers of contaminated land must not contain information if, in the opinion of the Secretary of State, the publication of that information would be contrary to the interests of national security (EPA 1990, s. 78S). This might be the case, for instance, where the contaminated land in question had been the site of a government research station. The Secretary of State may by directions given to enforcing authorities specify information, or descriptions of information, which is to be excluded from the register on this ground or which should be referred to him for a decision as to whether or not it is to be excluded and which in the meantime is not to be included in the register. Any person who considers that any particular information may fall into the excluded category may apply to the Secretary of State to determine whether or not it is to be registered, in which case the information cannot be included in the register until a direction is made.

Where information is excluded from the register in pursuance of a direction from the Secretary of State, the enforcing authority must notify the Secretary of State.

These provisions are similar to equivalent provisions applying to registers dealing with integrated pollution control and waste licensing in the EPA 1990, as amended by the Environment Act.

16.10.3 Exclusion of commercially confidential information

The general principle laid down by EPA 1990, s. 78T is that information relating to the affairs of any individual or business cannot be included in the register without the consent of the individual or person carrying on the business if and so long as the information is commercially confidential. Information is to be regarded as commercially confidential if its publication in the register would prejudice to an unreasonable degree the commercial interests of the individual or person concerned (s. 78T(10)).

However, information relating only to the ownership or occupation of the contaminated land in question or to its value is not to be regarded as confidential (s. 78T(11)). This exception has no equivalent in the provisions contained in EPA 1990 which protect commercially confidential information in the case of the registers dealing with integrated pollution control and waste licensing. This deliberate difference was explained by the Minister in standing committee in the House of Commons:

> One of the major purposes of the contaminated land registers is to inform potential purchasers of land. It would be perverse if precisely the kind of information that would benefit them most were to be excluded from the registers on grounds of commercial confidentiality. The new [s. 78T(11)] will prevent that from happening. (Hansard, HC Standing Committee B, 23 May 1995, Mr Atkins at cols. 381–2.)

Whether any particular information should be excluded on grounds of commercial confidentiality falls to be decided not by the interested person but by the enforcing authority subject to appeal to the Secretary of State. If the enforcing authority considers that any particular information might be commercially confidential, it must give the interested person an opportunity of objecting to the inclusion of the information in the register on those grounds and of making representations to the authority to justify the objections. If the enforcing authority decides that the information is commercially confidential it will be excluded from the register. If not, the interested person may appeal to the Secretary of State within 21 days of the decision. The information cannot be entered in the register until the expiry of that period or, if an appeal is brought, within seven days after the appeal is determined or withdrawn. If either party wishes, or if the Secretary of State so decides, the appeal to the Secretary of State must take the form of a hearing which must be held in private.

Information excluded from the register on the grounds of commercial confidentiality will remain protected for four years from the date of the determination by the enforcing authority or the Secretary of State. After that period it will be eligible for inclusion in the register unless the person who gave the information makes a successful application to the enforcing authority for the exclusion to remain in force. The procedure for determining an application for continuance of the exclusion is the same as on the original application (s. 78T(8), (9)).

The Secretary of State may override the confidentiality exemption by giving a direction that specified information, or descriptions of information, is to be included in the register if he considers it to be in the public interest (s. 78T(7)).

Draft guidance was issued by the DoE (DoE News Release No. 56, 30 January 1990) on the application of the commercial confidentiality exemption in the case of the register kept under EPA 1990, s. 20 for integrated pollution control and the same principles will probably be applied in this case.

16.11   REPORTS AND GUIDANCE BY THE AGENCIES

The EA and SEPA are under a duty to prepare and publish reports on the state of contaminated land in their parts of Britain (EPA 1990, s. 78U) from time to time or when the Secretary of State requests.

Both the EA and SEPA, as appropriate, may under s. 78V(1) issue site-specific guidance to any local authority with respect to the exercise of the authority's functions to which the authority must have regard unless (s. 78V(2)) the guidance is inconsistent with any guidance issued by the Secretary of State under the new EPA 1990, Pt. IIA.

Local authorities must comply with any request by each Agency for information which the Agency may need to compile reports or issue guidance provided the information has been, or may reasonably be, obtained by the local authority in the exercise of its functions relating to contaminated land (ss. 78U(2), (3) and 78V(3), (4)).

In preparing any such reports or issuing site specific guidance the Agency concerned must have regard to any guidance issued by the Secretary of State (see 16.12 below).

16.12   GUIDANCE BY THE SECRETARY OF STATE

There are several provisions in the new Part IIA of the EPA 1990 inserted by the Environment Act which specifically refer to guidance to be issued by the Secretary of State. These have been mentioned in 16.2.2, 16.3, 16.4, 16.5.3, 16.6.2, 16.7.3, 16.8.1, 16.8.2 and 16.11 above. In addition to these specific powers, the Secretary of State is given a general power by s. 78W to issue guidance to the EA and SEPA with respect to the exercise of their functions.

An interesting distinction is drawn in Part IIA between cases where the enforcing authority is 'to have regard' to any guidance issued by the Secretary of State and cases where the more stringent duty 'to act in accordance with' such guidance is imposed. That this distinction is deliberate can be seen in s. 78W which requires the EA or SEPA 'to have regard to' the Secretary of State's guidance but without prejudice to any duty imposed by any other provision of Part IIA 'to act in accordance with' guidance. The duty 'to have regard to' does not require the authority to follow the guidance concerned, so that it may in an appropriate case depart from the guidance provided it has first considered it fully; see *De Falco* v *Crawley Borough Council* [1980] QB 460, CA; *Eastleigh Borough Council* v *Betts* [1983] 2 AC 613, HL.

The cases in which the more exacting duty — 'to act in accordance with' — is imposed are guidance on the manner in which local authorities are to determine whether land appears to be contaminated (see s. 78A(2) and 16.3 above), guidance on the determination of questions relevant to whether land is to be regarded as contaminated (see s. 78A(5) and 16.2 above), guidance on the carrying out of inspections by local authorities of their areas to identify contaminated land (see s. 78B(2) and 16.3 above), guidance, in a case where there is more than one appropriate person, on exonerating one or more of them from liability and/or apportioning the costs of remediation between them (see s. 78F(6) and (7) and 16.6.2 above), and guidance to the appropriate Agency on reviewing the condition of, and terminating the designation of, special sites (see s. 78Q(6) and 16.4 above).

It can therefore be seen that guidance under the new Part IIA will play an important role in supplementing the statutory provisions and in providing an indication to interested persons as to how the new regime will be operated in practice. That importance is recognised in the requirement in s. 78YA that any proposed guidance is to be subject to negative Parliamentary procedure, i.e., a draft must be laid before each House of Parliament and the guidance cannot be issued if either House resolves that it should not be issued. Before issuing guidance, the Secretary of State must consult with the EA, SEPA and any other bodies or persons he considers appropriate.

At the time of writing, no guidance had been issued but draft guidance on the determination of whether land is contaminated had been circulated (see 16.2 above).

16.13   FUNCTIONS OF A LOCAL AUTHORITY IN RELATION TO LAND OUTSIDE ITS AREA

A local authority may exercise its functions under the new EPA 1990, Part IIA in relation to contaminated land which is outside but adjoining or adjacent to its area if it appears to the authority that significant harm is being caused within its area, or there is a significant possibility of such harm being caused, or that pollution of controlled waters is being, or is likely to be, caused within its area (EPA 1990, s. 78X(2)).

The functions are exercisable concurrently with the local authority in whose area the contaminated land is in fact situated.

16.14   INTERACTION WITH OTHER CLEAN-UP REGIMES

16.14.1   General

EPA 1990, s. 78YB contains provision which is intended to prevent overlap between the new regime in Part IIA of the EPA 1990 and other powers relating to cleaning up. The Government's stated objective was to avoid increasing the regulatory burden on landowners and others by securing that only one cleaning up regime would apply to any particular case.

16.14.2 Integrated pollution control under Part I of the Environmental Protection Act 1990

A remediation notice may not be served if and to the extent that it appears to the enforcing authority that the EA or SEPA has power under EPA 1990, s. 27 in relation to the harm or pollution concerned (EPA 1990, s. 78YB(1)). Section 27 empowers the EA or SEPA to remedy any harm caused by breaches of the integrated pollution control provisions in EPA 1990, Pt. I and to recover the cost from the offender.

16.14.3 Licensing of sites for waste under Part II of the Environmental Protection Act 1990

The provisions in the new EPA 1990, Pt. IIA do not apply in relation to land which is regulated by a site licence granted under EPA 1990, Pt. II authorising the keeping or disposal of waste in or on the land (EPA 1990, s. 78YB(2)). This exemption does not apply if the harm or pollution concerned is not attributable to activities authorised by the licence or by breaches of the conditions of the licence (in which latter case the enforcement provisions in EPA 1990, Pt. II will apply). EPA 1990, s. 78YB(2) has the effect of removing land subject to a waste site licence from the scope of the new regulatory regime for contaminated land and so ensures that persons such as the authority that granted the licence, those that carry on waste disposal activities in accordance with the licence or the landowner who granted a lease for that purpose cannot be held responsible under the new EPA 1990, Part IIA as having caused or knowingly permitted the presence on the land of any contaminative substance if its presence is authorised by the site licence.

16.14.4 Fly-tipping

EPA 1990, s. 59 confers powers on a waste regulation authority or waste collection authority to require the removal of controlled waste which has been unlawfully deposited or to arrange for the removal of the waste itself and to recover the costs of doing so from the responsible person (if any). Where land is contaminated by reason of the unlawful deposit of waste, no remediation notice may be served under the new EPA 1990, Pt. IIA if and to the extent that it appears to the enforcing authority that the powers under s. 59 are exercisable (s. 78YB(3)).

This exemption was introduced following an undertaking given by the Government at the report stage in the House of Lords (Hansard, HL 7 March 1995, cols 181–3). It is significant since its effect is to protect landowners from paying for cleaning up where the presence of the contaminative substances on the land in question has been caused by fly-tipping.

16.14.5 Discharges into controlled waters authorised under the Water Resources Act 1991 or the Control of Pollution Act 1974

A remediation notice may not require a person to do anything if the effect of doing so would be to impede or prevent the making of any discharge into controlled waters for which consent has been given by a licence granted under the WRA 1991, Pt. III, Chapter II or, in Scotland, the CPA 1974, Pt. II (EPA 1990, s. 78YB(4)).

This exemption, together with the provision made by the new EPA 1990, s. 78J, ensures that there is no inconsistency between the obligations imposed by the new EPA 1990, Pt. IIA and those imposed under the WRA 1991. See 16.6.4 above.

16.15   RADIOACTIVE CONTAMINATION

Dealing with radioactivity is considered by the Government to raise special technical and administrative issues and, for that reason, issues relating to radioactivity have to date been dealt with by specific legislation such as the RSA 1993 rather than being included in general legislation such as the EPA 1990 and the WRA 1991.

However, in the case of contaminated land, the Government considers that the regime in the new EPA 1990, Pt. IIA will provide a suitable basis for dealing with any radioactive contamination on former industrial sites such as old radium luminising works. But it is felt that modifications to the general regime may be required to deal with the particular scientific issues which arise with respect to the identification of radioactive contamination and the development of decontamination strategies. The Government also considers that it may be appropriate to place greater direct reliance on the EA and SEPA, particularly in view of the expertise that those Agencies have inherited from HMIP and HMIPI, than is necessary for other types of contamination. (See Mr Atkins, Hansard, HC Standing Committee B, 23 May 1995, col. 386.)

Accordingly, EPA 1990, s. 78YC provides that the provisions relating to contaminated land do not in themselves apply in relation to harm, or pollution of controlled waters, so far as attributable to radioactivity. But regulations may be made applying those provisions to such harm or pollution with modifications. Section 78YC is similar to EPA 1990, s. 78 which excludes radioactive waste from the provisions relating to waste control in EPA, Pt. II but enables regulations to be made applying those provisions with modifications to radioactive waste.

Chapter 17
Contamination from Mines

17.1 INTRODUCTION

The provisions in the Environment Act relating to abandoned mines were prompted by widespread public concern over problems of contamination caused by the leakage of mine water from abandoned mines when pumping stops.

As is explained in 17.2 below, the owner of an abandoned mine currently enjoys a specific exemption from the offences under s. 85 of the WRA 1991 which relate to the pollution of controlled waters. It follows that if the relevant authority (formerly the NRA in England and Wales, or any river purification authority in Scotland, and now the EA or SEPA) takes measures to remedy pollution of waters caused by an abandoned mine the authority cannot recover the costs of doing so from the owner of the abandoned mine. This exemption has become increasingly controversial with the recent closure of large numbers of mines and as anxieties over contamination from abandoned mines increase.

In March 1994 the Government published a consultation paper on the review of contaminated land and liabilities, *Paying for our Past*, stating that it would reassess the justification for the unique statutory exemptions for abandoned mines. In response, the NRA published a report, *Abandoned Mines and the Water Environment* (March 1994) which set out the extent of the problem and recommended that the abandonment of a mine should carry with it a corresponding duty to execute works to ameliorate the environmental effects of the abandonment.

The issue was given further prominence by the privatisation of British Coal. During the passage through Parliament of the Bill for the Coal Industry Act 1994, the point was repeatedly made in both Houses of Parliament that special safeguards with respect to abandoned mines were needed. Cases such as the Durham Coalfield were cited as examples giving rise to concern. Although the Government resisted all amendments to the Bill which would have imposed specific obligations on the newly formed Coal Authority, assurances were given on behalf of the Government by Lord Strathclyde that the issue would not be exacerbated by privatisation:

I should like there to be no doubt that so far as water pollution or potential water pollution is concerned the Government will not be content for the Authority to rest on the present effect of the exemptions. On the contrary, we will expect it to go beyond the minimum standards of environmental responsibility which are set by its legal duties in these areas and to seek the best environmental result which can be secured from the use of the resources available to it for these purposes.

The Authority will naturally have to set priorities for its activities in these areas. We will expect it to do this in consultation with the NRA and the appropriate river purification boards. (Hansard, HL, 26 April 1994, col. 541).

He stated that the Coal Authority would become the owner of existing abandoned coal mines throughout Great Britain irrespective of when they had been worked and would discharge its legal obligations with regard to those mines. In addition, the Authority would have 'a specific budget earmarked for these purposes and that this will enable it to carry forward in full the role and activities of British Coal in this area' (Hansard, HL, 26 April 1994, col. 542).

In *Framework for Contaminated Land* (DoE, November 1994), para. 5, the Government announced that it would propose legislative amendments to remove the existing statutory defence and exemptions for mines abandoned on or after 1 January 2000 so that the newly formed EA and SEPA (the successors to the NRA and river purification boards) would have the same powers in respect of those mines as for other discharges into controlled waters. In addition, a new duty would be conferred on mine operators to give the new environmental agencies six months' notice of any proposed abandonment with the object of providing 'an additional safeguard to ensure that when mines are abandoned this is done in a responsible manner with full regard to the effects on the water environment' (para. 5.3).

At the time of writing the provisions of the Environment Act referred to in this chapter had not been brought into force except in so far as they confer power on the Secretary of State to make supplementary provision, such as regulations, relating to them.

17.2 LIABILITY FOR PERMITTING WATER FROM AN ABANDONED MINE TO ENTER CONTROLLED WATERS

17.2.1. Offences of polluting controlled waters

The offences of polluting controlled waters are laid down in s. 85(1) to (5) of the WRA 1991, re-enacting provisions formerly in s. 107 of the WA 1989, itself largely based on ss. 31 and 32 of the CPA 1974:

(1) A person contravenes this section if he causes or knowingly permits any poisonous, noxious or polluting matter or any solid waste matter to enter any controlled waters.

(2) A person contravenes this section if he causes or knowingly permits any matter, other than trade effluent or sewage effluent, to enter controlled waters by being discharged from a drain or sewer in contravention of a prohibition imposed under s. 86 below.

(3) A person contravenes this section if he causes or knowingly permits any trade effluent or sewage effluent to be discharged—

(a)   into any controlled waters; or

(b)   from land in England and Wales, through a pipe, into the sea outside the seaward limits of controlled waters.

(4)   A person contravenes this section if he causes or knowingly permits any trade effluent or sewage effluent to be discharged, in contravention of any prohibition imposed under s. 86 below, from a building or from any fixed plant—

(a)   on to or into any land; or

(b)   into any waters of a lake or pond which are not inland freshwaters.

(5)   A person contravenes this section if he causes or knowingly permits any matter whatever to enter any inland freshwaters so as to tend (either directly or in combination with other matter which he or another person causes or permits to enter those waters) to impede the proper flow of the waters in a manner leading, or likely to lead, to a substantial aggravation of—

(a)   pollution due to other causes; or

(b)   the consequences of such pollution.

These offences are all punishable, on summary conviction, with imprisonment for a term not exceeding three months or to a fine not exceeding £20,000 or both or, on indictment, to imprisonment for a term not exceeding two years or to an unlimited fine or to both. The fine on summary conviction was increased from the statutory maximum (currently £5,000) to £20,000 by s. 145(1) of the EPA 1990.

Under WRA 1991,s. 104 the references in WRA 1991, s. 85 to 'controlled waters' are references to waters of any of the following classes:

(a)   relevant territorial waters, that is to say, . . . the waters which extend seaward for three miles from the baselines from which the breadth of the territorial sea adjacent to England and Wales is measured;

(b)   coastal waters, that is to say, any waters which are within the area which extends landward from those baselines as far as—

(i)   the limit of the highest tide; or

(ii)   in the case of the waters of any relevant river or watercourse [i.e., any river or watercourse, including an underground river or watercourse and an artificial river or watercourse, which is neither a public sewer nor a sewer or drain which drains into a public sewer], the freshwater limit of the river or watercourse,

together with the waters of any enclosed dock which adjoins waters within that area;

(c)   inland freshwaters, that is to say, the waters of any relevant lake or pond [i.e., any lake or pond which, whether it is natural or artificial or above or below ground, discharges into a relevant river or watercourse or into another lake or pond which is itself a relevant lake or pond] or of so much of any relevant river or watercourse as is above the freshwater limit;

(d)   ground waters, that is to say, any waters contained in underground strata [i.e., strata adjacent to the surface of any land].

The expression 'the waters of' any lake or pond or of any river or watercourse includes the bottom, channel or bed of any lake, pond, river or, as the case may be, watercourse which is for the time being dry (WRA 1991, s. 104(2)).

It can be seen from the above that the expression 'controlled water' is very wide, and includes, in particular, waters in underground strata.

The offences particularly relevant to the escape of polluted water from mines are those in WRA 1991, s. 85(1), (2) and (3)(a). It is, however, doubtful whether the offence in s. 85(3) which relates to the discharge of 'trade effluent' has any application in relation to an abandoned, as opposed to an active, mine. 'Trade effluent' is defined in WRA 1991, s. 221 as 'including any effluent which is discharged from premises used for carrying on any trade or industry other than surface water and domestic sewage'. It is arguable that effluent from an abandoned mine does not fall within this definition since the premises in question (i.e., the mine) are no longer used for trade or industry.

17.2.2 Exemption for abandoned mines

A working mine is the responsibility of its owner who is criminally liable under WRA 1991, s. 85 if he causes or knowingly permits polluted water from the mine to enter controlled waters. In contrast, a specific exemption is provided for the owner of an abandoned mine by WRA 1991, s. 89(3) which states:

A person shall not be guilty of an offence under s. 85 above by reason only of his permitting water from an abandoned mine to enter controlled waters.

The special exemption for mine owners was not introduced by the WRA 1991 but has a long history. The modern law of water pollution can be traced back to the Rivers Pollution Prevention Act 1876 which prohibited causing the falling or flowing of poisonous, noxious or polluting liquid into streams but expressly exempted causing the falling or flowing into streams from a mine of 'water in the same condition as that in which it has been drained or raised from such mine' (s. 5). The 1876 Act was replaced by the Rivers (Prevention of Pollution) Act 1951 which broadened the offences of polluting streams but, again, provided an exemption (subject to ministerial order) for 'the discharge of water raised or drained from any underground part of a mine into a stream in the same condition in which it is raised or drained from underground' (s. 2(4)). An exemption in identical terms contained in s. 1(2) of the Rivers (Prevention of Pollution) Act 1961 which extended the scope of the 1951 Act.

The current exemption in WRA 1991, s. 89(3) derives from the identically worded provision in s. 31(2) of the CPA 1974. The current exemption is narrower than the former exemption provided by the 1951 and 1961 Acts in three significant ways:

    (a)   The current exemption is restricted to water from abandoned mines. It does not exonerate owners of working mines from criminal liability.

    (b)   The current exemption relates only to permitting water *to enter* controlled waters. The former provision permitted the *discharge* of water from mines. Thus it appears that WRA 1991, s. 89(3) does not provide a defence to the offence under WRA 1991, s. 85(2) of permitting matter to enter controlled waters by being discharged from a drain or sewer in contravention of a prohibition imposed under s. 86. The owner of an abandoned mine is not, it is submitted, given *carte blanche* by s. 89(3) to pump out contaminated water from the mine and to discharge it into controlled waters.

(c)   The exemption only operates where the person concerned has *permitted* the entry into controlled waters of the polluted waters from the abandoned mine. It would not exonerate someone who *caused* such polluted water to enter controlled waters. It would, however, be difficult to show that the owner of an abandoned mine had 'caused' the escape of polluted water. Polluted water will inevitably escape from a mine unless preventive measures such as pumping are carried out. So, in practice, it is the cessation of pumping or other preventive measures which triggers the escape of water. For the owner to be liable under s. 85(1) it would have to be argued that he had 'caused' the entry of the polluted water into controlled waters by stopping pumping operations; in other words, that the owner had 'caused' the water to escape not by a positive act but by an omission. Such an argument would run counter to judicial dicta to the effect that the expression 'causes' in criminal provisions assumes some degree of dominance or control, or some express or positive mandate from the person 'causing' (*McLeod* v *Buchanan* [1940] 2 All ER 179 at p. 187 per Lord Wright). See also 16.6.1 above.

17.2.3   Effect of the Environment Act on exemption

Section 60 of the Environment Act removes the exemption in s. 89(3) of the WRA 1991 (explained in 17.2.2 above) but only in the case of mines which become abandoned on or after 1 January 2000. Thus, the exemption will still operate to protect the owners and occupiers of mines which were abandoned before the Environment Act was passed or of mines which were working at that time but which become abandoned before 1 January 2000. The owners of such mines will be able to stop pumping operations with impunity.

The Government has made no secret of the fact that the delay in the repeal of the exemption afforded by WRA 1991, s. 89(3) was motivated by its desire not to prejudice the privatisation of British Coal. This policy was revealed in the Explanatory and Financial Memorandum for the Bill for the Environment Act as presented to the House of Commons (which set out the effect of the Bill on public expenditure):

> For abandoned mines in the ownership of the Coal Authority there could be an increase in public expenditure, since the cost of any action taken, including pumping of mine water, would fall on the Authority. Since these proposals are coming forward in parallel with the privatisation of the coal industry, there could be some adverse effect on proceeds to the Government. Accordingly, the removal of the statutory protection is being timed to reduce any possible effect.

Hardly surprisingly, this proved one of the most politically controversial issues raised by the Environment Bill. Members of both Houses of Parliament argued that the retention of the exemption for mines abandoned before 1 January 2000 could not be justified on environmental grounds. They pointed out that only some 32 mines are still in operation while about 936 have been closed since nationalisation in 1947 and many more mines that were closed prior to 1947 still have significant pollution potential (Llew Smith MP Hansard, HC, 18 April 1995, col. 100).

Furthermore they feared that the long delay in the repeal of the exemption would actively encourage successor companies taking over mines on privatisation to close mines before 1 January 2000 in order to escape liability for eternal pumping (Paddy Tipping MP, Hansard, HC Standing Committee B, 23 May 1995, col. 418). The government's response was that privatisation was not the principal reason for choosing 31 December 1999 as the date after which the amended regime would take effect but that the Government had considered that the mining activities should have an adequate period to adapt to, and make provision for, the new liabilities (Robert Atkins MP, Hansard, HC Standing Committee B, 23 May 1995, col. 418).

Specific provision is made, for the first time, for the abandonment of a part (as opposed to the whole) of a mine. Environment Act, s. 60(1) amends WRA 1991, s. 89(3) to read 'A person shall not be guilty of an offence under s. 85 above by reason only of his permitting water from an abandoned mine *or an abandoned part of a mine* to enter controlled waters' (the italic words being the words inserted by Environment Act, s. 60(1)). This recognises that mines are often interlinked and that where a vein has been exhausted and so is closed it may be difficult to determine whether the closure is to be classified as the closure of an entire mine. The amendment makes such an exercise unnecessary. References to the abandonment of a part of a mine are carried into the provision which disapplies the exemption. So the exemption is removed from cases where parts of mines are abandoned after 31 December 1999 as well as from those where the whole of a mine has been abandoned after that date.

The possibility of an abandoned mine (or part of a mine) being reopened and then, subsequently, abandoned for a second or even third time is catered for in the new subss. (3B) and (3C) inserted in WRA 1991, s. 89 by Environment Act, s. 60(2). In such a case each 'abandonment' must be looked at separately to see if the exemption applies. Similarly each part of the mine must be looked at separately. The examples below illustrate how the provisions will work.

Example 1   Mine A was closed in 1990 (the first abandonment). In 1996 pumping stops and water from the mine pollutes controlled waters. In 1998 the mine is reopened and pumping recommences. In 2010 the mine is again closed. Under WRA 1991, s. 89(3) the owner is exempted from liability in respect of the incident in 1996 which occurred while the mine was abandoned. However, the owner would be liable if any polluted water from the mine entered controlled waters after the second abandonment because that occurred after 31 December 1999 (see WRA 1991, s. 89(3A) and (3B)). He still remains exempt in respect of the 1996 incident (see WRA 1991, s. 89(3B)).

Example 2   Mine B was closed in 1990 and pumping stopped. In 2005 a part of the mine (seam X) is reopened and worked until 2025 when it is abandoned. After 2025 water from the mine pollutes controlled waters. Under WRA 1991, s. 89(3) the owner is exempted from liability in so far as the escape of the water is attributable to those parts of the mine which were abandoned in 1990 and were not re-opened (that being a date that falls before 1 January 2000). However, the owner will be liable to the extent that the escape of water is attributable to seam X, the part of the mine which was abandoned in 2025 (that being a date which falls after

31 December 1999) (WRA 1991, s. 89(3A) and (3B)). Furthermore, the abandonment of seam X, the only part of the mine that is in use, in 2025 will not be regarded as constituting the abandonment of the whole of mine B but only that part of it (WRA 1991, s. 89(3C)).

WRA 1991, s. 161 enables the EA (formerly the NRA) to carry out certain preventative and remedial works and operations where it appears to the Agency that any poisonous, noxious or polluting matter or any solid waste matter is likely to enter, or to be or to have been present in, any controlled waters. The Agency can recover the expenses reasonably incurred in carrying out such works and operations from any person who:

(a)   caused or knowingly permitted the matter in question to be present at the place from which it was likely, in the opinion of the Agency, to enter any controlled waters, or
(b)   caused or knowingly permitted the matter in question to be present in any controlled waters,

those being the persons who would be potentially liable under WRA 1991, s. 85.

However, such expenses are not recoverable from a person for works or operations in respect of water from an abandoned mine (see s. 161(4)). This exemption is, of course, a logical extension of that in WRA 1991, s. 89(3). As one would expect, the Environment Act provides (s. 60(6)) that the exemption in WRA 1991, s. 161(4) will not apply to a mine or part of a mine which becomes abandoned after 31 December 1999. The provisions explained above relating to mines or parts of mines which are abandoned, restored and subsequently abandoned again also apply to the exemption in WRA 1991, s. 161(4). (See WRA 1991, s. 161(4B) inserted by Environment Act, s. 60(6)).

17.2.4   Other effects of the Environment Act

The provisions of the Environment Act, s. 60(3) to (5) extend the anti-pollution works and operations which the EA has power to carry out under WRA 1991, s. 161. Where water pollution is taking place, the EA is empowered to carry out investigations to establish the source of the matter in question and the identity of the person who has caused or knowingly permitted it to be present in controlled waters or at a place from which it was likely, in the EA's opinion, to enter controlled waters. Where those investigations identify the culprit, the EA may recover the cost of the investigations from him.

17.2.5   Position in Scotland

For Scotland the offences relating to water pollution are to be found in the CPA 1974. Those offences are now repealed and replaced by new sections inserted into CPA 1974 by Environment Act, sch. 16 which amalgamates the Scottish water pollution offence provisions in CPA 1974, ss. 31 and 32 to bring all the relevant criminal offences into a single section (the new s. 30F inserted into the CPA 1974 by Environment Act, sch. 16, para. 2) which is broadly in line with the corresponding provisions for England and Wales contained in the WRA 1991. Defences are provided by the new CPA 1974, ss. 30I and 30J. These include (in s. 30J(3)) an exemption in respect of abandoned mines corresponding to that in WRA 1991, s. 89(3) explained in 17.2.2 above.

The provisions limiting the exemptions to mines, or parts of mines, abandoned on or before 31 December 1999 are the same as those for England and Wales contained in the new subss. (3A) to (3C) inserted into WRA 1991, s. 89 by Environment Act, s. 60(2). See 17.2.3 above.

17.3 NOTIFICATION OF ABANDONMENT OF MINES

17.3.1 Introduction

Sections 58 and 59 of the Environment Act insert a new Chapter IIA into Part III of the WRA 1991 for England and Wales and a similar new Part IA into the CPA 1974 for Scotland, which impose duties to give notice of the abandonment of any mine. The purpose of these provisions is to ensure that the EA, or in Scotland SEPA, and local authorities are given adequate notice of any abandonment of work at mines which may cause water pollution so as to enable proper consideration to be given to whether any, and if so what, preventative operations should be undertaken. The protection afforded by those provisions is, however, limited because no duty is imposed on the operator of the mine, the relevant Agency, or the local authority to carry out any preventative operations which may be needed.

17.3.2 Duty to notify

The new WRA 1991, s. 91(B) (or, in Scotland, CPA 1974, s. 30Z) imposes a duty on the operator of a mine to give at least six months' notice of any proposed abandonment of the mine to the EA (or, in Scotland, SEPA). The notice must contain information to be prescribed by regulations which may include information about the operator's opinion as to the consequences of the abandonment. Failure to give such notice is an offence punishable, on summary conviction, by a fine not exceeding the statutory maximum (currently £5,000) or, on indictment, by an unlimited fine. But it is sufficient to give notice as soon as reasonably practicable after the abandonment has happened where the abandonment has taken place in an emergency in order to avoid danger to life or health.

Once the Agency concerned has received a notice under WRA 1991, s. 91(B) (or CPA 1974, s. 30Z) or learns of an abandonment or proposed abandonment of a mine in some other way, it must inform the local authority in whose area the land is situated if it considers that any land has, or is likely to, become contaminated land in consequence of the abandonment or proposed abandonment.

The operator's statutory duty to notify the relevant Agency applies in any case where the abandonment is to take place after the period of six months beginning on the day in which the provision imposing the obligation comes into force (WRA 1991, s. 91B(1) and (8); CPA 1974, s. 30Z(1) and (8)). So, if the provision comes into force on 1 January 1996, and the operator of a mine is aware that it is to be abandoned on 2 July 1996 he will be under an immediate duty to serve six months' notice. Since there is no similar transitional provision in respect of the Agency's duty to notify the appropriate local authority, the Agency will, as soon as the provision comes into force, be obliged to notify the local authority of any proposed abandonment of a mine of which it is aware.

In England and Wales, a 'local authority' means a unitary authority (i.e., a county council of an area for which there are no district councils, a district council for an area for which there is no county council, a London borough council or a county borough council in Wales), a district council (if not a unitary authority) and the Common Council of the City of London, the Sub-Treasurer of the Inner Temple and the Under-Treasurer of the Middle Temple (WRA 1991, s. 91B(8)). In Scotland 'local authority' means a council constituted under s. 2 of the Local Government etc. (Scotland) Act 1994 (CPA 1974, s. 30Z(8)).

17.3.3   Meaning of 'mine' and 'abandonment'

By WRA 1991, s. 91A(2), 'mine' for the purposes of the above provisions has the meaning given by s. 180 of the Mines and Quarries Act 1954 where it is defined as meaning:

> an excavation or system of excavations, including all such excavations to which a common system of ventilation is provided, made for the purpose of, or in connection with, the getting, wholly or substantially by means involving the employment of persons below ground, of minerals (whether in their natural state or in solution or suspension) or products of minerals.

The mine operators' statutory obligation is intended to ensure that the relevant Agency is given notice of any cessation of working of a mine or of operations for removing water from a mine which may give rise to water pollution if preventative measures are not taken. 'Abandonment' is therefore defined very widely for the purposes of the new WRA 1991, s. 91B in s. 91A(1) and for the new CPA 1974, s. 30Z in s. 30Y(1). In addition to the cessation of working of the mine, it includes the cessation of working of any seam, vein or vein-system forming part of the mine, the cessation of use of any shaft or outlet of the mine and the discontinuance of any or all of the operations for the removal of water from the mine. In the case of a mine in which activities other than mining are carried on, it also includes the discontinuance of some or all of those other activities or any substantial change in the operations for the removal of water from the mine. It should, however, be noted that this extended definition of 'abandonment' only applies for the purposes of the obligation to give notice and not for the purposes of the exemption in WRA 1991, s. 89(3) or, in Scotland, CPA 1974, s. 30J(3) referred to in 17.2.2 and 17.2.5 above.

Chapter 18
National Parks

18.1 INTRODUCTION

Part III of the Environment Act makes fundamental changes to the system of care and control of National Parks. These changes result from a major review carried out by the National Parks Review Panel, which was established in 1989 by the Countryside Commission under the Chairmanship of Professor Ron Edwards (who is now a member of the board of the EA — see 2.7.1) in order 'to identify the main factors, including likely developments in the future, which affect the ability of the National Parks to achieve their purposes; to assess the ways in which these purposes might most effectively be achieved in the future; and to recommend how these ways should be put into practical effect'. The Panel's Report, entitled *Fit for the Future* but referred to here as the Edwards Report, was published in March 1991 by the Countryside Commission (CCP334). The government responded in detail to the report, in generally favourable terms, in January 1992, stating that, when Parliamentary time allowed, a National Parks Bill would be introduced to implement those (major) recommendations of the report which required to be implemented by means of primary legislation (*Fit for the Future: A Statement by the Government on Policies for the National Parks* (Department of the Environment/Welsh Office, 1992)). In the absence of any legislative proposals from the government on the subject in the 1993–94 Parliamentary Session, Lord Norrie introduced his National Parks Bill into the House of Lords. Although the Bill had government support, and passed the House of Lords, it was blocked in the House of Commons and failed to reach the statute book. The opportunity was finally taken in the Environment Act to bring about the necessary legislative changes.

18.1.1 History and nature of National Parks

In order to understand the Edwards recommendations, and the changes made by the Environment Act, it is necessary to describe in outline the history and nature of the system of National Parks in England and Wales (there being no National Parks in Scotland). Although concern over the public's ability to enjoy some of our wilder scenic areas had grown between the wars, finding expression in acts of organised mass trespass on certain moorlands in the 1930s, the creation of the 10 existing National Parks arose directly from the Dower Report of 1945 and the Hobhouse Report of 1947. Dower established the case for National Parks to be designated, proposing a number of suitable candidates. Dower considered a National Park should be 'an extensive area of beautiful and relatively wild country' and that 'the concern of national parks must be broadly confined to relatively wild country, for, generally speaking, it is only in such country that the public at large either desires or can satisfactorily be given a wide measure of recreational access' (see Edwards Report ch. 2.2). The Hobhouse Committee refined the concept, concluding that:

> the essential requirements of a national park are that it should have great natural beauty, a high value for open-air recreation and substantial continuous extent. Further, the distribution of selected areas should as far as practicable be such that at least one of them is quickly accessible from each of the main centres of population in England and Wales. (Ibid., loc. cit.).

The Hobhouse Report led directly to the National Parks and Access to the Countryside Act 1949 (NPACA 1949). This Act established a National Parks Commission, and charged it with the task of designating suitable areas as National Parks. Section 5(1) of the Act sets out the purposes of National Parks as:

(a)   preserving and enhancing the natural beauty of the areas; and
(b)   promoting their enjoyment by the public.

These purposes effectively followed the recommendations of Dower and Hobhouse and, as the Edwards Report observes, it is not surprising that the areas which were designated by the Commission between 1951 and 1957 were those listed in the earlier reports as appropriate candidates because of their outstanding landscape qualities and suitability for public access and extensive recreation.

The existing National Parks are as follows:-

National Park	Year of designation	Area sq. km. (1990)	Population (1981)
Peak District	1951	1,404	37,400
Lake District	1951	2,292	40,000
Snowdonia	1951	2,171	23,800
Dartmoor	1951	945	29,100
Pembrokeshire Coast	1952	583	23,000
North York Moors	1952	1,432	27,000
Yorkshire Dales	1954	1,760	18,600
Exmoor	1954	686	10,000
Northumberland	1956	1,031	2,200
Brecon Beacons	1957	1,344	32,200

Although the Norfolk and Suffolk Broads are, in many respects, a National Park in all but name, the relatively recent establishment of the Broads Authority under the Norfolk and Suffolk Broads Act 1988, together with the particular constitution of that authority, reflecting the individual character of the area, were considered by the government to warrant delaying making any changes in its case along the lines of those proposed for the National Parks themselves. Part III of the Environment Act does not, therefore, deal with the Broads.

Of the 10 National Parks, the Peak District and the Lake District were each placed in the hands of boards, legally separate from their respective county councils, although dependent on them for funding. The other eight National Parks were administered by county council committees. The National Park bodies exercised certain town and country planning functions, as well as seeking to secure access for the public to open land in the Parks, e.g., by entering into access agreements with landowners under NPACA 1949, s. 64. The National Parks Commission was replaced by the Countryside Commission, established by the Countryside Act 1968, which also extended the limited powers of the boards or committees responsible for the National Parks to provide, e.g., refreshments, campsites and car parks so as to cover such matters as the provision of study centres and other facilities (s. 12) and the control of boats, etc. on lakes (s. 13). Following the passing of the Countryside Act 1968 ranger services were established in each of the National Parks, and efforts were made to add generally to the enjoyment of the Parks by providing information to visitors, not to mention such (now taken for granted) facilities as public conveniences and litter bins (s. 12(2)).

The general increase in wealth, leisure and mobility which occurred in the 1960s led to the realisation that situations could arise in which the second purpose of National Parks — the promotion of their enjoyment by the public — would be in conflict with the first purpose, namely, preserving and enhancing their natural beauty. Lord Sandford's *Review of National Park Policies* in 1974 produced a recommendation — now known as the 'Sandford principle' — that where conflict between the first and second purposes becomes acute, the first one must prevail.

At the same time as the negative aspects of public access to the National Parks were becoming recognised, informed observers (including Sandford) were also starting to voice concerns at the effect of changes in agricultural practices.

Under the Local Government Act 1972 the newly formed county councils were required to form single National Park committees for each National Park to which development control functions were delegated. National Parks acquired their own support staffs, headed by National Park officers, and, as the Edwards Report acknowledges, the National Parks system gained in confidence as a result. Notwithstanding this, National Park bodies were still predominately concerned with controlling development within their areas, but the 1980s saw this change to encompass a degree of land management, with the agricultural notification scheme (1980) and the Wildlife and Countryside Act 1981. The latter contains provisions (*inter alia*) enabling the ploughing up etc. of moors and heaths within a National Park to be controlled (s. 42), and permitting the National Park body to give financial assistance to a person to help conserve and enhance the natural beauty of the Park or promote its enjoyment by the public (i.e., the first and second purposes — see above) (s. 44).

Despite these changes, the Edwards Report considered that the enormous changes which have taken place in the countryside since the 1940s necessitated a radical reassessment of the National Parks system:

There has been a shift from conserving natural beauty alone to the conservation of the whole environment. A more discriminating approach to meeting recreation demands is also evident. The importance of local history and culture is increasingly acknowledged. As the quality of our countryside is eroded, and as urban life becomes more artificial and technologically driven, so the value of the qualities represented by our National Parks has grown. We now recognise more clearly that the whole of our countryside has special qualities, but the National Parks still contain the greatest tracts of open countryside, the strongest sense of remoteness, and the grandest and most dramatic scenery, where nature seems to be most about us. Furthermore, as remoteness and wildness become rarer, the recreational importance of our National Parks as a source of physical challenge and spiritual refreshment, and as a place of study and learning, has increased.

The softer and less remote areas of our National Parks also exemplify, at their best, a harmonious interaction between humanity and the natural world. We see this in farms, barns and stone walls, and in the villages. This part of the National Park scene, where man's hand is most in evidence, is no less an integral element. (Edwards Report, ch. 2.2.)

The Edwards Report concluded that National Park authorities:

have faced serious impediments in pursuing their aims, and . . . the parks themselves have often not lived up to the expectations of their founders. Notwithstanding their many achievements we saw evidence within the parks of deteriorating environmental quality, permanent damage to the landscape and poor local relationships.

In order to overcome these and other difficulties, Edwards recommended reformulating the purposes of National Parks, putting more emphasis on 'the overall environmental imperative' and redefining the objective of public enjoyment, in order to deal with problems caused by noisy and otherwise potentially antisocial activities — such as jet-skiing, motorcycle scrambling and microlight aircraft flying — which have appeared in National Parks in recent years.

A redefined set of objectives for National Parks must also, the Report considered, address the role which National Park authorities should play in relation to their local communities.

In order to enable National Parks to fulfil the vision of their founders and tackle the wider environmental and social problems which have arisen in the past 40 years — including problems caused by the Parks' very popularity — the Edwards Report recommended that National Parks should be administered by newly formed autonomous authorities, in all cases independent of county council control, with appointments to those authorities designed to ensure more effective representation.

Amongst other recommendations which the Report acknowledged would require primary legislation was an extension of National Park authorities' powers.

18.1.2 An overview of Environment Act, Part III

Environment Act, s. 61 replaces the first and second purposes in NPACA 1949, s. 5 with a new set of purposes, whilst s. 62 deals with the economic and social well-being of local communities within the National Parks and imposes a general duty on government and other public bodies to have regard to the National Park purposes. Section 63 and sch. 7 enable the Secretary of State to establish an authority (a 'National Park authority') for an existing or new National Park, whilst s. 76 provides for the transfer of property etc. from existing bodies to the new authorities. Sections 65 to 70 deal with the functions of National Park authorities, including their planning functions (ss. 67 and 68). Sections 71 to 74 concern finances of National Park authorities.

18.2 PURPOSES OF NATIONAL PARKS

The Edwards Report recommended that:

> the purposes of National Parks should be defined in a new National Parks Act as:
>   (i)   to protect, maintain and enhance the scenic beauty, natural systems and land forms, and the wildlife and cultural heritage of the area;
>   (ii)   to promote the quiet enjoyment and understanding of the area, in so far as it is not in conflict with the primary purpose of conservation. (Edwards Report, ch. 3.1.)

18.2.1 The first purpose

Edwards considered that the first purpose in NPACA 1949, s. 5(1), namely, preserving and enhancing the natural beauty of the areas, had tended to be interpreted as a largely visual concept, and endorsed the view that the environmental concerns of the National Parks should enhance much more than the conservation of fine scenery. The new National Park authorities 'must take an active interest in all of the environmental attributes and cultural traditions which contribute to the high quality of their areas and should seek to ensure their proper protection and management' (ch. 3).

Environment Act, s. 61(1) inserts a new s. 5(1) into the NPACA 1949. New s. 5(1)(a) defines the first purpose as 'conserving and enhancing the natural beauty, wildlife and cultural heritage of the areas' of National Parks. Despite some criticism during the Bill's passage that the government's wording is less comprehensive than that in the Edwards Report, new s. 5(1)(a) in fact precisely covers the Edwards formulation, since the expression 'natural beauty' covers scenic beauty, natural systems and land forms (see Hansard, HL, 2 February 1995, col. 1593).

18.2.2 The second purpose and quiet enjoyment

18.2.2.1 The Edwards Report's recommendations The Edwards Report concluded that the second purpose of National Parks — promoting their enjoyment by the public — required amendment in order to take account of the difficulties which the Review Panel perceived to have arisen recently as a result of the growth in the number of visitors and the introduction of a wider range of recreational pursuits, some of which can be damaging to the physical structure of the Parks themselves and detrimental to the enjoyment of other visitors:

We consider that the unique qualities of the Parks, with their opportunities for both physical and spiritual refreshment, and for physical challenge, are particularly precious in a crowded island such as ours. It is vitally important that these qualities should be sustained without impairment. . . . the public's enjoyment of National Parks is, and should be, derived from the special qualities of the Parks. This means, in our opinion, promoting only the quiet enjoyment of the Parks and particularly the activities that depend upon the special qualities and natural resources of these areas. Intrusive activities should be discouraged.

We recognise the intrusion caused by several noisy sports, by motorcycle scrambling, by four-wheel-drive vehicles away from highways, by trail bikes, powerboats and microlight aircraft. While we do not support their total prohibition in National Parks, they should only take place on the rare sites where they do not cause undue annoyance to other Park users or damage the fabric of the Parks themselves. In most cases, there may be more appropriate sites outside the Parks, and recreational provision of this kind should be determined on a regional scale. (Edwards Report, ch. 5.)

Accordingly, Edwards proposed a reformulation of the second purpose which expressly acknowledged the concept of quiet enjoyment in the following terms:

to promote the quiet enjoyment and understanding of the area, in so far as it is not in conflict with the primary purpose of conservation.

18.2.2.2 The government's response In their statement of January 1992 on policies for the National Parks, the Department of the Environment and the Welsh Office welcomed the proposed references to quiet enjoyment and understanding as having special relevance to National Parks (para. 2.3). The Bill, as introduced into Parliament, did not, however, contain any express reference to quiet enjoyment. It proposed a new s. 5(1) for NPACA 1949, in which para. (b) would set out the new second purpose as 'promoting opportunities for the understanding and enjoyment of the special qualities of those areas by the public'.

At committee stage in the House of Lords the government was defeated and the Bill amended to substitute for the words 'understanding and enjoyment' the words 'quiet enjoyment and understanding'.

Why had the government itself not used these words in the Bill, when it had previously indicated its acceptance of them? During the debate which culminated in the government's defeat, the Minister (Viscount Ullswater) pointed out that, whilst the 1992 policy statement accepted that the second National Park purpose should refer to 'quiet enjoyment' it:

also recognised that the Parks should provide a wide range of experiences for the visitor and that there are activities which are in conflict with the concept of quiet enjoyment. It also made clear that cooperation is the best means of encouraging sensitive uses of the Parks while recognising that those experiences which are unique to them — and which are largely related to the quiet enjoyment of these areas — should be protected and fostered. So, while our policy statement reflected the importance of the term 'quiet enjoyment', it also recognised that the issue was not as clear-cut as might at first glance be supposed. Since then, we have also found that there are difficulties in using that specific term. (Hansard, HL, 2 February 1995, col. 1608.)

These difficulties were highlighted in the same debate by Lord Ackner. Speaking as a judge, he considered that:

> the amendment will require the definition of what is meant by 'quiet' in relation to the word 'enjoyment'. One achieves nothing by having 'quiet' on its own. In fact, one achieves a possible complication because it is a term of art in landlord and tenant work, as it is in vendor and purchaser work.
>
> . . . you do not establish any principle until you define what you mean by 'quiet'. The landlord and tenant aspect is important because it is a term of art which relates only to physical interference. It has no acoustic connotation at all.
> . . . Is the principle to be that there is an obligation to make no noise, or only the noise which would be the subject-matter of a successful action in nuisance — in which case one does not need the clause? Or is it to be specific activities — in which case I submit that the specific activities ought to be defined and stated, so that one knows exactly what one is dealing with? (Hansard, HL, 2 February 1995, cols. 1602–3.)

Following its defeat in the House of Lords, the government re-examined the question, receiving the views of nature conservation interests and those representing field sports and motor rallying interests. Eventually, at report stage in the House of Commons, the government successfully moved an amendment to restore its original wording. It had been a hard decision, as the Minister (Robert Atkins MP) acknowledged:

> . . . A Law Lord said, following the passing of the amendment adding 'quiet' to 'enjoyment', that that was bad law, that it was capable of misinterpretation or many interpretations and that an amendment was required to define what 'quiet' meant. We tried. We considered it carefully, and my officials and Parliamentary Counsel struggled to find ways and means whereby we could assuage the anxieties that were expressed to me by a variety of organisations.
> . . . I considered several variations on many amendments. We even nearly reached the stage of tabling one, but grave anxieties continued to be expressed to me by the motor sports industry.
> . . . we tried extremely hard to find a way of defining 'quiet' and, in the final analysis, were unable to do so. It seemed to me that, in the circumstances, the best thing to do was to revert to what was the case when the Bill was presented in another place. (Hansard, HC, 28 June 1995, col. 975.)

The government's decision alarmed conservationists, and several National Park officers, who argued that because the second purpose is expressed in terms of 'promoting', rather than 'prohibiting', the absence of an express reference to 'quiet enjoyment' would make it impossible to ban noisy activities in National Parks. It is, however, reasonably clear that the government listened to the views of the motor sports industry, and others, who were concerned that, because the second purpose overlies and colours all that the National Park authorities must do —

including exercising their planning functions — such an express reference could have had tangible effects on the ground. It will be interesting to see to what extent the National Park authorities will seek to apply NPACA 1949, new s. 5(1)(b), bearing in mind that, even without the word 'quiet', the wording hardly covers the promotion of 'unwelcome' recreational pursuits — for example, can motorcycle scrambling in a National Park on a hillside which is not in itself special or unusual be said to concern the understanding and enjoyment of the 'special qualities' of that Park?

18.2.3   Relationship between the two National Park purposes

Reference has been made earlier (18.1.1) to the Sandford principle, that in cases of conflict between the two National Park purposes (as originally enacted) the first purpose — preserving and enhancing the natural beauty of the areas — should prevail.

This principle is given a form of statutory authority by Environment Act, s. 62(1) which inserts a new s. 11A into the NPACA 1949. Section 11A(2) provides that, in exercising or performing any functions in relation to, or so as to affect, land in a National Park, any relevant authority shall have regard to the purposes in NPACA 1949, new s. 5(1) and, 'if it appears that there is a conflict between those purposes, shall attach greater weight to the purpose of conserving and enhancing the natural beauty, wildlife and cultural heritage of the area comprised in the National Park'.

This new statutory requirement was cited by the government, during the debates on 'quiet enjoyment', as a reason why those who were worried at losing that expression from new s. 5(1)(b) should not in fact be concerned.

18.2.4   Commencement of the new purposes

The majority of Part III of the Environment Act, including s. 61, came into force on 19 September 1995 (Environment Act, s. 125(2)). However, subss. (3) to (5) of s. 61 ensure that, in relation to any National Park, existing enactments which confer functions etc. on National Park bodies etc. by reference to the purposes set out in NPACA, s. 5(1), are to continue to be read as referring to s. 5(1) as originally enacted, until such time as the new National Park authority has become the local planning authority for that Park under Environment Act, s. 67 (see below). For example, the Countryside Act 1968, s. 13(4) requires a National Park body, when making byelaws controlling vessels on lakes, to have regard to the fulfilment of the objects set out in NPACA 1949, s. 5. So an existing National Park board must make byelaws by reference to the original purposes set out in NPACA, s. 5(1), until it is replaced by a new National Park authority.

18.3   ECONOMIC AND SOCIAL WELL-BEING OF COMMUNITIES IN NATIONAL PARKS

The Edwards Report considered the question of whether what they called a 'third purpose' should be established for National Parks:

There was wide recognition of the special needs and problems of Park communities, and a consensus that National Park authorities must have a concern for these needs. Many expressed the view that one of the purposes of National Parks should be the promotion of the social and economic well-being of Park communities, the justification being that a sound rural economy is a prerequisite for effective conservation measures and for the provision of facilities for public enjoyment. However, others stressed that the promotion of the social and economic well-being should focus clearly on those actions that are supportive of the existing National Park purposes, which should always take priority. (Edwards Report, ch. 3.)

The Panel accepted the latter approach, recommending that, in pursuance of the first and second purposes, National Park authorities 'should support the appropriate agencies in fostering the social and economic well-being of the communities within the National Park, in ways which are compatible with the purposes for which National Parks are designated'. The Panel noted that National Park authorities need not 'incur substantial expenditure' in supporting such economic and social well-being. Rather 'they should be concerned with facilitating the efforts of other bodies already active in these areas'.

Although the Edwards recommendations were broadly accepted by the government, the Bill as introduced was criticised on the grounds that it merely required National Park authorities 'to have regard to the economic and social well-being of local communities within the National Park' (clause 59(1)). In response to this criticism, the government brought forward an amendment at third reading in the House of Lords, which reflects much more closely the Edwards recommendations. As a result, NPACA 1949, new s. 11A(1) (inserted by Environment Act, s. 62(1)) requires a National Park authority, in pursuing the first and second purposes in new s. 5(1), to:

> seek to foster the economic and social well-being of local communities within the National Park, but without incurring significant expenditure in doing so, and shall for that purpose cooperate with local authorities and public bodies whose functions include the promotion of economic or social development within the area of the National Park.

Introducing the amendment, the Minister (Viscount Ullswater) claimed that it:

> . . . paved the way for a more positive attitude on the part of the new authorities which will ensure that they both take these responsibilities seriously and are seen to do so. . . .
>
> Nor does the revised duty in any way undermine these primary purposes for which the Parks exist. On the contrary, I believe it enhances and reinforces those purposes, the achievement of which will be impossible without active and wholehearted cooperation between the National Park authorities and those who live and work in the Parks. (Hansard, HL, 20 March 1995, cols. 1065, 1066.)

The new s. 11A(1) duty takes effect in the case of a particular National Park from the time when the new National Park authority becomes the local planning authority for the Park (Environment Act, s. 62(3)).

18.4 GENERAL DUTY TO FURTHER NATIONAL PARK PURPOSES

The Edwards Report recommended that 'there should be a statutory duty placed upon all Ministers, government departments and public bodies, in the exercise of their duties as they affect National Parks, to further National Park purposes' (12.2.5).

The result is NPACA 1949, new s. 11A(2) to (6) (inserted by Environment Act, s. 62(1)). A duty is imposed upon any 'relevant authority' to have regard to the main s. 5(1) purposes, in exercising or performing any functions in relation to, or so as to affect, land in a National Park, and, in cases of conflict between the 'first' and 'second' purposes, to give greater weight to the first (the 'Sandford principle', see18.2.3). 'Relevant authority' means Ministers, public bodies, statutory undertakers and anyone holding public office. 'Public body' includes any local authority, joint board or joint committee and any National Park authority (s. 11A(3), (4)).

18.5 NEW NATIONAL PARK AUTHORITIES

18.5.1 Introduction

When the Edwards Panel reported, the Peak District was administered as a National Park by the Peak Park Joint Planning Board and the Lake District by the Lake District Special Planning Board, each constituted under the Local Government Act 1972, sch. 17. The remaining eight National Parks were administered by committees of the councils of the counties in which the Parks were situated. Edwards noted that 'the status of National Park authorities, and in particular whether they should form part of, or be independent of, the structure of local government, is regarded as a critical issue in giving future steer and thrust to the achievement of National Park purposes'. Over 70% of those giving evidence to Edwards favoured independence from other local government bodies. The majority considered that independent status would induce greater self-confidence in fulfilling Park purposes and that the 'committee' Parks could be 'constrained by their parent county councils, particularly over staff appointments, budgets, capital expenditure and committee practices' (Edwards Report, 12.1). Edwards became convinced 'that there was a strong case for a reform of the existing administrative arrangements for national parks'. Four options were identified:

(a) a single, centrally run, National Parks agency,

(b) directly elected National Park authorities,

(c) independent bodies with members appointed by central and local government,

(d) local authority committees with members appointed by central and local government.

Option (a) was rejected, since such an agency would have difficulty convincing local communities of its responsiveness to their needs and concerns. Option (b) was rejected because, although directly elected authorities would be locally accountable, they would be unlikely to serve the long-term, national interest. The choice came down to one between, in effect, the Peak and Lake Districts concept of an independent board, and the system of local authority committees. The advantages of independence included clarity of vision and self-confidence, a higher profile, freedom to manage finances, personnel, etc., independent officer advice and freedom from county council spending policies and responsibilities. Perceived disadvantages included loss of local accountability, separation from local services (e.g., highways, housing and economic development) and the need to employ separate specialist services (e.g., lawyers).

The Edwards Report concluded that:

> the balance of advantage clearly lies with organisations of independent status for all Parks. We also suggest that the independent authorities should be formally entitled National Park authorities.
>
> Our decision was influenced to some degree by evident administrative difficulties and inefficiencies of long standing in some Parks, resulting from existing county council procedures. However, an important consideration in arriving at our judgment has been the need for Park authorities to make decisions in support of Park purposes unconstrained by the sometimes conflicting priorities of their parent county councils and freed of the possible pressures felt by senior staff from divided allegiances. (Edwards Report, 12.1).

In September 1991 the government announced that it was minded to accept the key recommendation that independent authorities should be established for all National Parks, having accepted Edwards's conclusions as to the advantages to be gained by such a move.

18.5.2 Establishment of National Park authorities

Environment Act, s. 63 (which came into force on 19 September 1995) enables the Secretary of State by order to establish 'a National Park authority' in place of the existing authority for an existing National Park or following the designation of a new National Park. The order may provide for the existing authority to cease to have any functions as from the time when the new National Park authority becomes the local planning authority. Provision is made for the order to be able to transfer such functions (if any) which would not become the functions of the new authority to the person who would have them if the area were not a National Park. The existing authority would then cease to exist or be dissolved (s. 63(2)).

Special provision is required in the case of Wales, as a result of the process of reorganisation of local government in the principality which, at the time of the passing of the Environment Act, was being carried out in pursuance of the Local Government (Wales) Act 1994. That Act amended sch. 17 to the Local Government Act 1972 so as to permit the creation of National Park planning boards for the areas of existing National Parks in Wales (namely, Snowdonia, the Pembrokeshire Coast and the Brecon Beacons). Notwithstanding the provisions in the Environment Act for creating new National Park authorities, the government apprehended that it might be necessary to create planning boards under the amended sch. 17 in the autumn of 1995.

Accordingly, Environment Act, s. 64 provides for any such board to be converted into a new National Park authority, without a change in its corporate status. Section 64(3) enables work done in preparation for the establishment of a planning board for a Welsh National Park to count as if it had been done in preparation for the creation of a new National Park Authority.

18.5.3   Membership of National Park authorities

18.5.3.1   The Edwards recommendations   In considering the question of membership of the new National Park authorities, the Edwards Panel paid particular attention to the balance between Secretary of State and local authority appointees. Whilst understanding the case for increasing the proportion of members appointed by the Secretary of State in order to give greater recognition to the national importance of National Parks, Edwards concluded that, on balance, the proportion of Secretary of State appointed members should remain at one third. Instead, the issue of representing the national interest more effectively would be achieved largely by changes in the selection and appointment process. As for local authority appointments, the Report recommended an increase in the proportion of district council members, as a means of enhancing local responsiveness and as a recognition of the responsibilities of district councils in relation to the social and economic needs of Park communities. Edwards therefore recommended a three-way split, with one third of appointments being made by the Secretary of State, one third by county councils and one-third by district councils (Edwards Report, 12.1).

18.5.3.2   The government's stance   The Environment Bill basically reflected the Edwards recommendations just described (bearing in mind the advent of one-tier local government in certain areas, including Wales). Order-making powers would determine the precise size of National Park authorities and the identity of the appointing councils.

However, during the passage of the Bill, there were calls for the new authorities to be more locally accountable than would be the case under the Edwards recommendations and on 22 May 1995 the government announced that it was consulting on a proposal which would increase the proportion of Secretary of State appointees so as to enable him to make appointments from members of parish councils in the Parks. Although the proposals were (not unexpectedly) welcomed by parish councils, they drew criticism from the National Parks themselves and others who were concerned that the proposals, if implemented, would destroy the 'delicate balance' which the Edwards Report had arrived at. Professor Edwards himself was quoted at report stage in the House of Commons on 28 June 1995 as having told the Secretary of State that his proposal was 'counterproductive both in producing a sensibly balanced pluralism on Park authorities and, politically, being perceived as moving from bodies with a clear majority of democratically elected representatives towards quangos which are currently viewed with deep suspicion. And for what?' (Hansard, HL, 28 June 1995, col. 1015.)

18.5.3.3   Membership under the Act   Notwithstanding these criticisms, the Environment Bill was amended to give effect to the government's proposals. Accordingly, the membership of the new National Park authorities to be established in England under Environment Act s. 63 and sch. 7 will be as follows:

(a)   one half of the authority's members plus one will be appointed by local authorities with land in the Park;

(b)   the remainder will be appointed by the Secretary of State of whom one half minus one will be drawn from parishes.

Thus, in the case of a National Park authority having a total of 22 members, 12 would be appointed by local authorities and 10 by the Secretary of State. Of those 10, six would be appointed directly to represent the national interest and four would be drawn from relevant parishes. Where there is a two-tier system of local government in the Park, the government has said that it will ensure there is equal representation among the two tiers (i.e., county council and district councils).

Environment Act, sch. 7, para. 2 requires the Secretary of State to consult the local authorities before making an order as to the precise number of local authority members, the local authorities which are to be appointing bodies and the precise numbers to be appointed by each local authority. A person is not eligible to be a local authority member unless he is a member of a principal council for an area which is wholly or partly within the Park concerned. In making its appointments, the principal council must have regard to the desirability of appointing members who represent wards or (in Wales) electoral divisions, situated wholly or partly within the Park.

Appointment of parish members by the Secretary of State is governed by sch. 7, para. 3. A person may not be appointed as a parish member unless he is either a member of the parish council for a parish which is wholly or partly in the Park or the chairman of the parish meeting of a parish which does not have a separate parish council but which, again, is wholly or partly in the Park.

The government has stated that nominations to the Secretary of State for parish members will be sought from any or all of the following: the National Association of Local Councils, groupings of parishes within the Parks or individual parishes. The Secretary of State will 'encourage parish interests to provide agreed nominations' although it is accepted that nominations could also come from other sources, including individuals with an interest in Park affairs.

The position as regards the composition of National Park authorities in Wales basically remains as in the Environment Bill. The government decided that, because of commitments which had already been made in respect of the membership of National Park boards under the Local Government (Wales) Act 1994 (see above), the changes made for England have not been adopted in the case of Wales. Accordingly, the two-thirds/one-third split between local authority and the Secretary of State remains in the case of new National Park authorities in Wales, without any parish involvement.

Various provisions of the Local Government Act 1972 are applied by Environment Act, sch. 7 in the case of National Park authorities, in order to deal with such matters as disqualification of members, vacation of office, codes of conduct, restrictions on voting on account of interests, allowances and procedure for meetings. Schedule 7, para. 14 requires every National Park authority to have a National Park officer.

18.6   FUNCTIONS OF NEW NATIONAL PARK AUTHORITIES

18.6.1   General purposes and powers

Although Environment Act, s. 65 deals with the general purposes and powers of National Park authorities, it provides that the whole of Part III of the Act (including

s. 65) has effect for the 'first' and 'second' purposes set out in NPACA 1949, s. 5 (see 18.2).

During the period (if any) from the establishment of a National Park authority to the time when it becomes the local planning authority for the Park concerned, the authority's functions are confined to the taking of such steps as the authority considers appropriate for securing that it is able properly to carry out its functions after that time. Before taking such steps, the authority must consult with the Secretary of State and any existing National Park body (Environment Act, s. 65(3)).

Section 65(2) ensures that National Park authorities, in carrying out their functions under the NPACA 1949, the Countryside Act 1968 and the Wildlife and Countryside Act 1981 will have due regard to the needs of agriculture and forestry and to the economic and social interests of rural areas. It also ensures that, in exercising their functions under the NPACA 1949 and the Countryside Act 1968, the authorities will have due regard to the pollution of certain waters.

National Park authorities may do anything which, in their opinion, is calculated to facilitate, or is conducive or incidental to, the accomplishment of the purposes in NPACA 1949, s. 5(1) or the carrying out of any functions conferred on them by virtue of any other enactment, provided it is not in contravention of any statutory restriction on the powers of the authorities, or concerns certain powers to raise money (s. 65(5), (6)).

18.6.2   National Park management plans

Existing National Park bodies (whether they be joint planning boards, special planning boards or county council committees) are required by the Local Government Act 1972, sch. 17, para. 18 to prepare management plans for their Parks. Environment Act, s. 66 imposes a similar requirement upon new National Park authorities. Such an authority must prepare and publish a 'National Park Management Plan' within three years of its becoming the local planning authority. There is an exception from this requirement if, within six months of becoming the local planning authority, the National Park authority adopts the existing plan prepared and published by the predecessor body under the Local Government Act 1972, sch. 17, para. 18, as its National Park Management Plan, and publishes notice that it has done so (Environment Act, s. 66(2)). In such a case, the National Park authority may review the existing plan, and shall do so if the plan would otherwise have been due for review under sch. 17 (Environment Act, s. 66(3)). A National Park authority shall review its Management Plan within five years of becoming the local planning authority (s. 66(4)). If an adopted plan has not been reviewed at the time of adoption, it must be reviewed not later than the time when it would otherwise have fallen due for review (s. 66(5)). The adoption or review of a plan must be preceded by notification of local authorities, the Countryside Commission and nature conservancy bodies, whose observations must be taken into account by the National Park authority (s. 66(7)).

A National Park Management Plan must formulate the policy of the National Park authority for the management of its Park and for the carrying out of its functions in relation to that Park (s. 66(1)). It is important to appreciate that these Management Plans are not the same as development plans to be prepared by

National Park authorities in their capacity as local planning authorities (see below). The Edwards Report, ch. 11, quoted from Circular guidance which stated the purposes of the plans prepared under LGA 1972, sch. 17 as follows:

(a) to set out the objectives for the National Park

(b) to describe the management policies of the National Park authority

(c) to form the basis for coordination of management policies of other bodies, public and private, to achieve park objectives

(d) to provide the framework for organisation of the work and staff of the National Park authority

(e) to provide a basis for the coordination of management policies within the area of the Park with those operating outside

(f) to provide a basis for programming the implementation of management policies

(g) to provide a basis for financial estimates related to management policies

(h) to provide a means of informing the public and involving them in management policy for the Park.

As well as suggesting that the Management Plan should be physically combined with the Park development plan in a single document, Edwards believed that the role of Management Plans would be:

> much enhanced if our proposals for environmental inventories and vision statements for each Park are adopted. The former would assist the preparation of more informed policies for environmental conservation and public enjoyment; the latter would identify the long-term goals which the policies must be designed to achieve (Edwards Report, ch. 11.).

18.6.3   National Park authority as planning authority

Although National Park regulation was conceived as operating through the town and country planning system, the Edwards Panel found the situation in the late 1980s to be less than satisfactory. In the case of the two 'board' Parks — the Peak District and the Lake District — the boards were responsible as of right for development plans, although the structure plan in the case of the Lake District was prepared jointly with Cumbria County Council, so as to cover the whole county. In the eight Parks administered by county council committees, Edwards found that all the relevant county councils had either delegated their responsibilities for local plans to the National Park committees, or were expecting soon to do so. However, none had delegated responsibility for structure plans. Edwards recommended that the existing arrangements for structure planning for the Peak and Lake District Parks should remain but that, for the other eight Parks, county structure plans should be prepared jointly between the constituent counties and the National Park authorities (Edwards Report, 11.3).

As to development control, Edwards recommended that National Park authorities should be responsible for all aspects of the development control process. Certain concerns of the Panel have in fact been met as a result of the Planning and Compensation Act 1991 which enabled National Park bodies to receive and process planning applications. The Edwards Report also highlighted certain forms of development which, the Panel considered, should be more tightly controlled within National Parks. Examples included fish farming, clay pigeon shooting, war games, motorcycle scrambling and the erection of satellite dishes. The government has gone some way towards dealing with some of these matters in the Town and Country Planning (General Permitted Development) Order 1995 (SI 1995/418) (see, e.g., the withdrawal of permitted development rights under sch. 2, part 4 for clay pigeon shooting and war games within sites of special scientific interest). The 1995 Order also withdraws most permitted development rights in cases where an environmental assessment would be required in the event of a planning application being made in respect of that development. This change is particularly relevant to National Parks, as the government acknowledged in its policy statement issued in response to the Edwards Report, 'because of possible effects on conservation and opportunities for public enjoyment in their areas, National Park authorities could be expected to require environmental impact assessments for a higher proportion of schedule 2 proposals than are necessary for the wider countryside' (5.22). (The reference is to sch. 2 to the Town and Country Planning (Assessment of Environmental Effects) Regulations 1988 (SI 1988/1199).)

In the Environment Act, the government decided to create a system which would, where appropriate, enable National Park authorities to assume total responsibility for all planning functions, to the exclusion of both county and district councils, whilst at the same time allowing for a more limited approach in relation to development plan functions if particular circumstances warrant. Accordingly, Environment Act, s. 67(1) inserts a new s. 4A into the Town and Country Planning Act 1990, whereby the Secretary of State, in establishing a new National Park authority, can by order provide for that authority to be the sole planning authority and mineral planning authority for the area of the Park, and to exclude the Park from the area of any other planning authority (s. 4A(2)). Section 4A(3) provides that, where a provision of planning legislation confers functions, in relation to different areas, on the county or district planning authority and on councils, those functions are to be treated as conferred on the councils as the local planning authority for their areas. In this way s. 4A(2) will ensure that the functions concerned will be exercisable by the National Park authority.

Subsections (4) and (5) of s. 4A ensure that, where a National Park or part thereof is served by a district council, the provisions of the Town and Country Planning Act 1990 relating to tree preservation orders, replacement of trees and preservation of trees in conservation areas will be exercisable concurrently by the district council and the National Park authority.

Subsections (2) and (3) of Environment Act, s. 67 deal with the question of development plans. They ensure that the Secretary of State will be able to make appropriate adjustments to the development plan system for National Parks, in the light of the changes to local government in England which are being wrought under the Local Government Act 1992. This flexibility is such that, even after the establishment of the new National Park authorities, the Secretary of State will be able to preserve the existing development plan system in those eight Parks which are currently administered by county council committees. Under that system, county councils have responsibility for structure plans (see above).

In Wales, the unitary development plan system will apply from 1 April 1996, and each National Park in Wales will be treated as a planning area in its own right (see s. 20 of the Local Government (Wales) Act 1994).

Environment Act, s. 67(5) deals with purchase notices. Under this system a landowner may serve a notice on the appropriate local authority requiring it to buy the land if he considers that his property has become incapable of reasonably beneficial use in its existing condition, and planning permission for its development has been refused. Section 67(5) enables a National Park authority to become a body on whom a purchase notice can be served. This is achieved by inserting a new s. 147A in the Town and Country Planning Act 1990.

18.6.4   Planning functions under National Parks legislation

Existing National Park bodies exercise various functions as local planning authorities, under the NPACA 1949 and the Countryside Act 1968. Environment Act, s. 68 ensures that National Park authorities which have become local planning authorities assume the functions conferred on local planning authorities by or under NPACA 1949 and the Countryside Act 1968, to the exclusion of any other authority.

Environment Act, s. 68(3) precludes duplication between NPACA, s. 11 and Environment Act, s. 65 (see 18.6.1) by disapplying the former provision in the case of a new National Park authority. The ability of a National Park authority to provide facilities such as accommodation, meals etc. under NPACA 1949, s. 12 outside (but in the neighbourhood of) its Park is exercisable only with the agreement of the relevant local planning authority (s. 68(4)).

In the case of English National Parks where there are district councils, the functions of tree planting and treatment of derelict land (under NPACA 1949, s. 89) and the provision of camping and picnic sites (under Countryside Act 1968, s. 10) will be exercisable concurrently by the National Park authority and the council, which may also continue to make byelaws controlling such sites (Environment Act s. 68(6) to (8)).

18.6.5   Planning functions under Wildlife and Countryside Act 1981

Where a National Park authority has become the local planning authority for its Park, Environment Act, s. 69 provides that the authority shall exercise the functions in respect of the Park which are conferred on a planning authority under the Wildlife and Countryside Act 1981 (Environment Act s. 69(1), (2)). The provisions in the Wildlife and Countryside Act 1981, s. 43 regarding maps in National Parks showing certain areas of moor or heath are revised by Environment Act, s. 69(3) so as to permit the consolidation of maps, as well as to deal with the possibility of new National Park designations.

18.6.6   Other powers and functions

Schedules 8 and 9 to the Environment Act confer upon new National Park authorities various supplemental powers and functions. The authorities are, for example, given powers of compulsory acquisition based upon the powers enjoyed by local authorities. They may promote private Bills in Parliament (provided these do not modify the authority's area or constitution etc.). They are also subjected to requirements regarding competitive tendering which apply to local authorities, and to the same restrictions on publicity (sch. 8). Schedule 9 enables various functions of local authorities to apply to National Park authorities — e.g., in respect of common land, caravan sites, country parks and ancient monuments and archaeological areas.

18.7 FINANCES OF NATIONAL PARK AUTHORITIES

Environment Act, s. 71 enables National Park authorities to issue levies every financial year to the local councils who appoint members to that authority.

Environment Act, s. 72 empowers the Secretary of State to make grants to a National Park authority for such purposes, of such amounts and on such terms and conditions as he thinks fit. The consent of the Treasury is required to the making of a grant.

Environment Act, s. 74 deals with a difficulty which occurred in respect of the National Parks Supplementary Grant ('NPSG') paid under the Local Government Act 1974, s. 7. The Local Government, Planning and Land Act 1980 provided that no payment of NPSG could be made until the amount had been prescribed in a Rate Support Grant Report, approved by the House of Commons. Since the abolition of Rate Support Grant in 1990 it has not been possible to meet this requirement. Environment Act, s. 74 accordingly retrospectively validates payments of NPSG made between 1 April 1990 and 31 March 1996.

CHAPTER 19
Air Quality

19.1 INTRODUCTION

The recurrence in the Summer of 1994 of ozone episodes, the publication of Department of Health commissioned research into the effect of the smog episode of December 1991 and the increasing incidence of asthma in children widely attributed to vehicle emissions have raised public concern about air quality. To meet that concern, the Government published a consultation paper, *Improving Air Quality* (March 1994) and, subsequently, a paper setting out its proposals, *Air Quality: Meeting the Challenge* (January 1995). Part IV of the Environment Act contains provisions intended to implement the proposals in that consultation paper. Parallel developments are occurring in Europe. On the enactment of the Environment Act, John Gummer, the Secretary of State for the Environment, issued a press release stating—

Because air pollution can be a problem which crosses international boundaries, we have been pushing for a European framework for tackling air pollution. We achieved this with our European partners at [the June 1995] EU Environment Council. The framework complements closely our newly-enacted national air quality management framework.

Part IV of the Environment Act provides for action at both national and local level. Duties are conferred on the Secretary of State to publish a national strategy to include standards and targets for the main pollutants and a timetable for their achievement. Local authorities are placed under a duty to carry out regular assessments of air quality in their area, to create air quality management areas where levels do not meet targets and to direct action to those areas.

The Act provides the statutory framework for the new system. It is intended that detailed local arrangements will be provided under regulations made by the Secretary of State under the Act and in accordance with guidance to be given by the Secretary of State.

The Government has stated that it is establishing with the local authority associations a committee to review what powers may be needed, and any resources implications.

19.2   THE NATIONAL AIR QUALITY STRATEGY

When the Environment Act, s. 80 is brought into force the Secretary of State will be placed under an immediate duty to publish, as soon as possible, a national air quality strategy, that is to say a statement of policies with respect to the assessment or management of the quality of air including, if he wishes, policies for implementing any relevant EC or other international obligations. The strategy may consist of more than one document but must cover the whole of England, Wales and Scotland.

The strategy will include standards relating to the quality of air, objectives for the restriction of the levels at which particular substances are present in the air and the measures which are to be taken by local authorities and others to achieve those objectives. The Government plans to publish the national strategy by the end of 1995 and has stated that the objectives will cover the pollutants which are of most concern, including small particles.

Before publishing the strategy the Secretary of State must consult the EA, in relation to England and Wales, and the SEPA, in relation to Scotland, bodies representative of local government or the interests of industry and any other bodies or persons he considers appropriate. He must also publish a draft of the proposed strategy inviting representations and take any such representations into account.

Once published, the policy in the national strategy must be kept under review and the strategy modified if necessary. The procedures set out above as to consultation and publication of draft documents also apply in relation to any modification of the strategy.

The EA and SEPA are each placed under a duty to have regard to the national strategy in exercising their pollution control functions (Environment Act, s. 81).

19.3   LOCAL AUTHORITY REVIEWS, AIR QUALITY MANAGEMENT AREAS AND ACTION PLANS

Under Environment Act, s. 82 each local authority must cause a review to be conducted from time to time of the present and likely future air quality within its area. The authority must also cause an assessment to be made of whether the air quality standards and objectives to be prescribed by regulations (see 19.6 below) are being achieved or are likely to be achieved within the period prescribed by regulations. For the purposes of these provisions 'local authority' is defined, in relation to England and Wales, as any unitary authority, any district council so far as it is not a unitary authority, the Common Council of the City of London and, as respects the Temples, the Sub-Treasurer of the Inner Temple and the Under-Treasurer of the Middle Temple. In relation to Scotland, 'local authority' means a council for an area constituted under s. 2 of the Local Government etc. (Scotland) Act 1994 (s. 91(1)).

If a local authority considers that the prescribed air quality standards and objectives are not likely to be achieved within the prescribed period in relation to any part of its area, the authority must make an order under s. 83 designating that part as an air quality management area. A s. 83 order may be varied or, if it subsequently appears that the prescribed air quality standards and objectives are likely to be achieved, may be revoked.

The designating of an air quality management area triggers other duties on the part of the local authority which are set out in s. 84. Within 12 months of the coming into operation of an order designating an air quality management area, a further air quality assessment must be made in relation to the area and a report on that assessment prepared. Most importantly, the local authority must prepare a written action plan setting out the measures to be taken by the authority in exercise of its powers in order to achieve the air quality standards and objectives in that area together with a timetable within which those measures will be implemented (s. 84(2)(b) and (3)). An action plan may be revised.

The provisions of the Environment Act only set out the functions of local authorities in outline. More detailed provision will be contained in regulations to be made by the Secretary of State under s. 87 which will include, amongst other matters, provision as to the making, publication, scope, content and form of air quality reviews, assessments, action plans and the measures which are to be taken by local authorities (see further 19.6 below).

In carrying out any of the above functions, a local authority must consult the Secretary of State, the EA (or, in Scotland, SEPA), every local authority whose area is contiguous with the authority's area and the other bodies listed in Environment Act, sch. 11, para. 1. Local authorities must make available to the public, for inspection or sale, copies of reports on the results of any air quality review or assessment, any air quality management area designation, any action plan, any proposals submitted by the county council and any directions given by the Secretary of State. (sch. 11, para. 4).

19.4   NON-UNITARY AUTHORITIES

The main duties of Part IV of the Environment Act to review areas, identify and designate air quality management areas and implement action plans with respect to those areas are conferred on district councils in areas for which there is a county council. Where a district council is preparing an action plan, the county council must prepare and submit to the district council its own action plan, that is to say its proposals, with a timetable, for the exercise of the county council's air quality functions conferred under Part IV (s. 86(3) and (4)).

The county council may make recommendations to the district council with respect to any particular air quality review, assessment or action plan being prepared by the district council which must then take those recommendations into account (s. 86(2)). If the district council and the county council disagree about the contents of a proposed action plan (or any revision to it) either of them may refer the matter to the Secretary of State who may confirm the action plan with or without modifications or reject it and exercise any of the reserve powers mentioned in 19.5 below (s. 84(5)).

Under sch. 11, para. 2 the district council and county council must exchange all information that the other may reasonably require for carrying out its air quality functions under Part IV.

Part IV of the Environment Act provides only a framework for the county council's action plan, the more detailed requirements being left to regulations to be made under the Act (see 19.6 below).

19.5   DEFAULT POWERS OF THE SECRETARY OF STATE OR SEPA

Environment Act, s. 85 confers on the Secretary of State reserve powers in relation to England and Wales. The reserve powers enable the Secretary of State himself to exercise the functions of district councils mentioned in 19.3 above of conducting local reviews, making assessments and identifying areas which should be designated as air quality management areas.

Wide powers are given to the Secretary of State (ss. 85 and 86) to give directions to local authorities where air quality targets are not being achieved, where there has been any failure to discharge the functions mentioned in 19.3 or 19.4 above or where he considers that those functions are being exercised inappropriately. The Secretary of State may, for example, direct a local authority to cause a fresh air quality review to be conducted, to make or modify an action plan, to designate an area as an air quality management area or to take steps for the implementation of any EC or international obligations. It is the duty of a local authority to which such a direction is given to comply with it.

In Scotland, these default powers are exercisable not by the Secretary of State but by SEPA.

Any direction must be published in the *London Gazette* or, in Scotland, the *Edinburgh Gazette* and copies must be made available to the public.

19.6   REGULATIONS

It has already been explained that Part IV of the Environment Act only sets out the framework of the new air quality control regime. The detailed provision is to be made by regulations under s. 87 which is in very wide terms. Local authorities will have to wait for these regulations to be made before they will be able to exercise their functions under Part IV.

The regulations will, in particular, confer powers on local authorities intended to enable them to secure that the prescribed air quality targets are met. It is thought that these powers will include the issuing of fixed penalty notices in the case of any fixed penalty offences created by the regulations (sch. 11, para. 5). The sorts of powers that could be conferred on local authorities by regulations include power to prohibit or restrict certain vehicles from access to specified areas and power to exercise spot checks on vehicle emissions.

Before the regulations are made, consultation is to take place with the EA or SEPA, bodies representing local government, bodies representing the interests of industry and any other appropriate persons or bodies. Because of the importance of the regulations, they are subject to affirmative Parliamentary procedure, that is to say they must be approved by resolution of each House of Parliament (s. 87(8)).

19.7   GUIDANCE

The Secretary of State is to issue guidance to local authorities in connection with the exercise of any powers conferred, or the discharge of any duty imposed, on them under Part IV of the Environment Act to which the authorities must have regard in carrying out those functions (s. 88).

CHAPTER 20

Waste Strategy and Producer Responsibility

20.1 NATIONAL WASTE STRATEGY

20.1.1 Introduction

The EC 'Waste Framework Directive' (75/442/EEC, as amended by 91/156/EEC on waste and the Standardised Reporting Directive 91/692/EEC) requires the drawing up, as soon as possible, of one or more waste management plans. These plans must, in particular, relate to:

(a) the type, quantity and origin of waste to be recovered or disposed of;
(b) general technical requirements;
(c) any special arrangements for particular waste; and
(d) suitable disposal sites or installations.

Waste management plans are also required to implement the objectives set out in the Waste Framework Directive.

These requirements were formerly intended to be implemented jointly through local waste management plans under s. 50 of the EPA 1990 required to be drawn up by waste regulation authorities and the development plans which planning authorities are required to draw up under Part II of the Town and Country Planning Act 1990 or Part II of the Town and Country Planning (Scotland) Act 1972. In addition, sch. 4 to the Waste Management Licensing Regulations 1994 (SI 1994/1056) makes provision for Ministers to draw up an offshore waste management plan. (See DOE Circular 11/94 and Welsh Circular 26/94 on the Environmental Protection Act 1990: Part II, Waste Management Licensing and the Framework Directive on Waste, April 1994.)

The element of the implementation of the Waste Framework Directive which has hitherto been dealt with by local waste management plans under EPA 1990, s. 50 is now to be replaced by national waste strategies to be drawn up for England and Wales by the Secretary of State and for Scotland by SEPA under EPA 1990, ss. 44A and 44B, inserted by Environment Act, s. 92. See also 8.1.5 above.

At the time of writing no order has been made bringing s. 92 into force. As an interim measure, a consultation draft waste strategy for England and Wales was issued by the Government in January 1995. This brought together policies on the hierarchy of waste management options (reduction, recycling, reuse, disposal), the management of different waste streams and the role of householders, industry and local government. It was intended to set out a framework of policies to achieve sustainable waste management in line with *Sustainable Development — the UK Strategy* (DoE, December 1994) (Viscount Ullswater, Hansard, HL, 9 February 1995, cols. 337–8). The final version of the waste strategy due to be issued shortly after the time of writing will eventually be superseded by the national waste strategies provided for by the new EPA 1990, ss. 44A and 44B.

20.1.2 The new provisions

Section 44A of EPA 1990 requires the Secretary of State to prepare one or more written statements, referred to as a 'strategy', containing his policies in relation to the recovery and disposal of waste in England and Wales. The strategy must, as a minimum, include the matters required to be covered by the Waste Framework Directive, i.e., the type, quantity and origin of waste to be recovered or disposed of, general technical requirements and any special requirements for particular wastes. The fourth matter — suitable disposal sites or installations — specified in the Directive will continue to be covered by development plans (see 20.1.1 above). The strategy must set out the Secretary of State's policies for attaining the objectives specified in the new EPA 1990, sch. 2A (set out in Environment Act, sch. 12) which are the same as those contained in the Waste Framework Directive. These include the objectives of:

(a) ensuring that waste is recovered or disposed of without endangering human health or causing nuisance or other adverse effects;
(b) establishing an integrated and adequate network of waste disposal installations, taking account of the best available technology not involving excessive costs;
(c) ensuring self-sufficiency in waste disposal;
(d) encouraging the prevention or reduction of waste production and its harmfulness; and
(e) encouraging the recovery of waste by means of recycling, reuse or reclamation and the use of waste as a source of energy.

In preparing the strategy or any modification of it, the Secretary of State is required to consult the EA, bodies or persons representative of the interests of local government and bodies or persons representative of the interests of industry, and may consult others.

Directions may be given by the Secretary of State to the EA requiring it to advise him on the policies which are to be included in the strategy or to carry out surveys or investigations to assist in the preparation of the strategy or any modification including surveys or investigations into the kinds or quantities of waste in England and Wales and the waste facilities needed. Before carrying out such a survey or investigation, the EA must consult bodies or persons representative of local planning authorities and persons or bodies representative of the interests of industry and must make its findings available to those authorities.

Similar provision is made for Scotland under EPA 1990, s. 44B, inserted by Environment Act, s. 92. But in the case of Scotland the strategy is to be prepared not by the Secretary of State but by SEPA. Like the Secretary of State, SEPA must consult appropriate bodies or persons representative of the interests of industry but, instead of consulting persons or bodies 'representative of the interests of local government', SEPA must consult 'such local authorities as appear to it to be likely to be affected by the strategy or modification'. Like the Secretary of State, SEPA may consult other bodies or persons if it considers it appropriate. The Secretary of State is given the same power to give directions to SEPA as to the EA but, in addition, he may give directions as to the policies which are to be included in the strategy. In carrying out any such direction, SEPA is under the same duty to consult and to make its findings available as is the EA.

20.2 PRODUCER RESPONSIBILITY

20.2.1 Introduction

Sections 93 to 95 of the Environment Act are enabling provisions which concern the new area of producer responsibility for waste. These provisions came into force on 21 September 1995.

The policy underlying the provisions was explained by Viscount Ullswater at the committee stage of the Bill in the House of Lords:

Producer responsibility is an instrument which seeks to encourage those who are responsible for placing goods on the market to assume an increased share of the responsibility for dealing with the waste which arises from these products. In other words, it seeks to increase the environmental awareness of producers by placing some of the costs of waste disposal onto those who produce products. It gives as much scope as possible for a market-based response.

The initiative has generally operated by means of a challenge from government to key industries. Our general approach has been to seek to offer the maximum scope to industry to organise itself to respond to the challenge. In this way, our objectives will be achieved in the most cost-effective manner.

There are seven separate waste streams involved in the first tranche of the initiative and the most prominent of these is the packaging chain — namely, those companies involved in manufacturing and using packaging. The general response from industry has been very encouraging. In the background to our discussions on packaging waste has been the EC Directive on Packaging and Packaging Waste, which was adopted, with UK support, in December.

In November, the former Producer Responsibility Group finalised its report on increasing the level of recovery and recycling of packaging waste. Key among its recommendations was that government should introduce legislation to eliminate the potential problem of 'free-riders', namely those companies which might seek to gain a competitive advantage by refusing to accept their share of the responsibility to act.

In bringing forward these clauses, we are responding to that request, and propose to put in place a mechanism which will allow us to legislate in respect of any waste stream, where this proves necessary and appropriate. In this way, we can assure that the policy area is capable of further development and that we can incorporate additional waste streams, if appropriate. With this in mind, our aim is to introduce the minimum legislative structure which is consistent with effective enforcement, in support of the objective of more sustainable waste management practices. (Hansard, HL, 9 February 1995, cols. 351–2.)

20.2.2 Producer responsibility regulations

Section 93 of the Environment Act empowers the Secretary of State to make regulations imposing producer responsibility obligations on persons to be specified in the regulations in respect of products or materials to be specified in the regulations. The purpose for which the regulations may be made is the promotion or securing of an increase in the reuse, recovery or recycling of products or materials. The regulations will require the relevant persons to take specified steps to secure attainment of specified targets. To take a hypothetical example, persons in a particular industry could be required to recycle a fixed percentage of specified packaging waste by the year 2000.

Because of the potential burden which may be imposed on industries covered by the regulations, s. 93 provides for three safeguards.

(1)   The regulations will be subject to affirmative Parliamentary procedure, i.e., they are required to be approved by resolution of each House of Parliament (s. 93(10)).

(2)   Before making the regulations the Secretary of State must consult with bodies or persons appearing to him to be representative of bodies or persons whose interests are, or are likely to be, substantially affected by the proposed regulations (s. 93(2)).

(3)   The regulations can only be made if, after consultation, the Secretary of State is satisfied as to the matters specified in s. 93(6). These are:

(a)   that the regulations would be likely to result in an increase in the re-use, recovery or recycling of the products or materials in question;

(b)   that the increase would produce environmental or economic benefits;

(c)   that those benefits are significant as against the likely costs resulting from the imposition of the proposed producer responsibility obligation;

(d)   that the burdens imposed on businesses by the regulations are the minimum necessary to secure those benefits; and

(e)   that those burdens are imposed on persons most able to make a contribution to the achievement of the relevant targets:

(i)   having regard to the desirability of acting fairly between persons who manufacture, process, distribute or supply products or materials; and

(ii)   taking account of the need to ensure that the proposed producer responsibility obligation is so framed as to be effective in achieving the purposes for which it is to be imposed.

There is, however, an express power for the regulations to impose an obligation on a class or description of person to the exclusion of others. In addition, the

Secretary of State has a duty to secure that the regulations do not, except to the extent necessary to achieve the environmental or economic benefits in question, restrict, distort or prevent competition (s. 93(7)).

Great care will have to be taken in the procedures leading up to the making of any regulations under s. 93. The Secretary of State will have to be able to show that full consultation took place and to justify the grounds on which he is satisfied as to the matters in s. 93(6) if his decisions are not to be successfully challenged in the courts.

The above provisions as to consultation etc. are modified where the regulations are made to implement EC or international obligations.

The detailed matters for which the regulations may make provision are set out in s. 94. As mentioned above, the regulations may specify the classes or descriptions of persons on whom any producer responsibility obligation is to be imposed, the classes or descriptions of products or materials in respect of which the obligation applies and the recycling targets which are to be achieved. Provision may be made for the registration and monitoring by the EA or SEPA of approved exemption schemes. It is envisaged that industries will be encouraged to set up and apply for the registration of their own approved voluntary schemes and that persons who are members of such schemes will be exempt from the statutory requirements imposed by regulations. The exemption schemes will be subject to scrutiny to ensure that they do not have the effect of restricting, distorting or preventing competition except to the extent necessary to achieve the environmental or economic benefits in question.

In the case of persons who are not members of exemption schemes, compliance with statutory obligations will be monitored by the EA or SEPA by the issue of certificates of compliance. The regulations may confer enforcement powers on the new Agencies including powers of entry and inspection and may make provision for appeals and for the payment of fees.

Failure to comply with regulations may be made an offence punishable on summary conviction with a fine not exceeding the statutory maximum (currently £5,000) or, on indictment, with an unlimited fine (s. 95(1)). Provision may be made for an officer or manager of a body corporate to be made criminally liable in respect of an offence committed by the body corporate if it is proved to have been committed with his consent or connivance or to have been attributable to his neglect (s. 95(2) to (4)).

CHAPTER 21
Review of Mineral Planning Permissions

21.1 INTRODUCTION

The Environment Act builds on the process begun by the Town and Country Planning (Minerals) Act 1981 and continued by the Planning and Compensation Act 1991 to update planning controls on mineral workings.

Before 1981 mineral workings were controlled by the same planning regimes as applied generally to all development. However, mineral workings constitute a unique form of 'development' in that, by definition, the extraction of minerals breaks down the substance of the land concerned rather than bringing the land to a more advanced state. During the 1970s it became generally acknowledged that special provision should be made for additional controls over and above the general planning regime. Other forms of land development can be adequately controlled by a 'once and for all' system of control: the main purpose of a planning permission for (say) the construction of a building is to define the authorised development and control the way in which it is carried out. Once the construction is completed the planning permission has served its purpose. In the case of mineral workings, on the other hand, the authorised activity is carried out over many years and long-term controls are needed to ensure that as little harm as possible is caused to the environment. Furthermore, planning and environmental standards are considerably higher today than when modern planning controls were established by the Town and Country Planning Act 1947, and mineral planning consents have become subject to ever more stringent and sophisticated conditions. It follows that in many cases mineral extraction undertaken under old consents is not subject to the same controls as are thought essential today and that there is an ever widening gap between the standards required by modern consents and those required by old consents.

The need to review and update mineral planning permissions was recognised by the report of the Stevens Committee, *Planning Control over Mineral Working* (HMSO, 1976), whose recommendations were partly implemented by the Town and Country Planning (Minerals) Act 1981. Amongst other measures, the 1981 Act provided that all *new* planning permissions for minerals development were to have a limited duration — 60 years unless the mineral planning authority prescribed a different period. Powers were conferred on mineral planning authorities to impose restoration and aftercare conditions to secure that, after operations for the winning and working of minerals have been completed, the site will be restored and brought to the required standard for agriculture, forestry or amenity. Mineral planning authorities were also given a duty to review the terms on which the development was carried out under *existing* consents and power to modify those terms, subject in some cases to the payment of compensation.

The Planning and Compensation Act 1991 made further provision for the strengthening of planning controls on mining. In particular, consents for mineral working granted by interim development orders, i.e., permissions predating the Town and Country Planning Act 1947, were brought under the control of mineral planning authorities for the first time. The interim development order regime was unsatisfactory in two ways. First, there was no system of registration of pre-1947 consents so their number was not known and, secondly, there was no power to impose on pre-1947 permissions conditions to protect the environment such as restoration and aftercare conditions. The 1991 Act sought to cure these defects by requiring all pre-1947 permissions to be registered and empowering the mineral planning authorities to impose on such permissions any conditions which could be imposed on a new application for planning permission. Although the mineral planning authorities were placed under a duty to review mineral sites in their areas and to make orders updating old permissions as necessary, the provision made in the 1991 Act has not proved very effective mainly because no time limits were imposed for carrying out the review.

The Environment Act extends the process begun by the 1991 Act by tackling the updating of post-1948 mineral planning permissions. The government's proposals were foreshadowed in a consultation paper, *The Reform of Old Mineral Permissions 1948–1981* published by the Department of the Environment in March 1994. In that paper the government stated that the policy behind the proposed changes was not only to ensure that mineral operators keep up with rising environmental standards but also to even out the distortion of the market which occurs when older mineral permissions operate to lower standards than those applied to more recent permissions.

21.2 THE NEW UPDATING REGIME IN OUTLINE

The broad effect of Environment Act, sch. 13 is to provide for an initial review of mineral planning permissions granted after 1948 but before 1982. The identification of all sites to be included in the initial review must take place within three months of the coming into force of sch. 13. Phase I of the initial review must be begun within a further period of three years and the mineral sites to be reviewed in Phase I (active 'Phase I sites') are active sites which are either wholly or mainly controlled by pre-1969 planning permissions or are situated in sensitive areas such as National Parks. Phase II of the initial review — to begin within six years of the identification of the sites — will cover the remaining active sites (active 'Phase II sites') i.e., active sites wholly or mainly controlled by planning permissions granted after 1969 but before 1982 which are not situated in sensitive areas. In the case of a dormant site, all relevant planning permissions which relate to the site, cease to have effect on the coming into force of sch. 13 unless and until an application for the permissions to be reviewed has been determined.

The first stage in the review process is the preparation by each mineral planning authority of a list of mineral sites in their area indicating whether they are active Phase I sites, active Phase II sites or dormant sites. The authority must also designate — either in that first list or in a second list — the date by which the owner of the site or of mineral rights in the site must apply for the planning conditions relating to that site to be updated. The onus then shifts to the owner to make an application in accordance with the sch. 13 procedures to the mineral planning authority to determine the conditions to which the planning permissions relating to the site are to be subject. Relevant planning permissions relating to Phase I or Phase II sites will cease to have effect (except in so far as they impose restoration or aftercare conditions) unless the site is included in the list and an application is properly made for the planning conditions to be reviewed. It can therefore be seen that it is crucial for owners of mineral sites or of mineral rights to ensure that their sites are included in the list and that proper and timely applications under sch. 13 are made.

Compensation is payable in the limited circumstances described in 21.8.4 below.

The effect of the first review provided for by sch. 13, taken with the provisions of the 1991 Act, is that all pre-1982 planning permissions will have been updated or replaced within the timetable prescribed by that schedule. Thereafter, all mineral planning permissions are to be reviewed at 15-year intervals (see 21.13 below).

21.3 INITIAL REVIEW: SITES TO BE INCLUDED

Each mineral planning authority is to conduct an initial review of the mineral sites in their area which will be phased in two periods; the first dealing with the period 1 July 1948 to 31 March 1969 (or, in Scotland, 7 December 1969), and the second dealing with the period 1 April 1969 (or, in Scotland, 8 December 1969) to 21 February 1982. The 1969 cut-off date was chosen because the Town and Country Planning Act 1968, as modified by the Town and Country Planning (Minerals) Regulations 1971, provided that in the case of mineral permissions granted or deemed to be granted before 1 April 1969 where development had not been begun before 1 January 1968, development had to have been begun no later than 1 April 1969 for the permission to remain valid. Similar provision was made for Scotland. The government therefore considered that many supposedly extant pre-1969 permissions would, on closer examination, be found to have lapsed. The second phase is concluded by 21 February 1982 because the Town and Country Planning (Minerals) Act 1981 enabled aftercare conditions to be imposed on permissions granted after that date and it was assumed that permissions granted after that date do not require to be included in the initial review since they will already be subject to appropriate conditions.

Although it is individual planning permissions which are to be reviewed this will be done on a site-by-site basis. Mineral sites are often the subject of a number of permissions granted at different times and it is intended that all the permissions (whenever granted) relating to a particular site will be reviewed together. The only permissions which are exempted from the initial review are those granted under interim development orders or by a development order under section 59 of the Town and Country Planning Act 1990. (See the definition of 'relevant planning permission' in Environment Act, sch. 13, para. 1(1).) Interim development orders were updated by the Planning and Compensation Act 1991 and it is envisaged that permission granted by a development order will be dealt with by provision similar to sch. 13 or 14 to the Environment Act to be made by a new development order (see Environment Act, s. 96(5)).

The sites to be included in the initial review are all mineral sites except where the whole or greater part of the site is governed by post-1982 permissions (i.e., permissions granted after 21 February 1982) (see sch. 13. para. 2(2)).

The sites are divided into Phase I sites (those to be reviewed first) and Phase II sites (those to be reviewed later). The Phase I sites are sites in sensitive areas, i.e., where the whole or part of the site is situated in a National Park, a site of special scientific interest under s. 28 of the Wildlife and Countryside Act 1981, an area of outstanding natural beauty under s. 87 of the NPACA 1949, a National Scenic Area under s. 262C of the Town and Country Planning (Scotland) Act 1972 or a Natural Heritage Area under s. 6 of the NH(S)A 1991 or sites the whole or greater part of which are governed by planning permissions granted on or before 31 March 1969 (or, in Scotland, 7 December 1969). All sites to be included in the initial review which are not Phase I sites, i.e., those not in sensitive areas or wholly or mainly governed by pre-1982 permissions granted after 31 March 1969 (or, in Scotland, 7 December 1969) are Phase II sites (see Environment Act, sch. 13, para. 2).

21.4 PHASE I OF INITIAL REVIEW: THE FIRST LIST

The first step in the initial review is the preparation by the mineral planning authority of the 'first list', that is to say, a complete list of all the Phase I and Phase II sites in their area (Environment Act, sch. 13, para. 3). The list must be completed and published within three months of the coming into force of sch. 13 (sch. 13, paras 3(6) and 5(4)). The list must indicate, in the case of each site, whether it is an active Phase I site, an active Phase II site or a dormant site, that is to say, a Phase I or Phase II site on or under which no minerals development has been carried out to any substantial extent at any time in the period between 22 February 1982 and 6 June 1995 (except by a permission granted by an interim development order or a development order) (see sch. 13, para. 1(1)).

In the case of each Phase I site the list must also specify the date by which the owner of the site or person entitled to the mineral rights in the site must make an application to the mineral planning authority to determine the conditions to which the planning permissions relating to the site are to be subject. This date, which is referred to in this chapter as 'the application deadline', is of key importance to the review process because if no application is made by the application deadline (as specified in the list or as extended by agreement) the planning permissions concerned will lapse (see further 21.9 below). Different application deadlines may be specified for different Phase I sites but all such dates must be no earlier than one year from the publication of the first list and no later than three years from the date on which sch. 13 comes into force (sch. 13, para. 3(5)).

It can therefore be seen that the first list serves a dual purpose:

(a) It constitutes a preliminary stage for both Phase I and Phase II of the initial review since it identifies all the sites which are to be reviewed.

(b) The publication of the first list triggers Phase I of the initial review since, by specifying the application deadlines, it lays down the timetable by which the Phase I sites are to be considered by the mineral planning authority.

Unless a Phase I or Phase II site is included in the first list, each planning permission (other than one granted by an interim development order or development order) which relates to the site will cease to have effect (see 21.9 below and sch. 13, para. 12(4)). It follows that it is essential for owners of mineral sites or mineral rights to make sure that the sites with which they are concerned are included in the first list. Schedule 13 makes provision for any such person to apply, within 3 months from the publication of the list, to the mineral planning authority for a site or mineral interest omitted from the first list to be included and for the list to be amended accordingly (sch. 13, para. 6). If the mineral planning authority do not amend the list as requested or do not give a decision within eight weeks (or such extended period of time as may be agreed), the owner concerned may appeal to the Secretary of State within six months of the decision or the end of that period (sch. 13, para. 6(11) to (13)). Where the first list is amended, an application deadline will be specified for the site in question — by the first list if the site is a Phase I site or by the second list if the site is a Phase II site (see 21.5 below). The application deadline must be at least one year from the date on which the application is dealt with (sch. 13, para. 6(6) to (9)). Subject to that, the application deadline must be within three years of the coming into force of sch. 13 if the site is a Phase I site or within six years if the site is a Phase II site.

21.5   PHASE II OF INITIAL REVIEW: THE SECOND LIST

Following the preparation and publication of the first list, the mineral planning authority must prepare and publish a second list, i.e., a list of the active Phase II sites in their area, and indicate the application deadline for each of those sites (the date by which the owner of the site or of mineral rights must apply to the mineral planning authority to determine the conditions to which the planning permissions relating to that site are to be subject). The second list must be prepared within three years of the coming into force of Environment Act, sch. 13 (or such longer period as the Secretary of State may by order specify) (sch. 13, paras 4(7) and 5(5)).

As with Phase I sites, the application deadline may be different for different sites but must be no later than one year from the publication of the second list. However, the latest time which may be specified as the application deadline is six years from the date on which sch. 13 comes in force as compared to three years in the case of Phase I sites (sch. 13, para. 4(4)). The period of six years may be extended by order made by the Secretary of State (sch. 13, para. 4(5)).

As in the case of the first list, the publication of the second list triggers Phase II of the initial review by laying down the timetable by which the Phase II sites are to be considered by the mineral planning authority.

21.6   PUBLICATION OF FIRST AND SECOND LISTS

Both the first list and the second list must be advertised in local newspapers by a notice containing statutory information explaining the effect of the relevant provisions in Environment Act, sch. 13 (sch. 13, para. 5). In addition, the mineral planning authority must serve individual notices on every person appearing to them to be the owner of any land (as defined in sch. 13, para. 1(1)), or entitled to any mineral, included within a mineral site which has been included in the first or second list and such notice must be served not later than the time when the list in question is first advertised (sch. 13, para. 8). Under sch. 13, para. 8 the notice must specify the application deadline applicable to the site in question, explain the consequences which will occur if the application is not made by that date and explain the right to apply to have the date postponed. If no application has been made in relation to the site eight weeks before the application deadline, a further notice must be served on each person concerned four weeks before the deadline. Provision is made for notices to be displayed on the land in question in cases where the name and address of the persons concerned cannot be ascertained (sch. 13, para. 8(7) to (10)).

21.7   UPDATING OF PLANNING CONDITIONS

The review of the planning permissions relating to a Phase I or II site is initiated by an application made to the mineral planning authority by the owner of the site or person entitled to minerals in the site. It is a key feature of the statutory regime that the mineral planning authority have no duty to review planning permissions unless such an application is made. It is crucial that the owner of a Phase I or II site or of mineral rights relating to such a site makes the necessary application before the relevant application deadline since the consequence of not doing so is that the planning permissions relating to the site will lapse (see 21.9 below).

An application may be made in respect of any Phase I or Phase II site (whether active or dormant). Although an application may not be made after the relevant application deadline prescribed by the first or second list (or such later date as may be agreed between the applicant and the authority), there does not appear to be any bar to an application being made before the publication of the first or second list provided it is made after sch. 13 has come into force. The application must be in writing and must contain the information prescribed by sch. 13, para. 9(2). In particular, it must identify the mineral site to which the application relates, identify the relevant planning permissions relating to the site (i.e., all permissions for mineral development other than those granted on or before 30 June 1948 or by an interim development order or a development order) and set out the conditions to which the applicant proposes that those permissions should be subject. It must be accompanied by the usual certificate required for planning applications that the applicant is either the sole owner of the land and mineral rights in question or has given notice to all other persons having a notifiable interest.

On receipt of the application, the mineral planning authority must determine the conditions to which each relevant planning permission relating to the site is to be subject. Once a determination has been made, the planning permissions have effect subject to those conditions (sch. 13, para. 9(6)). The new conditions may be in addition to, or in substitution for, any existing planning conditions and may include any conditions, such as aftercare conditions, which could have been imposed on a new grant of planning permission for minerals development (sch.13, para. 9(7)).

The determination should be made within three months of the application, which time may be extended by agreement between the applicant and the authority, unless the authority require further details to determine the application. In that case, the authority may serve a notice on the applicant within one month of the receipt of the application specifying any details they reasonably require which may include information, plans, drawings or evidence verifying the details supplied by the applicant (sch. 13, para. 9(10), (11)). If such a request is made, the three-month period does not run until the details requested by the authority have been received by them. If the authority do not notify their determination to the applicant within the three-month period or the agreed extended period, the permissions will on the expiry of that period have effect subject to the conditions proposed by the applicant in the application and those conditions are treated as having been determined by the authority.

An appeal lies to the Secretary of State where the conditions determined by the mineral planning authority differ in any respect from those proposed in the application. Notice of appeal must be given within six months of the date on which the authority gave notice to the applicant of their determination (sch. 13, para. 11).

Since there will often be several persons having an interest in a mineral site entitling them to make apply to have the planning conditions relating to the site reviewed, the Environment Act provides (sch. 13, para. 14) that where two or more applications are duly made to a mineral planning authority in respect of a site and the determination has not yet been made, they shall be treated as a single application received by the authority on the date on which the latest application was received. However, it is unclear how sch. 13, para. 9(9) is to apply to such a case. That provides that if the authority do not make a determination within three months from the receipt of an application, the planning permission in question shall have effect subject to the conditions proposed in the application. Difficulties would arise where (say) two applications are made in relation to the same site proposing different planning permissions. Furthermore, since the right to compensation can only arise where the conditions determined by the mineral planning authority are different from those proposed in an application, it is important for the applicants to be clear which of the planning conditions are to be treated for that purpose as being the conditions proposed in the application. It is assumed that this precondition for the payment of compensation would only be satisfied if the conditions determined by the authority were different from each of the sets of conditions proposed. It is therefore desirable for all persons interested in a mineral site to consult together before any application is made so as to avoid any such confusion.

An applicant may only make one application in respect of a site and, after a determination has been made for that site, no further application from any other applicant may be made (sch. 13, para. 14(1)).

21.8 PROTECTION WHERE PLANNING CONDITIONS ARE IMPOSED WHICH AFFECT THE ASSET VALUE OF A SITE

21.8.1 Introduction

The Planning and Compensation Act 1991 empowered mineral planning authorities to update conditions subject to which planning permissions granted prior to 1 June 1948 under interim development orders ('IDOs') were to have effect. The 1991 Act did not provide for any compensation for the cost of complying with any new conditions imposed. However, ministerial guidance in MPG9, 'Planning and Compensation Act 1991: Interim Development Order Permissions (IDOs) — Conditions' advised that whilst it would be appropriate to impose modern conditions for dormant sites, for active sites a distinction should be made between conditions which deal with the environment, amenity, restoration and aftercare ('sensory conditions') which would be acceptable, and conditions affecting asset values (e.g., those that fundamentally alter the amount of mineral that can be extracted and the rate of output), which would not.

In its consultation paper, *Review of the Town and Country Planning (Minerals) Act 1981: the Reform of Old Mineral Permissions 1948–1981* (March 1994), the Government declared that it saw no case for departing from the general principles established for IDOs. A distinction was again drawn between the imposition of modern sensory conditions and conditions affecting asset values. In the case of the former, the recommendation was that the mineral operator should bear the cost of the imposition without compensation in accordance with the 'polluter pays' principle. However, in the case of the latter, compensation should be payable for conditions imposed on active sites.

These principles have, broadly speaking, been implemented in the Environment Act. Compensation will only be payable where planning conditions are imposed (whether by the mineral planning authority or by the Secretary of State) in respect of an active Phase I or II site which restricts working rights in respect of the site and where the effect of the restriction is such as to prejudice adversely to an unreasonable degree the economic viability of operating the site or the asset value of the site. Compensation is not payable unless that condition is fulfilled. It will be seen that compensation is never payable in respect of a dormant site.

21.8.2   Paragraph 10 notice to be given where planning conditions are imposed which restrict working rights

In order to determine whether compensation is payable, provision is made in Environment Act, sch. 13, para. 10 for the person determining the application (whether the mineral planning authority or the Secretary of State) to issue a formal notice stating whether, in the opinion of the authority, the effect of that restriction of working rights would be such as to prejudice adversely to an unreasonable degree the economic viability of operating the site or the asset value of the site.

The duty to make a para. 10 statement arises where the mineral planning authority (or the Secretary of State on a referred application — see 21.11 below) determine conditions which differ in any respect from those proposed in the application and the effect of those conditions (other than restoration and aftercare conditions), as compared with the effect of the conditions (other than any restoration or aftercare conditions) to which the relevant planning permissions in question were subject immediately prior to the determination, is to restrict working rights in respect of the site. For this purpose working rights are taken to be restricted in respect of the site if any of the following is restricted or reduced in respect of the site in question:

(a)   the size of the area which may be used for the winning and working of minerals or the depositing of mineral waste;

(b)   the depth to which operations for the winning and working of minerals may extend;

(c)   the height of any deposit of mineral waste;

(d)   the rate at which any particular mineral may be extracted;

(e)   the rate at which any particular mineral waste may be deposited;

(f)   the period at the expiry of which any winning or working of minerals or depositing of mineral waste is to cease; or

(g)   the total quantity of minerals which may be extracted from, or of mineral waste which may be deposited on, the site (see sch. 13, para. 1(6).)

A para. 10 notice must be given at the same time as the notice of conditions determined by the mineral planning authority (or Secretary of State). The notice must:

(a)   state that the conditions determined by the authority differ in some respect from the proposed conditions set out in the application;

(b)   state that the effect of the conditions, other than any restoration or aftercare conditions, determined, as compared with the effect of the conditions, other than any restoration or aftercare conditions, to which the relevant planning permissions relating to the site in question were subject immediately prior to the determination, is to restrict working rights in respect of the site;

(c)   identify the working rights so restricted; and

(d)   state whether, in the opinion of the authority (or Secretary of State), the effect of that restriction of working rights would be such as to prejudice adversely to an unreasonable degree the economic viability of operating the site or the asset value of the site.

It is the statement in (d) which is crucial to whether or not compensation is payable under sch. 13, para. 11.

Guidance will be issued by the Secretary of State to which mineral planning authorities are to have regard in determining whether the effect of any restriction of working rights would or would not fall within para. (d).

21.8.3   Appeals against para. 10 notices

If a mineral planning authority issue a para. 10 notice but do not include a para. 10(2)(d) statement that the restriction of working rights in question would, in their opinion, prejudice adversely to an unreasonable degree the economic viability of operating the site or the asset value of the site, the applicant may within six months appeal to the Secretary of State (sch. 13, para. 11(1)(b) and (2)).

21.8.4   Compensation

Under Environment Act, sch. 13, para. 15, compensation is payable only if the following conditions are fulfilled:

(a)   The conditions in respect of a Phase I or II site have been finally determined on a sch. 13 application, whether by the mineral planning authority or by the Secretary of State on appeal or on a referred application (see 21.11 below).

(b)   The site is an active site.

(c)   No appeal is pending.

(d)   The conditions which have been determined differ in some respect from those proposed by the applicant.

(e)   The effect of the conditions, other than restoration or aftercare conditions, so determined, as compared with the effect of the conditions, other than any restoration or aftercare conditions, to which the relevant planning permissions in question were subject immediately prior to the determination, is to restrict working rights in respect of the site.

(f)   A statement has been given that the effect of that restriction of working rights would be such as to prejudice adversely to an unreasonable degree the economic viability of operating the site or the asset value of the site. That statement may be given either in a para. 10 notice given by the mineral planning authority or by the Secretary of State or on an appeal (see 21.8.3 above).

Where compensation is payable, the amount of compensation is determined under Parts IV and IX of the Town and Country Planning Act 1990 (or, in Scotland, Parts VIII and IX of the Town and Country Planning (Scotland) Act 1972). Those provisions have effect as if the determination to vary the conditions had been made under s. 97 of the 1990 Act (or, in Scotland, s. 42 of the 1972 Act) (Environment Act, sch. 13, para. 15(4)).

Compensation is only payable for the restriction of working rights effected by the new conditions and not, for example, for any imposition of restoration and aftercare conditions (sch. 13, para. 15(5)).

A detailed explanation of the compensation provisions of the Town and Country Planning Act is beyond the scope of this work. But, broadly, compensation will be payable to a person interested in the mineral site or minerals in respect of expenditure incurred by him in carrying out work which is rendered abortive by the imposition of the new conditions or in respect of loss or damage otherwise sustained by him which is directly attributable to the imposition of the conditions. The special modifications of compensation provisions in respect of mineral works contained in s. 116 of the 1990 Act (or, in Scotland, s. 167A of the 1972 Act) do not apply (sch. 13, para. 15(6)).

21.9   PERMISSIONS CEASING TO HAVE EFFECT

The sanction underlying the review regime in Environment Act, sch. 13 is that relevant planning permissions relating to Phase I or II sites will cease to have effect unless they are reviewed. Relevant planning permissions are defined in sch. 13, para. 1(1) as including all planning permissions granted after 30 June 1948 except those granted under interim development orders or development orders.

A distinction is drawn between dormant sites (i.e., sites on or under which no minerals development has been carried out under any relevant planning permission to any substantial extent during the period from 22 February 1982 to 6 June 1995 inclusive) and active sites. In the case of a dormant site, all relevant planning permissions which relate to the site cease to have effect on the coming into force of sch. 13 unless and until an application for the permissions to be reviewed made under sch. 13, para. 9 has been determined under para. 9(6) (sch. 13, para. 12(3)). Although para. 12(3) does not specifically mention deemed determinations under para. 9(9), it is submitted that that provision does apply so that where an application is made in respect of a dormant site which the mineral planning authority do not determine within the three-month period, the planning permissions in question have effect subject to the conditions imposed by the applicant.

Planning permissions relating to active Phase I or II sites, on the other hand, continue to have effect until the day following the date specified in the first or second list (as the case may be) as the deadline for applying to review the conditions unless an application has been made by that date — or such later date as may be agreed between the applicant and the mineral planning authority (sch. 13, para. 12(1), (2)).

Where a Phase I or II site has not been included in the first list, any relevant planning permission ceases to have effect on the day following the date on which an interested person could apply for the site to be included in the list under sch. 13, para. 6(1) (see 21.4 above) unless such an application has been made. If an application is made, the planning permission will cease to have effect when proceedings on the application have been finally determined unless the site is added to the list (sch. 13, para. 12(4)).

Where planning permissions cease to have effect, no further development is authorised under those permissions. However, any restoration and aftercare conditions will, nonetheless, continue to have effect.

21.10   POSTPONEMENT OF DEADLINE FOR APPLICATION WHERE EXISTING CONDITIONS ARE SATISFACTORY

Environment Act, sch. 13, para. 7 makes provision for deadlines to be postponed in the case of active sites where the existing planning conditions are satisfactory. The postponement is achieved by the owner of any land, or of any interest in any mineral, comprised in an active Phase I or II site making a successful written application to the mineral planning authority.

In the case of a Phase I active site, such an application must be made within three months from the time that the first list is first advertised. In the case of an active Phase II site, the application must be made within three months from the time that the second list is first advertised. If, in either case, the list in question did not originally include the site in question but was subsequently amended so as to include it (see 21.4 above), the period of three months runs from the time that notice was given of the decision to amend the list.

The application must be in writing and must set out the conditions to which each relevant planning permission relating to the site is subject, the applicant's reasons for considering the conditions to be satisfactory and the date which is proposed as the extended deadline. It must be accompanied by the certificate usually required for planning applications that the applicant is either the sole owner of the land concerned or has given notice of the application to all other persons with a notifiable interest.

If the mineral planning authority agree that the conditions are satisfactory, they must postpone the deadline, determine a new deadline and amend the first or, as the case may be, second list. If they do not agree, they must refuse the application. In either case they must notify the applicant of their decision. If the authority do not notify the applicant of their decision within three months (or such later date as they may agree with the applicant) they will be treated as having agreed to the deadline being postponed to the date proposed by the applicant and the appropriate list must be amended accordingly.

21.11 REFERENCE OF APPLICATIONS TO THE SECRETARY OF STATE

Environment Act, sch. 13, para. 13 empowers the Secretary of State to give directions requiring applications under para. 9 to the mineral planning authority to be referred to him for determination instead of being dealt with by the authority. Such a direction may provide for a particular application to be referred to the Secretary of State or may relate to all applications falling within a class specified in the direction.

The same rules apply in relation to a referred application as apply to applications falling to be determined by the mineral planning authority. But before determining a referred application, the Secretary of State must, if either the applicant or the mineral planning authority wish, give each of them an opportunity of appearing before and being heard by a person appointed by him.

The appeal provisions in sch. 13, para. 11 do not apply to a determination made by the Secretary of State which is final.

21.12 APPEALS

Where an appeal to the Secretary of State is provided for by Environment Act, sch. 13 (see 21.4, 21.7 and 21.8.3 above) the appeal must be made on a prescribed form and giving, so far as reasonably practicable, the information required by that form (sch. 13, para. 16(2)). The Secretary of State's decision on the appeal is final. He has power to allow or dismiss the appeal or reverse or vary any part of the decision of the mineral planning authority (whether the appeal relates to that part of it or not) and may deal with the application as if it had been made to him at first instance. Both the applicant and the mineral planning authority must, if they wish, be given an opportunity of appearing before and being heard by a person appointed by the Secretary of State before a decision on the appeal is made. If the Secretary of State at any time considers that the appellant is responsible for undue delay in the process of the appeal, he may give the appellant notice that the appeal is to be dismissed unless he takes specified steps within a specified period. If those steps are not taken within that period, the Secretary of State may dismiss the appeal (Planning and Compensation Act 1991, sch. 2, para. 6 as applied by Environment Act, sch. 13, para. 16(3)).

The provisions restricting any challenge to the validity of planning decisions contained in the Town and Country Planning Act 1990 or, in Scotland, the Town and Country Planning (Scotland) Act 1972 are applied by Environment Act, sch. 13, para. 16(4) and (6) to any decisions by the Secretary of State whether on an appeal or on an application referred to him (see 21.11 above). The effect of this is that such a decision of the Secretary of State may only be challenged in the manner provided by s. 288 of the 1990 Act (or, in Scotland, s. 233 of the 1972 Act), under which an aggrieved person may challenge the validity of an action by the Secretary of State by making an application to the High Court (or, in Scotland, the Court of Session) within six weeks from the date on which the action is taken on the grounds that the action is not within the powers of the Act or that any of the relevant requirements have not been complied with in relation to the action. Subject to that, the validity of any action by the Secretary of State may not be questioned in any legal proceedings whatsoever (see s. 284 of the 1990 Act (or, in Scotland, s. 231 of the 1972 Act)).

21.13 PERIODIC REVIEWS FOLLOWING INITIAL REVIEWS

21.13.1 Duty to carry out periodic reviews

Each mineral planning authority are given a duty by the Environment Act, sch. 14, para. 1 to carry out periodic reviews of the mineral permissions relating to the mining sites in their area. Each site is to be reviewed every 15 years. The procedures for carrying out the reviews, which are laid down by sch. 14, are very similar to the procedures applying to the interim reviews of Phase I and Phase II sites explained above.

The reviews must be carried out on a site-by-site basis. For this purpose a mining site is any land to which a planning permission for mineral development relates other than a planning permission granted by a development order (sch. 14, para. 2(1)). However, a mineral planning authority may treat the aggregate of land to which any two or more mineral permissions relate as a single site if they think it expedient having regard to any guidance issued by the Secretary of State (sch. 14, para. 2(1), (2)).

21.13.2 The first review date

The first review date is separately determined for each mineral site under the rules set out in sch. 14, para. 3. The underlying principle is that the review must take place 15 years from the time the planning permissions relating to that site were brought up to date.

Where a mining site is a Phase I or Phase II site within the meaning of Environment Act, sch. 13, the first review date is 15 years after the determination under sch. 13 of the planning conditions to which the relevant planning permissions relating to the site are subject (see 21.7 above). If a mineral site is not a Phase I or Phase II site and includes an 'old mining permission' which fell to be reviewed under sch. 2 to the Planning and Compensation Act 1991 or, in Scotland, sch. 2 to the Town and Country Planning (Scotland) Act 1972 then the first review date is 15 years after the conditions to which the old mineral planning permission or permissions is subject were determined under the 1991 Act or the 1972 Act (see 21.1 above). If a mining site is not a Phase I or Phase II site or a site with an old mining permission, the first review date is 15 years after the date when the most recent mineral permission which relates to the site was granted. However, if the most recent mineral permission relates only to part of the site, the mineral planning authority may take the date of another planning permission as the base date for determining the first review date if they consider it expedient having regard to any guidance issued by the Secretary of State (sch. 13, para. 3(4), (5)).

Where one or more orders under s. 97 of the Town and Country Planning Act 1990 or s. 42 of the Town and Country Planning (Scotland) Act 1972 have been made, the first review date is 15 years after the date on which the order, or the last of the orders, took effect.

If two or more of the above dates apply to a mining site, the first review date is the latest of those dates (sch. 13, para. 3(7)).

21.13.3 Service of notice of first review

The process of review is started by the mineral planning authority serving a notice under sch. 14, para. 4 on each person appearing to them to be the owner of the land (as defined in sch. 14, para. 2(1)) or entitled to an interest in any mineral in the site. The provisions relating to the notice are similar to those relating to the notice required to be given of the initial review of Phase I and Phase II sites (see 21.6 above). The notice must specify the mining rights, identify the mineral permissions relating to the site, state the first review date, state that an application must be made for the approval of the relevant planning permission by that date and the consequences of not making such an application and explain the right to apply for a postponement of the first review date.

If no application is made in relation to the site eight weeks before the first review date, a written reminder must be served on each person concerned not less than four weeks before the first review date. Provision is made for notices to be displayed on the land in question in cases where the name and address of the persons concerned cannot be ascertained (sch. 14, para. 4(5) to (8)).

21.13.4 Application for postponement of the first review date

Environment Act, sch. 14, para. 5 makes provision for the first review date to be postponed in the case of sites where the existing planning conditions are satisfactory. The provision is similar to that made by sch. 13, para. 7 for the postponement of deadlines for making applications for reviewing the planning conditions relating to Phase I and Phase II sites (see 21.10 above).

The owner of any land, or of any interest in any mineral, comprised in a mining site may make an application for the postponement of the first review date within three months from the service of the notice served on him by the mineral planning authority.

The application must be in writing and must set out the conditions to which each mineral permission relating to the site is subject, the applicant's reasons for considering those conditions to be satisfactory and the date which the applicant wishes to have substituted as the postponed review date.

If the mineral planning authority agree that the conditions are satisfactory they must postpone the first review date to a new date determined by them. If they do not agree, they must refuse the application. In either case they must notify the applicant of their decision. If the authority do not notify the applicant of their decision within three months (or such later date as they may agree with the applicant) they will be treated as having agreed to the first review date being postponed to the date proposed by the applicant.

21.13.5 Updating of planning conditions

As in the case of the initial review of planning permissions relating to Phase I or Phase II sites (see 21.7 above), the review of the planning permissions on subsequent reviews is initiated by an application made to the mineral planning authority by the owner of the site or person entitled to an interest in a mineral in the site. If no such application is made before the first review date (or any extended time agreed with the mineral planning authority) then each planning permission relating to the site identified in the notice served by the mineral planning authority under sch. 14, para. 4 (see 21.13.3 above) will lapse on the day following the first review date except in so far as it imposes any restoration or aftercare condition (sch. 14, para. 7).

The application must be in writing and must contain the information prescribed by sch. 14, para. 6(2). In particular, it must identify the mineral site to which the application relates, identify the mineral permissions relating to the site and set out the conditions to which the applicant proposes those permissions should be subject. It must be accompanied by the usual certificate required for planning applications that the applicant is either the sole owner of the land and mineral rights in question or has given notice to all other persons having a notifiable interest.

On receipt of the application, the mineral planning authority must determine the conditions to which each mineral permission relating to the site is to be subject. Once the application is made (or, if there is an appeal, the appeal has been determined) the mineral permissions have effect subject to the conditions as so determined (sch. 14, para. 10)).

The new conditions may include any condition which may be imposed on a grant of planning permission for mineral development and may be in addition to, or in substitution for, any existing conditions to which the permission in question is subject (sch. 14, para. 6(6)).

The determination should be made within three months of the application, which time may be extended by agreement between the applicant and the authority, unless the authority require further details to determine the application. In that case, the authority may serve a notice on the applicant within one month of the application specifying any details which they may reasonably require. The three-month period does not run until the details requested by the authority have been received by them (sch. 14, para. 6(9)).

If the authority do not notify their determination to the applicant within the three-month period or any agreed extended period, any permission in question will have effect on the expiry of that period subject to the conditions proposed by the applicant in the application and those conditions are treated as having been determined by the authority (sch. 14, para. 6(8)).

21.13.6 Reference of applications to the Secretary of State

Environment Act, sch. 14, para. 8 empowers the Secretary of State to give directions requiring applications to the mineral planning authority for the review of mineral permissions to be referred to him for determination instead of being dealt with by the authority. Such directions may provide for a particular application to be referred to the Secretary of State or may relate to all applications falling within a specified class.

The same rules apply in relation to a referred application as apply to applications falling to be determined by the mineral planning authority. But before determining a referred application, the Secretary of State must give the applicant and the mineral planning authority the opportunity of appearing before and being heard by a person appointed by the Secretary of State.

These provisions are similar to those applying in relation to the reference to the Secretary of State of applications for the review of planning permissions for Phase I and Phase II sites. See 21.11 above.

21.13.7 Appeals

An appeal lies to the Secretary of State where the mineral planning authority determine conditions that differ in any respect from the proposed conditions set out in the application (sch. 14, para. 9(1)). No appeal lies from the decision of the Secretary of State under a referred application (see 21.13.6 above) which is final (sch. 14, para. 8(3)(c)).

The procedure relating to appeals is the same as for appeals against the determination of mineral planning conditions relating to Phase I and Phase II sites on an initial review (see sch. 14, para. 9 and 21.12 above).

21.13.8   Two or more applications

As in the case of initial reviews of Phase I and Phase II sites, there will often be several persons having an interest in a mining site which entitles them each to make an application to have the mineral planning conditions relating to the site reviewed. Sch. 14, para. 11 provides that where two or more applications are made relating to the same site they will be treated as a single application made on the date on which the latest application was made. No person may make more than one application in respect of the same site and no further application can be made once the planning conditions have been determined. These provisions are similar to those relating to initial reviews of Phase I and Phase II sites which are more fully discussed in 21.7 above.

21.13.9   Compensation

Enviroment Act, sch. 14, para. 13 provides for compensation to be payable in cases where the conditions relating to the site determined under sch. 14 are different from those proposed by the applicant if the effect of the new conditions as compared with the effect of the existing conditions is to restrict working rights. For this purpose restoration or aftercare conditions are disregarded.

The expression 'restriction of working rights' is defined in sch. 14, para. 13(3) and has the same meaning as in the compensation provisions relating to the determination of planning conditions for Phase I or Phase II sites on an initial review (see 21.8.2 above). Where compensation is payable the amount of compensation is similar to that payable under sch. 13 where conditions are imposed on an initial review of a Phase I or Phase II site (see 13.8.2 above). However, unlike sch. 13, it is not a precondition for the payment of compensation that the effect of the restriction of working rights would, in the opinion of the authority, be such as to prejudice adversely to an unreasonable degree the economic viability of operating the site or the asset value of the site.

21.13.10   Second and subsequent periodic reviews

After the first review, subsequent reviews are to be made at 15-year intervals. The provisions relating to the first review described in 21.13.1 to 21.13.9 above apply equally to second and subsequent reviews (sch. 13, para. 12).

CHAPTER 22
Hedgerows and the Conservation of the Countryside

22.1 INTRODUCTION

The importance of hedges in providing habitat for wildlife and in conserving the beauty of the countryside has been given increasing recognition. In agricultural land, hedges act as linear landscape features providing migration and travel routes for animals which are particularly necessary in open countryside where wildlife habitats would otherwise be isolated. Hedgerows often mark ancient boundaries and are frequently the oldest visible features in the countryside.

There is, however, a tension between the interests of conservation and those of agriculture: hedges restrict the area of open farm fields and so may be thought to impede the ability to farm land in the most efficient and cost-effective manner; farmers sometimes blame hedges for harbouring weeds, pests and diseases that affect crops and birds and small mammals that feed on crops; proper conservation of hedges requires the expenditure of resources which farmers may be unable or unwilling to allocate to this purpose.

Most agricultural and countryside activities are not controlled by the town and country planning legislation because they do not amount to 'development' for the purposes of that legislation. Although there is provision for tree preservation orders to be made for the protection of specified trees, hedges are not covered.

The political interest in countryside conservation matters, and particularly in hedgerows, caused the Department of the Environment to commission a report from the Institute of Terrestrial Ecology and Institute of Freshwater Ecology. The report, *The Countryside Survey 1990*, was published in 1993 though the hedgerow results were published some two years earlier. The report revealed a net decrease in hedgerows by 23 per cent between 1984 and 1990, amounting to a loss of 53,000 miles of hedgerows. Although the report found that most of that loss was due to a change in form such as the replacement of a hedge with a line of trees, 10 per cent was complete loss.

The Government's response to concern over diminishing hedgerows has been a mixture of stick and carrot. In July 1992 the Hedgerow Incentive Scheme was introduced by the Government with £550,000 funding in 1992–3 offering grants towards the cost of maintaining hedges (Countryside Commission Press Release NR/93/2, 21 January 1993 and Department of the Environment, *This Common*

Inheritance: the Second Year Report: Britain's Environmental Strategy (Cm. 2068) (London: HMSO, 1992)). Legislation to preserve hedgerows of particular importance was promised.

Attempts were made to protect hedges by introducing into Parliament two separate private members' Bills. Peter Ainsworth MP introduced his Hedgerows Bill in the 1992–3 session which would have made it an offence to destroy or reduce the quality of hedgerows on certain types of land unless planning permission had been granted. The Bill, which was opposed by members representing farming and land-owning interests, ran out of Parliamentary time but was supported by the Government. A second Hedgerows Bill was introduced by Peter Hardy MP in the 1993–4 session but this too made no progress.

The Government subsequently stated that, partly due to the Countryside Stewardship and Environmentally Sensitive Area Schemes, the rate of hedgerow removal had decreased to a loss of 3,600 km per year between 1990 and 1993 and that the rate of removal was being exceeded by the rate of new planting (Hansard, HC, 21 July 1994, col. 470). Nevertheless, the Government made it clear that it remained committed to protecting hedges of key importance.

Sections 97 to 99 of the Environment Act were enacted to implement this policy. They are enabling provisions and were brought into force on 21 September 1995.

22.2 PROTECTION OF HEDGEROWS

The provision for the protection of hedgerows is not set out in the Environment Act itself but s. 97 confers power to make regulations for 'the protection of important hedgerows in England or Wales'. It should be noted that this power does not extend to Scotland.

The protection is to be confined to 'important' hedgerows and what is or is not to be important for this purpose is to be determined in accordance with criteria prescribed by the regulations. The regulations may make it an offence to remove protected hedgerows or to carry out prescribed acts in relation to them. The regulations may apply provisions of the planning Acts (as defined in the Town and Country Planning Act 1990, s. 336(1)), with or without modifications.

During the second reading debate in the House of Lords, Viscount Ullswater gave an indication of the scheme envisaged by the Government:

Our aim is to introduce a scheme which is fair, reasonable and practical; and which minimises the burden both on those who are subject to these controls and those who administer them. We consider that these aims are best met through a notification scheme. Land managers would be required to give notice of their intention to remove hedgerows to the local planning authority who would have 28 days in which to refuse a proposal. If the land manager hears nothing within the 28-day period, the proposed work may go ahead.

We plan to limit the requirement to notify to rural hedges. The results of our surveys show that widespread removal in the countryside is not the problem it was, but significant numbers of rural hedges are still being removed. Newly planted hedges will be excluded so as not to discourage new planting. We regard it as essential that controls are focused only on the most important hedges; for example, the ancient parish boundary hedge for which no amount of replanting can substitute. We propose, therefore, that local planning authorities should be required to make their decisions in accordance with statutory criteria, prescribed in regulations. We have research in hand to develop and test workable criteria.

We propose that there should be a right of appeal against a local planning authority's refusal of a notice to [the Secretary of State for the Environment], in respect of England, and to the Secretary of State for Wales, in respect of Wales. (Hansard, HL, 15 December 1994, col. 1379.)

The regulations will prove controversial because of the inevitable conflict between environmental and conservation interests and the interests of farmers and landowners. Before making the regulations Ministers must consult bodies representative of business interests likely to be affected by the regulations (e.g., the National Farmers Union), bodies representative of interests of owners or occupiers of land (e.g., the Country Landowners Association), bodies representing the interests of local authorities and statutory bodies, such as the Countryside Commission, the Nature Conservancy Council for England and the Historic Buildings and Monuments Commission for England, whose functions include the provision to Government of advice on matters relating to the conservation in England and Wales of natural beauty or amenity, or flora or fauna, or features of archaeological or historic interest. The regulations will be subject to affirmative Parliamentary procedure, i.e., they will require to be approved by resolution of each House of Parliament.

Viscount Ullswater declined to give a commitment on when the regulations would be made but stated that it is the Government's intention to have the hedgerows regulations in place as soon as possible allowing time for consultation and for securing the approval of both Houses of Parliament (Hansard, HL, 9 February 1995, col. 397).

During the passage of s. 97 through Parliament attempts were made to extend its scope to cover stone walls (or, in Scotland, dykes) and ponds. While affirming their interest in the preservation of these features of the countryside the Government was not persuaded that statutory protection was required.

22.3   GRANTS FOR PURPOSES CONDUCIVE TO CONSERVATION

While the hedgerow regulations to be made under Environment Act, s. 97 will apply the stick, the carrot will be provided by grants to be made under s. 98. That section confers powers on Ministers to make regulations establishing schemes for England, Wales and Scotland for the payment of grants to persons who do, or undertake to do, things which are conducive to the conservation or enhancement of the natural beauty or amenity of the countryside (including its flora and fauna and geological and physiographical features) or of any features of archaeological interest there or the promotion of the enjoyment of the countryside by the public.

The grants may be made subject to conditions and may be required to be repaid if such conditions are breached.

22.4   CONSULTATION BEFORE MAKING CERTAIN SUBORDINATE CONSERVATION LEGISLATION

Under Environment Act, s. 99 the Minister of Agriculture, Fisheries and Food is required to consult the Secretary of State, the Countryside Commission, the Nature Conservancy Council for England and the Historic Buildings and Monuments Commission for England before making the schemes and regulations listed in s. 99(3) and (4). Broadly speaking, the schemes and regulations concern the management of land and their purpose is the promotion of the conservation or enhancement of the natural beauty or amenity of the countryside (including its flora and fauna and geological and physiographical features) or of any features of archaeological interest there or the enjoyment of the countryside by the public.

The purpose of this provision, which is confined to English subordinate legislation, is to coordinate the activities of the Government agencies and statutory bodies having functions in this area.

CHAPTER 23
Scottish Statutory Nuisances

The legislation for the control of statutory nuisances in England and Wales is contained in Part III of the EPA 1990, as amended by the Noise and Statutory Nuisance Act 1993. The Environment Act extends those provisions to Scotland by repealing EPA 1990, s. 83 which had previously provided that they were not to apply there. The Environment Act, sch. 17 makes the technical modifications to the provisions which are required to make them consistent with general legislation, and the system for the administration of justice, in Scotland.

A detailed exposition of Part III of the EPA 1990 would be beyond the scope of this work. Briefly, each local authority is placed under a duty to cause its area to be inspected to detect statutory nuisances. 'Statutory nuisances' are defined in EPA 1990, s. 79(1) and may include things such as premises being in a state prejudicial to health, smoke, fumes, gas, dust, smells, effluvia, deposits and noise.

The local authority may serve an abatement notice for any statutory nuisance on the person responsible requiring the nuisance to be abated or prohibiting or restricting its recurrence and/or requiring the execution of works or the taking of any other appropriate steps. There are special provisions relating to abatement notices which relate to noise in streets. Subject to rights of appeal, non-compliance with an abatement notice is a criminal offence but in most cases it is a defence to prove that the best practicable means were used to prevent, or to counteract the effects of, the nuisance. Where an abatement notice is not complied with, the local authority may, in addition to taking criminal or civil proceedings, abate the nuisance itself, recover the reasonable expenses of doing so from the person responsible and make charging orders.

Any person aggrieved by a statutory nuisance is given the right to make complaints to the magistrates' court (or, in Scotland, the sheriff) who may make orders for the abatement etc. of the nuisance. No equivalent right is conferred by the provisions relating to contaminated land contained in the new EPA 1990, Pt. IIA and described in chapter 16 above.

The provisions relating to statutory nuisance in EPA 1990, Pt. III no longer apply to the extent that the statutory nuisance consists of, or is caused by, land being in a contaminated state (see 16.1.3 above).

At the time of writing no order has been made to bring into force the provisions in the Environment Act extending the statutory nuisance regime to Scotland.

Environment Act 1995

ARRANGEMENT OF SECTIONS

PART I

THE ENVIRONMENT AGENCY AND THE SCOTTISH ENVIRONMENT PROTECTION AGENCY

CHAPTER I

THE ENVIRONMENT AGENCY

Establishment of the Agency

CHAPTER II

THE SCOTTISH ENVIRONMENT PROTECTION AGENCY

Establishment of SEPA

CHAPTER III

MISCELLANEOUS, GENERAL AND SUPPLEMENTAL PROVISIONS RELATING TO THE NEW AGENCIES

Additional general powers and duties

PART II

CONTAMINATED LAND AND ABANDONED MINES

PART III

NATIONAL PARKS

Purposes of National Parks

Establishment of National Park authorities

Functions of National Park authorities

Finances of National Park authorities

Supplemental provisions

PART IV

AIR QUALITY

PART V

MISCELLANEOUS, GENERAL AND SUPPLEMENTAL PROVISIONS

Waste

Mineral planning permissions

Hedgerows etc.

Drainage

Fisheries

New provisions for Scotland

Environment Act 1995

An Act to provide for the establishment of a body corporate to be known as the Environment Agency and a body corporate to be known as the Scottish Environment Protection Agency; to provide for the transfer of functions, property, rights and liabilities to those bodies and for the conferring of other functions on them; to make provision with respect to contaminated land and abandoned mines; to make further provision in relation to National Parks; to make further provision for the control of pollution, the conservation of natural resources and the conservation or enhancement of the environment; to make provision for imposing obligations on certain persons in respect of certain products or materials; to make provision in relation to fisheries; to make provision for certain enactments to bind the Crown; to make provision with respect to the application of certain enactments in relation to the Isles of Scilly; and for connected purposes.   [19 July 1995]

BE IT ENACTED by the Queen's most Excellent Majesty, by and with the advice and consent of the Lords Spiritual and Temporal, and Commons, in this present Parliament assembled, and by the authority of the same, as follows:—

PART I

THE ENVIRONMENT AGENCY AND THE SCOTTISH ENVIRONMENT PROTECTION AGENCY

CHAPTER I

THE ENVIRONMENT AGENCY

Establishment of the Agency

1. The Environment Agency

   (1)   There shall be a body corporate to be known as the Environment Agency or, in Welsh, Asiantaeth yr Amgylchedd (in this Act referred to as 'the Agency'), for the purpose of carrying out the functions transferred or assigned to it by or under this Act.

   (2)   The Agency shall consist of not less than eight nor more than fifteen members of whom—

   (a)   three shall be appointed by the Minister; and

   (b)   the others shall be appointed by the Secretary of State.

   (3)   The Secretary of State shall designate—

   (a)   one of the members as the chairman of the Agency, and

   (b)   another of them as the deputy chairman of the Agency.

   (4)   In appointing a person to be a member of the Agency, the Secretary of State or, as the case may be, the Minister shall have regard to the desirability of appointing a person

who has experience of, and has shown capacity in, some matter relevant to the functions of the Agency.

(5) Subject to the provisions of section 36 below, the Agency shall not be regarded—

(a) as the servant or agent of the Crown, or as enjoying any status, immunity or privilege of the Crown; or

(b) by virtue of any connection with the Crown, as exempt from any tax, duty, rate, levy or other charge whatsoever, whether general or local;

and the Agency's property shall not be regarded as property of, or property held on behalf of, the Crown.

(6) The provisions of Schedule 1 to this Act shall have effect with respect to the Agency.

Transfer of functions, property etc. to the Agency

2. Transfer of functions to the Agency

(1) On the transfer date there shall by virtue of this section be transferred to the Agency—

(a) the functions of the National Rivers Authority, that is to say—

(i) its functions under or by virtue of Part II (water resources management) of the Water Resources Act 1991 (in this Part referred to as 'the 1991 Act');

(ii) its functions under or by virtue of Part III of that Act (control of pollution of water resources);

(iii) its functions under or by virtue of Part IV of that Act (flood defence) and the Land Drainage Act 1991 and the functions transferred to the Authority by virtue of section 136(8) of the Water Act 1989 and paragraph 1(3) of Schedule 15 to that Act (transfer of land drainage functions under local statutory provisions and subordinate legislation);

(iv) its functions under or by virtue of Part VII of the 1991 Act (land and works powers);

(v) its functions under or by virtue of the Diseases of Fish Act 1937, the Sea Fisheries Regulation Act 1966, the Salmon and Freshwater Fisheries Act 1975, Part V of the 1991 Act or any other enactment relating to fisheries;

(vi) the functions as a navigation authority, harbour authority or conservancy authority which were transferred to the Authority by virtue of Chapter V of Part III of the Water Act 1989 or paragraph 23(3) of Schedule 13 to that Act or which have been transferred to the Authority by any order or agreement under Schedule 2 to the 1991 Act;

(vii) its functions under Schedule 2 to the 1991 Act;

(viii) the functions assigned to the Authority by or under any other enactment, apart from this Act;

(b) the functions of waste regulation authorities, that is to say, the functions conferred or imposed on them by or under—

(i) the Control of Pollution (Amendment) Act 1989, or

(ii) Part II of the Environmental Protection Act 1990 (in this Part referred to as 'the 1990 Act'),

or assigned to them by or under any other enactment, apart from this Act;

(c) the functions of disposal authorities under or by virtue of the waste regulation provisions of the Control of Pollution Act 1974;

(d) the functions of the chief inspector for England and Wales constituted under section 16(3) of the 1990 Act, that is to say, the functions conferred or imposed on him by or under Part I of that Act or assigned to him by or under any other enactment, apart from this Act;

(e) the functions of the chief inspector for England and Wales appointed under section 4(2)(a) of the Radioactive Substances Act 1993, that is to say, the functions conferred or imposed on him by or under that Act or assigned to him by or under any other enactment, apart from this Act;

(f)   the functions conferred or imposed by or under the Alkali, &c, Works Regulation Act 1906 (in this section referred to as 'the 1906 Act') on the chief, or any other, inspector (within the meaning of that Act), so far as exercisable in relation to England and Wales;

(g)   so far as exercisable in relation to England and Wales, the functions in relation to improvement notices and prohibition notices under Part I of the Health and Safety at Work etc. Act 1974 (in this section referred to as 'the 1974 Act') of inspectors appointed under section 19 of that Act by the Secretary of State in his capacity as the enforcing authority responsible in relation to England and Wales for the enforcement of the 1906 Act and section 5 of the 1974 Act; and

(h)   the functions of the Secretary of State specified in subsection (2) below.

(2)   The functions of the Secretary of State mentioned in subsection (1)(h) above are the following, that is to say—

(a)   so far as exercisable in relation to England and Wales, his functions under section 30(1) of the Radioactive Substances Act 1993 (power to dispose of radioactive waste);

(b)   his functions under Chapter III of Part IV of the Water Industry Act 1991 in relation to special category effluent, within the meaning of that Chapter, other than any function of making regulations or of making orders under section 139 of that Act;

(c)   so far as exercisable in relation to England and Wales, the functions conferred or imposed on him by virtue of his being, for the purposes of Part I of the 1974 Act, the authority which is by any of the relevant statutory provisions made responsible for the enforcement of the 1906 Act and section 5 of the 1974 Act;

(d)   so far as exercisable in relation to England and Wales, his functions under, or under regulations made by virtue of, section 9 of the 1906 Act (registration of works), other than any functions of his as an appellate authority or any function of making regulations;

(e)   so far as exercisable in relation to England and Wales, his functions under regulations 7(1) and 8(2) of, and paragraph 2(2)(c) of Schedule 2 to, the Sludge (Use in Agriculture) Regulations 1989 (which relate to the provision of information and the testing of soil).

(3)   The National Rivers Authority and the London Waste Regulation Authority are hereby abolished.

3.   Transfer of property, rights and liabilities to the Agency

(1)   On the transfer date—

(a)   the property, rights and liabilities—

(i)   of the National Rivers Authority, and

(ii)   of the London Waste Regulation Authority,

shall, by virtue of this paragraph, be transferred to and vested in the Agency;

(b)   any property, rights or liabilities which are the subject of—

(i)   a scheme made under the following provisions of this section by the Secretary of State, or

(ii)   a scheme made under those provisions by a body which is a waste regulation authority and approved (with or without modifications) under those provisions by the Secretary of State,

shall be transferred to and vested in the Agency by and in accordance with the scheme.

(2)   The Secretary of State may, before the transfer date, make a scheme for the transfer to the Agency of such of—

(a)   his property, rights and liabilities, or

(b)   the property, rights and liabilities of any of the inspectors or chief inspectors mentioned in subsection (1) of section 2 above,

as appear to the Secretary of State appropriate to be so transferred in consequence of the transfer of any functions to the Agency by virtue of any of paragraphs (d) to (h) of that subsection.

(3)   It shall be the duty of every body which is a waste regulation authority, other than the London Waste Regulation Authority—

(a) to make a scheme, after consultation with the Agency, for the transfer to the Agency of such of the body's property, rights and liabilities as appear to the body appropriate to be so transferred in consequence of the transfer of any functions to the Agency by virtue of section 2(1)(b) or (c) above; and

(b) to submit that scheme to the Secretary of State for his approval before such date as he may direct.

(4) Any body preparing a scheme in pursuance of subsection (3) above shall take into account any guidance given by the Secretary of State as to the provisions which he regards as appropriate for inclusion in the scheme.

(5) Where a scheme under subsection (3) above is submitted to the Secretary of State, he may—

(a) approve the scheme;

(b) approve the scheme subject to such modifications as he considers appropriate; or

(c) reject the scheme;

but the power conferred on the Secretary of State by paragraph (b) above shall only be exercisable after consultation with the body which submitted the scheme to him and with the Agency.

(6) The Secretary of State may, in the case of any body which is required to make a scheme under subsection (3) above, himself make a scheme for the transfer to the Agency of such of the body's property, rights or liabilities as appear to him appropriate to be so transferred in consequence of the transfer of any functions to the Agency by virtue of section 2(1)(b) or (c) above, if—

(a) the body fails to submit a scheme under subsection (3) above to him for approval before the due date; or

(b) the Secretary of State rejects a scheme under that subsection submitted to him by that body;

but nothing in this subsection shall prevent the Secretary of State from approving any scheme which may be submitted to him after the due date.

(7) The Secretary of State may, at any time before the transfer date, modify any scheme made or approved by him under this section but only after consultation with the Agency and, in the case of a scheme which was approved by him (with or without modifications), after consultation with the body which submitted the scheme to him for approval.

(8) Schedule 2 to this Act shall have effect in relation to transfers by or under this section.

4. Principal aim and objectives of the Agency

(1) It shall be the principal aim of the Agency (subject to and in accordance with the provisions of this Act or any other enactment and taking into account any likely costs) in discharging its functions so to protect or enhance the environment, taken as a whole, as to make the contribution towards attaining the objective of achieving sustainable development mentioned in subsection (3) below.

(2) The Ministers shall from time to time give guidance to the Agency with respect to objectives which they consider it appropriate for the Agency to pursue in the discharge of its functions.

(3) The guidance given under subsection (2) above must include guidance with respect to the contribution which, having regard to the Agency's responsibilities and resources, the Ministers consider it appropriate for the Agency to make, by the discharge of its functions, towards attaining the objective of achieving sustainable development.

(4) In discharging its functions, the Agency shall have regard to guidance given under this section.

(5) The power to give guidance to the Agency under this section shall only be exercisable after consultation with the Agency and such other bodies or persons as the Ministers consider it appropriate to consult in relation to the guidance in question.

(6)   A draft of any guidance proposed to be given under this section shall be laid before each House of Parliament and the guidance shall not be given until after the period of 40 days beginning with the day on which the draft was so laid or, if the draft is laid on different days, the later of the two days.

(7)   If, within the period mentioned in subsection (6) above, either House resolves that the guidance, the draft of which was laid before it, should not be given, the Ministers shall not give that guidance.

(8)   In reckoning any period of 40 days for the purposes of subsection (6) or (7) above, no account shall be taken of any time during which Parliament is dissolved or prorogued or during which both Houses are adjourned for more than four days.

(9)   The Ministers shall arrange for any guidance given under this section to be published in such manner as they consider appropriate.

5.   General functions with respect to pollution control

(1)   The Agency's pollution control powers shall be exercisable for the purpose of preventing or minimising, or remedying or mitigating the effects of, pollution of the environment.

(2)   The Agency shall, for the purpose—

(a)   of facilitating the carrying out of its pollution control functions, or

(b)   of enabling it to form an opinion of the general state of pollution of the environment, compile information relating to such pollution (whether the information is acquired by the Agency carrying out observations or is obtained in any other way).

(3)   If required by either of the Ministers to do so, the Agency shall—

(a)   carry out assessments (whether generally or for such particular purpose as may be specified in the requirement) of the effect, or likely effect, on the environment of existing or potential levels of pollution of the environment and report its findings to that Minister; or

(b)   prepare and send to that Minister a report identifying—

(i)   the options which the Agency considers to be available for preventing or minimising, or remedying or mitigating the effects of, pollution of the environment, whether generally or in cases or circumstances specified in the requirement; and

(ii)   the costs and benefits of such options as are identified by the Agency pursuant to sub-paragraph (i) above.

(4)   The Agency shall follow developments in technology and techniques for preventing or minimising, or remedying or mitigating the effects of, pollution of the environment.

(5)   In this section, 'pollution control powers' and 'pollution control functions', in relation to the Agency, mean respectively its powers or its functions under or by virtue of the following enactments, that is to say—

(a)   the Alkali, &c, Works Regulation Act 1906;

(b)   Part I of the Health and Safety at Work etc. Act 1974;

(c)   Part I of the Control of Pollution Act 1974;

(d)   the Control of Pollution (Amendment) Act 1989;

(e)   Parts I, II and IIA of the 1990 Act (integrated pollution control etc, waste on land and contaminated land);

(f)   Chapter III of Part IV of the Water Industry Act 1991 (special category effluent);

(g)   Part III and sections 161 to 161D of the 1991 Act (control of pollution of water resources);

(h)   the Radioactive Substances Act 1993;

(j)   regulations made by virtue of section 2(2) of the European Communities Act 1972, to the extent that the regulations relate to pollution.

6.   General provisions with respect to water

(1)   It shall be the duty of the Agency, to such extent as it considers desirable, generally to promote—

(a) the conservation and enhancement of the natural beauty and amenity of inland and coastal waters and of land associated with such waters;

(b) the conservation of flora and fauna which are dependent on an aquatic environment; and

(c) the use of such waters and land for recreational purposes;

and it shall be the duty of the Agency, in determining what steps to take in performance of the duty imposed by virtue of paragraph (c) above, to take into account the needs of persons who are chronically sick or disabled.

This subsection is without prejudice to the duties of the Agency under section 7 below.

(2) It shall be the duty of the Agency to take all such action as it may from time to time consider, in accordance with any directions given under section 38 below, to be necessary or expedient for the purpose—

(a) of conserving, redistributing or otherwise augmenting water resources in England and Wales; and

(b) of securing the proper use of water resources in England and Wales;

but nothing in this subsection shall be construed as relieving any water undertaker of the obligation to develop water resources for the purpose of performing any duty imposed on it by virtue of section 37 of the Water Industry Act 1991 (general duty to maintain water supply system).

(3) The provisions of the 1991 Act relating to the functions of the Agency under Chapter II of Part II of that Act and the related water resources provisions so far as they relate to other functions of the Agency shall not apply to so much of any inland waters as—

(a) are part of the River Tweed;

(b) are part of the River Esk or River Sark at a point where either of the banks of the river is in Scotland; or

(c) are part of any tributary stream of the River Esk or the River Sark at a point where either of the banks of the tributary stream is in Scotland.

(4) Subject to section 106 of the 1991 Act (obligation to carry out flood defence functions through committees), the Agency shall in relation to England and Wales exercise a general supervision over all matters relating to flood defence.

(5) The Agency's flood defence functions shall extend to the territorial sea adjacent to England and Wales in so far as—

(a) the area of any regional flood defence committee includes any area of that territorial sea; or

(b) section 165(2) or (3) of the 1991 Act (drainage works for the purpose of defence against sea water or tidal water, and works etc to secure an adequate outfall for a main river) provides for the exercise of any power in the territorial sea.

(6) It shall be the duty of the Agency to maintain, improve and develop salmon fisheries, trout fisheries, freshwater fisheries and eel fisheries.

(7) The area in respect of which the Agency shall carry out its functions relating to fisheries shall be the whole of England and Wales, together with—

(a) such part of the territorial sea adjacent to England and Wales as extends for six miles from the baselines from which the breadth of that sea is measured, and

(b) in the case of—

(i) the Diseases of Fish Act 1937,

(ii) the Salmon and Freshwater Fisheries Act 1975,

(iii) Part V of the 1991 Act (general control of fisheries), and

(iv) subsection (6) above,

so much of the River Esk, with its banks and tributary streams up to their source, as is situated in Scotland, and

(c) in the case of sections 31 to 34 and 36(2) of the Salmon and Freshwater Fisheries Act 1975 as applied by section 39(1B) of that Act, so much of the catchment area of the River Esk as is situated in Scotland, but, in the case of the enactments specified in paragraph (b) above, excluding the River Tweed.

(8)   In this section—

'miles' means international nautical miles of 1,852 metres;

'the related water resources provisions' has the same meaning as it has in the 1991 Act;

'the River Tweed' means 'the river' within the meaning of the Tweed Fisheries Amendment Act 1859 as amended by byelaws.

7.   General environmental and recreational duties

(1) It shall be the duty of each of the Ministers and of the Agency, in formulating or considering—

(a)   any proposals relating to any functions of the Agency other than its pollution control functions, so far as may be consistent—

(i)   with the purposes of any enactment relating to the functions of the Agency,

(ii)   in the case of each of the Ministers, with the objective of achieving sustainable development,

(iii)   in the case of the Agency, with any guidance under section 4 above,

(iv)   in the case of the Secretary of State, with his duties under section 2 of the Water Industry Act 1991,

so to exercise any power conferred on him or it with respect to the proposals as to further the conservation and enhancement of natural beauty and the conservation of flora, fauna and geological or physiographical features of special interest;

(b)   any proposals relating to pollution control functions of the Agency, to have regard to the desirability of conserving and enhancing natural beauty and of conserving flora, fauna and geological or physiographical features of special interest;

(c)   any proposal relating to any functions of the Agency—

(i)   to have regard to the desirability of protecting and conserving buildings, sites and objects of archaeological, architectural, engineering or historic interest;

(ii)   to take into account any effect which the proposals would have on the beauty or amenity of any rural or urban area or on any such flora, fauna, features, buildings, sites or objects; and

(iii)   to have regard to any effect which the proposals would have on the economic and social well-being of local communities in rural areas.

(2)   Subject to subsection (1) above, it shall be the duty of each of the Ministers and of the Agency, in formulating or considering any proposals relating to any functions of the Agency,—

(a)   to have regard to the desirability of preserving for the public any freedom of access to areas of woodland, mountains, moor, heath, down, cliff or foreshore and other places of natural beauty;

(b)   to have regard to the desirability of maintaining the availability to the public of any facility for visiting or inspecting any building, site or object of archaeological, architectural, engineering or historic interest; and

(c)   to take into account any effect which the proposals would have on any such freedom of access or on the availability of any such facility.

(3)   Subsections (1) and (2) above shall apply so as to impose duties on the Agency in relation to—

(a)   any proposals relating to the functions of a water undertaker or sewerage undertaker,

(b)   any proposals relating to the management, by the company holding an appointment as such an undertaker, of any land for the time being held by that company for any purpose whatever (whether or not connected with the carrying out of the functions of a water undertaker or sewerage undertaker), and

(c)   any proposal which by virtue of section 156(7) of the Water Industry Act 1991 (disposals of protected land) falls to be treated for the purposes of section 3 of that Act as a proposal relating to the functions of a water undertaker or sewerage undertaker, ˙

as they apply in relation to proposals relating to the Agency's own functions, other than its pollution control functions.

(4)   Subject to obtaining the consent of any navigation authority, harbour authority or conservancy authority before doing anything which causes obstruction of, or other interference with, navigation which is subject to the control of that authority, it shall be the duty of the Agency to take such steps as are—

(a)   reasonably practicable, and

(b)   consistent with the purposes of the enactments relating to the functions of the Agency,

for securing, so long as the Agency has rights to the use of water or land associated with water, that those rights are exercised so as to ensure that the water or land is made available for recreational purposes and is so made available in the best manner.

(5)   It shall be the duty of the Agency, in determining what steps to take in performance of any duty imposed by virtue of subsection (4) above, to take into account the needs of persons who are chronically sick or disabled.

(6)   Nothing in this section, the following provisions of this Act or the 1991 Act shall require recreational facilities made available by the Agency to be made available free of charge.

(7)   In this section—

'building' includes structure;

'pollution control functions', in relation to the Agency, has the same meaning as in section 5 above.

8.   Environmental duties with respect to sites of special interest

(1)   Where the Nature Conservancy Council for England or the Countryside Council for Wales is of the opinion that any area of land in England or, as the case may be, in Wales—

(a)   is of special interest by reason of its flora, fauna or geological or physiographical features, and

(b)   may at any time be affected by schemes, works, operations or activities of the Agency or by an authorisation given by the Agency,

that Council shall notify the fact that the land is of special interest for that reason to the Agency.

(2)   Where a National Park authority or the Broads Authority is of the opinion that any area of land in a National Park or in the Broads—

(a)   is land in relation to which the matters for the purposes of which sections 6(1) and 7 above (other than section 7(1)(c)(iii) above) have effect are of particular importance, and

(b)   may at any time be affected by schemes, works, operations or activities of the Agency or by an authorisation given by the Agency,

the National Park authority or Broads Authority shall notify the Agency of the fact that the land is such land, and of the reasons why those matters are of particular importance in relation to the land.

(3)   Where the Agency has received a notification under subsection (1) or (2) above with respect to any land, it shall consult the notifying body before carrying out or authorising any works, operations or activities which appear to the Agency to be likely—

(a)   to destroy or damage any of the flora, fauna, or geological or physiographical features by reason of which the land is of special interest; or

(b)   significantly to prejudice anything the importance of which is one of the reasons why the matters mentioned in subsection (2) above are of particular importance in relation to that land.

(4)   Subsection (3) above shall not apply in relation to anything done in an emergency where particulars of what is done and of the emergency are notified to the Nature Conservancy Council for England, the Countryside Council for Wales, the National Park

authority in question or, as the case may be, the Broads Authority as soon as practicable after that thing is done.

(5)   In this section—

'authorisation' includes any consent or licence;

'the Broads' has the same meaning as in the Norfolk and Suffolk Broads Act 1988; and

'National Park authority', subject to subsection (6) below, means a National Park authority established under section 60 below which has become the local planning authority for the National Park in question.

(6)   As respects any period before a National Park authority established under section 60 below in relation to a National Park becomes the local planning authority for that National Park, any reference in subsections (1) to (4) above to a National Park authority shall be taken as a reference to the National Park Committee or joint or special planning board for that National Park.

9.   Codes of practice with respect to environmental and recreational duties

(1)   Each of the Ministers shall have power by order to approve any code of practice issued (whether by him or by another person) for the purpose of—

(a)   giving practical guidance to the agency with respect to any of the matters for the purposes of which sections 6(1), 7 and 8 above have effect, and

(b)   promoting what appear to him to be desirable practices by the Agency with respect to those matters,

and may at any time by such an order approve a modification of such a code or withdraw his approval of such a code or modification.

(2)   In discharging its duties under section 6(1), 7 or 8 above, the Agency shall have regard to any code of practice, and any modifications of a code of practice, for the time being approved under this section.

(3)   Neither of the Ministers shall make an order under this section unless he has first consulted—

(a)   the Agency;

(b)   the Countryside Commission, the Nature Conservancy Council for England and the Countryside Council for Wales;

(c)   the Historic Buildings and Monuments Commission for England;

(d)   the Sports Council and the Sports Council for Wales; and

(e)   such other persons as he considers it appropriate to consult.

(4)   The power of each of the Ministers to make an order under this section shall be exercisable by statutory instrument; and any statutory instrument containing such an order shall be subject to annulment in pursuance of a resolution of either House of Parliament.

10.   Incidental functions of the Agency

(1)   This section has effect—

(a)   for the purposes of section 35(1) below, as it applies in relation to the Agency; and

(b)   for the construction of any other enactment which, by reference to the functions of the Agency, confers any power on or in relation to the Agency;

and any reference in this section to 'the relevant purposes' is a reference to the purposes described in paragraphs (a) and (b) above.

(2)   For the relevant purposes, the functions of the Agency shall be taken to include the protection against pollution of—

(a)   any waters, whether on the surface or underground, which belong to the Agency or any water undertaker or from which the Agency or any water undertaker is authorised to take water;

(b)   without prejudice to paragraph (a) above, any reservoir which belongs to or is operated by the Agency or any water undertaker or which the Agency or any water undertaker is proposing to acquire or construct for the purpose of being so operated; and

(c) any underground strata from which the Agency or any water undertaker is for the time being authorised to abstract water in pursuance of a licence under Chapter II of Part II of the 1991 Act (abstraction and impounding).

(3) For the relevant purposes, the functions of the Agency shall be taken to include joining with or acting on behalf of one or more relevant undertakers for the purpose of carrying out any works or acquiring any land which at least one of the undertakers with which it joins, or on whose behalf it acts, is authorised to carry out or acquire for the purposes of—

(a) any function of that undertaker under any enactment; or

(b) any function which is taken to be a function of that undertaker for the purposes to which section 217 of the Water Industry Act 1991 applies.

(4) For the relevant purposes, the functions of the Agency shall be taken to include the provision of supplies of water in bulk, whether or not such supplies are provided for the purposes of, or in connection with, the carrying out of any other function of the Agency.

(5) For the relevant purposes, the functions of the Agency shall be taken to include the provision of houses and other buildings for the use of persons employed by the Agency and the provision of recreation grounds for persons so employed.

(6) In this section—

'relevant undertaker' means a water undertaker or sewerage undertaker; and

'supply of water in bulk' means a supply of water for distribution by a water undertaker taking the supply.

Advisory committees

11. Advisory committee for Wales

(1) The Secretary of State shall establish and maintain a committee for advising him with respect to matters affecting, or otherwise connected with, the carrying out in Wales of the Agency's functions.

(2) The committee shall consist of such persons as may from time to time be appointed by the Secretary of State.

(3) The committee shall meet at least once a year.

(4) The Secretary of State may pay to the members of the committee such sums by way of reimbursement (whether in whole or in part) for loss of remuneration, for travelling expenses and for other out-of-pocket expenses as he may determine.

12. Environment protection advisory committees

(1) It shall be the duty of the Agency—

(a) to establish and maintain advisory committees, to be known as Environment Protection Advisory Committees, for the different regions of England and Wales;

(b) to consult the advisory committee for any region as to any proposals of the Agency relating generally to the manner in which the Agency carries out its functions in that region; and

(c) to consider any representations made to it by the advisory committee for any region (whether in response to consultation under paragraph (b) above or otherwise) as to the manner in which the Agency carries out its functions in that region.

(2) The advisory committee for any region shall consist of—

(a) a chairman appointed by the Secretary of State; and

(b) such other members as the Agency may appoint in accordance with the provisions of the approved membership scheme for that region.

(3) In appointing the chairman of any advisory committee, the Secretary of State shall have regard to the desirability of appointing a person who has experience of, and has shown capacity in, some matter relevant to the functions of the committee.

(4) The members of advisory committees appointed by virtue of subsection (2)(b) above—

(a) must not be members of the Agency; but

(b)   must be persons who appear to the Agency to have a significant interest in matters likely to be affected by the manner in which the Agency carries out any of its functions in the region of the advisory committee in question.

(5)   The duty imposed by subsection (1)(a) above to establish and maintain advisory committees is a duty to establish and maintain an advisory committee for each area which the Agency considers it appropriate for the time being to regard as a region of England and Wales for the purposes of this section.

(6)   It shall be the duty of the Agency, in determining the regions for which advisory committees are established and maintained under this section, to ensure that one of those regions consists wholly or mainly of, or of most of, Wales.

(7)   For the purposes of this section, functions of the Agency which are carried out in any area of Scotland, or of the territorial sea which is adjacent to any region for which an advisory committee is maintained, shall be regarded as carried out in that region.

(8)   Schedule 3 to this Act shall have effect with respect to advisory committees.

(9)   In this section—

'advisory committee' means an advisory committee under this section;

'approved membership scheme' means a scheme, as in force for the time being, prepared by the Agency and approved (with or without modification) by the Secretary of State under Schedule 3 to this Act which makes provision with respect to the membership of the advisory committee for a region.

13.   Regional and local fisheries advisory committees

(1)   It shall be the duty of the Agency—

(a)   to establish and maintain advisory committees of persons who are not members of the Agency but appear to it to be interested in salmon fisheries, trout fisheries, freshwater fisheries or eel fisheries in the different parts of the controlled area; and

(b)   to consult those committees as to the manner in which the Agency is to perform its duty under section 6(6) above.

(2)   If the Agency, with the consent of the Ministers, so determines, it shall also be under a duty to consult those committees, or such of them as may be specified or described in the determination, as to—

(a)   the manner in which it is to perform its duties under or by virtue of such of the enactments relating to recreation, conservation or navigation as may be the subject of the determination, or

(b)   such matters relating to recreation, conservation or navigation as may be the subject of the determination.

(3)   Where, by virtue of subsection (2) above, the Agency is under a duty to consult those committees or any of them, there may be included among the members of the committees in question persons who are not members of the Agency but who appear to it to be interested in matters—

(a)   likely to be affected by the manner in which it performs the duties to which the determination in question relates, or

(b)   which are the subject of the determination,

if the Ministers consent to the inclusion of persons of that description.

(4)   The duty to establish and maintain advisory committees imposed by subsection (1) above is a duty to establish and maintain—

(a)   a regional advisory committee for each such region of the controlled area as the Agency considers it appropriate for the time being to regard as a region of that area for the purposes of this section; and

(b)   such local advisory committees as the Agency considers necessary to represent—

(i)   the interests referred to in subsection (1)(a) above, and

(ii)   where persons may be appointed members of those committees by virtue of subsection (3) above by reference to any such interests as are mentioned in that subsection, the interests in question, in the different parts of each such region.

(5) It shall be the duty of the Agency in determining the regions for which regional advisory committees are established and maintained under this section to ensure that one of those regions consists (apart from territorial waters) wholly or mainly of, or of most of, Wales.

(6) In addition to any members appointed under the foregoing provisions of this section, there shall, in the case of each regional advisory committee established and maintained under this section, also be a chairman appointed—

(a) by the Secretary of State, in the case of the committee established and maintained for the region described in subsection (5) above; or

(b) by the Minister, in any other case.

(7) There shall be paid by the Agency—

(a) to the chairman of any regional or local advisory committee established and maintained under this section such remuneration and such travelling and other allowances; and

(b) to any other members of that committee such sums by way of reimbursement (whether in whole or in part) for loss of remuneration, for travelling expenses or for any other out-of-pocket expenses,

as may be determined by one of the Ministers.

(8) In this section 'the controlled area' means the area specified in section 6(7) above in respect of which the Agency carries out functions under section 6(6) above and Part V of the 1991 Act.

Flood defence committees

14. Regional flood defence committees

(1) There shall be committees, known as regional flood defence committees, for the purpose of carrying out the functions which fall to be carried out by such committees by virtue of this Act and the 1991 Act.

(2) Subject to Schedule 4 to this Act (which makes provision for the alteration of the boundaries of and the amalgamation of the areas of regional flood defence committees)—

(a) there shall be a regional flood defence committee for each of the areas for which there was an old committee immediately before the transfer date; but

(b) where under section 165(2) or (3) of the 1991 Act any function of the Agency falls to be carried out at a place beyond the seaward boundaries of the area of any regional flood defence committee, that place shall be assumed for the purposes of this Act and the 1991 Act to be within the area of the regional flood defence committee to whose area the area of sea where that place is situated is adjacent.

(3) The Agency shall maintain a principal office for the area of each regional flood defence committee.

(4) In this section 'old committee' means a regional flood defence committee for the purposes of section 9 of the 1991 Act.

15. Composition of regional flood defence committees

(1) Subject to subsection (2) below, a regional flood defence committee shall consist of the following, none of whom shall be a member of the Agency, that is to say—

(a) a chairman and a number of other members appointed by the relevant Minister;

(b) two members appointed by the Agency;

(c) a number of members appointed by or on behalf of the constituent councils.

(2) Any person who immediately before the transfer date is, by virtue of his appointment—

(a) by a Minister of the Crown,

(b) by or on behalf of any council, or

(c) by the National Rivers Authority,

the chairman or a member of an old committee which, by virtue of section 14 above, is replaced by a new committee shall be treated, on and after that date, for the remainder of the period for which he would, under the terms of his appointment, have held office in relation to the old committee, as if he had been appointed as the chairman or, as the case may be, a member of the new committee, and on the same terms, by that Minister or, as the case may be, by or on behalf of that council or, in the case of a person appointed by the National Rivers Authority, by the Agency.

(3) Subject to section 16 below and to any order under Schedule 4 to this Act amalgamating the areas of any two or more regional flood defence committees—

(a) the total number of members of a new committee for any area shall be the same as the total number of members of the old committee for that area immediately before the transfer date;

(b) the number of members to be appointed to a new committee for any area by or on behalf of each of the constituent councils or, as the case may be, jointly by or on behalf of more than one of them shall be the same as the number of members of the old committee for that area which fell to be so appointed immediately before the transfer date.

(4) In any case where—

(a) the appointment of one or more members of a regional flood defence committee is (by virtue of subsection (3) above or an order under section 16(5) below), to be made jointly by more than one constituent council, and

(b) the councils by whom that appointment is to be made are unable to agree on an appointment,

the member or members in question shall be appointed by the relevant Minister on behalf of those councils.

(5) In appointing a person to be the chairman or a member of a regional flood defence committee under subsection (1)(a) or (c) or (4) above the relevant Minister or, as the case may be, a constituent council shall have regard to the desirability of appointing a person who has experience of, and has shown capacity in, some matter relevant to the functions of the committee.

(6) The councils of every county, county borough, metropolitan district or London borough any part of which is in the area of a regional flood defence committee shall be the constituent councils for the regional flood defence committee for that area, and the Common Council of the City of London shall be a constituent council for the regional flood defence committee for any area which comprises any part of the City.

(7) In this section—

'old committee' has the same meaning as in section 14 above;

'new committee' means a regional flood defence committee established under section 14 above;

'the relevant Minister'—

(a) in relation to the regional flood defence committee for an area the whole or the greater part of which is in Wales, means the Secretary of State; and

(b) in relation to any other regional flood defence committee, means the Minister.

16. Change of composition of regional flood defence committee

(1) The Agency may, in accordance with the following provisions of this section, from time to time make a determination varying the total number of members of a regional flood defence committee.

(2) The Agency shall submit any determination under subsection (1) above to the relevant Minister.

(3) For the purposes of this section—

(a) the total number of members of a regional flood defence committee shall not be less than eleven; and

(b) any determination by the Agency under subsection (1) above that a regional flood defence committee should consist of more than seventeen members shall be provisional and shall take effect only if the relevant Minister makes an order under subsection (4) below.

(4) If the Agency submits a provisional determination to the relevant Minister with respect to any regional flood defence committee and he considers that the committee should consist of more than seventeen members, he may by order made by statutory instrument—

(a) confirm it; or

(b) substitute for the number of members determined by the Agency some other number not less than seventeen.

(5) Subject to the following provisions of this section, whenever—

(a) the total number of members of a regional flood defence committee is varied under this section, or

(b) the relevant Minister considers it necessary or expedient to make an order under this subsection,

the relevant Minister shall by order made by statutory instrument specify the number of members to be appointed to the committee by each of the constituent councils.

(6) An order under subsection (5) above shall relate—

(a) where paragraph (a) of that subsection applies, to times after the coming into force of the variation; and

(b) where paragraph (b) of that subsection applies, to such times as are specified in the order.

(7) An order under subsection (5) above shall be so framed that the total number of members appointed under section 15(1)(a) and (b) above is one less than the number of those appointed by or on behalf of constituent councils.

(8) For the purpose of determining for the purposes of subsection (5) above the number of persons to be appointed to a regional flood defence committee by or on behalf of each constituent council, the relevant Minister—

(a) if he considers it to be inappropriate that that council should appoint a member of the committee, or

(b) if he considers that one or more members should be appointed jointly by that council and one or more other constituent councils,

may include provision to that effect in the order.

(9) In this section—

'member', in relation to a regional flood defence committee, includes the chairman of the committee;

'the relevant Minister' has the same meaning as in section 15 above.

17. Local flood defence schemes and local flood defence committees

(1) A scheme, known as a local flood defence scheme, may be made by the Agency, in accordance with the following provisions of this section—

(a) for the creation in the area of a regional flood defence committee of one or more districts, to be known as local flood defence districts; and

(b) for the constitution, membership, functions and procedure of a committee for each such district, to be known as the local flood defence committee for that district.

(2) Any local flood defence scheme which was made under the 1991 Act or continued in force by virtue of paragraph 14(1) of Schedule 2 to the Water Consolidation (Consequential Provisions) Act 1991 and which, immediately before the transfer date, is in force in relation to the area of a regional flood defence committee, shall on and after that date have effect, and may be amended or revoked, as if it were a local flood defence scheme made under this section in relation to that area; and, accordingly, subject to any such amendment or revocation—

(a) any local flood defence district created by that scheme and in being immediately before that date shall be treated, on and after that date, as a local flood defence district created by a scheme under this section in relation to the area of that regional flood defence committee; and

(b) any local flood defence committee created by that scheme for any such district and in being immediately before that date shall be treated, on and after that date, as the local flood defence committee for that district.

(3) A regional flood defence committee may at any time submit to the Agency—

(a) a local flood defence scheme for any part of their area for which there is then no such scheme in force; or

(b) a scheme varying a local flood defence scheme or revoking such a scheme and, if the committee think fit, replacing it with another such scheme;

and references in the following provisions of this section and in section 18 below to local flood defence schemes are references to schemes under either of paragraphs (a) and (b) above.

(4) Before submitting a scheme to the Agency under subsection (3) above, a regional flood defence committee shall consult—

(a) every local authority any part of whose area will fall within the area to which the scheme is proposed to relate; and

(b) such organisations representative of persons interested in flood defence (within the meaning of Part IV of the 1991 Act) or agriculture as the regional flood defence committee consider to be appropriate.

(5) It shall be the duty of the Agency to send any scheme submitted to it under subsection (3) above to one of the Ministers.

(6) A local flood defence scheme may define a local flood defence district—

(a) by reference to the districts which were local land drainage districts immediately before 1st September 1989;

(b) by reference to the area of the regional flood defence committee in which that district is situated;

(c) by reference to a map;

or partly by one of those means and partly by another or others.

(7) A local flood defence scheme may contain incidental, consequential and supplementary provisions.

(8) Either of the Ministers may approve a local flood defence scheme with or without modifications; and any scheme approved under this subsection shall come into force on a date fixed by the Minister approving it.

18. Composition of local flood defence committees

(1) Subject to subsections (2) and (3) below, a local flood defence scheme shall provide that any local flood defence committee to which it relates shall consist of not less than eleven and not more than fifteen members.

(2) A regional flood defence committee may include in a local flood defence scheme which they submit to the Agency a recommendation that a committee to which the scheme relates should consist of a number of members greater than fifteen; and a scheme so submitted shall be taken to provide for the number of members of a committee if it contains a recommendation under this subsection relating to that committee.

(3) The power conferred on each of the Ministers by section 17(8) above shall include power to direct that a committee to which a recommendation under subsection (2) above relates shall consist either of the recommended number of members or of some other number of members greater than fifteen.

(4) A local flood defence committee shall consist of—

(a) a chairman appointed from among their own members by the regional flood defence committee;

(b) other members appointed by that committee; and

(c) members appointed, in accordance with and subject to the terms of the local flood defence scheme, by or on behalf of constituent councils.

(5) The number of members appointed to a local flood defence committee by or on behalf of constituent councils shall be one more than the total number of members appointed by the regional flood defence committee.

(6) In appointing a person to be a member of a local flood defence committee, the regional flood defence committee shall have regard to the desirability of appointing a person

who has experience of, and has shown capacity in, some matter relevant to the functions of the committee to which he is appointed.

(7) Any person who, immediately before the transfer date is, by virtue of an appointment by an old regional committee or by or on behalf of any council, the chairman or a member of a local flood defence committee which is continued in force by virtue of section 17(2) above shall be treated, on and after that date, for the remainder of the period for which he would, under the terms of his appointment, have held office in relation to the local flood defence committee—

(a) as if he had been appointed as such under this section by the regional flood defence committee or, as the case may be be, by or on behalf of that council; and

(b) in the case of the chairman, as if he were a member of the regional flood defence committee.

(8) The councils of every county, county borough, metropolitan district or London borough any part of which is in a local flood defence district shall be the constituent councils for the local flood defence committee for that district, and the Common Council of the City of London shall be a constituent council for the local flood defence committee of any local flood defence district which comprises any part of the City.

(9) In this section 'old regional committee' means a regional flood defence committee for the purposes of section 9 of the 1991 Act.

19. Membership and proceedings of flood defence committees
Schedule 5 to this Act shall have effect in relation to regional flood defence committees and local flood defence committees.

CHAPTER II

THE SCOTTISH ENVIRONMENT PROTECTION AGENCY

Establishment of SEPA

20. The Scottish Environment Protection Agency
(1) There shall be a body to be known as the Scottish Environment Protection Agency (in this Act referred to as 'SEPA'), for the purpose of carrying out the functions transferred or assigned to it by or under this Act.

(2) Schedule 6 to this Act shall have effect with respect to SEPA.

Transfer of functions, property etc. to SEPA

21. Transfer of functions to SEPA
(1) On the transfer date there shall by virtue of this section be transferred to SEPA—

(a) the functions of river purification authorities, that is to say—

(i) their functions with respect to water resources under or by virtue of Part III of the Rivers (Prevention of Pollution) (Scotland) Act 1951 (in this Part referred to as 'the 1951 Act') and Part II of the Natural Heritage (Scotland) Act 1991;

(ii) their functions with respect to water pollution under or by virtue of Part III of the 1951 Act, the Rivers (Prevention of Pollution) (Scotland) Act 1965 and Part II of the Control of Pollution Act 1974;

(iii) their functions as enforcing authority, in relation to releases of substances into the environment, under or by virtue of Part I of the 1990 Act;

(iv) their functions with respect to flood warning systems under or by virtue of Part VI of the Agriculture Act 1970; and

(v) the functions assigned to them by or under any other enactment apart from this Act;

(b) the functions of waste regulation authorities, that is to say, the functions conferred or imposed on them by or under—

    (i)   the Control of Pollution (Amendment) Act 1989; or

    (ii)   Part II of the 1990 Act,

or assigned to them by or under any other enactment apart from this Act;

    (c)   the functions of disposal authorities under or by virtue of sections 3 to 10, 16, 17(1)(a) and 17(2)(b) to (d) of the Control of Pollution Act 1974;

    (d)   the functions of the chief inspector for Scotland constituted under section 16(3) of the 1990 Act, that is to say, the functions conferred or imposed on him by or under Part I of that Act or assigned to him by or under any other enactment apart from this Act;

    (e)   the functions of the chief inspector for Scotland appointed under section 4(2)(b) of the Radioactive Substances Act 1993, that is to say, the functions conferred or imposed on him by or under that Act or assigned to him by or under any other enactment apart from this Act;

    (f)   the functions conferred or imposed by or under the Alkali, &c, Works Regulation Act 1906 (in this section referred to as 'the 1906 Act') on the chief, or any other, inspector (within the meaning of that Act), so far as exercisable in relation to Scotland;

    (g)   so far as exercisable in relation to Scotland, the functions in relation to improvement notices and prohibition notices under Part I of the Health and Safety at Work etc. Act 1974 (in this section referred to as 'the 1974 Act') of inspectors appointed under section 19 of that Act by the Secretary of State in his capacity as enforcing authority responsible in relation to Scotland for the enforcement of the 1906 Act and section 5 of the 1974 Act;

    (h)   the functions of local authorities as enforcing authority, in relation to releases of substances into the air, under or by virtue of Part I of the 1990 Act; and

    (i)   the functions of the Secretary of State specified in subsection (2) below.

(2) The functions of the Secretary of State mentioned in subsection (1)(i) above are, so far as exercisable in relation to Scotland—

    (a)   the functions conferred or imposed on him by virtue of his being, for the purposes of Part I of the 1974 Act, the authority which is by any of the relevant statutory provisions made responsible for the enforcement of the 1906 Act and section 5 of the 1974 Act;

    (b)   his functions under, or under regulations made by virtue of, section 9 of the 1906 Act (registration of works), other than any functions of his as an appellate authority or any function of making regulations;

    (c)   his functions under section 19 of the Clean Air Act 1993 with respect to the creation of smoke control areas by local authorities; and

    (d)   his functions under section 30(1) of the Radioactive Substances Act 1993 (power to dispose of radioactive waste).

(3) River purification boards shall be dissolved on the transfer date.

22. Transfer of property, rights and liabilities to SEPA

    (1)   On the transfer date—

    (a)   the property, rights and liabilities of every river purification board shall, by virtue of this paragraph, be transferred to and vested in SEPA;

    (b)   any property, rights and liabilities which are the subject of a scheme under this section—

    (i)   made by the Secretary of State; or

    (ii)   made by a local authority and approved by the Secretary of State, shall be transferred to and vested in SEPA by and in accordance with the scheme.

    (2)   The Secretary of State may, before the transfer date, make a scheme for the transfer to SEPA of such of—

    (a)   his property, rights and liabilities; or

    (b)   the property, rights and liabilities of any of the inspectors or chief inspectors mentioned in subsection (1) of section 21 above,

as appear to the Secretary of State appropriate to be so transferred in consequence of the transfer of any functions to SEPA by virtue of that subsection.

(3)   It shall be the duty of every local authority to make a scheme, after consultation with SEPA, for the transfer to SEPA of—

(a)   such of the authority's property and rights as are held by it for the purposes of its functions as—

(i)   a waste regulation authority;

(ii)   a disposal authority under or by virtue of the provisions mentioned in section 21(1)(c) above;

(iii)   enforcing authority, in relation to releases of substances into the air, by virtue of Part I of the 1990 Act; and

(iv)   in the case of an islands council, a river purification authority; and

(b)   such of its liabilities as are liabilities to which it is subject by virtue of its being an authority mentioned in paragraph (a)(i) to (iv) above,

and to submit that scheme to the Secretary of State for his approval before such date as he may direct.

(4)   Any local authority preparing a scheme in pursuance of subsection (3) above shall take into account any guidance given by the Secretary of State as to the provisions which he regards as appropriate for inclusion in the scheme.

(5)   Where a scheme under subsection (3) above is submitted to the Secretary of State, he may—

(a)   approve the scheme;

(b)   approve the scheme subject to such modifications as he considers appropriate; or

(c)   reject the scheme;

but the power conferred on the Secretary of State by paragraph (b) above shall be exercisable only after consultation with the local authority which submitted the scheme to him and with SEPA.

(6)   The Secretary of State may, in the case of any local authority which is required to make a scheme under subsection (3) above, himself make a scheme for the transfer to SEPA of such of the body's property, rights or liabilities as are mentioned in paragraph (a) or (b) of that subsection, if—

(a)   the authority fails to submit a scheme under that subsection to him for his approval before the due date; or

(b)   the Secretary of State rejects a scheme under that subsection submitted to him by the authority;

but nothing in this subsection shall prevent the Secretary of State from approving any scheme which may be submitted to him after the due date.

(7)   Where the Secretary of State makes a transfer scheme under subsection (6) above, he may recover his reasonable expenses in doing so, or such proportion of those expenses as he thinks fit, from the local authority in question by such means as appear to him to be appropriate including, without prejudice to that generality, setting off the expenses payable by the local authority against revenue support grant or non-domestic rate income payable by the Secretary of State to the local authority under paragraph 3 of Schedule 12 to the Local Government Finance Act 1992.

(8)   The Secretary of State may, at any time before the transfer date, modify any scheme made or approved by him under this section but only after consultation with SEPA and, in the case of a scheme which was approved by him (with or without modifications), after consultation with the local authority which submitted the scheme to him for approval.

(9)   Schedule 2 to this Act shall have effect in relation to transfers by or under this section.

23.   Functions of staff commission

The functions of the staff commission established under section 12 of the Local Government etc. (Scotland) Act 1994 shall include—

(a)   considering and keeping under review the arrangements for the transfer to SEPA, in consequence of this Act or of any scheme made under it, of staff employed by local authorities;

(b) considering such staffing problems arising out of, consequential on or connected with any provision of, or scheme made under, this Act as may be referred to them by the Secretary of State or by any local authority;

(c) advising the Secretary of State as to the steps necessary to safeguard the interests of the staff referred to in paragraph (a) above.

Other functions etc. of SEPA

24. Consultation with respect to drainage works

(1) Subject to subsection (2) below, any person proposing to carry out drainage works shall—

(a) before commencing such works, consult SEPA as to precautions to be taken to prevent pollution to controlled waters as a result of the works; and

(b) in carrying out such works, take account of SEPA's views.

(2) The Secretary of State may, by regulations made by statutory instrument subject to annulment in pursuance of a resolution of either House of Parliament, prescribe types of drainage works in relation to which subsection (1) above shall not apply.

(3) In this section, 'drainage works' has the same meaning as in the Land Drainage (Scotland) Act 1958 and 'controlled waters' has the same meaning as in the Control of Pollution Act 1974.

25. Assessing flood risk

(1) Without prejudice to section 92 of the Agriculture Act 1970 (provision of flood warning systems), SEPA shall have the function of assessing, as far as it considers it appropriate, the risk of flooding in any area of Scotland.

(2) If requested by a planning authority to do so, SEPA shall, on the basis of such information as it holds with respect to the risk of flooding in any part of the authority's area, provide the authority with advice as to such risk.

26. Power of SEPA to purchase land compulsorily

(1) The Secretary of State may authorise SEPA, for the purpose of any of its functions, to purchase land compulsorily.

(2) The Acquisition of Land (Authorisation Procedure) (Scotland) Act 1947 shall apply in relation to the compulsory purchase of land under this section as if this section had been in force immediately before the commencement of that Act and, in relation to such purchase of land, SEPA shall be treated as if it were a local authority within the meaning of that Act.

27. Power of SEPA to obtain information about land

(1) Where, with a view to performing a function conferred on it by any enactment, SEPA considers that it ought to have information connected with any land, it may serve on one or more of the persons mentioned in subsection (2) below a notice—

(a) specifying the land, the function and the enactment; and

(b) requiring the recipient of the notice to furnish to SEPA, within such period of not less than 14 days from the date of service of the notice as is specified in the notice—

(i) the nature of his interest in the land; and

(ii) the name and address of each person whom he believes is, as respects the land, a person mentioned in subsection (2) below.

(2) The persons referred to in subsection (1) above are—

(a) the occupier of the land;

(b) any person—

(i) who has an interest in the land as owner, creditor in a heritable security or lessee; or

(ii) who directly or indirectly receives rent for the land; and

(c) any person who, in pursuance of an agreement between himself and a person interested in the land, is authorised to manage the land or to arrange for the letting of it.

(3)   A person who—

(a)   fails to comply with the requirements of a notice served on him in pursuance of subsection (1) above; or

(b)   in furnishing any information in compliance with such a notice makes a statement which he knows to be false in a material particular or recklesssly makes a statement which is false in a material particular,

shall be guilty of an offence and liable on summary conviction to a fine not exceeding level 5 on the standard scale.

28.   Power of SEPA to promote or oppose private legislation

(1)   SEPA may, where it is satisfied that it is expedient to do so—

(a)   with the consent of the Secretary of State, petition for the issue of a provisional order under the Private Legislation Procedure (Scotland) Act 1936; or

(b)   oppose any private legislation in Parliament.

(2)   An application for the consent mentioned in paragraph (a) of subsection (1) above shall be accompanied by a concise summary of the purposes of the order petitioned for.

(3)   In paragraph (b) of subsection (1) above, 'private legislation in Parliament' includes—

(a)   a provisional order and a Confirmation Bill relating to such an order; and

(b)   any local or personal Bill.

29.   Procedure relating to making of byelaws

The following provisions of the Local Government (Scotland) Act 1973—

(a)   section 202 (procedure etc for byelaws);

(b)   section 202C (revocation of byelaws);

(c)   section 204 (evidence of byelaws),

shall apply in relation to SEPA as they apply in relation to a local authority, provided that in the application of the said section 202 to SEPA for subsection (13) there shall be substituted—

'(13) The Scottish Environment Protection Agency shall send a copy of any byelaws made by it to the proper officer of the local authority for any area to the whole or any part of which the byelaws will apply.'.

30.   Records held by SEPA

(1)   Subject to subsection (3) below—

(a)   this section applies to all records (in whatever form or medium)—

(i)   transferred to and vested in SEPA by or under section 22 above;

(ii)   created or acquired by it in the exercise of any of its functions; or

(iii)   otherwise in its keeping;

(b)   SEPA shall ensure that the records, other than such as are mentioned in paragraph (c) below, are preserved and managed in accordance with such arrangements as it, after consulting the Keeper of the Records of Scotland, shall put into effect;

(c)   records which in SEPA's opinion are not worthy of preservation may be disposed of by it;

(d)   SEPA may from time to time revise the arrangements mentioned in paragraph (b) above but before making any material change to those arrangements shall consult the Keeper; and

(e)   SEPA—

(i)   shall secure that the Keeper has, at all reasonable hours, unrestricted access to the records preserved by it;

(ii)   may afford members of the public, free of charge or on payment of reasonable charges, facilities for inspecting and for obtaining copies or extracts from those records.

(2)   Nothing in subsection (1)(e)(ii) above permits infringement of copyright or contravention of conditions subject to which records are in SEPA's keeping.

(3) Insofar as any provision of any enactment, being a provision which relates to records of a specific kind, is (but for this subsection) inconsistent with subsection (1) above, that subsection is subject to the provision in question.

General powers and duties

31. Guidance on sustainable development and other aims and objectives

(1) The Secretary of State shall from time to time give guidance to SEPA with respect to aims and objectives which he considers it appropriate for SEPA to pursue in the performance of its functions.

(2) The guidance given under subsection (1) above must include guidance with respect to the contribution which, having regard to SEPA's responsibilities and resources, the Secretary of State considers it appropriate for SEPA to make, by the performance of its functions, towards attaining the objective of achieving sustainable development.

(3) In performing its functions, SEPA shall have regard to guidance given under this section.

(4) The power to give guidance to SEPA under this section shall be exercisable only after consultation with SEPA and such other bodies or persons as the Secretary of State considers it appropriate to consult in relation to the guidance in question.

(5) A draft of any guidance proposed to be given under this section shall be laid before each House of Parliament and the guidance shall not be given until after the period of 40 days beginning with the day on which the draft was so laid or, if the draft is laid on different days, the later of the two days.

(6) If, within the period mentioned in subsection (5) above, either House resolves that the guidance, the draft of which was laid before it, should not be given, the Secretary of State shall not give that guidance.

(7) In reckoning any period of 40 days for the purposes of subsection (5) or (6) above, no account shall be taken of any time during which Parliament is dissolved or prorogued or during which both Houses are adjourned for more than four days.

(8) The Secretary of State shall arrange for any guidance given under this section to be published in such manner as he considers appropriate.

32. General environmental and recreational duties

(1) It shall be the duty of the Secretary of State and of SEPA, in formulating or considering any proposals relating to any functions of SEPA—

(a) to have regard to the desirability of conserving and enhancing the natural heritage of Scotland;

(b) to have regard to the desirability of protecting and conserving buildings, sites and objects of archaeological, architectural, engineering or historic interest;

(c) to take into account any effect which the proposals would have on the natural heritage of Scotland or on any such buildings, sites or objects; and

(d) to have regard to the social and economic needs of any area or description of area of Scotland and, in particular, to such needs of rural areas.

(2) Subject to subsection (1) above, it shall be the duty of the Secretary of State and of SEPA, in formulating or considering any proposals relating to any functions of SEPA—

(a) to have regard to the desirability of preserving for the public any freedom of access (including access for recreational purposes) to areas of forest, woodland, mountains, moor, bog, cliff, foreshore, loch or reservoir and other places of natural beauty;

(b) to have regard to the desirability of maintaining the availability to the public of any facility for visiting or inspecting any building, site or object of archaeological, architectural, engineering or historic interest; and

(c) to take into account any effect which the proposals would have on any such freedom of access or on the availability of any such facility.

(3) In this section—

'building' includes structure; and
'the natural heritage of Scotland' has the same meaning as in section 1(3) of the Natural
Heritage (Scotland) Act 1991.

33. General duties with respect to pollution control

(1)   SEPA's pollution control powers shall be exercisable for the purpose of preventing
or minimising, or remedying or mitigating the effects of, pollution of the environment.

(2)   SEPA shall, for the purpose—

(a)   of facilitating the carrying out of its pollution control functions; or

(b)   of enabling it to form an opinion of the general state of pollution of the
environment,
compile information relating to such pollution (whether the information is acquired by
SEPA carrying out observations or is obtained in any other way).

(3)   If required by the Secretary of State to do so, SEPA shall—

(a)   carry out assessments (whether generally or for such particular purpose as may be
specified in the requirement) of the effect, or likely effect, on the environment of existing
or potential levels of pollution of the environment and report its findings to the Secretary
of State; or

(b)   prepare and send to the Secretary of State a report identifying—

(i)   the options which SEPA considers to be available for preventing or minimising, or remedying or mitigating the effects of, pollution of the environment, whether
generally or in cases or circumstances specified in the requirement; and

(ii)   the costs and benefits of such options as are identified by SEPA pursuant to
sub-paragraph (i) above.

(4)   SEPA shall follow developments in technology and techniques for preventing or
minimising, or remedying or mitigating the effects of, pollution of the environment.

(5)   In this section, 'pollution control powers' and 'pollution control functions' in
relation to SEPA, mean respectively its powers or its functions under or by virtue of—

(a)   the Alkali, &c. Works Regulation Act 1906;

(b)   Part III of the 1951 Act, the Rivers (Prevention of Pollution) (Scotland) Act 1965
and Parts I, IA and II of the Control of Pollution Act 1974;

(c)   Part I of the Health and Safety at Work etc Act 1974;

(d)   the Control of Pollution (Amendment) Act 1989;

(e)   Parts I, II and IIA of the 1990 Act;

(f)   section 19 of the Clean Air Act 1993;

(g)   the Radioactive Substances Act 1993; and

(h)   regulations made by virtue of section 2(2) of the European Communities Act
1972, to the extent that the regulations relate to pollution.

34. General duties with respect to water

(1)   It shall be the duty of SEPA—

(a)   to promote the cleanliness of—

(i)   rivers, other inland waters and ground waters in Scotland; and

(ii)   the tidal waters of Scotland; and

(b)   to conserve so far as practicable the water resources of Scotland.

(2)   Without prejudice to section 32 above, it shall be the duty of SEPA, to such extent
as it considers desirable, generally to promote—

(a)   the conservation and enhancement of the natural beauty and amenity of inland
and coastal waters and of land associated with such waters; and

(b)   the conservation of flora and fauna which are dependent on an aquatic environment.

(3)   Subsection (1) above is without prejudice to section 1 of the Water (Scotland) Act
1980 (general duties of Secretary of State and water authorities as respects water resources
and supplies).

(4)   In subsection (1) above, 'tidal waters' means any part of the sea or the tidal part of any river, watercourse or inland water (whether natural or artificial) and includes the waters of any enclosed dock which adjoins tidal waters.

35.   Environmental duties as respects Natural Heritage Areas and sites of special interest

(1)   Where an area of land—

(a)   has been designated, under section 6(2) of the Natural Heritage (Scotland) Act 1991 (in this section referred to as 'the 1991 Act') as a Natural Heritage Area; or

(b)   is, in the opinion of Scottish Natural Heritage (in this section referred to as 'SNH'), of special interest by reason of its flora, fauna or geological or physiographical features,

and SNH consider that it may at any time be affected by schemes, works, operations or activities of SEPA or by an authorisation given by SEPA, SNH shall give notice to SEPA in accordance with subsection (2) below.

(2)   A notice under subsection (1) above shall specify—

(a)   in the case of an area of land mentioned in paragraph (a) of that subsection, SNH's reasons for considering that the area is of outstanding value to the natural heritage of Scotland;

(b)   in the case of an area of land mentioned in paragraph (b) of that subsection, SNH's reasons for holding the opinion there mentioned; and

(3)   Where SNH has given notice under subsection (1) above in respect of an area of land and—

(a)   in the case of an area of land mentioned in paragraph (a) of that subsection, the designation is cancelled or varied under section 6(7) of the 1991 Act; or

(b)   in the case of an area of land mentioned in paragraph (b) of that subsection, SNH ceases to be of the opinion there mentioned, SNH shall forthwith notify SEPA of that fact.

(4)   Where SEPA has received notice under subsection (1) above with respect to any area of land, it shall (unless SNH has given notice under subsection (3) above with respect to the land) consult SNH before carrying out or authorising any schemes, works, operations or activities which appear to SEPA to be likely—

(a)   in the case of an area of land mentioned in subsection (1)(a), significantly to prejudice the value of the land, or any part of it, as a Natural Heritage Area; and

(b)   in the case of an area of land mentioned in subsection (1)(b), to destroy or damage any of the flora or fauna or features by reason of which SNH formed the opinion there mentioned.

(5)   Subsection (4) above shall not apply in relation to anything done in an emergency if particulars of what is done and of the emergency are notified by SEPA to SNH as soon as practicable after the thing is done.

(6)   In this section, 'authorisation' includes any consent, licence or permission.

(7)   Any expression used in this section and in Part I of the 1991 Act and not defined in this Act shall be construed in accordance with that Part.

36.   Codes of practice with respect to environmental and recreational duties

(1)   The Secretary of State shall have power by order to approve any code of practice issued (whether by him or by another person) for the purpose of—

(a)   giving practical guidance to SEPA with respect to any of the matters for the purposes of which sections 32, 34(2) and 35 above have effect; and

(b)   promoting what appear to him to be desirable practices by SEPA with respect to those matters,

and may at any time by such an order approve a modification of such a code or withdraw his approval of such a code or modification.

(2)   In discharging its duties under section 32, 34(2) or 35 above, SEPA shall have regard to any code of practice, and any modifications of a code of practice, for the time being approved under this section.

(3) The Secretary of State shall not make an order under this section unless he has first consulted—

(a) SEPA;

(b) Scottish Natural Heritage;

(c) Scottish Enterprise;

(d) Highlands and Islands Enterprise;

(e) the East of Scotland Water Authority;

(f) the West of Scotland Water Authority;

(g) the North of Scotland Water Authority; and

(h) such other persons as he considers it appropriate to consult.

(4) The power of the Secretary of State to make an order under this section shall be exercisable by statutory instrument; and any statutory instrument containing such an order shall be subject to annulment in pursuance of a resolution of either House of Parliament.

CHAPTER III

MISCELLANEOUS, GENERAL AND SUPPLEMENTAL PROVISIONS RELATING TO THE NEW AGENCIES

Additional general powers and duties

37. Incidental general functions

(1) Each new Agency (that is to say, in this Part, the Agency or SEPA)—

(a) may do anything which, in its opinion, is calculated to facilitate, or is conducive or incidental to, the carrying out of its functions; and

(b) without prejudice to the generality of that power, may, for the purposes of, or in connection with, the carrying out of those functions, acquire and dispose of land and other property and carry out such engineering or building operations as it considers appropriate; and the Agency may institute criminal proceedings in England and Wales.

(2) It shall be the duty of each new Agency to provide the Secretary of State or the Minister with such advice and assistance as he may request.

(3) Subject to subsection (4) below, each new Agency may provide for any person, whether in or outside the United Kingdom, advice or assistance, including training facilities, as respects any matter in which that new Agency has skill or experience.

(4) Without prejudice to any power of either new Agency apart from subsection (3) above to provide advice or assistance of the kind mentioned in that subsection, the power conferred by that subsection shall not be exercised in a case where the person for whom the advice or assistance is provided is outside the United Kingdom, except with the consent in writing of the appropriate Minister which consent may be given subject to such conditions as the Minister giving it thinks fit.

(5) Each new Agency—

(a) shall make arrangements for the carrying out of research and related activities (whether by itself or by others) in respect of matters to which its functions relate; and

(b) may make the results of any such research or related activities available to any person in return for payment of such fee as it considers appropriate.

(6) Subsection (5) above shall not be taken as preventing a new Agency from making the results of any research available to the public free of charge whenever it considers it appropriate to do so.

(7) Each new Agency may by agreement with any person charge that person a fee in respect of work done, or services or facilities provided, as a result of a request made by him for advice or assistance, whether of a general or specific character, in connection with any matter involving or relating to environmental licences.

(8) Subsection (7) above—

(a) is without prejudice to the generality of the powers of either new Agency to make charges; but

(b) is subject to any such express provision with respect to charging by the new Agency in question as is contained in the other provisions of this Part or in any other enactment.

(9) In this section 'engineering or building operations', without prejudice to the generality of that expression, includes—

(a) the construction, alteration, improvement, maintenance or demolition of any building or structure or of any reservoir, watercourse, dam, weir, well, borehole or other works; and

(b) the installation, modification or removal of any machinery or apparatus.

38. Delegation of functions by Ministers etc. to the new Agencies

(1) Agreements may be made between—

(a) any Minister of the Crown, and

(b) a new Agency,

authorising the new Agency (or any of its employees) to exercise on behalf of that Minister, with or without payment, any eligible function of his.

(2) An agreement under subsection (1) above shall not authorise the new Agency (or any of its employees) to exercise on behalf of a Minister of the Crown any function which consists of a power to make regulations or other instruments of a legislative character or a power to fix fees or charges.

(3) An agreement under this section may provide for any eligible function to which it relates to be exercisable by the new Agency in question (or any of its employees)—

(a) either wholly or to such extent as may be specified in the agreement;

(b) either generally or in such cases or areas as may be so specified; or

(c) either unconditionally or subject to the fulfilment of such conditions as may be so specified.

(4) Subsection (5) below applies where, by virtue of an agreement under this section, a new Agency (or any of its employees) is authorised to exercise any function of a Minister of the Crown.

(5) Subject to subsection (6) below, anything done or omitted to be done by the new Agency (or an employee of the new Agency) in, or in connection with, the exercise or purported exercise of the function shall be treated for all purposes as done or omitted to be done by that Minister in his capacity as such.

(6) Subsection (5) above shall not apply—

(a) for the purposes of so much of any agreement made between that Minister and the new Agency as relates to the exercise of the function; or

(b) for the purposes of any criminal proceedings brought in respect of anything done or omitted to be done as mentioned in that subsection.

(7) An agreement under this section shall not prevent a Minister of the Crown exercising any function to which the agreement relates.

(8) Where a Minister of the Crown has power to include, in any arrangements which he makes in relation to the performance by him of an eligible function, provision for the making of payments to him—

(a) by other parties to the arrangements, or

(b) by persons who use any facilities or services provided by him pursuant to the arrangements or in relation to whom the function is otherwise exercisable,

he may include in any such arrangements provision for the making of such payments to him or a new Agency in cases where the new Agency (or any of its employees) acts on his behalf by virtue of an agreement under this section.

(9) The power conferred on a Minister of the Crown by subsection (1) above is in addition to any other power by virtue of which functions of his may be exercised by other persons on his behalf.

(10) In this section—

'eligible function' means any function of a Minister of the Crown which the Secretary of State, having regard to the functions conferred or imposed upon the new Agency in question under or by virtue of this Act or any other enactment, considers can appropriately be exercised by that new Agency (or any of its employees) on behalf of that Minister;

'Minister of the Crown' has the same meaning as in the Ministers of the Crown Act 1975.

39. General duty of the new Agencies to have regard to costs and benefits in exercising powers

(1) Each new Agency—

(a) in considering whether or not to exercise any power conferred upon it by or under any enactment, or

(b) in deciding the manner in which to exercise any such power,

shall, unless and to the extent that it is unreasonable for it to do so in view of the nature or purpose of the power or in the circumstances of the particular case, take into account the likely costs and benefits of the exercise or non-exercise of the power or its exercise in the manner in question.

(2) The duty imposed upon a new Agency by subsection (1) above does not affect its obligation, nevertheless, to discharge any duties, comply with any requirements, or pursue any objectives, imposed upon or given to it otherwise than under this section.

40. Ministerial directions to the new Agencies

(1) The appropriate Minister may give a new Agency directions of a general or specific character with respect to the carrying out of any of its functions.

(2) The appropriate Minister may give a new Agency such directions of a general or specific character as he considers appropriate for the implementation of—

(a) any obligations of the United Kingdom under the Community Treaties, or

(b) any international agreement to which the United Kingdom is for the time being a party.

(3) Any direction under subsection (2) above shall be published in such manner as the Minister giving it considers appropriate for the purpose of bringing the matters to which it relates to the attention of persons likely to be affected by them; and—

(a) copies of the direction shall be made available to the public; and

(b) notice shall be given—

(i) in the case of a direction given to the Agency, in the London Gazette, or

(ii) in the case of a direction given to SEPA, in the Edinburgh Gazette,

of the giving of the direction and of where a copy of the direction may be obtained.

(4) The provisions of subsection (3) above shall have effect in relation to any direction given to a new Agency under an enactment other than subsection (2) above for the implementation of—

(a) any obligations of the United Kingdom under the Community Treaties, or

(b) any international agreement to which the United Kingdom is for the time being a party,

as those provisions have effect in relation to a direction given under subsection (2) above.

(5) In determining—

(a) any appeal against, or reference or review of, a decision of a new Agency, or

(b) any application transmitted from a new Agency,

the body or person making the determination shall be bound by any direction given by a Minister of the Crown to the new Agency to the same extent as the new Agency.

(6) Any power to give a direction under this section shall be exercisable, except in an emergency, only after consultation with the new Agency concerned.

(7) Any power of the appropriate Minister to give directions to a new Agency otherwise than by virtue of this section shall be without prejudice to any power to give directions conferred by this section.

(8)   It is the duty of a new Agency to comply with any direction which is given to that new Agency by a Minister of the Crown under this section or any other enactment.

Charging schemes

41. Power to make schemes imposing charges

(1)   Subject to the following provisions of this section and section 40 below—

(a)   in the case of any particular licence under Chapter II of Part II of the 1991 Act (abstraction and impounding), the Agency may require the payment to it of such charges as may from time to time be prescribed;

(b)   in relation to other environmental licences, there shall be charged by and paid to a new Agency such charges as may from time to time be prescribed; and

(c)   as a means of recovering costs incurred by it in performing functions conferred by regulations under section 62 of the 1990 Act (dangerous or intractable waste) each of the new Agencies may require the payment to it of such charges as may from time to time be prescribed;

and in this section 'prescribed' means specified in, or determined under, a scheme (in this section referred to as a 'charging scheme') made under this section by the new Agency in question.

(2)   As respects environmental licences, charges may be prescribed in respect of—

(a)   the grant or variation of an environmental licence, or any application for, or for a variation of, such a licence;

(b)   the subsistence of an environmental licence;

(c)   the transfer (where permitted) of an environmental licence to another person, or any application for such a transfer;

(d)   the renewal (where permitted) of an environmental licence, or any application for such a renewal;

(e)   the surrender (where permitted) of an environmental licence, or any application for such a surrender; or

(f)   any application for the revocation (where permitted) of an environmental licence.

(3)   A charging scheme may, for the purposes of subsection (2)(b) above, impose—

(a)   a single charge in respect of the whole of any relevant licensed period;

(b)   separate charges in respect of different parts of any such period; or

(c)   both such a single charge and such separate charges.

and in this subsection 'relevant licensed period' means the period during which an environmental licence is in force or such part of that period as may be prescribed.

(4)   Without prejudice to subsection (7)(a) below, a charging scheme may, as respects environmental licences, provide for different charges to be payable according to—

(a)   the description of environmental licence in question;

(b)   the description of authorised activity in question;

(c)   the scale on which the authorised activity in question is carried on;

(d)   the description or amount of the substance to which the authorised activity in question relates;

(e)   the number of different authorised activities carried on by the same person.

(5)   A charging scheme—

(a)   shall specify, in relation to any charge prescribed by the scheme, the description of person who is liable to pay the charge; and

(b)   may provide that it shall be a condition of an environmental licence of any particular description that any charge prescribed by a charging scheme in relation to an environmental licence of that description is paid in accordance with the scheme.

(6)   Without prejudice to subsection (5)(b) above, if it appears to a new Agency that any charges due and payable to it in respect of the subsistence of an environmental licence have not been paid, it may, in accordance with the appropriate procedure, suspend or revoke the environmental licence to the extent that it authorises the carrying on of an authorised activity.

(7)   A charging scheme may—

(a)   make different provision for different cases, including different provision in relation to different persons, circumstances or localities;

(b)   provide for the times at which, and the manner in which, the charges prescribed by the scheme are to be paid;

(c)   revoke or amend any previous charging scheme;

(d)   contain supplemental, incidental, consequential or transitional provision for the purposes of the scheme.

(8)   If and to the extent that a charging scheme relates to licences under Chapter II of Part II of the 1991 Act (abstraction and impounding), the scheme shall have effect subject to any provision made by or under sections 125 to 130 of that Act (exemption from charges, imposition of special charges for spray irrigation, and charges in respect of abstraction from waters of the British Waterways Board).

(9)   A new Agency shall not make a charging scheme unless the provisions of the scheme have been approved by the Secretary of State under section 42 below.

(10)   In this section—

'the appropriate procedure' means such procedure as may be specified or described in regulations made for the purpose by the Secretary of State;

'authorised activity' means any activity to which an environmental licence relates.

(11)   Any power to make regulations under this section shall be exercisable by statutory instrument; and a statutory instrument containing any such regulations shall be subject to annulment pursuant to a resolution of either House of Parliament.

42.   Approval of charging schemes

(1)   Before submitting a proposed charging scheme to the Secretary of State for his approval, a new Agency shall, in such manner as it considers appropriate for bringing it to the attention of persons likely to be affected by the scheme, publish a notice—

(a)   setting out its proposals; and

(b)   specifying the period within which representations or objections with respect to the proposals may be made to the Secretary of State.

(2)   Where any proposed charging scheme has been submitted to the Secretary of State for his approval, he shall, in determining whether or not to approve the scheme or to approve it subject to modifications,—

(a)   consider any representations or objections duly made to him and not withdrawn; and

(b)   have regard to the matter specified in subsection (3) below.

(3)   The matter mentioned in subsection (2)(b) above is the desirability of ensuring that, in the case of each of the descriptions of environmental licence specified in the paragraphs of the definition of that expression in section 56 below, the amounts recovered by the new Agency in question by way of charges prescribed by charging schemes are the amounts which, taking one year with another, need to be recovered by that new Agency to meet such of the costs and expenses (whether of a revenue or capital nature)—

(a)   which it incurs in carrying out its functions,

(b)   in the case of environmental licences which are authorisations under section 13(1) of the Radioactive Substances Act 1993—

(i)   which the Minister incurs in carrying out his functions under or in consequence of that Act, and

(ii)   which the Secretary of State incurs under that Act in carrying out in relation to Scotland or Wales such of his functions under or in consequence of that Act as are exercised by the Minister in relation to England,

as the Secretary of State may consider it appropriate to attribute to the carrying out of those functions in relation to activities to which environmental licences of the description in question relate.

(4) Without prejudice to the generality of the expression 'costs and expenses', in determining for the purposes of subsection (3) above the amounts of the costs and expenses which the Secretary of State considers it appropriate to attribute to the carrying out of a new Agency's or the Minister's or the Secretary of State's functions in relation to the activities to which environmental licences of any particular description relate, the Secretary of State—

(a) shall take into account any determination of the new Agency's financial duties under section 44 below; and

(b) may include amounts in respect of the depreciation of, and the provision of a return on, such assets as are held by the new Agency, the Minister or the Secretary of State, as the case may be, for purposes connected with the carrying out of the functions in question.

(5) If and to the extent that a charging scheme relates to any licence under Chapter II of Part II of the 1991 Act (abstraction and impounding), the Secretary of State may consider it appropriate to attribute to the carrying out of the Agency's functions in relation to activities to which such a licence relates any costs and expenses incurred by the Agency in carrying out any of its functions under Part II of that Act or under section 6(2) above.

(6) Subsection (5) above is without prejudice to what costs and expenses the Secretary of State may consider it appropriate to attribute to the carrying out of any functions of a new Agency, the Minister or the Secretary of State in relation to activities to which environmental licences of any particular description relate.

(7) The consent of the Treasury shall be required for the giving of approval to a charging scheme and, if and to the extent that the scheme relates to authorisations by the Agency under section 13 of the Radioactive Substances Act 1993 (disposal of radioactive waste), the consent of the Minister shall also be required.

(8) It shall be the duty of a new Agency to take such steps as it considers appropriate for bringing the provisions of any charging scheme made by it which is for the time being in force to the attention of persons likely to be affected by them.

(9) If and to the extent that any sums recovered by a new Agency by way of charges prescribed by charging schemes may fairly be regarded as so recovered for the purpose of recovering the amount required to meet (whether in whole or in part—

(a) such of the costs and expenses incurred by the Secretary of State as fall within subsection (3) above, or

(b) such of the costs and expenses incurred by the Minister as fall within that subsection,

those sums shall be paid by that new Agency to the Secretary of State or, as the case may be, to the Minister.

(10) For the purposes of subsection (9) above, any question as to the extent to which any sums may fairly be regarded as recovered for the purpose of recovering the amount required to meet the costs and expenses falling within paragraph (a) or paragraph (b) of that subsection shall be determined—

(a) in the case of costs and expenses falling within paragraph (a) of that subsection, by the Secretary of State; and

(b) in the case of costs and expenses falling within paragraph (b) of that subsection, by the Secretary of State and the Minister.

(11) In this section 'charging scheme' has the same meaning as in section 39 above.

Incidental power to impose charges

43. Incidental power of the new Agencies to impose charges
Without prejudice to the generality of its powers by virtue of section 37(1)(a) above and subject to any such express provision with respect to charging by a new Agency as is contained in the preceding provisions of this Chapter or any other enactment, each new Agency shall have the power to fix and recover charges for services and facilities provided in the course of carrying out its functions.

General financial provisions

44. General financial duties

(1)   The appropriate Ministers may—

   (a)   after consultation with a new Agency, and

   (b)   with the approval of the Treasury,

determine the financial duties of that new Agency; and different determinations may be made for different functions and activities of the new Agency.

(2)   The appropriate Ministers shall give a new Agency notice of every determination of its financial duties under this section, and such a determination may—

   (a)   relate to a period beginning before, on, or after, the date on which it is made;

   (b)   contain supplemental provisions; and

   (c)   be varied by a subsequent determination.

(3)   The appropriate Minister may, after consultation with the Treasury and a new Agency, give a direction to that new Agency requiring it to pay to him an amount equal to the whole or such part as may be specified in the direction of any sum, or any sum of a description, so specified which is or has been received by that new Agency.

(4)   Where it appears to the appropriate Minister that a new Agency has a surplus, whether on capital or revenue account, he may, after consultation with the Treasury and the new Agency, direct the new Agency to pay to him such amount not exceeding the amount of that surplus as may be specified in the direction.

(5)   In the case of the Agency—

   (a)   subsection (1) above is subject to section 118 of the 1991 Act (special duties with respect to flood defence revenue);

   (b)   subsection (3) above is subject to sections 118(1)(a) and 119(1) of the 1991 Act (special duties with respect to flood defence revenue and funds raised for fishery purposes under local enactments); and

   (c)   subsection (4) above is subject to sections 118(1)(b) and 119(2) of the 1991 Act (which provide for flood defence revenue and certain funds raised under local enactments to be disregarded in determining whether there is a surplus).

45. Accounts and records

(1)   Each new Agency shall—

   (a)   keep proper accounts and proper accounting records; and

   (b)   prepare in respect of each accounting year a statement of accounts giving a true and fair view of the state of affairs and the income and expenditure of the new Agency.

(2)   Every statement of accounts prepared by a new Agency in accordance with this section shall comply with any requirement which the appropriate Ministers have, with the consent of the Treasury, notified in writing to the new Agency and which relates to any of the following matters, namely—

   (a)   the information to be contained in the statement;

   (b)   the manner in which that information is to be presented;

   (c)   the methods and principles according to which the statement is to be prepared.

(3)   In this section—

'accounting records', in the case of a new Agency, includes all books, papers and other records of the new Agency relating to, or to matters dealt with in, the accounts required to be kept by virtue of this section;

'accounting year', subject to subsection (4) below, means, in relation to a new Agency, a financial year.

(4)   If the Secretary of State so directs in relation to any accounting year of either new Agency, that accounting year shall end with such date other than the next 31st March as may be specified in the direction; and, where the Secretary of State has given such a direction, the following accounting year shall begin with the day after the date so specified

and, subject to any further direction under this subsection, shall end with the next 31st March.

46. Audit

(1) The accounts of each new Agency shall be audited by an auditor appointed for each accounting year by the Secretary of State.

(2) A person shall not be qualified for appointment under subsection (1) above unless—

(a) he is eligible for appointment as a company auditor under Part II of the Companies Act 1989; and

(b) he would not be ineligible for appointment as company auditor of the new Agency in question by virtue of section 27 of that Act (ineligibility on ground of lack of independence), if that new Agency were a body to which section 384 of the Companies Act 1985 (duty to appoint auditor) applies.

(3) A copy of—

(a) any accounts of a new Agency which are audited under subsection (1) above, and

(b) the report made on those accounts by the auditor,

shall be sent to each of the appropriate Ministers as soon as reasonably practicable after the report is received by the new Agency; and the Secretary of State shall lay before each House of Parliament a copy of those accounts and that report.

(4) The Comptroller and Auditor General—

(a) shall be entitled to inspect the contents of all accounts and accounting records of a new Agency; and

(b) may report to the House of Commons the results of any inspection carried out by him under paragraph (a) above;

and section 6 of the National Audit Act 1983 (examinations of economy, efficiency and effectiveness) accordingly applies to each new Agency.

(5) In this section—

'accounting records' has the same meaning as in section 45 above;

'accounting year' has the same meaning as in section 45 above;

'accounts', in relation to the Agency, includes any statement under section 45 above.

47. Grants to the new Agencies

The appropriate Minister may, with the approval of the Treasury, make to a new Agency grants of such amounts, and on such terms, as he thinks fit.

48. Borrowing powers

(1) Each new Agency shall be entitled to borrow in accordance with the following provisions of this section, but not otherwise.

(2) Subject to subsection (5) below, each new Agency may—

(a) with the consent of the appropriate Minister, and

(b) with the approval of the Treasury,

borrow temporarily in sterling, by way of overdraft or otherwise, from persons other than the appropriate Ministers, such sums as it may require for meeting its obligations and carrying out its functions.

(3) Subject to subsection (5) below, each new Agency may borrow from the appropriate Minister, by way of temporary loan or otherwise, such sums in sterling as it may require for meeting its obligations and carrying out its functions.

(4) Any consent under subsection (2)(a) above may be granted subject to conditions.

(5) The aggregate amount outstanding in respect of the principal of sums borrowed under this section by a new Agency shall not at any time exceed—

(a) in the case of the Agency, £100 million or such greater sum, not exceeding £160 million, as the Ministers may by order specify; or

(b) in the case of SEPA, £5 million or such greater sum, not exceeding £10 million, as the Secretary of State may by order specify.

(6) The power to make an order under subsection (5) above shall be exercisable by statutory instrument; but no order shall be made under that subsection unless a draft of the order has been laid before, and approved by a resolution of, the House of Commons.

49. Government loans to the new Agencies

(1) The appropriate Minister may, with the approval of the Treasury, lend to a new Agency any sums which it has power to borrow under section 48(3) above.

(2) Any loan made under this section by one of the appropriate Ministers shall be repaid to him at such times and by such methods, and interest on the loan shall be paid to him at such rates and at such times, as that Minister may with the approval of the Treasury from time to time determine.

(3) If in any financial year any of the appropriate Ministers lends any sums to a new Agency under this section, he shall—

    (a) prepare in respect of that financial year an account of the sums so lent by him; and

    (b) send that account to the Comptroller and Auditor General before the end of September in the following financial year;

and the form of the account and the manner of preparing it shall be such as the Treasury may direct.

(4) The Comptroller and Auditor General shall examine, certify and report on each account sent to him under this section and shall lay copies of it and of his report before each House of Parliament.

(5) The Treasury may issue to any of the appropriate Ministers—

    (a) out of the National Loans Fund, or

    (b) out of money provided by Parliament,

such sums as are necessary to enable him to make loans to a new Agency under this section; and any sums received by a Minister of the Crown in pursuance of subsection (2) above shall be paid into the National Loans Fund or, as the case may be, the Consolidated Fund.

50. Government guarantees of a new Agency's borrowing

(1) The appropriate Minister may, with the consent of the Treasury, guarantee, in such manner and on such conditions as he may think fit, the repayment of the principal of, the payment of interest on, and the discharge of any other financial obligation in connection with, any sum which a new Agency borrows from any person.

(2) A Minister who gives a guarantee under this section shall forthwith lay a statement of the guarantee before each House of Parliament.

(3) Where any sum is paid out for fulfilling a guarantee under this section, the Minister who gave the guarantee shall, as soon as reasonably practicable after the end of each financial year (beginning with that in which the sum is paid out and ending with that in which all liability in respect of the principal of the sum and in respect of interest on it is finally discharged), lay before each House of Parliament a statement relating to that sum.

(4) If any sums are paid out in fulfilment of a guarantee under this section, the new Agency which borrowed the sum by reference to which the guarantee was given shall make to the Minister who gave the guarantee, at such times and in such manner as he may from time to time direct,—

    (a) payments of such amounts as he may so direct in or towards repayment of the sums so paid out; and

    (b) payments of interest, at such rate as he may so direct, on what is outstanding for the time being in respect of sums so paid out;

and the consent of the Treasury shall be required for the giving of a direction under this subsection.

Information

51. Provision of information by the new Agencies

(1) A new Agency shall furnish the appropriate Minister with all such information as he may reasonably require relating to—

(a)   the new Agency's property;

(b)   the carrying out and proposed carrying out of its functions; and

(c)   its responsibilities generally.

(2)   Information required under this section shall be furnished in such form and manner, and be accompanied or supplemented by such explanations, as the appropriate Minister may reasonably require.

(3)   The information which a new Agency may be required to furnish to the appropriate Minister under this section shall include information which, although it is not in the possession of the new Agency or would not otherwise come into the possession of the new Agency, is information which it is reasonable to require the new Agency to obtain.

(4)   A requirement for the purposes of this section shall be contained in a direction which—

(a)   may describe the information to be furnished in such manner as the Minister giving the direction considers appropriate; and

(b)   may require the information to be furnished on a particular occasion, in particular circumstances or from time to time.

(5)   For the purposes of this section a new Agency shall—

(a)   permit any person authorised for the purpose by the appropriate Minister to inspect and make copies of the contents of any accounts or other records of the new Agency; and

(b)   give such explanation of them as that person or the appropriate Minister may reasonably require.

52.   Annual report

(1)   As soon as reasonably practicable after the end of each financial year, each new Agency shall prepare a report on its activities during that year and shall send a copy of that report to each of the appropriate Ministers.

(2)   Every such report shall set out any directions under section 40 above which have been given to the new Agency in question during the year to which the report relates, other than directions given under subsection (1) of that section which are identified to that new Agency in writing by the appropriate Minister as being directions the disclosure of which would, in his opinion, be contrary to the interests of national security.

(3)   The Secretary of State shall lay a copy of every such report before each House of Parliament and shall arrange for copies of every such report to be published in such manner as he considers appropriate.

(4)   A new Agency's annual report shall be in such form and contain such information as may be specified in any direction given to the new Agency by the appropriate Ministers.

Supplemental provisions

53.   Inquiries and other hearings

(1)   Without prejudice to any other provision of this Act or any other enactment by virtue of which an inquiry or other hearing is authorised or required to be held, the appropriate Minister may cause an inquiry or other hearing to be held if it appears to him expedient to do so—

(a)   in connection with any of the functions of a new Agency; or

(b)   in connection with any of his functions in relation to a new Agency.

(2)   Subsections (2) to (5) of section 250 of the Local Government Act 1972 (which contain supplementary provisions with respect to local inquiries held in pursuance of that section) shall apply to inquiries or other hearings under this section or any other enactment—

(a)   in connection with any of the functions of the Agency, or

(b)   in connection with any functions of the Secretary of State or the Minister in relation to the Agency, as they apply to inquiries under that section, but taking the reference in subsection (4) of that section to a local authority as including a reference to the Agency.

(3) The provisions of subsections (2) to (8) of section 210 of the Local Government (Scotland) Act 1973 (which relate to the holding of local inquiries) shall apply to inquiries or other hearings held under this section or any other enactment—

(a) in connection with any of the functions of SEPA, or

(b) in connection with any functions of the Secretary of State in relation to SEPA,

as they apply to inquiries held under that section.

54. Appearance in legal proceedings

In England and Wales, a person who is authorised by the Agency to prosecute on its behalf in proceedings before a magistrates' court shall be entitled to prosecute in any such proceedings although not of counsel or a solicitor.

55. Continuity of exercise of functions: the new Agencies

(1) The abolition of—

(a) the National Rivers Authority,

(b) the London Waste Regulation Authority, or

(c) a river purification board,

shall not affect the validity of anything done by that Authority or board before the transfer date.

(2) Anything which, at the transfer date, is in the process of being done by or in relation to a transferor in the exercise of, or in connection with, any of the transferred functions may be continued by or in relation to the transferee.

(3) Anything done by or in relation to a transferor before the transfer date in the exercise of, or otherwise in connection with, any of the transferred functions, shall, so far as is required for continuing its effect on and after that date, have effect as if done by or in relation to the transferee.

(4) Subsection (3) above applies in particular to—

(a) any decision, determination, declaration, designation, agreement or instrument made by a transferor;

(b) any regulations or byelaws made by a transferor;

(c) any licence, permission, consent, approval, authorisation, exemption, dispensation or relaxation granted by or to a transferor;

(d) any notice, direction or certificate given by or to a transferor;

(e) any application, request, proposal or objection made by or to a transferor;

(f) any condition or requirement imposed by or on a transferor;

(g) any fee or charge paid by or to a transferor;

(h) any appeal allowed by or in favour of or against a transferor;

(j) any proceedings instituted by or against a transferor.

(5) Any reference in the foregoing provisions of this section to anything done by or in relation to a transferor includes a reference to anything which, by virtue of any enactment, is treated as having been done by or in relation to that transferor.

(6) Any reference to a transferor in any document constituting or relating to anything to which the foregoing provisions of this section apply shall, so far as is required for giving effect to those provisions, be construed as a reference to the transferee.

(7) The foregoing provisions of this section—

(a) are without prejudice to any provision made by this Act in relation to any particular functions; and

(b) shall not be construed as continuing in force any contract of employment made by a transferor;

and the Secretary of State may, in relation to any particular functions, by order exclude, modify or supplement any of the foregoing provisions of this section or make such other transitional provisions as he thinks necessary or expedient.

(8) Where, by virtue of any provision of Schedule 15 to this Act, the Minister is the transferor in the case of any functions, he shall have the same powers under subsection (7) above in relation to those functions as the Secretary of State.

(9) The power to make an order under subsection (7) above shall be exercisable by statutory instrument; and any statutory instrument containing such an order shall be subject to annulment pursuant to a resolution of either House of Parliament.

(10) In this section—

'the transferee', in the case of any transferred functions, means the new Agency whose functions they become by virtue of any provision made by or under this Act;

'transferred functions' means any functions which, by virtue of any provision made by or under this Act, become functions of a new Agency; and

'transferor' means any body or person any or all of whose functions become, by virtue of any provision made by or under this Act, functions of a new Agency.

56. Interpretation of Part I

(1) In this Part of this Act, except where the context otherwise requires—

'the 1951 Act' means the Rivers (Prevention of Pollution) (Scotland) Act 1951;

'the 1990 Act' means the Environmental Protection Act 1990;

'the 1991 Act' means the Water Resources Act 1991;

'the appropriate Minister'—

    (a) in the case of the Agency, means the Secretary of State or the Minister; and

    (b) in the case of SEPA, means the Secretary of State;

'the appropriate Ministers'—

    (a) in the case of the Agency, means the Secretary of State and the Minister; and

    (b) in the case of SEPA, means the Secretary of State;

'conservancy authority' has the meaning given by section 221 (1) of the 1991 Act;

'costs' includes—

    (a) costs to any person; and

    (b) costs to the environment;

'disposal authority'—

    (a) in the application of this Part in relation to the Agency, has the same meaning as it has in Part I of the Control of Pollution Act 1974 by virtue of section 30(1) of that Act; and

    (b) in the application of this Part in relation to SEPA, has the meaning assigned to it by section 30(2) of that Act;

'the environment' has the same meaning as in Part I of the 1990 Act;

'environmental licence', in the application of this Part in relation to the Agency, means any of the following—

    (a) registration of a person as a carrier of controlled waste under section 2 of the Control of Pollution (Amendment) Act 1989,

    (b) an authorisation under Part I of the 1990 Act, other than any such authorisation granted by a local enforcing authority,

    (c) a waste management licence under Part II of that Act,

    (d) a licence under Chapter II of Part II of the 1991 Act,

    (e) a consent for the purposes of section 88(1)(a), 89(4)(a) or 90 of that Act,

    (f) registration under the Radioactive Substances Act 1993,

    (g) an authorisation under that Act,

    (h) registration of a person as a broker of controlled waste under the Waste Management Licensing Regulations 1994,

    (j) registration in respect of an activity falling within paragraph 45(1) or (2) of Schedule 3 to those Regulations,

    so far as having effect in relation to England and Wales;

'environmental licence', in the application of this Part in relation to SEPA, means any of the following—

(a) a consent under Part II of the Control of Pollution Act 1974,

(b) registration of a person as a carrier of controlled waste under section 2 of the Control of Pollution (Amendment) Act 1989,

(c) an authorisation under Part I of the 1990 Act,

(d) a waste management licence under Part II of that Act,

(e) a licence under section 17 of the Natural Heritage (Scotland) Act 1991,

(f) registration under the Radioactive Substances Act 1993,

(g) an authorisation under that Act, or

(h) registration of a person as a broker of controlled waste under the Waste Management Licensing Regulations 1994,

(j) registration in respect of an activity falling within paragraph 45(1) or (2) of Schedule 3 to those Regulations,

so far as having effect in relation to Scotland;

'flood defence functions', in relation to the Agency, has the same meaning as in the 1991 Act;

'harbour authority' has the meaning given by section 221(1) of the 1991 Act;

'local authority', in the application of this Part in relation to SEPA, means a district or islands council in Scotland;

'the Minister' means the Minister of Agriculture, Fisheries and Food;

'the Ministers' means the Secretary of State and the Minister;

'navigation authority' has the meaning given by section 221(1) of the 1991 Act;

'new Agency' means the Agency or SEPA;

'river purification authority' means a river purification authority within the meaning of the 1951 Act;

'river purification board' means a river purification board established by virtue of section 135 of the Local Government (Scotland) Act 1973;

'the transfer date' means such date as the Secretary of State may by order made by statutory instrument appoint as the transfer date for the purposes of this Part; and different dates may be appointed for the purposes of this Part—

(i) as it applies for or in connection with transfers under or by virtue of Chapter I above, and

(ii) as it applies for or in connection with transfers under or by virtue of Chapter II above;

'waste regulation authority'—

(a) in the application of this Part in relation to the Agency, means any authority in England or Wales which, by virtue of section 30(1) of the 1990 Act, is a waste regulation authority for the purposes of Part II of that Act; and

(b) in the application of this Part in relation to SEPA, means any council which, by virtue of section 30(1)(g) of the 1990 Act, is a waste regulation authority for the purposes of Part II of that Act.

(2) In relation to any time on or after 1st April 1996—

(a) subsection (1) above shall have effect as if, in the definition of 'local authority', for the words 'district or islands council in Scotland' there were substituted the words 'council constituted under section 2 of the Local Government etc. (Scotland) Act 1994'; and

(b) in section 22(3)(a)(iv) above the reference to an islands council shall be construed as a reference to a council mentioned in section 3(1) of the Local Government etc. (Scotland) Act 1994.

(3) Where by virtue of any provision of this Part any function of a Minister of the Crown is exercisable concurrently by different Ministers, that function shall also be exercisable jointly by any two or more of those Ministers.

PART II

CONTAMINATED LAND AND ABANDONED MINES

54. Contaminated land

After section 78 of the Environmental Protection Act 1990 there shall be inserted—

'PART IIA

CONTAMINATED LAND

78A. Preliminary

(1) The following provisions have effect for the interpretation of this Part.

(2) ''Contaminated land'' is any land which appears to the local authority in whose area it is situated to be in such a condition, by reason of substances in, on or under the land, that—

(a) significant harm is being caused or there is a significant possibility of such harm being caused; or

(b) pollution of controlled waters is being, or is likely to be, caused;

and, in determining whether any land appears to be such land, a local authority shall, subject to subsection (5) below, act in accordance with guidance issued by the Secretary of State in accordance with section 78YA below with respect to the manner in which that determination is to be made.

(3) A ''special site'' is any contaminated land—

(a) which has been designated as such a site by virtue of section 78C(7) or 78D(6) below; and

(b) whose designation as such has not been terminated by the appropriate Agency under section 78Q(4) below.

(4) ''Harm'' means harm to the health of living organisms or other interference with the ecological systems of which they form part and, in the case of man, includes harm to his property.

(5) The questions—

(a) what harm is to be regarded as ''significant'',

(b) whether the possibility of significant harm being caused is ''significant'',

(c) whether pollution of controlled waters is being, or is likely to be, caused,

shall be determined in accordance with guidance issued for the purpose by the Secretary of State in accordance with section 78YA below.

(6) Without prejudice to the guidance that may be issued under subsection (5) above, guidance under paragraph (a) of that subsection may make provision for different degrees of importance to be assigned to, or for the disregard of,—

(a) different descriptions of living organisms or ecological systems;

(b) different descriptions of places; or

(c) different descriptions of harm to health or property, or other interference;

and guidance under paragraph (b) of that subsection may make provision for different degrees of possibility to be regarded as ''significant'' (or as not being ''significant'') in relation to different descriptions of significant harm.

(7) ''Remediation'' means—

(a) the doing of anything for the purpose of assessing the condition of—

(i) the contaminated land in question;

(ii) any controlled waters affected by that land; or

(iii) any land adjoining or adjacent to that land;

(b) the doing of any works, the carrying out of any operations or the taking of any steps in relation to any such land or waters for the purpose—

(i) of preventing or minimising, or remedying or mitigating the effects of, any significant harm, or any pollution of controlled waters, by reason of which the contaminated land is such land; or

(ii)   of restoring the land or waters to their former state; or

(c)   the making of subsequent inspections from time to time for the purpose of keeping under review the condition of the land or waters;

and cognate expressions shall be construed accordingly.

(8)   Controlled waters are "affected by" contaminated land if (and only if) it appears to the enforcing authority that the contaminated land in question is, for the purposes of subsection (2) above, in such a condition, by reason of substances in, on or under the land, that pollution of those waters is being, or is likely to be caused.

(9)   The following expressions have the meaning respectively assigned to them—

"the appropriate Agency" means—

(a)   in relation to England and Wales, the Environment Agency;

(b)   in relation to Scotland, the Scottish Enviromment Protection Agency;

"appropriate person" means any person who is an appropriate person, determined in accordance with section 78F below, to bear responsibility for any thing which is to be done by way of remediation in any particular case;

"charging notice" has the meaning given by section 78(3)(b) below;

"controlled waters"

(a)   in relation to England and Wales, has the same meaning as in Part III of the Water Resources Act 1991, and

(b)   in relation to Scotland, has the same meaning as in section 30A of the Control of Pollution Act 1974;

"creditor" has the same meaning as in the Conveyancing and Feudal Reform (Scotland) Act 1970;

"enforcing authority" means—

(a)   in relation to a special site, the appropriate Agency;

(b)   in relation to contaminated land other than a special site, the local authority in whose area the land is situated;

"heritable security" has the same meaning as in the Conveyancing and Feudal Reform (Scotland) Act 1970;

"local authority" in relation to England and Wales means—

(a)   any unitary authority;

(b)   any district council, so far as it is not a unitary authority;

(c)   the Common Council of the City of London and, as respects the Temples, the Sub-Treasurer of the Inner Temple and the Under-Treasurer of the Middle Temple respectively;

and in relation to Scotland means a council for an area constituted under section 2 of the Local Government etc. (Scotland) Act 1994;

"notice" means notice in writing;

"notification" means notification in writing;

"owner", in relation to any land in England and Wales, means a person (other than a mortgagee not in possession) who, whether in his own right or as trustee for any other person, is entitled to receive the rack rent of the land, or, where the land is not let at a rack rent, would be so entitled if it were so let;

"owner", in relation to any land in Scotland, means a person (other than a creditor in a heritable security not in possession of the security subjects) for the time being entitled to receive or who would, if the land were let, be entitled to receive, the rents of the land in connection with which the word is used and includes a trustee, factor, guardian or curator and in the case of public or municipal land includes the persons to whom the management of the land is entrusted;

"pollution of controlled waters" means the entry into controlled waters of any poisonous, noxious or polluting matter or any solid waste matter;

"prescribed" means prescribed by regulations;

"regulations" means regulations made by the Secretary of State;

"remediation declaration" has the meaning given by section 78H(6) below;

"remediation notice" has the meaning given by section 78E(1) below;

"remediation statement" has the meaning given by section 78H(7) below;

"required to be designated as a special site" shall be construed in accordance with section 78C(8) below;

"substance" means any natural or artificial substance, whether in solid or liquid form or in the form of a gas or vapour;

"unitary authority" means—

(a)   the council of a county, so far as it is the council of an area for which there are no district councils;

(b)   the council of any district comprised in an area for which there is no county council;

(c)   the council of a London borough;

(d)   the council of a county borough in Wales;

78B.   Identification of contaminated land

(1)   Every local authority shall cause its area to be inspected from time to time for the purpose—

(a)   of identifying contaminated land; and

(b)   of enabling the authority to decide whether any such land is land which is required to be designated as a special site.

(2)   In performing its functions under subsection (1) above a local authority shall act in accordance with any guidance issued for the purpose by the Secretary of State in accordance with section 78YA below.

(3)   If a local authority identifies any contaminated land in its area, it shall give notice of that fact to—

(a)   the appropriate Agency;

(b)   the owner of the land;

(c)   any person who appears to the authority to be in occupation of the whole or any part of the land; and

(d)   each person who appears to the authority to be an appropriate person;

and any notice given under this subsection shall state by virtue of which of paragraphs (a) to (d) above it is given.

(4)   If, at any time after a local authority has given any person a notice pursuant to subsection (3)(d) above in respect of any land, it appears to the enforcing authority that another person is an appropriate person, the enforcing authority shall give notice to that other person—

(a)   of the fact that the local authority has identified the land in question as contaminated land; and

(b)   that he appears to the enforcing authority to be an appropriate person.

78C.   Identification and designation of special sites

(1)   If at any time it appears to a local authority that any contaminated land in its area might be land which is required to be designated as a special site, the authority—

(a)   shall decide whether or not the land is land which is required to be so designated; and

(b)   if the authority decides that the land is land which is required to be so designated, shall give notice of that decision to the relevant persons.

(2)   For the purposes of this section 'the relevant persons' at any time in the case of any land are the persons who at that time fall within paragraphs (a) to (d) below that is to say—

(a)   the appropriate Agency;

(b)   the owner of the land;

(c)   any person who appears to the local authority concerned to be in occupation of the whole or any part of the land; and

(d)   each person who appears to that authority to be an appropriate person.

(3)   Before making a decision under paragraph (a) of subsection (1) above in any particular case, a local authority shall request the advice of the appropriate Agency, and in making its decision shall have regard to any advice given by that Agency in response to the request.

(4)   If at any time the appropriate Agency considers that any contaminated land is land which is required to be designated as a special site, that Agency may give notice of that fact to the local authority in whose area the land is situated.

(5)   Where notice under subsection (4) above is given to a local authority, the authority shall decide whether the land in question—

(a)   is land which is required to be designated as a special site, or

(b)   is not land which is required to be so designated,

and shall give notice of that decision to the relevant persons.

(6)   Where a local authority makes a decision falling within subsection (1)(b) or 5(a) above, the decision shall, subject to section 78D below, take effect on the day after whichever of the following events first occurs, that is to say—

(a)   the expiration of the period of twenty-one days beginning with the day on which the notice required by virtue of subsection (1)(b) or, as the case may be, (5)(a) above is given to the appropriate Agency; or

(b)   if the appropriate Agency gives notification to the local authority in question that it agrees with the decision, the giving of that notification;

and where a decision takes effect by virtue of this subsection, the local authority shall give notice of that fact to the relevant persons.

(7)   Where a decision that any land is land which is required to be designated as a special site takes effect in accordance with subsection (6) above, the notice given under subsection (1)(b) or, as the case may be, (5)(a) above shall have effect, as from the time when the decision takes effect, as the designation of that land as such a site.

(8)   For the purposes of this Part, land is required to be designated as a special site if, and only if, it is land of a description prescribed for the purposes of this subsection.

(9)   Regulations under subsection (8) above may make different provision for different cases or circumstances or different areas or localities and may, in particular, describe land by reference to the area or locality in which it is situated.

(10)   Without prejudice to the generality of his power to prescribe any description of land for the purposes of subsection (8) above, the Secretary of State, in deciding whether to prescribe a particlar description of contaminated land for those purposes, may, in particular, have regard to—

(a)   whether land of the description in question appears to him to be land which is likely to be in such a condition, by reason of substances in, on or under the land that—

(i)   serious harm would or might be caused, or

(ii)   serious pollution of controlled waters would be, or would be likely to be, caused; or

(b)   whether the appropriate Agency is likely to have expertise in dealing with the kind of significant harm, or pollution of controlled waters, by reason of which land of the description in question is contaminated land.

78D.   Referral of special site decisions to the Secretary of State

(1)   In any case where—

(a)   a local authority gives notice of a decision to the appropriate Agency pursuant to subsection (1)(b) or (5)(b) of section 78C above, but

(b) before the expiration of the period of twenty-one days beginning with the day on which that notice is so given, that Agency gives the local authority notice that it disagrees with the decision, together with a statement of its reasons for disagreeing, the authority shall refer the decision to the Secretary of State and shall send to him a statement of its reasons for reaching the decision.

(2) Where the appropriate Agency gives notice to a local authority under paragraph (b) of subsection (1) above, it shall also send to the Secretary of State a copy of the notice and of the statement given under that paragraph.

(3) Where a local authority refers a decision to the Secretary of State under subsection (1) above, it shall give notice of that fact to the relevant persons.

(4) Where a decision of a local authority is referred to the Secretary of State under subsection (1) above, he—

(a) may confirm or reverse the decision with respect to the whole or any part of the land to which it relates; and

(b) shall give notice of this decision on the referral—

(i) to the relevant persons; and

(ii) to the local authority.

(5) Where a decision of a local authority is referred to the Secretary of State under subsection (1) above, the decision shall not take effect until the day after that on which the Secretary of State gives the notice required by subsection (4) above to the persons there mentioned and shall then take effect as confirmed or reversed by him.

(6) Where a decision which takes effect in accordance with subsection (5) above is to the effect that at least some land is land which is required to be designated as a special site, the notice given under subsection (4)(b) above shall have effect, as from the time when the decision takes effect, as the designation of that land as such a site.

(7) In this section ''the relevant persons'' has the same meaning as in section 78C above.

78E. Duty of enforcing authority to require remediation of contaminated land etc.

(1) In any case where—

(a) any land has been designated as a special site by virtue of section 78C(7) or 78D(6) above, or

(b) a local authority has identified any contaminated land (other than a special site) in its area,

the enforcing authority shall, in accordance with such procedure as may be prescribed and subject to the following provisions of this Part, serve on each person who is an appropriate person a notice (in this Part referred to as a 'remediation notice') specifying what that person is to do by way of remediation and the periods within which he is required to do each of the things so specified.

(2) Different remediation notices requiring the doing of different things by way of remediation may be served on different persons in consequence of the presence of different substances in, on or under any land or waters.

(3) Where two or more persons are appropriate persons in relation to any particular thing which is to be done by way of remediation, the remediation notice served on each of them shall state the proportion, determined under section 78F(7) below, of the cost of doing that thing which each of them respectively is liable to bear.

(4) The only things by way of remediation which the enforcing authority may do, or require to be done, under or by virtue of this Part are things which it considers reasonable, having regard to—

(a) the cost which is likely to be involved; and

(b) the seriousness of the harm, or pollution of controlled waters, in question.

(5) In determining for any purpose of this Part—

(a)   what is to be done (whether by an appropriate person, the enforcing authority or any other person) by way of remediation in any particular case,

(b)   the standard to which any land is, or waters are, to be remediated pursuant to the notice, or

(c)   what is, or is not, to be regarded as reasonable for the purposes of subsection (4) above,

the enforcing authority shall have regard to any guidance issued for the purpose by the Secretary of State.

(6)   Regulations may make provision for or in connection with—

(a)   the form or content of remediation notices; or

(b)   any steps of a procedural nature which are to be taken in connection with, or in consequence of, the service of a remediation notice.

78F. Determination of the appropriate person to bear responsibility for remediation

(1)   This section has effect for the purpose of determining who is the appropriate person to bear responsibility for any particular thing which the enforcing authority determines is to be done by way of remediation in any particular case.

(2)   Subject to the following provisions of this section, any person, or any of the persons, who caused or knowingly permitted the substances, or any of the substances, by reason of which the contaminated land in question is such land to be in, on or under that land is an appropriate person.

(3)   A person shall only be an appropriate person by virtue of subsection (2) above in relation to things which are to be done by way of remediation which are to any extent referable to substances which he caused or knowingly permitted to be present in, on or under the contaminated land in question.

(4)   If no person has, after reasonable inquiry, been found who is by virtue of subsection (2) above an appropriate person to bear responsibility for the things which are to be done by way of remediation, the owner or occupier for the time being of the contaminated land in question is an appropriate person.

(5)   If, in consequence of subsection (3) above, there are things which are to be done by way of remediation in relation to which no person has, after reasonable inquiry, been found who is an appropriate person by virtue of subsection (2) above, the owner or occupier for the time being of the contaminated land in question is an appropriate person in relation to those things.

(6)   Where two or more persons would, apart from this subsection, be appropriate persons in relation to any particular thing which is to be done by way of remediation, the enforcing authority shall determine in accordance with guidance issued for the purpose by the Secretary of State whether any, and if so which, of them is to be treated as not being an appropriate person in relation to that thing.

(7)   Where two or more persons are appropriate persons in relation to any particular thing which is to be done by way of remediation, they shall be liable to bear the cost of doing that thing in proportions determined by the enforcing authority in accordance with guidance issued for the purpose by the Secretary of State.

(8)   Any guidance issued for the purposes of subsection (6) or (7) above shall be issued in accordance with section 78YA below.

(9)   A person who has caused or knowingly permitted any substance ("substance A") to be in, or under any land shall also be taken for the purposes of this section to have caused or knowingly permitted there to be in, on or under that land any substance which is there as a result of a chemical reaction or biological process affecting substance A.

(10)   A thing which is to be done by way of remediation may be regarded for the purposes of this Part as referable to the presence of any substance notwithstanding that the thing in question would not have to be done—

(a)   in consequence only of the presence of that substance in any quantity; or

(b)   in consequence only of the quantity of that substance which any particular person caused or knowingly permitted to be present.

78G.   Grant of, and compensation for, rights of entry etc.

(1)   A remediation notice may require an appropriate person to do things by way of remediation, notwithstanding that he is not entitled to do those things.

(2)   Any person whose consent is required before any thing required by a remediation notice may be done shall grant, or join in granting, such rights in relation to any of the relevant land or waters as will enable the appropriate person to comply with any requirements imposed by the remediation notice.

(3)   Before serving a remediation notice, the enforcing authority shall reasonably endeavour to consult every person who appears to the authority—

(a)   to be the owner or occupier of any of the relevant land or waters, and

(b)   to be a person who might be required by subsection (2) above to grant, or join in granting, any rights,

concerning the rights which that person may be so required to grant.

(4)   Subsection (3) above shall not preclude the service of a remediation notice in any case where it appears to the enforcing authority that the contaminated land in question is in such a condition, by reason of substances in, on or under the land, that there is imminent danger of serious harm or serious pollution of controlled waters, being caused.

(5)   A person who grants, or joins in granting, any rights pursuant to subsection (2) above shall be entitled, on making an application within such period as may be prescribed and in such manner as may be prescribed to such person as may be prescribed, to be paid by the appropriate person compensation of such amount as may be determined in such manner as may be prescribed.

(6)   Without prejudice to the generality of the regulations that may be made by virtue of subsection (5) above, regulations by virtue of that subsection may make such provision in relation to compensation under this section as may be made by regulations by virtue of subsection (4) of section 35A above in relation to compensation under that section.

(7)   In this section, "relevant land or waters" means—

(a)   the contaminated land in question;

(b)   any controlled waters affected by that land; or

(c)   any land adjoining or adjacent to that land or those waters.

78H.   Restrictions and prohibitions on serving remediation notices

(1)   Before serving a remediation notice, the enforcing authority shall reasonably endeavour to consult—

(a)   the person on whom the notice is to be served,

(b)   the owner of any land to which the notice relates,

(c)   any person who appears to that authority to be in occupation of the whole or any part of the land, and

(d)   any person of such other description as may be prescribed,

concerning what is to be done by way of remediation.

(2)   Regulations may make provision for, or in connection with, steps to be taken for the purposes of subsection (1) above.

(3)   No remediation notice shall be served on any person by reference to any contaminated land during any of the following periods, that is to say—

(a)   the period—

(i)   beginning with the identification of the contaminated land in question pursuant to section 78B(1) above, and

(ii)   ending with the expiration of the period of three months beginning with the day on which the notice required by subsection (3)(d) or, as the case may be, (4) of section 78B above is given to that person in respect of that land;

(b)   if a decision falling within paragraph (b) of section 78C(1) above is made in relation to the contaminated land in question, the period beginning with the making of the decision and ending with the expiration of the perod of three months beginning with—

(i)   in a case where the decision is not referred to the Secretary of State under section 78D above, the day on which the notice required by section 78C(6) above is given, or

(ii)   in a case where the decision is referred to the Secretary of State under section 78D above, the day on which he gives the notice required by subsection (4)(b) of that section;

(c)   if the appropriate Agency gives a notice under subsection (4) of section 78C above to a local authority in relation to the contaminated land in question, the period beginning with the day on which that notice is given and ending with the expiration of the period of three months beginning with—

(i)   in a case where notice is given under subsection (6) of that section, the day on which that notice is given;

(ii)   in a case where the authority makes a decision falling within subsection (5)(b) of that section and the appropriate Agency fails to give notice under paragraph (b) of section 78D(1) above, the day following the expiration of the period of twenty-one days mentioned in that paragraph; or

(iii) in a case where the authority makes a decision falling within section 78C(5)(b) above which is referred to the Secretary of State under section 78D above, the day on which the Secretary of State gives the notice required by subsection (4)(b) of that section.

(4)   Neither subsection (1) nor subsection (3) above shall preclude the service of a remediation notice in any case where it appears to the enforcing authority that the land in question is in such a condition, by reason of substances in, on or under the land, that there is imminent danger of serious harm, or serious pollution of controlled waters, being caused.

(5)   The enforcing authority shall not serve a remediation notice on a person if and so long as any one or more of the following conditions is for the time being satisfied in the particular case, that is to say—

(a)   the authority is satisfied, in consequence of section 78E(4) and (5) above, that there is nothing by way of remediation which could be specified in a remediation notice served on that person;

(b)   the authority is satisfied that appropriate things are being, or will be, done by way of remediation without the service of a remediation notice on that person;

(c)   it appears to the authority that the person on whom the notice would be served is the authority itself; or

(d)   the authority is satisfied that the powers conferred on it by section 78N below to do what is appropriate by way of remediation are exercisable.

(6)   Where the enforcing authority is precluded by virtue of section 78E(4) or (5) above from specifying in a remediation notice any particular thing by way of remediation which it would otherwise have specified in such a notice, the authority shall prepare and publish a document (in this Part referred to as a "remediation declaration") which shall record—

(a)   the reasons why the authority would have specified that thing; and

(b)   the grounds on which the authority is satisfied that it is precluded from specifying that thing in such a notice.

(7)   In any case where the enforcing authority is precluded, by virtue of paragraph (b), (c) or (d) of subsection (5) above, from serving a remediation notice, the responsible person shall prepare and publish a document (in this Part referred to as a "remediation statement") which shall record—

(a)   the things which are being, have been, or are expected to be, done by way of remediation in the particular case;

(b)   the name and address of the person who is doing, has done, or is expected to do, each of those things; and

(c)   the periods within which each of those things is being, or is expected to be, done.

(8)   For the purposes of subsection (7) above, the "responsible person" is—

(a)   in a case where the condition in paragraph (b) of subsection (5) above is satisfied, the person who is doing or has done, or who the enforcing authority is satisfied will do, the things there mentioned; or

(b)   in a case where the condition in paragraph (c) or (d) of that subsection is satisfied, the enforcing authority.

(9)   If a person who is required by virtue of subsection (8)(a) above to prepare and publish a remediation statement fails to do so within a reasonable time after the date on which a remediation notice specifying the things there mentioned could, apart from subsection (5) above, have been served, the enforcing authority may itself prepare and publish the statement and may recover its reasonable costs of doing so from that person.

(10)   Where the enforcing authority has been precluded by virtue only of subsection (5) above from serving a remediation notice on an appropriate person but—

(a)   none of the conditions in that subsection is for the time being satisified in the particular case, and

(b)   the authority is not precluded by any other provison of this Part from serving a remediation notice on that appropriate person,

the authority shall serve a remediation notice on that person; and any such notice may be so served without any further endeavours by the authority to consult persons pursuant to subsection (1) above, if and to the extent that that person has been consulted pursuant to that subsection concerning the things which will be specified in the notice.

78J.   Restrictions on liability relating to the pollution of controlled waters

(1)   This section applies where any land is contaminated land by virtue of paragraph (b) of subsection (2) of section 78A above (whether or not the land is also contaminated land by virtue of paragraph (a) of that subsection).

(2)   Where this section applies, no remediation notice given in consequence of the land in question being contaminated land shall require a person who is an appropriate person by virtue of section 78F(4) or (5) above to do anything by way of remediation to that or any other land, or any waters, which he could not have been required to do by such a notice had paragraph (b) of section 78A(2) above (and all other references to pollution of controlled waters) been omitted from this Part.

(3)   If, in a case where this section applies, a person permits, has permitted, or might permit, water from an abandoned mine or part of a mine—

(a)   to enter any controlled waters, or

(b)   to reach a place from which it is or, as the case may be, was likely, in the opinion of the enforcing authority, to enter such waters,

no remediation notice shall require him in consequence to do anything by way of remediation (whether to the contaminated land in question or to any other land or waters) which he could not have been required to do by such a notice had paragraph (b) of section 78A(2) above (and all other references to pollution of controlled waters) been omitted from this Part.

(4)   Subsection (3) above shall not apply to the owner or former operator of any mine or part of a mine if the mine or part in question became abandoned after 31st December 1999.

(5)   In determining for the purposes of subsection (4) above whether a mine or part of a mine became abandoned before, on or after 31st December 1999 in a case where the mine or part has become abandoned on two or more occasions, of which—

(a)   at least one falls on or before that date, and

(b)   at least one falls after that date,

the mine or part shall be regarded as becoming abandoned after that date (but without prejudice to the operation of subsection (3) above in relation to that mine or part at, or in relation to, any time before the first of those occasions which fall after that date).

(6)   Where, immediately before a part of a mine becomes abandoned, that part is the only part of the mine not falling to be regarded as abandoned for the time being, the abandonment of that part shall not be regarded for the purposes of subsection (4) or (5) above as constituting the abandonment of the mine, but only of that part of it.

(7)   Nothing in subsection (2) or (3) above prevents the enforcing authority from doing anything by way of remediation under section 78N below which it could have done apart from that subsection, but the authority shall not be entitled under section 78P below to recover from any person any part of the cost incurred by the authority in doing by way of remediation anything which it is precluded by subsection (2) or (3) above from requiring that person to do.

(8)   In this section "mine" has the same meaning as in the Mines and Quarries Act 1954.

78K.   Liability in respect of contaminating substances which escape to other land

(1)   A person who has caused or knowingly permitted any substances to be in, on or under any land shall also be taken for the purposes of this Part to have caused or, as the case may be, knowingly permitted those substances to be in, on or under any other land to which they appear to have escaped.

(2)   Subsections (3) and (4) below apply in any case where it appears that any substances are or have been in, on or under any land (in this section referred to as "land A") as a result of their escape, whether directly or indirectly from other land in, on or under which a person caused or knowingly permitted them to be.

(3)   Where this subsection applies, no remediation notice shall require a person—

(a)   who is the owner or occupier of land A, and

(b)   who has not caused or knowingly permitted the substances in question to be in, on or under that land,

to do anything by way of remediation to any land or waters (other than land or waters of which he is the owner or occupier) in consequence of land A appearing to be in such a condition, by reason of the presence of those substances in, on or under it, that significant harm is being caused, or there is a significant possibility of such harm being caused, or that pollution of controlled waters is being, or is likely to be caused.

(4)   Where this subsection applies, no remediation notice shall require a person—

(a)   who is the owner or occupier of land A, and

(b)   who has not caused or knowingly permitted the substances in question to be in, on or under that land,

to do anything by way of remediation in consequence of any further land in, on or under which those substances or any of them appear to be or to have been present as a result of their escape from land A ("land B") appearing to be in such a condition, by reason of the presence of those substances in, on or under it, that significant harm is being caused, or there is a significant possibility of such harm being caused, or that pollution of controlled waters is being, or is likely to be caused, unless he is also the owner or occupier of land B.

(5)   In any case where—

(a)   a person ("person A") has caused or knowingly permitted any substances to be in, on, or under any land,

(b)   another person ("person B") who has not caused or knowingly permitted those substances to be in, or under that land becomes the owner or occupier of that land, and

(c)   the substances, or any of the substances, mentioned in paragraph (a) above appear to have escaped to other land,

no remediation notice shall require person B to do anything by way of remediation to that other land in consequence of the apparent acts or omissions of person A, except to the extent that person B caused or knowingly permitted the escape.

(6)   Nothing in subsection (3), (4) or (5) above prevents the enforcing authority from doing anything by way of remediation under section 78N below which it could have done apart from that subsection, but the authority shall not be entitled under section 78P below to recover from any person any part of the cost incurred by the authority in doing by way of remediation anything which it is precluded by subsection (3), (4) or (5) above from requiring that person to do.

(7)   In this section, "appear" means appear to the enforcing authority, and cognate expressions shall be construed accordingly.

78L.   Appeals against remediation notices

(1)   A person on whom a remediation notice is served may, within the period of twenty-one days beginning with the day on which the notice is served, appeal against the notice—

(a)   if it was served by a local authority, to a magistrates' court or, in Scotland, to the sheriff by way of summary application; or

(b)   if it was served by the appropriate Agency, to the Secretary of State;

and in the following provisions of this section "the appellate authority" means the magistrates' court, the sheriff or the Secretary of State, as the case may be.

(2)   On any appeal under subsection (1) above the appellate authority—

(a)   shall quash the notice, if it is satisfied that there is a material defect in the notice; but

(b)   subject to that, may confirm the remediation notice, with or without modification, or quash it.

(3)   Where an appellate authority confirms a remediation notice, with or without modification, it may extend the period specified in the notice for doing what the notice requires to be done.

(4)   Regulations may make provision with respect to—

(a)   the grounds on which appeals under subsection (1) above may be made;

(b)   the cases in which, grounds on which, court or tribunal to which, or person at whose instance, an appeal against a decision of a magistrates' court or sheriff court in pursuance of an appeal under subsection (1) above shall lie; or

(c)   the procedure on an appeal under subsection (1) above or on an appeal by virtue of paragraph (b) above.

(5)   Regulations under subsection (4) above may (among other things)—

(a)   include provisions comparable to those in section 290 of the Public Health Act 1936 (appeals against notices requiring the execution of works);

(b)   prescribe the cases in which a remediation notice is, or is not, to be suspended until the appeal is decided, or until some other stage in the proceedings;

(c)   prescribe the cases in which the decision on an appeal may in some respects be less favourable to the appellant than the remediation notice against which he is appealing;

(d)   prescribe the cases in which the appellant may claim that a remediation notice should have been served on some other person and prescribe the procedure to be followed in those cases;

(e)   make provision as respects—

      (i)   the particulars to be included in the notice of appeal;

      (ii)   the persons on whom notice of appeal is to be served and the particulars, if any, which are to accompany the notice; and

      (iii) the abandonment of an appeal;

    (f)   make different provision for different cases or classes of case.

(6) This section, so far as relating to appeals to the Secretary of State, is subject to section 114 of the Environment Act 1995 (delegation or reference of appeals etc).

78M. Offences of not complying with a remediation notice

(1) If a person on whom an enforcing authority serves a remediation notice fails, without reasonable excuse, to comply with any of the requirements of the notice, he shall be guilty of an offence.

(2) Where the remediation notice in question is one which was required by section 78E(3) above to state, in relation to the requirement which has not been complied with, the proportion of the cost involved which the person charged with the offence is liable to bear, it shall be a defence for that person to prove that the only reason why he has not complied with the requirement is that one or more of the other persons who are liable to bear a proportion of that cost refused, or was not able, to comply with the requirement.

(3) Except in a case falling within subsection (4) below, a person who commits an offence under subsection (1) above shall be liable, on summary conviction, to a fine not exceeding level 5 on the standard scale and to a further fine of an amount equal to one-tenth of level 5 on the standard scale for each day on which the failure continues after conviction of the offence and before the enforcing authority has begun to exercise its powers by virtue of section 78N(3)(c) below.

(4) A person who commits an offence under subsection (1) above in a case where the contaminated land to which the remediation notice relates is industrial, trade or business premises shall be liable on summary conviction to a fine not exceeding £20,000 or such greater sum as the Secretary of State may from time to time by order substitute and to a further fine of an amount equal to one-tenth of that sum for each day on which the failure continues after conviction of the offence and before the enforcing authority has begun to exercise its powers by virtue of section 78N(3)(c) below.

(5) If the enforcing authority is of the opinion that proceedings for an offence under this section would afford an ineffectual remedy against a person who has failed to comply with any of the requirements of a remediation notice which that authority has served on him, that authority may take proceedings in the High Court or, in Scotland, in any court of competent jurisdiction, for the purpose of securing compliance with the remediation notice.

(6) In this section 'industrial, trade or business premises' means premises used for any industrial, trade or business purposes or premises not so used on which matter is burnt in connection with any industrial, trade or business process, and premises are used for industrial purposes where they are used for the purposes of any treatment or process as well as where they are used for the purpose of manufacturing.

(7) No order shall be made under subsection (4) above unless a draft of the order has been laid before, and approved by a resolution of, each House of Parliament.

78N. Powers of the enforcing authority to carry out remediation

(1) Where this section applies, the enforcing authority shall itself have power, in a case falling within paragraph (a) or (b) of section 78E(1) above, to do what is appropriate by way of remediation to the relevant land or waters.

(2) Subsection (1) above shall not confer power on the enforcing authority to do anything by way of remediation if the authority would, in the particular case, be

precluded by section 78YB below from serving a remediation notice requiring that thing to be done.

(3)   This section applies in each of the following cases, that is to say—

(a)   where the enforcing authority considers it necessary to do anything itself by way of remediation for the purpose of preventing the occurrence of any serious harm, or serious pollution of controlled waters, of which there is imminent danger;

(b)   where an appropriate person has entered into a written agreement with the enforcing authority for that authority to do, at the cost of that person, that which he would otherwise be required to do under this Part by way of remediation;

(c)   where a person on whom the enforcing authority serves a remediation notice fails to comply with any of the requirements of the notice;

(d)   where the enforcing authority is precluded by section 78J or 78K above from including something by way of remediation in a remediation notice;

(e)   where the enforcing authority considers that, were it to do some particular thing by way of remediation, it would decide, by virtue of subsection (2) of section 78P below or any guidance issued under that subsection,—

(i)   not to seek to recover under subsection (1) of that section any of the reasonable cost incurred by it in doing that thing; or

(ii)   to seek so to recover only a portion of that cost;

(f)   where no person has, after reasonable inquiry, been found who is an appropriate person in relation to any particular thing.

(4)   Subject to section 78E(4) and (5) above, for the purposes of this section, the things which it is appropriate for the enforcing authority to do by way of remediation are—

(a)   in a case falling within paragraph (a) of subsection (3) above, anything by way of remediation which the enforcing authority considers necessary for the purpose mentioned in that paragraph;

(b)   in a case falling within paragraph (b) of that subsection, anything specified in, or determined under, the agreement mentioned in that paragraph;

(c)   in a case falling within paragraph (c) of that subsection, anything which the person mentioned in that paragraph was required to do by virtue of the remediation notice;

(d)   in a case falling within paragraph (d) of that subsection, anything by way of remediation which the enforcing authority is precluded by section 78J or 78K above from including in a remediation notice;

(e)   in a case falling within paragraph (e) or (f) of that subsection, the particular thing mentioned in the paragraph in question.

(5)   In this section "the relevant land or waters" means—

(a)   the contaminated land in question;

(b)   any controlled waters affected by that land; or

(c)   any land adjoining or adjacent to that land or those waters.

78P. Recovery of, and security for, the cost of remediation by the enforcing authority

(1)   Where, by virtue of section 78N(3)(a), (c), (e) or (f) above, the enforcing authority does any particular thing by way of remediation, it shall be entitled, subject to section 78J(7) and 78K(6) above, to recover the reasonable cost incurred in doing it from the appropriate person or, if there are two or more appropriate persons in proportions determined pursuant to section 78F(7) above.

(2)   In deciding whether to recover the cost, and, if so, how much of the cost, which it is entitled to recover under subsection (1) above, the enforcing authority shall have regard—

(a)   to any hardship which the recovery may cause to the person from whom the cost is recoverable; and

(b) to any guidance issued by the Secretary of State for the purposes of this subsection.

(3) Subsection (4) below shall apply in any case where—

(a) any cost is recoverable under subsection (1) above from a person—

(i) who is the owner of any premises which consist of or include the contaminated land in question; and

(ii) who caused or knowingly permitted the substances, or any of the substances, by reason of which the land is contaminated land to be in, on or under the land; and

(b) the enforcing authority serves a notice under this subsection (in this Part referred to as a 'charging notice') on that person.

(4) Where this subsection applies—

(a) the cost shall carry interest, at such reasonable rate as the enforcing authority may determine, from the date of service of the notice until the whole amount is paid; and

(b) subject to the following provisions of this section, the cost and accrued interest shall be a charge on the premises mentioned in subsection (3)(a)(i) above.

(5) A charging notice shall—

(a) specify the amount of the cost which the enforcing authority claims is irrecoverable;

(b) state the effect of subsection (4) above and the rate of interest determined by the authority under that subsection; and

(c) state the effect of subsections (7) and (8) below.

(6) On the date on which an enforcing authority serves a charging notice on a person, the authority shall also serve a copy of the notice on every other person who, to the knowledge of the authority, has an interest in the premises capable of being affected by the charge.

(7) Subject to any order under subsection (9)(b) or (c) below, the amount of any cost specified in a charging notice and the accrued interest shall be a charge on the premises—

(a) as from the end of the period of twenty-one days beginning with the service of the charging notice, or

(b) where an appeal is brought under subsection (8) below, as from the final determination or (as the case may be) the withdrawal, of the appeal, until the cost and interest are recovered.

(8) A person served with a charging notice or a copy of a charging notice may appeal against the notice to a county court within the period of twenty-one days beginning with the date of service.

(9) On an appeal under subsection (8) above, the court may—

(a) confirm the notice without modification;

(b) order that the notice is to have effect with the substitution of a different amount for the amount originally specified in it; or

(c) order that the notice is to be of no effect.

(10) Regulations may make provision with respect to—

(a) the grounds on which appeals uner this section may be made; or

(b) the procedure on any such appeal.

(11) An enforcing authority shall, for the purpose of enforcing a charge under this section, have all the same powers and remedies under the Law of Property Act 1925, and otherwise, as if it were a mortgagee by deed having powers of sale and lease, of accepting surrenders of leases and of appointing a receiver.

(12) Where any cost is a charge on premises under this section, the enforcing authority may by order declare the cost to be payable with interest by instalments within the specified period until the whole amount is paid.

(13) In subsection (12) above—

"interest" means interest at the rate determined by the enforcing authority under subsection (4) above; and

"the specified period" means such period of thirty years or less from the date of service of the charging notice as is specified in the order.

(14) Subsections (3) to (13) above do not extend to Scotland.

78Q. Special sites

(1) If, in a case where a local authority has served a remediation notice, the contaminated land in question becomes a special site, the appropriate Agency may adopt the remediation notice and, if it does so,—

(a) it shall give notice of its decision to adopt the remediation notice to the appropriate person and to the local authority;

(b) the remediation notice shall have effect, as from the time at which the appropriate Agency decides to adopt it, as a remediation notice given by that Agency; and

(c) the validity of the remediation notice shall not be affected by—

(i) the contaminated land having become a special site;

(ii) the adoption of the remediation notice by the appropriate Agency; or

(iii) anything in paragraph (b) above.

(2) Where a local authority has, by virtue of section 78N above, begun to do anything, or any series of things, by way of remediation—

(a) the authority may continue doing that thing, or that series of things, by virtue of that section, notwithstanding that the contaminated land in question becomes a special site; and

(b) section 78P above shall apply in relation to the reasonable cost incurred by the authority in doing that thing or those things as if that authority were the enforcing authority.

(3) If and so long as any land is a special site, the appropriate Agency may from time to time inspect that land for the purpose of keeping its condition under review.

(4) If it appears to the appropriate Agency that a special site is no longer land which is required to be designated as such a site, the appropriate Agency may give notice—

(a) to the Secretary of State, and

(b) to the local authority in whose area the site is situated,

terminating the designation of the land in question as a special site as from such date as may be specified in the notice.

(5) A notice under subsection (4) above shall not prevent the land, or any of the land, to which the notice relates being designated as a special site on a subsequent occasion.

(6) In exercising its functions under subsection (3) or (4) above, the appropriate Agency shall act in accordance with any guidance given for the purpose by the Secretary of State.

78R. Registers

(1) Every enforcing authority shall maintain a register containing prescribed particulars of or relating to—

(a) remediation notices served by that authority;

(b) appeals against any such remediation notices;

(c) remediation statements or remediation declarations prepared and published under section 78H above;

(d) in relation to an enforcing authority in England and Wales, appeals against charging notices served by that authority;

(e) notices under subsection (1)(b) or (5)(a) of section 78C above which have effect by virtue of subsection (7) of that section as the designation of any land as a special site;

(f) notices under subsection (4)(b) of section 78D above which have effect by virtue of subsection (6) of that section as the designation of any land as a special site;

(g) notices given by or to the enforcing authority under section 78Q(4) above terminating the designation of any land as a special site;

(h) notifications given to that authority by persons—

    (i) on whom a remediation notice has been served, or

    (ii) who are or were required by virtue of section 78H(8)(a) above to prepare and publish a remediation statement,

of what they claim has been done by them by way of remediation;

(j) notifications given to that authority by owners or occupiers of land—

    (i) in respect of which a remediation notice has been served, or

    (ii) in respect of which a remediation statement has been prepared and published,

of what they claim has been done on the land in question by way of remediation;

(k) convictions for such offences under section 78M above as may be prescribed;

(l) such other matters relating to contaminated land as may be prescribed;

but that duty is subject to sections 78S and 78T below.

(2) The form of, and the descriptions of information to be contained in, notifications for the purposes of subsection (1)(h) or (j) above may be prescribed by the Secretary of State.

(3) No entry made in a register by virtue of subsection (1)(h) or (j) above constitutes a repesentation by the body maintaining the register or, in a case where the entry is made by virtue of subsection (6) below, the authority which sent the copy of the particulars in question pursuant to subsection (4) or (5) below—

(a) that what is stated in the entry to have been done has in fact been done; or

(b) as to the manner in which it has been done.

(4) Where any particulars are entered on a register maintained under this section by the appropriate Agency, the appropriate Agency shall send a copy of those particulars to the local authority in whose area is situated the land to which the particulars relate.

(5) In any case where—

(a) any land is treated by virtue of section 78X(2) below as situated in the area of a local authority other than the local authority in whose area it is in fact situated, and

(b) any particulars relating to that land are entered on the register maintained under this section by the local authority in whose area the land is so treated as situated,

that authority shall send a copy of those particulars to the local authority in whose area the land is in fact situated.

(6) Where a local authority receives a copy of any particulars sent to it pursuant to subsection (4) or (5) above, it shall enter those particulars on the register maintained by it under this section.

(7) Where information of any description is excluded by virtue of section 78T below from any register maintained under this section, a statement shall be entered in the register indicating the existence of information of that description.

(8) It shall be the duty of each enforcing authority—

(a) to secure that the registers maintained by it under this section are available, at all reasonable times, for inspection by the public free of charge; and

(b) to afford to members of the public facilities for obtaining copies of entries, on payment of reasonable charges;

and, for the purposes of this subsection, places may be prescribed by the Secretary of State at which any such registers or facilities as are mentioned in paragraph (a) or (b) above are to be available or afforded to the public in pursuance of the paragraph in question.

(9) Registers under this section may be kept in any form.

78S. Exclusion from registers of information affecting national security

(1) No information shall be included in a register maintained under section 78R above if and so long as, in the opinion of the Secretary of State, the inclusion in the register of that information, or information of that description, would be contrary to the interests of national security.

(2) The Secretary of State may, for the purpose of securing the exclusion from registers of information to which subsection (1) above applies, give to enforcing authorities directions—

(a) specifying information, or descriptions of information, to be excluded from their registers; or

(b) specifying descriptions of information to be referred to the Secretary of State for his determination;

and no information referred to the Secretary of State in pursuance of paragraph (b) above shall be in any such register until the Secretary of State determines that it should be so included.

(3) The enforcing authority shall notify the Secretary of State of any information which it excludes from the register in pursuance of directions under subsection (2) above.

(4) A person may, as respects any information which appears to him to be information to which subsection (1) above may apply, give a notice to the Secretary of State specifying the information and indicating its apparent nature; and, if he does so—

(a) he shall notify the enforcing authority that he has done so; and

(b) no information so notified to the Secretary of State shall be included in any such register until the Secretary of State has determined that it should be so included.

78T. Exclusion from registers of certain confidential information

(1) No information relating to the affairs of any individual or business shall be included in a register maintained under section 78R above, without the consent of that individual or the person for the time being carrying on that business, if and so long as the information—

(a) is, in relation to him, commercially confidential; and

(b) is not required to be included in the register in pursuance of directions under subsection (7) below;

but information is not commercially confidential for the purposes of this section unless it is determined under this section to be so by the enforcing authority or, on appeal, by the Secretary of State.

(2) Where it appears to an enforcing authority that any information which has been obtained by the authority under or by virtue of any provision of this Part might be commercially confidential, the authority shall—

(a) give to the person to whom or whose business it relates notice that that information is required to be included in the register unless excluded under this section; and

(b) give him a reasonable opportunity—

(i) of objecting to the inclusion of the information on the ground that it is commercially confidential; and

(ii) of making representations to the authority for the purpose of justifying any such objection;

and, if any representations are made, the enforcing authority shall, having taken the representations into account, determine whether the information is or is not commercially confidential.

(3) Where, under subsection (2) above, an authority determines that information is not commercially confidential—

(a) the information shall not be entered in the register until the end of the period of twenty-one days beginning with the date on which the determination is notified to the person concerned;

(b) that person may appeal to the Secretary of State against the decision;

and, where an appeal is brought in respect of any information, the information shall not be entered in the register until the end of the period of seven days following the day on which the appeal is finally determined or withdrawn.

(4) An appeal under subsection (3) above shall, if either party to the appeal so requests or the Secretary of State so decides, take or continue in the form of a hearing (which must be held in private).

(5) Subsection (10) of section 15 above shall apply in relation to an appeal under subsection (3) above as it applies in relation to an appeal under that section.

(6) Subsection (3) above is subject to section 114 of the Environment Act 1995 (delegation or reference of appeals etc).

(7) The Secretary of State may give to the enforcing authorities directions as to specified information, or descriptions of information, which the public interest requires to be included in registers maintained under section 78R above notwithstanding that the information may be commercially confidential.

(8) Information excluded from a register shall be treated as ceasing to be commercially confidential for the purposes of this section at the expiry of the period of four years beginning with the date of the determination by virtue of which it was excluded; but the person who furnished it may apply to the authority for the information to remain excluded from the register on the ground that it is still commercially confidential and the authority shall determine whether or not that is the case.

(9) Subsections (3) to (6) above shall apply in relation to a determination under subsection (8) above as they apply in relation to a determination under subsection (2) above.

(10) Information is, for the purposes of any determination under this section, commercially confidential, in relation to any individual or person, if its being contained in the register would prejudice to an unreasonable degree the commercial interests of that individual or person.

(11) For the purposes of subsection (10) above, there shall be disregarded any prejudice to the commercial interests of any individual or person so far as relating only to the value of the contaminated land in question or otherwise to the ownership or occupation of that land.

78U. Reports by the appropriate Agency on the state of contaminated land

(1) The appropriate Agency shall—

(a) from time to time, or

(b) if the Secretary of State at any time so requests,

prepare and publish a report on the state of contaminated land in England and Wales or in Scotland, as the case may be.

(2) A local authority shall, at the written request of the appropriate Agency, furnish the appropriate Agency with such information to which this subsection applies as the appropriate Agency may require for the purpose of enabling it to perform its functions under subsection (1) above.

(3) The information to which subsection (2) above applies is such information as the local authority may have, or may reasonably be expected to obtain, with respect to the condition of contaminated land in its area, being information which the authority has acquired or may acquire in the exercise of its functions under this Part.

78V. Site-specific guidance by the appropriate Agency concerning contaminated land

(1) The appropriate Agency may issue guidance to any local authority with respect to the exercise or performance of the authority's powers or duties under this Part in relation to any particular contaminated land; and in exercising or performing those powers or duties in relation to that land the authority shall have regard to any such guidance so issued.

(2) If and to the extent that any guidance issued under subsection (1) above to a local authority is inconsistent with any guidance issued under this Part by the Secretary of State, the local authority shall disregard the guidance under that subsection.

(3) A local authority shall, at the written request of the appropriate Agency, furnish the appropriate Agency with such information to which this subsection applies as the approprate Agency may require for the purpose of enabling it to issue guidance for the purposes of subsection (1) above.

(4) The information to which subsection (3) above applies is such information as the local authority may have, or may reasonably be expected to obtain, with respect to any contaminated land in its area, being information which the authority has acquired, or may acquire, in the exercise of its functions under this Part.

78W. The appropriate Agency to have regard to guidance given by the Secretary of State

(1) The Secretary of State may issue guidance to the appropriate Agency with respect to the exercise or performance of that Agency's powers or duties under this Part; and in exercising or performing those powers or duties the appropriate Agency shall have regard to any such guidance so issued.

(2) The duty imposed on the appropriate Agency by subsection (1) above is without prejudice to any duty imposed by any other provision of this Part on that Agency to act in accordance with guidance issued by the Secretary of State.

78X. Supplementary provisions

(1) Where it appears to a local authority that two or more different sites, when considered together, are in such a condition, by reason of substances in, on or under the land, that—

(a) significant harm is being caused or there is a significant possibility of such harm being caused, or

(b) pollution of controlled waters is being, or is likely to be, caused,

this Part shall apply in relation to each of those sites, whether or not the condition of the land at any of them, when considered alone, appears to the authority to be such that significant harm is being caused, or there is a significant possibility of such harm being caused, or that pollution of controlled waters is being or is likely to be caused.

(2) Where it appears to a local authority that any land outside, but adjoining or adjacent to, its area is in such a condition, by reason of substances in, on or under the land, that significant harm is being caused, or there is a significant possibility of such harm being caused, or that pollution of controlled waters is being, or is likely to be, caused within its area—

(a) the authority may, in exercising its functions under this Part, treat that land as if it were land situated within its area; and

(b) except in this subsection, any reference—

(i) to land within the area of a local authority, or

(ii) to the local authority in whose area any land is situated,

shall be construed accordingly;

but this subsection is without prejudice to the functions of the local authority in whose area the land is in fact situated.

(3)   A person acting in a relevant capacity—

(a)   shall not thereby be personally liable, under this Part, to bear the whole or any part of the cost of doing any thing by way of remediation, unless that thing is to any extent referable to substances whose presence in, on or under the contaminated land in question is a result of any act done or omission made by him which it was unreasonable for a person acting in that capacity to do or make; and

(b)   shall not thereby be guilty of an offence under or by virtue of section 78M above unless the requirement which has not been complied with is a requirement to do some particular thing for which he is personally liable to bear the whole or any part of the cost.

(4)   In subsection (3) above, "person acting in a relevant capacity" means—

(a)   a person acting as an insolvency practitioner, within the meaning of section 388 of the Insolvency Act 1986 (includng that section as it applies in relation to an insolvent partnership by virtue of any order made under section 421 of that Act);

(b)   the official receiver acting in a capacity in which he would be regarded as acting as an insolvency practitioner within the meaning of section 388 of the Insolvency Act 1986 if subsection (5) of that section were disregarded;

(c)   the official receiver acting as receiver or manager;

(d)   a person acting as a special manager under section 177 or 370 of the Insolvency Act 1986;

(e)   the Accountant in Bankruptcy acting as permanent or interim trustee in a sequestration (within the meaning of the Bankruptcy (Scotland) Act 1985);

(f)   a person acting as a receiver or receiver and manager—

(i)   under or by virtue of any enactment; or

(ii)   by virtue of his appointment as such by an order of a court or by any other instrument.

(5)   Regulations may make different provision for different cases or circumstances.

78Y.   Application to the Isles of Scilly

(1)   Subject to the provisions of any order under this section, this Part shall not apply in relation to the Isles of Scilly.

(2)   The Secretary of State may, after consultation with the Council of the Isles of Scilly, by order provide for the application of any provisions of this Part to the Isles of Scilly; and any such order may provide for the application of those provisions to those Isles with such modifications as may be specified in the order.

(3)   An order under this section may—

(a)   make different provision for different cases, including different provision in relation to different persons, circumstances or localities; and

(b)   contain such supplemental, consequential and transitional provision as the Secretary of State considers appropriate, including provision saving provision repealed by or under any enactment.

78YA.   Supplementary provisions with respect to guidance by the Secretary of State

(1)   Any power of the Secretary of State to issue guidance under this Part shall only be exercisable after consultation with the appropriate Agency and such other bodies or persons as he may consider it appropriate to consult in relation to the guidance in question.

(2)   A draft of any guidance proposed to be issued under section 78A(2) or (5), 78B(2) or 78F(6) or (7) above shall be laid before each House of Parliament and the guidance shall not be issued until after the period of 40 days beginning with the day

on which the draft was so laid or, if the draft is laid on different days, the later of the two days.

(3) If, within the period mentioned in subsection (2) above, either House resolves that the guidance, the draft of which was laid before it, should not be issued, the Secretary of State shall not issue that guidance.

(4) In reckoning any period of 40 days for the purposes of subsection (2) or (3) above, no account shall be taken of any time during which Parliament is dissolved or prorogued or during which both Houses are adjourned for more than four days.

(5) The Secretary of State shall arrange for any guidance issued by him under this Part to be published in such manner as he considers appropriate.

78YB. Interaction of this Part with other enactments

(1) A remediation notice shall not be served if and to the extent that it appears to the enforcing authority that the powers of the appropriate Agency under section 27 above may be exercised in relation to—

    (a)   the significant harm (if any), and

    (b)   the pollution of controlled waters (if any),

by reason of which the contaminated land in question is such land.

(2) Nothing in this Part shall apply in relation to any land in respect of which there is for the time being in force a site licence under Part II above, except to the extent that any significant harm, or pollution of controlled waters, by reason of which that land would otherwise fall to be regarded as contaminated land is attributable to causes other than—

    (a)   breach of the conditions of the licence; or

    (b)   the carrying on, in accordance with the conditions of the licence, of any activity authorised by the licence.

(3) If, in a case falling within subsection (1) or (7) of section 59 above, the land in question is contaminated land, or becomes such land by reason of the deposit of the controlled waste in question, a remediation notice shall not be served in respect of that land by reason of that waste or any consequences of its deposit, if and to the extent that it appears to the enforcing authority that the powers of a waste regulation authority or waste collection authority under that section may be exercised in relation to that waste or the consequences of its deposit.

(4) No remediation notice shall require a person to do anything the effect of which would be to impede or prevent the making of a discharge in pursuance of a consent given under Chapter II of Part III of the Water Resources Act 1991 (pollution offences) or, in relation to Scotland, in pursuance of a consent given under Part II of the Control of Pollution Act 1974.

78YC. This Part and radioactivity

Except as provided by regulations, nothing in this Part applies in relation to harm, or pollution of controlled waters, so far as attributable to any radioactivity possessed by any substance; but regulations may—

    (a)   provide for prescribed provisions of this Part to have effect with such modifications as the Secretary of State considers appropriate for the purpose of dealing with harm, or pollution of controlled waters, so far as attributable to any radioactivity possessed by any substances; or

    (b)   make such modifications of the Radioactive Substances Act 1993 or any other Act as the Secretary of State considers appropriate.'

58. Abandoned mines: England and Wales

After Chapter II of Part III of the Water Resources Act 1991 (pollution offences) there shall be inserted—

'CHAPTER IIA
ABANDONED MINES

91A. Introductory

(1) For the purposes of this Chapter, "abandonment", in relation to a mine,—

(a) subject to paragraph (b) below, includes—

(i) the discontinuance of any or all of the operations for the removal of water from the mine;

(ii) the cessation of working of any relevant seam, vein or vein-system;

(iii) the cessation of use of any shaft or outlet of the mine;

(iv) in the case of a mine in which activities other than mining activities are carried on (whether or not mining activities are also carried on in the mine)—

(A) the discontinuance of some or all of those other activities in the mine; and

(B) any substantial change in the operations for the removal of water from the mine; but

(b) does not include—

(i) any disclaimer under section 178 or 315 of the Insolvency Act 1986 (power of liquidator, or trustee of a bankrupt's estate, to disclaim onerous property) by the official receiver acting in a compulsory capacity; or

(ii) the abandonment of any rights, interests or liabilities by the Accountant in Bankruptcy acting as permanent or interim trustee in a sequestration (within the meaning of the Bankruptcy (Scotland) Act 1985);

and cognate expressions shall be construed accordingly.

(2) In this Chapter, except where the context otherwise requires—

"the 1954 Act" means the Mines and Quarries Act 1954;

"acting in a compulsory capacity", in the case of the official receiver, means acting as—

(a) liquidator of a company;

(b) receiver or manager of a bankrupt's estate, pursuant to section 287 of the Insolvency Act 1986;

(c) trustee of a bankrupt's estate;

(e) trustee of an insolvent partnership;

(f) trustee, or receiver or manager, of the insolvent estate of a deceased person;

"mine" has the same meaning as in the 1954 Act;

"the official receiver" has the same meaning as it has in the Insolvency Act 1986 by virtue of section 399(1) of that Act;

"prescribed" means prescribed in regulations;

"regulations" means regulations made by the Secretary of State;

"relevant seam, vein or vein-system", in the case of any mine, means any seam, vein or vein-system for the purpose of, or in connection with, whose working any excavation constituting or comprised in the mine was made.

91B. Mine operators to give the Agency six months' notice of any proposed abandonment

(1) If, in the case of any mine, there is to be an abandonment at any time after the expiration of the initial period, it shall be the duty of the operator of the mine to give notice of the proposed abandonment to the Agency at least six months before the abandonment takes effect.

(2) A notice under subsection (1) above shall contain such information (if any) as is prescribed for the purpose, which may include information about the operator's opinion as to any consequences of the abandonment.

(3) A person who fails to give the notice required by subsection (2) above shall be guilty of an offence and liable—

    (a)   on summary conviction, to a fine not exceeding the statutory maximum;

    (b)   on conviction on indictment, to a fine.

    (4)   A person shall not be guilty of an offence under subsection (3) above if—

    (a)   the abandonment happens in an emergency in order to avoid danger to life or health; and

    (b)   notice of the abandonment, containing such information as may be prescribed, is given as soon as reasonably practicable after the abandonment has happened.

    (5)   Where the operator of a mine is—

    (a)   the official receiver acting in a compulsory capacity, or

    (b)   the Accountant in Bankruptcy acting as permanent or interim trustee in a sequestration (within the meaning of the Bankruptcy (Scotland) Act 1985),

he shall not be guilty of an offence under subsection (3) above by reason of any failure to give the notice required by subsection (1) above if, as soon as reasonably practicable (whether before or after the abandonment), he gives to the Agency notice of the abandonment or proposed abandonment, containing such information as may be prescribed.

    (6)   Where a person gives notice under subsection (1), (4)(b) or (5) above, he shall publish prescribed particulars of, or relating to, the notice in one or more local newspapers circulating in the locality where the mine is situated.

    (7)   Where the Agency—

    (a)   receives notice under this section or otherwise learns of the abandonment or proposed abandonment of any mine, and

    (b)   considers that, in consequence of the abandonment or proposed abandonment taking effect, any land has or is likely to become contaminated land, within the meaning of Part IIA of the Environmental Protection Act 1990,

it shall be the duty of the Agency to inform the local authority in whose area that land is situated of the abandonment or proposed abandonment.

    (8)   In this section—

"the initial period" means the period of six months beginning with the day on which subsection (1) above comes into force;

"local authority" means-

    (a)   any unitary authority;

    (b)   any district council, so far as it is not a unitary authority;

    (c)   the Common Council of the City of London and, as respects the Temples, the Sub-Treasurer of the Inner Temple and the Under-Treasurer of the Middle Temple respectively;

"unitary authority" means—

    (a)   the council of a county, so far as it is the council of an area for which there are no district councils;

    (b)   the council of any district comprised in an area for which there is no county council;

    (c)   the council of a London borough;

    (d)   the council of a county borough in Wales.'

59. Abandoned mines: Scotland

After Part I of the Control of Pollution Act 1974 (waste on land) there shall be inserted—

'PART IA

ABANDONED MINES

30Y. Introductory

    (1)   For the purposes of this Part, "abandonment", in relation to a mine,—

    (a)   Subject to paragraph (b) below, includes—

(i)   the discontinuance of any or all of the operations for the removal of water from the mine;

(ii)   the cessation of working of any relevant seam, vein or vein-system;

(iii)   the cessation of use of any shaft or outlet of the mine;

(iv)   in the case of a mine in which activities other than mining activities are carried on (whether or not mining activities are also carried on in the mine)—

(A)   the discontinuance of some or all of those other activities in the mine; and

(B)   any substantial change in the operations for the removal of water from the mine; but

(b)   does not include—

(i)   the abandonment of any rights, interests or liabilities by the Accountant in Bankruptcy acting as permanent or interim trustee in a sequestration (within the meaning of the Bankruptcy (Scotland) Act 1985); or

(ii)   any disclaimer under section 178 or 315 of the Insolvency Act 1986 (power of liquidator, or trustee of bankrupt's estate, to disclaim onerous property) by the official receiver acting in a compulsory capacity;

and cognate expressions shall be construed accordingly.

(2)   In this Part, except where the context otherwise requires—

"acting in a compulsory capacity", in the case of the official receiver, means acting as—

(a)   liquidator of a company

(b)   receiver or manager of a bankrupt's estate, pursuant to section 287 of the Insolvency Act 1986;

(c)   trustee of a bankrupt's estate;

(d)   liquidator of an insolvent partnership;

(e)   trustee of an insolvent partnership;

(f)   trustee, or receiver or manager, of the insolvent estate of a deceased person;

"the official receiver" has the same meaning as it has in the Insolvency Act 1986 by virtue of section 399(1) of that Act;

"relevant seam, vein or vein-system", in the case of any mine, means any seam, vein or vein-system for the purpose of, or in connection with, whose working any excavation constituting or comprised in the mine was made.

(3)   This Part extends only to Scotland.

30Z. Mine operators to give SEPA six months' notice of any proposed abandonment.

(1)   If, in the case of any mine, there is to be an abandonment at any time after the expiration of the initial period, it shall be the duty of the operator of the mine to give notice of the proposed abandonment to SEPA at least six months before the abandonment takes effect.

(2)   A notice under subsection (1) above shall contain such information (if any) as is prescribed for the purpose, which may include information about the operator's opinion as to any consequences of the abandonment.

(3)   A person who fails to give the notice required by subsection (1) above shall be guilty of an offence and liable—

(a)   on summary conviction, to a fine not exceeding the statutory maximum;

(b)   on conviction on indictment, to a fine.

(4)   A person shall not be guilty of an offence under subsection (3) above if—

(a)   the abandonment happens in an emergency in order to avoid danger to life or health; and

(b)   notice of the abandonment, containing such information as may be prescribed, is given as soon as reasonably practicable after the abandonment has happened.

(5)   Where the operator of a mine is—

(a)   the Accountant in Bankruptcy acting as permanent or interim trustee in a sequestration (within the meaning of the Bankruptcy (Scotland) Act 1985); or

(b)   the official receiver acting in a compulsory capacity,

he shall not be guilty of an offence under subsection (3) above by reason of any failure to give the notice required by subsection (1) above if, as soon as is reasonably practicable (whether before or after the abandonment), he gives to SEPA notice of the abandonment or proposed abandonment, containing such information as may be prescribed.

(6)   Where a person gives notice under subsection (1) (4)(b) or (5) above, he shall publish particulars of, or relating to, the notice in one or more local newspapers circulating in the locality where the mine is situated.

(7)   Where SEPA—

(a)   receives notice under this section or otherwise learns of an abandonment or proposed abandonment in the case of any mine, and

(b)   considers that, in consequence of the abandonment or proposed abandonment taking effect, any land has or is likely to become contaminated land, within the meaning of Part IIA of the Environmental Protection Act 1990,

it shall be the duty of SEPA to inform the local authority in whose area that land is situated of the abandonment or proposed abandonment.

(8)   In this section—

"the initial period" means the period of six months beginning with the day on which subsection (1) above comes into force;

"local authority" means a council constituted under section 2 of the Local Government etc. (Scotland) Act 1994.'

60.   Amendments to sections 89 and 161 of the Water Resources Act 1991

(1)   In section 89 of the Water Resources Act 1991 (defences) in subsection (3) (person not to be guilty of an offence under section 85 by reason only of permitting water from an abandoned mine to enter controlled waters) after the words 'an abandoned mine' there shall be inserted the words 'or an abandoned part of a mine'.

(2)   After that subsection there shall be inserted—

'(3A)   Subsection (3) above shall not apply to the owner or former operator of any mine or part of a mine if the mine or part in question became abandoned after 31st December 1999.

(3B)   In determining for the purposes of subsection (3A) above whether a mine or part of a mine became abandoned before, on or after 31st December 1999 in a case where the mine or part has become abandoned on two or more occasions, of which—

(a)   at least one falls on or before that date, and

(b)   at least one falls after that date,

the mine or part shall be regarded as becoming abandoned after that date (but without prejudice to the operation of subsection (3) above in relation to that mine or part at, or in relation to, any time before the first of those occasions which falls after that date).

(3C)   Where, immediately before a part of a mine becomes abandoned, that part is the only part of the mine not falling to be regarded as abandoned for the time being, the abandonment of that part shall not be regarded for the purposes of subsection (3A) or (3B) above as constituting the abandonment of the mine, but only of that part of it.'

(3)   In section 161 of that Act (anti-pollution works and operations) in subsection (1), after paragraph (b) there shall be inserted the words—

'and, in either case, the Agency shall be entitled to carry out investigations for the purpose of establishing the source of the matter and the identity of the person who has caused or knowingly permitted it to be present in controlled waters or at a place from which it was likely, in the opinion of the Agency, to enter controlled waters.'

(4)   In subsection (3) of that section (Agency entitled to recover expenses of works or operations from the person responsible for the pollution) for the words 'or operations' there shall be substituted the words 'operations or investigations'.

(5)   In subsection (4) of that section (exception for expenses of works or operations in respect of water from an abandoned mine)—

(a)   for the words 'or operations' there shall be substituted the words 'operations or investigations'; and

(b)   after the words 'an abandoned mine' there shall be inserted the words 'or an abandoned part of a mine'.

(6)   After that subsection there shall be inserted—

'(4A)   Subsection (4) above shall not apply to the owner or former operator of any mine or part of a mine if the mine or part in question became abandoned after 31st December 1999.

(4B)   Subsections (3B) and (3C) of section 89 above shall apply in relation to subsections (4) and (4A) above as they apply in relation to subsections (3) and (3A) of that section.'

(7)   In subsection (6) of that section (definitions), after the definition of 'controlled waters' there shall be inserted—

'"expenses" includes costs;'.

PART III

NATIONAL PARKS

Purposes of National Parks

61.   Purposes of National Parks

(1)   In section 5 of the National Parks and Access to the Countryside Act 1949 (National Parks) for subsection (1) (which provides that Part II of that Act has effect for the purpose of preserving and enhancing the natural beauty of the areas specified in subsection (2) of that section and for the purpose of promoting their enjoyment by the public) there shall be substituted—

'(1)   The provisions of this Part of this Act shall have effect for the purpose—

(a)   of conserving and enhancing the natural beauty, wildlife and cultural heritage of the areas specified in the next following subsection; and

(b)   of promoting opportunities for the quiet enjoyment and understanding of the special qualities of those areas by the public.'

(2)   The amendment made by subsection (1) above is without prejudice to the continuing validity of any designation of an area as a National Park under subsection (3) of that section.

(3)   The following enactments (which refer to the purposes specified in section 5(1) of the National Parks and Access to the Countryside Act 1949), that is to say—

(a)   sections 6(3) and (4)(g), 11 and 101 (3) of that Act, and

(b)   sections 2(5)(b) and 13(4) of the Countryside Act 1968,

shall have effect in accordance with subsection (4) below.

(4)   In the application of any provision specified in subsection (3) above, any reference to the purposes specified in subsection (1) of section 5 of the National Parks and Access to the Countryside Act 1949—

(a)   in relation to any particular National Park, shall be construed as a reference to the substituted purposes as from the time when a National Park authority becomes the local planning authority for that Park; and

(b)   in relation to National Parks generally, shall be construed as a reference—

(i)   to the original purposes, so far as relating to National Parks in the case of which the National Park authority has not become the local planning authority since the coming into force of this section, and

(ii)   to the substituted purposes, so far as relating to National Parks in the case of which the National Park authority has become the local planning authority since the coming into force of this section.

(5)   In subsection (4) above—
'original purposes' means the purposes specified in subsection (1) of section 5 of that Act, as originally enacted;
'substituted purposes' means the purposes specified in that subsection as substituted by subsection (1) above.

62.   Duty of certain bodies and persons to have regard to the purposes for which National Parks are designated

(1)   After section 11 of the National Parks and Access to the Countryside Act 1949 (general powers of local planning authorities in relation to National Parks) there shall be inserted—

11A.   'Duty of certain bodies and persons to have regard to the purposes for which National Parks are designated

(1)   A National Park authority, in pursuing in relation to the National Park the purposes specified in subsection (1) of section five of this Act, shall seek to foster the economic and social well-being of local communities within the National Park, but without incurring significant expenditure in doing so, and shall for that purpose co-operate with local authorities and public bodies whose functions include the promotion of economic or social development within the area of the National Park.

(2)   In exercising or performing any functions in relation to, or so as to affect, land in a National Park, any relevant authority shall have regard to the purposes specified in subsection (1) of section five of this Act and, if it appears that there is a conflict between those purposes, shall attach greater weight to the purpose of conserving and enhancing the natural beauty, wildlife and cultural heritage of the area comprised in the National Park.

(3)   For the purposes of this section "relevant authority" means—
    (a)   any Minister of the Crown,
    (b)   any public body,
    (c)   any statutory undertaker, or
    (d)   any person holding public office.

(4)   In subsection (3) of this section—
"public body" includes—
    (a)   any local authority, joint board or joint committee;
    (b)   any National Park authority;
"public office" means—
    (a)   an office under Her Majesty;
    (b)   an office created or continued in existence by a public general Act of Parliament; or
    (c)   an office the remuneration in respect of which is paid out of money provided by Parliament.

(5)   In subsection (4) of this section, "joint board" and "joint committee" mean—
    (a)   a joint or special planning board for a National Park reconstituted by order under paragraph 1 or 3 of Schedule 17 to the Local Government Act 1972, or a joint planning board within the meaning of section 2 of the Town and Country Planning Act 1990;
    (b)   a joint committee: appointed under section 102(1)(b) of the Local Government Act 1972.

(6)   In this section, "local authority"—
    (a)   in relation to England, means a county council, district council or parish council;
    (b)   in relation to Wales, means a county council, county borough council, district council or community council.'

(2)   The duty imposed by subsection (1) of the section 11A inserted by subsection (1) above shall take effect, in the case of any particular National Park, as from the time when a National Park authority becomes the local planning authority for that Park.

Establishment of National Park authorities

63. Establishment of National Park authorities

(1) The Secretary of State may—

    (a) in the case of any National Park for which there is an existing authority, or

    (b) in connection with the designation. of any area as a new such Park,

by order establish an authority (to be known as 'a National Park authority') to carry out in relation to that Park the functions conferred on such an authority by or under this Part.

(2) An order under this section may provide, in relation to any National Park for which there is an existing authority—

    (a) for the existing authority to cease to have any functions in relation to that Park as from the time when a National Park authority becomes the local planning authority, for that Park;

    (b) for such (if any) of the functions of the existing authority as, by virtue of this Part, are not as from that time to be functions of the National Park authority for that Park to become functions of the person on whom they would be conferred if the area in question were not in a National Park; and

    (c) for the winding up of the existing authority and for that authority to cease to exist, or to be dissolved, as from such time as may be specified in the order.

(3) Subject to any order under subsection (4) below, where there is a variation of the area of a National Park for which there is or is to be a National Park authority, the Park for which that authority is or is to be the authority shall be deemed, as from the time when the variation takes effect, to be that area as varied.

(4) Where provision is made for the variation of the area of a National Park for which there is or is to be a National Park authority, the Secretary of State may by order make such transitional provision as he thinks fit with respect to—

    (a) any functions which, in relation to any area that becomes part of the National Park, are by virtue of the variation to become functions of that authority; and

    (b) any functions which, in relation to any area that ceases to be part of the National Park, are by virtue of the variation to become functions of a person other than that authority.

(5) Schedule 7 to this Act shall have effect with respect to National Park authorities.

64. National Park authorities in Wales

(1) Where a National Park planning board has been constituted for the area of any particular existing National Park in Wales, the Secretary of State may exercise his power under section 63 above to establish a National Park authority in relation to that National Park by making an order under that section designating for the body corporate constituted as that board a date earlier than 31st March 1997 on which that body—

    (a) shall cease to be a National Park planning board, and

    (b) shall be constituted the National Park authority in relation to that National Park,

without affecting its corporate status (and an order made under or by virtue of that section may make provision re-naming that body accordingly).

(2) Any order under—

    (a) paragraph 3A of Schedule 17 to the 1972 Act (special planning boards), or

    (b) section 2(1B) of the Town and Country Planning Act 1990 (joint planning boards),

relating to the body corporate constituted as the National Park planning board in question shall have effect on and after the designated date for that body as an order under section 63 above relating to that body in its capacity as the National Park authority in relation to the National Park in question.

(3) For the purposes of any order establishing a National Park authority under section 60 above by virtue of subsection (1) above, or any order which, by virtue of subsection (2) above, has effect as an order under that section—

    (a) the requirements of paragraph 2(3) of Schedule 7 to this Act with respect to consultation with councils for principal areas shall, by virtue of the establishment of the

National Park planning board, be deemed to have been complied with as respects any provision of the order;

(b)   in the case of any member of the National Park planning board immediately before the designated date who was holding that office by virtue of his appointment as such by the Secretary of State under and in accordance with paragraph 11 of Schedule 17 to the 1972 Act (which requires prior consultation), the appointment shall, on and after the designated date, have effect for the remainder of the period for which it was made as an appointment as a member of the National Park authority made by the Secretary of State in accordance with paragraph 3(1) of Schedule 7 to this Act;

(c)   in the case of any other member of the National Park planning board immediately before the designated date who is on that date a member of a principal council for an area which includes the whole or any part of the National Park in question, his appointment as a member of that board shall, on and after the designated date, have effect for the remainder of the period for which it was made as an appointment as a local authority member of the National Park authority made in accordance with paragraph 2 of that Schedule; and

(d)   any other requirement, whether statutory or otherwise, which must be complied with in connection with the establishment of a National Park authority shall be deemed to have been complied with by virtue of the establishment of the National Park planning board; and, except as provided by paragraphs (b) and (c) above, no person who is a member of the National Park planning board immediately before the designated date shall, by virtue of the order, become a member of the National Park authority.

(4)   The functions of a National Park planning board shall include the duty to take such steps as it considers necessary to enable it (that is to say, the body corporate constituted as that board) on being constituted the National Park authority in relation to the National Park in question by an order made by virtue of subsection (1) above, to perform its functions as a National Park authority on and after the designated date; and the functions conferred on such a board by this subsection—

(a)   shall be exercisable before (as well as on or after) 1st April 1996; and

(b)   are in addition to any other functions which are exercisable by such a board before that date by virtue of paragraph 13 of Schedule 17 to the Local Government (Wales) Act 1994.

(5)   The functions of a principal council for an area which includes the whole or any part of the area of a National Park planning board shall include the duty to take such steps as it considers necessary to enable the body corporate constituted as that board, on being constituted the National Park authority in relation to the National Park in question by an order made by virtue of subsection (1) above, to perform those functions which would, apart from the order, be exercisable by a principal council but which will become functions of that body, as the National Park authority, on the designated date.

(6)   Where the Secretary of State—

(a)   has taken any steps with a view to, or otherwise in connection with, the establishment of a National Park planning board for the area of an existing National Park in Wales ('the proposed board'), but

(b)   decides not to proceed with the establishment of the proposed board and to establish instead a National Park authority in relation to that National Park ('the proposed authority'), and

(c)   the proposed authority is, or is to be, established before 31st March 1997,

the doing of anything by or in relation to the Secretary of State (other than the making by the Secretary of State of an instrument of a legislative character) with a view to, or otherwise in connection with, establishing the proposed board shall be treated, as respects the proposed authority, as the doing of any corresponding or reasonably similar thing falling to be done for the purposes of, or otherwise in connection with, the establishment of that authority.

(7)   Without prejudice to the generality of subsection (6) above, in any case falling within paragraphs (a) to (c) of that subsection—

(a)   any consultation with a principal council after 15th December 1994 by the Secretary of State as respects the proposed board (whether or not required by or under any enactment) shall be deemed, as respects the proposed authority, to have been carried out for the purposes of the consultation with councils for principal areas required by paragraph 2(3) of Schedule 7 to this Act;

(b)   anything done by or in relation to the Secretary of State for the purposes of the consultation required by paragraph 11 of Schedule 17 to the 1972 Act (appointment of members by Secretary of State) preparatory to the appointment of a person as a member of the proposed board shall be deemed, as respects the proposed authority, to have been done for the purposes of the consultation required by paragraph 4(1) of Schedule 7 to this Act preparatory to the appointment of that person as a member of that authority;

(c)   anything done by or in relation to the Secretary of State (other than the making by the Secretary of State of an instrument of a legislative character) for the purposes of, or otherwise in connection with, any other requirement, whether statutory or otherwise, of a consultative or procedural nature—

    (i)   which relates to a National Park planning board, and

    (ii)   for which there is a corresponding or reasonably similar requirement which relates to a National Park authority,

shall be treated, as respects the proposed authority, as done for the purposes of, or otherwise in connection with, that other corresponding or reasonably similar requirement.

(8)   Section 54 of the Local Government (Wales) Act 1994 (powers to make incidental, consequential, transitional or supplemental provision) shall have effect as if this Part were contained in that Act, except that subsection (2)(e) of that section shall have effect as if this Part were contained in an Act passed in the same Session as that Act.

(9)   In this section—

'the designated date', in the case of any body corporate constituted as a National Park planning board which becomes, or is to become, a National Park authority by virtue of this section, means the date designated by virtue of subsection (1) above in the order relating to that body;

'existing National Park' means a National Park in respect of which there was in force on 15th December 1994 an order under section 5 of the National Parks and Access to the Countryside Act 1949 (designation of areas as National Parks);

'National Park planning board' means—

    (a)   a special planning board constituted by order under paragraph 3A of Schedule 17 to the 1972 Act to discharge, as respects the area of a National Park in Wales, the functions to which Part I of that Schedule applies, or

    (b)   a joint planning board constituted by order under subsection (1B) of section 2 of the Town and Country Planning Act 1990 for a united district comprising the area of a National Park in Wales.

Functions of National Park authorities

65. General purposes and powers

(1)   This Part so far as it relates to the establishment and functions of National Park authorities shall have effect for the purposes specified in section 5(1) of the National Parks and Access to the Countryside Act 1949 (purposes of conserving and enhancing the natural beauty, wildlife and cultural heritage of National Parks and of promoting opportunities for the understanding and enjoyment of the special qualities of those Parks by the public).

(2)   Sections 37 and 38 of the Countryside Act 1968 (general duties as to the protection of interests of the countryside and the avoidance of pollution) shall apply to National Park authorities as they apply to local authorities.

(3)   The functions of a National Park authority in the period (if any) between the time when it is established and the time when it becomes the local planning authority for the

relevant Park shall be confined to the taking of such steps as the authority, after consultation with the Secretary of State and any existing authority for that Park, considers appropriate for securing that it is able properly to carry out its functions after that time.

(4)   In the application of subsection (3) above in the case of a National Park authority established in relation to a National Park in Wales, the reference to any existing authority for that Park shall have effect as respects consultation carried out during so much of that period as falls before 1st April 1996 as including a reference to any principal council whose area is wholly or partly comprised in that Park.

(5)   The powers of a National Park authority shall include power to do anything which, in the opinion of that authority, is calculated to facilitate, or is conducive or incidental to—

(a)   the accomplishment of the purposes mentioned in subsection (1) above; or

(b)   the carrying out of any functions conferred on it by virtue of any other enactment.

(6)   The powers conferred on a National Park authority by subsection (5) above shall not include either—

(a)   power to do anything in contravention of any restriction imposed by virtue of this Part in relation to any express power of the authority; or

(b)   a power to raise money (whether by borrowing or otherwise) in a manner which is not authorised apart from that subsection;

but the things that may be done in exercise of those powers shall not be treated as excluding anything by reason only that it involves the expenditure, borrowing or lending of money or the acquisition or disposal of any property or rights.

(7)   Schedule 8 to this Act shall have effect with respect to the supplemental and incidental powers of a National Park authority.

66.   National Park Management Plans

(1)   Subject to subsection (2) below, every National Park authority shall, within three years after its operational date, prepare and publish a plan, to be known as a National Park Management Plan, which formulates its policy for the management of the relevant Park and for the carrying out of its functions in relation to that Park.

(2)   A National Park authority for a Park wholly or mainly comprising any area which, immediately before the authority's operational date, was or was included in an area for which there was a National Park Plan prepared and published under paragraph 18 of Schedule 17 to the 1972 Act (National Park plans) shall not be required to prepare a Management Plan under subsection (1) above if, within six months of that date, it adopts the existing National Park Plan as its Management Plan and publishes notice that it has done so.

(3)   Where a National Park authority is proposing to adopt a plan under subsection (2) above, it may review the plan before adopting it and shall do so if the plan would have fallen to be reviewed under paragraph 18 of Schedule 17 to the 1972 Act in the period of twelve months beginning with the authority's operational date.

(4)   A National Park authority shall review its National Park Management Plan within the period of five years of its operational date and, after the first review, at intervals of not more than five years.

(5)   Where a National Park authority has adopted a plan under subsection (2) above as its National Park Management Plan and has not reviewed that Plan before adopting it, the first review of that Plan under subsection (4) above shall take place no later than the time when the adopted plan would otherwise have fallen to be reviewed under paragraph 18 of Schedule 17 to the 1972 Act.

(6)   Where a National Park authority reviews any plan under this section, it shall—

(a)   determine on that review whether it would be expedient to amend the plan and what (if any) amendments would be appropriate;

(b)   make any amendments that it considers appropriate; and

(c)   publish a report on the review specifying any amendments made.

(7) A National Park authority which is proposing to publish, adopt or review any plan under this section shall—

(a) give notice of the proposal to every principal council whose area is wholly or partly comprised in the relevant Park and, according to whether that Park is in England or in Wales, to the Countryside Commission and the Nature Conservancy Council for England or to the Countryside Council for Wales;

(b) send a copy of the plan, together (where appropriate) with any proposed amendments of the plan, to every body to which notice of the proposal is required to be given by paragraph (a) above; and

(c) take into consideration any observations made by any such body.

(8) A National Park authority shall send to the Secretary of State a copy of every plan, notice or report which it is required to publish under this section.

(9) In this section 'operational date', in relation to a National Park authority, means the date on which the authority becomes the local planning authority for the relevant Park.

67. National Park authority to be local planning authority

(1) After section 4 of the Town and Country Planning Act 1990 (National Parks) there shall be inserted—

'4A. National Parks with National Park authorities

(1) Where a National Park authority has been established for any area, this section, instead of section 4(1) to (4), shall apply, as from such time as may be specified for the purposes of this section in the order establishing that authority, in relation to the Park for which it is the authority.

(2) Subject to subsections (4) and (5) below, the National Park authority for the Park shall be the sole local planning authority for the area of the Park and, accordingly—

(a) functions conferred by or under the planning Acts on a planning authority of any description (including the functions of a mineral planning authority under those Acts and under the Planning and Compensation Act 1991) shall, in relation to the Park, be functions of the National Park authority, and not of any other authority; and

(b) so much of the area of any other authority as is included in the Park shall be treated as excluded from any area for which that other authority is a planning authority of any description.

(3) For the purposes of subsection (2) above functions under the planning Acts which (apart from this section) are conferred—

(a) in relation to some areas on the county or district planning authorities for those areas, and

(b) in relation to other areas on the councils for those areas,

shall be treated, in relation to those other areas, as conferred on each of those councils as the local planning authority for their area.

(4) The functions of a local planning authority by virtue of sections 198 to 201, 206 to 209 and 211 to 215, so far as they are functions of a National Park authority by virtue of this section, shall be exercisable as respects any area which is or is included in an area for which there is a district council, concurrently with the National Park authority, by that council.

(5) For the purposes of any enactment relating to the functions of a district planning authority, the functions of a district council by virtue of subsection (4) above shall be deemed to be conferred on them as a district planning authority and as if the district were the area for which they are such an authority.'

(2) The Secretary of State may by order make provision—

(a) for applying Chapter I of Part II of that Act of 1990 (unitary development plans), instead of provisions of Chapter II of that Part (structure and local plans), in relation to the area of any National Park; or

(b) for applying Chapter II of that Part in relation to the area of such a Park—

(i)   as if functions under that Chapter of a planning authority of any description were functions of such public authority as may be specified in the order (and not of the National Park authority); and

(ii)   as if that Part had effect with such other modifications as may be so specified in relation to the carrying out of those functions by an authority so specified.

(3)   Without prejudice to any power conferred by virtue of section 75 below, the Secretary of State shall have power by order, for the purposes of any provision made by virtue of this section, to modify the provisions of Part II of that Act of 1990 (development plans) in relation to any such area of a local planning authority as, but for any exclusion by virtue of section 4A of that Act, would include the whole or any part of a National Park.

(4)   References in this section to provisions of Part II of that Act of 1990 include references to any provisions for modifying those provisions which are contained in any enactment passed after this Act.

(5)   Before section 148 of that Act of 1990 (interpretation of provisions relating to purchase notices) there shall be inserted—

'147A.   Application of Chapter I to National Parks

This Chapter shall have effect as if—

(a)   the bodies on whom a purchase notice may be served under section 137 included any National Park authority which is the local planning authority for the area in which the land is situated; and

(b)   a National Park authority were a local authority for the purposes of this Act and the National Park for which it is the local planning authority were its area;

and the references in this Chapter and in section 288(10)(a) to a council and to a local authority shall be construed accordingly.'

68.   Planning authority functions under National Parks legislation etc.

(1)   Where a National Park authority is the local planning authority for any National Park, section 184 of the 1972 Act and paragraph 37 of Schedule 17 to that Act (functions under certain legislation relating to the National Parks and the countryside) shall not apply as respects that Park in relation to any of the functions conferred by or under—

(a)   the National Parks and Access to the Countryside Act 1949 ('the 1949 Act'), or

(b)   the Countryside Act 1968 ('the 1968 Act'),

on a planning authority of any description.

(2)   In consequence of subsection (1) above, but subject to subsections (3) to (7) below—

(a)   functions which are conferred on a local planning authority by or under the 1949 Act or the 1968 Act, and the functions conferred on a county planning authority (or, in relation to Wales, a local planning authority) by section 69 of the 1949 Act (suspension of access to avoid risk of fire), shall, as respects the whole or any part of a National Park for which a National Park authority is the local planning authority, be functions of that authority and not of any other authority;

(b)   references in those Acts to a local planning authority whose area consists of or includes the whole or any part of a National Park shall be construed, in relation to any National Park for which a National Park authority is the local planning authority, as references to the National Park authority; and

(c)   other references in those Acts to a local planning authority and

the references to a local authority in section 103 of the 1949 Act and sections 10 and 43 to 45 of the 1968 Act (which contain provision applying in relation to local authorities in their capacity as local planning authorities) shall have effect accordingly.

(3)   Section 11 of the 1949 Act (which makes provision in relation to a local planning authority that corresponds to provision made by section 65 above in relation to a National Park authority) shall not apply in relation to any National Park authority.

(4)   The functions conferred by or under section 12 of the 1949 Act or section 12 of the 1968 Act (facilities for National Parks) which are exercisable by virtue of this section by a National Park authority in a National Park—

(a)   shall be exercisable by that authority outside the relevant Park on any land in the neighbourhood of that Park; but

(b)   shall be so exercisable only under arrangements made with the local planning authority for the area where they are exercised.

(5)   Sections 61 to 63 of the 1949 Act (survey of access requirements and action in response to the survey) shall have effect in accordance with subsection (2) above as respects the area of any National Park for which a National Park authority has become the local planning authority—

(a)   in the case of a Park designated after the commencement of this section, as if section 61(1) applied with the substitution for the reference to the commencement of that Act of a reference to the time when that authority became the local planning authority for that Park;

(b)   as if no area were required by virtue of subsection (3) of section 61 of that Act, or of any previous review under that section, to be excluded from any area to be reviewed by virtue of paragraph (a) above; and

(c)   in the case of a Park designated before the commencement of this section, as if—

(i)   the power (if any) to make a resolution for the purposes of the proviso to that subsection (3) as respects any part of the area of the Park which has not previously been reviewed under that section; and

(ii)   the functions which, where such a resolution has been so made, are conferred on the authority which made it or on any authority which has conducted a review in pursuance of the resolution,

were a power or, as the case may be, functions of the National Park authority, and not of any other authority.

(6)   The following functions, so far as exercisable by a National Park authority in relation to land or countryside in a National Park in England for which that authority is the local planning authority, that is to say—

(a)   those conferred by or under section 89 of the 1949 Act (planting of trees and treatment of derelict land), and

(b)   those conferred by section 10 of the 1968 Act (camping and picnic sites), shall be exercisable in relation to so much of that Park as is comprised in a district for which there is a district council, concurrently with the National Park authority, by that district council.

(7)   For the purposes of any enactment relating to the functions of a district planning authority, the functions of a district council by virtue of subsection (6) above shall be deemed to be conferred on them as a district planning authority and as if the district were the area for which they are such an authority.

(8)   The following powers, that is to say—

(a)   those conferred on a local authority by or under section 92 of the 1949 Act (wardens), and

(b)   those conferred on a local authority by or under section 41 of the 1968 Act (byelaws),

so far as they are conferred in relation to any of the functions which by virtue of this section are functions of a National Park authority as respects the relevant Park, shall be exercisable by that authority and also, in the case of those conferred by or under section 41 of the 1968 Act, by a district council in relation to that council's functions by virtue of subsection (6)(b) above, but not by any other authority.

(9)   Section 104 of the 1949 Act (general provisions as to appropriation and disposal of land), except subsection (11), shall have effect as if references in that section to a local authority included references to a National Park authority.

(10)   For the purposes of any functions conferred on a National Park authority by virtue of this section references in any enactment to the area of the authority shall be construed as references to the relevant Park.

69. Planning authority functions under the Wildlife and Countryside Act 1981

(1) A National Park authority which is the local planning authority for any National Park, and not any other authority, shall have all the functions under the Wildlife and Countryside Act 1981 which are conferred as respects that Park on a planning authority of any description.

(2) Accordingly—

(a) a National Park authority shall be the relevant authority for the purposes of sections 39, 41 and 50 of that Act (management agreements and duties of agriculture Ministers in relation to the countryside) as respects any land in any National Park for which that authority is the local planning authority; and

(b) section 52(2) of that Act (construction of references to a local planning authority) shall not apply as respects any National Park for which a National Park authority is the local planning authority.

(3) Section 43 of that Act (maps of National Parks) shall have effect in accordance with the preceding provisions of this section—

(a) in the case of a National Park designated after the commencement of this section, as if the relevant date for the purposes of that section were the date on which a National Park authority becomes the local planning authority for the Park; and

(b) in any other case, as if the function of reviewing and revising any map of a part of the Park in question included a power, in pursuance of the review and revisions, to consolidate that map with other maps prepared under that section as respects other parts of that Park.

(4) In section 44 of that Act (grants and loans for purposes of National Parks), after subsection (1) there shall be inserted the following subsection—

'(1A) Subsection (1) above shall not apply in relation to any National Park for which a National Park authority is the local planning authority; but the National Park authority for such a Park may give financial assistance by way of grant or loan, or partly in one way and partly in the other, to any person in respect of expenditure incurred by him in doing anything which, in the opinion of the authority, is conducive to the attainment in the Park in question of any of the purposes mentioned in section 5(1) of the 1949 Act (purposes of conserving and enhancing the natural beauty, wildlife and cultural heritage of National Parks and of promoting opportunities for the understanding and enjoyment of the special qualities of those Parks by the public).'

70. Other statutory functions

In addition to its functions under the enactments mentioned in sections 67 to 69 above and to such of its functions under any other enactment as are conferred by virtue of its being a local planning authority within the meaning of the Town and Country Planning Act 1990, a National Park authority shall have the further miscellaneous functions conferred on it by virtue of Schedule 9 to this Act.

Finances of National Park authorities

71. National Park authorities to be levying bodies

(1) A National Park authority shall have power in respect of every financial year beginning after the establishment of that authority to issue levies to the councils by whom the local authority members of that authority fall to be appointed.

(2) Subject to the following provisions of this section, a levy issued by virtue of this section shall be issued in accordance with regulations under section 74 of the Local Government Finance Act 1988 (power to make regulations authorising a levying body to issue a levy); and, accordingly, a National Park authority shall be deemed to be a levying body within the meaning of that section.

(3) Subject to any maximum specified in or determined in accordance with any regulations under that section 74, the amount of the levies issued by a National Park

authority in respect of any financial year shall be equal to the sum by which the aggregate of the amounts specified in subsection (4) below is exceeded by the aggregate of the sums which it estimates it will require in respect of that year for the following purposes, that is to say—

(a)   meeting the expenditure of the authority which will fall to be charged for that year to any revenue account;

(b)   making such provision as may be appropriate for meeting contingencies the expenditure on which would fall to be so charged;

(c)   securing the availability to the authority of adequate working balances on its revenue accounts; and

(d)   providing the authority with the funds required for covering any deficit carried forward from a previous financial year in any revenue account.

(4)   The amounts mentioned in subsection (3) above in relation to any financial year are—

(a)   any amounts to be received by the authority in respect of that year by way of grant under section 72 below;

(b)   the authority's estimate of the amounts which are likely for that year to be credited to any revenue account in respect of sums payable to the authority for things done in the course of, or in connection with, the carrying out of its functions; and

(c)   the authority's estimate of the amounts not falling within paragraph (a) or (b) above which apart from this section are, or are likely to be, available to it for that year for the purposes mentioned in subsection (3) above.

(5)   Where agreement as to the apportionment of the amount to be raised by a National Park authority in respect of any financial year by way of levies is entered into, before 1st December in the immediately preceding financial year, by all the authorities to whom the levies in respect of that year may be issued by that authority, that amount shall be apportioned between those authorities in accordance with the agreement, instead of in accordance with any provision made by virtue of that section 74.

(6)   Regulations under that section 74 may include provision for requiring an authority to anticipate a levy by virtue of this section when making any calculations which fall, for the financial year following that in which any National Park authority is established, to be made (whether originally or by way of substitute) under section 32 or 43 of the Local Government Finance Act 1992 (calculation of budget requirement).

(7)   A National Park authority shall not by virtue of this section be a local authority within the meaning of the Town and Country Planning Act 1990.

72. National Park grant

(1)   The Secretary of State may make grants to a National Park authority for such purposes, of such amounts and on such terms and conditions as he thinks fit.

(2)   Before determining the amount of any grant which he proposes to make to a National Park authority under this section, or the purpose for which it is to be made, the Secretary of State shall consult, according to whether the relevant Park is in England or in Wales, either the Countryside Commission or the Countryside Council for Wales.

(3)   The consent of the Treasury shall be required for the making of a grant under this section.

73. Capital finances and borrowing

In section 39(1) of the Local Government and Housing Act 1989 (which specifies the authorities to which the provisions of Part IV of that Act relating to capital accounts and borrowing powers apply), after paragraph (i) there shall be inserted—

'(ia) a National Park authority;'.

74. Validation of certain grants paid to local authorities in respect of expenditure relating to National Parks

(1)   No payment made for any year beginning on or after 1st April 1990 and ending on or before 31st March 1996 by the Secretary of State by way of grant to the council of a

county or a metropolitan district in respect of the council's expenditure or estimated expenditure in connection with National Parks shall be regarded as made otherwise than under and in accordance with the relevant enactments by reason only of—

(a) the aggregate amount of such grants for the year to such councils not having been duly prescribed;

(b) the method of determining the proportion of such aggregate amount payable to that council not having been duly prescribed; or

(c) payment of the grant being, or having been, made—

(i) otherwise than in accoradance with an approved Rate Support Grant Report or such a Report as varied by an approved supplementary report for the year; or

(ii) without there being an approved Rate Support Grant Report for the year.

(2) Any reference in this section to a payment by way of grant made under and in accordance with the relevant enactments is a reference to a payment of grant made under section 7 of the Local Government Act 1974 (supplementary grants towards expenditure with respect to National Parks) in accordance with the provisions of that section and those of section 60 or 61 of the Local Government, Planning and Land Act 1980 (rate support grant reports and supplementary reports) as they apply in relation to grants under the said section 7.

(3) In this section—

'approved Rate Support Grant Report' means a Rate Support Grant Report which has been laid before and approved by a resolution of the House of Commons;

'approved supplementary report' means a supplementary report which has been laid before and approved by a resolution of the House of Commons;

'duly prescribed' means prescribed by a Rate Support Grant Report or a supplementary report;

'Rate Support Grant Report' means a Rate Support Grant Report made under section 60 of the Local Government, Planning and Land Act 1980;

'supplementary report' means a supplementary report made under section 61 of that Act; and

'year' means a period of 12 months beginning with 1st April.

Supplemental provisions

75. Powers to make orders

(1) This section applies to every power of the Secretary of State under the preceding provisions of this Part to make an order.

(2) The powers to which this section applies shall, in each case, be exercisable by statutory instrument; and, except in the case of a statutory instrument made by virtue of section 64 above which only—

(a) designates a date,

(b) specifies a time for the purposes of section 4A of the Town and Country Planning Act 1990,

(c) renames a body,

(d) makes provision under paragraph 2(3) of Schedule 7 to this Act—

(i) for excluding a council from the councils by whom the local authority members of a National Park authority are to be appointed, or

(ii) for so increasing the number of local authority members of a National Park authority to be appointed by any council as to secure that the number of local authority members of that authority remains unchanged notwithstanding any such exclusion of a council, or

(e) makes provision under section 60(2) above,

any such statutory instrument shall be subject to annulment in pursuance of a resolution of either House of Parliament.

(3) The powers to which this section applies shall, in each case, include power to make such incidental, supplemental, consequential and transitional provision as the Secretary of State thinks necessary or expedient.

(4) A power of the Secretary of State by an order under this Part to make incidental, supplemental, consequential or transitional provision shall include power for any incidental, supplemental, consequential or, as the case may be, transitional purpose—

(a) to apply with or without modifications,

(b) to extend, exclude or modify, or

(c) to repeal or revoke with or without savings,

any enactment or any instrument made under any enactment.

(5) The provision that may be made for incidental, supplemental, consequential or transitional purposes in the case of any order under this Part which—

(a) establishes a National Park authority or winds up the existing authority for any National Park, or

(b) otherwise has the effect of transferring functions from one person to another or of providing for functions to become exercisable concurrently by two or more persons or to cease to be so exercisable,

shall include provision for the transfer of property, rights and liabilities from one person to another.

(6) A power of the Secretary of State under this Part to provide by order for the transfer of any property, rights or liabilities, or to make transitional provision in connection with any such transfer or with any order by which functions become or cease to be exercisable by any authority, shall include power to provide, in particular—

(a) for the management and custody of any transferred property (whether real or personal);

(b) for any liabilities transferred to include liabilities under any enactment;

(c) for legal proceedings commenced by or against any person to be continued by or against a person to whom property, rights or liabilities are transferred or, as the case may be, any authority by whom any functions are to become exercisable;

(d) for the transfer of staff, compensation for loss of office, pensions and other staffing matters; and

(e) for treating any person to whom a transfer of property, rights or liabilities is made or, as the case may be, by whom any functions are to become exercisable as, for some or all purposes, the same person in law as the person from whom the transfer is made or the authority by whom the functions have previously been exercisable.

(7) The powers to which this section applies shall, in each case, include power to make different provision for different cases, including different provision for different areas or localities and for different authorities.

(8) The powers to which this section applies shall be without prejudice to any powers conferred by Part II of the Local Government Act 1992 or any other enactment.

(9) In this section 'enactment' includes an enactment contained in an Act passed after this Act.

76. Agreements as to incidental matters

(1) Any public authorities affected by an order under this Part may from time to time make agreements with respect to—

(a) any property, income, rights, liabilities or expenses (so far as affected by the order) of the parties to the agreement; or

(b) any financial relations between those parties.

(2) Such an agreement may provide—

(a) for the transfer or retention of any property, rights and liabilities, with or without conditions, and for the joint use of any property;

(b)   for the making of payments by any party to the agreement in respect of—
    (i)   property, rights and liabilities transferred or retained,
    (ii)   the joint use of any property, or
    (iii)   remuneration or compensation payable to any person; and
(c)   for the making of any such payment either by way of a capital sum or of a terminable annuity.

(3)   In default of agreement as to any disputed matter, the matter shall be referred to the arbitration of a single arbitrator agreed on by the parties or, in default of agreement, appointed by the Secretary of State; and the award of the arbitrator may make any provision that might be contained in an agreement under this section.

(4)   In subsection (3) above 'disputed matter' means any matter which—
(a)   might be the subject of provision contained in an agreement under this section; and
(b)   is the subject of such a dispute between two or more public authorities as is not resolved by or under provision contained in any order under this Part.

77.   Isles of Scilly
(1)   This Part shall have effect in relation to the Isles of Scilly subject to any such modifications as may be provided for by the Secretary of State by order made by statutory instrument.

(2)   Before making an order under this section the Secretary of State shall consult with the Council of the Isles of Scilly.

(3)   The power to make an order under this section shall include power to make such incidental, supplemental, consequential or transitional provision as the Secretary of State thinks necessary or expedient.

78.   Minor and consequential amendments relating to National Parks
The enactments mentioned in Schedule 10 to this Act shall have effect subject to the amendments contained in that Schedule (being minor amendments and consequential amendments in connection with the provisions of this Part).

79.   Interpretation of Part III
(1)   In this Part, except in so far as the context otherwise requires—
'the 1972 Act' means the Local Government Act 1972;
'existing authority', in relation to a National Park, means—
(a)   any such joint or special planning board for that Park or for any area wholly or partly comprised in that Park as was reconstituted by an order under paragraph 1 or 3 of Schedule 17 to the 1972 Act or constituted by an order under paragraph 3A of that Schedule or section 2(1B) of the Town and Country Planning Act 1990; or
(b)   any National Park Committee for that Park or for any such area;
'liability', in relation to the transfer of liabilities from one person to another, does not include any criminal liability;
'principal council' and 'principal area' have the same meanings as in the 1972 Act;
'public authority' means any local authority within the meaning of the 1972 Act (including any such authority in their capacity as a local planning authority), any National Park authority, any existing authority for a National Park, any joint authority or residuary body established under Part II of the Local Government Act 1992, any joint authority established under section 34 of the Local Government (Wales) Act 1994 or the Residuary Body for Wales established by section 39 of that Act;
'the relevant Park', in relation to a National Park authority, means the area for which that authority is or is to be the National Park authority.

(2)   Where—

(a)   any enactment that is applied by virtue of this Part in relation to National Park authorities refers, or falls to be construed as referring, to any other enactment, and

(b)   that other enactment is also one which is so applied,

the reference shall be construed (so far as it would not be so construed apart from this subsection) as including a reference to the other enactment as it is applied in relation to National Park authorities.

PART IV

AIR QUALITY

80.   National air quality strategy

(1)   The Secretary of State shall as soon as possible prepare and publish a statement (in this Part referred to as 'the strategy') containing policies with respect to the assessment or management of the quality of air.

(2)   The strategy may also contain policies for implementing—

(a)   obligations of the United Kingdom under the Community Treaties, or

(b)   international agreements to which the United Kingdom is for the time being a party,

so far as relating to the quality of air.

(3)   The strategy shall consist of or include—

(a)   a statement which relates to the whole of Great Britain; or

(b)   two or more statements which between them relate to every part of Great Britain.

(4)   The Secretary of State—

(a)   shall keep under review his policies with respect to the quality of air; and

(b)   may from time to time modify the strategy.

(5)   Without prejudice to the generality of what may be included in the strategy, the strategy must include statements with respect to—

(a)   standards relating to the quality of air;

(b)   objectives for the restriction of the levels at which particular substances are present in the air; and

(c)   measures which are to be taken by local authorities and other persons for the purpose of achieving those objectives.

(6)   In preparing the strategy or any modification of it, the Secretary of State shall consult—

(a)   the appropriate new Agency;

(b)   such bodies or persons appearing to him to be representative of the interests of local government as he may consider appropriate;

(c)   such bodies or persons appearing to him to be representative of the interests of industry as he may consider appropriate; and

(d)   such other bodies or persons as he may consider appropriate.

(7)   Before publishing the strategy or any modification of it, the Secretary of State—

(a)   shall publish a draft of the proposed strategy or modification, together with notice of a date before which, and an address at which, representations may be made to him concerning the draft so published; and

(b)   shall take into account any such representations which are duly made and not withdrawn.

81.   Functions of the new Agencies

(1)   In discharging its pollution control functions, each new Agency shall have regard to the strategy.

(2)   In this section 'pollution control functions', in relation to a new Agency, means—

(a)   in the case of the Agency, the functions conferred on it by or under the enactments specified in section 5(5) above; or

(b)   in the case of SEPA, the functions conferred on it by or under the enactments specified in section 33(5) above.

82. Local authority reviews

(1) Every local authority shall from time to time cause a review to be conducted of the quality for the time being, and the likely future quality within the relevant period, of air within the authority's area.

(2) Where a local authority causes a review under subsection (1) above to be conducted, it shall also cause an assessment to be made of whether air quality standards and objectives are being achieved, or are likely to be achieved within the relevant period, within the authority's area.

(3) If, on an assessment under subsection (2) above, it appears that any air quality standards or objectives are not being achieved, or are not likely within the relevant period to be achieved, within the local authority's area, the local authority shall identify any parts of its area in which it appears that those standards or objectives are not likely to be achieved within the relevant period.

83. Designation of air quality management areas

(1) Where, as a result of an air quality review, it appears that any air quality standards or objectives are not being achieved, or are not likely within the relevant period to be achieved, within the area of a local authority, the local authority shall by order designate as an air quality management area (in this Part referred to as a 'designated area') any part of its area in which it appears that those standards or objectives are not being achieved, or are not likely to be achieved within the relevant period.

(2) An order under this section may, as a result of a subsequent air quality review,—

    (a) be varied by a subsequent order; or

    (b) be revoked by such an order, if it appears on that subsequent air quality review that the air quality standards and objectives are being achieved, and are likely throughout the relevant period to be achieved, within the designated area.

84. Duties of local authorities in relation to designated areas

(1) Where an order under section 83 above comes into operation, the local authority which made the order shall, for the purpose of supplementing such information as it has in relation to the designated area in question, cause an assessment to be made of—

    (a) the quality for the time being, and the likely future quality within the relevant period, of air within the designated area to which the order relates; and

    (b) the respects (if any) in which it appears that air quality standards or objectives are not being achieved, or are not likely within the relevant period to be achieved, within that designated area.

(2) A local authority which is required by subsection (1) above to cause an assessment to be made shall also be under a duty—

    (a) to prepare, before the expiration of the period of twelve months beginning with the coming into operation of the order mentioned in that subsection, a report of the results of that assessment; and

    (b) to prepare, in accordance with the following provisions of this Part, a written plan (in this Part referred to as an 'action plan') for the exercise by the authority, in pursuit of the achievement of air quality standards and objectives in the designated area, of any powers exercisable by the authority.

(3) An action plan shall include a statement of the time or times by or within which the local authority in question proposes to implement each of the proposed measures comprised in the plan.

(4) A local authority may from time to time revise an action plan.

(5) This subsection applies in any case where the local authority preparing an action plan or a revision of an action plan is the council of a district in England which is comprised in an area for which there is a county council; and if, in a case where this subsection applies, the county council disagrees with the authority about the contents of the proposed action plan or revision of the action plan—

(a) either of them may refer the matter to the Secretary of State;

(b) on any such reference the Secretary of State may confirm the authority's proposed action plan or revision of the action plan, with or without modifications (whether or not proposed by the county council) or reject it and, if he rejects it, he may also exercise any powers of his under section 85 below; and

(c) the authority shall not finally determine the content of the action plan, or the revision of the action plan, except in accordance with his decision on the reference or in pursuance of directions under section 85 below.

85. Reserve powers of the Secretary of State or SEPA

(1) In this section, 'the appropriate authority' means—

(a) in relation to England and Wales, the Secretary of State; and

(b) in relation to Scotland, SEPA acting with the approval of the Secretary of State.

(2) The appropriate authority may conduct or make, or cause to be conducted or made,—

(a) a review of the quality for the time being, and the likely future quality within the relevant period, of air within the area of any local authority;

(b) an assessment of whether air quality standards and objectives are being achieved, or are likely to be achieved within the relevant period, within the area of a local authority;

(c) an identification of any parts of the area of a local authority in which it appears that those standards or objectives are not likely to be achieved within the relevant period; or

(d) an assessment of the respects (if any) in which it appears that air quality standards or objectives are not being achieved, or are not likely within the relevant period to be achieved, within the area of a local authority or within a designated area.

(3) If it appears to the appropriate authority—

(a) that air quality standards or objectives are not being achieved, or are not likely within the relevant period to be achieved, within the area of a local authority,

(b) that a local authority has failed to discharge any duty imposed on it under or by virtue of this Part,

(c) that the actions, or proposed actions, of a local authority in purported compliance with the provisions of this Part are inappropriate in all the circumstances of the case, or

(d) that developments in science or technology, or material changes in circumstances, have rendered inappropriate the actions or proposed actions of a local authority in pursuance of this Part,

the appropriate authority may give directions to the local authority requiring it to take such steps as may be specified in the directions.

(4) Without prejudice to the generality of subsection (3) above, directions under that subsection may, in particular, require a local authority—

(a) to cause an air quality review to be conducted under section 82 above in accordance with the directions;

(b) to cause an air quality review under section 82 above to be conducted afresh, whether in whole or in part, or to be so conducted with such differences as may be specified or described in the directions;

(c) to make an order under section 83 above designating as an air quality management area an area specified in, or determined in accordance with, the directions;

(d) to revoke, or modify in accordance with the directions, any order under that section;

(e) to prepare in accordance with the directions an action plan for a designated area;

(f) to modify, in accordance with the directions, any action plan prepared by the authority; or

(g) to implement, in accordance with the directions, any measures in an action plan.

(5) The Secretary of State shall also have power to give directions to local authorities requiring them to take such steps specified in the directions as he considers appropriate for the implementation of—

(a)   any obligations of the United Kingdom under the Community Treaties, or

(b)   any international agreement to which the United Kingdom is for the time being a party,

so far as relating to the quality of air.

(6)   Any direction given under this section shall be published in such manner as the body or person giving it considers appropriate for the purpose of bringing the matters to which it relates to the attention of persons likely to be affected by them; and—

(a)   copies of the direction shall be made available to the public; and

(b)   notice shall be given—

(i)   in the case of a direction given to a local authority in England and Wales, in the London Gazette, or

(ii)   in the case of a direction given to a local authority in Scotland, in the Edinburgh Gazette,

of the giving of the direction and of where a copy of the direction may be obtained.

(7)   It is the duty of a local authority to comply with any direction given to it under or by virtue of this Part.

86.   Functions of county councils for areas for which there are district councils

(1)   This section applies in any case where a district in England for which there is a district council is comprised in an area for which there is a county council; and in this paragraph—

(a)   any reference to the county council is a reference to the council of that area; and

(b)   any reference to a district council is a reference to the council of a district comprised in that area.

(2)   The county council may make recommendations to a district council with respect to the carrying out of—

(a)   any particular air quality review,

(b)   any particular assessment under section 82 or 84 above, or

(c)   the preparation of any particular action plan or revision of an action plan,

and the district council shall take into account any such recommendations.

(3)   Where a district council is preparing an action plan, the county council shall, within the relevant period, submit to the district council proposals for the exercise (so far as relating to the designated area) by the county council, in pursuit of the achievement of air quality standards and objectives, of any powers exercisable by the county council.

(4)   Where the county council submits proposals to a district council in pursuance of subsection (3) above, it shall also submit a statement of the time or times by or within which it proposes to implement each of the proposals.

(5)   An action plan shall include a statement of—

(a)   any proposals submitted pursuant to subsection (3) above; and

(b)   any time or times set out in the statement submitted pursuant to subsection (4) above.

(6)   If it appears to the Secretary of State—

(a)   that air quality standards or objectives are not being achieved, or are not likely within the relevant period to be achieved, within the area of a district council,

(b)   that the county council has failed to discharge any duty imposed on it under or by virtue of this Part,

(c)   that the actions, or proposed actions, of the county council in purported compliance with the provisions of this Part are inappropriate in all the circumstances of the case, or

(d)   that developments in science or technology, or material changes in circumstances, have rendered inappropriate the actions or proposed actions of the county council in pursuance of this Part,

the Secretary of State may give directions to the county council requiring it to take such steps as may be specified in the directions.

(7) Without prejudice to the generality of subsection (6) above, directions under that subsection may, in particular, require the county council—

(a) to submit, in accordance with the directions, proposals pursuant to subsection (3) above or a statement pursuant to subsection (4) above;

(b) to modify, in accordance with the directions, any proposals or statement submitted by the county council pursuant to subsection (3) or (4) above;

(c) to submit any proposals or statement so modified to the district council in question pursuant to subsection (3) or (4) above; or

(d) to implement, in accordance with the directions, any measures included in an action plan.

(8) The Secretary of State shall also have power to give directions to county councils for areas for which there are district councils requiring them to take such steps specified in the directions as he considers appropriate for the implementation of—

(a) any obligations of the United Kingdom under the Community Treaties, or

(b) any international agreement to which the United Kingdom is for the time being a party,

so far as relating to the quality of air.

(9) Any direction given under this section shall be published in such manner as the Secretary of State considers appropriate for the purpose of bringing the matters to which it relates to the attention of persons likely to be affected by them; and—

(a) copies of the direction shall be made available to the public; and

(b) notice of the giving of the direction, and of where a copy of the direction may be obtained, shall be given in the London Gazette.

(10) It is the duty of a county council for an area for which there are district councils to comply with any direction given to it under or by virtue of this Part.

87. Regulations for the purposes of Part IV

(1) Regulations may make provision—

(a) for, or in connection with, implementing the strategy;

(b) for, or in connection with, implementing—

(i) obligations of the United Kingdom under the Community Treaties, or

(ii) international agreements to which the United Kingdom is for the time being a party,

so far as relating to the quality of air; or

(c) otherwise with respect to the assessment or management of the quality of air.

(2) Without prejudice to the generality of subsection (1) above, regulations under that subsection may make provision—

(a) prescribing standards relating to the quality of air;

(b) prescribing objectives for the restriction of the levels at which particular substances are present in the air;

(c) conferring powers or imposing duties on local authorities;

(d) for or in connection with—

(i) authorising local authorities (whether by agreements or otherwise) to exercise any functions of a Minister of the Crown on his behalf,

(ii) directing that functions of a Minister of the Crown shall be exercisable concurrently with local authorities; or

(iii) transferring functions of a Minister of the Crown to local authorities;

(e) prohibiting or restricting, or for or in connection with prohibiting or restricting,—

(i) the carrying on of prescribed activities, or

(ii) the access of prescribed vehicles or mobile equipment to prescribed areas, whether generally or in prescribed circumstances;

(f) for or in connection with the designation of air quality management areas by orders made by local authorities in such cases or circumstances not falling within section 83 above as may be prescribed;

(g) for the application, with or without modifications, of any provisions of this Part in relation to areas designated by virtue of paragraph (f) above or in relation to orders made by virtue of that paragraph;

(h) with respect to—

(i) air quality reviews;

(ii) assessments under this Part;

(iii) orders designating air quality management areas; or

(iv) action plans;

(j) prescribing measures which are to be adopted by local authorities (whether in action plans or otherwise) or other persons in pursuance of the achievement of air quality standards or objectives;

(k) for or in connection with the communication to the public of information relating to quality for the time being, or likely future quality, of the air;

(l) for or in connection with the obtaining by local authorities from any person of information which is reasonably necessary for the discharge of functions conferred or imposed on them under or by virtue of this Part;

(m) for or in connection with the recovery by a local authority from prescribed persons in prescribed circumstances, and in such manner as may be prescribed, of costs incurred by the authority in discharging functions conferred or imposed on the authority under or by virtue of this Part;

(n) for a person who contravenes, or fails to comply with, any prescribed provision of the regulations to be guilty of an offence and liable on summary conviction to a fine not exceeding level 5 on the standard scale or such lower level on that scale as may be prescribed in relation to the offence;

(o) for or in connection with arrangements under which a person may discharge any liability to conviction for a prescribed offence by payment of a penalty of a prescribed amount;

(p) for or in connection with appeals against determinations or decisions made, notices given or served, or other things done under or by virtue of the regulations.

(3) Without prejudice to the generality of paragraph (h) of subsection (2) above, the provision that may be made by virtue of that paragraph includes provision for or in connection with any of the following, that is to say—

(a) the scope or form of a review or assessment;

(b) the scope, content or form of an action plan;

(c) the time at which, period within which, or manner in which a review or assessment is to be carried out or an action plan is to be prepared;

(d) the methods to be employed—

(i) in carrying out reviews or assessments; or

(ii) in monitoring the effectiveness of action plans;

(e) the factors to be taken into account in preparing action plans;

(f) the actions which must be taken by local authorities or other persons in consequence of reviews, assessments or action plans;

(g) requirements for consultation;

(h) the treatment of representations or objections duly made;

(j) the publication of, or the making available to the public of, or of copies of,—

(i) the results, or reports of the results, of reviews or assessments; or

(ii) orders or action plans;

(k) requirements for—

(i) copies of any such reports, orders or action plans, or

(ii) prescribed information, in such form as may be prescribed, relating to reviews or assessments,

to be sent to the Secretary of State or to the appropriate new Agency.

(4) In determining—

(a) any appeal against, or reference or review of, a decision of a local authority under or by virtue of regulations under this Part, or

(b) any application transmitted from a local authority under or by virtue of any such regulations,

the body or person making the determination shall be bound by any direction given by a Minister of the Crown or SEPA to the local authority to the same extent as the local authority.

(5) The provisions of any regulations under this Part may include—

(a) provision for anything that may be prescribed by the regulations to be determined under the regulations and for anything falling to be so determined to be determined by such persons, in accordance with such procedure and by reference to such matters, and to the opinion of such persons, as may be prescribed;

(b) different provision for different cases, including different provision in relation to different persons, circumstances, areas or localities; and

(c) such supplemental, consequential, incidental or transitional provision (including provision amending any enactment or any instrument made under any enactment) as the Secretary of State considers appropriate.

(6) Nothing in regulations under this Part shall authorise any person other than a constable in uniform to stop a vehicle on any road.

(7) Before making any regulations under this Part, the Secretary of State shall consult—

(a) the appropriate new Agency;

(b) such bodies or persons appearing to him to be representative of the interests of local government as he may consider appropriate;

(c) such bodies or persons appearing to him to be representative of the interests of industry as he may consider appropriate; and

(d) such other bodies or persons as he may consider appropriate.

(8) Any power conferred by this Part to make regulations shall be exercisable by statutory instrument; and no statutory instrument containing regulations under this Part shall be made unless a draft of the instrument has been laid before, and approved by a resolution of, each House of Parliament.

(9) If, apart from this subsection, the draft of an instrument containing regulations under this Part would be treated for the purposes of the Standing Orders of either House of Parliament as a hybrid instrument, it shall proceed in that House as if it were not such an instrument.

88. Guidance for the purposes of Part IV

(1) The Secretary of State may issue guidance to local authorities with respect to, or in connection with, the exercise of any of the powers conferred, or the discharge of any of the duties imposed, on those authorities by or under this Part.

(2) A local authority, in carrying out any of its functions under or by virtue of this Part, shall have regard to any guidance issued by the Secretary of State under this Part.

(3) This section shall apply in relation to county councils for areas for which there are district councils as it applies in relation to local authorities.

89. Application of Part IV to the Isles of Scilly

(1) Subject to the provisions of any order under this section, this Part, other than section 80, shall not apply in relation to the Isles of Scilly.

(2) The Secretary of State may, after consultation with the Council of the Isles of Scilly, by order provide for the application of any provisions of this Part (other than section 80) to the Isles of Scilly; and any such order may provide for the application of those provisions to those Isles with such modifications as may be specified in the order.

(3) An order under this section may—

(a) make different provision for different cases, including different provision in relation to different persons, circumstances or localities; and

(b)   contain such supplemental, consequential and transitional provision as the Secretary of State considers appropriate, including provision saving provision repealed by or under any enactment.

(4)   The power of the Secretary of State to make an order under this section shall be exercisable by statutory instrument; and a statutory instrument containing such an order shall be subject to annulment in pursuance of a resolution of either House of Parliament.

90. Supplemental provisions

Schedule 11 to this Act shall have effect.

91   Interpretation of Part IV

(1)   In this Part—

'action plan' shall be construed in accordance with section 84(2)(b) above;

'air quality objectives' means objectives prescribed by virtue of section 87(2)(b) above;

'air quality review' means a review under section 82 or 85 above;

'air quality standards' means standards prescribed by virtue of section 87(2)(a) above;

'the appropriate new Agency' means—

(a)   in relation to England and Wales, the Agency;

(b)   in relation to Scotland, SEPA;

'designated area' has the meaning given by section 83(1) above;

'local authority', in relation to England and Wales, means—

(a)   any unitary authority,

(b)   any district council, so far as it is not a unitary authority,

(c)   the Common Council of the City of London and, as respects the Temples, the Sub-Treasurer of the Inner Temple and the Under-Treasurer of the Middle Temple respectively,

and, in relation to Scotland, means a council for an area constituted under section 2 of the Local Government etc. (Scotland) Act 1994;

'new Agency' means the Agency or SEPA;

'prescribed' means prescribed, or of a description prescribed, by or under regulations;

'regulations' means regulations made by the Secretary of State;

'the relevant period', in the case of any provision of this Part, means such period as may be prescribed for the purposes of that provision;

'the strategy' has the meaning given by section 80(1) above;

'unitary authority' means—

(a)   the council of a county, so far as it is the council of an area for which there are no district councils;

(b)   the council of any district comprised in an area for which there is no county council;

(c)   the council of a London borough;

(d)   the council of a county borough in Wales.

(2)   Any reference in this Part to it appearing that any air quality standards or objectives are not likely within the relevant period to be achieved includes a reference to it appearing that those standards or objectives are likely within that period not to be achieved.

PART V

MISCELLANEOUS, GENERAL AND SUPPLEMENTAL PROVISIONS

Waste

92. National waste strategy

(1)   Before section 45 of the Environmental Protection Act 1990 there shall be inserted—

'44A. National waste strategy: England and Wales

(1) The Secretary of State shall as soon as possible prepare a statement ('the strategy') containing his policies in relation to the recovery and disposal of waste in England and Wales.

(2) The strategy shall consist of or include—

(a) a statement which relates to the whole of England and Wales; or

(b) two or more statements which between them relate to the whole of England and Wales.

(3) The Secretary of State may from time to time modify the strategy.

(4) Without prejudice to the generality of what may be included in the strategy, the strategy must include—

(a) a statement of the Secretary of State's policies for attaining the objectives specified in Schedule 2A to this Act;

(b) provisions relating to each of the following, that is to say—

(i) the type, quantity and origin of waste to be recovered or disposed of;

(ii) general technical requirements; and

(iii) any special requirements for particular wastes.

(5) In preparing the strategy or any modification of it, the Secretary of State—

(a) shall consult the Environment Agency,

(b) shall consult—

(i) such bodies or persons appearing to him to be representative of the interests of local government, and

(ii) such bodies or persons appearing to him to be representative of the interests of industry,

as he may consider appropriate, and

(c) may consult such other bodies or persons as he considers appropriate,

(6) Without prejudice to any power to give directions conferred by section 38 of the Environment Act 1995, the Secretary of State may give directions to the Environment Agency requiring it—

(a) to advise him on the policies which are to be included in the strategy;

(b) to carry out a survey of or investigation into—

(i) the kinds or quantities of waste which it appears to that Agency is likely to be situated in England and Wales,

(ii) the facilities which are or appear to that Agency likely to be available or needed in England and Wales for recovering or disposing of any such waste,

(iii) any other matter upon which the Secretary of State wishes to be informed in connection with his preparation of the strategy or any modification of it, and to report its findings to him.

(7) A direction under subsection (6)(b) above—

(a) shall specify or describe the matters or the areas which are to be the subject of the survey or investigation; and

(b) may make provision in relation to the manner in which—

(i) the survey or investigation is to be carried out, or

(ii) the findings are to be reported or made available to other persons.

(8) Where a direction is given under subsection (6)(b), the Environment Agency shall, in accordance with any requirement of the direction,—

(a) before carrying out the survey or investigation, consult—

(i) such bodies or persons appearing to it to be representative of local planning authorities, and

(ii) such bodies or persons appearing to it to be representative of the interests of industry,

as it may consider appropriate; and

(b)   make its findings available to those authorities.

(9)   In this section—

"local planning authority" has the same meaning as in the Town and Country Planning Act 1990;

"strategy" includes the strategy as modified from time to time and "statement" shall be construed accordingly.

(10)   This section makes provision for the purpose of implementing Article 7 of the directive of the Council of the European Communities, dated 15th July 1975, on waste, as amended by—

(a)   the directive of that Council, dated 18th March 1991, amending directive 75/442/EEC on waste; and

(b)   the directive of that Council, dated 23rd December 1991, standardising and rationalising reports on the implementation of certain Directives relating to the environment.

44B.   National waste strategy: Scotland

(1)   SEPA shall as soon as possible prepare a statement ("the strategy") containing its policies in relation to the recovery and disposal of waste in Scotland.

(2)   SEPA may from time to time modify the strategy.

(3)   Without prejudice to the generality of what may be included in the strategy, the strategy must include—

(a)   a statement of SEPA's policies for attaining the objectives specified in Schedule 2A to this Act;

(b)   provisions relating to each of the following, that is to say—

(i)   the type, quantity and origin of waste to be recovered or disposed of;

(ii)   general technical requirements; and

(iii)   any special requirements for particular wastes.

(4)   In preparing the strategy or any modification of it SEPA shall consult—

(a)   such bodies or persons appearing to it to be representative of the interests of industry as it may consider appropriate;

(b)   such local authorities as appear to it to be likely to be affected by the strategy or modification,

and may consult such other bodies or persons as it considers appropriate.

(5)   Without prejudice to any power to give directions conferred by section 40 of the Environment Act 1995, the Secretary of State may give directions to SEPA—

(a)   as to the policies which are to be included in the strategy;

(b)   requiring it to carry out a survey or investigation into—

(i)   the kinds or quantities of waste which it appears to it is likely to be situated in Scotland,

(ii)   the facilities which are or appear to it likely to be available or needed in Scotland for recovering or disposing of any such waste,

(iii)   any other matter which the Secretary of State considers appropriate in connection with its preparation of the strategy or any modifications of it.

(6)   A direction under subsection (5)(b) above—

(a)   shall specify or describe the matters or the areas which are to be the subject of the survey or investigation; and

(b)   may make provision in relation to the manner in which—

(i)   the survey or investigation is to be carried out, or

(ii)   the findings are to be reported or made available to other persons.

(7)   Where a direction is given under subsection (5)(b) above SEPA shall, in accordance with any requirement of the direction—

(a)   before carrying out the survey or investigation, consult—

(i)   such bodies or persons appearing to it to be representative of planning authorities, and

(ii)   such bodies or persons appearing to it to be representative of the interests of industry,

as it may consider appropriate; and

(b)   make its findings available to those authorities.

(8)   In this section—

"planning authority" means an authority within the meaning of section 172 of the Local Government (Scotland) Act 1973;

"strategy" includes the strategy as modified from time to time and "statement" shall be construed accordingly.

(9)   This section makes provision for the purpose of implementing Article 7 of the directive of the Council of the European Communities dated 15th July 1975 on waste, as amended by—

(a)   the directive of that Council dated 18th March 1991 amending directive 75/442/EEC on waste; and

(b)   the directive of that Council dated 23rd December 1991 standardising and rationalising reports on the implementation of certain Directives relating to the environment.'

(2)   After Schedule 2 to that Act there shall be inserted the Schedule set out in Schedule 12 to this Act.

93. Producer responsibility: general

(1)   For the purpose of promoting or securing an increase in the re-use, recovery or recycling of products or materials, the Secretary of State may by regulations make provision for imposing producer responsibility obligations on such persons, and in respect of such products or materials, as may be prescribed.

(2)   The power of the Secretary of State to make regulations shall be exercisable only after consultation with bodies or persons appearing to him to be representative of bodies or persons whose interests are, or are likely to be, substantially affected by the regulations which he proposes to make.

(3)   Except in the case of regulations for the implementation of—

(a)   any obligations of the United Kingdom under the Community Treaties, or

(b)   any international agreement to which the United Kingdom is for the time being a party,

the power to make regulations shall be exercisable only where the Secretary of State, after such consultation as is required by subsection (2) above, is satisfied as to the matters specified in subsection (6) below.

(4)   The powers conferred by subsection (1) above shall also be exercisable, in a case falling within paragraph (a) or (b) of subsection (3) above, for the purpose of sustaining at least a minimum level of (rather than promoting or securing an increase in) re-use, recovery or recycling of products or materials.

(5)   In making regulations by virtue of paragraph (a) or (b) of subsection (3) above, the Secretary of State shall have regard to the matters specified in subsection (6) below; and in its application in relation to the power conferred by virtue of subsection (4) above, subsection (6) below shall have effect as if—

(a)   any reference to an increase in the re-use, recovery or recycling of products or materials were a reference to the sustaining of at least a minimum level of re-use, recovery or recycling of the products or materials in question, and

(b)   any reference to the production of environmental or economic benefits included a reference to the sustaining of at least a minimum level of any such existing benefits,

and any reference in this section or section 94 below to securing or achieving any such benefits shall accordingly include a reference to sustaining at least a minimum level of any such existing benefits.

(6)   The matters mentioned in subsections (3) and (5) above are—

(a) that the proposed exercise of the power would be likely to result in an increase in the re-use, recovery or recycling of the products or materials in question;

(b) that any such increase would produce environmental or economic benefits;

(c) that those benefits are significant as against the likely costs resulting from the imposition of the proposed producer responsibility obligation;

(d) that the burdens imposed on businesses by the regulations are the minimum necessary to secure those benefits; and

(e) that those burdens are imposed on persons most able to make a contribution to the achievement of the relevant targets—

    (i) having regard to the desirability of acting fairly between persons who manufacture, process, distribute or supply products or materials; and

    (ii) taking account of the need to ensure that the proposed producer responsibility obligation is so framed as to be effective in achieving the purposes for which it is to be imposed;

but nothing in sub-paragraph (i) of paragraph (e) above shall be taken to prevent regulations imposing a producer responsibility obligation on any class or description of person to the exclusion of any others.

(7) The Secretary of State shall have a duty to exercise the power to make regulations in the manner which he considers best calculated to secure that the exercise does not have the effect of restricting, distorting or preventing competition or, if it is likely to have any such effect, that the effect is no greater than is necessary for achieving the environmental or economic benefits mentioned in subsection (6) above.

(8) In this section—

'prescribed' means prescribed in regulations;

'product' and 'material' include a reference to any product or material (as the case may be) at a time when it becomes, or has become, waste;

'producer responsibility obligation' means the steps which are required to be taken by relevant persons of the classes or descriptions to which the regulations in question apply in order to secure attainment of the targets specified or described in the regulations;

'recovery', in relation to products or materials, includes—

(a) composting, or any other form of transformation by biological process, of products or materials; or

(b) the obtaining, by any means, of energy from products or materials;

'regulations' means regulations under this section;

'relevant persons', in the case of any regulations or any producer responsibility obligation, means persons of the class or description to which the producer responsibility obligation imposed by the regulations applies;

'relevant targets' means the targets specified or described in the regulations imposing the producer responsibility obligation in question;

and regulations may prescribe, in relation to prescribed products or materials, activities, or the activities, which are to be regarded for the purposes of this section and sections 94 and 95 below or any regulations as re-use, recovery or recycling of those products or materials.

(9) The power to make regulations shall be exercisable by statutory instrument.

(10) Subject to the following provisions of this section, a statutory instrument containing regulations shall not be made unless a draft of the instrument has been laid before and approved by a resolution of each House of Parliament.

(11) Subsection (10) above shall not apply to a statutory instrument by reason only that it contains regulations varying any relevant targets.

(12) A statutory instrument which, by virtue of subsection (11) above, is not subject to any requirement that a draft of the instrument be laid before and approved by a resolution of each House of Parliament shall be subject to annulment in pursuance of a resolution of either House of Parliament.

94. Producer responsibility: supplementary provisions

(1) Without prejudice to the generality of section 93 above, regulations may, in particular, make provision for or with respect to—

(a) the classes or descriptions of person to whom the producer responsibility obligation imposed by the regulations applies;

(b) the classes or descriptions of products or materials in respect of which the obligation applies;

(c) the targets which are to be achieved with respect to the proportion (whether by weight, volume or otherwise) of the products or materials in question which are to be re-used, recovered or recycled, whether generally or in any prescribed way;

(d) particulars of the obligation imposed by the regulations;

(e) the registration of persons who are subject to a producer responsibility obligation and who are not members of registered exemption schemes, the imposition of requirements in connection with such registration, the variation of such requirements, the making of applications for such registration, the period for which any such registration is to remain in force and the cancellation of any such registration;

(f) the approval, or withdrawal of approval, of exemption schemes by the Secretary of State;

(g) the imposition of requirements on persons who are not members of registered exemption schemes to furnish certificates of compliance to the appropriate Agency;

(h) the approval of persons by the appropriate Agency for the purpose of issuing certificates of compliance;

(j) the registration of exemption schemes, the imposition of conditions in connection with such registration, the variation of such conditions, the making of applications for such registration and the period for which any such registration is to remain in force;

(k) the requirements which must be fulfilled, and the criteria which must be met, before an exemption scheme may be registered;

(l) the powers of the appropriate Agency in relation to applications received by it for registration of exemption schemes;

(m) the cancellation of the registration of an exemption scheme;

(n) competition scrutiny of registered exemption schemes or of exemption schemes in whose case applications for registration have been received by the appropriate Agency;

(o) the exclusion or modification of any provision of the Restrictive Trade Practices Acts 1976 and 1977 in relation to exemption schemes or in relation to agreements where at least one of the parties is an operator of an exemption scheme;

(p) the fees, or the method of determining the fees, which are to be paid to the appropriate Agency—

(i) in respect of the approval of persons for the purpose of issuing certificates of compliance;

(ii) on the making of an application for registration of an exemption scheme;

(iii) in respect of the subsistence of the registration of that scheme;

(iv) on submission to the appropriate Agency of a certificate of compliance;

(v) on the making of an application for, or for the renewal of, registration of a person required to register under the regulations,

(vi) in respect of the renewal of the registration of that person;

(q) appeals against the refusal of registration, the imposition of conditions in connection with registration, or the cancellation of the registration, of any exemption scheme;

(r) the procedure on any such appeal;

(s) cases, or classes of case,—

(i) in which an exemption scheme is, or is not, to be treated as registered, or

(ii) in which a person is, or is not, to be treated as a member of a registered exemption scheme, pending the determination or withdrawal of an appeal, and otherwise with respect to the position of persons and exemption schemes pending such determination or withdrawal;

(t)   the imposition on the appropriate Agency of a duty to monitor compliance with any of the obligations imposed by the regulations;

(u)   the imposition on prescribed persons of duties to maintain records, and furnish to the Secretary of State or to the appropriate Agency returns, in such form as may be prescribed of such information as may be prescribed for any purposes of, or for any purposes connected with, or related to, sections 93 to 95 of this Act or any regulations;

(w)   the imposition on the appropriate Agency of a duty to maintain, and make available for inspection by the public, a register containing prescribed information relating to registered exemption schemes or persons required to register under the regulations;

(y)   the powers of entry and inspection which are exercisable by a new Agency for the purposes of its functions under the regulations.

(ya) the conferring on prescribed persons of power to require, for the purposes of or otherwise in connection with competition scrutiny, the provision by any person of any information which he has, or which he may at any future time acquire, relating to any exemption scheme or to any acts or omissions of an operator of such a scheme or of any person dealing with such an operator.

(2)   If it appears to the Secretary of State—

(a)   that any action proposed to be taken by the operator of a registered exemption scheme would be incompatible with—

(i)   any obligations of the United Kingdom under the Community Treaties, or

(ii)   any international agreement to which the United Kingdom is for the time being a party, or

(b)   that any action which the operator of such a scheme has power to take is required for the purpose of implementing any such obligations or agreement,

he may direct that operator not to take or, as the case may be, to take the action in question.

(3)   Regulations may make provision as to which of the new Agencies is the appropriate Agency for the purposes of any function conferred or imposed by or under this section or section 93 above, or for the purposes of the exercise of that function in relation to the whole or a prescribed part of Great Britain, and may make provision for things done or omitted to be done by either new Agency in relation to any part of Great Britain to be treated for prescribed purposes as done or omitted to be done by the other of them in relation to some other part of Great Britain.

(4)   Persons issuing certificates of compliance shall act in accordance with guidance issued for the purpose by the appropriate Agency, which may include guidance as to matters which are, or are not, to be treated as evidence of compliance or as evidence of non-compliance.

(5)   In making any provision in relation to fees, regard shall be had to the desirability of securing that the fees received by each new Agency under the regulations are sufficient to meet the costs and expenses incurred by that Agency in the performance of its functions under the regulations.

(6)   In this section—

'the appropriate Agency', subject to regulations made by virtue of subsection (3) above, means—

(a)   in relation to England and Wales, the Agency;

(b)   in relation to Scotland, SEPA;

'certificate of compliance' means a certificate issued by a person approved for the purpose by the appropriate Agency to the effect that that person is satisfied that the person in respect of whom the certificate is issued is complying with any producer responsibility obligation to which he is subject;

'competition scrutiny', in the case of any scheme, means scrutiny of the scheme for the purpose of enabling the Secretary of State to satisfy himself—

(i)   whether or not the scheme has or is likely to have the effect of restricting, distorting or preventing competition or, if it appears to him that the scheme has or is likely to have any such effect, that the effect is or is likely to be no greater than is necessary for achieving the environmental or economic benefits mentioned in section 93(6) above; or

(ii)   whether or not the scheme leads or is likely to lead to an abuse of market power;
'exemption scheme' means a scheme which is (or, if it were to be registered in accordance with the regulations, would be) a scheme whose members for the time being are, by virtue of the regulations and their membership of that scheme, exempt from the requirement to comply with the producer responsibility obligation imposed by the regulations;
'new Agency' means the Agency or SEPA;
'operator', in relation to an exemption scheme, includes any person responsible for establishing, maintaining or managing the scheme;
'registered exemption scheme' means an exemption scheme which is registered pursuant to regulations;
and expressions used in this section and in section 93 above have the same meaning in this section as they have in that section.

(7)   Regulations—

(a)   may make different provision for different cases;

(b)   without prejudice to the generality of paragraph (a) above, may impose different producer responsibility obligations in respect of different classes or descriptions of products or materials and for different classes or descriptions of person or exemption scheme;

(c)   may include incidental, consequential, supplemental or transitional provision.

(8)   Any direction under this section—

(a)   may include such incidental, consequential, supplemental or transitional provision as the Secretary of State considers necessary or expedient; and

(b)   shall, on the application of the Secretary of State, be enforceable by injunction or, in Scotland, by interdict or by an order for specific performance under section 45 of the Court of Session Act 1988.

95.   Producer responsibility: offences

(1)   Regulations may make provision for a person who contravenes a prescribed requirement of the regulations to be guilty of an offence and liable—

(a)   on summary conviction, to a fine not exceeding the statutory maximum;

(b)   on conviction on indictment, to a fine.

(2)   Where an offence under any provision of the regulations committed by a body corporate is proved to have been committed with the consent or connivance of, or to have been attributable to any neglect on the part of, any director, manager, secretary or other similar officer of the body corporate or a person who was purporting to act in any such capacity, he as well as the body corporate shall be guilty of that offence and shall be liable to be proceeded against and punished accordingly.

(3)   Where the affairs of a body corporate are managed by its members, subsection (2) above shall apply in relation to the acts or defaults of a member in connection with his functions of management as if he were a director of the body corporate.

(4)   Where the commission by any person of an offence under the regulations is due to the act or default of some other person, that other person may be charged with and convicted of the offence by virtue of this section whether or not proceedings for the offence are taken against the first-mentioned person.

(5)   Expressions used in this section and in section 93 or 94 above have the same meaning in this section as they have in that section.

Mineral planning permissions

96.   Mineral planning permissions

(1)   Schedules 13 and 14 to this Act shall have effect.

(2)   This section, those Schedules as they apply to England and Wales, and the 1990 Act shall have effect as if this section and those Schedules (as so applying) were included in Part III of that Act.

(3)   This section, those Schedules as they apply to Scotland, and the 1972 Act shall have effect as if this section and those Schedules (as so applying) were included in Part III of that Act.

(4)   Section 105 of the 1990 Act and section 251A of the 1972 Act shall cease to have effect.

(5)   Without prejudice to the generality of sections 59 to 61 of the 1990 Act or, as the case may be, section 21 of the 1972 Act, a development order may make, in relation to any planning permission which is granted by a development order for minerals development, provision similar to any provision made by Schedule 13 or 14 to this Act.

(6)   In this section and those Schedules—

'the 1972 Act' means the Town and Country Planning (Scotland) Act 1972;

'the 1990 Act' means the Town and Country Planning Act 1990;

'the 1991 Act' means the Planning and Compensation Act 1991; and

'minerals development' means development consisting of the winning and working of minerals, or involving the depositing of mineral waste.

Hedgerows etc.

97.   Hedgerows

(1)   The appropriate Ministers may by regulations make provision for, or in connection with, the protection of important hedgerows in England or Wales.

(2)   The question whether a hedgerow is or is not 'important' for the purposes of this section shall be determined in accordance with prescribed criteria.

(3)   For the purpose of facilitating the protection of important hedgerows, regulations under subsection (1) above may also make provision in relation to other hedgerows in England or Wales.

(4)   Without prejudice to the generality of subsections (1) to (3) above, regulations under subsection (1) above may provide for the application (with or without modifications) of, or include provision comparable to, any provision contained in the planning Acts and may, in particular, make provision—

(a)   prohibiting, or for prohibiting, the removal of, or the carrying out of prescribed acts in relation to, a hedgerow except in prescribed cases;

(b)   for or with respect to appeals against determinations or decisions made, or notices given or served, under or by virtue of the regulations, including provision authorising or requiring any body or person to whom an appeal lies to consult prescribed persons with respect to the appeal in prescribed cases;

(c)   for a person who contravenes, or fails to comply with, any prescribed provision of the regulations to be guilty of an offence;

(d)   for a person guilty of an offence by virtue of paragraph (c) above which consists of the removal, in contravention of the regulations, of a hedgerow of a description prescribed for the purposes of this paragraph to be liable—

(i)   on summary conviction, to a fine not exceeding the statutory maximum, or

(ii)   on conviction on indictment, to a fine;

(e)   for a person guilty of any other offence by virtue of paragraph (c) above to be liable on summary conviction to a fine not exceeding such level on the standard scale as may be prescribed.

(5)   Regulations under this section may make different provision for different cases, including different provision in relation to different descriptions of hedgerow, different descriptions of person, different areas or localities or different circumstances.

(6)   Before making any regulations under this section the appropriate Ministers shall consult—

(a)   such bodies appearing to them to be representative of persons whose business interests are likely to be affected by the proposed regulations,

(b)   such bodies appearing to them to be representative of the interests of owners or occupiers of land,

(c)   such bodies appearing to them to be representative of the interests of local authorities,

(d)   such bodies whose statutory functions include the provision to Ministers of the Crown of advice concerning matters relating to environmental conservation, and

(e)   such bodies not falling within paragraphs (a) to (d) above,

as the appropriate Ministers may consider appropriate.

(7)   No statutory instrument containing regulations under this section shall be made unless a draft of the instrument has been laid before, and approved by a resolution of, each House of Parliament.

(8)   In this section—

'the appropriate Ministers' means—

(a)   as respects England, the Secretary of State and the Minister of Agriculture, Fisheries and Food;

(b)   as respects Wales, the Secretary of State;

'environmental conservation' means conservation—

(a)   of the natural beauty or amenity, or flora or fauna, of England or Wales; or

(b)   of features of archaeological or historic interest in England or Wales;

'hedgerow' includes any stretch of hedgerow;

'local authority' means—

(a)   the council of a county, county borough, district, London borough, parish or community;

(b)   the Common Council of the City of London;

(c)   the Council of the Isles of Scilly;

'the planning Acts' has the same meaning as it has in the Town and Country Planning Act 1990 by virtue of section 336(1) of that Act;

'prescribed' means specified, or of a description specified, in regulations;

'regulations' means regulations made by statutory instrument;

'remove', in relation to a hedgerow, means uproot or otherwise destroy, and cognate expressions shall be construed accordingly;

'statutory functions' means functions conferred or imposed by or under any enactment.

(9)   Any reference in this section to removing, or carrying out an act in relation to, a hedgerow includes a reference to causing or permitting another to remove, or (as the case may be) carry out an act in relation to, a hedgerow.

98.   Grants for purposes conducive to conservation

(1)   The appropriate Minister, with the consent of the Treasury, may by regulations make provision for and in connection with the making of grants to persons who do, or who undertake to that Minister that they will do, anything which in the opinion of that Minister is conducive to—

(a)   the conservation or enhancement of the natural beauty or amenity of the countryside (including its flora and fauna and geological and physiographical features) or of any features of archaeological interest there; or

(b)   the promotion of the enjoyment of the countryside by the public.

(2)   Regulations under this section may—

(a)   make different provision for different cases or classes of case or for different areas;

(b)   provide for grants to be made subject to conditions;

(c)   confer power on the appropriate Minister to modify, in any particular case, the conditions to which a grant would otherwise be subject, if he is satisfied that the making of that grant, subject to the conditions as so modified, is consistent with the purposes for which the regulations are made;

(d)   make provision for or in connection with the recovery of any sums paid by way of grant, or the withholding of any further payments of grant, in cases where the applicant for the grant—

(i)   in making the application, or in furnishing any information in connection with the application, has made a statement which was false or misleading in a material respect;

(ii)   has failed to do something which he undertook to do if the grant was made; or

(iii)   is in breach of any condition subject to which the grant was made.

(3)   The power to make regulations under this section shall be exercisable by statutory instrument; and a statutory instrument containing any such regulations shall be subject to annulment pursuant to a resolution of either House of Parliament.

(4)   The powers conferred by this section are in addition to any other powers of the Secretary of State or the Minister of Agriculture, Fisheries and Food.

(5)   In this section 'the appropriate Minister' means—

(a)   as respects England, the Minister of Agriculture, Fisheries and Food;

(b)   as respects Wales, the Secretary of State;

(c)   as respects Scotland, the Secretary of State.

99.   Consultation before making or modifying certain subordinate legislation for England

(1)   The Minister shall consult the bodies and persons specified in subsection (2) below before—

(a)   making any legislation to which this section applies (other than a modification of any such legislation);

(b)   modifying any such legislation in a way which changes the purpose of the legislation in question; or

(c)   modifying any such legislation in a way which modifies, in a respect which he considers material, any conditions subject to which grants or other payments are payable under that legislation.

(2)   The bodies and persons mentioned in subsection (1) above are—

(a)   the Secretary of State;

(b)   the Countryside Commission;

(c)   the Nature Conservancy Council for England;

(d)   the Historic Buildings and Monuments Commission for England.

(3)   The legislation to which this section applies is—

(a)   any order under section 18 of the Agriculture Act 1986 (orders establishing environmentally sensitive areas);

(b)   any regulations under section 98 above;

(c)   any statutory instrument specified in subsection (4) below;

(d)   any other statutory instrument which concerns the management of land and whose primary purpose is the promotion of—

(i)   the conservation or enhancement of the natural beauty or amenity of the countryside (including its flora and fauna and geological and physiographical features) or of any features of archaeological interest there; or

(ii)   the enjoyment of the countryside by the public.

(4)   The statutory instruments mentioned in subsection (3)(c) above are—

(a)   the Farm Woodlands Premium Scheme 1992;

(b)   the Habitat (Water Fringe) Regulations 1994;

(c)   the Habitat (Former Set-Aside Land) Regulations 1994;

(d)   the Habitat (Salt Marsh) Regulations 1994;

(e)   the Organic Farming (Aid) Regulations 1994;

(f)   the Nitrate Sensitive Areas Regulations 1994;

(g) the Countryside Access Regulations 1994.

(h) the Moorland (Livestock Extensification) Regulations 1995.

(5) In this section, 'the Minister' means the Minister of Agriculture, Fisheries and Food.

(6) This section applies in relation to any legislation only so far as relating to land in England.

Drainage

100. Meaning of 'drainage' in certain enactments

(1) In the definition of 'drainage' in section 113(1) of the Water Resources Act 1991, after paragraph (c) there shall be added the words 'and

(d) the carrying on, for any purpose, of any other practice which involves management of the level of water in a watercourse;'.

(2) For the definition of 'drainage' in section 72(1) of the Land Drainage Act 1991 there shall be substituted—

' "drainage" includes—

(a) defence against water (including sea water);

(b) irrigation, other than spray irrigation;

(c) warping; and

(d) the carrying on, for any purpose, of any other practice which involves management of the level of water in a watercourse;'.

101. Grants in connection with drainage works

(1) In section 147 of the Water Resources Act 1991 (grants for drainage works) in subsection (4), after the words 'expenditure properly incurred by it with a view to' there shall be inserted '(a)' and at the end of that subsection there shall be added—

'(b) enabling it to determine in any particular case whether drainage works, or drainage works of any particular description, should or should not be carried out;

(c) obtaining or organising information, including information about natural processes affecting the coastline, to enable it to formulate or develop its plans with respect to the defence against sea water of any part of the coastline; or

(d) obtaining, at any time after the carrying out of drainage works, information with respect to—

(i) the quality or effectiveness, or the effect on the environment, of those works; or

(ii) any matter of a financial nature relating to those works.

(4A) Paragraphs (b) to (d) of subsection (4) above are without prejudice to any power—

(a) to make any grant under subsection (1) or (4)(a) above, or

(b) to impose any condition under subsection (2) above,

which could be made or imposed apart from those paragraphs.'

(2) In section 59 of the Land Drainage Act 1991 (grants to drainage bodies) in subsection (4), after the words 'expenditure properly incurred by them with a view to' there shall be inserted '(a)' and at the end of that subsection there shall be added—

'(b) enabling them to determine in any particular case whether drainage works, or drainage works of any particular description, should or should not be carried out;

(c) obtaining or organising information, including information about natural processes affecting the coastline, to enable them to formulate or develop their plans with respect to the defence against sea water of any part of the coastline; or

(d) obtaining, at any time after the carrying out of drainage works, information with respect to—

(i) the quality or effectiveness, or the effect on the environment, of those works; or

(ii) any matter of a financial nature relating to those works.

(4A) Paragraphs (b) to (d) of subsection (4) above are without prejudice to any power—
    (a)   to make any grant under subsection (1) or (4)(a) above, or
    (b)   to impose any condition under subsection (2) above,
which could be made or imposed apart from those paragraphs.'

Fisheries

102. Sea fisheries

(1) The Sea Fisheries Regulation Act 1966 shall be amended in accordance with the following provisions of this section.

(2) In section 2 (constitution of local fisheries committees) in subsection (2) (which includes provision for the members appointed by the Minister to be persons acquainted with the needs and opinions of the fishing interests of that district) after the words 'of that district' there shall be added the words 'or as being persons having knowledge of, or expertise in, marine environmental matters'.

(3) After that subsection there shall be inserted—

'(2A) In addition to the members appointed as mentioned in subsection (1) above, a local fisheries committee may appoint such number of persons with knowledge of or expertise in marine environmental matters as it thinks fit as further members of the committee for those occasions on which it is considering any proposed byelaw under section 5 below by virtue of section 5A below, or any proposed amendment or revocation of such a byelaw,'.

(4) At the end of that section there shall be added—

'(7) In this section "marine environmental matters" means—
    (a)   the conservation or enhancement of the natural beauty or amenity of marine or coastal areas (including their geological or physiographical features) or of any features of archaeological or historic interest in such areas; or
    (b)   the conservation of flora or fauna which are dependent on, or associated with, a marine or coastal environment.'

(5) After section 5 (byelaws for regulation etc of sea fisheries) there shall be inserted—

'5A. Byelaws under section 5 for marine environmental purposes.

(1) Any power to make byelaws conferred by section 5 above may be exercised for marine environmental purposes.

(2) The power to make byelaws under section 5 above by virtue of this section is in addition to, and not in derogation from, the power to make byelaws under that section otherwise than by virtue of this section.

(3) Byelaws under section 5 above by virtue of this section shall be submitted for confirmation under section 7 below—
    (a)   in the case of a byelaw which is to have effect in England, only after consultation with the Nature Conservancy Council for England;
    (b)   in the case of a byelaw which is to have effect in Wales, only after consultation with the Countryside Council for Wales.

(4) In this section "marine environmental purposes" means the purposes—
    (a)   of conserving or enhancing the natural beauty or amenity of marine or coastal areas (including their geological or physiographical features) or of any features of archaeological or historic interest in such areas; or
    (b)   of conserving flora or fauna which are dependent on, or associated with, a marine or coastal environment.'

(6) In section 8 (power of Minister to revoke byelaws if it appears necessary or desirable for the maintenance or improvement of fisheries) after the words 'maintenance or improvement of fisheries' there shall be inserted the words 'or for marine environmental purposes, within the meaning of section 5A above,'.

103. Other marine or aquatic environmental conservation powers

(1) After section 5 of the Sea Fish (Conservation) Act 1967 (power to restrict fishing for sea fish) there shall be inserted—

'5A. Powers to restrict fishing for marine environmental purposes.

(1) Any power to make an order under section 5 above may be exercised for marine environmental purposes.

(2) The power to make an order under section 5 above by virtue of this section is in addition to, and not in derogation from, the power to make an order under that section otherwise than by virtue of this section.

(3) In this section "marine environmental purposes" means the purposes—

    (a) of conserving or enhancing the natural beauty or amenity of marine or coastal areas (including their geological or physiographical features) or of any features of archaeological or historic interest in such areas; or

    (b) of conserving flora or fauna which are dependent on, or associated with, a marine or coastal environment.'

(2) After section 2 of the Inshore Fishing (Scotland) Act 1984 there shall be inserted—

'2A. Powers to restrict fishing, or to prohibit the carriage of specified types of net, for marine environmental purposes

(1) Any power to make an order under section 1 or 2 above may be exercised for marine environmental purposes.

(2) The power to make an order under section 1 or 2 above by virtue of this section is in addition to, and not in derogation from, the power to make an order under that section otherwise than by virtue of this section.

(3) In this section "marine environmental purposes" means the purposes—

    (a) of conserving or enhancing the natural beauty or amenity of marine or coastal areas (including their geological or physiographical features) or of any features of archaeological or historic interest in such areas; or

    (b) of conserving flora or fauna which are dependent on, or associated with, a marine or coastal environment.'

(3) In Schedule 25 to the Water Resources Act 1991 (byelaw making powers) after paragraph 6 (byelaws for purposes of fisheries functions) there shall be inserted—

'Fisheries byelaws for marine or aquatic environmental purposes

6A.—(1) Any power to make byelaws conferred by paragraph 6 above may be exercised for marine or aquatic environmental purposes.

(2) The power to make byelaws under paragraph 6 above by virtue of this paragraph is in addition to, and not in derogation from, the power to make byelaws under that paragraph otherwise than by virtue of this paragraph.

(3) In this paragraph "marine or aquatic environmental purposes" means—

    (a) the conservation or enhancement of the natural beauty or amenity of marine or coastal, or aquatic or waterside, areas (including their geological or physiographical features) or of any features of archaeological or historic interest in such areas; or

    (b) the conservation of flora or fauna which are dependent on, or associated with, a marine or coastal, or aquatic or waterside, environment.'

104. Fixed penalty system for certain fisheries offences

(1) After section 37 of the Salmon and Freshwater Fisheries Act 1975 there shall be inserted—

'37A. Fixed penalty notices for certain offences

(1) Where on any occasion a water bailiff or other officer of the Agency finds a person who he has reason to believe is committing, or has on that occasion committed, a fixed penalty offence, he may give to that person a notice (in this section referred to as a "fixed penalty notice") offering him the opportunity of discharging any liability to conviction for that offence by payment of a fixed penalty.

(2) Where a person is given a fixed penalty notice in respect of a fixed penalty offence—

(a) no proceedings shall be instituted for that offence before the expiration of the period for paying the fixed penalty; and

(b) he shall not be convicted of that offence if the fixed penalty is paid before the expiration of that period.

(3) The Agency may extend the period for paying the fixed penalty in any particular case if it considers it appropriate to do so in all the circumstances of the case.

(4) If, in any particular case, the Agency considers that a fixed penalty notice which has been given ought not to have been given, it may give to the person to whom the fixed penalty notice was given a notice withdrawing the fixed penalty notice; and where notice under this subsection is given—

(a) the Agency shall repay any amount which has been paid by way of fixed penalty in pursuance of the fixed penalty notice; and

(b) no proceedings shall be instituted or continued against that person for the offence in question.

(5) The amount by which the sums received by the Agency by way of fixed penalties exceed the sums repaid by it under subsection (4)(a) above shall be paid into the Consolidated Fund.

(6) In any proceedings, a certificate purporting to be signed by or on behalf of the Chief Executive of the Agency and stating either—

(a) that payment of a fixed penalty was, or (as the case may be) was not, received by the Agency on or before a date specified in the certificate, or

(b) that an envelope containing an amount sent by post in payment of a fixed penalty was marked as posted on a date specified in the certificate,

shall be received as evidence of the matters so stated and shall be treated, without further proof, as being so signed unless the contrary is shown.

(7) A fixed penalty notice shall give such reasonable particulars of the circumstances alleged to constitute the fixed penalty offence to which the notice relates as are necessary for giving reasonable information of the offence and shall state—

(a) the monetary amount of the fixed penalty which may be paid;

(b) the person to whom and the address at which—

(i) the fixed penalty may be paid, and

(ii) any correspondence relating to the fixed penalty notice may be sent;

(c) the method or methods by which payment of the fixed penalty may be made;

(d) the period for paying the fixed penalty;

(e) the consequences of the fixed penalty not being paid before the expiration of that period.

(8) A fixed penalty notice may also contain such other information relating to, or for the purpose of facilitating, the administration of the fixed penalty system as the Agency considers necessary or desirable.

(9) Regulations may—

(a) make provision with respect to the giving of fixed penalty notices, including, in particular, provision with respect to—

(i) the methods by which,

(ii) the officers, servants or agents by, to or on whom, and

(iii) the places at which,

fixed penalty notices may be given by, or served on behalf of, a water bailiff or other officer of the Agency;

(b) prescribe the method or methods by which fixed penalties may be paid;

(c) make provision for or with respect to the issue of prescribed documents to persons to whom fixed penalty notices are or have been given.

(10) In this section—

"fixed penalty" means a penalty of such amount as may be prescribed (whether by being specified in, or made calculable under, regulations);

"fixed penalty offence" means, subject to subsection (11) below, any offence—

    (a)   under this Act,

    (b)   under the Salmon Act 1986,

    (c)   under or by virtue of regulations or orders made under section 115, 116 or 142 of the Water Resources Act 1991, or

    (d)   under section 211(3) of that Act, so far as relating to byelaws made by virtue of paragraph 6 of Schedule 25 to that Act,

which is for the time being prescribed for the purpose;

"the fixed penalty system" means the system implementing this section and regulations made under it;

"the Ministers" means the Secretary of State and the Minister;

"notice" means notice in writing;

"the period for paying", in relation to any fixed penalty, means such period as may be prescribed for the purpose;

"prescribed" means prescribed by regulations;

"regulations" means regulations made under this section by the Ministers.

(11) The provision that may be made by regulations prescribing fixed penalty offences includes provision for an offence to be a fixed penalty offence—

    (a)   only if it is committed in such circumstances or manner as may be prescribed; or

    (b)   except if it is committed in such circumstances or manner as may be prescribed.

(12) Regulations may provide for any offence which is a fixed penalty offence to cease to be such an offence.

(13) An offence which, in consequence of regulations made by virtue of subsection (12) above, has ceased to be a fixed penalty offence shall be eligible to be prescribed as such an offence again.

(14) Regulations may—

    (a)   make different provision in relation to different cases or classes of case; or

    (b)   provide for such exceptions, limitations and conditions, or make such incidental, supplemental, consequential or transitional provision, as the Ministers consider necessary or expedient.

(15) Any power to make regulations under this section shall be exercisable by statutory instrument made by the Ministers; and a statutory instrument containing any such regulations shall be subject to annulment pursuant to a resolution of either House of Parliament.'

(2) In section 35 of that Act (which, among other things, creates an offence of failing to state one's name and address when required to do so under that section) in subsection (1) (water bailiffs and constables), for the words from 'A water bailiff' to 'any constable' there shall be substituted the words 'A water bailiff or other officer of the Agency, or any constable,'.

(3) After that subsection there shall be inserted—

'(1A) Without prejudice to subsection (1) above, a water bailiff or other officer of the Agency who on any occasion finds a person who he has reason to believe is committing, or has on that occasion committed, a fixed penalty offence, within the meaning of section 37A below, may require that person to state his name and address.'

(4) In section 41(1) of that Act (definitions), before the definition of 'authorised officer' there shall be inserted—

'"the Agency" means the Environment Agency;'.

105. Minor and consequential amendments relating to fisheries

Schedule 15 to this Act (which makes minor and consequential provision in relation to fisheries) shall have effect.

New provisions for Scotland

106. Control of pollution of water in Scotland
Schedule 16 to this Act (which amends the Control of Pollution Act 1974 as respects the control of pollution of rivers and coastal waters in Scotland) shall have effect.

107. Statutory nuisances: Scotland
Schedule 17 to this Act (which makes provision with respect to statutory nuisances in Scotland) shall have effect.

Powers of entry

108. Powers of enforcing authorities and persons authorised by them
(1) A person who appears suitable to an enforcing authority may be authorised in writing by that authority to exercise, in accordance with the terms of the authorisation, any of the powers specified in subsection (4) below for the purpose—

(a) of determining whether any provision of the pollution control enactments in the case of that authority is being, or has been, complied with;

(b) of exercising or performing one or more of the pollution control functions of that authority; or

(c) of determining whether and, if so, how such a function should be exercised or performed.

(2) A person who appears suitable to the Agency or SEPA may be authorised in writing by the Agency or, as the case may be, SEPA to exercise, in accordance with the terms of the authorisation, any of the powers specified in subsection (4) below for the purpose of enabling the Agency or, as the case may be, SEPA to carry out any assessment or prepare any report which the Agency or, as the case may be, SEPA is required to carry out or prepare under section 5(3) or 33(3) above.

(3) Subsection (2) above only applies where the Minister who required the assessment to be carried out, or the report to be prepared, has, whether at the time of making the requirement or at any later time, notified the Agency or, as the case may be, SEPA that the assessment or report appears to him to relate to an incident or possible incident involving or having the potential to involve—

(a) serious pollution of the environment,

(b) serious harm to human health, or

(c) danger to life or health.

(4) The powers which a person may be authorised to exercise under subsection (1) or (2) above are—

(a) to enter at any reasonable time (or, in an emergency, at any time and, if need be, by force) any premises which he has reason to believe it is necessary for him to enter;

(b) on entering any premises by virtue of paragraph (a) above, to take with him—

(i) any other person duly authorised by the enforcing authority and, if the authorised person has reasonable cause to apprehend any serious obstruction in the execution of his duty, a constable; and

(ii) any equipment or materials required for any purpose for which the power of entry is being exercised;

(c) to make such examination and investigation as may in any circumstances be necessary;

(d) as regards any premises which he has power to enter, to direct that those premises or any part of them, or anything in them, shall be left undisturbed (whether generally or in particular respects) for so long as is reasonably necessary for the purpose of any examination or investigation under paragraph (c) above;

(e) to take such measurements and photographs and make such recordings as he considers necessary for the purpose of any examination or investigation under paragraph (c) above;

(f)   to take samples, or cause samples to be taken, of any articles or substances found in or on any premises which he has power to enter, and of the air, water or land in, on, or in the vicinity of, the premises;

(g)   in the case of any article or substance found in or on any premises which he has power to enter, being an article or substance which appears to him to have caused or to be likely to cause pollution of the environment or harm to human health, to cause it to be dismantled or subjected to any process or test (but not so as to damage or destroy it, unless that is necessary);

(h)   in the case of any such article or substance as is mentioned in paragraph (g) above, to take possession of it and detain it for so long as is necessary for all or any of the following purposes, namely—

(i)   to examine it, or cause it to be examined, and to do, or cause to be done, to it anything which he has power to do under that paragraph;

(ii)   to ensure that it is not tampered with before examination of it is completed;

(iii)   to ensure that it is available for use as evidence in any proceedings for an offence under the pollution control enactments in the case of the enforcing authority under whose authorisation he acts or in any other proceedings relating to a variation notice, enforcement notice or prohibition notice under those enactments;

(j)   to require any person whom he has reasonable cause to believe to be able to give any information relevant to any examination or investigation under paragraph (c) above to answer (in the absence of persons other than a person nominated by that person to be present and any persons whom the authorised person may allow to be present) such questions as the authorised person thinks fit to ask and to sign a declaration of the truth of his answers;

(k)   to require the production of, or where the information is recorded in computerised form, the furnishing of extracts from, any records—

(i)   which are required to be kept under the pollution control enactments for the enforcing authority under whose authorisation he acts, or

(ii)   which it is necessary for him to see for the purposes of an examination or investigation under paragraph (c) above,

and to inspect and take copies of, or of any entry in, the records;

(l)   to require any person to afford him such facilities and assistance with respect to any matters or things within that person's control or in relation to which that person has responsibilities as are necessary to enable the authorised person to exercise any of the powers conferred on him by this section;

(m)   any other power for—

(i)   a purpose falling within any paragraph of subsection (1) above, or

(ii)   any such purpose as is mentioned in subsection (2) above,

which is conferred by regulations made by the Secretary of State.

(5)   The powers which by virtue of subsections (1) and (4) above are conferred in relation to any premises for the purpose of enabling an enforcing authority to determine whether any provision of the pollution control enactments in the case of that authority is being, or has been, complied with shall include power, in order to obtain the information on which that determination may be made,—

(a)   to carry out experimental borings or other works on those premises; and

(b)   to install, keep or maintain monitoring and other apparatus there.

(6)   Except in an emergency, in any case where it is proposed to enter any premises used for residential purposes, or to take heavy equipment on to any premises which are to be entered, any entry by virtue of this section shall only be effected—

(a)   after the expiration of at least seven days' notice of the proposed entry given to a person who appears to the authorised person in question to be in occupation of the premises in question, and

(b)   either—

    (i)   with the consent of a person who is in occupation of those premises; or

    (ii)   under the authority of a warrant by virtue of Schedule 18 to this Act.

(7)   Except in an emergency, where an authorised person proposes to enter any premises and—

    (a)   entry has been refused and he apprehends on reasonable grounds that the use of force may be necessary to effect entry, or

    (b)   he apprehends on reasonable grounds that entry is likely to be refused and that the use of force may be necessary to effect entry,

any entry on to those premises by virtue of this section shall only be effected under the authority of a warrant by virtue of Schedule 18 to this Act.

(8)   In relation to any premises belonging to or used for the purposes of the United Kingdom Atomic Energy Authority, subsections (1) to (4) above shall have effect subject to section 6(3) of the Atomic Energy Authority Act 1954 (which restricts entry to such premises where they have been declared to be prohibited places for the purposes of the Official Secrets Act 1911).

(9)   The Secretary of State may by regulations make provision as to the procedure to be followed in connection with the taking of, and the dealing with, samples under subsection (4)(f) above.

(10)   Where an authorised person proposes to exercise the power conferred by subsection (4)(g) above in the case of an article or substance found on any premises, he shall, if so requested by a person who at the time is present on and has responsibilities in relation to those premises, cause anything which is to be done by virtue of that power to be done in the presence of that person.

(11)   Before exercising the power conferred by subsection (4)(g) above in the case of any article or substance, an authorised person shall consult—

    (a)   such persons having duties on the premises where the article or substance is to be dismantled or subjected to the process or test, and

    (b)   such other persons,

as appear to him appropriate for the purpose of ascertaining what dangers, if any, there may be in doing anything which he proposes to do or cause to be done under the power.

(12)   No answer given by a person in pursuance of a requirement imposed under subsection (4)(j) above shall be admissible in evidence in England and Wales against that person in any proceedings, or in Scotland against that person in any criminal proceedings.

(13)   Nothing in this section shall be taken to compel the production by any person of a document of which he would on grounds of legal professional privilege be entitled to withhold production on an order for discovery in an action in the High Court or, in relation to Scotland, on an order for the production of documents in an action in the Court of Session.

(14)   Schedule 18 to this Act shall have effect with respect to the powers of entry and related powers which are conferred by this section.

(15) In this section—

'authorised person' means a person authorised under subsection (1) or (2) above;

'emergency' means a case in which it appears to the authorised person in question—

    (a)   that there is an immediate risk of serious pollution of the environment or serious harm to human health, or

    (b)   that circumstances exist which are likely to endanger life or health,

and that immediate entry to any premises is necessary to verify the existence of that risk or those circumstances or to ascertain the cause of that risk or those circumstances or to effect a remedy;

'enforcing authority' means—

    (a)   the Secretary of State;

    (b)   the Agency;

    (c)   SEPA; or

    (d)   a local enforcing authority;

'local enforcing authority' means—

    (a)   a local enforcing authority, within the meaning of Part I of the Environmental Protection Act 1990;

    (b)   a local authority, within the meaning of Part IIA of that Act, in its capacity as an enforcing authority for the purposes of that Part;

    (c)   a local authority for the purposes of Part IV of this Act or regulations under that Part;

'mobile plant' means plant which is designed to move or to be moved whether on roads or otherwise;

'pollution control enactments', in relation to an enforcing authority, means the enactments and instruments relating to the pollution control functions of that authority;

'pollution control functions', in relation to the Agency or SEPA, means the functions conferred on it by or under—

    (a)   the Alkali, &c, Works Regulation Act 1906;

    (b)   Part III of the Rivers (Prevention of Pollution) (Scotland) Act 1951;

    (c)   the Rivers (Prevention of Pollution) (Scotland) Act 1965;

    (d)   Part I of the Health and Safety at Work etc Act 1974;

    (e)   Parts I, IA and II of the Control of Pollution Act 1974;

    (f)   the Control of Pollution (Amendment) Act 1989;

    (g)   Parts I, II and IIA of the Environmental Protection Act 1990 (integrated pollution control, waste on land and contaminated land);

    (h)   Chapter III of Part IV of the Water Industry Act 1991 (special category effluent);

    (j)   Part III and sections 161 to 161D of the Water Resources Act 1991;

    (k)   section 19 of the Clean Air Act 1993;

    (l)   the Radioactive Substances Act 1993;

    (m)   regulations made by virtue of section 2(2) of the European Communities Act 1972, to the extent that the regulations relate to pollution;

'pollution control functions', in relation to a local enforcing authority, means the functions conferred or imposed on, or transferred to, that authority—

    (a)   by or under Part I or IIA of the Environmental Protection Act 1990;

    (b)   by or under regulations made by virtue of Part IV of this Act; or

    (c)   by or under regulations made by virtue of section 2(2) of the European Communities Act 1972, to the extent that the regulations relate to pollution;

'pollution control functions', in relation to the Secretary of State, means any functions which are conferred or imposed upon him by or under any enactment or instrument and which relate to the control of pollution;

'premises' includes any land, vehicle, vessel or mobile plant.

    (16)   Any power to make regulations under this section shall be exercisable by statutory instrument; and a statutory instrument containing any such regulations shall be subject to annulment pursuant to a resolution of either House of Parliament.

109.   Power to deal with cause of imminent danger of serious pollution etc.

    (1)   Where, in the case of any article or substance found by him on any premises which he has power to enter, an authorised person has reasonable cause to believe that, in the circumstances in which he finds it, the article or substance is a cause of imminent danger of serious pollution of the environment or serious harm to human health, he may seize it and cause it to be rendered harmless (whether by destruction or otherwise).

    (2)   As soon as may be after any article or substance has been seized and rendered harmless under this section, the authorised person shall prepare and sign a written report giving particulars of the circumstances in which the article or substance was seized and so dealt with by him, and shall—

(a)   give a signed copy of the report to a responsible person at the premises where the article or substance was found by him; and

(b)   unless that person is the owner of the article or substance, also serve a signed copy of the report on the owner;

and if, where paragraph (b) above applies, the authorised person cannot after reasonable inquiry ascertain the name or address of the owner, the copy may be served on him by giving it to the person to whom a copy was given under paragraph (a) above.

(3)   In this section, 'authorised person' has the same meaning as in section 108 above.

110. Offences

(1)   It is an offence for a person intentionally to obstruct an authorised person in the exercise or performance of his powers or duties.

(2)   It is an offence for a person, without reasonable excuse,—

(a)   to fail to comply with any requirement imposed under section 108 above;

(b)   to fail or refuse to provide facilities or assistance or any information or to permit any inspection reasonably required by an authorised person in the execution of his powers or duties under or by virtue of that section; or

(c)   to prevent any other person from appearing before an authorised person, or answering any question to which an authorised person may require an answer, pursuant to subsection (4) of that section.

(3)   It is an offence for a person falsely to pretend to be an authorised person.

(4)   A person guilty of an offence under subsection (1) above shall be liable—

(a)   in the case of an offence of obstructing an authorised person in the execution of his powers under section 109 above—

(i)   on summary conviction, to a fine not exceeding the statutory maximum;

(ii)   on conviction on indictment, to a fine or to imprisonment for a term not exceeding two years, or to both;

(b)   in any other case, on summary conviction, to a fine not exceeding level 5 on the standard scale.

(5)   A person guilty of an offence under subsection (2) or (3) above shall be liable on summary conviction to a fine not exceeding level 5 on the standard scale.

(6)   In this section—

'authorised person' means a person authorised under section 108 above and includes a person designated under paragraph 2 of Schedule 18 to this Act;

'powers and duties' includes powers or duties exercisable by virtue of a warrant under Schedule 18 to this Act.

Evidence

111. Evidence in connection with certain pollution offences

(1)   The following provisions (which restrict the admissibility in evidence of information obtained from samples) shall cease to have effect—

(a)   section 19(2) to (2B) of the Rivers (Prevention of Pollution) (Scotland) Act 1951;

(b)   section 49 of the Sewerage (Scotland) Act 1968;

(c)   section 171(4) and (5) of the Water Industry Act 1991; and

(d)   section 209(1), (2) and (4) of the Water Resources Act 1991.

(2)   Information provided or obtained pursuant to or by virtue of a condition of a relevant licence (including information so provided or obtained, or recorded, by means of any apparatus) shall be admissible in evidence in any proceedings, whether against the person subject to the condition or any other person.

(3)   For the purposes of subsection (2) above, apparatus shall be presumed in any proceedings to register or record accurately, unless the contrary is shown or the relevant licence otherwise provides.

(4)   Where—

(a) by virtue of a condition of a relevant licence, an entry is required to be made in any record as to the observance of any condition of the relevant licence, and

(b) the entry has not been made,

that fact shall be admissible in any proceedings as evidence that that condition has not been observed.

(5) In this section—

'apparatus' includes any meter or other device for measuring, assessing, determining, recording or enabling to be recorded, the volume, temperature, radioactivity, rate, nature, origin, composition or effect of any substance, flow, discharge, emission, deposit or abstraction;

'condition of a relevant licence' includes any requirement to which a person is subject under, by virtue of or in consequence of a relevant licence;

'environmental licence' has the same meaning as it has in Part I above as it applies in relation to the Agency or SEPA, as the case may be;

'relevant licence' means—

(a) any environmental licence;

(b) any consent under Part II of the Sewerage (Scotland) Act 1968 to make discharges of trade effluent;

(c) any agreement under section 37 of that Act with respect to, or to any matter connected with, the reception, treatment or disposal of such effluent;

(d) any consent under Chapter III of Part IV of the Water Industry Act 1991 to make discharges of special category effluent; or

(e) any agreement under section 129 of that Act with respect to, or to any matter connected with, the reception or disposal of such effluent.

(6) In section 25 of the Environmental Protection Act, after subsection (2) (which makes similar provision to subsection (4) above) there shall be inserted—

'(3) Subsection (2) above shall not have effect in relation to any entry required to be made in any record by virtue of a condition of a relevant licence, within the meaning of section 111 of the Environment Act 1995 (which makes corresponding provision in relation to such licences).'

Offences

112. Amendment of certain offences relating to false or misleading statements or false entries

Schedule 19 to this Act shall have effect.

Information

113. Disclosure of information

(1) Notwithstanding any prohibition or restriction imposed by or under any enactment or rule of law, information of any description may be disclosed—

(a) by a new Agency to a Minister of the Crown, the other new Agency or a local enforcing authority,

(b) by a Minister of the Crown to a new Agency, another Minister of the Crown or a local enforcing authority, or

(c) by a local enforcing authority to a Minister of the Crown, a new Agency or another local enforcing authority,

for the purpose of facilitating the carrying out by either of the new Agencies of any of its functions, by any such Minister of any of his environmental functions or by any local enforcing authority of any of its relevant functions; and no person shall be subject to any civil or criminal liability in consequence of any disclosure made by virtue of this subsection.

(2) Nothing in this section shall authorise the disclosure to a local enforcing authority by a new Agency or another local enforcing authority of information—

(a)   disclosure of which would, in the opinion of a Minister of the Crown, be contrary to the interests of national security; or

(b)   which was obtained under or by virtue of the Statistics of Trade Act 1947 and which was disclosed to a new Agency or any of its officers by the Secretary of State.

(3)   No information disclosed to any person under or by virtue of this section shall be disclosed by that person to any other person otherwise than in accordance with the provisions of this section, or any provision of any other enactment which authorises or requires the disclosure, if that information is information—

(a)   which relates to a trade secret of any person or which otherwise is or might be commercially confidential in relation to any person; or

(b)   whose disclosure otherwise than under or by virtue of this section would, in the opinion of a Minister of the Crown, be contrary to the interests of national security.

(4)   Any authorisation by or under this section of the disclosure of information by or to any person shall also be taken to authorise the disclosure of that information by or, as the case may be, to any officer of his who is authorised by him to make the disclosure or, as the case may be, to receive the information.

(5)   In this section—

'new Agency' means the Agency or SEPA;

'the environment' has the same meaning as in Part I of the Environmental Protection Act 1990;

'environmental functions', in relation to a Minister of the Crown, means any function of that Minister, whether conferred or imposed under or by virtue of any enactment or otherwise, relating to the environment; and

'local enforcing authority' means—

(a)   any local authority within the meaning of Part IIA of the Environmental Protection Act 1990, and the 'relevant functions' of such an authority are its functions under or by virtue of that Part;

(b)   any local authority within the meaning of Part IV of this Act, and the 'relevant functions' of such an authority are its functions under or by virtue of that Part;

(c)   in relation to England, any county council for an area for which there are district councils, and the 'relevant functions' of such a county council are its functions under or by virtue of Part IV of this Act; or

(d)   in relation to England and Wales, any local enforcing authority within the meaning of section 1(7) of the Environmental Protection Act 1990, and the 'relevant functions' of such an authority are its functions under or by virtue of Part I of that Act.

Appeals

114.   Power of Secretary of State to delegate his functions of determining, or to refer matters involved in, appeals

(1)   The Secretary of State may—

(a)   appoint any person to exercise on his behalf, with or without payment, any function to which this paragraph applies; or

(b)   refer any item to which this paragraph applies to such person as the Secretary of State may nominate for the purpose, with or without payment.

(2) The functions to which paragraph (a) of subsection (1) above applies are any of the Secretary of State's functions of determining—

(a)   an appeal under—

    (i)   section 31A(2)(b), 42B(5) or 49B of the Control of Pollution Act 1974,

    (ii)   section 4 of the Control of Pollution (Amendment) Act 1989,

    (iii)   section 15, 22(5), 43, 62(3)(c), 66(5) or 78G of the Environmental Protection Act 1990,

    (iv)   paragraph 2 or paragraph 3(3) of Schedule 6 to the Natural Heritage (Scotland) Act 1991,

(v)   section 43, 91, 92, 96, 161C or 19IB(5) of the Water Resources Act 1991,

(vi)   section 26 of the Radioactive Substances Act 1993 against any decision of, or notice served by, SEPA;

(vii)   paragraph 6 of Schedule 5 to the Waste Management Licensing Regulations 1994,

or any matter involved in such an appeal;

(b)   the questions, or any of the questions, which fall to be determined by the Secretary of State under section 39(1) or section 49(4) of the Control of Pollution Act 1974.

(3)   The items to which paragraph (b) of subsection (1) above applies are—

(a)   any matter involved in an appeal falling within subsection (2)(a) above;

(b)   any of the questions which fall to be determined by the Secretary of State under section 39(1) or section 49(4) of the Control of Pollution Act 1974.

(4)   Schedule 20 to this Act shall have effect with respect to appointments under subsection (1)(a) above.

Crown application

115.   Application of this Act to the Crown

(1)   Subject to the provisions of this section, this Act shall bind the Crown.

(2)   Part III of this Act and any amendments, repeals and revocations made by other provisions of this Act (other than those made by Schedule 21, which shall bind the Crown) bind the Crown to the extent that the enactments to which they relate bind the Crown.

(3)   No contravention by the Crown of any provision made by or under this Act shall make the Crown criminally liable; but the High Court or, in Scotland, the Court of Session may, on the application of the Agency or, in Scotland, SEPA, declare unlawful any act or omission of the Crown which constitutes such a contravention.

(4)   Notwithstanding anything in subsection (3) above, any provision made by or under this Act shall apply to persons in the public service of the Crown as it applies to other persons.

(5)   If the Secretary of State certifies that it appears to him, as respects any Crown premises and any powers of entry exercisable in relation to them specified in the certificate, that it is requisite or expedient that, in the interests of national security, the powers should not be exercisable in relation to those premises, those powers shall not be exercisable in relation to those premises; and in this subsection 'Crown premises' means premises held or used by or on behalf of the Crown.

(6)   Nothing in this section shall be taken as in any way affecting Her Majesty in her private capacity; and this subsection shall be construed as if section 38(3) of the Crown Proceedings Act 1947 (interpretation of references to Her Majesty in her private capacity) were contained in this Act.

116.   Application of certain other enactments to the Crown

Schedule 21 to this Act shall have effect.

Isles of Scilly

117.   Application of this Act to the Isles of Scilly

(1)   Subject to sections 77, 80 and 89 above and the provisions of any order under this section or section 89 above, nothing in this Act shall require or authorise any function, duty or power to be carried out, performed or exercised in relation to the Isles of Scilly by the Agency; and references in the other provisions of this Act (apart from Part III) to England and Wales shall not include references to those Isles.

(2)   The Secretary of State may, after consultation with the Council of the Isles of Scilly, by order make provision with respect to the carrying out in those Isles of functions (other than functions under or by virtue of Part III or IV of this Act) failing to be carried out in relation to other parts of England and Wales by the Agency.

(3)   Without prejudice to the generality of the power conferred by subsection (2) above, an order under this section may apply any provision of this Act (other than a provision contained in Part III or IV) in relation to the Isles of Scilly with or without modifications.

(4)   An order under this section may—

(a)   make different provision for different cases, including different provision in relation to different persons, circumstances or localities; and

(b)   contain such supplemental, consequential and transitional provision as the Secretary of State considers appropriate, including provision saving provision repealed by or under any enactment.

(5)   The power of the Secretary of State to make an order under this section shall be exercisable by statutory instrument; and a statutory instrument containing such an order shall be subject to annulment in pursuance of a resolution of either House of Parliament.

118.   Application of certain other enactments to the Isles of Scilly

(1)   After section 10 of the Control of Pollution (Amendment) Act 1989 there shall be inserted—

'10A.   Application to the Isles of Scilly

(1)   Subject to the provisions of any order under this section, this Act shall not apply in relation to the Isles of Scilly.

(2)   The Secretary of State may, after consultation with the Council of the Isles of Scilly, by order provide for the application of any provisions of this Act to the Isles of Scilly; and any such order may provide for the application of those provisions to those Isles with such modifications as may be specified in the order.

(3)   An order under this section may—

(a)   make different provision for different cases, including different provision in relation to different persons, circumstances or localities; and

(b)   contain such supplemental, consequential and transitional provision as the Secretary of State considers appropriate, including provision saving provision repealed by or under any enactment.

(4)   The power of the Secretary of State to make an order under this section shall be exercisable by statutory instrument; and a statutory instrument containing such an order shall be subject to annulment in pursuance of a resolution of either House of Parliament.'

(2)   In section 11 of that Act, subsection (3) (which provides for section 107 of the Control of Pollution Act 1974 to have effect in relation to the application and modification of that Act to the Isles of Scilly) shall cease to have effect.

(3)   For section 76 of the Environmental Protection Act 1990 (which provides for Part II of that Act to have effect in its application to the Isles of Scilly with modifications specified by order) there shall be substituted—

'76.   Application to the Isles of Scilly

(1)   Subject to the provisions of any order under this section, this Part shall not apply in relation to the Isles of Scilly.

(2)   The Secretary of State may, after consultation with the Council of the Isles of Scilly, by order provide for the application of any provisions of this Part to the Isles of Scilly; and any such order may provide for the application of those provisions to those Isles with such modifications as may be specified in the order.

(3)   An order under this section may—

(a)   make different provision for different cases, including different provision in relation to different persons, circumstances or localities; and

(b)   contain such supplemental, consequential and transitional provision as the Secretary of State considers appropriate, including provision saving provision repealed by or under any enactment.'

(4)   For section 222 of the Water Industry Act 1991 (application to the Isles of Scilly) there shall be substituted—

'222. Application to the Isles of Scilly

(1) Subject to the provisions of any order under this section, this Act shall not apply in relation to the Isles of Scilly.

(2) The Secretary of State may, after consultation with the Council of the Isles of Scilly, by order provide for the application of any provisions of this Act to the Isles of Scilly; and any such order may provide for the application of those provisions to those Isles with such modifications as may be specified in the order.

(3) An order under this section may—

    (a) make different provision for different cases, including different provision in relation to different persons, circumstances or localities; and

    (b) contain such supplemental, consequential and transitional provision as the Secretary of State considers appropriate, including provision saving provision repealed by or under any enactment.

(4) The power of the Secretary of State to make an order under this section shall be exercisable by statutory instrument subject to annulment in pursuance of a resolution of either House of Parliament.'

(5) For section 224 of the Water Resources Act 1991 (application to the Isles of Scilly) there shall be substituted—

'224. Application to the Isles of Scilly

(1) Subject to the provisions of any order under this section, this Act shall not apply in relation to the Isles of Scilly.

(2) The Secretary of State may, after consultation with the Council of the Isles of Scilly, by order provide for the application of any provisions of this Act to the Isles of Scilly; and any such order may provide for the application of those provisions to those Isles with such modifications as may be specified in the order.

(3) An order under this section may—

    (a) make different provision for different cases, including different provision in relation to different persons, circumstances or localities; and

    (b) contain such supplemental, consequential and transitional provision as the Secretary of State considers appropriate, including provision saving provision repealed by or under any enactment.

(4) The power of the Secretary of State to make an order under this section shall be exercisable by statutory instrument subject to annulment in pursuance of a resolution of either House of Parliament.'

(6) For section 75 of the Land Drainage Act 1991 (application to the Isles of Scilly) there shall be substituted—

'75. Application to the Isles of Scilly

(1) Subject to the provisions of any order under this section, this Act shall not apply in relation to the Isles of Scilly.

(2) The Secretary of State may, after consultation with the Council of the Isles of Scilly, by order provide for the application of any provisions of this Act to the Isles of Scilly; and any such order may provide for the application of those provisions to those Isles with such modifications as may be specified in the order.

(3) An order under this section may—

    (a) make different provision for different cases, including different provision in relation to different persons, circumstances or localities; and

    (b) contain such supplemental, consequential and transitional provision as the Secretary of State considers appropriate, including provision saving provision repealed by or under any enactment.

(4) The power of the Secretary of State to make an order under this section shall be exercisable by statutory instrument subject to annulment in pursuance of a resolution of either House of Parliament.'

Miscellaneous and supplemental

119. Stamp duty

(1) No transfer effected by Part I of this Act shall give rise to any liability to stamp duty.

(2) Stamp duty shall not be chargeable—

(a) on any transfer scheme; or

(b) on any instrument or agreement which is certified to the Commissioners of Inland Revenue by the Secretary of State as made in pursuance of a transfer scheme.

(3) No transfer scheme, and no instrument which is certified as mentioned in subsection (2)(b) above, shall be taken to be duly stamped unless—

(a) it has, in accordance with section 12 of the Stamp Act 1891, been stamped with a particular stamp denoting that it is not chargeable with that duty or that it is duly stamped; or

(b) it is stamped with the duty to which it would be liable, apart from this section.

(4) In this section 'transfer scheme' means a scheme made or approved by the Secretary of State under section 3 or 22 above for the transfer of property, rights or liabilities to the Agency or to SEPA.

120. Minor and consequential amendments, transitional and transitory provisions, savings and repeals

(1) The enactments mentioned in Schedule 22 to this Act shall have effect with the amendments there specified (being minor amendments and amendments consequential on provisions of this Act); and, without prejudice to any power conferred by any other provision of this Act, the Secretary of State and the Minister shall each have power by regulations to make such additional consequential amendments—

(a) of public general enactments passed before, or in the same Session as, this Act; and

(b) of subordinate legislation made before the passing of this Act,

as he considers necessary or expedient by reason of the coming into force of any provision of this Act.

(2) The transitional provisions, transitory provisions and savings contained in Schedule 23 to this Act shall have effect; but those provisions are without prejudice to sections 16 and 17 of the Interpretation Act 1978 (effect of repeals).

(3) The enactments mentioned in Schedule 24 to this Act (which include some that are spent or no longer of practical utility) are hereby repealed to the extent specified in the third column of that Schedule.

(4) The power to make regulations under subsection (1) above shall be exercisable by statutory instrument; and a statutory instrument containing any such regulations shall be subject to annulment in pursuance of a resolution of either House of Parliament.

(5) The power to make regulations under subsection (1) above includes power to make such incidental, supplemental, consequential and transitional provision as the Secretary of State or the Minister thinks necessary or expedient.

(6) In this section—

'the Minister' means the Minister of Agriculture, Fisheries and Food;

'subordinate legislation' has the same meaning as in the Interpretation Act 1978.

121. Local statutory provisions: consequential amendments etc.

(1) If it appears to the Secretary of State or the Minister to be appropriate to do so—

(a) for the purposes of, or in consequence of, the coming into force of any enactment contained in this Act; or

(b) in consequence of the effect or operation at any time after the transfer date of any such enactment or of anything done under any such enactment, he may by order repeal, amend or re-enact (with or without modifications) any local statutory provision, including, in the case of an order by virtue of paragraph (b) above, a provision amended by virtue of paragraph (a) above.

(2) An order made by the Secretary of State or the Minister under subsection (1) above may—

(a) make provision applying generally in relation to local statutory provisions of a description specified in the order;

(b) make different provision for different cases, including different provision in relation to different persons, circumstances or localities;

(c) contain such supplemental, consequential and transitional provision as the Secretary of State or, as the case may be, the Minister considers appropriate; and

(d) in the case of an order made after the transfer date, require provision contained in the order to be treated as if it came into force on that date.

(3) The power under this section to repeal or amend a local statutory provision shall include power to modify the effect in relation to any local statutory provision of any provision of Schedule 23 to this Act.

(4) Nothing in any order under this section may abrogate or curtail the effect of so much of any local statutory provision as confers any right of way or confers on or preserves for the public—

(a) any right of enjoyment of air, exercise or recreation on land; or

(b) any right of access to land for the purposes of exercise or recreation.

(5) The power to make an order under subsection (1) above shall be exercisable by statutory instrument subject to annulment in pursuance of a resolution of either House of Parliament.

(6) The power to make an order under subsection (1) above shall be without prejudice to any power conferred by any other provision of this Act.

(7) In this section—

'local statutory provision' means—

(a) a provision of a local Act (including an Act confirming a provisional order);

(b) a provision of so much of any public general Act as has effect with respect to a particular area, with respect to particular persons or works or with respect to particular provisions falling within any paragraph of this definition;

(c) a provision of an instrument made under any provision falling within paragraph (a) or (b) above; or

(d) a provision of any other instrument which is in the nature of a local enactment;

'the Minister' means the Minister of Agriculture, Fisheries and Food;

'the transfer date' has the same meaning as in Part I of this Act.

122. Directions

(1) Any direction given under this Act shall be in writing.

(2) Any power conferred by this Act to give a direction shall include power to vary or revoke the direction.

(3) Subsections (4) and (5) below apply to any direction given—

(a) to the Agency or SEPA under any provision of this Act or any other enactment, or

(b) to any other body or person under any provision of this Act,

being a direction to any extent so given for the purpose of implementing any obligations of the United Kingdom under the Community Treaties.

(4) A direction to which this subsection applies shall not be varied or revoked unless, notwithstanding the variation or revocation, the obligations mentioned in subsection (3) above, as they have effect for the time being, continue to be implemented, whether by directions or any other instrument or by any enactment.

(5) Any variation or revocation of a direction to which this subsection applies shall be published in such manner as the Minister giving it considers appropriate for the purpose of

bringing the matters to which it relates to the attention of persons likely to be affected by them; and—

(a) copies of the variation or revocation shall be made available to the public; and

(b) notice of the variation or revocation, and of where a copy of the variation or revocation may be obtained, shall be given—

(i) if the direction has effect in England and Wales, in the London Gazette;

(ii) if the direction has effect in Scotland, in the Edinburgh Gazette.

123. Service of documents

(1) Without prejudice to paragraph 17(2)(d) of Schedule 7 to this Act, any notice required or authorised by or under this Act to be served (whether the expression 'serve' or the expression 'give' or 'send' or any other expression is used) on any person may be served by delivering it to him, or by leaving it at his proper address, or by sending it by post to him at that address.

(2) Any such notice may—

(a) in the case of a body corporate, be served on the secretary or clerk of that body;

(b) in the case of a partnership, be served on a partner or a person having the control or management of the partnership business.

(3) For the purposes of this section and of section 7 of the Interpretation Act 1978 (service of documents by post) in its application to this section, the proper address of any person on whom any such notice is to be served shall be his last known address, except that—

(a) in the case of a body corporate or their secretary or clerk, it shall be the address of the registered or principal office of that body;

(b) in the case of a partnership or person having the control or the management of the partnership business, it shall be the principal office of the partnership;

and for the purposes of this subsection the principal office of a company registered outside the United Kingdom or of a partnership carrying on business outside the United Kingdom shall be their principal office within the United Kingdom.

(4) If the person to be served with any such notice has specified an address in the United Kingdom other than his proper address within the meaning of subsection (3) above as the one at which he or someone on his behalf will accept notices of the same description as that notice, that address shall also be treated for the purposes of this section and section 7 of the Interpretation Act 1978 as his proper address.

(5) Where under any provision of this Act any notice is required to be served on a person who is, or appears to be, in occupation of any premises then—

(a) if the name or address of such a person cannot after reasonable inquiry be ascertained, or

(b) if the premises appear to be or are unoccupied,

that notice may be served either by leaving it in the hands of a person who is or appears to be resident or employed on the premises or by leaving it conspicuously affixed to some building or object on the premises.

(6) This section shall not apply to any notice in relation to the service of which provision is made by rules of court.

(7) The preceding provisions of this section shall apply to the service of a document as they apply to the service of a notice.

(8) In this section—

'premises' includes any land, vehicle, vessel or mobile plant;

'serve' shall be construed in accordance with subsection (1) above.

124. General interpretation

(1) In this Act, except in so far as the context otherwise requires—

'the Agency' means the Environment Agency;

'financial year' means a period of twelve months ending with 31st March;

'functions' includes powers and duties;

'modifications' includes additions, alterations and omissions and cognate expressions shall be construed accordingly;

'notice' means notice in writing;

'records', without prejudice to the generality of the expression, includes computer records and any other records kept otherwise than in a document;

'SEPA' means the Scottish Environment Protection Agency.

(2) The amendment by this Act of any provision contained in subordinate legislation shall not be taken to have prejudiced any power to make further subordinate legislation amending or revoking that provision.

(3) In subsection (2) above, 'subordinate legislation' has the same meaning as in the Interpretation Act 1978.

125. Short title, commencement, extent, etc

(1) This Act may be cited as the Environment Act 1995.

(2) Part III of this Act, except for section 78, paragraph 7(2) of Schedule 7 and Schedule 10, shall come into force at the end of the period of two months beginning with the day on which this Act is passed.

(3) Except as provided in subsection (2) above and except for this section, section 74 above and paragraphs 76(8)(a) and 135 of Schedule 22 to this Act (which come into force on the passing of this Act) and the repeal of sub-paragraph (1) of paragraph 22 of Schedule 10 to this Act (which comes into force in accordance with sub-paragraph (7) of that paragraph) this Act shall come into force on such day as the Secretary of State may specify by order made by statutory instrument; and different days may be so specified for different provisions or for different purposes of the same provision.

(4) Without prejudice to the provisions of Schedule 23 to this Act, an order under subsection (3) above may make such transitional provisions and savings as appear to the Secretary of State necessary or expedient in connection with any provision brought into force by the order.

(5) The power conferred by subsection (4) above includes power to modify any enactment contained in this or any other Act.

(6) An Order in Council under paragraph 1(1)(b) of Schedule 1 to the Northern Ireland Act 1974 (legislation for Northern Ireland in the interim period) which states that it is made only for purposes corresponding to those of section 98 of this Act—

(a) shall not be subject to paragraph 1(4) and (5) of that Schedule (affirmative resolution of both Houses of Parliament); but

(b) shall be subject to annulment in pursuance of a resolution of either House of Parliament.

(7) Except for this section and any amendment or repeal by this Act of any provision contained in—

(a) the Parliamentary Commissioner Act 1967,

(b) the Sea Fish (Conservation) Act 1967,

(c) the House of Commons Disqualification Act 1975, or

(d) the Northern Ireland Assembly Disqualification Act 1975,

this Act shall not extend to Northern Ireland.

(8) Part III of this Act, and Schedule 24 to this Act so far as relating to that Part, extends to England and Wales only.

(9) Section 106 of, and Schedule 16 to, this Act extend to Scotland only.

(10) Subject to the foregoing provisions of this section and to any express provision made by this Act to the contrary, any amendment, repeal or revocation made by this Act shall have the same extent as the enactment or instrument to which it relates.

SCHEDULES

SCHEDULE 1

THE ENVIRONMENT AGENCY

Membership

1.—(1) Subject to the following provisions of this paragraph, a member shall hold and vacate office in accordance with the terms of his appointment and shall, on ceasing to be a member, be eligible for re-appointment.

(2) A member may at any time resign his office by giving notice to the appropriate Minister.

(3) The appropriate Minister may remove a member from that office if he is satisfied—

(a) that the member has been absent from meetings of the Agency for a period of more than three months without the permission of the Agency;

(b) that the member has been adjudged bankrupt, that his estate has been sequestrated or that he has made a composition or arrangement with, or granted a trust deed for, his creditors; or

(c) that the member is unable or unfit to carry out the functions of a member.

Chairman and deputy chairman

2. The chairman or deputy chairman of the Agency shall hold office as such unless and until—

(a) he resigns that office by giving notice to the Secretary of State, or

(b) he ceases to be a member,

and shall, on ceasing to be the chairman or deputy chairman, be eligible for further designation as such in accordance with section 1(3) of this Act at any time when he is a member.

Remuneration, pensions, etc.

3.—(1) The Agency shall pay to its members such remuneration, and such travelling and other allowances, as may be determined by the appropriate Minister.

(2) The Agency shall, if so required by the appropriate Minister,—

(a) pay such pension, allowances or gratuities as may be determined by that Minister to or in respect of a person who is or has been a member;

(b) make such payments as may be determined by that Minister towards provision for the payment of a pension, allowances or gratuities to or in respect of a person who is or has been a member; or

(c) provide and maintain such schemes (whether contributory or not) as may be determined by that Minister for the payment of pensions, allowances or gratuities to or in respect of persons who are or have been members.

(3) If, when any member ceases to hold office, the appropriate Minister determines that there are special circumstances which make it right that that member should receive compensation, the Agency shall pay to him a sum by way of compensation of such amount as may be so determined.

Staff

4.—(1) The Agency may appoint such officers and employees as it may determine.

(2) No member or other person shall be appointed by the Agency to act as chief executive of the Agency unless the Secretary of State has consented to the appointment of that person.

(3) The Agency may—

(a) pay such pensions, allowances or gratuities to or in respect of any persons who are or have been its officers or employees as it may, with the approval of the Secretary of State, determine;

(b) make such payments as it may so determine towards provision for the payment of pensions, allowances or gratuities to or in respect of any such persons;

(c) provide and maintain such schemes as it may so determine (whether contributory or not) for the payment of pensions, allowances or gratuities to or in respect of any such persons.

(4) Any reference in sub-paragraph (3) above to pensions, allowances or gratuities to or in respect of any such persons as are mentioned in that sub-paragraph includes a reference to pensions, allowances or gratuities by way of compensation to or in respect of any of the Agency's officers or employees who suffer loss of office or employment or loss or diminution of emoluments.

Proceedings of the Agency

5. Subject to the following provisions of this Schedule and to section 106 of the 1991 Act (obligation to carry out flood defence functions through committees), the Agency may regulate its own procedure (including quorum).

Delegation of powers

6. Subject to section 106 of the 1991 Act, anything authorised or required by or under any enactment to be done by the Agency may be done—

(a) by any member, officer or employee of the Agency who has been authorised for the purpose, whether generally or specially, by the Agency; or

(b) by any committee or sub-committee of the Agency which has been so authorised.

Members' interests

7.—(1) A member who is in any way directly or indirectly interested in any matter that is brought up for consideration at a meeting of the Agency shall disclose the nature of his interest to the meeting; and, where such a disclosure is made—

(a) the disclosure shall be recorded in the minutes of the meeting; and

(b) the member shall not take any part in any deliberation or decision of the Agency, or of any of its committees or sub-committees, with respect to that matter.

(2) For the purposes of sub-paragraph (1) above, a general notification given at a meeting of the Agency by a member to the effect that he—

(a) is a member of a specified company or firm, and

(b) is to be regarded as interested in any matter involving that company or firm, shall be regarded as a sufficient disclosure of his interest in relation to any such matter.

(3) A member need not attend in person at a meeting of the Agency in order to make a disclosure which he is required to make under this paragraph if he takes reasonable steps to secure that the disclosure is made by a notice which is read and considered at the meeting.

(4) The Secretary of State may, subject to such conditions as he considers appropriate, remove any disability imposed by virtue of this paragraph in any case where the number of members of the Agency disabled by virtue of this paragraph at any one time would be so great a proportion of the whole as to impede the transaction of business.

(5) The power of the Secretary of State under sub-paragraph (4) above includes power to remove, either indefinitely or for any period, a disability which would otherwise attach to any member, or members of any description, by reason of such interests, and in respect of such matters, as may be specified or described by the Secretary of State.

(6) Nothing in this paragraph precludes any member from taking part in the consideration or discussion of, or voting on, any question whether an application should be made to the Secretary of State for the exercise of the power conferred by sub-paragraph (4) above.

(7) Any reference in this paragraph to a meeting of the Agency includes a reference to a meeting of any committee or sub-committee of the Agency.

Vacancies and defective appointments

8. The validity of any proceedings of the Agency shall not be affected by a vacancy amongst the members or by a defect in the appointment of a member.

Minutes

9.—(1) Minutes shall be kept of proceedings of the Agency, of its committees and of its sub-committees.

(2) Minutes of any such proceedings shall be evidence of those proceedings if they are signed by a person purporting to have acted as chairman of the proceedings to which the minutes relate or of any subsequent proceedings in the course of which the minutes were approved as a correct record.

(3) Where minutes of any such proceedings have been signed as mentioned in sub-paragraph (2) above, those proceedings shall, unless the contrary is shown, be deemed to have been validly convened and constituted.

Application of seal and proof of instruments

10.—(1) The application of the seal of the Agency shall be authenticated by the signature of any member, officer or employee of the Agency who has been authorised for the purpose, whether generally or specially, by the Agency.

(2) In this paragraph the reference to the signature of a person includes a reference to a facsimile of a signature by whatever process reproduced; and, in paragraph 11 below, the word 'signed' shall be construed accordingly.

Documents served etc. by or on the Agency

11.—(1) Any document which the Agency is authorised or required by or under any enactment to serve, make or issue may be signed on behalf of the Agency by any member, officer or employee of the Agency who has been authorised for the purpose, whether generally or specially, by the Agency.

(2) Every document purporting to be an instrument made or issued by or on behalf of the Agency and to be duly executed under the seal of the Agency, or to be signed or executed by a person authorised by the Agency for the purpose, shall be received in evidence and be treated, without further proof, as being so made or issued unless the contrary is shown.

(3) Any notice which is required or authorised, by or under any provision of any other Act, to be given, served or issued by, to or on the Agency shall be in writing.

Interpretation

12. In this Schedule—

'the appropriate Minister', in relation to any person who is or has been a member, means the Minister or the Secretary of State, according to whether that person was appointed as a member by the Minister or by the Secretary of State; and

'member', except where the context otherwise requires, means any member of the Agency (including the chairman and deputy chairman).

SCHEDULE 2

TRANSFERS OF PROPERTY ETC: SUPPLEMENTAL PROVISIONS

PART I

INTRODUCTORY

Interpretation

1. In this Schedule—
   'the chief inspector'—

(a)   in the application of this Schedule in relation to transfers by or under section 3 of this Act, means any of the inspectors or chief inspectors mentioned in section 2(1) of this Act;

(b)   in the application of this Schedule in relation to transfers by or under section 22 of this Act, means any of the inspectors or chief inspectors mentioned in section 21(1) of this Act;

and any reference to the chief inspector for England and Wales or the chief inspector for Scotland shall be construed accordingly;

'the relevant new Agency' means—

(a)   in the application of this Schedule in relation to transfers by or under section 3 of this Act, the Agency; and

(b)   in the application of this Schedule in relation to transfers by or under section 22 of this Act, SEPA;

'transfer scheme' means a scheme under section 3 or 22 of this Act;

'the transferor', in relation to transfers by or under section 3 of this Act, means—

(a)   in the case of any transfer by section 3(1)(a) of this Act, the National Rivers Authority or the London Waste Regulation Authority, as the case may be; or

(b) in the case of any transfer scheme, or any transfer by transfer scheme—

(i)   the Secretary of State,

(ii)   the chief inspector, or

(iii)   any waste regulation authority,

(as the case may be) from whom any property, rights or liabilities are, or are to be, transferred by that scheme;

'the transferor', in relation to transfers by or under section 22 of this Act, means—

(a)   in the case of any transfer by section 22(1)(a) of this Act, the river purification board in question; or

(b)   in the case of any transfer scheme, or any transfer by transfer scheme—

(i)   the Secretary of State;

(ii)   the chief inspector; or

(iii)   any local authority,

(as the case may be) from whom any property, rights or liabilities are, or are to be, transferred by that scheme; and, as respects any such local authority which is a district or islands council, includes, in relation to any time on or after 1st April 1996, the council for any local government area named in column 1 of Schedule 1 to the Local Government etc. (Scotland) Act 1994 which is wholly or partly conterminous with the area of that council.

The property etc. which may be transferred

2.—(1)   The property, rights and liabilities which are transferred by, or may be transferred by transfer scheme under, section 3 or 22 of this Act include—

(a)   property, rights and liabilities that would not otherwise be capable of being transferred or assigned by the transferor;

(b)   in the case of a transfer scheme, such property, rights and liabilities to which the transferor may become entitled or subject after the making of the scheme and before the transfer date as may be specified in the scheme;

(c)   property situated anywhere in the United Kingdom or elsewhere;

(d)   rights and liabilities under enactments;

(e)   rights and liabilities under the law of any part of the United Kingdom or of any country or territory outside the United Kingdom.

(2)   The transfers authorised by paragraph (a) of sub-paragraph (1) above include transfers which, by virtue of that paragraph, are to take effect as if there were no such contravention, liability or interference with any interest or right as there would be, in the case of a transfer or assignment otherwise than by or under section 3 or 22 of this Act, by

reason of any provision having effect (whether under any enactment or agreement or otherwise) in relation to the terms on which the transferor is entitled or subject to the property, right or liability in question.

(3) This paragraph is subject to paragraph 3 below.

Contracts of employment

3.—(1) The rights and liabilities that may be transferred by and in accordance with a transfer scheme include (subject to the following provisions of this paragraph) any rights or liabilities of the employer under the contract of employment of any person—

    (a) who is employed—
        (i) in the civil service of the State;
        (ii) by a body which is a waste regulation authority in England or Wales; or
        (iii) by a local authority in Scotland;
    (b) who appears to the appropriate authority to be employed for the purposes of, or otherwise in connection with, functions which are by virtue of this Act to become functions of a new Agency; and
    (c) whom the appropriate authority considers it necessary or expedient to transfer into the employment of that new Agency;

and in the following provisions of this paragraph any reference to a 'qualifying employee' is a reference to such a person.

(2) A transfer scheme which provides for the transfer of rights or liabilities under the contracts of employment of qualifying employees must identify those employees—

    (a) by specifying them;
    (b) by referring to persons of a description specified in the scheme (with or without exceptions); or
    (c) partly in the one way and partly in the other.

(3) A transfer scheme shall not operate to transfer rights or liabilities under so much of a contract of employment as relates to an occupational pension scheme, other than any provisions of such a pension scheme which do not relate to benefits for old age, invalidity or survivors.

(4) Where a transfer scheme provides for the transfer of rights or liabilities under the contract of employment of a qualifying employee—

    (a) all the employer's rights, powers, duties and liabilities under or in connection with the contract of employment shall be transferred to the relevant new Agency on the transfer date by and in accordance with the scheme, and
    (b) anything done by or in relation to the employer in respect of the qualifying employee before the transfer date shall be treated on and after that date as done by or in relation to the relevant new Agency,

except in a case where objection is made by the qualifying employee as mentioned in sub-paragraph (8)(b) below.

(5) Sub-paragraphs (6) and (7) below shall have effect in any case where rights or liabilities under the contract of employment of a qualifying employee are transferred by and in accordance with a transfer scheme.

(6) In a case falling within sub-paragraph (5) above—

    (a) the transfer shall be regarded for the purposes of section 84 of the Employment Protection (Consolidation) Act 1978 (renewal of contract or re-engagement) as a renewal of the qualifying employee's contract of employment, or a re-engagement of the qualifying employee, falling within subsection (1) of that section; and
    (b) the qualifying employee shall accordingly not be regarded as having been dismissed by virtue of the transfer.

(7) In a case falling within sub-paragraph (5) above, for the purposes of Schedule 13 to the Employment Protection (Consolidation) Act 1978 (ascertainment of the length of an employee's period of employment and whether that employment is continuous)—

(a) so much of the qualifying employee's period of continuous employment as ends with the day preceding the transfer date shall be treated on and after that date as a period of employment with the relevant new Agency; and

(b) the continuity of the period of employment of the qualifying employee shall be treated as not having been broken by the transfer.

(8) Sub-paragraph (9) below shall have effect in any case where—

(a) a transfer scheme contains provision for the transfer of rights or liabilities under the contract of employment of a qualifying employee, but

(b) the qualifying employee informs the appropriate authority or the relevant new Agency that he objects to becoming employed by that new Agency.

(9) In a case falling within sub-paragraph (8) above—

(a) the transfer scheme—

(i) shall not operate to transfer any rights, powers, duties or liabilities under or in connection with the contract of employment; but

(ii) shall operate so as to terminate that contract on the day preceding the transfer date; and

(b) the qualifying employee shall not, by virtue of that termination, be treated for any purpose as having been dismissed.

(10) In this paragraph—

'the appropriate authority' means—

(a) in the case of a person employed in the civil service of the State, the Secretary of State;

(b) in the case of a transfer scheme under section 3 of this Act and a person employed by a body which is a waste regulation authority, that body;

(c) in the case of a transfer scheme under section 22 of this Act and a person employed by a local authority, that authority;

'occupational pension scheme' has the meaning given by section 1 of the Pension Schemes Act 1993.

(11) This paragraph shall apply in relation to any qualifying employee as if, as respects any time before the transfer date,—

(a) any reference to a person's contract of employment included a reference to his employment in the civil service of the State or to the terms of that employment, as the case may require; and

(b) any reference to the dismissal of a person included a reference to the termination of his employment in that service.

PART II

TRANSFER SCHEMES

Description of the property etc. to be transferred by scheme

4. A transfer scheme may define the property, rights and liabilities to be transferred by the scheme—

(a) by specifying or describing the property, rights and liabilities in question;

(b) by referring to all (or all but so much as may be excepted) of the property, rights and liabilities comprised in a specified part of the undertaking of the transferor; or

(c) partly in the one way and partly in the other.

Division of property etc. to be transferred by scheme: creation of new rights and interests

5.—(1) For the purpose of making any division of property, rights or liabilities which it is considered appropriate to make in connection with the transfer of property, rights and liabilities by and in accordance with a transfer scheme, any such scheme may—

(a)   create in favour of the transferor an interest in, or right over, any property transferred by the scheme;

(b)   create in favour of the relevant new Agency an interest in, or right over, any property retained by the transferor;

(c)   create new rights and liabilities as between the relevant new Agency and the transferor; or

(d)   in connection with any provision made by virtue of paragraph (a), (b) or (c) above, make incidental provision as to the interests, rights and liabilities of persons other than the transferor and the relevant new Agency with respect to the subject-matter of the transfer scheme;

and references in the other provisions of Part I of this Act to the transfer of property, rights or liabilities (so far as relating to transfers by and in accordance with transfer schemes) shall accordingly be construed as including references to the creation of any interest, right or liability by virtue of paragraph (a), (b) or (c) above or the making of provision by virtue of paragraph (d) above.

(2)   The provision that may be made by virtue of paragraph (c) of sub-paragraph (1) above includes—

(a)   provision for treating any person who is entitled by virtue of a transfer scheme to possession of a document as having given another person an acknowledgement in writing of the right of that other person to the production of the document and to delivery of copies of it; and

(b)   in the case of a transfer scheme under section 3 of this Act, provision applying section 64 of the Law of Property Act 1925 (production and safe custody of documents) in relation to any case in relation to which provision falling within paragraph (a) above has effect.

Transfer schemes: incidental, supplemental and consequential provision

6.—(1)   A transfer scheme may make such incidental, supplemental and consequential provision—

(a)   as the Secretary of State considers appropriate, in the case of a scheme made by him,

(b)   as a body which is a waste regulation authority considers appropriate, in the case of a scheme made by that body under section 3 of this Act, or

(c)   as a local authority considers appropriate, in the case of a scheme made by that authority under section 22 of this Act.

(2)   Without prejudice to the generality of sub-paragraph (1) above, a transfer scheme may provide—

(a)   that disputes as to the effect of the scheme between the transferor and the relevant new Agency are to be referred to such arbitration as may be specified in or determined under the transfer scheme;

(b)   that determinations on such arbitrations and certificates given jointly by the transferor and the relevant new Agency as to the effect of the scheme as between them are to be conclusive for all purposes.

Modification of transfer schemes

7.—(1)   If at any time after a transfer scheme has come into force the Secretary of State considers it appropriate to do so, he may by order provide that the scheme shall for all purposes be deemed to have come into force with such modifications as may be specified in the order.

(2)   An order under sub-paragraph (1) above—

(a)   may make, with effect from the coming into force of the transfer scheme in question, such provision as could have been made by the scheme; and

(b)   in connection with giving effect to that provision from that time, may contain such supplemental, consequential or transitional provision as the Secretary of State considers appropriate.

(3)   The Secretary of State shall not make an order under sub-paragraph (1) above except after consultation with—

    (a)   the relevant new Agency; and

    (b)   if the transfer scheme in question is—

        (i)   a scheme under section 3 of this Act which transferred property, rights or liabilities of a waste regulation authority, or

        (ii)   a scheme under section 22 of this Act which transferred property, rights or liabilities of a local authority,

the body which was the transferor in the case of that scheme.

(4)   The power to make an order under sub-paragraph (1) above shall be exercisable by statutory instrument; and a statutory instrument containing any such order shall be subject to annulment in pursuance of a resolution of either House of Parliament.

Provision of information and assistance to the Secretary of State and the new
Agencies in connection with transfer schemes

8.—(1)   It shall be the duty of each of the following, that is to say—

    (a)   the chief inspector for England and Wales,

    (b)   any body which is a waste regulation authority in England or Wales, and

    (c)   any officer of such a body,

to provide the Secretary of State or the Agency with such information or assistance as the Secretary of State or, as the case may be, the Agency may reasonably require for the purposes of, or in connection with, the exercise of any powers of the Secretary of State or the Agency in relation to transfer schemes.

(2)   It shall be the duty of each of the following, that is to say—

    (a)   the chief inspector for Scotland,

    (b)   any local authority, and

    (c)   any officer of a local authority,

to provide the Secretary of State or SEPA with such information or assistance as the Secretary of State or, as the case may be, SEPA may reasonably require for the purposes of, or in connection with, the exercise of any powers of the Secretary of State or SEPA in relation to transfer schemes.

PART III

GENERAL PROVISIONS WITH RESPECT TO TRANSFERS BY OR UNDER SECTION 3 OR 22

Consideration

9.   No consideration shall be provided in respect of the transfer of any property, rights or liabilities by or under section 3 or 22 of this Act; but—

    (a)   a transfer scheme may contain provision for consideration to be provided by the relevant new Agency in respect of the creation of interests, rights or liabilities by means of the transfer scheme; and

    (b)   any such provision shall be enforceable in the same way as if the interests, rights or liabilities had been created, and (if the case so requires) had been capable of being created, by agreement between the parties.

Continuity

10.—(1)   This paragraph applies in relation to—

    (a)   any transfer of property, rights or liabilities by section 3 or 22 of this Act; or

(b) subject to any provision to the contrary in the transfer scheme in question, any transfer of property, rights or liabilities by a transfer scheme.

(2) Where this paragraph applies in relation to a transfer, then, so far as may be necessary for the purposes of, or in connection with, the transfer—

(a) any agreements made, transactions effected or other things done by or in relation to the transferor shall be treated as made, effected or done by or in relation to the relevant new Agency;

(b) references (whether express or implied and, if express, however worded) to the transferor in any agreement (whether in writing or not) or in any deed, bond, instrument or other document relating to the property, rights or liabilities transferred shall, as respects anything falling to be done on or after the transfer date, have effect as references to the relevant new Agency.

Remedies

11.—(1) Without prejudice to the generality of paragraph 10 above, a new Agency and any other person shall, as from the transfer date, have the same rights, powers and remedies (and, in particular, the same rights and powers as to the taking or resisting of legal proceedings or the making or resisting of applications to any authority) for ascertaining, perfecting or enforcing any right or liability transferred to that new Agency by or under this Act as that new Agency or that person would have had if that right or liability had at all times been a right or liability of that new Agency.

(2) Without prejudice to the generality of paragraph 10 above, any legal proceedings or applications to any authority pending immediately before the transfer date by or against a transferor, in so far as they relate to any property, right or liability transferred to the relevant new Agency by or under this Act or to any agreement relating to any such property, right or liability, shall be continued by or against the relevant new Agency to the exclusion of the transferor.

Perfection of vesting of foreign property, rights and liabilities

12.—(1) This paragraph applies in the case of any transfer by or under section 3 or 22 of this Act of any foreign property, rights or liabilities.

(2) It shall be the duty of the transferor and the relevant new Agency to take, as and when that new Agency considers it appropriate, all such steps as may be requisite to secure that the vesting in that new Agency by, or by transfer scheme under, section 3 or 22 of this Act of any foreign property, right or liability is effective under the relevant foreign law.

(3) Until the vesting in the relevant new Agency by, or by transfer scheme under, section 3 or 22 of this Act of any foreign property, right or liability is effective under the relevant foreign law, it shall be the duty of the transferor to hold that property or right for the benefit of, or to discharge that liability on behalf of, the relevant new Agency.

(4) Nothing in sub-paragraphs (2) and (3) above shall be taken as prejudicing the effect under the law of any part of the United Kingdom of the vesting in the relevant new Agency by, or by transfer scheme under, section 3 or 22 of this Act of any foreign property, right or liability.

(5) The transferor shall have all such powers as may be requisite for the performance of his duty under this paragraph, but it shall be the duty of the relevant new Agency to act on behalf of the transferor (so far as possible) in performing the duty imposed on the transferor by this paragraph.

(6) References in this paragraph to any foreign property, right or liability are references to any property, right or liability as respects which any issue arising in any proceedings would have been determined (in accordance with the rules of private international law) by reference to the law of a country or territory outside the United Kingdom.

(7) Duties imposed on the transferor or the relevant new Agency by this paragraph shall be enforceable in the same way as if the duties were imposed by a contract between the transferor and that new Agency.

(8)   Any expenses reasonably incurred by the transferor under this paragraph shall be met by the relevant new Agency.

SCHEDULE 3
ENVIRONMENT PROTECTION ADVISORY COMMITTEES

Introductory

1.—(1)   In this Schedule, 'scheme' means a scheme prepared under this Schedule.

(2)   Subject to sub-paragraph (1) above, expressions used in this Schedule and in section 12 of this Act have the same meaning in this Schedule as they have in that section.

Duty of Agency to prepare and submit schemes for each region

2.—(1)   It shall be the duty of the Agency, in accordance with such guidance as may be given for the purpose by the Secretary of State,—

(a)   to prepare, in respect of each region, a scheme with respect to the appointment of persons as members of the advisory committee for that region; and

(b)   to submit that scheme to the Secretary of State for his approval before such date as may be specified in the guidance.

(2)   Every scheme shall—

(a)   specify descriptions of bodies which, or persons who, appear to the Agency likely to have a significant interest in matters likely to be affected by the manner in which it carries out its functions in the region to which the scheme relates;

(b)   indicate how the membership of the advisory committee is to reflect the different descriptions of bodies or persons so specified;

(c)   specify or describe bodies which, and persons whom, the Agency proposes to consult in connection with appointments of persons as members of the advisory committee; and

(d)   make provision with respect to such other matters as the Agency considers relevant to the membership of the advisory committee.

Approval of schemes

3.—(1)   A scheme shall not come into force unless it has been approved by the Secretary of State or until such date as he may specify for the purpose in giving his approval.

(2)   Where the Agency submits a scheme to the Secretary of State for his approval, it shall also submit to him—

(a)   a statement of the Agency's reasons for considering that the scheme is one which it is appropriate for him to approve; and

(b)   such information in support of those reasons as it considers necessary.

(3)   On submitting a scheme to the Secretary of State for his approval, the Agency shall publish the scheme, in such manner as it considers appropriate for bringing it to the attention of persons likely to be interested in it, together with a notice specifying the period within which representations or objections with respect to the scheme may be made to the Secretary of State.

(4)   Where a scheme has been submitted to the Secretary of State for his approval, it shall be the duty of the Secretary of State, in determining whether to—

(a)   approve the scheme,

(b)   reject the scheme, or

(c)   approve the scheme subject to modifications,

to consider any representations or objections made to him within the period specified pursuant to sub-paragraph (3) above and not withdrawn.

(5)   Where the Secretary of State approves a scheme, with or without modifications, it shall be the duty of the Agency to take such steps as it considers appropriate for bringing

the scheme as so approved to the attention of persons whom it considers likely to be interested in it.

Replacement and variation of approved membership schemes

4.—(1) The Agency may from time to time, and if required to do so by the Secretary of State shall,—

(a) prepare in accordance with paragraph 2 above a fresh scheme with respect to the appointment of persons as members of the advisory committee for any particular region; and

(b) submit that scheme to the Secretary of State for his approval;

and paragraph 3 above shall have effect accordingly in relation to any such scheme.

(2) An approved membership scheme may from time to time be varied by the Agency with the approval of the Secretary of State.

(3) The provisions of paragraph 3 above shall have effect in relation to any variation of an approved membership scheme as they have effect in relation to a scheme.

Appointment of members

5.—(1) Before appointing a person to be a member of an advisory committee, the Agency—

(a) shall consult such of the associates for that advisory committee as it considers appropriate in the particular case; and

(b) may, if it considers it appropriate to do so, also consult bodies or persons who are not associates for that advisory committee.

(2) In this paragraph, 'associates', in the case of any advisory committee, means those bodies and persons specified or described in the approved membership scheme for that advisory committee pursuant to paragraph 2(2)(c) above.

Vacancies, defective appointments etc.

6. The validity of any proceedings of an advisory committee shall not be affected by—

(a) any vacancy amongst the members;

(b) any defect in the appointment of a member; or

(c) any temporary breach of the terms of the approved membership scheme for the advisory committee.

Remuneration and allowances

7.—(1) The Agency shall pay to the chairman of an advisory committee such remuneration, and such travelling and other allowances, as the Secretary of State may determine.

(2) The Agency shall pay to the members of an advisory committee other than the chairman such sums by way of reimbursement (whether in whole or in part) for loss of remuneration, for travelling expenses and for other out-of-pocket expenses as the Secretary of State may determine.

SCHEDULE 4

BOUNDARIES OF REGIONAL FLOOD DEFENCE AREAS

Power to make order

1.—(1) The relevant Minister may by order made by statutory instrument—

(a) alter the boundaries of the area of any regional flood defence committee; or

(b) provide for the amalgamation of any two or more such areas.

(2) Where an order under this Schedule makes provision by reference to anything shown on a main river map, that map shall be conclusive evidence for the purposes of the order of what is shown on the map.

(3) The power to make an order under this Schedule shall include power to make such supplemental, consequential and transitional provision as the relevant Minister considers appropriate.

(4) In the case of an order under this Schedule amalgamating the areas of any two or more regional flood defence committees, the provision made by virtue of sub-paragraph (3) above may include provision determining—

    (a)   the total number of members of the amalgamated committee; and

    (b)   the total number of such members to be appointed by the constituent councils of that committee;

and subsections (7) and (8) of section 16 of this Act shall apply in relation to so much of an order under this Schedule as is made by virtue of this sub-paragraph as they apply in relation to an order under subsection (5) of that section.

(5) In this paragraph and the following paragraphs of this Schedule 'the relevant Minister' —

    (a)   in relation to any alteration of the boundaries of an area where the whole or any part of that area is in Wales, means the Ministers;

    (b)   in relation to the amalgamation of any two or more areas where the whole or any part of any one of those areas is in Wales, means the Ministers; and

    (c)   in any other case, means the Minister.

(6) In this paragraph—

'main river' means a main river within the meaning of Part IV of the 1991 Act; and 'main river map' has, subject to section 194 of the 1991 Act, the meaning given by section 193(2) of that Act.

Consultation and notice of intention to make order

2.—(1) Before making an order under this Schedule, the relevant Minister shall—

    (a)   consult such persons or representative bodies as he considers it appropriate to consult at that stage;

    (b)   prepare a draft order;

    (c)   publish a notice complying with sub-paragraph (2) below in the London Gazette and in such other manner as he considers appropriate for bringing the draft order to the attention of persons likely to be affected by it if it is made.

(2) A notice for the purposes of sub-paragraph (1)(c) above with respect to a draft order shall—

    (a)   state the relevant Minister's intention to make the order and its general effect;

    (b)   specify the places where copies of the draft order and of any map to which it refers may be inspected by any person free of charge at all reasonable times during the period of twenty-eight days beginning with the date on which the notice is first published otherwise than in the London Gazette; and

    (c)   state that any person may within that period by notice in writing to the relevant Minister object to the making of the order.

(3) The relevant Minister shall also cause copies of the notice and of the draft order to be served on every person carrying out functions under any enactment who appears to him to be concerned.

Objections to draft order and making of order

3.—(1) Before making an order under this Schedule, the relevant Minister—

    (a)   shall consider any representations or objections which are duly made with respect to the draft order and are not withdrawn; and

    (b)   may, if he thinks fit, cause a local inquiry to be held with respect to any such representations or objections.

(2) Where notice of a draft order has been published and given in accordance with paragraph 2 above and any representations or objections considered under sub-paragraph (1)

above, the relevant Minister may make the order either in the terms of the draft or in those terms as modified in such manner as he thinks fit, or may decide not to make the order.

(3)   The relevant Minister shall not make a modification of a draft order in so far as the modification is such as to include in the area of any regional flood defence committee any tidal waters which, if the order had been made in the form of the draft, would have been outside the area of every regional flood defence committee.

Procedure for making of order

4.—(1)   Where the relevant Minister makes an order under this Schedule, he shall serve notice of the making of the order on every person (if any) who—

(a)   is a person on whom notice is required to have been served under paragraph 2(3) above; and

(b)   has duly made an objection to the making of the order that has not been withdrawn.

(2)   Where a notice is required to be served under sub-paragraph (1) above with respect to any order, the order shall not have effect before the end of a period of twenty-eight days from the date of service of the last notice served under that sub-paragraph.

(3)   If before an order takes effect under sub-paragraph (2) above—

(a)   any person who has been served with a notice under sub-paragraph (1) above with respect to that order serves notice objecting to the order on the Minister (or, in the case of an order made jointly by the Ministers, on either of them), and

(b)   the objection is not withdrawn,

the order shall be subject to special parliamentary procedure.

(4)   A statutory instrument containing an order under this Schedule which is not subject to special parliamentary procedure under sub-paragraph (3) above shall be subject to annulment in pursuance of a resolution of either House of Parliament.

Notice after making of order

5.—(1)   Subject to sub-paragraph (2) below, after making an order under this Schedule, the relevant Minister shall publish in the London Gazette, and in such other manner as he considers appropriate for bringing the order to the attention of persons likely to be affected by it, a notice—

(a)   stating that the order has been made; and

(b)   naming the places where a copy of the order may be inspected at all reasonable times.

(2)   In the case of an order to which sub-paragraph (2) of paragraph 4 above applies, the notice—

(a)   shall not be published until the end of the period of twenty-eight days referred to in that sub-paragraph; and

(b)   shall state whether or not the order is to be subject to special parliamentary procedure.

Questioning of order in courts

6.—(1)   Subject to sub-paragraph (3) below, if any person desires to question the validity of an order under this Schedule on the ground—

(a)   that it is not within the powers of this Schedule, or

(b)   that any requirement of this Schedule has not been complied with,

he may, within six weeks after the date of the first publication of the notice required by paragraph 5 above, make an application for the purpose to the High Court.

(2)   On an application under this paragraph the High Court, if satisfied—

(a)   that the order is not within the powers of this Schedule, or

(b)   that the interests of the applicant have been substantially prejudiced by a failure to comply with any of the requirements of this Schedule,

may quash the order either generally or in so far as it affects the applicant.

(3)   Sub-paragraph (1) above—

(a)   shall not apply to any order which is confirmed by Act of Parliament under section 6 of the Statutory Orders (Special Procedure) Act 1945; and

(b)   shall have effect in relation to any other order which is subject to special parliamentary procedure by virtue of the provisions of this Schedule as if the reference to the date of the first publication of the notice required by paragraph 5 above were a reference to the date on which the order becomes operative under that Act of 1945.

(4)   Except as provided by this paragraph the validity of an order under this Schedule shall not, either before or after the order has been made, be questioned in any legal proceedings whatsoever.

SCHEDULE 5

MEMBERSHIP AND PROCEEDINGS OF REGIONAL AND LOCAL FLOOD DEFENCE COMMITTEES

PART I

MEMBERSHIP OF FLOOD DEFENCE COMMITTEES

Terms of membership

1.—(1)   Members of a flood defence committee (that is to say a regional flood defence committee or a local flood defence committee), other than those appointed by or on behalf of one or more constituent councils, shall hold and vacate office in accordance with the terms of their appointment.

(2)   The first members of a local flood defence committee appointed by or on behalf of any one or more constituent councils—

(a)   shall come into office on the day on which the committee comes into existence or, in the case of a member who is for any reason appointed after that day, on the day on which the appointment is made; and

(b)   subject to the following provisions of this Schedule, shall hold office until the end of May in such year as may be specified for the purposes of this paragraph in the scheme establishing the committee.

(3)   Any members of a flood defence committee appointed by or on behalf of any one or more constituent councils who are not members to whom sub-paragraph (2) above applies—

(a)   shall come into office at the beginning of the June next following the day on which they are appointed; and

(b)   subject to the following provisions of this Schedule, shall hold office for a term of four years.

(4)   If for any reason any such member as is mentioned in sub-paragraph (3) above is appointed on or after the day on which he ought to have come into office, he shall—

(a)   come into office on the day on which he is appointed; and

(b)   subject to the following provisions of this Schedule, hold office for the remainder of the term.

(5)   References in this paragraph and the following provisions of this Schedule to a member of a flood defence committee include references to the chairman of such a committee.

Membership of constituent council as qualification for membership of committee

2.—(1)   Members of a flood defence committee appointed by or on behalf of any one or more constituent councils may be members of that council, or one of those councils, or other persons.

(2) Any member of a flood defence committee appointed by or on behalf of a constituent council who at the time of his appointment was a member of that council shall, if he ceases to be a member of that council, also cease to be a member of the committee with whichever is the earlier of the following—

(a) the end of the period of three months beginning with the date when he ceases to be a member of the council; and

(b) the appointment of another person in his place.

(3) For the purposes of sub-paragraph (2) above a member of a council shall not be deemed to have ceased to be a member of the council by reason of retirement if he has been re-elected a member of the council not later than the date of his retirement.

Disqualification for membership of committee

3.—(1) Subject to the following provisions of this paragraph, a person shall be disqualified for appointment as a member of a flood defence committee if he—

(a) is a paid officer of the Agency; or

(b) is a person who has been adjudged bankrupt, or whose estate has been sequestrated or who has made a composition or arrangement with, or granted a trust deed for, his creditors; or

(c) within the period of five years before the day of his appointment, has been convicted, in the United Kingdom, the Channel Islands or the Isle of Man, of any offence and has had passed on him a sentence of imprisonment (whether suspended or not) for a period of not less than three months without the option of a fine; or

(d) is disqualified for being elected or for being a member of a local authority under Part III of the Local Government Finance Act 1982 (accounts and audit) or Part III of the Representation of the People Act 1983 (legal proceedings).

(2) Where a person is disqualified under sub-paragraph (1) above by reason of having been adjudged bankrupt, the disqualification shall cease—

(a) unless the bankruptcy order made against that person is previously annulled, on his discharge from bankruptcy; and

(b) if the bankruptcy order is so annulled, on the date of the annulment.

(3) Where a person is disqualified under sub-paragraph (1) above by reason of having had his estate sequestrated, the disqualification shall cease—

(a) unless the sequestration is recalled or reduced, on the person's discharge under section 54 of the Bankruptcy (Scotland) Act 1985; and

(b) if the sequestration is recalled or reduced, on the date of the recall or reduction.

(4) Where a person is disqualified under sub-paragraph (1) above by reason of his having made a composition or arrangement with, or having granted a trust deed for, his creditors, the disqualification shall cease—

(a) if he pays his debts in full, on the date on which the payment is completed; and

(b) in any other case, at the end of five years from the date on which the terms of the deed of composition or arrangement, or of the trust deed, are fulfilled.

(5) For the purposes of sub-paragraph (1)(c) above the date of the conviction shall be taken to be—

(a) the ordinary date on which the period allowed for making an appeal or application with respect to the conviction expires; or

(b) if such an appeal or application is made, the date on which it is finally disposed of or abandoned or fails by reason of non-prosecution.

(6) Section 92 of the Local Government Act 1972 (proceedings for disqualification) shall apply in relation to disqualification under this paragraph for appointment as a member of a flood defence committee as it applies in relation to disqualification for acting as a member of a local authority.

Vacation of office by disqualifying event

4.—(1) The office of a member of a flood defence committee shall become vacant upon the fulfilment of any of the following conditions, that is to say—

(a) the person holding that office is adjudged bankrupt, is a person whose estate is sequestrated or makes a composition or arrangement with, or grants a trust deed for, his creditors;

(b) that person is convicted, in the United Kingdom, the Channel Islands or the Isle of Man, of any offence and has passed on him a sentence of imprisonment (whether suspended or not) for a period of not less than three months without the option of a fine;

(c) that person is disqualified for being elected or for being a member of a local authority under Part III of the Local Government Finance Act 1982 (accounts and audit) or Part Ill of the Representation of the People Act 1983 (legal proceedings); or

(d) that person has, for a period of six consecutive months been absent from meetings of the committee, otherwise than by reason of illness or some other cause approved during the period by the committee.

(2) For the purposes of sub-paragraph (1)(d) above, the attendance of a member of a flood defence committee—

(a) at a meeting of any sub-committee of the committee of which he is a member, or

(b) at any joint committee to which he has been appointed by that committee,

shall be treated as attendance at a meeting of the committee.

Resignation of office by members of regional committee

5.—(1) The chairman of a regional flood defence committee may resign his office at any time by giving notice to the chairman of the Agency and to one of the Ministers.

(2) Any other member of such a committee may resign his office at any time by giving notice to the chairman of the committee and also, if he was appointed by one of the Ministers, to that Minister.

Resignation of office by members of local committee

6.—(1) The chairman of a local flood defence committee may resign his office at any time by giving notice to the chairman of the regional flood defence committee.

(2) Any other member of a local flood defence committee may resign his office at any time by giving notice to the chairman of that local flood defence committee.

Appointments to fill casual vacancies

7.—(1) Where, for any reason whatsoever, the office of a member of a flood defence committee becomes vacant before the end of his term of office, the vacancy—

(a) shall, if the unexpired portion of the term of office of the vacating member is six months or more, be filled by the appointment of a new member; and

(b) may be so filled in any other case.

(2) A person appointed by virtue of sub-paragraph (1) above to fill a casual vacancy shall hold office for so long only as the former member would have held office.

Eligibility of previous members for re-appointment

8. Subject to the provisions of this Schedule, a member of a flood defence committee shall be eligible for reappointment.

Appointment of deputies

9.—(1) Subject to the following provisions of this paragraph, a person nominated by one or more constituent councils may act as deputy for a member of a flood defence committee appointed by or on behalf of that council or those councils and may, accordingly, attend and vote at a meeting of the committee, instead of that member.

(2)   A person nominated under sub-paragraph (1) above as deputy for a member of a flood defence committee may, by virtue of that nomination, attend and vote at a meeting of a sub-committee of that committee which—

(a)   has been appointed, by that committee under Part II of this Schedule; and

(b)   is a committee to which the member for whom he is a deputy belongs.

(3)   A person acting as deputy for a member of a flood defence committee shall be treated for the purposes for which he is nominated as a member of that committee.

(4)   A person shall not act as deputy for a member of a flood defence committee unless his nomination has been notified to such officer of the Agency as is appointed to receive such nominations.

(5)   A nomination under this paragraph shall be in writing and may apply either to a particular meeting or to all meetings during a stated period or until the nomination is revoked.

(6)   A person shall not act as deputy for more than one member of a flood defence committee.

(7)   Nothing in this paragraph shall entitle a person to attend and vote at a meeting of a local flood defence committee by reason of his nomination as deputy for a member of a regional flood defence committee.

Payments to past and present chairmen and to members

10.—(1)   The Agency shall pay to any person who is a chairman of a flood defence committee such remuneration and allowances as may be determined by the relevant Minister.

(2)   If the relevant Minister so determines in the case of any person who is or has been chairman of a flood defence committee, the Agency shall pay or make arrangements for the payment of a pension in relation to that person in accordance with the determination.

(3)   If a person ceases to be chairman of a flood defence committee and it appears to the relevant Minister that there are special circumstances which make it right that that person should receive compensation in respect of his ceasing to be chairman, the relevant Minister may require the Agency to pay to that person a sum of such amount as that Minister may determine.

(4)   The Agency may pay to any person who is a member of a flood defence committee such allowances as may be determined by the relevant Minister.

(5)   In this paragraph—

'pension', in relation to any person, means a pension (whether contributory or not) of any kind payable to or in respect of him, and includes an allowance, gratuity or lump sum so payable and a return of contributions with or without interest or any other addition; and 'the relevant Minister'—

(a)   in relation to the regional flood defence committee for an area the whole or the greater part of which is in Wales and in relation to any local flood defence committee for any district comprised in the area of such a regional flood defence committee, means the Secretary of State; and

(b)   in relation to any other flood defence committee, means the Minister.

PART II

PROCEEDINGS OF FLOOD DEFENCE COMMITTEES

Appointment of sub-committees, joint sub-committees etc.

11.—(1)   For the purpose of carrying out any functions in pursuance of arrangements under paragraph 12 below—

(a)   a flood defence committee may appoint a sub-committee of the committee;

(b)   two or more regional or two or more local flood defence committees may appoint a joint sub-committee of those committees;

(c)   any sub-committee may appoint one or more committees of that sub-committee ('under sub-committees').

(2)   The number of members of any sub-committee and their terms of office shall be fixed by the appointing committee or committees or, in the case of an under sub-committee, by the appointing sub-committee.

(3)   A sub-committee appointed under this paragraph may include persons who are not members of the appointing committee or committees or, in the case of an under sub-committee, the committee or committees of whom they are an under sub-committee; but at least two thirds of the members appointed to any such sub-committee shall be members of that committee or those committees, as the case may be.

(4)   A person who is disqualified for being a member of a flood defence committee shall be disqualified also for being a member of a sub-committee or under sub-committee appointed under this paragraph.

Delegation of functions to sub-committees etc.

12.—(1)   Subject to section 106 of the 1991 Act and to any other express provision contained in any enactment, a flood defence committee may arrange for the carrying out of any of their functions—

(a)   by a sub-committee, or an under sub-committee of the committee or an officer of the Agency; or

(b)   by any other regional or, as the case may be, local flood defence committee; and two or more regional or two or more local flood defence committees may arrange to carry out any of their functions jointly or may arrange for the carrying out of any of their functions by a joint sub-committee of theirs.

(2)   where by virtue of this paragraph any functions of a flood defence committee or of two or more such committees may be carried out by a sub-committee, then, unless the committee or committees otherwise direct, the sub-committee may arrange for the carrying out of any of those functions by an under sub-committee or by an officer of the Agency.

(3)   Where by virtue of this paragraph any functions of a flood defence committee or of two or more such committees may be carried out by an under sub-committee, then, unless the committee or committees or the sub-committee otherwise direct, the under sub-committee may arrange for the carrying out of any of those functions by an officer of the Agency.

(4)   Any arrangements made by a flood defence committee under this paragraph for the carrying out of any function shall not prevent the committee from discharging their functions themselves.

(5)   References in the preceding provisions of this paragraph to the carrying out of any functions of a flood defence committee include references to the doing of anything which is calculated to facilitate, or is conducive or incidental to, the carrying out of any of those functions.

(6)   A regional flood defence committee shall not, under this paragraph, make arrangements for the carrying out in a local flood defence district of any functions which fall to be carried out there by the local flood defence committee.

Rules of procedure

13.—(1)   A flood defence committee may, with the approval of the relevant Minister, make rules for regulating the proceedings of the committee.

(2)   Nothing in section 6(4) of this Act or section 105 or 106 of the 1991 Act shall entitle the Agency to make any arrangements or give any directions for regulating the proceedings of any flood defence committee.

(3)   In this paragraph 'the relevant Minister' has the same meaning as in paragraph 10 above.

Declarations of interest etc.

14.—(1)   Subject to the following provisions of this paragraph, the provisions of sections 94 to 98 of the Local Government Act 1972 (pecuniary interests of members of local authorities) shall apply in relation to members of a flood defence committee as those provisions apply in relation to members of local authorities.

(2)   In their application by virtue of this paragraph those provisions shall have effect in accordance with the following provisions—

(a)   for references to meetings of the local authority there shall be substituted references to meetings of the committee;

(b)   in section 94(4), for the reference to provision being made by standing orders of a local authority there shall be substituted a reference to provisions being made by directions of the committee;

(c)   in section 96, for references to the proper officer of the local authority there shall be substituted a reference to an officer of the Agency appointed for the purposes of this paragraph; and

(d)   section 97 shall apply as it applies to a local authority other than a parish or community council.

(3)   Subject to sub-paragraph (4) below, a member of a flood defence committee shall be disqualified, for so long as he remains such a member and for twelve months after he ceases to be such a member, for appointment to any paid office by the Agency or any regional flood defence committee.

(4)   Sub-paragraph (3) above shall not disqualify any person for appointment to the office of chairman of a local flood defence committee.

Authentication of documents

15.—(1)   Any notice or other document which a flood defence committee are required or authorised to give, make or issue by or under any enactment may be signed on behalf of the committee by any member of the committee or any officer of the Agency who is generally or specifically authorised for that purpose by a resolution of the committee.

(2)   Any document purporting to bear the signature of a person expressed to be authorised as mentioned in sub-paragraph (1) above shall be deemed, unless the contrary is shown, to be duly given, made or issued by authority of the committee.

(3)   In this paragraph 'signature' includes a facsimile of a signature by whatever process reproduced.

Proof and validity of proceedings

16.—(1)   A minute of the proceedings of a meeting of a flood defence committee, purporting to be signed at that or the next ensuing meeting by—

(a)   the chairman of the meeting to the proceedings of which the minute relates, or

(b)   by the chairman of the next ensuing meeting,

shall be evidence of the proceedings and shall be received in evidence without further proof.

(2)   Where a minute has been signed as mentioned in sub-paragraph (1) above in respect of a meeting of a committee or sub-committee, then, unless the contrary is shown—

(a)   the meeting shall be deemed to have been duly convened and held;

(b)   all the proceedings had at any such meeting shall be deemed to have been duly had; and

(c)   that committee or sub-committee shall be deemed to have been duly constituted and have had power to deal with the matters referred to in the minute.

(3)   The validity of any proceedings of a flood defence committee shall not be affected by any vacancy among the members of the committee or by any defect in the appointment of such a member.

SCHEDULE 6

THE SCOTTISH ENVIRONMENT PROTECTION AGENCY

Status

1.   SEPA shall be a body corporate with a common seal.
2.   Subject to section 36 of this Act, SEPA shall not—
     (a)   be regarded as a servant or agent of the Crown;
     (b)   have any status, immunity or privilege of the Crown;
     (c)   by virtue of its connection with the Crown, be exempt from any tax, duty, rate, levy or other charge whatsoever whether general or local,
and its property shall not be regarded as property of, or held on behalf of, the Crown.

Membership

3.   SEPA shall consist of not less than eight, nor more than twelve, members appointed by the Secretary of State.
4.   In making appointments under paragraph 3 above, the Secretary of State shall have regard to the desirability of appointing persons who have knowledge or experience in some matter relevant to the functions of SEPA.
5.   Subject to paragraphs 7 and 8 below, each member—
     (a)   shall hold and vacate office in accordance with the terms of his appointment;
     (b)   may, by giving notice to the Secretary of State, resign his office; and
     (c)   after ceasing to hold office shall be eligible for reappointment as a member.
6.   The Secretary of State may, by order made by statutory instrument subject to annulment in pursuance of a resolution of either House of Parliament, amend paragraph 3 above so as to substitute for the numbers for the time being specified as, respectively, the minimum and maximum membership such other numbers as he thinks fit.
7.   The Secretary of State may remove a member from office if he is satisfied that the member—
     (a)   has been absent from meetings of SEPA for a period longer than three months without the permission of SEPA; or
     (b)   has been adjudged bankrupt, has made an arrangement with his creditors, has had his estate sequestrated or has granted a trust deed for his creditors or a composition contract; or
     (c)   is unable or unfit to carry out the functions of a member.

Chairman and deputy chairman

8.—(1)   The Secretary of State shall appoint one of the members of SEPA to be chairman and another of those members to be deputy chairman.
     (2)   The chairman and deputy chairman shall hold and vacate office in terms of their appointments.
     (3)   A member who is chairman or deputy chairman may resign his office by giving notice to the Secretary of State; but if the chairman or deputy chairman ceases to be a member (whether or not on giving notice under paragraph 5(b) above) he shall cease to be chairman or, as the case may be, deputy chairman.
     (4)   A person who ceases to be chairman or deputy chairman shall be eligible for reappointment as such under sub-paragraph (1) above at any time when he is a member.

Remuneration, pensions, etc.

9.—(1)   SEPA shall—
(a)   pay to its members such remuneration and such travelling and other allowances (if any); and
(b)   as regards any member or former member in whose case the Secretary of State may so determine—
(i)   pay such pension, allowance or gratuity to or in respect of him;
(ii)   make such payments towards the provision of such pension, allowance or gratuity; or
(iii)   provide and maintain such schemes (whether contributory or not) for the payment of pensions, allowances or gratuities,
as the Secretary of State may determine.

(2)   If a person ceases to be a member, and it appears to the Secretary of State that there are special circumstances which make it right that he should receive compensation, the Secretary of State may require SEPA to pay to that person a sum of such amount as the Secretary of State may determine.

Staff

10.—(1)   There shall be a chief officer of SEPA.
(2)   The Secretary of State shall, after consultation with the chairman or person designated to be chairman (if there is a person holding or designated to hold that office), make the first appointment of chief officer on such terms and conditions as he may determine; and thereafter SEPA may, with the approval of the Secretary of State, make subsequent appointments to that office on such terms and conditions as it may with such approval determine.

11.   SEPA may appoint such other employees as it thinks fit.

12.—(1)   SEPA shall, in the case of such of its employees or former employees as it may, with the approval of the Secretary of State, determine—
(a)   pay such pensions, allowances or gratuities to or in respect of those employees;
(b)   make such payments towards provision of such pensions, allowances or gratuities; or
(c)   provide and maintain such schemes (whether contributory or not) for the payment of such pensions, allowances or gratuities,
as it may, with the approval of the Secretary of State, determine.

(2)   References in sub-paragraph (1) above to pensions, allowances or gratuities in respect of employees of SEPA include references to pensions, allowances or gratuities by way of compensation to or in respect of any such employee who suffers loss of office or employment.

Proceedings

13.—(1)   SEPA may regulate its own procedure and that of any committee established by it (including making provision in relation to the quorum for its meetings and the meetings of any such committee).
(2)   The proceedings of SEPA and of any committee established by it shall not be invalidated by any vacancy amongst its members or the members of such committee or by any defect in the appointment of such member.

Committees

14.—(1)   SEPA may appoint persons who are not members of it to be members of any committee established by it, but at least one member of any such committee shall be a member of SEPA.

(2) SEPA shall pay to a person so appointed such remuneration and allowances (if any) as the Secretary of State may determine.

(3) Any committee established by SEPA shall comply with any directions given to them by it.

Delegation of powers

15.—(1) Anything authorised or required by or under any enactment to be done by SEPA may be done by any of its committees which, or by any of its members or employees who, is authorised (generally or specifically) for the purpose by SEPA.

(2) Nothing in sub-paragraph (1) above shall prevent SEPA from doing anything that a committee, member or employee has been authorised or required to do.

Regional Boards

16.—(1) Without prejudice to the generality of its power to establish committees, SEPA shall establish committees (to be known as 'Regional Boards') for the purposes of discharging in relation to such areas as it may, with the approval of the Secretary of State, determine, such of its functions as it may, with such approval, determine.

(2) A Regional Board shall have a chairman who shall be a member of SEPA and appointed to that office by SEPA.

(3) It shall be the duty of SEPA to comply with such guidance as the Secretary of State may from time to time give as to—

(a) the number of persons to be appointed to a Regional Board;

(b) the qualifications and experience which persons (other than members of SEPA) should have to be eligible for appointment to a Regional Board;

(c) the descriptions of bodies which, or persons who, have a significant interest in matters likely to be affected by the discharge by a Regional Board of its functions; and

(d) how the membership of a Regional Board is to reflect the different descriptions of bodies or persons referred to in paragraph (c) above.

(4) Anything authorised or required to be done by a Regional Board by virtue of sub-paragraph (1) above may be done by any member of the Board, or by any employee of SEPA, who is authorised (generally or specifically) for the purpose by the Board.

(5) Nothing in sub-paragraph (4) above shall prevent a Regional Board doing anything that a member or employee has been authorised or required to do.

Members' interests

17.—(1) A member who is in any way directly or indirectly interested in any matter that is brought up for consideration at a meeting of SEPA shall disclose the nature of his interest to the meeting; and, where such a disclosure is made—

(a) the disclosure shall be recorded in the minutes of the meeting; and

(b) the member shall not take any part in any deliberation or decision of SEPA or of any of its committees with respect to that matter.

(2) For the purposes of sub-paragraph (1) above, a general notification given at a meeting of SEPA by a member to the effect that he—

(a) is a member of a specified company or firm, and

(b) is to be regarded as interested in any matter involving that company or firm,

shall be regarded as a sufficient disclosure of his interest in relation to any such matter.

(3) A member need not attend in person at a meeting of SEPA in order to make a disclosure which he is required to make under this paragraph if he takes reasonable steps to secure that the disclosure is made by a notice which is read and considered at the meeting.

(4) The Secretary of State may, subject to such conditions as he considers appropriate, remove any disability imposed by virtue of this paragraph in any case where the number of

members of SEPA disabled by virtue of this paragraph at any one time would be so great a proportion of the whole as to impede the transaction of business.

(5)   The power of the Secretary of State under sub-paragraph (4) above includes power to remove, either indefinitely or for any period, a disability which would otherwise attach to any member, or members of any description, by reason of such interests, and in respect of such matters, as may be specified or described by the Secretary of State.

(6)   Nothing in this paragraph precludes any member from taking part in the consideration or discussion of, or voting on, any question whether an application should be made to the Secretary of State for the exercise of the power conferred by sub-paragraph (4) above.

(7)   In this paragraph—
  (a)   any reference to a meeting of SEPA includes a reference to a meeting of any of SEPA's committees; and
  (b)   any reference to a member includes a reference to a person who is not a member of SEPA but who is a member of any such committee.

Minutes

18.—(1)   Minutes shall be kept of proceedings of SEPA and of its committees.

(2)   Minutes of any such proceedings shall be evidence of those proceedings if they are signed by a person purporting to have acted as chairman of the proceedings to which the minutes relate or of any subsequent proceedings in the course of which the minutes were approved as a correct record.

(3)   Where minutes of any such proceedings have been signed as mentioned in sub-paragraph (2) above, those proceedings shall, unless the contrary is shown, be deemed to have been validly convened and constituted.

SCHEDULE 7

NATIONAL PARK AUTHORITIES

Status and constitution of authorities

1.—(1)   A National Park authority shall be a body corporate.

(2)   A National Park authority shall consist of—
  (a)   such number of local authority members as may be specified in the relevant order; and
  (b)   such number of members to be appointed by the Secretary of State as may be so specified.

(3)   In the case of a National Park authority for a National Park in England, such number as may be specified in the relevant order of the number of members of the authority to be appointed by the Secretary of State shall be parish members.

(4)   The number specified in the relevant order for any National Park authority as the number of members of that authority who are to be appointed by the Secretary of State shall—
  (a)   as respects any National Park authority for a National Park in England, be two less than the number of local authority members specified in the order; and
  (b)   as respects any National Park authority for a National Park in Wales, be equal to half the number of local authority members specified in the order.

(5)   As respects any National Park authority for a National Park in England, the number specified in the relevant order as the number of parish members to be appointed by the Secretary of State shall be one less than one half of the total number of the members of the authority to be appointed by the Secretary of State.

(6)   Accordingly—
  (a)   in the case of a National Park authority for a National Park in England, the effect of the relevant order shall be such that the total number of members of the authority will be an even number which is not a whole number multiple of four; and

(b)   in the case of a National Park authority for a National Park in Wales, the number of local authority members specified in the relevant order shall be an even number.

Local authority members

2.—(1)   The local authority members of a National Park authority shall be appointed by such of the councils for the principal areas wholly or partly comprised in the relevant Park as may be specified in or determined under the relevant order.

(2)   Each of the councils who are to appoint the local authority members of a National Park authority shall be entitled to appoint such number of those members as may be so specified or determined and to make any appointment required by reason of a vacancy arising in respect of a member appointed by that council.

(3)   Before making any provision by the relevant order as to—

(a)   the number of members of a National Park authority who are to be local authority members,

(b)   the councils by whom the local authority members of a National Park authority are to be appointed, or

(c)   the number of members to be appointed by each such council,

the Secretary of State shall consult the council for every principal area the whole or any part of which is comprised in the relevant Park; and the Secretary of State may make provision for excluding the council for any such area from the councils by whom the local authority members of a National Park authority are to be appointed only at the request of that council.

(4)   A person shall not be appointed as a local authority member of a National Park authority unless he is a member of a principal council the area of which is wholly or partly comprised in the relevant Park; and, in appointing local authority members of a National Park authority, a principal council shall have regard to the desirability of appointing members of the council who represent wards, or (in Wales) electoral divisions, situated wholly or partly within the relevant Park.

(5)   Subject to the following provisions of this Schedule, where a person who qualifies for his appointment by virtue of his membership of any council is appointed as a local authority member of a National Park authority—

(a)   he shall hold office from the time of his appointment until he ceases to be a member of that council; but

(b)   his appointment may, before any such cessation, be terminated for the purposes of, and in accordance with, sections 15 to 17 of the Local Government and Housing Act 1989 (political balance).

(6)   Sub-paragraph (5)(a) above shall have effect so as to terminate the term of office of a person who, on retiring from any council, immediately becomes such a member again as a newly elected councillor; but a person who so becomes a member again shall be eligible for re-appointment to the National Park authority.

(7)   The appointment of any person as a local authority member of a National Park authority may provide that he is not to be treated for the purposes of sub-paragraph (5) above as qualifying for his appointment by virtue of his membership of any council other than that specified in the appointment.

(8)   In paragraph 2(1) of Schedule 1 to the Local Government and Housing Act 1989 (bodies to which appointments have to be made taking account of political balance), after paragraph (b) there shall be inserted the following paragraph—

'(ba)   a National Park authority;'.

Parish members of English National Park authorities

3.—(1)   The parish members of an English National Park authority shall be appointed by the Secretary of State.

(2) A person shall not be appointed as a parish member of an English National Park authority unless he is—

    (a) a member of the parish council for a parish the whole or any part of which is comprised in the relevant Park; or

    (b) the chairman of the parish meeting of a parish—

        (i) which does not have a separate parish council; and

        (ii) the whole or any part of which is comprised in the relevant Park.

(3) Subject to the following provisions of this Schedule, where a person who qualifies for his appointment by virtue of his membership of a parish council is appointed as a parish member of an English National Park authority, he shall hold office from the time of his appointment until he ceases to be a member of that parish council.

(4) Sub-paragraph (3) above shall have effect so as to terminate the term of office of a person who on retiring from any parish council immediately becomes such a member again as a newly elected councillor; but a person who so becomes a member again shall be eligible for re-appointment to the National Park authority.

(5) Subject to the following provisions of this Schedule, where a person who qualifies for his appointment by virtue of his being the chairman of a parish meeting is appointed as a parish member of an English National Park authority, he shall hold office from the time of his appointment until he ceases to be the chairman of that parish meeting.

(6) Sub-paragraph (5) above shall have effect so as to terminate the term of office of a person who is elected to succeed himself as chairman of any parish meeting; but a person who so becomes the chairman again shall be eligible for re-appointment to the National Park authority.

(7) Subject to the provisions of this Schedule, a parish member of an English National Park authority shall hold office in accordance with the terms of his appointment.

(8) In this paragraph, 'English National Park authority' means a National Park authority for a National Park in England.

Members (other than parish members) appointed by the Secretary of State

4.—(1) Before appointing any person as a member of a National Park authority the Secretary of State shall consult, according to whether the relevant Park is in England or in Wales, either the Countryside Commission or the Countryside Council for Wales.

(2) Subject to the following provisions of this Schedule, a person appointed as a member of a National Park authority by the Secretary of State—

    (a) shall hold office for such period of not less than one year nor more than three years as may be specified in the terms of his appointment; but

    (b) on ceasing to hold office shall be eligible for re-appointment.

(3) The term of office of a person appointed by the Secretary of State to fill such a vacancy in the membership of a National Park authority as occurs where a person appointed by the Secretary of State ceases to be a member of the authority before the end of his term of office may be for a period of less than one year if it is made to expire with the time when the term of office of the person in respect of whom the vacancy has arisen would have expired.

(4) Subject to the provisions of this Schedule, a member of a National Park authority appointed by the Secretary of State shall hold office in accordance with the terms of his appointment.

(5) This paragraph shall not apply to persons appointed as parish members of a National Park authority for a National Park in England or to their appointment as such members.

Chairman and deputy chairman

5.—(1) The members of a National Park authority shall elect, from amongst their members, both a chairman and a deputy chairman of the authority.

(2)   Subject to sub-paragraphs (3) and (4) below, the chairman and deputy chairman of a National Park authority shall be elected for a period not exceeding one year; but a person so elected shall, on ceasing to hold office at the end of his term of office as chairman or deputy chairman, be eligible for re-election.

(3)   A person shall cease to hold office as chairman or deputy chairman of a National Park authority if he ceases to be a member of the authority.

(4)   Where a vacancy occurs in the office of chairman or deputy chairman of a National Park authority, it shall be the duty of the members of that authority to secure that that vacancy is filled as soon as possible.

Removal of members

6.—(1)   The Secretary of State may, by giving a local authority member of a National Park authority such written notice of the termination of his appointment as the Secretary of State considers appropriate, remove that member from office; but he shall do so only where he considers it appropriate to remove that member from office in consequence of the provisions of any order for varying either the area of the relevant Park or the number of local authority members of that authority.

(2)   The Secretary of State may remove from office any member of a National Park authority appointed by him, other than any parish member of a National Park authority for a National Park in England, either—

(a)   by giving that member three months' written notice of the termination of the appointment; or

(b)   in such other manner as may be provided for in the terms of that member's appointment.

(3)   The Secretary of State may remove from office any parish member of a National Park authority for a National Park in England either—

(a)   by giving that member such written notice of the termination of his appointment as the Secretary of State considers appropriate; or

(b)   in such other manner as may be provided for in the terms of that member's appointment;

but a parish member shall only be removed from office in the manner mentioned in paragraph (a) above where the Secretary of State considers it appropriate to do so in consequence of the provisions of any order for varying either the area of the relevant Park or the number of parish members of the National Park authority in question.

Disqualification of members

7.—(1)   A person is disqualified for becoming or remaining a member of a National Park authority if he holds any paid office or employment appointments to which are or may be made or confirmed by—

(a)   the authority itself or any council by whom a local authority member of the authority is appointed;

(b)   any committee or sub-committee of the authority or of any such council;

(c)   any joint committee on which the authority or any such council is represented; or

(d)   as respects a National Park authority for a National Park in England—

(i)   any parish council for, or parish meeting of, a parish the whole or any part of which is comprised in the relevant Park;

(ii) any committee or sub-committee of any such parish council or any committee of any such parish meeting; or

(iii)   any joint committee on which any such parish council or parish meeting is represented; or

(e)   any person himself holding an office or employment which disqualifies him for becoming a member of the authority.

(2)   A person is also disqualified for becoming or remaining a member of a National Park authority if he holds any employment in a company which, in accordance with Part V of the Local Government and Housing Act 1989 other than section 73, is under the control of that authority.

(3)   Section 92 of the 1972 Act (proceedings for disqualification) shall have effect in relation to a person who acts or claims to be entitled to act as a member of a National Park authority as it applies in relation to a person who acts or claims to be entitled to act as a member of a local authority, but as if—

(a)   references in that section to a local government elector for the area concerned were references to a local government elector for any principal area the whole or any part of which is comprised in the relevant Park; and

(b)   in subsection (6)(b) of that section (failure to deliver declaration of acceptance of office), the words from 'failure' to 'or by reason' were omitted.

(4)   Sections 1 to 3 of the Local Government and Housing Act 1989 (disqualification of persons holding politically restricted posts) shall have effect as if a National Park authority were a local authority for the purposes of Part I of that Act.

(5)   In Part III of Schedule 1 to the House of Commons Disqualification Act 1975 (other disqualifying offices), in the entry inserted by section 1(2) of that Act of 1989 (politically restricted post), after 'that Part' there shall be inserted 'or a National Park authority'.

Vacation of office for failure to attend meetings

8.   Section 85 of the 1972 Act (failure to attend meetings) shall have effect in relation to a National Park authority as it has effect in relation to a local authority.

Code of conduct for members

9.   Section 31 of the Local Government and Housing Act 1989 (code of conduct for members of local authorities) shall have effect as if a National Park authority were a local authority for the purposes of that section.

Restrictions on voting on account of interests etc.

10.—(1)   Sections 94 to 98 of the 1972 Act (restrictions on voting) shall have effect in relation to meetings of a National Park authority as they have effect in relation to meetings of a local authority.

(2)   Section 19 of the Local Government and Housing Act 1989 (members' interests) shall have effect as if a National Park authority were a local authority for the purposes of Part I of that Act.

Allowances and time off for members

11.—(1)   A National Park authority shall be a body to which sections 174 to 176 of the 1972 Act (allowances for travelling, conferences and visits) shall apply and shall also be deemed to be a relevant authority for the purposes of section 18 of the Local Government and Housing Act 1989 (basic attendance and special responsibility allowances).

(2)   For the purposes of sub-paragraph (1) above references in section 18 of that Act of 1989 to a member of an authority who is a councillor shall be deemed, in relation to a National Park authority, to include references to a member of that authority who is appointed as such a member by the Secretary of State.

(3)   In section 29(1) of the Employment Protection (Consolidation) Act 1978 (time off for public duties), after paragraph (b) there shall be inserted the following paragraph—

'(ba)   a National Park authority;'

but section 10 of that Act of 1989 (limit on paid leave for local authority duties) shall have effect as if a National Park authority were a relevant council for the purposes of that section.

Meetings and proceedings of the authority

12.—(1) The following provisions, that is to say—

(a) the provisions of Part VI of Schedule 12 to the 1972 Act (proceedings and meetings of local authorities) and of section 99 of that Act so far as it relates to that Part of that Schedule; and

(b) the provisions of section 100 of that Act (admission of the public and press), shall have effect as if a National Park authority were a local authority for the purposes of those provisions.

(2) In section 100J of the 1972 Act (bodies in addition to principal councils to which provisions as to access to meetings etc. apply)—

(a) in subsection (1), after paragraph (cc) there shall be inserted the following paragraph—

'(cd) a National Park authority;'

(b) in subsection (3), after '(cc)' there shall be inserted '(cd)'; and

(c) in subsection (4)(aa)—

(i) after 'Navigation Committee' there shall be inserted 'or any National Park authority'; and

(ii) for 'body which' there shall be substituted 'person who'.

(3) Section 20 of the Local Government and Housing Act 1989 (power to require adoption of certain procedural standing orders) shall have effect as if a National Park authority were a relevant authority for the purposes of that section.

(4) The validity of any proceedings of a National Park authority shall not be affected by a vacancy amongst its members, by any defect in the appointment of a member of the authority or by the want of qualification, or the disqualification, of any such member.

Committees and sub-committees and officers

13.—(1) Sections 101 to 106 of the 1972 Act (arrangements for committees and sub-committees) shall have effect as if a National Park authority were a local authority for the purposes of those sections.

(2) Accordingly, section 13 of the Local Government and Housing Act 1989 (voting rights of members of certain committees) shall have effect as if a National Park authority were a relevant authority for the purposes of that section.

(3) It shall be the duty of a National Park authority, in relation to any committee or sub-committee to which this sub-paragraph applies, to secure—

(a) that the membership of the committee or sub-committee consists of or includes both local authority members of the authority and at least one member appointed to the authority by the Secretary of State;

(b) that the division of members of the authority who are members of the committee or sub-committee between—

(i) local authority members, and

(ii) members appointed to the authority by the Secretary of State, is (as nearly as possible using whole numbers) in the same proportions as required, by virtue of paragraph 1(2) above, in the case of the authority itself; and

(c) that the quorum of the committee or sub-committee includes at least one local authority member of the authority and at least one member appointed to the authority by the Secretary of State.

(4) Sub-paragraph (3) above applies in the case of any National Park authority to the following committees and sub-committees, except those appointed under section 102(4) or (4A) of the 1972 Act (advisory committees), that is to say—

(a) any committee or sub-committee of the authority;

(b) any joint committee on which the authority is represented; and

(c) any sub-committee of such a joint committee.

(5) The proceedings of a committee or sub-committee to which sub-paragraph (3) above applies shall not be invalidated by any failure of a National Park authority to perform its duty under that sub-paragraph.

(6) The provisions of sections 112 to 119 and 151 of the 1972 Act (staff of local authorities) and of section 30 of the Local Government (Miscellaneous Provisions) Act 1976 (power to forgo repayment of remuneration) shall have effect as if a National Park authority were a local authority for the purposes of those provisions.

(7) The following provisions of the Local Government and Housing Act 1989 shall apply in relation to a National Park authority as they apply in relation to the authorities which are relevant authorities for the purposes of those provisions, that is to say—

    (a) section 4 (designation and reports of head of paid service);

    (b) section 5 (designation and reports of monitoring officer); and

    (c) with the omission of subsection (4)(d) (assistants for political groups), section 8 (standing orders with respect to staff);

and section 7 of that Act (staff to be appointed on merit) shall apply to any appointment to paid office or employment under a National Park authority as it applies to an appointment to paid office or employment under a body which is a local authority for the purposes of Part I of that Act.

(8) Section 12 of that Act of 1989 (conflict of interest in staff negotiations) shall have effect as if references in that section to a local authority included references to a National Park authority.

National Park Officer

14.—(1) Every National Park authority for a National Park shall secure that there is at all times an officer appointed by that authority to be responsible to the authority for the manner in which the carrying out of its different functions is co-ordinated.

(2) For the purposes of this paragraph a National Park authority may adopt—

    (a) any appointment which an existing authority has made under paragraph 15 of Schedule 17 to the 1972 Act in relation to any area wholly or partly comprised in the relevant Park; or

    (b) if the relevant Park is in Wales, any appointment—

        (i) which was made under that paragraph in relation to any such area, and

        (ii) which was adopted by a National Park planning board, as defined in section 64 of this Act, by virtue of an order under paragraph 3A of Schedule 17 to the 1972 Act or section 2(1B) of the Town and Country Planning Act 1990.

(3) Before making or adopting an appointment under this paragraph or assigning additional responsibilities to a person holding such an appointment, a National Park authority shall consult, according to whether the Park in question is in England or in Wales, either the Countryside Commission or the Countryside Council for Wales.

(4) Sub-paragraph (3) above shall not apply in relation to the adoption of an appointment under this paragraph in relation to a National Park in Wales in any case where—

    (a) the National Park authority in question is the National Park authority in relation to that National Park by virtue of an order under section 63 of this Act made by virtue of section 64(1) of this Act;

    (b) the appointment in question was made or adopted by the body corporate which has so become that National Park authority, but in its capacity as the National Park planning board, as defined in section 64 of this Act, for the area of the National Park in question; and

    (c) no additional responsibilities are, on the occasion of the adoption of the appointment, to be assigned to the person holding the appointment.

(5) A person who holds office with a National Park authority by virtue of an appointment made or adopted under this paragraph—

    (a) may at the same time hold the office of head of that authority's paid service, the office of monitoring officer in relation to that authority or both those offices; but

(b) shall not at the same time be that authority's chief finance officer (within the meaning of section 5 of the Local Government and Housing Act 1989) or hold any office under any principal council.

(6) An officer holding office with a National Park authority by virtue of an appointment made or adopted under this paragraph shall be known as a National Park officer.

Personal liability of members and officers

15. Section 265 of the Public Health Act 1875 (personal liability of members and officers of certain authorities) shall have effect as if—

(a) a National Park authority were an authority such as is mentioned in that section;
(b) the references in that section to a member of the authority included, in relation to a National Park authority, references to any person who is not such a member but for the time being serves as a member of a committee or sub-committee of such an authority;
(c) the references in that section to the purpose of executing that Act and to the purposes of that Act were each, in relation to a National Park authority, references to the purpose of carrying out the functions of that authority by virtue of Part III of this Act; and
(d) the words 'or rate' were omitted.

Liaison with parish and community councils

16. A National Park authority shall make arrangements—

(a) in the case of a National Park in England, with each parish council the area of which is comprised wholly or partly within the Park, or
(b) in the case of a National Park in Wales, with each community council the area of which is so comprised,
for the purpose of informing and consulting that council about the authority's discharge of its functions.

Documents, notices, records, byelaws etc.

17.—(1) The Local Government (Records) Act 1962 shall have effect in relation to a National Park authority as if that authority were a local authority for the purposes of that Act.

(2) Subject to sub-paragraph (3) below, the following provisions of the 1972 Act, that is to say—

(a) sections 224 and 225(1) (custody and deposit of documents with a proper officer of the local authority),
(b) sections 228 and 229 (inspection of documents and photocopies),
(c) section 230 (reports and returns),
(d) sections 231 to 234 (service and authentication of documents), and
(e) without prejudice to their application by virtue of any other provision of Part III of this Act, sections 236 to 238 (byelaws),
shall have effect as if for the purposes of those provisions a National Park authority were a local authority or, in the case of section 224, a principal council.

(3) References in section 228 of the 1972 Act to a local government elector shall have effect for the purposes of that section as applied by sub-paragraph (2) above as if, in relation to a National Park authority, they were references to a local government elector for any principal area the whole or any part of which is comprised in the relevant Park.

(4) Section 41 of the Local Government (Miscellaneous Provisions) Act 1976 (evidence of resolutions and minutes of proceedings) shall have effect as if a National Park authority were a local authority for the purposes of that Act.

(5) Where a National Park authority has made any byelaws and those byelaws have been confirmed, that authority shall send a copy of the byelaws as confirmed to every council for a principal area the whole or any part of which is comprised in the relevant Park.

Investigation in connection with maladministration etc.

18.—(1)   In section 25(1) of the Local Government Act 1974 (bodies subject to investigation under Part III of that Act), after paragraph (aa) there shall be inserted the following
paragraph—

'(ab)   a National Park authority;'.

(2)   In section 26(7) of that Act (no investigation where complaint relates to all or most
of the inhabitants of an area), before paragraph (a) there shall be inserted the following
paragraph—

'(aa)   where the complaint relates to a National Park authority, the area of the Park
for which it is such an authority;'.

(3)   In section 34(1) of that Act (interpretation), in the definition of 'member', after 'the
joint board' there shall be inserted 'and in relation to a National Park authority, includes a
member of any of the councils by whom a local authority member of the authority is
appointed'.

Audit by Audit Commission auditor etc.

19.—(1)   In section 12(2) of the Local Government Finance Act 1982 (bodies whose
accounts are subject to audit), after paragraph (ff) there shall be inserted the following
paragraph—

'(fg)   a National Park authority;'

and sections 1 to 7 of the Local Government Act 1992 (performance standards and further
provisions relating to audit) shall have effect accordingly.

(2)   Sections 19 and 20 of that Act of 1982 (unlawful payments etc.) shall have effect
as if references in those sections to a local authority included references to a National Park
authority.

(3)   In section 36 of that Act of 1982 (interpretation), after subsection (3) there shall be
inserted the following subsection—

'(3A)   In the application of Part III of this Act in relation to a National Park authority,
any reference to a local government elector for the area of the authority shall be construed
as a reference to a local government elector for any area the whole or any part of which
is comprised in the Park for which that authority is the local planning authority.'

Meaning of 'relevant order'

20.   In this Schedule 'the relevant order', in relation to a National Park authority,
means—

(a)   the order under section 60 of this Act establishing that authority;

(b)   any order under that section relating to that authority; or

(c)   any order made in relation to that authority in exercise of the power to amend an
order under that section.

SCHEDULE 8

SUPPLEMENTAL AND INCIDENTAL POWERS OF NATIONAL PARK
AUTHORITIES

Powers in relation to land etc.

1.—(1)   Subject to sub-paragraph (2) below, the following provisions, that is to say—

(a)   sections 120, 122 and 123 of the 1972 Act (powers of local authorities to acquire
and dispose of land), and

(b)   sections 128 to 131 of that Act (general provisions in relation to land transactions),
shall have effect as if, for the purposes of those provisions, a National Park authority were
a principal council and the relevant Park were the authority's area.

(2)   The following provisions of the Local Government (Miscellaneous Provisions) Act 1976, that is to say—

    (a)   section 13 (compulsory acquisition of rights over land),

    (b)   section 15 (survey of land for the purposes of compulsory purchase),

    (c)   section 16 (obtaining information about land), and

    (d)   section 29 (repayment of unclaimed compensation),

shall apply in relation to a National Park authority as if the authority were a local authority for the purposes of that Act.

(3)   Section 33 of the Local Government (Miscellaneous Provisions) Act 1982 (enforceability by local authorities of certain covenants relating to land) shall have effect as if references to a principal council included references to a National Park authority and as if the relevant Park were that authority's area; and for the purposes of this paragraph the reference in subsection (1) of that section to section 111 of the 1972 Act shall have effect as a reference to section 65 of this Act.

(4)   This paragraph shall be without prejudice to any power conferred on a National Park authority by virtue of paragraph 2 below.

2.—(1)   After section 244 of the Town and Country Planning Act 1990 (powers of joint planning boards) there shall be inserted the following section—

'244A.   Powers of National Park authorities under Part IX

    (1)   A National Park authority shall, on being authorised to do so by the Secretary of State, have the same power to acquire land compulsorily as the local authorities to whom section 226 applies have under that section.

    (2)   A National Park authority shall have the same power to acquire land by agreement as the local authorities mentioned in subsection (1) of section 227 have under that subsection.

    (3)   Sections 226(1) and (7), 227, 229, 230, 232, 233 and 235 to 242 shall apply with the necessary modifications as if a National Park authority were a local authority to which those sections applied and as if the Park in relation to which it carries out functions were the authority's area.'

(2)   Every such reference in that Act to the acquisition or appropriation of land for planning purposes as falls to be construed in accordance with section 246 of that Act shall be taken (so far as it would not otherwise do so) to include a reference to an acquisition or appropriation of land under any power conferred by virtue of sub-paragraph (1) above.

(3)   The following provisions of that Act, that is to say—

    (a)   sections 251(1), 258(1), 260(1), 261, 271, 272 and 274 (extinguishing rights of way and other rights),

    (b)   sections 275 and 276 (extension and modification of functions of statutory undertakers), and

    (c) section 324(6) (rights of entry).

shall have effect as if a National Park authority were a local authority for the purposes of that Act.

(4)   The reference to a local authority in section 66(2) of the Planning (Listed Buildings and Conservation Areas) Act 1990 (which refers to the powers of a local authority under sections 232, 233 and 235(1) of the Town and Country Planning Act 1990) shall include a reference to a National Park authority.

Miscellaneous transactions and powers

3.—(1)   The following provisions of the 1972 Act shall also have effect as if a National Park authority were a principal council for the purposes of that Act and as if the relevant Park were the authority's area, that is to say—

    (a)   section 132 (use of premises);

    (b)   section 135 (contracts of local authorities);

(c)   section 136 (contributions towards expenditure on concurrent functions);

(d)   section 139 (acceptance of gifts of property);

(e)   sections 140, 140A and 140C (insurance);

(f)   section 143 (subscriptions to local government associations); and

(g)   sections 222 and 223 (conduct of prosecutions and participation in other legal proceedings).

(2)   Section 38 of the Local Government (Miscellaneous Provisions) Act 1976 (use of spare capacity of local authority computers) shall have effect as if a National Park authority were a local authority for the purposes of that Act.

(3)   Section 41 of the Local Government (Miscellaneous Provisions) Act 1982 (lost property) shall have effect as if a National Park authority were a local authority for the purposes of that Act.

(4)   Section 45 of that Act of 1982 (arrangements under the Employment and Training Act 1973) shall have effect as if a National Park authority were a local authority to which that section applies.

Transfer of securities on alteration of area

4.   Section 146 of the 1972 Act (transfer of securities on alteration of area) shall have effect as if a National Park authority were a local authority for the purposes of that Act and as if the reference in subsection (1)(b) of that section to an enactment similar to a provision of the 1972 Act included a reference to any provision of Part III of this Act.

The Local Authorities (Goods and Services) Act 1970

5.   The Local Authorities (Goods and Services) Act 1970 (supply of goods and services by local authorities) shall have effect as if a National Park authority were both a local authority and a public body for the purposes of that Act.

Power to execute works outside Park

6.   Any power to execute works which is conferred on a National Park authority by virtue of Part III of this Act or any other enactment shall be taken, except in so far as the contrary intention appears, to include power, for the purposes of the carrying out of the authority's functions in relation to the relevant Park, to execute works of the relevant description outside, as well as inside, that Park.

Power to promote Bills

7.—(1)   Section 239 of the 1972 Act (power of local authority to promote local or personal Bills) shall have effect in relation to a National Park authority as if it were a local authority for the purposes of that Act and as if the relevant Park were the authority's area.

(2)   A National Park authority shall have no power by virtue of Part III of this Act to promote a Bill for—

(a)   modifying the area of any National Park or any local government area;

(b)   modifying the authority's own constitution or that of any other National Park authority; or

(c)   modifying the status or the electoral arrangements of any such local government area.

(3)   In sub-paragraph (2) above—

'electoral arrangements' means any electoral arrangements within the meaning of section 14(4) of the Local Government Act 1992 or any corresponding arrangements in relation to any area in Wales; and

'local government area' means any local government area within the meaning of that Act or any area in Wales for which any council carries out functions of local government.

Competitive tendering etc

8.—(1) Part III of the Local Government, Planning and Land Act 1980 (direct labour organisations) shall have effect in relation to a National Park authority as if such an authority were a local authority for the purposes of that Part.

(2) In section 1(l) of the Local Government Act 1988 (defined authorities for the purposes of the provisions of that Act relating to competition), after paragraph (a) there shall be inserted the following paragraph—

'(aa) a National Park authority;'.

(3) In Schedule 2 to that Act of 1988 (bodies to which Part II of that Act applies), after the entry relating to the Broads Authority there shall be inserted—

'Any National Park authority'.

(4) In section 18 of that Act of 1988 (race relations matters), after subsection (7) there shall be inserted the following subsection—

'(7A) Any reference in this section to a local authority shall be deemed to include a reference to a National Park authority.'

(5) In section 33(3)(c) of that Act of 1988 (definition of 'relevant public body' for the purposes of provisions relating to contracts with associated companies),
after 'within' there shall be inserted 'paragraph (aa) or'.

(6) References in sections 8 to 10 of the Local Government Act 1992 (competition) to any provisions of that Act of 1980 or of that Act of 1988 shall include references to those provisions as they have effect by virtue of this paragraph.

Restrictions on publicity

9. Part II of the Local Government Act 1986 (restrictions on publicity) shall have effect as if a National Park authority were a local authority for the purposes of that Part.

Provisions applying in relation to companies in which authorities have interests

10. In section 67(3) of the Local Government and Housing Act 1989 (local authorities for the purposes of Part V of that Act), after paragraph (m) there shall be inserted the following paragraph—

'(ma) a National Park authority;'.

Provisions as to charges

11. In section 152(2) of that Act of 1989 (provisions as to charges), after paragraph (j) there shall be inserted the following paragraph—

'(ja) a National Park authority;'
and section 151 of that Act (power to amend existing provisions as to charges) shall have effect as if references to an existing provision included references to any such provision as applied by Part III of this Act.

Service agency agreements

12. Section 25 of the Local Government (Wales) Act 1994 (service agency agreements) shall have effect as if a National Park authority for any National Park in Wales were a new principal council for the purposes of that section.

Contracting out

13. Part II of the Deregulation and Contracting Out Act 1994 (contracting out) shall have effect as if a National Park authority were a local authority for the purposes of that Part.

SCHEDULE 9

MISCELLANEOUS STATUTORY FUNCTIONS OF NATIONAL PARK AUTHORITIES

Common land etc.

1.—(1) The enactments specified in sub-paragraph (2) below shall have effect in relation to any registered common which—

(a) is within any National Park for which a National Park authority is the local planning authority, and

(b) is not owned by, or vested in, any other body which is a local authority,

as if the National Park authority were a local authority for the purposes of those enactments and as if the relevant Park were that authority's area.

(2) The enactments mentioned in sub-paragraph (1) above are—

(a) section 1 of the Commons Act 1899 (scheme for regulation);

(b) section 194(2) of the Law of Property Act 1925 (application for removal of works);

(c) section 23 of and Schedule 2 to the Caravan Sites and Control of Development Act 1960 (power of district council to prohibit caravans on commons); and

(d) section 9 of the Commons Registration Act 1965 (protection of unclaimed common land).

(3) In the Commons Act 1899 references to the council by which a scheme is made under section 1 of that Act shall be construed accordingly; and the powers conferred by sections 7 and 12 of that Act (acquisition of land and contributions to expenses) shall be exercisable by a National Park authority in relation to the relevant Park as they are exercisable by a district council in relation to their district.

(4) A National Park authority shall have the same power to make an application under section 18 of the Commons Act 1899 (modification of provisions for recreation grounds) as a local authority.

(5) References in this paragraph, in relation to an enactment specified in sub-paragraph (2) above or to any enactment contained in section 18 of the Commons Act 1899, to a local authority are references to any such local authority, within the meaning of the 1972 Act, as has functions conferred on it by or by virtue of that enactment.

(6) In this paragraph 'registered common' means any land registered as common land or as a town or village green under the Commons Registration Act 1965.

Open spaces

2. The Open Spaces Act 1906 shall have effect as if references in that Act to a local authority included references to a National Park authority.

Nature reserves

3. Sections 21 and 22 of the National Parks and Access to the Countryside Act 1949 (establishment of nature reserves and application of enactments to local authority reserves) shall have effect as if the bodies on whom powers are conferred by section 21 of that Act included every National Park authority and as if the relevant Park were the authority's area; and references in those sections to a local authority and to their area shall be construed accordingly.

Caravan sites

4. In the Caravan Sites and Control of Development Act 1960—

(a) section 24 (power to provide sites for caravans), and

(b)   paragraph 11 of Schedule 1 to that Act (no licence required for land occupied by a local authority),
shall have effect as if a National Park authority were a local authority for the purposes of that Act and as if the relevant Park were that authority's area.

Country Parks

5.   The Countryside Act 1968 shall have effect as if a National Park authority were a local authority for the purposes of—
    (a)   sections 6 to 8 of that Act (country parks);
    (b)   section 9 of that Act (powers exercisable over or near common land); and
    (c)   section 41 of that Act (byelaws) in so far as it has the effect in relation to—
        (i)   any country park provided under section 7 of that Act, or
        (ii)   any land as respects which any powers under section 9 of that Act have been exercised,
of conferring powers on a local authority or of applying provisions of section 92 of the National Parks and Access to the Countryside Act 1949 (wardens);
and the references to a local authority in sections 43 to 45 of that Act of 1968 (general provisions as to the powers of local authorities) shall have effect accordingly.

Provision of information and encouragement of visitors

6.   Sections 142 and 144 of the 1972 Act (provision of information about local services and encouragement of visitors) shall have effect (subject to paragraph 9 of Schedule 8 to this Act) as if a National Park authority were a local authority for the purposes of that Act and as if the relevant Park were the authority's area.

Derelict land etc.

7.   The provisions of section 16 of the Welsh Development Agency Act 1975 and of section 1 of the Derelict Land Act 1982 (powers for the improvement of land) shall have effect in relation to land in a National Park for which a National Park authority is the local planning authority as if references in those provisions to a local authority included references to the National Park authority and as if the relevant Park were the authority's area.

Recreational facilities

8.   Section 19 of the Local Government (Miscellaneous Provisions) Act 1976 (recreational facilities) shall have effect as if the powers conferred by that section on local authorities were also conferred, so as to be exercisable within a National Park for which a National Park authority is the local planning authority, on that authority.

Refuse Disposal

9.—(1)   Subject to sub-paragraph (2) below, references to a local authority in the Refuse Disposal (Amenity) Act 1978 shall have effect in relation to land in a National Park for which a National Park authority is the local planning authority as if they included references to that authority and as if the relevant Park were the authority's area.

(2)   Sub-paragraph (1) above shall not apply, in relation to any time before the coming into force of the repeal of section 1 of that Act, to any reference in that section.

Ancient Monuments and Archaeological Areas

10.—(1)   Subject to sub-paragraph (2) below, Parts I and II of the Ancient Monuments and Archaeological Areas Act 1979 shall have effect as if in relation—
    (a)   to any monument in a National Park for which a National Park authority is the local planning authority, or
    (b)   to any area the whole or any part of which is comprised in such a Park,

the references in those Parts to a local authority included references to that National Park authority.

(2) Section 35 of that Act (notice of operations affecting area of archaeological importance) shall have effect in relation to land in such a National Park as is mentioned in sub-paragraph (1) above as if—

(a) any notice required to be served on a local authority under that section were required, instead, to be served on the National Park authority; and

(b) the functions conferred on a local authority by virtue of that section had been conferred instead on the National Park authority.

(3) Section 45(2) and (3) of that Act (assistance for archaeological investigations) shall have effect as if a National Park authority were a local authority for the purposes of that Act and as if the relevant Park were the authority's area.

Footpaths and bridleways

11. The following provisions of the the Highways Act 1980, that is to say—

(a) sections 25 to 29 (footpaths and bridleways),

(b) section 72(2) (widening of public paths),

(c) sections 118 to 121 (stopping up and diversion of public paths), and

(d) Schedule 6 (procedure for orders),

shall have effect as if references in those sections to a local authority or council included references to a National Park authority and as if the relevant Park were the authority's area.

Litter

12. The following provisions, that is to say—

(a) section 4 of the Litter Act 1983 (consultations and proposals for the abatement of litter), and

(b) section 88 of the Environmental Protection Act 1990 (fixed penalty notices for leaving litter),

shall have effect as if a National Park authority were a litter authority for the purposes of those provisions, as if the relevant Park were the authority's area and as if the reference in that section 4 to the authority's area were a reference to any part of the relevant Park.

Listed and historic buildings

13.—(1) In the case of a building situated in a National Park for which a National Park authority is the local planning authority, that authority and no other authority shall be the appropriate authority for the purposes of sections 47 to 51 of the Planning (Listed Buildings and Conservation Areas) Act 1990 (purchase of listed buildings etc in need of repair); and the reference to a local authority in section 88(5) of that Act (rights of entry) and in section 6 of the Historic Buildings and Ancient Monuments Act 1953 (under which grants for the acquisition of buildings in Wales may be made) shall have effect accordingly.

(2) In relation to any building or land in any such National Park, the powers conferred on a county council or county borough council by section 52 of that Act of 1990 (power to acquire building and land by agreement) shall be exercisable by the National Park authority, and not (without prejudice to their powers apart from that section) by any other authority; and subsection (2) of that section shall have effect accordingly.

(3) Section 53(1) of that Act (management of listed buildings etc. acquired under the Act) shall apply in relation to the powers conferred by virtue of this paragraph on a National Park authority as it applies in relation to the powers conferred by sections 47 and 52 of that Act on a local authority.

(4) That Act shall have effect as if a National Park authority were a local authority for the purposes of—

(a) sections 54 and 55 of that Act (urgent works to preserve listed buildings etc.), and

(b) sections 57 and 58 of that Act (power of local authorities to contribute towards preservation of listed buildings etc.),
and, in relation to those provisions, as if the relevant Park were the authority's area.

(5) In relation to the powers conferred on a National Park authority by virtue of this paragraph, section 88 of that Act (powers of entry) shall have effect as if references in that section to a local authority included references to a National Park authority.

(6) References to a local authority in section 90(1) to (4) of that Act (financial provisions) shall be deemed to include references to a National Park authority.

Hazardous substances

14.—(1) For the purposes of the Planning (Hazardous Substances) Act 1990, where a National Park authority is the local planning authority for any National Park, that authority, and no other authority, shall be the hazardous substances authority for land in the relevant Park.

(2) References to a local authority in sections 12 and 38(1) to (4) of that Act (government consent to local authority activities and financial provisions) shall be deemed to include references to a National Park authority.

Local Charities

15. Sections 76 to 78 of the Charities Act 1993 (local charities) shall have effect as if the references to a council for any area included references to a National Park authority and as if the relevant Park were the authority's area.

Overseas Assistance

16. The Local Government (Overseas Assistance) Act 1993 shall have effect as if a National Park authority were a local authority for the purposes of that Act.

SCHEDULE 10

MINOR AND CONSEQUENTIAL AMENDMENTS RELATING TO NATIONAL PARKS

The Finance Act 1931 (c. 28)

1. In Schedule 2 to the Finance Act 1931 (requirements in connection with production of instruments of transfer), in paragraph (viii), for 'local authority' there shall be substituted 'local planning authority'.

The National Parks and Access to the Countryside Act 1949 (c. 97)

2.—(1) In section 6 of the National Parks and Access to the Countryside Act 1949 (general duties of Countryside Commission and the Countryside Council for Wales as respects the National Parks)—

(a) in subsection (3)—

(i) in paragraph (a), before 'local authorities' there shall be inserted 'National Park authorities and'; and

(ii) in paragraph (b), before 'local authority' there shall be inserted 'National Park authority';

and

(b) in subsection (6), after 'means' there shall be inserted the words 'a National Park authority or'.

(2) In section 7 of that Act—

(a) in subsection (5) (bodies consulted about variation of the area of a National Park), after 'consult with' there shall be inserted 'any National Park authority for the Park in question and with'; and

(b) in subsection (6) (notices), after 'as the case may be' there shall be inserted 'at the offices (where the order is for the variation of an order designating a Park) of any National Park authority for the Park in question'.

(3) In section 9(1) of that Act (local planning authority to consult Countryside Commission or Countryside Council for Wales about proposals for a development plan affecting a National Park), for 'the local planning authority' there shall be substituted 'the authority or authorities who are required to prepare the plan or, as the case may be, who are entitled to alter or add to it'.

(4) In section 12(1) of that Act (provision in a National Park of facilities) for 'provision in' there shall be substituted 'provision for'.

(5) In subsection (4) of section 51 of that Act (consultation as to proposals for a long distance route)—

(a) after the word 'every', in the first place where it occurs, there shall be inserted 'National Park authority,';

(b) after 'whose' there shall be inserted 'Park or'; and

(c) after 'every such' there shall be inserted 'authority,';

and in subsection (5) of that section (report to contain estimates of capital outlay by local authorities), after 'local authorities' there shall be inserted 'and National Park authorities'.

(6) In section 52(2) of that Act (notice of determination as to any proposals on long distance routes)—

(a) after 'every' there shall be inserted 'National Park authority'; and

(b) after 'whose' there shall be inserted 'Park or'.

(7) For section 88 of that Act (application to areas of outstanding natural beauty of provisions relating to National Parks) there shall be substituted—

'88. Functions of certain bodies in relation to areas of outstanding natural beauty

(1) The following provisions of this Act, that is to say—

(a) paragraph (e) of subsection (4) of section six,

(b) section nine,

(c) subsection (1) of section sixty-two,

(d) subsection (5) of section sixty-four, and

(e) subsections (5) and (5A) of section sixty-five,

shall apply in relation to areas of outstanding natural beauty as they apply in relation to National Parks.

(2) In paragraph (e) of subsection (4) of section six of this Act as it applies by virtue of the last foregoing subsection, the expression ''appropriate planning authority'' means a local planning authority whose area consists of or includes the whole or any part of an area of outstanding natural beauty and includes a local authority, not being a local planning authority, by whom any powers of a local planning authority as respects an area of outstanding natural beauty are exercisable, whether under this Act or otherwise.

(3) The provisions of section 4A of this Act shall apply to the provisions mentioned in paragraphs (a) and (b) of subsection (1) of this section for the purposes of their application to areas of outstanding natural beauty as the provisions of the said section 4A apply for the purposes of Part II of this Act.

(4) A local planning authority whose area consists of or includes the whole or any part of an area of outstanding natural beauty shall have power, subject to the following provisions of this section, to take all such action as appears to them expedient for the accomplishment of the purpose of conserving and enhancing the natural beauty of the area of outstanding natural beauty or so much thereof as is included in their area.

(5) Nothing in this Act shall be construed as limiting the generality of the last foregoing subsection; but in so far as the provisions of this Act confer specific powers falling within that subsection those powers shall be exercised in accordance with those provisions and subject to any limitations expressed or implied therein.

(6)   Without prejudice to the powers conferred by this Act, subsection (4) of this section shall have effect only for the purpose of removing any limitation imposed by law on the capacity of a local planning authority by virtue of its constitution, and shall not authorise any act or omission on the part of such an authority which apart from that subsection would be actionable at the suit of any person on any ground other than such a limitation.'

(8)   In section 114(2) of that Act (construction of references to the preservation of the natural beauty of an area) after the word 'preservation'—

(a)   in the first place where it occurs, there shall be inserted the words ', or the conservation,', and

(b)   in the second place where it occurs, there shall be inserted the words 'or, as the case may be, the conservation'.

(9)   In Schedule 1 to that Act (procedure for certain orders)—

(a)   in paragraph 1, after sub-paragraph (3) there shall be inserted the following sub-paragraph—

'(3A)   Where under this paragraph any notice is required to be given by any person in respect of any land which is already in a National Park for which a National Park authority is the local planning authority, that person shall serve a copy of that notice on that authority.';

(b)   in paragraph 2(5), after 'the Council' there shall be inserted 'a National Park authority,';

(c)   in paragraph 3(a), after 'under sub-paragraph' there shall be inserted '(3A) or'; and

(d)   after paragraph 3 there shall be inserted the following paragraph—

'3A.   An order designating a National Park shall have effect as from such time as may be determined by the Minister and specified in the notice of the confirmation of that order.'

The Landlord and Tenant Act 1954 (c. 56)

3.   In section 69(1) of the Landlord and Tenant Act 1954 (interpretation), in the definition of 'local authority', for the words from 'has the same meaning' to 'Broads Authority' there shall be substituted 'means any local authority within the meaning of the Town and Country Planning Act 1990, any National Park authority, the Broads Authority or'.

The Land Compensation Act 1961 (c. 33)

4.—(1)   Paragraph 55(2) of Schedule 16 to the 1972 Act (which relates to the operation of section 17 of the Land Compensation Act 1961 in a National Park) shall not apply in the case of a National Park for which a National Park authority is the local planning authority.

(2)   In section 39(1) of that Act of 1961 (interpretation), for the definition of 'local planning authority' there shall be substituted the following definition—

'"local planning authority" shall be construed in accordance with Part I of the Town and Country Planning Act 1990;'.

The Trustee Investments Act 1961 (c. 62)

5.   In section 11 of the Trustee Investments Act 1961 (local authority investment schemes), in subsection (4)(a), after 'the Broads Authority' there shall be inserted 'a National Park authority'.

The Agriculture Act 1967 (c. 22)

6.   In section 50(3) of the Agriculture Act 1967 (bodies transfers to whom are not subject to section 49), after paragraph (a) there shall be inserted the following paragraph—

'(aa)   a National Park authority;'.

The Leasehold Reform Act 1967 (c. 88)

7.   In section 28 of the Leasehold Reform Act 1967 (retention or resumption of land required for public purposes), in subsection (5), after paragraph (aa) there shall be inserted the following paragraph—
'(ab)   to any National Park authority; and'.

The Countryside Act 1968 (c. 41)

8.—(1)   In section 4(1) of the Countryside Act 1968 (experimental projects and schemes) after 'local authorities' there shall be inserted 'National Park authorities'.
(2)   In section 12(1) of that Act (provision in National Park of facilities), for 'provision in' there shall be substituted 'provision for'.
(3)   In section 13(12) of that Act (enforcement of byelaws), for 'in the area of that other local authority' there shall be substituted 'for an area that includes any part of the National Park in question'.

The Employers Liability (Compulsory Insurance) Act 1969 (c. 57)

9.   In section 3 of the Employers Liability (Compulsory Insurance) Act 1969 (employers exempted from insurance), in subsection (2), after 'the Broads Authority' there shall be inserted 'a National Park authority'.

The 1972 Act

10.—(1)   In subsection (1)(a) of section 80 of the 1972 Act (disqualification for persons holding appointments made or confirmed by a local authority or connected authority), after 'joint committee' there shall be inserted 'or National Park authority'; and after subsection (2) of that section there shall be inserted the following subsections—
'(2A)   Subsection (2) above shall have effect as if the reference to a joint board included a reference to a National Park authority.
(2B)   For the purposes of this section a local authority shall be treated as represented on a National Park authority if it is entitled to make any appointment of a local authority member of the National Park authority.'
(2)   In section 184 of the 1972 Act (functions under countryside legislation)—
(a)   at the beginning of subsection (1) there shall be inserted the words 'Subject to section 68 of the Environment Act 1995 (planning authority functions under National Parks legislation to be functions of National Park authorities in certain cases),'; and
(b)   in paragraph (b) of that subsection, for the words 'subsections (6) to (8) below' there shall be substituted the words 'subsections (7) and (8) below'.
(3)   In subsection (3) of that section, for the words 'sections 9 and 11' there shall be substituted the words 'section 9'.

The Employment Agencies Act 1973 (c. 35)

11.   In section 13(7) of the Employment Agencies Act 1973 (cases in which Act does not apply), after paragraph (ff) there shall be inserted the following paragraph—
'(fg) the exercise by a National Park authority of any of its functions;'.

The Health and Safety at Work etc. Act 1974 (c. 37)

12.   In section 28 of the Health and Safety at Work etc. Act 1974 (restrictions on disclosure of information), for subsection (10) there shall be substituted the following subsection—
'(10)   The Broads Authority and every National Park authority shall be deemed to be local authorities for the purposes of this section.'

The Welsh Development Agency Act 1975 (c. 70)

13.—(1) In section 1(14) of the Welsh Development Agency Act 1975 (consultation by
Agency with local authorities and other bodies), after 'local authorities' there shall be
inserted 'National Park authorities'.

(2) In subsections (1) and (2) of section 5 of that Act (assistance to the Agency from
other bodies), after 'local authority', in each case, there shall be inserted 'a National Park
authority'.

(3) In section 15(1) of that Act (which refers to consultation under section 1(14)), after
'local authorities' there shall be inserted 'National Park authorities'.

Local Land Charges Act 1975 (c. 76)

14. In sections 1 and 2 of the Local Land Charges Act 1975 (obligations that are and are
not local land charges), after the words 'local authority', in each place where they occur,
there shall be inserted 'or National Park authority'.

The Race Relations Act 1976 (c. 74)

15.—(1) In section 19A of the Race Relations Act 1976 (discrimination in planning), in
subsection (2)(a) (definition of 'planning authority'), after 'the Broads Authority' there shall
be inserted 'a National Park authority or'.

(2) In section 71 of that Act (general statutory duty of local authorities), after 'the
Broads Authority' there shall be inserted 'and every National Park authority'.

The Development of Rural Wales Act 1976 (c. 75)

16.—(1) In section 1(4) of the Development of Rural Wales Act 1976 (consultation as to
orders varying area for which the Board is responsible), after paragraph (b) there shall be
inserted the following paragraph—
    '(ba) every National Park authority which is the local planning authority for a
National Park any part of which will be included in the area for which the Board is
responsible if the order is made or which (whether the proposal is for an order under
subsection (2) or for an order under subsection (3)) is included in the area for which it is
responsible at the time of the proposal;'.

(2) In section 4(1)(d)(i) of that Act (power to finance measures taken by local
authorities), after 'local authority' there shall be inserted 'National Park authority'.

(3) In subsections (1) and (3) of section 8 of that Act (assistance to the Board from
other bodies), after 'local authority', in each case, there shall be inserted 'National Park
authority'.

(4) In paragraph 3(3) of Schedule 1 to that Act (consultation as to membership of
Board), after paragraph (a) there shall be inserted the following paragraph—
    '(aa) every National Park authority which is the local planning authority for a
National Park any part of which is included in the area for which the Board is responsible;
and'.

(5) In Schedule 3 to that Act (the New Towns code), in paragraph 14 (special
parliamentary procedure for compulsory purchase of local authority property), after the
words 'local authority', in each place where they occur, there shall be inserted 'or National
Park authority'.

The Rent (Agriculture) Act 1976 (c. 80)

17. In section 5(3) of the Rent (Agriculture) Act 1976 (no statutory tenancy where
landlord's interest belongs to Crown or local authority etc.), after paragraph (bc) there shall
be inserted the following paragraph—
    '(bd) any National Park authority;'.

The Rent Act 1977 (c. 42)

18.   In section 14 of the Rent Act 1977 (exemption from protection for lettings by local authorities etc.), after paragraph (bb) there shall be inserted the following paragraph—
      '(bc)   a National Park authority;'.

The Justices of the Peace Act 1979 (c. 55)

19.   In section 64 of the Justices of the Peace Act 1979 (which disqualifies in certain circumstances justices who are members of local authorities), in subsection (2A), for the words 'shall be treated as a local authority' there shall be substituted 'and every National Park authority shall be deemed to be local authorities.'

The Local Government, Planning and Land Act 1980 (c. 65)

20.—(1)   In section 103 of the Local Government, Planning and Land Act 1980—
      (a)   in subsection (2)(c) (consultation with local authorities as to acquisition of land by the Land Authority for Wales), the word 'and' immediately preceding sub-paragraph (ii) shall be omitted and after that sub-paragraph there shall be inserted 'and
            (iii)   any National Park authority which is the local planning authority for a National Park in which the land, or any part of the land, is situated';
and
      (b)   after subsection (8) there shall be inserted the following subsection—
      '(8A)   Subsections (6) to (8) above shall have effect as if any reference to a council included a reference to a National Park authority for a National Park in Wales and the references to the area of a council were to be construed accordingly.'
   (2)   In paragraph 1 of Schedule 19 to that Act (public authorities who may be assisted by that Authority), after sub-paragraph (f) there shall be inserted the following sub-paragraph—
      '(fa)   a National Park authority;'.
   (3)   In paragraph 4 of Schedule 20 to that Act (notice to and objections by local authorities in the case of compulsory purchase by that Authority), at the end there shall be inserted—
      'For the purposes of this paragraph the references to a local authority within whose area the land is situated shall be deemed to include references to any National Park authority which is the local planning authority for a National Park in which the land is situated.'
   (4)   In paragraph 9 of Schedule 21 to that Act (notice of planning applications) in sub-paragraph (1), after 'Wales' there shall be inserted 'and every National Park authority for a National Park in Wales'.

The Acquisition of Land Act 1981 (c. 67)

21.—(1)   In section 17(3) of the Acquisition of Land Act 1981 (special Parliamentary procedure not to apply to compulsory acquisition by certain bodies), after 'subsection (4) below)' there shall be inserted ', a National Park authority'.
   (2)   In paragraph 4(3) of Schedule 3 to that Act (which makes similar provision in relation to the acquisition of rights), after 'sub-paragraph (4) below)' there shall be inserted ', a National Park authority'.

The Wildlife and Countryside Act 1981 (c. 69)

22.—(1)   In section 39(5)(a) of the Wildlife and Countryside Act 1981 (definition of 'relevant authority'), before 'in a National Park' there shall be inserted 'which is not in an area for which a National Park authority is the local planning authority but is'.
   (2)   In section 41(5A) of that Act (duties of agriculture Ministers with respect to the countryside to have effect in relation to the Broads as if the Broads were a National Park),

at the end there shall be inserted '(and, as respects land within the Broads, any reference in this section to the relevant authority is accordingly a reference to the Broads Authority).'

(3) In section 42 of that Act (notification of agricultural operations on moor and heath), for the words 'local planning authority', wherever they occur, there shall be substituted 'National Park authority'.

(4) In section 44 of that Act (grants and loans for National Parks purposes)—

(a) in subsection (2), for 'a local planning authority' there shall be substituted 'the authority in question';

(b) in subsection (3), for 'A local planning authority' there shall be substituted 'The authority in question'; and

(c) in subsection (4), for the words from 'county planning authority' onwards there shall be substituted 'National Park authority and the Broads as a National Park for which it is the local planning authority'.

(5) In section 51(2)(c) of that Act (definition of 'relevant authority' in relation to the exercise of powers of entry for the purposes of section 42), for 'local planning authority' there shall be substituted 'National Park authority'.

(6) In section 52(2) of that Act (construction of references to a local planning authority), after 'except as respects' there shall be inserted 'a National Park for which a National Park authority is the local planning authority,'.

(7) Sub-paragraph (1) above shall cease to have effect with the coming into force of the repeal by this Act of section 39(5)(a) of that Act of 1981.

The County Courts Act 1984 (c. 28)

23. In section 60(3) of the County Courts Act 1984 (right of audience for proper officer of local authority in certain circumstances), after 'the Broads Authority' there shall be inserted 'any National Park authority,'.

The Housing Act 1985 (c. 68)

24.—(1) In section 43 of the Housing Act 1985 (consent of the Secretary of State required for certain disposals by local authorities), after subsection (5) there shall be inserted the following subsection—

'(5A) References in this section and in section 44 to a local authority shall include references to a National Park authority.'

(2) In section 45(2)(b) of that Act (definition of 'public sector authority' for the purposes of provisions relating to service charges after disposal), after 'a local authority' there shall be inserted—

'a National Park authority'.

(3) In section 573 of that Act (definition of 'public sector authority' for the purposes of assisting the owners of defective housing), after the entry relating to joint boards there shall be inserted the following entry—

'a National Park authority (or a predecessor of such an authority),'.

The Landlord and Tenant Act 1985 (c. 70)

25.—(1) In sections 14(4) and 26(1) of, and in paragraph 9(1) of the Schedule to, the Landlord and Tenant Act 1985 (provisions excluding operation of certain provisions in the case of public sector housing), after 'a local authority', in each case, there shall be inserted—

'a National Park authority'.

(2) In section 28(6) of that Act (meaning of 'qualified accountant' in the case of public sector landlords), after 'local authority' there shall be inserted 'National Park authority'.

(3) In section 31(3) of that Act (reserve powers to limit rents), in the definition of 'rent', after 'local authorities' there shall be inserted 'National Park authorities'.

The Landlord and Tenant Act 1987 (c. 31)

26. In section 58(1) of the Landlord and Tenant Act 1987 (exempt landlords), after paragraph (dd) there shall be inserted the following paragraph—
'(de) a National Park authority;'.

The Norfolk and Suffolk Broads Act 1988 (c. 4)

27. In Schedule 3 to the Norfolk and Suffolk Broads Act 1988 (functions of the Broads authority), in paragraph 43, for the words from 'as a local authority' onwards there shall be substituted 'for the purposes of the Derelict Land Act 1982 as a National Park authority and the Broads as a National Park for which it is the local planning authority'.

The Housing Act 1988 (c. 50)

28. In paragraph 12(2) of Schedule 1 to the Housing Act 1988 (meaning of 'local authority' for the purposes of determining the tenancies to be treated as local authority tenancies), after paragraph (d) there shall be inserted the following paragraph—
'(da) a National Park authority;'.

The Road Traffic Act 1988 (c. 52)

29. In section 144(2)(a)(i) of the Road Traffic Act 1988 (exemptions from requirement of third party insurance or security), after 'London borough' there shall be inserted 'a National Park authority'.

The Electricity Act 1989 (c. 29)

30.—(1) Paragraph 2(6) of Schedule 8 to the Electricity Act 1989 (definition of 'relevant planning authority' for the purposes of consents under that Act) shall be amended in accordance with the following provisions of this paragraph.

(2) In this paragraph 'the 1994 amendment' means the omission of the words 'and Wales' in paragraph (a) of the said paragraph 2(6) by paragraph 22 of Schedule 6 to the Local Government (Wales) Act 1994.

(3) If the 1994 amendment comes into force after this paragraph, then—
(a) in paragraph (a) of the said paragraph 2(6), for the words 'England and Wales' there shall be substituted the words 'land in England and Wales which is not in a National Park for which a National Park authority is the local planning authority';
(b) after that paragraph (a) there shall be inserted the following paragraph—
'(aa) in relation to land in England and Wales which is in a National Park for which a National Park authority is the local planning authority, means that National Park authority; and'; and
(c) the 1994 amendment shall have effect in relation to the said paragraph (a) as amended by paragraph (a) above, and on the coming into force of the 1994 amendment the words 'and Wales' shall also be omitted from the paragraph (aa) inserted by paragraph (b) above.

(4) If the 1994 amendment comes into force before this paragraph, then—
(a) in paragraph (a) of the said paragraph 2(6), for the word 'England' there shall be substituted the words 'land in England which is not in a National Park for which a National Park authority is the local planning authority'; and
(b) after that paragraph (a) there shall be inserted the following paragraph—
'(aa) in relation to land in England which is in a National Park for which a National Park authority is the local planning authority, means that National Park authority; and'.

(5) If the 1994 amendment comes into force on the same day as this paragraph, the 1994 amendment shall be deemed to have come into force immediately before this paragraph (and sub-paragraph (4) above shall have effect accordingly).

(6) The paragraph (aa) inserted by paragraph 22 of Schedule 6 to the Local Government (Wales) Act 1994 shall be re-numbered '(ab)'.

The Local Government and Housing Act 1989 (c. 42)

31.—(1) In section 21(1) of the Local Government and Housing Act 1989 (interpretation of Part I) the word 'and' immediately preceding paragraph (m) shall be omitted and after that paragraph there shall be added 'and

(n) a joint planning board constituted for an area in Wales outside a National Park by an order under section 2(1B) of the Town and Country Planning Act 1990.'

(2) In section 39(1) of that Act (application of Part IV), after paragraph (h) there shall be inserted—

'(hh) a joint planning board constituted for an area in Wales outside a National Park by an order under section 2(1B) of the Town and Country Planning Act 1990;'.

(3) In section 67(3) of that Act (local authorities for the purposes of Part V) the word 'and' at the end of paragraph (o) shall be omitted and after that paragraph there shall be inserted—

'(oo) a joint planning board constituted for an area in Wales outside a National Park by an order under section 2(1B) of the Town and Country Planning Act 1990; and'.

(4) In section 152(2) of that Act (relevant authorities for the purposes of imposing certain charges) the word 'and' immediately preceding paragraph (1) shall be omitted and after that paragraph there shall be added 'and

(m) a joint planning board constituted for an area in Wales outside a National Park by an order under section 2(1B) of the Town and Country Planning Act 1990.'

(5) In paragraph 2(1)(b) of Schedule 1 to that Act (bodies to which appointments are made taking account of political balance) for 'paragraphs (k) and (m)' there shall be substituted 'paragraphs (k), (m) and (n)'.

The Town and Country Planning Act 1990 (c. 8)

32.—(1) In paragraph (a) of section 1(5) of the Town and Country Planning Act 1990 (provisions to which subsections (1) to (4) are subject)—

(a) for 'sections 5 to' there shall be substituted 'sections 4A to'; and

(b) at the end there shall be inserted 'and'.

(2) In section 2 of that Act (joint planning boards), before subsection (2) of that section there shall be inserted the following subsection—

'(1D) The areas that may be constituted as a united district for the purposes of this section shall not include the whole or any part of an area which is comprised in a National Park for which there is a National Park authority.'

(3) In section 4 of that Act (National Parks), after subsection (4) there shall be inserted the following subsection—

'(5) This section shall have effect subject to section 4A below.'

(4) In sections 90(1) and 101(2)(c) of that Act (development with government authorisation), after the words 'local authority', in each place where they occur, there shall be inserted 'or National Park authority'.

(5) In sections 169 and 170(2)(b) of that Act (provisions in relation to blighted land), after 'local authority' there shall be inserted 'National Park authority'.

(6) In section 209(5) of that Act (regulations for charging expenses of a local authority which is a local planning authority on land), after 'local authority' there shall be inserted 'or National Park authority'.

(7) In section 252 of that Act (procedure for making certain orders)—

(a) in subsection (2) (bodies to be given notice), after paragraph (a) there shall be inserted the following paragraph—

'(aa) on any National Park authority which is the local planning authority for the area in which any highway or, as the case may be, any land to which the order relates is situated, and';

(b) in subsection (4) (objections), after 'local authority' there shall be inserted 'National Park authority'.

(8) In section 253(2)(a) of that Act (procedure in anticipation of planning permission)—

(a) in subsections (2)(a) and (3)(a), after 'local authority', in each case, there shall be inserted 'National Park authority'; and

(b) in subsection (4), after 'London borough' there shall be inserted 'a National Park authority'.

(9) In section 305(1)(a) of that Act (contribution by Ministers towards compensation paid by local authorities), after 'local authority' there shall be inserted 'or National Park authority'.

(10) In section 306 of that Act (contributions by local authorities and statutory undertakers), after subsection (5) there shall be inserted the following subsection—

'(6) This section shall have effect as if the references to a local authority included references to a National Park authority.'

(11) In section 330 of that Act (power to require information as to interests in land), after subsection (5) there shall be inserted the following subsection—

'(6) This section shall have effect as if the references to a local authority included references to a National Park authority.'

(12) In section 333(1) of that Act (regulations as to form of notice etc.), after 'local authority' there shall be inserted 'or National Park authority'.

(13) In section 336(1) of that Act (interpretation), in the definition of 'local authority' after 'subsection (10)' there shall be inserted 'below and section 71(7) of the Environment Act 1995'.

(14) In Schedule 1 to that Act (distribution of planning functions)—

(a) in paragraph 4(2) (consultation with district planning authorities)—

(i) after 'determined by a' there shall be inserted 'National Park authority or'; and

(ii) before 'the district planning authority' there shall be inserted 'any authority which (but for section 4A) would be or, as the case may be, which is'; and

(b) in paragraph 13(1), for 'A county planning authority' there shall be substituted 'In the case of any area for which there is both a district planning authority and a county planning authority, the county planning authority';

(c) in sub-paragraph (2) of paragraph 19, after 'Park' there shall be inserted 'to which section 4 applies', and after that sub-paragraph there shall be inserted the following sub-paragraph—

'(2A) As respects the area of any National Park for which a National Park authority is the local planning authority those functions shall be exercised by that authority.'

(d) in paragraph 20(4)—

(i) in paragraph (a), for 'outside a metropolitan county' there shall be substituted 'which is land in an area the local planning authority for which comprises both a county planning authority and a district planning authority'; and

(ii) in paragraph (b), for 'elsewhere' there shall be substituted 'other land in an area the local planning authority for which comprises both a county planning authority and a district planning authority'.

(15) In paragraph 4(5)(b) of Schedule 8 to that Act (which refers to directions under section 90(1) of that Act), after 'local authority' there shall be inserted 'National Park authority'.

(16) In Schedule 13 to that Act (blighted land), in paragraph 1(a)(i), after 'local authority' there shall be inserted 'National Park authority'.

(17) In Schedule 14 to that Act (procedure for footpaths and bridleways orders)—

(a) after paragraph 1(2)(b)(ii) (persons on whom notice served) there shall be inserted the following sub-paragraph—

'(iia) any National Park authority for a National Park which includes any of that land; and';

(b) in paragraph 1(6) (cases where owner, occupier or lessee is local authority), after 'local authority' there shall be inserted 'National Park authority'; and

(c) in paragraph 3(2) (local inquiry to be held if objection by local authority), after 'local authority' there shall be inserted 'or a National Park authority'.

(18) So much of any provision of this paragraph as amends an enactment repealed by this Act shall cease to have effect with the coming into force of the repeal.

The Planning (Listed Buildings and Conservation Areas) Act 1990 (c. 9)

33.—(1) The Planning (Listed Buildings and Conservation Areas) Act 1990 shall be amended as follows.

(2) In section 32 (purchase notice), after subsection (4) there shall be inserted the following subsection—

'(4A) This section and sections 33 to 37 shall have effect as if—

(a) the bodies on whom a listed building purchase notice may be served under this section included any National Park authority which is the local planning authority for the area in which the building and land in question are situated; and

(b) a National Park authority were a local authority for the purposes of this Act and the Park for which it is the local planning authority were its area;

and the references in those sections and in section 63(7)(a) to a council and to a local authority shall be construed accordingly.'

(3) In subsection (3) of section 79 (definition of 'local authority' for the purposes of town scheme agreements), after paragraph (c) there shall be inserted the following paragraph—

'(ca) in relation to any building in a National Park for which a National Park authority is the local planning authority, that authority;'.

(4) In section 93(1)(a) (regulations as to form of notice etc.), after 'local authority' there shall be inserted 'or National Park authority'.

(5) In paragraph 4 of Schedule 2, after sub-paragraph (3) (expenses of various persons and bodies with respect to listed building enforcement) there shall be inserted the following sub-paragraph—

'(4) The reference to a local authority in sub-paragraph (3) above includes a reference to any National Park authority which is the local planning authority for any area.'

(6) In paragraph 2 of Schedule 4 (provision as to exercise of functions by different authorities), after '4' there shall be inserted '4A'.

(7) In paragraph 3 of Schedule 4—

(a) after 'determined by a' there shall be inserted 'National Park authority or'; and

(b) in sub-paragraph (a), before 'the district planning authority' there shall be inserted 'any authority which (but for section 4A) would be or, as the case may be, which is';

(c) in sub-paragraph (b), for 'the district planning' there shall be substituted 'any such'.

(8) In paragraph 4 of Schedule 4—

(a) in sub-paragraph (1)—

(i) in paragraph (a), after 'a metropolitan county' there shall be inserted 'or in any National Park for which a National Park authority is the local planning authority'; and

(ii) in paragraph (b), for 'outside a metropolitan county' there shall be substituted 'to which paragraph (a) above does not apply'; and

(b) in sub-paragraph (2), after 'county planning authority' there shall be inserted 'or National Park authority'.

Water consolidation legislation

34.—(1) The references to a National Park authority in the following provisions (which impose environmental duties), that is to say—

(a) section 4 of the Water Industry Act 1991,

(b) section 17 of the Water Resources Act 1991, and

(c)   section 61C of the Land Drainage Act 1991,
shall have effect, until the coming into force of the repeal by this Act of the definition for the purposes of those provisions of the expression 'National Park authority', as if they included references to a National Park authority established under Part III of this Act which has become the local planning authority for the National Park in question; and thereafter those references shall have effect as if they were references to a National Park authority so established.

(2)   The references to a National Park planning authority—
(a)   in sections 34 and 45 of the Water Resources Act 1991 (regulations with respect to notice to be given of particulars of certain licence applications), and
(b)   in any regulations under those sections,
shall have effect, until the coming into force of the repeal by this Act of subsection (5) of section 34 of that Act, as if they included references to a National Park authority established under Part III of this Act which has become the local planning authority for the National Park in question; and thereafter those references shall have effect as if they were references to a National Park authority so established.

The Local Government Finance Act 1992 (c. 14)

35.   In section 35 of the Local Government Finance Act 1992 (definition of 'special items') in subsection (5) (expenses of a billing authority not to be special expenses if they are expenses of meeting a levy from a National Park planning board) paragraphs (a) and (b) shall be omitted and at the end of that subsection there shall be added the words 'or
(c)   a National Park authority in relation to a National Park in Wales.'

The Local Government (Overseas Assistance) Act 1993 (c. 25)

36.   In section 1(10) of the Local Government (Overseas Assistance) Act 1993 (certain bodies on which powers are conferred by the Act), at the end there shall be added—
'(h)   a joint planning board constituted for an area in Wales outside a National Park by an order under section 2(1B) of the Town and Country Planning Act 1990.'

The Welsh Language Act 1993 (c. 38)

37.   In section 6(1) of the Welsh Language Act 1993 (bodies which are public bodies for the purposes of the provisions of that Act about Welsh language schemes), after paragraph (c) there shall be inserted the following paragraph—
'(ca) a National Park authority;'.

The Local Government (Wales) Act 1994 (c. 19)

38.—(1)   In Schedule 6 to the Local Government (Wales) Act 1994 (minor and consequential amendments relating to planning) in paragraph 1, at the beginning of the subsection which that paragraph substitutes for subsection (1) of section 184 of the 1972 Act, there shall be inserted the words 'Subject to section 68 of the Environment Act 1995 (planning authority functions under National Parks legislation to be functions of National Park authorities in certain cases),'.

(2)   In paragraph 2 of that Schedule, for the words 'paragraphs 3 to 14' there shall be substituted the words 'paragraphs 13 and 14'.

SCHEDULE 11

AIR QUALITY: SUPPLEMENTAL PROVISIONS

Consultation requirements

1.—(1)   A local authority in carrying out its functions in relation to—
(a)   any air quality review,

  (b) any assessment under section 82 or 84 of this Act, or

  (c) the preparation of an action plan or any revision of an action plan,

shall consult such other persons as fall within sub-paragraph (2) below.

  (2) Those persons are—

  (a) the Secretary of State;

  (b) the appropriate new Agency;

  (c) in England and Wales, the highway authority for any highway in the area to which the review or, as the case may be, the action plan or revision relates;

  (d) every local authority whose area is contiguous to the authority's area;

  (e) any county council in England whose area consists of or includes the whole or any part of the authority's area;

  (f) any National Park authority for a National Park whose area consists of or includes the whole or any part of the authority's area;

  (g) such public authorities exercising functions in, or in the vicinity of, the authority's area as the authority may consider appropriate;

  (h) such bodies appearing to the authority to be representative of persons with business interests in the area to which the review or action plan in question relates as the authority may consider appropriate;

  (j) such other bodies or persons as the authority considers appropriate.

  (3) In this paragraph 'National Park authority', subject to sub-paragraph (4) below, means a National Park authority established under section 63 of this Act which has become the local planning authority for the National Park in question.

  (4) As respects any period before a National Park authority established under section 63 of this Act in relation to a National Park becomes the local planning authority for that National Park, any reference in sub-paragraph (2) above to a National Park authority shall be taken as a reference to the National Park Committee or joint or special planning board for that National Park.

Exchange of information with county councils in England

2.—(1) This paragraph applies in any case where a district in England for which there is a district council is comprised in an area for which there is a county council; and in this paragraph—

  (a) any reference to the county council is a reference to the council of that area; and

  (b) any reference to a district council is a reference to the council of a district comprised in that area.

  (2) It shall be the duty of the county council to provide a district council with all such information as is reasonably requested by the district council for purposes connected with the carrying out of its functions under or by virtue of this Part.

  (3) It shall be the duty of a district council to provide the county council with all such information as is reasonably requested by the county council for purposes connected with the carrying out of any of its functions relating to the assessment or management of the quality of air.

  (4) Information provided to a district council or county council under sub-paragraph (2) or (3) above shall be provided in such form and in such manner and at such times as the district council or, as the case may be, the county council may reasonably require.

  (5) A council which provides information under sub-paragraph (2) or (3) above shall be entitled to recover the reasonable cost of doing so from the council which requested the information.

  (6) The information which a council may be required to provide under this paragraph shall include information which, although it is not in the possession of the council or would not otherwise come into the possession of the council, is information which it is reasonable to require the council to obtain.

Joint exercise of local authority functions

3.—(1)   The appropriate authority may give directions to any two or more local authorities requiring them to exercise the powers conferred by—

(a)   section 101(5) of the Local Government Act 1972 (power of two or more local authorities to discharge functions jointly), or

(b)   section 56(5) of the Local Government (Scotland) Act 1973 (which makes similar provision for Scotland),

in relation to functions under or by virtue of this Part in accordance with the directions.

(2)   The appropriate authority may give directions to a local authority requiring it—

(a)   not to exercise those powers, or

(b)   not to exercise those powers in a manner specified in the directions,

in relation to functions under or by virtue of this Part.

(3)   Where two or more local authorities have exercised those powers in relation to functions under or by virtue of this Part, the appropriate authority may give them directions requiring them to revoke, or modify in accordance with the directions, the arrangements which they have made.

(4)   In this paragraph, 'the appropriate authority' means—

(a)   in relation to England and Wales, the Secretary of State; and

(b)   in relation to Scotland, SEPA acting with the approval of the Secretary of State.

Public access to information about air quality

4.—(1)   It shall be the duty of every local authority—

(a)   to secure that there is available at all reasonable times for inspection by the public free of charge a copy of each of the documents specified in sub-paragraph (2) below; and

(b)   to afford to members of the public facilities for obtaining copies of those documents on payment of a reasonable charge.

(2)   The documents mentioned in sub-paragraph (1)(a) above are—

(a)   a report of the results of any air quality review which the authority has caused to be conducted;

(b)   a report of the results of any assessment which the authority has caused to be made under section 82 or 84 of this Act;

(c)   any order made by the authority under section 83 of this Act;

(d)   any action plan prepared by the authority;

(e)   any proposals or statements submitted to the authority pursuant to subsection (3) or (4) of section 86 of this Act;

(f)   any directions given to the authority under this Part;

(g)   in a case where section 86 of this Act applies, any directions given to the county council under this Part.

Fixed penalty offences

5.—(1)   Without prejudice to the generality of paragraph (o) of subsection (2) of section 87 of this Act, regulations may, in particular, make provision—

(a)   for the qualifications, appointment or authorisation of persons who are to issue fixed penalty notices;

(b)   for the offences in connection with which, the cases or circumstances in which, the time or period at or within which, or the manner in which fixed penalty notices may be issued;

(c)   prohibiting the institution, before the expiration of the period for paying the fixed penalty, of proceedings against a person for an offence in connection with which a fixed penalty notice has been issued;

(d)   prohibiting the conviction of a person for an offence in connection with which a fixed penalty notice has been issued if the fixed penalty is paid before the expiration of the period for paying it;

(e)   entitling, in prescribed cases, a person to whom a fixed penalty notice is issued to give, within a prescribed period, notice requesting a hearing in respect of the offence to which the fixed penalty notice relates;

(f)   for the amount of the fixed penalty to be increased by a prescribed amount in any case where the person liable to pay the fixed penalty fails to pay it before the expiration of the period for paying it, without having given notice requesting a hearing in respect of the offence to which the fixed penalty notice relates;

(g)   for or in connection with the recovery of an unpaid fixed penalty as a fine or as a civil debt or as if it were a sum payable under a county court order;

(h)   for or in connection with execution or other enforcement in respect of an unpaid fixed penalty by prescribed persons;

(j)   for a fixed penalty notice, and any prescribed proceedings or other prescribed steps taken by reference to the notice, to be rendered void in prescribed cases where a person makes a prescribed statutory declaration, and for the consequences of any notice, proceedings or other steps being so rendered void (including extension of any time limit for instituting criminal proceedings);

(k)   for or in connection with the extension, in prescribed cases or circumstances, by a prescribed person of the period for paying a fixed penalty;

(l)   for or in connection with the withdrawal, in prescribed circumstances, of a fixed penalty notice, including—

(i)   repayment of any amount paid by way of fixed penalty in pursuance of a fixed penalty notice which is withdrawn; and

(ii)   prohibition of the institution or continuation of proceedings for the offence in connection with which the withdrawn notice was issued;

(m)   for or in connection with the disposition of sums received by way of fixed penalty;

(n)   for a certificate purporting to be signed by or on behalf of a prescribed person and stating either—

(i)   that payment of a fixed penalty was, or (as the case may be) was not, received on or before a date specified in the certificate, or

(ii)   that an envelope containing an amount sent by post in payment of a fixed penalty was marked as posted on a date specified in the certificate,

to be received as evidence of the matters so stated and to be treated, without further proof, as being so signed unless the contrary is shown;

(o)   requiring a fixed penalty notice to give such reasonable particulars of the circumstances alleged to constitute the fixed penalty offence to which the notice relates as are necessary for giving reasonable information of the offence and to state—

(i)   the monetary amount of the fixed penalty which may be paid;

(ii)   the person to whom, and the address at which, the fixed penalty may be paid and any correspondence relating to the fixed penalty notice may be sent;

(iii)   the method or methods by which payment of the fixed penalty may be made;

(iv)   the period for paying the fixed penalty;

(v)   the consequences of the fixed penalty not being paid before the expiration of that period;

(p)   similar to any provision made by section 79 of the Road Traffic Offenders Act 1988 (statements by constables in fixed penalty cases);

(q)   for presuming, in any proceedings, that any document of a prescribed description purporting to have been signed by a person to whom a fixed penalty notice has been issued has been signed by that person;

(r)   requiring or authorising a fixed penalty notice to contain prescribed information relating to, or for the purpose of facilitating, the administration of the fixed penalty system;

(s)   with respect to the giving of fixed penalty notices, including, in particular, provision with respect to—

    (i)   the methods by which,

    (ii)   the officers, servants or agents by, to or on whom, and

    (iii) the places at which,

fixed penalty notices may be given by, or served on behalf of, a prescribed person;

    (t)   prescribing the method or methods by which fixed penalties may be paid;

    (u)   for or with respect to the issue of prescribed documents to persons to whom fixed penalty notices are or have been given;

    (w) for a fixed penalty notice to be treated for prescribed purposes as if it were an information or summons or any other document of a prescribed description.

    (2)   The provision that may be made by regulations prescribing fixed penalty offences includes provision for an offence to be a fixed penalty offence—

    (a)   only if it is committed in such circumstances or manner as may be prescribed; or

    (b)   except if it is committed in such circumstances or manner as may be prescribed.

    (3)   Regulations may provide for any offence which is a fixed penalty offence to cease to be such an offence.

    (4)   An offence which, in consequence of regulations made by virtue of sub-paragraph (3) above, has ceased to be a fixed penalty offence shall be eligible to be prescribed as such an offence again.

    (5)   Regulations may make provision for such exceptions, limitations and conditions as the Secretary of State considers necessary or expedient.

    (6)   In this paragraph—

'fixed penalty' means a penalty of such amount as may be prescribed (whether by being specified in, or made calculable under, regulations);

'fixed penalty notice' means a notice offering a person an opportunity to discharge any liability to conviction for a fixed penalty offence by payment of a penalty of a prescribed amount;

'fixed penalty offence' means, subject to sub-paragraph (2) above, any offence (whether under or by virtue of this Part or any other enactment) which is for the time being prescribed as a fixed penalty offence;

'the fixed penalty system' means the system implementing regulations made under or by virtue of paragraph (o) of subsection (2) of section 87 of this Act;

'the period for paying', in relation to any fixed penalty, means such period as may be prescribed for the purpose;

'regulations' means regulations under or by virtue of paragraph (o) of subsection (2) of section 87 of this Act.

SCHEDULE 12

SCHEDULE 2A TO THE ENVIRONMENTAL PROTECTION ACT 1990

'SCHEDULE 2A

OBJECTIVES FOR THE PURPOSES OF THE NATIONAL WASTE STRATEGY

1.   Ensuring that waste is recovered or disposed of without endangering human health and without using processes or methods which could harm the environment and, in particular, without—

    (a)   risk to water, air, soil, plants or animals;

    (b)   causing nuisance through noise or odours; or

    (c)   adversely affecting the countryside or places of special interest.

2.   Establishing an integrated and adequate network of waste disposal installations, taking account of the best available technology not involving excessive costs:

3. Ensuring that the network referred to in paragraph 2 above enables—

(a) the European Community as a whole to become self-sufficient in waste disposal, and the Member States individually to move towards that aim, taking into account geographical circumstances or the need for specialised installations for certain types of waste; and

(b) waste to be disposed of in one of the nearest appropriate installations, by means of the most appropriate methods and technologies in order to ensure a high level of protection for the environment and public health.

4. Encouraging the prevention or reduction of waste production and its harmfulness, in particular by—

(a) the development of clean technologies more sparing in their use of natural resources;

(b) the technical development and marketing of products designed so as to make no contribution or to make the smallest possible contribution, by the nature of their manufacture, use or final disposal, to increasing the amount or harmfulness of waste and pollution hazards; and

(c) the development of appropriate techniques for the final disposal of dangerous substances contained in waste destined for recovery.

5. Encouraging—

(a) the recovery of waste by means of recycling, re-use or reclamation or any other process with a view to extracting secondary raw materials; and

(b) the use of waste as a source of energy.'

SCHEDULE 13
REVIEW OF OLD MINERAL PLANNING PERMISSIONS

Interpretation

1.—(1) In this Schedule—

'dormant site' means a Phase I or Phase II site in, on or under which no minerals development has been carried out to any substantial extent at any time in the period beginning on 22nd February 1982 and ending with 6th June 1995 otherwise than by virtue of a planning permission which is not a relevant planning permission relating to the site;

'first list', in relation to a mineral planning authority, means the list prepared by them pursuant to paragraph 3 below;

'mineral planning authority'—

(a) as respects England and Wales, means a mineral planning authority within the meaning of the 1990 Act, and

(b) as respects Scotland, means a planning authority for the purposes of the 1972 Act;

'mineral site' has the meaning given by sub-paragraph (2) below;

'National Park' means an area designated as such under section 5(3) of the National Parks and Access to the Countryside Act 1949;

'old mining permission' has the meaning given—

(a) as respects England and Wales, by section 22(1) of the 1991 Act, and

(b) as respects Scotland, by section 49H(1) of the 1972 Act;

'owner', in relation to any land—

(a) as respects England and Wales, means any person who—

(i) is the estate owner in respect of the fee simple, or

(ii) is entitled to a tenancy granted or extended for a term of years certain of which not less than seven years remains unexpired; and

(b) as respects Scotland, has the meaning given by paragraph 10(1) of Schedule 10A to the 1972 Act;

'Phase I site' and 'Phase II site' have the meaning given by paragraph 2 below;
'relevant planning permission' means any planning permission, other than an old mining permission or a planning permission granted by a development order, granted after 30th June 1948 for minerals development; and
'second list', in relation to a mineral planning authority, means the list prepared by them pursuant to paragraph 4 below.

(2) For the purposes of this Schedule, but subject to sub-paragraph (3) below, 'mineral site' means—

(a) in a case where it appears to the mineral planning authority to be expedient to treat as a single site the aggregate of the land to which any two or more relevant planning permissions relate, the aggregate of the land to which those permissions relate; and

(b) in any other case, the land to which a relevant planning permission relates.

(3) In determining whether it appears to them to be expedient to treat as a single site the aggregate of the land to which two or more relevant planning permissions relate a mineral planning authority shall have regard to any guidance issued for the purpose by the Secretary of State.

(4) Any reference (however expressed) in this Schedule to an old mining permission or a relevant planning permission relating to a mineral site is a reference to the mineral site, or some part of it, being the land to which the permission relates; and where any such permission authorises the carrying out of development consisting of the winning and working of minerals but only in respect of any particular mineral or minerals, that permission shall not be taken, for the purposes of this Schedule, as relating to any other mineral in, on or under the land to which the permission relates.

(5) For the purposes of this Schedule, a mineral site which is a Phase I site or a Phase II site is active if it is not a dormant site.

(6) For the purposes of this Schedule, working rights are restricted in respect of a mineral site if any of—

(a) the size of the area which may be used for the winning and working of minerals or the depositing of mineral waste;

(b) the depth to which operations for the winning and working of minerals may extend;

(c) the height of any deposit of mineral waste;

(d) the rate at which any particular mineral may be extracted;

(e) the rate at which any particular mineral waste may be deposited;

(f) the period at the expiry of which any winning or working of minerals or depositing of mineral waste is to cease; or

(g) the total quantity of minerals which may be extracted from, or of mineral waste which may be deposited on, the site,

is restricted or reduced in respect of the mineral site in question.

(7) For the purposes of this Schedule, where an application is made under paragraph 9 below for the determination of the conditions to which the relevant planning permissions relating to the mineral site to which the application relates are to be subject, those conditions are finally determined when—

(a) the proceedings on the application, including any proceedings on or in consequence of an application under section 288 of the 1990 Act or, as the case may be, section 233 of the 1972 Act, have been determined, and

(b) any time for appealing under paragraph 11(1) below, or applying or further applying under paragraph 9 below, (where there is a right to do so) has expired.

Phase I and II sites

2.—(1) This paragraph has effect for the purposes of determining which mineral sites are Phase I sites, which are Phase II sites, and which are neither Phase I nor Phase II sites.

(2) A mineral site is neither a Phase I site nor a Phase II site where—

(a) all the relevant planning permissions which relate to the site have been granted after 21st February 1982; or

(b) some only of the relevant planning permissions which relate to the site have been granted after 21st February 1982, and the parts of the site to which those permissions relate constitute the greater part of that site.

(3) With the exception of those mineral sites which, by virtue of sub-paragraph (2) above, are neither Phase I nor Phase II sites, every mineral site is either a Phase I site or a Phase II site.

(4) Subject to sub-paragraph (2) above, where any part of a mineral site is situated within—

(a) a National Park;

(b) a site in respect of which a notification under section 28 of the Wildlife and Countryside Act 1981 (sites of special scientific interest) is in force;

(c) an area designated under section 87 of the National Parks and Access to the Countryside Act 1949 as an area of outstanding natural beauty;

(d) an area designated as a National Scenic Area under section 262C of the 1972 Act; or

(e) an area designated as a Natural Heritage Area under section 6 of the Natural Heritage (Scotland) Act 1991,

that site is a Phase I site.

(5) Subject to sub-paragraphs (2) and (4) above, where—

(a) all the relevant planning permissions which relate to a mineral site, and which were not granted after 21st February 1982, were granted after the relevant day in 1969; or

(b) the parts of a mineral site to which relate such of the relevant planning permissions relating to the site as were granted after the relevant day in 1969 but before 22nd February 1982 constitute a greater part of the site than is constituted by those parts of the site to which no such relevant planning permission relates but to which a relevant planning permission granted on or before the relevant day in 1969 does relate,

the mineral site is a Phase II site.

(6) In sub-paragraph (5) above, 'the relevant day in 1969' means—

(a) as respects England and Wales, 31st March 1969; and

(b) as respects Scotland, 7th December 1969.

(7) Every other mineral site, that is to say any mineral site other than one—

(a) which is, by virtue of sub-paragraph (2) above, neither a Phase I nor a Phase II site; or

(b) which is a Phase I site by virtue of sub-paragraph (4) above; or

(c) which is a Phase II site by virtue of sub-paragraph (5) above,

is a Phase I site.

(8) In ascertaining, for the purposes of sub-paragraph (2) or (5) above, whether any parts of a mineral site constitute the greater part of that site, or whether a part of a mineral site is greater than any other part, that mineral site shall be treated as not including any part of the site—

(a) to which an old mining permission relates; or

(b) which is a part where minerals development has been (but is no longer being) carried out and which has, in the opinion of the mineral planning authority, been satisfactorily restored;

but no part of a site shall be treated, by virtue of paragraph (b) above, as being not included in the site unless the mineral planning authority are satisfied that any aftercare conditions which relate to that part have, so far as relating to that part, been complied with.

The 'first list'

3.—(1) A mineral planning authority shall, in accordance with the following provisions of this paragraph, prepare a list of mineral sites in their area ('the first list').

(2)   A site shall, but shall only, be included in the first list if it is a mineral site in the area of the mineral planning authority and is either—

(a)   an active Phase I site;

(b)   an active Phase II site; or

(c)   a dormant site.

(3)   In respect of each site included in the first list, the list shall indicate whether the site is an active Phase I site, an active Phase II site or a dormant site.

(4)   In respect of each active Phase I site included in the first list, that list shall specify the date by which an application is to be made to the mineral planning authority under paragraph 9 below.

(5)   Any date specified pursuant to sub-paragraph (4) above shall be a date—

(a)   not earlier than the date upon which expires the period of 12 months from the date on which the first list is first advertised in accordance with paragraph 5 below, and

(b)   not later than the date upon which expires the period of three years from the date upon which the provisions of this Schedule come into force.

(6)   The preparation of the first list shall be completed before the day upon which it is first advertised in accordance with paragraph 5 below.

The 'second list'

4.—(1)   A mineral planning authority shall, in accordance with the following provisions of this paragraph, prepare a list of the active Phase II sites in their area ('the second list').

(2)   The second list shall include each mineral site in the mineral planning authority's area which is an active Phase II site.

(3)   In respect of each site included in the second list, that list shall indicate the date by which an application is to be made to the mineral planning authority under paragraph 9 below.

(4)   Subject to paragraph (5) below, any date specified pursuant to sub-paragraph (3) above shall be a date—

(a)   not earlier than the date upon which expires the period of 12 months from the date on which the second list is first advertised in accordance with paragraph 5 below, and

(b)   not later than the date upon which expires the period of six years from the date upon which the provisions of this Schedule come into force.

(5)   The Secretary of State may by order provide that sub-paragraph (4)(b) above shall have effect as if for the period of six years referred to in that paragraph there were substituted such longer period specified in the order.

(6)   The power of the Secretary of State to make an order under sub-paragraph (5) above shall be exercisable by statutory instrument; and any statutory instrument containing such an order shall be subject to annulment in pursuance of a resolution of either House of Parliament.

(7)   The preparation of the second list shall be completed before the day upon which it is first advertised in accordance with paragraph 5 below.

Advertisement of the first and second lists

5.—(1)   This paragraph makes provision for the advertisement of the first and second lists prepared by a mineral planning authority.

(2)   The mineral planning authority shall advertise each of the first and second lists by causing to be published, in each of two successive weeks, in one or more newspapers circulating in its area, notice of the list having been prepared.

(3)   In respect of each of those lists, such notice shall—

(a)   state that the list has been prepared by the authority; and

(b)   specify one or more places within the area of the authority at which the list may be inspected, and in respect of each such place specify the times (which shall be reasonable times) during which facilities for inspection of the list will be afforded.

(4) In respect of the first list, such notice shall—

(a) be first published no later than the day upon which expires the period of three months from the date upon which the provisions of this Schedule come into force;

(b) explain the general effect of a mineral site being classified as a dormant site or, as the case may be, as an active Phase I site or an active Phase II site;

(c) explain the consequences which will occur if no application is made under paragraph 9 below in respect of an active Phase I site included in the list by the date specified in the list for that site;

(d) explain the effects for any dormant or active Phase I or II site not included in the list of its not being included in the list and—

(i) set out the right to make an application to the authority for that site to be included in the list;

(ii) set out the date by which such an application must be made; and

(iii) state that the owner of such a site has a right of appeal against any decision of the authority upon such an application; and

(e) explain that the owner of an active Phase I site has a right to apply for postponement of the date specified in the list for the making of an application under paragraph 9 below, and set out the date by which an application for such postponement must be made.

(5) In respect of the second list, such notice shall—

(a) be first published no later than the day upon which expires the period of three years, or such longer period as the Secretary of State may by order specify, from the date upon which the provisions of this Schedule come into force; and

(b) explain the consequences which will occur if no application is made under paragraph 9 below in respect of an active Phase II site included in the list by the date specified in the list for that site.

(6) The power of the Secretary of State to make an order under sub-paragraph (5) above shall be exercisable by statutory instrument; and any statutory instrument containing such an order shall be subject to annulment in pursuance of a resolution of either House of Parliament.

Applications for inclusion in the first list of sites not included in that list as originally prepared and appeals from decisions upon such applications

6.—(1) Any person who is the owner of any land, or is entitled to an interest in a mineral, may, if that land or interest is not a mineral site included in the first list and does not form part of any mineral site included in that list, apply to the mineral planning authority for that land or interest to be included in that list.

(2) An application under sub-paragraph (1) above shall be made no later than the day upon which expires the period of three months from the day when the first list was first advertised in accordance with paragraph 5 above.

(3) Where the mineral planning authority consider that—

(a) the land or interest is, or forms part of, any dormant or active Phase I or II site, they shall accede to the application; or

(b) part only of the land or interest is, or forms part of, any dormant or active Phase I or II site, they shall accede to the application so far as it relates to that part of the land or interest, but shall otherwise refuse the application.

(4) On acceding, whether in whole or in part, to an application made under sub-paragraph (1) above, the mineral planning authority shall amend the first list as follows—

(a) where they consider that the land or interest, or any part of the land or interest, is a dormant site or an active Phase I or II site, they shall add the mineral site consisting of the land or interest or, as the case may be, that part, to the first list and shall cause the list to indicate whether the site is an active Phase I site, an active Phase II site or a dormant site;

(b) where they consider that the land or interest, or any part of the land or interest, forms part of any mineral site included in the first list, they shall amend the entry in the first list for that site accordingly.

(5) Where the mineral planning authority amend the first list in accordance with sub-paragraph (4) above, they shall also—

(a) in a case where an active Phase I site is added to the first list pursuant to paragraph (a) of that sub-paragraph, cause that list to specify, in respect of that site, the date by which an application is to be made to the mineral planning authority under paragraph 9 below;

(b) in a case where—

(i) the entry for an active Phase I site included in the first list is amended pursuant to paragraph (b) of that sub-paragraph; and

(ii) the date specified in that list in respect of that site as the date by which an application is to be made to the mineral planning authority under paragraph 9 below is a date falling less than 12 months after the date upon which the authority make their decision upon the application in question,

cause that date to be amended so as to specify instead the date upon which expires the period of 12 months from the date on which the applicant is notified under sub-paragraph (10) below of the authority's decision upon his application.

(6) Any date specified pursuant to sub-paragraph (5)(a) above shall be a date—

(a) not earlier than the date upon which expires the period of 12 months from the date on which the applicant is notified under sub-paragraph (10) below of the mineral planning authority's decision upon his application, and

(b) not later than the later of—

(i) the date upon which expires the period of three years from the date upon which the provisions of this Schedule come into force; and

(ii) the date mentioned in paragraph (a) above.

(7) On acceding, whether in whole or in part, to an application made under sub-paragraph (1) above, the mineral planning authority shall, if the second list has been first advertised in accordance with paragraph 5 above prior to the time at which they make their decision on the application, amend the second list as follows—

(a) where they consider that the land or interest, or any part of the land or interest, is an active Phase II site, they shall add the mineral site consisting of the land or interest or, as the case may be, that part, to the second list;

(b) where they consider that the land or interest, or any part of the land or interest, forms part of any active Phase II site included in the second list, they shall amend the entry in that list for that site accordingly.

(8) Where the mineral planning authority amend the second list in accordance with sub-paragraph (7) above, they shall also—

(a) in a case where an active Phase II site is added to the second list pursuant to paragraph (a) of that sub-paragraph, cause that list to specify, in respect of that site, the date by which an application is to be made to the authority under paragraph 9 below;

(b) in a case where—

(i) the entry for an active Phase II site included in the second list is amended pursuant to paragraph (b) of that sub-paragraph; and

(ii) the date specified in that list in respect of that site as the date by which an application is to be made to the authority under paragraph 9 below is a date falling less than 12 months after the date upon which the authority make their decision upon the application in question,

cause that date to be amended so as to specify instead the date upon which expires the period of 12 months from the date on which the applicant is notified under sub-paragraph (10) below of the authority's decision upon his application.

(9) Any date specified pursuant to sub-paragraph (8)(a) above shall be a date—

(a)   not earlier than the date upon which expires the period of 12 months from the date on which the applicant is notified under sub-paragraph (10) below of the mineral planning authority's decision upon his application, and

(b)   not later than the later of—

(i)   the date upon which expires the period of six years from the date upon which the provisions of this Schedule come into force; and

(ii)   the date mentioned in paragraph (a) above.

(10)   When a mineral planning authority determine an application made under sub-paragraph (1) above, they shall notify the applicant in writing of their decision and, in a case where they have acceded to the application, whether in whole or in part, shall supply the applicant with details of any amendment to be made to the first or second list in accordance with sub-paragraph (4) or (8) above.

(11)   Where a mineral planning authority—

(a)   refuse an application made under sub-paragraph (1) above; or

(b)   accede to such an application only so far as it relates to part of the land or interest in respect of which it was made,

the applicant may by notice appeal to the Secretary of State.

(12)   A person who has made such an application may also appeal to the Secretary of State if the mineral planning authority have not given notice to the applicant of their decision on the application within eight weeks of their having received the application or within such extended period as may at any time be agreed upon in writing between the applicant and the authority.

(13) An appeal under sub-paragraph (11) or (12) above must be made by giving notice of appeal to the Secretary of State before the end of the period of six months beginning with—

(a)   in the case of an appeal under sub-paragraph (11) above, the determination; or

(b)   in the case of an appeal under sub-paragraph (12) above, the end of the period of eight weeks mentioned in that sub-paragraph or, as the case may be, the end of the extended period mentioned in that sub-paragraph.

Postponement of the date specified in the first or second list for review of the permissions relating to a Phase I or II site in cases where the existing conditions are satisfactory

7.—(1)   Any person who is the owner of any land, or of any interest in any mineral, comprised in—

(a)   an active Phase I site included in the first list; or

(b)   an active Phase II site included in the second list,

may apply to the mineral planning authority for the postponement of the date specified in that list in respect of that site as the date by which an application is to be made to the authority under paragraph 9 below (in this paragraph referred to as 'the specified date').

(2)   Subject to sub-paragraph (3) below, an application under sub-paragraph (1) above shall be made no later than the day upon which expires the period of three months from the day when—

(a)   in the case of an active Phase I site, the first list; or

(b)   in the case of an active Phase II site, the second list,

was first advertised in accordance with paragraph 5 above.

(3)   In the case of—

(a)   an active Phase I site—

(i)   added to the first list in accordance with paragraph 6(4)(a) above; or

(ii)   in respect of which the entry in the first list was amended in accordance with paragraph 6(4)(b) above; or

(b)   an active Phase II site—

(i)   added to the second list in accordance with paragraph 6(7)(a) above; or

(ii)   in respect of which the entry in the second list was amended in accordance with paragraph 6(7)(b) above,

an application under sub-paragraph (1) above shall be made no later than the day upon which expires the period of three months from the day on which notice was given under paragraph 6(10) above of the mineral planning authority's decision to add the site to or, as the case may be, so to amend the list in question.

(4)   An application under sub-paragraph (1) above shall be in writing and shall—

(a)   set out the conditions to which each relevant planning permission relating to the site is subject;

(b)   set out the applicant's reasons for considering those conditions to be satisfactory;

(c)   set out the date which the applicant wishes to be substituted for the specified date; and

(d)   be accompanied by the appropriate certificate (within the meaning of sub-paragraph (5) or (6) below).

(5)   For the purposes of sub-paragraph (4) above, as respects England and Wales the appropriate certificate is such a certificate—

(a)   as would be required, under section 65 of the 1990 Act (notice etc. of applications for planning permission) and any provision of a development order made by virtue of that section, to accompany the application if it were an application for planning permission for minerals development, but

(b)   with such modifications as are required for the purposes of this paragraph,

and section 65(6) of that Act (offences) shall also have effect in relation to any certificate purporting to be the appropriate certificate.

(6)   For the purposes of sub-paragraph (4) above, the appropriate certificate is, as respects Scotland, each of the certificates which would be required, under or by virtue of sections 23 and 24 of the 1972 Act (notice etc. of applications for planning permission), to accompany the application if it were an application for planning permission for minerals development, but with such modifications as are required for the purposes of this paragraph; and sections 23(3) and 24(5) of that Act (offences) shall have effect in relation to any certificate purporting to be the appropriate certificate.

(7)   Where the mineral planning authority receive an application made under sub-paragraph (1) above—

(a)   if they consider the conditions referred to in sub-paragraph (4)(a) above to be satisfactory they shall agree to the specified date being postponed in which event they shall determine the date to be substituted for that date;

(b)   in any other case they shall refuse the application.

(8)   Where the mineral planning authority agree to the specified date being postponed they shall cause the first or, as the case may be, the second list to be amended accordingly.

(9)   When a mineral planning authority determine an application made under sub-paragraph (1) above, they shall notify the applicant in writing of their decision and, in a case where they have agreed to the postponement of the specified date, shall notify the applicant of the date which they have determined should be substituted for the specified date.

(10)   Where, within three months of the mineral planning authority having received an application under sub-paragraph (1) above, or within such extended period as may at any time be agreed upon in writing between the applicant and the authority, the authority have not given notice, under sub-paragraph (9) above, to the applicant of their decision upon the application, the authority shall be treated as—

(a)   having agreed to the specified date being postponed; and

(b)   having determined that the date referred to in sub-paragraph (4)(c) above be substituted for the specified date,

and sub-paragraph (8) above shall apply accordingly.

Service on owners etc. of notice of preparation of the first and second lists

8.—(1) The mineral planning authority shall, no later than the date upon which the first list is first advertised in accordance with paragraph 5 above, serve notice in writing of the first list having been prepared on each person appearing to them to be the owner of any land, or entitled to an interest in any mineral, included within a mineral site included in the first list, but this sub-paragraph is subject to sub-paragraph (7) below.

(2) A notice required to be served by sub-paragraph (1) above shall—

(a) indicate whether the mineral site in question is a dormant site or an active Phase I or II site; and

(b) where that site is an active Phase I site—

(i) indicate the date specified in the first list in relation to that site as the date by which an application is to be made to the mineral planning authority under paragraph 9 below;

(ii) explain the consequences which will occur if such an application is not made by the date so specified; and

(iii) explain the right to apply to have that date postponed, and indicate the date by which such an application must be made.

(3) Where, in relation to any land or mineral included in an active Phase I site, the mineral planning authority—

(a) has served notice on any person under sub-paragraph (1) above; and

(b) has received no application under paragraph 9 below from that person by the date falling eight weeks before the date specified in the first list as the date by which such applications should be made in respect of the site in question,

the authority shall serve a written reminder on that person, and such a reminder shall—

(i) indicate that the land or mineral in question is included in an active Phase I site;

(ii) comply with the requirements of sub-paragraph (2)(b)(i) and (ii) above; and

(iii) be served on that person on or before the date falling four weeks before the date specified in the first list in respect of that site as the date by which an application is to be made to the authority under paragraph 9 below.

(4) The mineral planning authority shall, no later than the date upon which the second list is first advertised in accordance with paragraph 5 above, serve notice in writing of the second list having been prepared on each person appearing to them to be the owner of any land, or entitled to an interest in any mineral, included within an active Phase II site included in the second list, but this sub-paragraph is subject to sub-paragraph (7) below.

(5) A notice required to be served by sub-paragraph (4) above shall—

(a) indicate that the mineral site in question is an active Phase II site; and

(b) indicate the date specified in the second list in relation to that site as the date by which an application is to be made to the mineral planning authority under paragraph 9 below;

(c) explain the consequences which will occur if such an application is not made by the date so specified; and

(d) explain the right to apply to have that date postponed, and indicate the date by which such an application must be made.

(6) Where, in relation to any land or mineral included in an active Phase II site, the mineral planning authority—

(a) has served notice on any person under sub-paragraph (4) above; and

(b) has received no application under paragraph 9 below from that person by the date falling eight weeks before the date specified in the second list as the date by which such applications should be made in respect of the site in question,

the authority shall serve a written reminder on that person, and such a reminder shall—

(i)   comply with the requirements of sub-paragraph (5)(a) to (c) above; and

(ii)   be served on that person on or before the date falling four weeks before the date specified in the second list in respect of that site as the date by which an application is to be made to the authority under paragraph 9 below.

(7)   Sub-paragraph (1) or (4) above shall not require the mineral planning authority to serve notice under that sub-paragraph upon any person whose identity or address for service is not known to and cannot practicably, after reasonable inquiry, be ascertained by them, but in any such case the authority shall cause to be firmly affixed, to each of one or more conspicuous objects on the land or, as the case may be, on the surface of the land above the interest in question, a copy of the notice which they would (apart from the provisions of this sub-paragraph) have had to serve under that sub-paragraph on the owner of that land or interest.

(8)   If, in a case where sub-paragraph (7) above applies, no person makes an application to the authority under paragraph 9 below in respect of the active Phase I or II site which includes the land or interest in question by the date failing eight weeks before the date specified in the first or, as the case may be, the second list as the date by which such applications should be made in respect of that site, the authority shall cause to be firmly affixed, to each of one or more conspicuous objects on the land or, as the case may be, on the surface of the land above the interest in question, a copy of the written reminder that would, in a case not falling within sub-paragraph (7) above, have been served under sub-paragraph (3) or (6) above.

(9)   Where by sub-paragraph (7) or (8) above a copy of any notice is required to be affixed to an object on any land that copy shall—

(a)   be displayed in such a way as to be easily visible and legible;

(b)   be first displayed—

(i)   in a case where the requirement arises under sub-paragraph (7) above, no later than the date upon which the first or, as the case may be, the second list is first advertised in accordance with paragraph 5 above; or

(ii)   in a case where the requirement arises under sub-paragraph (8) above, no later than the date falling four weeks before the date specified in the first or, as the case may be, the second list in respect of the site in question as the date by which an application is to be made to the authority under paragraph 9 below; and

(c)   be left in position for at least the period of 21 days from the date when it is first displayed, but where the notice is, without fault or intention of the authority, removed, obscured or defaced before that period has elapsed, that requirement shall be treated as having been complied with if the authority has taken reasonable steps for protection of the notice and, if need be, its replacement.

(10)   In sub-paragraphs (7) and (8) above, any reference to a conspicuous object on any land includes, in a case where the person serving a notice considers that there are no or insufficient such objects on the land, a reference to a post driven into or erected upon the land by the person serving the notice for the purpose of having affixed to it the notice in question.

(11)   Where the mineral planning authority, being required—

(a)   by sub-paragraph (3) or (6) above to serve a written reminder on any person; or

(b)   by sub-paragraph (8) above to cause a copy of such a reminder to be displayed in the manner set out in that sub-paragraph,

fail to comply with that requirement by the date specified for the purpose, they may at any later time serve or, as the case may be, cause to be displayed, such a written reminder and, in any such case, the date by which an application in relation to the mineral site in question is to be made under paragraph 9 below is the date upon which expires the period of three months from the date when the reminder was served or posted in accordance with the provisions of this sub-paragraph.

Applications for approval of conditions and appeals in cases where the conditions approved are not those proposed

9.—(1)   Any person who is the owner of any land, or who is entitled to an interest in a mineral, may, if that land or mineral is or forms part of a dormant site or an active Phase I or II site, apply to the mineral planning authority to determine the conditions to which the relevant planning permissions relating to that site are to be subject.

(2)   An application under this paragraph shall be in writing and shall—

(a)   identify the mineral site to which the application relates;

(b)   specify the land or minerals comprised in the site of which the applicant is the owner or, as the case may be, in which the applicant is entitled to an interest;

(c)   identify any relevant planning permissions relating to the site;

(d)   identify, and give an address for, each other person that the applicant knows or, after reasonable inquiry, has cause to believe to be an owner of any land, or entitled to any interest in any mineral, comprised in the site;

(e)   set out the conditions to which the applicant proposes the permissions referred to in paragraph (c) above should be subject; and

(f)   be accompanied by the appropriate certificate (within the meaning of sub-paragraph (3) or (4) below).

(3)   For the purposes of sub-paragraph (2) above, as respects England and Wales the appropriate certificate is such a certificate—

(a)   as would be required, under section 65 of the 1990 Act (notice etc. of applications for planning permission) and any provision of a development order made by virtue of that section, to accompany the application if it were an application for planning permission for minerals development, but

(b)   with such modifications as are required for the purposes of this paragraph,

and section 65(6) of that Act (offences) shall also have effect in relation to any certificate purporting to be the appropriate certificate.

(4)   For the purposes of sub-paragraph (2) above, the appropriate certificate is, as respects Scotland, each of the certificates which would be required, under or by virtue of sections 23 and 24 of the 1972 Act (notice etc. of applications for planning permission), to accompany the application if it were an application for planning permission for minerals development, but with such modifications as are required for the purposes of this paragraph; and sections 23(3) and 24(5) of that Act (offences) shall have effect in relation to any certificate purporting to be the appropriate certificate.

(5)   Section 65 of the 1990 Act or, as respects Scotland, section 24 of the 1972 Act (by virtue of which a development order may provide for publicising applications for planning permission) shall have effect, with any necessary modifications, as if subsection (1) of that section also authorised a development order to provide for publicising applications under this paragraph.

(6)   Where the mineral planning authority receive an application under this paragraph in relation to a dormant site or an active Phase I or II site they shall determine the conditions to which each relevant planning permission relating to the site is to be subject; and any such permission shall, from the date when the conditions to which it is to be subject are finally determined, have effect subject to the conditions which are determined under this Schedule as being the conditions to which it is to be subject.

(7)   The conditions imposed by virtue of a determination under sub-paragraph (6) above—

(a)   may include any conditions which may be imposed on a grant of planning permission for minerals development;

(b)   may be in addition to, or in substitution for, any existing conditions to which the permission in question is subject.

(8)   In determining that a relevant planning permission is to be subject to any condition relating to development for which planning permission is granted by a development order,

the mineral planning authority shall have regard to any guidance issued for the purpose by the Secretary of State.

(9) Subject to sub-paragraph (10) below, where, within the period of three months from the mineral planning authority having received an application under this paragraph, or within such extended period as may at any time be agreed upon in writing between the applicant and the authority, the authority have not given notice to the applicant of their decision upon the application, the authority shall be treated as having at the end of that period or, as the case may be, that extended period, determined that the conditions to which any relevant planning permission to which the application relates is to be subject are those specified in the application as being proposed in relation to that permission; and any such permission shall, from that time, have effect subject to those conditions.

(10) Where a mineral planning authority, having received an application under this paragraph, are of the opinion that they are unable to determine the application unless further details are supplied to them, they shall within the period of one month from having received the application give notice to the applicant—

(a) stating that they are of such opinion; and

(b) specifying the further details which they require,

and where the authority so serve such a notice the period of three months referred to in sub-paragraph (9) above shall run not from the authority having received the application but from the time when the authority have received all the further details specified in the notice.

(11) Without prejudice to the generality of sub-paragraph (10) above, the further details which may be specified in a notice under that sub-paragraph include any—

(a) information, plans or drawings; or

(b) evidence verifying any particulars of details supplied to the authority in

respect of the application in question,

which it is reasonable for the authority to request for the purpose of enabling them to determine the application.

Notice of determination of conditions to be accompanied by additional information in certain cases

10.—(1) This paragraph applies in a case where—

(a) on an application made to the mineral planning authority under paragraph 9 above in respect of an active Phase I or II site the authority determine under that paragraph the conditions to which the relevant planning permissions relating to the site are to be subject;

(b) those conditions differ in any respect from the proposed conditions set out in the application; and

(c) the effect of the conditions, other than any restoration or aftercare conditions, so determined by the authority, as compared with the effect of the conditions, other than any restoration or aftercare conditions, to which the relevant planning permissions in question were subject immediately prior to the authority making the determination, is to restrict working rights in respect of the site.

(2) In a case where this paragraph applies, the mineral planning authority shall, upon giving to the applicant notice of the conditions determined by the authority under paragraph 9 above, also give to the applicant notice—

(a) stating that the conditions determined by the authority differ in some respect from the proposed conditions set out in the application;

(b) stating that the effect of the conditions, other than any restoration or aftercare conditions, determined by the authority, as compared with the effect of the conditions, other than any restoration or aftercare conditions, to which the relevant planning permissions relating to the site in question were subject immediately prior to the making of the authority's determination, is to restrict working rights in respect of the site;

(c) identifying the working rights so restricted; and

(d) stating whether, in the opinion of the authority, the effect of that restriction of working rights would be such as to prejudice adversely to an unreasonable degree—

    (i) the economic viability of operating the site; or

    (ii) the asset value of the site.

(3) In determining whether, in their opinion, the effect of that restriction of working rights would be such as is mentioned in sub-paragraph (2)(d) above, a mineral planning authority shall have regard to any guidance issued for the purpose by the Secretary of State.

(4) In this paragraph, 'the applicant' means the person who made the application in question under paragraph 9 above.

Right to appeal against mineral planning authority's determination of conditions etc.

11.—(1) Where the mineral planning authority—

    (a) on an application under paragraph 9 above determine under that paragraph conditions that differ in any respect from the proposed conditions set out in the application; or

    (b) give notice, under paragraph (d) of paragraph 10(2) above, stating that, in their opinion, the restriction of working rights in question would not be such as to prejudice adversely to an unreasonable degree either of the matters referred to in sub-paragraphs (i) and (ii) of the said paragraph (d),

the person who made the application may appeal to the Secretary of State.

(2) An appeal under sub-paragraph (1) above must be made by giving notice of appeal to the Secretary of State before the end of the period of six months beginning with the date on which the authority give notice to the applicant of their determination or, as the case may be, stating their opinion.

Permissions ceasing to have effect

12.—(1) Subject to paragraph 8(11) above, where no application under paragraph 9 above in respect of an active Phase I or II site has been served on the mineral planning authority by the date specified in the first or, as the case may be, the second list as the date by which applications under that paragraph in respect of that site are to be made, or by such later date as may at any time be agreed upon in writing between the applicant and the authority, each relevant planning permission relating to the site shall cease to have effect, except insofar as it imposes any restoration or aftercare condition, on the day following the last date on which such an application may be made.

(2) The reference in sub-paragraph (1) above to the date specified in the first or, as the case may be, the second list as the date by which applications under paragraph 9 above are to be made in respect of any Phase I or II site is a reference to the date specified for that purpose in respect of that site in that list as prepared by the mineral planning authority or, where that date has been varied by virtue of any provision of this Schedule, to that date as so varied.

(3) Subject to sub-paragraph (4) below, no relevant planning permission which relates to a dormant site shall have effect to authorise the carrying out of minerals development unless—

    (a) an application has been made under paragraph 9 above in respect of that site; and

    (b) that permission has effect in accordance with sub-paragraph (6) of that paragraph.

(4) A relevant planning permission which relates to a Phase I or II site not included in the first list shall cease to have effect, except insofar as it imposes any restoration or aftercare condition, on the day following the last date on which an application under sub-paragraph (1) of paragraph 6 above may be made in respect of that site unless an application has been made under that sub-paragraph by that date in which event, unless the site is added to that list, such a permission shall cease to have effect when the following conditions are met—

(a) the proceedings on that application, including any proceedings on or in consequence of the application under section 288 of the 1990 Act or, as the case may be, section 233 of the 1972 Act, have been determined, and

(b) any time for appealing under paragraph 6(11) or (12) above, or applying or further applying under paragraph 6(1) above, (where there is a right to do so) has expired.

Reference of applications to the Secretary of State

13.—(1) The Secretary of State may give directions requiring applications under paragraph 9 above to any mineral planning authority to be referred to him for determination instead of being dealt with by the authority.

(2) Any such direction may relate either to a particular application or to applications of a class specified in the direction.

(3) Where an application is referred to the Secretary of State in accordance with such a direction—

(a) subject to paragraph (b) below, the following provisions of this Schedule—
   (i)   paragraph 9(6) and (7),
   (ii) paragraph 10, and
   (iii) paragraph 14 so far as relating to applications under paragraph 9 above,
shall apply, with any necessary modifications, as they apply to applications which fall to be determined by the mineral planning authority;

(b) before determining the application the Secretary of State must, if either the applicant or the mineral planning authority so wish, give each of them an opportunity of appearing before and being heard by a person appointed by the Secretary of State for the purpose; and

(c) the decision of the Secretary of State on the application shall be final.

Two or more applicants

14.—(1) Where a mineral planning authority has received from any person a duly made application under paragraph 7(1) or 9 above—

(a) that person may not make any further application under the paragraph in question in respect of the same site; and

(b) if the application has been determined, whether or not in the case of an application under paragraph 9 above it has been finally determined, no other person may make an application under the paragraph in question in respect of the same site.

(2) Where—

(a) a mineral planning authority has received from any person in respect of a mineral site a duly made application under paragraph 7(1) or 9 above; and

(b) the authority receives from another person a duly made application under the paragraph in question in respect of the same site,
then for the purpose of the determination of the applications and any appeal against such a determination, this Schedule shall have effect as if the applications were a single application received by the authority on the date on which the later application was received by the authority and references to the applicant shall be read as references to either or any of the applicants.

Compensation

15.—(1) This paragraph applies in a case where—

(a) an application made under paragraph 9 above in respect of an active Phase I or II site is finally determined; and

(b) the requirements of either sub-paragraph (2) or (3) below are satisfied.

(2) The requirements, referred to in sub-paragraph (1)(b) above, of this sub-paragraph are—

(a)   that the conditions to which the relevant planning permissions relating to the site are to be subject were determined by the mineral planning authority;

(b)   no appeal was made under paragraph 11(1)(a) above in respect of that determination or any such appeal was withdrawn or dismissed; and

(c)   the authority gave notice under paragraph (d) of paragraph 10(2) above and either—

(i)   that notice stated that, in the authority's opinion, the restriction of working rights in question would be such as to prejudice adversely to an unreasonable degree either of the matters referred to in sub-paragraphs (i) and (ii) of the said paragraph (d); or

(ii)   that notice stated that, in the authority's opinion, the restriction in question would not be such as would so prejudice either of those matters but an appeal under paragraph 11(1) above in respect of the giving of the notice has been allowed.

(3)   The requirements, referred to in sub-paragraph (1)(b) above, of this sub-paragraph are that the conditions to which the relevant planning permissions are to be subject were determined by the Secretary of State (whether upon an appeal under paragraph 11(1)(a) above or upon a reference under paragraph 13 above) and—

(a)   in a case where those conditions were determined upon an appeal under paragraph 11(1)(a) above either—

(i)   the mineral planning authority gave notice under paragraph (d) of paragraph 10(2) above stating that, in their opinion, the restriction of working rights in question would be such as to prejudice adversely to an unreasonable degree either of the matters referred to in sub-paragraphs (i) and (ii) of the said paragraph (d), or

(ii)   the authority gave a notice under the said paragraph (d) stating that, in their opinion, the restriction in question would not be such as would so prejudice either of those matters but an appeal under paragraph 11(1)(b) above in respect of the giving of that notice has been allowed; or

(b)   in a case where those conditions were determined upon a reference under paragraph 13 above, the Secretary of State gave notice under paragraph (d) of paragraph 10(2) above stating that, in his opinion, the restriction of working rights in question would be such as to prejudice adversely to an unreasonable degree either of the matters referred to in sub-paragraphs (i) and (ii) of the said paragraph (d).

(4)   In a case to which this paragraph applies—

(a)   as respects England and Wales, Parts IV and XI of the 1990 Act, or

(b)   as respects Scotland, Parts VIII and XI of the 1972 Act,

shall have effect as if an order made under section 97 of the 1990 Act or, as the case may be, section 42 of the 1972 Act, had been confirmed by the Secretary of State under section 98 of the 1990 Act or, as the case may be, section 42 of the 1972 Act at the time when the application in question was finally determined and, as so confirmed, had effect to modify those permissions to the extent specified in sub-paragraph (5) below.

(5)   For the purposes of sub-paragraph (4) above, the order which is treated by virtue of that sub-paragraph as having been made under section 97 of the 1990 Act or section 42 of the 1972 Act is one whose only effect adverse to the interests of any person having an interest in the land or minerals comprised in the mineral site is to restrict working rights in respect of the site to the same extent as the relevant restriction.

(6)   For the purposes of section 116 of the 1990 Act and section 167A of the 1972 Act and of any regulations made under those sections, the permissions treated as being modified by the order mentioned in sub-paragraph (4) above shall be treated as if they were planning permissions for development which neither consists of nor includes any minerals development.

Appeals: general procedural provisions

16.—(1)   This paragraph applies to appeals under any of the following provisions of this Schedule—

(a)   paragraph 6(11) or (12) above; or

(b)   paragraph 11(1) above.

(2)   Notice of appeal in respect of an appeal to which this paragraph applies shall be given on a form supplied by or on behalf of the Secretary of State for use for that purpose, and giving, so far as reasonably practicable, the information required by that form.

(3)   Paragraph 6 of Schedule 2 to the 1991 Act (determination of appeals) shall, as respects England and Wales, apply to an appeal to which this paragraph applies as it applies to an appeal under paragraph 5 of that Schedule.

(4)   As respects England and Wales, sections 284 to 288 of the 1990 Act (validity of certain decisions and proceedings for questioning their validity) shall have effect as if the action mentioned in section 284(3) of that Act included any decision of the Secretary of State—

(a)   on an appeal to which this paragraph applies; or

(b)   on an application under paragraph 9 above referred to him under paragraph 13 above.

(5)   Paragraph 6 of Schedule 10A to the 1972 Act (determination of appeals) shall, as respects Scotland, apply to an appeal to which this paragraph applies as it applies to appeals under paragraph 5 of that Schedule.

(6)   As respects Scotland, sections 231 to 233 of the 1972 Act (validity of certain decisions and proceedings for questioning their validity) shall have effect as if the action mentioned in section 231(3) included any decision of the Secretary of State—

(a)   on an appeal to which this paragraph applies; or

(b)   on an application under paragraph 9 above referred to him under paragraph 13 above.

(7)   As respects Scotland, Schedule 7 to the 1972 Act shall apply to appeals to which this paragraph applies.

SCHEDULE 14
PERIODIC REVIEW OF MINERAL PLANNING PERMISSIONS

Duty to carry out periodic reviews

1.   The mineral planning authority shall, in accordance with the provisions of this Schedule, cause periodic reviews to be carried out of the mineral permissions relating to a mining site.

Interpretation

2.—(1)   For the purposes of this Schedule—

'first review date', in relation to a mining site, shall, subject to paragraph 5 below, be ascertained in accordance with paragraph 3 below;

'mineral permission' means any planning permission, other than a planning permission granted by a development order, for minerals development;

'mineral planning authority'—

(a)   as respects England and Wales, means a mineral planning authority within the meaning of the 1990 Act, and

(b)   as respects Scotland, means a planning authority for the purposes of the 1972 Act;

'mining site' means—

(a)   in a case where it appears to the mineral planning authority to be expedient to treat as a single site the aggregate of the land to which any two or more mineral permissions relate, the aggregate of the land to which those permissions relate; and

(b)   in any other case, the land to which a mineral permission relates;

'old mining permission' has the meaning given—

(a)   as respects England and Wales, by section 22(1) of the 1991 Act, and

(b)   as respects Scotland, by section 49H(1) of the 1972 Act; and
'owner', in relation to any land—
        (a)   as respects England and Wales, means any person who—
                (i)   is the estate owner in respect of the fee simple, or
                (ii)   is entitled to a tenancy granted or extended for a term of years certain of
which not less than seven years remains unexpired; and
        (b)   as respects Scotland, has the meaning given by paragraph 10(1) of Schedule
10A to the 1972 Act.

(2)   In determining whether it appears to them to be expedient to treat as a single site
the aggregate of the land to which two or more mineral permissions relate a mineral
planning authority shall have regard to any guidance issued for the purpose by the Secretary
of State.

(3)   Any reference (however expressed) in this Schedule to a mining site being a site to
which relates—
        (a)   an old mining permission; or
        (b)   a mineral permission,
is a reference to the mining site, or some part of it, being the land to which the permission
relates.

(4)   For the purposes of this Schedule, an application made under paragraph 6 below is
finally determined when—
        (a)   the proceedings on the application, including any proceedings on or in conse-
quence of an application under section 288 of the 1990 Act or section 233 of the 1972 Act,
have been determined, and
        (b)   any time for appealing under paragraph 9(1) below, or applying or further
applying under paragraph 6 below, (where there is a right to do so) has expired.

The first review date

3.—(1)   Subject to sub-paragraph (7) below, in a case where the mineral permissions
relating to a mining site include an old mining permission, the first review date means—
        (a)   the date falling fifteen years after the date upon which, pursuant to an application
made under paragraph 2 of Schedule 2 to the 1991 Act or, as the case may be, paragraph
2 of Schedule 10A to the 1972 Act, the conditions to which that old mining permission is
to be subject are finally determined under that Schedule; or
        (b)   where there are two or more old mining permissions relating to that site, and the
date upon which those conditions are finally determined is not the same date for each of
those permissions, the date falling fifteen years after the date upon which was made the last
such final determination to be so made in respect of any of those permissions,
and paragraph 10(2) of Schedule 2 to the 1991 Act or, as the case may be, paragraph 10(2)
of Schedule 10A to the 1972 Act (meaning of 'finally determined') shall apply for the
purposes of this sub-paragraph as it applies for the purposes of section 22 of and Schedule
2 to the 1991 Act or, as the case may be, section 49H of and Schedule 10A to the 1972 Act.

(2)   Subject to sub-paragraph (7) below, in the case of a mining site which is a Phase I
or II site within the meaning of Schedule 13 to this Act, the first review date means the date
failing fifteen years after the date upon which, pursuant to an application made under
paragraph 9 of that Schedule, there is determined under that paragraph the conditions to
which the relevant planning permissions (within the meaning of that Schedule) relating to
the site are to be subject.

(3)   Subject to sub-paragraphs (4) and (7) below, in the case of a mining site—
        (a)   which is not a Phase I or II site within the meaning of Schedule 13 to this Act; and
        (b)   to which no old mining permission relates,
the first review date is the date falling fifteen years after the date upon which was granted
the most recent mineral permission which relates to the site.

(4)   Where, in the case of a mining site falling within sub-paragraph (3) above, the most recent mineral permission relating to that site relates, or the most recent such permissions (whether or not granted on the same date) between them relate, to part only of the site, and in the opinion of the mineral planning authority it is expedient, for the purpose of ascertaining, under that sub-paragraph, the first review date in respect of that site, to treat that permission or those permissions as having been granted at the same time as the last of the other mineral permissions relating to the site, the first review date for that site shall be ascertained under that sub-paragraph accordingly.

(5)   A mineral planning authority shall, in deciding whether they are of such an opinion as is mentioned in sub-paragraph (4) above, have regard to any guidance issued by the Secretary of State for the purpose.

(6)   Subject to sub-paragraph (7) below, in the case of a mining site—

(a)   to which relates a mineral permission in respect of which an order has been made under section 97 of the 1990 Act or section 42 of the 1972 Act, or

(b)   in respect of which, or any part of which, an order has been made under paragraph 1 of Schedule 9 to the 1990 Act or section 49 of the 1972 Act,

the first review date shall be the date failing fifteen years after the date upon which the order took effect or, in a case where there is more than one such order, upon which the last of those orders to take effect took effect.

(7)   In the case of a mining site for which the preceding provisions of this paragraph have effect to specify two or more different dates as the first review date, the first review date shall be the latest of those dates.

Service of notice of first periodic review

4.—(1)   The mineral planning authority shall, in connection with the first periodic review of the mineral permissions relating to a mining site, no later than 12 months before the first review date, serve notice upon each person appearing to them to be the owner of any land, or entitled to an interest in any mineral, included in that site.

(2)   A notice required to be served under sub-paragraph (1) above shall—

(a)   specify the mining site to which it relates;

(b)   identify the mineral permissions relating to that site;

(c)   state the first review date;

(d)   state that the first review date is the date by which an application must be made for approval of the conditions to which the mineral permissions relating to the site are to be subject and explain the consequences which will occur if no such application is made by that date; and

(e)   explain the right to apply for postponement of the first review date and give the date by which such an application has to be made.

(3)   Where, in relation to any land or mineral included in a mining site, the mineral planning authority—

(a)   has served notice on any person under sub-paragraph (1) above; and

(b)   has received no application under paragraph 6 below from that person by the date failing eight weeks before the first review date,

the authority shall serve a written reminder on that person.

(4)   A reminder required to be served under sub-paragraph (3) above shall—

(a)   indicate that the land or mineral in question is included in a mining site;

(b)   comply with the requirements of sub-paragraph (2)(a) to (d) above; and

(c)   be served on the person in question on or before the date falling four weeks before the first review date.

(5)   Sub-paragraph (1) above shall not require the mineral planning authority to serve notice under that sub-paragraph upon any person whose identity or address for service is not known to and cannot practicably, after reasonable inquiry, be ascertained by them, but

in any such case the authority shall cause to be firmly affixed, to each of one or more conspicuous objects on the land or, as the case may be, on the surface of the land above the interest in question, a copy of the notice which they would (apart from the provisions of this sub-paragraph) have had to serve under that sub-paragraph on the owner of that land or interest.

(6) If, in a case where sub-paragraph (5) above applies, no person makes an application to the authority under paragraph 6 below in respect of the mining site which includes the land or interest in question by the date failing eight weeks before the first review date, the authority shall cause to be firmly affixed, to each of one or more conspicuous objects on the land or, as the case may be, on the surface of the land above the interest in question, a copy of the written reminder that would, in a case not failing within sub-paragraph (5) above, have been served under sub-paragraph (3) above.

(7) Where by sub-paragraph (5) or (6) above a copy of any notice is required to be affixed to an object on any land that copy shall—

(a)   be displayed in such a way as to be easily visible and legible;

(b)   be first displayed—

(i)   in a case where the requirement arises under sub-paragraph (5) above, no later than 12 months before the first review date; or

(ii)   in a case where the requirement arises under sub-paragraph (6) above, no later than the date falling four weeks before the first review date; and

(c)   be left in position for at least the period of 21 days from the date when it is first displayed, but where the notice is, without fault or intention of the authority, removed, obscured or defaced before that period has elapsed, that requirement shall be treated as having been complied with if the authority has taken reasonable steps for protection of the notice and, if need be, its replacement.

(8) In sub-paragraphs (5) and (6) above, any reference to a conspicuous object on any land includes, in a case where the person serving a notice considers that there are no or insufficient such objects on the land, a reference to a post driven into or erected upon the land by the person serving the notice for the purpose of having affixed to it a copy of the notice in question.

Application for postponement of the first review date

5.—(1) Any person who is the owner of any land, or of any interest in any mineral, comprised in a mining site may, no later than the day upon which expires the period of three months from the day upon which notice was served upon him under paragraph 4 above, apply under this paragraph to the mineral planning authority for the postponement of the first review date.

(2) An application under this paragraph shall be in writing and shall set out—

(a)   the conditions to which each mineral permission relating to the site is subject;

(b)   the applicant's reasons for considering those conditions to be satisfactory; and

(c)   the date which the applicant wishes to have substituted for the first review date.

(3) Where the mineral planning authority receive an application made under this paragraph—

(a)   if they consider the conditions referred to in sub-paragraph (2)(a) above to be satisfactory they shall agree to the first review date being postponed in which event they shall determine the date to be substituted for that date;

(b)   in any other case they shall refuse the application.

(4) When a mineral planning authority determine an application made under this paragraph, they shall notify the applicant in writing of their decision and, in a case where they have agreed to the postponement of the first review date, shall notify the applicant of the date which they have determined should be substituted for the first review date.

(5) Where, within the period of three months of the mineral planning authority having received an application under this paragraph, or within such extended period as may at any

time be agreed upon in writing between the applicant and the authority, the authority have not given notice, under sub–paragraph (4) above, to the applicant of their decision upon the application, the authority shall be treated as having, at the end of that period or, as the case may be, that extended period—

(a) agreed to the first review date being postponed; and

(b) determined that the date referred to in sub-paragraph (2)(c) above be substituted for the first review date.

Application to determine the conditions to which the mineral permissions relating to a mining site are to be subject

6.—(1) Any person who is the owner of any land, or who is entitled to an interest in a mineral, may, if that land or mineral is or forms part of a mining site, apply to the mineral planning authority to determine the conditions to which the mineral permissions relating to that site are to be subject.

(2) An application under this paragraph shall be in writing and shall—

(a) identify the mining site in respect of which the application is made and state that the application is made in connection with the first periodic review of the mineral permissions relating to that site;

(b) specify the land or minerals comprised in the site of which the applicant is the owner or, as the case may be, in which the applicant is entitled to an interest;

(c) identify the mineral permissions relating to the site;

(d) identify, and give an address for, each other person that the applicant knows or, after reasonable inquiry, has cause to believe to be an owner of any land, or entitled to any interest in any mineral, comprised in the site;

(e) set out the conditions to which the applicant proposes the permissions referred to in paragraph (c) above should be subject; and

(f) be accompanied by the appropriate certificate (within the meaning of sub-paragraph (3) or (4) below).

(3) For the purposes of sub-paragraph (2) above, as respects England and Wales the appropriate certificate is such a certificate—

(a) as would be required, under section 65 of the 1990 Act and any provision of a development order made by virtue of that section, to accompany the application if it were an application for planning permission for minerals development, but

(b) with such modifications as are required for the purposes of this paragraph, and section 65(6) of the 1990 Act shall also have effect in relation to any certificate purporting to be the appropriate certificate.

(4) For the purposes of sub-paragraph (2) above, the appropriate certificate is, as respects Scotland, each of the certificates which would be required, under or by virtue of sections 23 and 24 of the 1972 Act (notice etc. of applications for planning permission), to accompany the application if it were an application for planning permission for minerals development, but with such modifications as are required for the purposes of this paragraph; and sections 23(3) and 24(5) of that Act (offences) shall have effect in relation to any certificate purporting to be the appropriate certificate.

(5) Where the mineral planning authority receive an application under this paragraph in relation to a mining site they shall determine the conditions to which each mineral permission relating to the site is to be subject.

(6) The conditions imposed by virtue of a determination under sub-paragraph (5) above—

(a) may include any conditions which may be imposed on a grant of planning permission for minerals development;

(b) may be in addition to, or in substitution for, any existing conditions to which the permission in question is subject.

(7)   In determining that a mineral permission is to be subject to any condition relating to development for which planning permission is granted by a development order, the mineral planning authority shall have regard to any guidance issued for the purpose by the Secretary of State.

(8)   Subject to sub-paragraph (9) below, where, within the period of three months of the mineral planning authority having received an application under this paragraph, or within such extended period as may at any time be agreed upon in writing between the applicant and the authority, the authority have not given notice to the applicant of their decision upon the application, the authority shall be treated as having at the end of that period or, as the case may be, that extended period, determined that the conditions to which any mineral permission to which the application relates is to be subject are those specified in the application as being proposed in relation to that permission; and any such permission shall, from that time, have effect subject to those conditions.

(9)   Where a mineral planning authority, having received an application under this paragraph, are of the opinion that they are unable to determine the application unless further details are supplied to them, they shall within the period of one month from having received the application give notice to the applicant—

(a)   stating that they are of such opinion; and

(b)   specifying the further details which they require,

and where the authority so serve such a notice the period of three months referred to in sub-paragraph (8) above shall run not from the authority having received the application but from the time when the authority have received all the further details specified in the notice.

(10)   Without prejudice to the generality of sub-paragraph (9) above, the further details which may be specified in a notice under that sub-paragraph include any—

(a)   information, plans or drawings; or

(b)   evidence verifying any particulars of details supplied to the authority in respect of the application in question,

which it is reasonable for the authority to request for the purpose of enabling them to determine the application.

Permissions ceasing to have effect

7.   Where no application under paragraph 6 above in respect of a mining site has been served on the mineral planning authority by the first review date, or by such later date as may at any time be agreed upon in writing between the applicant and the authority, each mineral permission—

(a)   relating to the site; and

(b)   identified in the notice served in relation to the site under paragraph 4 above,

shall cease to have effect, except insofar as it imposes any restoration or aftercare condition, on the day following the first review date or, as the case may be, such later agreed date.

Reference of applications to the Secretary of State

8.—(1)   The Secretary of State may give directions requiring applications made under paragraph 6 above to any mineral planning authority to be referred to him for determination instead of being dealt with by the authority.

(2)   A direction under sub-paragraph (1) above may relate either to a particular application or to applications of a class specified in the direction.

(3)   Where an application is referred to the Secretary of State in accordance with a direction under sub-paragraph (1) above—

(a)   subject to paragraph (b) below, paragraph 6(5) and (6) above, and paragraph 11 below so far as relating to applications under paragraph 6 above, shall apply, with any necessary modifications, to his determination of the application as they apply to the determination of applications by the mineral planning authority;

(b)   before determining the application the Secretary of State must, if either the applicant or the mineral planning authority so wish, give each of them an opportunity of appearing before and being heard by a person appointed by the Secretary of State for the purpose; and

    (c)   the decision of the Secretary of State on the application shall be final.

Appeals

9.—(1)   Where on an application under paragraph 6 above the mineral planning authority determine conditions that differ in any respect from the proposed conditions set out in the application, the applicant may appeal to the Secretary of State.

    (2)   An appeal under sub-paragraph (1) above must be made by giving notice of appeal to the Secretary of State, before the end of the period of six months beginning with the determination, on a form supplied by or on behalf of the Secretary of State for use for that purpose, and giving, so far as reasonably practicable, the information required by that form.

    (3)   Paragraph 6 of Schedule 2 to the 1991 Act (determination of appeals) shall, as respects England and Wales, apply to appeals under sub-paragraph (1) above as it applies to appeals under paragraph 5 of that Schedule.

    (4)   As respects England and Wales, sections 284 to 288 of the 1990 Act shall have effect as if the action mentioned in section 284(3) of that Act included any decision of the Secretary of State—

    (a)   on an appeal under sub-paragraph (1) above; or

    (b)   on an application under paragraph 6 above referred to him under paragraph 8 above.

    (5)   Paragraph 6 of Schedule IOA to the 1972 Act (determination of appeals) shall, as respects Scotland, apply to appeals under sub-paragraph (1) above as it applies to appeals under paragraph 5 of that Schedule.

    (6)   As respects Scotland, sections 231 to 233 of the 1972 Act shall have effect as if the action mentioned in section 231(3) included any decision of the Secretary of State—

    (a)   on an appeal under sub-paragraph (1) above; or

    (b)   on an application under paragraph 6 above referred to him under paragraph 8 above.

    (7)   As respects Scotland, Schedule 7 to the 1972 Act shall apply to appeals under sub-paragraph (1) above.

Time from which conditions determined under this Schedule are to take effect

10.—(1)   Where an application has been made under paragraph 6 above in respect of a mining site, each of the mineral permissions relating to the site shall, from the time when the application is finally determined, have effect subject to the conditions to which it is determined under this Schedule that that permission is to be subject.

    (2)   Sub-paragraph (1) above is without prejudice to paragraph 6(8) above.

Two or more applicants

11.—(1)   Where a mineral planning authority have received from any person a duly made application under paragraph 5 or 6 above—

    (a)   that person may not make any further application under the paragraph in question in respect of the same site; and

    (b)   if the application has been determined, whether or not in the case of an application under paragraph 6 above it has been finally determined, no other person may make an application under the paragraph in question in respect of the same site.

    (2)   Where—

    (a)   a mineral planning authority have received from any person in respect of a mineral site a duly made application under paragraph 5 or 6 above; and

    (b)   the authority receives from another person a duly made application under the paragraph in question in respect of the same site,

then for the purpose of the determination of the applications and any appeal against such a determination, this Schedule shall have effect as if the applications were a single application received by the authority on the date on which the later application was received by the authority and references to the applicant shall be read as references to either or any of the applicants.

Second and subsequent periodic reviews

12.—(1) In this paragraph, in relation to a mining site, but subject to paragraph 5 above as applied by sub-paragraph (2) below, 'review date' means—

(a) in the case of the second periodic review, the date falling fifteen years after the date upon which was finally determined an application made under paragraph 6 above in respect of the site; and

(b) in the case of subsequent periodic reviews, the date falling fifteen years after the date upon which there was last finally determined under this Schedule an application made in respect of that site under paragraph 6 above as applied by sub-paragraph (2) below.

(2) Paragraphs 4 to 11 above shall apply in respect of the second or any subsequent periodic review of the mineral permissions relating to a mining site as they apply to the first such periodic review, but as if—

(a) any reference in those paragraphs to the 'first review date' were a reference to the review date; and

(b) the references in paragraphs 4(1) and 6(2)(a) above to the first periodic review were references to the periodic review in question.

Compensation

13.—(1) This paragraph applies where—

(a) an application made under paragraph 6 above in respect of a mining site is finally determined; and

(b) the conditions to which the mineral permissions relating to the site are to be subject, as determined under this Schedule, differ in any respect from the proposed conditions set out in the application; and

(c) the effect of the new conditions, except insofar as they are restoration or aftercare conditions, as compared with the effect of the existing conditions, except insofar as they were restoration or aftercare conditions, is to restrict working rights in respect of the site.

(2) For the purposes of this paragraph—

'the new conditions', in relation to a mining site, means the conditions, determined under this Schedule, to which the mineral permissions relating to the site are to be subject; and 'the existing conditions', in relation to a mining site, means the conditions to which the mineral permissions relating to the site were subject immediately prior to the final determination of the application made under paragraph 6 above in respect of that site.

(3) For the purposes of this paragraph, working rights are restricted in respect of a mining site if any of—

(a) the size of the area which may be used for the winning and working of minerals or the depositing of mineral waste;

(b) the depth to which operations for the winning and working of minerals may extend;

(c) the height of any deposit of mineral waste;

(d) the rate at which any particular mineral may be extracted;

(e) the rate at which any particular mineral waste may be deposited;

(f) the period at the expiry of which any winning or working of minerals or depositing of mineral waste is to cease; or

(g) the total quantity of minerals which may be extracted from, or of mineral waste which may be deposited on, the site,

is restricted or reduced in respect of the mining site in question.

(4) In a case to which this paragraph applies, but subject to sub-paragraph (6) below, as respects England and Wales, Parts IV and XI of the 1990 Act and, as respects Scotland,

Parts VIII and XI of the 1972 Act, shall have effect as if an order made under section 97 of the 1990 Act or, as the case may be, section 42 of the 1972 Act—

(a)   had been confirmed by the Secretary of State under section 98 of the 1990 Act or, as the case may be, section 42 of the 1972 Act at the time when the application in question was finally determined; and

(b)   as so confirmed, had effect to modify those permissions to the extent specified in sub-paragraph (6) below.

(5)   For the purposes of this paragraph, the order referred to in sub-paragraph (4) above is one whose only effect adverse to the interests of any person having an interest in the land or minerals comprised in the mineral site is to restrict working rights in respect of the site to the same extent as the relevant restriction.

(6)   For the purposes of section 116 of the 1990 Act and section 167A of the 1972 Act and of any regulations made under those sections, the permissions treated as being modified by the order mentioned in sub-paragraph (4) above shall be treated as if they were planning permissions for development which neither consists of nor includes any minerals development.

SCHEDULE 15

MINOR AND CONSEQUENTIAL AMENDMENTS RELATING TO FISHERIES

Interpretation

1.   In this Schedule—

'local statutory provision' means—

(a)   a provision of a local Act (including an Act confirming a provisional order);

(b)   a provision of so much of any public general Act as has effect with respect to particular persons or works or with respect to particular provisions falling within any paragraph of this definition;

(c)   a provision of an instrument made under any provision falling within paragraph (a) or (b) above;

(d)   a provision of any other instrument which is in the nature of a local enactment;

'the Minister' means the Minister of Agriculture, Fisheries and Food;

'subordinate legislation' has the same meaning as in the Interpretation Act 1978;

'the transfer date' has the same meaning as in Part I of this Act.

General modifications of references to the National Rivers Authority

2.—(1)   Subject to—

(a)   the following provisions of this Schedule,

(b)   the provisions of sections 102 to 104 of this Act, and

(c)   any repeal made by this Act,

any provision to which this paragraph applies which contains, or falls to be construed as containing, a reference (however framed and whether or not in relation to an area) to the National Rivers Authority shall have effect on and after the transfer date as if that reference were a reference to the Agency.

(2)   Sub-paragraph (1) above is subject to paragraph 1(2)(a) of Schedule 17 to the Water Act 1989 (references in certain local statutory provisions or subordinate legislation to the area of a particular water authority to have effect as references to the area which, immediately before the transfer date within the meaning of that Act, was the area of that authority for the purposes of their functions relating to fisheries).

(3)   Subject as mentioned in sub-paragraph (1) above, any provision to which this paragraph applies which contains, or falls to be construed as containing, a reference (however framed) to the whole area in relation to which the National Rivers Authority

carries out its functions in relation to fisheries shall have effect on and after the transfer date as if that reference were a reference to the whole area in relation to which the Agency carries out its functions relating to fisheries.

(4) The provisions to which this paragraph applies are the provisions of—

    (a)   the Sea Fisheries Regulation Act 1966;

    (b)   the Salmon and Freshwater Fisheries Act 1975; and

    (c)   any local statutory provision or subordinate legislation which is in force immediately before the transfer date and—

        (i)   relates to the carrying out by the National Rivers Authority of any function relating to fisheries; or

        (ii)   in the case of subordinate legislation, was made by virtue of any provision to which this paragraph applies or under the Diseases of Fish Act 1937.

(5) The modifications made by this paragraph shall be subject to any power by subordinate legislation to revoke or amend any provision to which this paragraph applies; and, accordingly, any such power, including the powers conferred by section 121 of this Act and paragraph 3 below, shall be exercisable so as to exclude the operation of this paragraph in relation to the provisions in relation to which the power is conferred.

Power to amend subordinate legislation etc.

3.—(1) If it appears to the Minister or the Secretary of State to be appropriate to do so for the purposes of, or in consequence of, the coming into force of any provision of this Schedule, he may by order revoke or amend any subordinate legislation.

(2) An order under this paragraph may—

    (a)   make different provision for different cases, including different provision in relation to different persons, circumstances or localities; and

    (b)   contain such supplemental, consequential and transitional provision as the Minister or the Secretary of State considers appropriate.

(3) The power conferred by virtue of this paragraph in relation to subordinate legislation made under any enactment shall be without prejudice to any other power to revoke or amend subordinate legislation made under that enactment, but—

    (a)   no requirement imposed with respect to the exercise of any such other power shall apply in relation to any revocation or amendment of that legislation by an order under this paragraph; and

    (b)   the power to make an order under this paragraph shall be exercisable (instead of in accordance with any such requirement) by statutory instrument subject to annulment in pursuance of a resolution of either House of Parliament.

The Diseases of Fish Act 1937

4.—(1) Subject to sub-paragraph (2) below, in the Diseases of Fish Act 1937—

    (a)   any reference which to any extent is, or falls to be construed as, a reference to the National Rivers Authority shall have effect, in relation to the area which by virtue of section 6(7) of this Act is the area in relation to which the Agency carries out functions under that Act, as a reference to the Agency; and

    (b)   references to an area (including references which fall to be construed as references to the area which by virtue of subsection (6) of section 2 of the Water Resources Act 1991 is the area in relation to which the National Rivers Authority carries out functions under the said Act of 1937), in relation to the Agency, shall have effect as references to the area described in paragraph (a) above.

(2) In section 8(3) of the said Act of 1937 (offences in relation to the Esk) for the words 'National Rivers Authority' there shall be substituted the words 'Environment Agency'.

(3) Nothing in this paragraph or in that Act shall authorise the Agency to take legal proceedings in Scotland in respect of any offence.

The Sea Fisheries Regulation Act 1966

5.—(1)   The provisions of section 1 of the Sea Fisheries Regulation Act 1966 (establishment of fisheries committees) which provide that an order under that section modifying a previous such order is to be made only on such an application and after such consultation as is mentioned in that section shall not apply to an order under that section which contains a statement that the only provision made by the order is provision which appears to the Minister making the order to be appropriate in consequence of any of the provisions of this Act.

(2)   In section 2(2) of that Act (constitution of local fisheries committee) for the words 'the National Rivers Authority' there shall be substituted the words 'the Environment Agency'.

(3)   In section 18(3) of that Act (provision where a water authority or harbour authority have the powers of a local fisheries committee) for the words 'National Rivers Authority)' there shall be substituted the words 'Environment Agency)'.

The Sea Fish (Conservation) Act 1967

6.   In section 18(1) of the Sea Fish (Conservation) Act 1967 (enforcement of orders relating to salmon and migratory trout)—

(a)   for the words 'subsection (6) of section 2 of the Water Resources Act 1991' there shall be substituted the words 'subsection (7) of section 6 of the Environment Act 1995'; and

(b)   for the words 'the National Rivers Authority' there shall be substituted the words 'the Environment Agency'.

The Salmon and Freshwater Fisheries Act 1975

7.   In section 5 of the Salmon and Freshwater Fisheries Act 1975 (prohibition of use of explosives, poisons, electrical devices etc) in subsection (2), the words following paragraph (b) (which require Ministerial approval for the giving of permission to use noxious substances) shall be omitted.

8.   In section 6(3) of that Act (definition of 'unauthorised fixed engine') in paragraph (d) for the words 'the National Rivers Authority' there shall be substituted the words 'the Agency'.

9.   In section 8(2) of that Act (fishing mill dams to have attached to them fish passes of form and dimensions approved by the Minister) for the words 'the Minister' there shall be inserted the words 'the Agency'.

10.   In section 9(1) of that Act (owner or occupier of certain dams or other obstructions to make fish passes of form and dimensions approved by the Minister) for the words 'the Minister' there shall be substituted the words 'the Agency'.

11.—(1)   In section 10 of that Act, in subsection (1) (power of the National Rivers Authority, with the written consent of the Minister, to construct and maintain fish passes of form and dimensions approved by the Minister)—

(a)   the words 'with the written consent of the Minister,' shall be omitted; and

(b)   for the words 'as the Minister may approve' there shall be substituted the words 'as it may determine'.

(2)   In subsection (2) of that section (power of the National Rivers Authority, with the consent of the Minister, to alter etc fish passes and free gaps) the words 'with the written consent of the Minister,' shall be omitted.

12.—(1)   In section 11 of that Act (Minister's consents and approvals for fish passes) for subsection (1) there shall be substituted—

'(1)   Any approval given by the Agency to or in relation to a fish pass may, if in giving it the Agency indicates that fact, be provisional until the Agency notifies the applicant for approval that the pass is functioning to its satisfaction.

(1A) The applicant for any such approval—

(a) shall be liable to meet any costs incurred (whether by him or by the Agency or any other person) for the purposes of, or otherwise in connection with, the performance of the Agency's function of determining for the purposes of subsection (1) above whether or not the fish pass in question is functioning to its satisfaction; and

(b) shall provide the Agency with such information or assistance as it may require for the purpose of performing that function.'

(2) In subsection (2) of that section (Minister's power to revoke approval or consent while still provisional)—

(a) for the words 'or consent is provisional, the Minister' there shall be substituted the words 'is provisional, the Agency'; and

(b) for the words from 'his intention' onwards there shall be substituted the words 'its intention to do so, revoke the approval'.

(3) In subsection (3) of that section (Minister's power, when revoking provisional approval, to extend period for making fish pass)—

(a) for the words 'the Minister' there shall be substituted the words 'the Agency'; and

(b) for the word 'he' there shall be substituted the word 'it'.

(4) In subsection (4) of that section (Minister's power to approve and certify fish pass if he is of the opinion that it is efficient)—

(a) for the words 'The Minister' there shall be substituted the words 'The Agency'; and

(b) for the word 'he' there shall be substituted the word 'it'.

(5) In subsection (5) of that section (fish passes approved by the Minister deemed to be in conformity with the Act) for the words 'the Minister' there shall be substituted the words 'the Agency'.

13. For section 14 of that Act (gratings) there shall be substituted—

'14. Screens

(1) This section applies in any case where—

(a) by means of any conduit or artificial channel, water is diverted from waters frequented by salmon or migratory trout; and

(b) any of the water so diverted is used for the purposes of a water or canal undertaking or for the purposes of any mill or fish farm;

and in this section 'the responsible person' means the owner of the water or canal undertaking or (as the case may be) the occupier of the mill or the owner or occupier of the fish farm.

(2) Where this section applies, the responsible person shall, unless an exemption from the obligation is granted by the Agency, ensure (at his own cost) that there is placed and maintained at the entrance of, or within, the conduit or channel a screen which—

(a) subject to subsection (4) below, prevents the descent of the salmon or migratory trout; and

(b) in a case where any of the water diverted is used for the purposes of a fish farm, prevents the egress of farmed fish from the fish farm by way of the conduit or channel.

(3) Where this section applies, the responsible person shall also, unless an exemption from the obligation is granted by the Agency, ensure (at his own cost) that there is placed and maintained across any outfall of the conduit or channel a screen which—

(a) prevents salmon or migratory trout from entering the outfall; and

(b) in a case where any of the water diverted is used for the purposes of a fish farm, prevents the egress of farmed fish from the fish farm by way of the outfall,

(4) Where a screen is placed within any conduit or channel pursuant to subsection (2) above, the responsible person shall ensure that a continuous by-wash is provided immediately upstream of the screen, by means of which salmon or migratory trout may

return by as direct a route as practicable to the waters from which they entered the conduit or channel (and accordingly nothing in subsection (2) or (3) above applies in relation to a by-wash provided for the purposes of this subsection).

(5)   Any screen placed, or by-wash provided, in pursuance of this section shall be so constructed and located as to ensure, so far as reasonably practicable, that salmon or migratory trout are not injured or damaged by it.

(6)   No such screen shall be so placed as to interfere with the passage of boats on any navigable canal.

(7)   Any exemption under subsection (2) or (3) above may be granted subject to conditions.

(8)   If any person who is required to do so by this section fails to ensure that a screen is placed or maintained, or that a by-wash is provided, in accordance with the provisions of this section, he shall be guilty of an offence.

(9)   In any proceedings for an offence under subsection (8) above, it shall, subject to subsection (10) below, be a defence for the person charged to prove that he took all reasonable precautions and exercised all due diligence to avoid the commission of the offence by himself or a person under his control.

(10)   If in any case the defence provided by subsection (9) above involves the allegation that the commission of the offence was due to an act or default of another person, or to reliance on information supplied by another person, the person charged shall not, without leave of the court, be entitled to rely on that defence unless—

(a)   at least seven clear days before the hearing, and

(b)   where he has previously appeared before a court in connection with the alleged offence, within one month of his first such appearance,

he has served on the prosecutor a notice in writing giving such information identifying or assisting in the identification of that other person as was then in his possession.

(11)   Any reference in subsection (10) above to appearing before a court includes a reference to being brought before a court.

(12)   The obligations imposed by subsections (2) to (6) above, except so far as relating to farmed fish, shall not be in force during such period (if any) in each year as may be prescribed by byelaw.

(13)   The obligations imposed by subsections (2) to (6) above on the occupier of a mill shall apply only where the conduit or channel was constructed on or after 18th July 1923.

(14)   Any reference in this section to ensuring that a screen is placed and maintained includes, in a case where the screen takes the form of apparatus the operation of which prevents the passage of fish of the descriptions in question, a reference to ensuring that the apparatus is kept in continuous operation.

(15)   In this section ''by-wash'' means a passage through which water flows.'

14.—(1)   In section 15 of that Act (power of National Rivers Authority, with the consent of the Minister, to use gratings etc. to limit movements of salmon and trout) for the word 'grating' or 'gratings', wherever occurring (including in the side-note), there shall be substituted respectively the word 'screen' or 'screens'.

(2)   In subsection (1) of that section (placing of gratings, deepening of channels etc.) the words 'with the written consent of the Minister' shall be omitted.

(3)   In subsection (3) of that section (use of such means as the Minister may approve for preventing ingress)—

(a)   the words 'with the written consent of the Minister' shall be omitted; and

(b)   for the words 'as the Minister may approve' there shall be substituted the words 'as in its opinion are necessary'.

(4)   At the end of that section there shall be added—

'(5)   In this section ''open'', in relation to a screen which consists of apparatus, includes the doing of anything which interrupts, or otherwise interferes with, the operation of the apparatus.'

15. In section 17 of that Act (restrictions on taking salmon or trout above or below an obstruction etc) in subsection (3) (section not to be enforced, in cases where the fish pass is approved by the Minister, until compensation has been paid) for the words 'approved by the Minister' there shall be substituted—

'(a) approved by the Agency, or

(b) constructed and maintained by the Agency in accordance with section 10(1) above,'.

16. In section 18 of that Act (provisions supplementary to Part II) for subsection (2) (notice of application for Ministerial consent to the doing of certain acts to be given to the owner and occupier of the dam etc in question) there shall be substituted—

'(2) The Agency shall not—

(a) construct, abolish or alter any fish pass, or abolish or alter any free gap, in pursuance of section 10 above, or

(b) do any work under section 15 above,

unless reasonable notice of its intention to do so (specifying the section in question) has been served on the owner and occupier of the dam, fish pass or free gap, watercourse, mill race, cut, leat, conduit or other channel, with a plan and specification of the proposed work; and the Agency shall take into consideration any objections by the owner or occupier, before doing the proposed work.'

17. In section 30 of that Act, the paragraph defining 'fish farm' (which is superseded by amendments made by this Schedule) shall be omitted.

18.—(1) In section 35 of that Act (power to require production of fishing licences) in subsection (3), for the words 'the National Rivers Authority' there shall be substituted the words 'the Agency'.

(2) For subsection (4) of that section (definition of 'the appropriate office of the National Rivers Authority') there shall be substituted—

'(4) In subsection (3) above, "the appropriate office of the Agency" means—

(a) in a case where the person requiring the production of the licence or other authority specifies a particular office of the Agency for its production, that office; and

(b) in any other case, any office of the Agency;

and for the purposes of that subsection where a licence or other authority which any person has been required to produce is sent by post to an office of the Agency that licence or other authority shall be treated as produced by that person at that office.'

19. After subsection (1A) of section 39 of that Act (application of Act to River Esk in Scotland) there shall be inserted—

'(1B) Sections 31 to 34 and 36(2) of this Act shall, subject to the modifications set out in subsection (1C) below, apply throughout the catchment area of the River Esk in Scotland but a water bailiff shall exercise his powers under those sections as so applied only in relation to an offence—

(a) against this Act;

(b) against section 1 of the Salmon and Freshwater Fisheries (Protection) (Scotland) Act 1951; or

(c) which is deemed to be an offence under this Act by virtue of section 211(6) of the Water Resources Act 1991,

which he has reasonable cause to suspect has been committed in a place to which this Act applies by virtue of subsection (1)(b) above.

(1C) The modifications referred to in subsection (1B) above are—

(a) references in sections 31 to 34 of this Act to "this Act" shall be construed as including references to section 1 of the Salmon and Freshwater Fisheries (Protection) (Scotland) Act 1951 (as applied to the River Esk by section 21 of that Act); and

(b)   in section 33—
(i)   references to a justice of the peace shall be construed as including references to a sheriff, and
(ii)   in subsection (2), the reference to an information on oath shall be construed as including a reference to evidence on oath.'.

20.   In section 41(1) of that Act (general definitions) the following definitions shall be inserted at the appropriate places, that is to say—
(a)   ' "fish farm" has the same meaning as in the Diseases of Fish Act 1937;'; and
(b)   ' "screen" means a grating or other device which, or any apparatus the operation of which, prevents—
(a)   the passage of salmon or migratory trout, and
(b)   if the screen is required in connection with a fish farm, the passage of any fish farmed at that fish farm,
or any combination of devices or apparatus which, taken together, achieve that result;';
and the definition of 'grating' shall be omitted.

21.   In subsection (3) of section 43 of that Act (extent of Act to Scotland), after the words '(1A)' there shall be inserted the words ', (1B), (1C)'.

22.   In paragraph 1 of Schedule 1 to that Act (close seasons and close times) for the words 'the National Rivers Authority' there shall be substituted the words 'the Agency'.

The Diseases of Fish Act 1983

23.   In section 9(1)(d) of the Diseases of Fish Act 1983 (disclosure of information for the purpose of enabling the National Rivers Authority to carry out any of its functions) for the words 'the National Rivers Authority' there shall be substituted the words 'the Environment Agency'.

The Salmon Act 1986

24.   In section 37(3) of the Salmon Act 1986 (byelaws requiring consent of the National Rivers Authority) for the words 'the National Rivers Authority has' there shall be substituted the words 'the Environment Agency has'.

The Water Resources Act 1991

25.   In section 115 of the Water Resources Act 1991, in subsection (1) (power by order to make provision in relation to an area defined by the order for the modification, in relation to the fisheries in that area, of the enactments specified in the paragraphs of that subsection) for paragraph (b) there shall be substituted—
'(b)   of section 142 or 156 below or paragraph 6 or 7 of Schedule 25 to this Act; or'

26.—(1)   In paragraph 6 of Schedule 25 to that Act (powers to make byelaws in relation to any part or parts of the area in relation to which the National Rivers Authority carries out its functions in relation to fisheries under Part V of that Act) in sub-paragraphs (1) to (5) for the words 'in relation to any part or parts', in each place where they occur, there shall be substituted the words 'in relation to the whole or any part or parts'.
(2)   In sub-paragraph (3)(c) of that paragraph (byelaws for the purpose of determining for the purposes of the Salmon and Freshwater Fisheries Act 1975 the period of the year during which gratings need not be maintained) for the word 'gratings' there shall be substituted the word 'screens'.

SCHEDULE 16

POLLUTION OF RIVERS AND COASTAL WATERS IN SCOTLAND: AMENDMENT OF THE CONTROL OF POLLUTION ACT 1974

1. The Control of Pollution Act 1974, as it has effect in Scotland, shall be amended in accordance with the following paragraphs.

2. After section 30E there shall be inserted the following sections—

'Control of entry of polluting matter and effluents into water

30F. Pollution offences

(1) A person contravenes this section if he causes or knowingly permits any poisonous, noxious or polluting matter or any solid waste matter to enter any controlled waters.

(2) A person contravenes this section if he causes or knowingly permits any matter, other than trade effluent or sewage effluent, to enter controlled waters by being discharged from a sewer or from a drain in contravention of a prohibition imposed under section 30G below.

(3) A person contravenes this section if he causes or knowingly permits any trade effluent or sewage effluent to be discharged—

(a) into any controlled waters; or

(b) from land in Scotland, through a pipe, into the sea outside the seaward limits of controlled waters.

(4) A person contravenes this section if he causes or knowingly permits any trade effluent or sewage effluent to be discharged, in contravention of any prohibition imposed under section 30G below, from a building or from any plant—

(a) on to or into any land; or

(b) into any waters of a loch or pond which are not inland waters.

(5) A person contravenes this section if he causes or knowingly permits any matter whatever to enter any inland waters so as to tend (either directly or in combination with other matter which he or another person causes or permits to enter those waters) to impede the proper flow of the waters in a manner leading, or likely to lead, to a substantial aggravation of—

(a) pollution due to other causes; or

(b) the consequences of such pollution.

(6) Subject to the following provisions of this Part, a person who contravenes this section shall be guilty of an offence and liable—

(a) on summary conviction, to imprisonment for a term not exceeding three months or to a fine not exceeding £20,000 or to both;

(b) on conviction on indictment, to imprisonment for a term not exceeding two years or to a fine or to both.

30G. Prohibition of certain discharges by notice or regulations

(1) For the purposes of section 30F above a discharge of any effluent or other matter is, in relation to any person, in contravention of a prohibition imposed under this section if, subject to the following provisions of this section—

(a) SEPA has given that person notice prohibiting him from making or, as the case may be, continuing the discharge; or

(b) SEPA has given that person notice prohibiting him from making or, as the case may be, continuing the discharge unless specified conditions are observed, and those conditions are not observed.

(2) For the purposes of section 30F above a discharge of any effluent or other matter is also in contravention of a prohibition imposed under this section if the effluent or matter discharged—

(a) contains a prescribed substance or a prescribed concentration of such a substance; or

(b) derives from a prescribed process or from a process involving the use of prescribed substances or the use of such substances in quantities which exceed the prescribed amounts.

(3) Nothing in subsection (1) above shall authorise the giving of a notice for the purposes of that subsection in respect of discharges from a vessel; and nothing in any regulations made by virtue of subsection (2) above shall require any discharge from a vessel to be treated as a discharge in contravention of a prohibition imposed under this section.

(4) A notice given for the purposes of subsection (1) above shall expire at such time as may be specified in the notice.

(5) The time specified for the purposes of subsection (4) above shall not be before the end of the period of three months beginning with the day on which the notice is given, except in a case where SEPA is satisfied that there is an emergency which requires the prohibition in question to come into force at such time before the end of that period as may be so specified.

(6) Where, in the case of such a notice for the purposes of subsection (1) above as (but for this subsection) would expire at a time at or after the end of the said period of three months, an application is made before that time for a consent in pursuance of section 34 of this Act in respect of the discharge to which the notice relates, that notice shall be deemed not to expire until the result of the application becomes final—

(a) on the grant or withdrawal of the application;

(b) on the expiration, without the bringing of an appeal with respect to the decision on the application, of any period prescribed by virtue of section 39(2) below as the period within which any such appeal must be brought; or

(c) on the withdrawal or determination of any such appeal.

30H. Discharges into and from sewers etc.

(1) For the purposes of section 30F above where—

(a) any sewage effluent is discharged as mentioned in subsection (3) or (4) of that section from any sewer or works—

(i) vested in a sewerage authority; or

(ii) vested in a person other than a sewerage authority and forming (or forming part of) a system provided by him such as is mentioned in section 98(1)(b) of the Local Government etc. (Scotland) Act 1994; and

(b) the authority or, as the case may be, the person did not cause or knowingly permit the discharge but was bound (either unconditionally or subject to conditions which were observed) to receive into the sewer or works matter included in the discharge,

the authority or person shall be deemed to have caused the discharge.

(2) A sewerage authority shall not be guilty of an offence under section 30F of this Act by reason only of the fact that a discharge from a sewer or works vested in the authority contravenes conditions of a consent relating to the discharge if—

(a) the contravention is attributable to a discharge which another person caused or permitted to be made into the sewer or works; and

(b) the authority either was not bound to receive the discharge into the sewer or works or was bound to receive it there subject to conditions but the conditions were not observed; and

(c) the authority could not reasonably have been expected to prevent the discharge into the sewer or works;

and a person shall not be guilty of such an offence in consequence of a discharge which he caused or permitted to be made into a sewer or works vested in a sewerage authority if the authority was bound to receive the discharge there either unconditionally or subject to conditions which were observed.

(3)   A person in whom any such sewer or works as is described in subsection (1)(a)(ii) above is vested (such person being in this subsection referred to as a ''relevant person'') shall not be guilty of an offence under section 30F of this Act by reason only of the fact that a discharge from the sewer or works contravenes conditions of a consent relating to the discharge if—

(a)   the contravention is attributable to a discharge which another person caused or permitted to be made into the sewer or works; and

(b)   the relevant person either was not bound to receive the discharge into the sewer or works or was bound to receive it there subject to conditions but the conditions were not observed; and

(c)   the relevant person could not reasonably have been expected to prevent the discharge into the sewer or works;

and another person shall not be guilty of such an offence in consequence of a discharge which he caused or permitted to be made into a sewer or works vested in a relevant person if the relevant person was bound to receive the discharge there either unconditionally or subject to conditions which were observed.

30I. Defence to principal offences in respect of authorised discharges

(1)   Subject to the following provisions of this section, a person shall not be guilty of an offence under section 30F above in respect of the entry of any matter into any waters or any discharge if the entry occurs or the discharge is made under and in accordance with, or as a result of, any act or omission under and in accordance with—

(a)   a consent in pursuance of section 34 of this Act or under Chapter II of Part III of the Water Resources Act 1991 (which makes corresponding provision for England and Wales);

(b)   an authorisation for a prescribed process designated for central control granted under Part I of the Environmental Protection Act 1990;

(c)   a waste management or disposal licence;

(d)   a licence granted under Part II of the Food and Environment Protection Act 1985;

(e)   section 33 of the Water (Scotland) Act 1980 (temporary discharge by authorities in connection with the construction of works);

(f)   any provision of a local Act or statutory order which expressly confers power to discharge effluent into water; or

(g)   any prescribed enactment.

(2)   Nothing in any disposal licence shall be treated for the purposes of subsection (1) above as authorising—

(a)   any such entry or discharge as is mentioned in subsections (2) to (4) of section 30F above; or

(b)   any act or omission so far as it results in any such entry or discharge.

(3)   In this section—

''disposal licence'' means a licence issued in pursuance of section 5 of this Act;

''local Act'' includes enactments in a public general Act which amend a local Act;

''statutory order'' means an order, byelaw, scheme or award made under an Act of Parliament, including an order or scheme confirmed by Parliament or brought into operation in accordance with special parliamentary procedure; and

''waste management licence'' means such a licence granted under Part II of the Environmental Protection Act 1990.

30J.   Other defences to principal offences

(1)   A person shall not be guilty of an offence under section 30F above in respect of the entry of any matter into any waters or any discharge if—

(a)   the entry is caused or permitted, or the discharge is made, in an emergency in order to avoid danger to life or health;

(b)   that person takes all such steps as are reasonably practicable in the circumstances for minimising the extent of the entry or discharge and of its polluting effects; and

(c)   particulars of the entry or discharge are furnished to SEPA as soon as reasonably practicable after the entry occurs.

(2)   A person shall not be guilty of an offence under section 30F above by reason of his causing or permitting any discharge of trade or sewage effluent from a vessel.

(3)   A person shall not be guilty of an offence under section 30F above by reason only of his permitting water from an abandoned mine or an abandoned part of a mine to enter controlled waters.

(4)   Subsection (3) above shall not apply to the owner or former operator of any mine or part of a mine if the mine or part in question became abandoned after 31st December 1999.

(5)   In determining for the purposes of subsection (4) above whether a mine or part of a mine became abandoned before, on or after 31st December 1999 in a case where the mine or part has become abandoned on two or more occasions, of which—

(a)   at least one falls on or before that date, and

(b)   at least one falls after that date,

the mine or part shall be regarded as becoming abandoned after that date (but without prejudice to the operation of subsection (3) above in relation to that mine or part at, or in relation to, any time before the first of those occasions which falls after that date).

(6)   Where, immediately before a part of a mine becomes abandoned, that part is the only part of the mine not failing to be regarded as abandoned for the time being, the abandonment of that part shall not be regarded for the purposes of subsection (4) or (5) above as constituting the abandonment of the mine, but only of that part of it.

(7)   A person shall not, otherwise than in respect of the entry of any poisonous, noxious or polluting matter into any controlled waters, be guilty of an offence under section 30F above by reason of his depositing the solid refuse of a mine or quarry on any land so that it falls or is carried into inland waters if—

(a)   he deposits the refuse on the land with the consent of SEPA;

(b)   no other site for the deposit is reasonably practicable; and

(c)   he takes all reasonably practicable steps to prevent the refuse from entering those inland waters.

(8)   A roads authority obliged or entitled to keep open a drain by virtue of section 31 of the Roads (Scotland) Act 1984 shall not be guilty of an offence under section 30F above by reason of its causing or permitting any discharge to be made from a drain kept open by virtue of that section unless the discharge is made in contravention of a prohibition imposed under section 30G above.'

3.   Sections 31(1), (2), (3), (7) and (10) (offences relating to pollution of rivers and coastal waters) and 32 (control of discharges of trade and effluent etc. into rivers and coastal waters etc.) shall cease to have effect.

4.   In section 31(8) (maximum penalties) for the words 'paragraphs (a) and (b) of the preceding subsection' there shall be substituted the words 'section 30F(6) above'.

5.   In section 31B(4)(d) (nitrate sensitive areas: maximum penalties) for the words 'subsection (7) of section 31 above' there shall be substituted the words 'subsection (6) of section 30F above'.

6.　In section 34(3) (consents for discharges of trade and effluent) for the words 'section 32(1)' there shall be substituted the words 'section 30F(2) to (4)'.

7.　In section 39(1)(a) (appeals to the Secretary of State) for the words 'section 31(3)' there shall be substituted the words 'section 30J(4)'.

8.　In section 56(1) (interpretation etc of Part II) the following definitions shall be inserted in the appropriate places—

　''"drain" has the same meaning as in the Sewerage (Scotland) Act 1968;'; and
　''"sewer" has the same meaning as in the Sewerage (Scotland) Act 1968;'.

9.　In section 87(3) (time-bar in relation to legal proceedings)—
　　(a)　the words from the beginning to 'offence; and' shall cease to have effect;
　　(b)　for the words 'section 23 of the Summary Jurisdiction (Scotland) Act 1954' there shall be substituted the words 'section 331 of the Criminal Procedure (Scotland) Act 1975';
　　(c)　for the words 'such offence' there shall be substituted the words 'offence under section 30F of this Act or regulations or byelaws made in pursuance of section 31 of this Act'; and
　　(d)　for the words 'subsection (2) of section 23 of the said Act of 1954' there shall be substituted the words 'subsection (3) of section 331 of the said Act of 1975';
　　(e)　the words 'in its application to Scotland' shall cease to have effect.

SCHEDULE 17

STATUTORY NUISANCES: SCOTLAND

Amendments of the Environmental Protection Act 1990

1.　The Environmental Protection Act 1990 shall be amended in accordance with the provisions of paragraphs 2 to 7 of this Schedule.

2.　In section 79 (statutory nuisances etc)—
　　(a)　in subsection (1)(ga) after the word 'street' there shall be inserted the words 'or in Scotland, road';
　　(b)　in subsection (7)—
　　　(i)　in the definition of 'local authority', before the word 'outside' in paragraph (b) there shall be inserted 'in England and Wales', the word 'and' after paragraph (b) shall cease to have effect, and after paragraph (c) there shall be inserted 'and
　　　(d)　in Scotland, a district or islands council or a council constituted under section 2 of the Local Government etc (Scotland) Act 1994;';
　　　(ii)　in the definition of 'premises' after the word 'and' where it second occurs there shall be inserted the words ', in relation to England and Wales,';
　　　(iii)　at the appropriate place there shall be inserted—
　''"road" has the same meaning as in Part IV of the New Roads and Street Works Act 1991;';
　　(c)　in subsection (8)—
　　　(i)　after the words 'port health district' where they first occur there shall be inserted the words 'or in Scotland where by an order under section 172 of the Public Health (Scotland) Act 1897 a port local authority or a joint port local authority has been constituted for the whole or part of a port,';
　　　(ii)　after the words 'port health authority' where they second occur there shall be inserted the words ', port local authority or joint port local authority, as the case may be';
　　(d)　in subsection (10) after the words 'or (e)' there shall be inserted 'and, in relation to Scotland, paragraph (g) or (ga),';
　　(e)　in subsection (11) after the words 'subsection (12) and' there shall be inserted the words ', in relation to England and Wales,'.

3. In section 80 (summary proceedings) in subsection (3) after the words 'magistrates' court' there shall be inserted the words 'or in Scotland, the sheriff';

4. In section 81 (supplementary provisions)—

(a) in subsection (2) after the words 'magistrates' court' there shall be inserted the words 'or in Scotland, the sheriff';

(b) in subsection (3) after the word 'offence' there shall be inserted the words 'or, in Scotland, whether or not proceedings have been taken for an offence,';

(c) in subsection (4) after the word 'court' where it first occurs there shall be inserted the words 'or sheriff' and after the words 'court consider' there shall be inserted the words 'or sheriff considers';

(d) in subsection (5) after the words 'High Court' there shall be inserted the words 'or, in Scotland, in any court of competent jurisdiction,'.

5. In section 81A at the end, as subsection (10), and in section 81B at the end, as subsection (6), there shall be added—

'( ) This section does not apply to Scotland.'.

6. In section 82 (proceedings by persons aggrieved)—

(a) in subsection (1) after the word 'complaint' there shall be inserted the words 'or, in Scotland, the sheriff may act under this section on a summary application,';

(b) in subsection (2)—

(i) after the words 'magistrates' court' there shall be inserted the words 'or, in Scotland, the sheriff';

(ii) after the word 'street' there shall be inserted the words 'or, in Scotland, road';

(iii) after the words 'the court' there shall be inserted the words 'or the sheriff';

(iv) in paragraph (a) after the word 'defendant' there shall be inserted the words 'or, in Scotland, defender';

(v) in paragraph (b) after the word 'defendant' there shall be inserted the words 'or defender';

(vi) after the word 'and' where it third occurs there shall be inserted the words ', in England and Wales,';

(c) in subsection (3), after the words 'magistrates' court' there shall be inserted the words 'or the sheriff' and after the words 'of the court' in both places where they occur there shall be inserted the words 'or of the sheriff';

(d) in subsection (11), after the words 'magistrates' court' there shall be inserted the words 'or the sheriff';

(e) in subsection (12) after the word 'complaint' there shall be inserted the words 'or summary application', after the words 'the court' in both places where they occur there shall be inserted the words 'or the sheriff' and for the words 'defendant (or defendants' there shall be substituted the words 'defendant or defender (or defendants or defenders)';

(f) in subsection (13), after the words 'magistrates' court' there shall be inserted the words 'or to the sheriff' and after the words 'the court' in both places where they occur there shall be inserted the words 'or the sheriff'.

7. In Schedule 3 (statutory nuisance: supplementary provisions)—

(a) after paragraph 1 there shall be inserted—

'Appeals to Sheriff

1A.—(1) This paragraph applies in relation to appeals to the sheriff under section 80(3) against an abatement notice.

(2) An appeal to which this paragraph applies shall be by way of a summary application.

(3) The Secretary of State may make regulations as to appeals to which this paragraph applies and the regulations may in particular include or prescribe any of the matters referred to in sub-paragraphs (4)(a) to (d) of paragraph 1 above.';

(b) in paragraph 2 at the end there shall be added—

'(8) In the application of this paragraph to Scotland, a reference to a justice of the peace or to a justice includes a reference to the sheriff.';

(c) in paragraph 2A(1)(b) after the word 'street' there shall be inserted the words 'or, in Scotland, road';

(d) in paragraph 4 at the end there shall be added—

'(9) This paragraph does not apply to Scotland.';

(e) in paragraph 6 after the words 'magistrates' court' there shall be inserted the words 'or, in Scotland, the sheriff'.

Amendments of the Radioactive Substances Act 1993

8. In the Radioactive Substances Act 1993, in Part II of Schedule 3—

(a) in paragraph 12, for the words 'Sections 16 and 17' there shall be substituted the words 'Section 16';

(b) at the end there shall be added—

'17A. Part III of the Environmental Protection Act 1990.'.

SCHEDULE 18

SUPPLEMENTAL PROVISIONS WITH RESPECT TO POWERS OF ENTRY

Interpretation

1.—(1) In this Schedule—

'designated person' means an authorised person, within the meaning of section 91 of this Act and includes a person designated by virtue of paragraph 2 below;

'relevant power' means a power conferred by section 108 of this Act, including a power exercisable by virtue of a warrant under this Schedule.

(2) Expressions used in this Schedule and in section 108 of this Act have the same meaning in this Schedule as they have in that section.

Issue of warrants

2.—(1) If it is shown to the satisfaction of a justice of the peace or, in Scotland, the sheriff or a justice of the peace, on sworn information in writing—

(a) that there are reasonable grounds for the exercise in relation to any premises of a relevant power; and

(b) that one or more of the conditions specified in sub-paragraph (2) below is fulfilled in relation to those premises,

the justice or sheriff may by warrant authorise an enforcing authority to designate a person who shall be authorised to exercise the power in relation to those premises, in accordance with the warrant and, if need be, by force.

(2) The conditions mentioned in sub-paragraph (1)(b) above are—

(a) that the exercise of the power in relation to the premises has been refused;

(b) that such a refusal is reasonably apprehended;

(c) that the premises are unoccupied;

(d) that the occupier is temporarily absent from the premises and the case is one of urgency; or

(e) that an application for admission to the premises would defeat the object of the proposed entry.

(3) In a case where subsection (6) of section 108 of this Act applies, a justice of the peace or sheriff shall not issue a warrant under this Schedule by virtue only of being satisfied

that the exercise of a power in relation to any premises has been refused, or that a refusal is reasonably apprehended, unless he is also satisfied that the notice required by that subsection has been given and that the period of that notice has expired.

(4)   Every warrant under this Schedule shall continue in force until the purposes for which the warrant was issued have been fulfilled.

Manner of exercise of powers

3.   A person designated as the person who may exercise a relevant power shall produce evidence of his designation and other authority before he exercises the power.

Information obtained to be admissible in evidence

4.—(1)   Subject to section 108(12) of this Act, information obtained in consequence of the exercise of a relevant power, with or without the consent of any person, shall be admissible in evidence against that or any other person.

(2)   Without prejudice to the generality of sub-paragraph (1) above, information obtained by means of monitoring or other apparatus installed on any premises in the exercise of a relevant power, with or without the consent of any person in occupation of the premises, shall be admissible in evidence in any proceedings against that or any other person.

Duty to secure premises

5.   A person who, in the exercise of a relevant power enters on any premises which are unoccupied or whose occupier is temporarily absent shall leave the premises as effectually secured against trespassers as he found them.

Compensation

6.—(1)   Where any person exercises any power conferred by section 108(4)(a) or (b) or (5) of this Act, it shall be the duty of the enforcing authority under whose authorisation he acts to make full compensation to any person who has sustained loss or damage by reason of—

    (a)   the exercise by the designated person of that power; or

    (b)   the performance of, or failure of the designated person to perform, the duty imposed by paragraph 5 above.

(2)   Compensation shall not be payable by virtue of sub-paragraph (1) above in respect of any loss or damage if the loss or damage—

    (a)   is attributable to the default of the person who sustained it; or

    (b)   is loss or damage in respect of which compensation is payable by virtue of any other provision of the pollution control enactments.

(3)   Any dispute as to a person's entitlement to compensation under this paragraph, or as to the amount of any such compensation, shall be referred to the arbitration of a single arbitrator or, in Scotland, arbiter appointed by agreement between the enforcing authority in question and the person who claims to have sustained the loss or damage or, in default of agreement, by the Secretary of State.

(4)   A designated person shall not be liable in any civil or criminal proceedings for anything done in the purported exercise of any relevant power if the court is satisfied that the act was done in good faith and that there were reasonable grounds for doing it.

SCHEDULE 19

OFFENCES RELATING TO FALSE OR MISLEADING STATEMENTS OR FALSE ENTRIES

The Control of Pollution Act 1974

1.—(1)   The Control of Pollution Act 1974 shall be amended in accordance with the following provisions of this paragraph.

(2) For subsection (5) of section 34 (offences relating to consents for discharge of effluent etc) there shall be substituted—

'(5) A person who, in an application for consent in pursuance of this section, makes any statement which he knows to be false or misleading in a material particular or recklessly makes any statement which is false or misleading in a material particular shall be guilty of an offence and shall be liable—

(a) on summary conviction, to a fine not exceeding the statutory maximum;

(b) on conviction on indictment, to a fine or to imprisonment for a term not exceeding two years, or to both.'.

(3) For subsection (3) of section 93 (offences relating to power of authorities to obtain information) there shall be substituted—

'(3) A person who—

(a) fails without reasonable excuse to comply with the requirements of a notice served on him in pursuance of this section; or

(b) in furnishing any information in compliance with such a notice, makes any statement which he knows to be false or misleading in a material particular or recklessly makes any statement which is false or misleading in a material particular,

shall be guilty of an offence.

(3A) A person guilty of an offence under this section shall be liable—

(a) on summary conviction, to a fine not exceeding the statutory maximum; or

(b) on conviction on indictment, to a fine or to imprisonment for a term not exceeding two years, or to both.'.

The Water (Scotland) Act 1980

2.—(1) The Water (Scotland) Act 1980 shall be amended in accordance with the following provisions of this paragraph.

(2) In section 93 (obtaining of information as to underground water) after subsection (7) there shall be inserted—

'(8) Any person who in keeping a journal under subsection (1) or in furnishing information under subsection (2) or (3) makes any statement which he knows to be false or misleading in a material particular or recklessly makes any statement which is false or misleading in a material particular shall be guilty of an offence and shall be liable—

(a) on summary conviction, to a fine not exceeding the statutory maximum;

(b) on conviction on indictment, to a fine or to imprisonment for a term not exceeding two years, or to both.'.

(3) In section 94 (false information) after the word 'Act' there shall be inserted the words '(other than by or under section 93)'.

The Control of Pollution (Amendment) Act 1989

3. In section 7(3)(b) of the Control of Pollution (Amendment) Act 1989 (offences of making false statements), after the word 'false' in each place where it occurs there shall be inserted the words 'or misleading'.

The Environmental Protection Act 1990

4.—(1) For section 44 of the Environmental Protection Act 1990 (offences of making false statements) there shall be substituted—

'44. Offences of making false or misleading statements or false entries

(1) A person who—

(a) in purported compliance with a requirement to furnish any information imposed by or under any provision of this Part, or

(b) for the purpose of obtaining for himself or another any grant of a licence, any modification of the conditions of a licence, any acceptance of the surrender of a licence or any transfer of a licence,

makes a statement which he knows to be false or misleading in a material particular, or recklessly makes any statement which is false or misleading in a material particular, commits an offence.

(2) A person who intentionally makes a false entry in any record required to be kept by virtue of a licence commits an offence.

(3) A person who commits an offence under this section shall be liable—

(a) on summary conviction, to a fine not exceeding the statutory maximum;

(b) on conviction on indictment, to a fine or to imprisonment for a term not exceeding two years, or to both.'

(2) In section 71(3) of that Act, paragraph (b) (offence of making false or misleading statements) shall cease to have effect.

The Water Resources Act 1991

5.—(1) Section 206 of the Water Resources Act 1991 (making of false statements etc) shall be amended in accordance with the following provisions of this paragraph.

(2) For subsection (1), there shall be substituted—

'(1) If, in furnishing any information or making any application under or for the purposes of any provision of this Act, any person makes a statement which he knows to be false or misleading in a material particular, or recklessly makes any statement which is false or misleading in a material particular, he shall be guilty of an offence under this section.'

(3) Subsection (2) (which is superseded by the amendment made by sub-paragraph (2) above) shall be omitted.

(4) After subsection (3) (offences relating to the use of meters in connection with licences under Chapter II of Part II) there shall be inserted—

'(3A) If a person intentionally makes a false entry in any record required to be kept by virtue of a licence under Chapter II of Part II of this Act, or a consent under Chapter II of Part III of this Act, he shall be guilty of an offence under this section.'

(5) For subsections (5) to (7) (which require consent to the prosecution of certain offences and provide different penalties for different offences) there shall be substituted—

'(5) A person who is guilty of an offence under this section shall be liable—

(a) on summary conviction, to a fine not exceeding the statutory maximum;

(b) on conviction on indictment, to a fine or to imprisonment for a term not exceeding two years, or to both.'

The Radioactive Substances Act 1993

6.—After section 34 of the Radioactive Substances Act 1993 (offences relating to disclosure of information about trade secrets etc) there shall be inserted—

'34A. Offences of making false or misleading statements or false entries

(1) Any person who—

(a) for the purpose of obtaining for himself or another any registration under section 7 or 10, any authorisation under section 13 or 14 or any variation of such an authorisation under section 17, or

(b) in purported compliance with a requirement to furnish information imposed under section 31(1)(d),

makes a statement which he knows to be false or misleading in a material particular, or recklessly makes a statement which is false or misleading in a material particular, shall be guilty of an offence.

(2) Any person who intentionally makes a false entry in any record—

(a)   which is required to be kept by virtue of a registration under section 7 or 10 or an authorisation under section 13 or 14, or

(b)   which is kept in purported compliance with a condition which must be complied with if a person is to have the benefit of an exemption under section 8, 11 or 15, shall be guilty of an offence.

(3)   A person guilty of an offence under this section shall be liable—

(a)   on summary conviction, to a fine not exceeding the statutory maximum;

(b)   on conviction on indictment, to a fine or to imprisonment for a term not exceeding two years, or to both.'

SCHEDULE 20
DELEGATION OF APPELLATE FUNCTIONS OF THE SECRETARY OF STATE

Interpretation

1.   In this Schedule—
'appointed person' means a person appointed under section 114(1)(a) of this Act; and 'appointment', in the case of any appointed person, means appointment under section 114(1)(a) of this Act.

Appointments

2.   An appointment under section 114(1)(a) of this Act must be in writing and—

(a)   may relate to any particular appeal, matters or questions specified in the appointment or to appeals, matters or questions of a description so specified;

(b)   may provide for any function to which it relates to be exercisable by the appointed person either unconditionally or subject to the fulfilment of such conditions as may be specified in the appointment; and

(c)   may, by notice in writing given to the appointed person, be revoked at any time by the Secretary of State in respect of any appeal, matter or question which has not been determined by the appointed person before that time.

Powers of appointed person

3.   Subject to the provisions of this Schedule, an appointed person shall, in relation to any appeal, matter or question to which his appointment relates, have the same powers and duties as the Secretary of State, other than—

(a)   any function of making regulations;

(b)   any function of holding an inquiry or other hearing or of causing an inquiry or other hearing to be held; or

(c)   any function of appointing a person for the purpose—

  (i)   of enabling persons to appear before and be heard by the person so appointed; or

  (ii)   of referring any question or matter to that person.

Holding of local inquiries and other hearings by appointed persons

4.—(1)   If either of the parties to an appeal, matter or question expresses a wish to appear before and be heard by the appointed person, the appointed person shall give both of them an opportunity of appearing and being heard.

(2)   Whether or not a party to an appeal, matter or question has asked for an opportunity to appear and be heard, the appointed person—

(a)   may hold a local inquiry or other hearing in connection with the appeal, matter or question, and

(b)   shall, if the Secretary of State so directs, hold a local inquiry in connection with the appeal, matter or question, but this sub-paragraph is subject to sub-paragraph (3) below.

(3)   No local inquiry shall be held by virtue of this Schedule in connection with an appeal under—

(a)   section 42B(5) of the Control of Pollution Act 1974,

(b)   section 22(5), 66(5) or 78T(3) of the Environmental Protection Act 1990, or

(c)   section 191B(5) of the Water Resources Act 1991,

(appeals against decisions that information is not commercially confidential), or any matter involved in such an appeal, and any hearing held by virtue of this Schedule in connection with any such appeal or matter must be held in private.

(4)   Where an appointed person holds a local inquiry or other hearing by virtue of this Schedule, an assessor may be appointed by the Secretary of State to sit with the appointed person at the inquiry or hearing and advise him on any matters arising, notwithstanding that the appointed person is to determine the appeal, matter or question.

(5)   Subject to paragraph 5 below, the costs of a local inquiry held under this Schedule shall be defrayed by the Secretary of State.

Local inquiries under this Schedule: evidence and costs

5.—(1)   In relation to England and Wales, subsections (2) to (5) of section 250 of the Local Government Act 1972 (local inquiries: evidence and costs) shall apply to local inquiries or other hearings held under this Schedule by an appointed person as they apply to inquiries caused to be held under that section by a Minister, but with the following modifications, that is to say—

(a)   with the substitution in subsection (2) (evidence) for the reference to the person appointed to hold the inquiry of a reference to the appointed person;

(b)   with the substitution in subsection (4) (recovery of costs of holding the inquiry) for the references to the Minister causing the inquiry to be held of references to the Secretary of State;

(c)   taking the reference in that subsection to a local authority as including the Agency; and

(d)   with the substitution in subsection (5) (orders as to the costs of the parties) for the reference to the Minister causing the inquiry to be held of a reference to the appointed person or the Secretary of State.

(2)   In relation to Scotland, subsections (3) to (8) of section 210 of the Local Government (Scotland) Act 1973 (which relate to the costs of and holding of local inquiries) shall apply to local inquiries or other hearings held under this Schedule as they apply to inquiries held under that section, but with the following modifications, that is to say—

(a)   with the substitution in subsection (3) (notice of inquiry) for the reference to the person appointed to hold the inquiry of a reference to the appointed person;

(b)   with the substitution in subsection (4) (evidence) for the reference to the person appointed to hold the inquiry and, in paragraph (b), the reference to the person holding the inquiry of references to the appointed person;

(c)   with the substitution in subsection (6) (expenses of witnesses etc.) for the references to the Minister causing the inquiry to be held of a reference to the appointed person or the Secretary of State;

(d)   with the substitution in subsection (7) (expenses) for the references to the Minister of references to the appointed person or the Secretary of State;

(e)   with the substitution in subsection (7A) (recovery of entire administrative expense)—

(i)   for the first reference to the Minister of a reference to the appointed person or the Secretary of State;

(ii)   in paragraph (a), for the reference to the Minister of a reference to the Secretary of State; and

(iii)   in paragraph (b), for the reference to the Minister holding the inquiry of a reference to the Secretary of State;

(f)   with the substitution in subsection (7B) (power to prescribe daily amount)—

(i)   for the first reference to the Minister of a reference to the Secretary of State;

(ii)   in paragraphs (a) and (c), for the references to the person appointed to hold the inquiry of references to the appointed person; and

(iii)   in paragraph (d), for the reference to the Minister of a reference to the appointed person or the Secretary of State; and

(g)   with the substitution in subsection (8) (certification of expenses) for the reference to the Minister, the reference to him and the reference to the Crown of references to the appointed person or the Secretary of State.

Revocation of appointments and making of new appointments

6.—(1)   Where under paragraph 2(c) above the appointment of the appointed person is revoked in respect of any appeal, matter or question, the Secretary of State shall, unless he proposes to determine the appeal, matter or question himself, appoint another person under section 114(i)(a) of this Act to determine the appeal, matter or question instead.

(2)   Where such a new appointment is made, the consideration of the appeal, matter or question, or any hearing in connection with it, shall be begun afresh.

(3)   Nothing in sub-paragraph (2) above shall require any person to be given an opportunity of making fresh representations or modifying or withdrawing any representations already made.

Certain acts and omissions of appointed person to be treated as those of
the Secretary of State

7.—(1)   Anything done or omitted to be done by an appointed person in, or in connection with, the exercise or purported exercise of any function to which the appointment relates shall be treated for all purposes as done or omitted to be done by the Secretary of State in his capacity as such.

(2)   Sub-paragraph (1) above shall not apply—

(a)   for the purposes of so much of any contract made between the Secretary of State and the appointed person as relates to the exercise of the function; or

(b)   for the purposes of any criminal proceedings brought in respect of anything done or omitted to be done as mentioned in that sub-paragraph.

SCHEDULE 21

APPLICATION OF CERTAIN ENACTMENTS TO THE CROWN

PART I
ENACTMENTS RELATING TO ENGLAND AND WALES

The Water Industry Act 1991

1.—(1)   For section 221 of the Water Industry Act 1991 (Crown application) there shall be substituted—

'221. Crown application

(1)   Subject to the provisions of this section, this Act shall bind the Crown.

(2)   No contravention by the Crown of any provision made by or under this Act shall make the Crown criminally liable; but the High Court may, on the application of the Environment Agency, a water undertaker or a sewerage undertaker, declare unlawful any act or omission of the Crown which constitutes such a contravention.

(3) Notwithstanding anything in subsection (2) above, any provision made by or under this Act shall apply to persons in the public service of the Crown as it applies to other persons.

(4) If the Secretary of State certifies that it appears to him, as respects any Crown premises and any powers of entry exercisable in relation to them specified in the certificate, that it is requisite or expedient that, in the interests of national security, the powers should not be exercisable in relation to those premises, those powers shall not be exercisable in relation to those premises.

(5) Nothing in this section shall be taken as in any way affecting Her Majesty in her private capacity; and this subsection shall be construed as if section 38(3) of the Crown Proceedings Act 1947 (interpretation of references to Her Majesty in her private capacity) were contained in this Act.

(6) Subject to subsections (4) and (5) above, the powers conferred by sections 155, 159, 161(2) and 167 above shall be exercisable in relation to land in which there is a Crown or Duchy interest only with the consent of the appropriate authority.

(7) In this section—

"the appropriate authority" has the same meaning as it has in Part XIII of the Town and Country Planning Act 1990 by virtue of section 293(2) of that Act;

"Crown or Duchy interest" means an interest which belongs to Her Majesty in right of the Crown or of the Duchy of Lancaster, or to the Duchy of Cornwall, or belonging to a government department or held in trust for Her Majesty for the purposes of a government department;

"Crown premises" means premises held by or on behalf of the Crown.

(8) The provisions of subsection (3) of section 293 of the Town and Country Planning Act 1990 (questions relating to Crown application) as to the determination of questions shall apply for the purposes of this section.'

The Water Resources Act 1991

2.—(1) The Water Resources Act 1991 shall be amended in accordance with the following provisions of this paragraph.

(2) In section 115 (fisheries orders) in subsection (7) (orders affecting Crown or Duchy property) in paragraph (a), after the words 'an order under this section' there shall be inserted the words 'making provision, by virtue of subsection (1)(b) above, for the modification of section 156 below in relation to fisheries in an area'.

(3) In section 142 (orders providing for the imposition and collection of fisheries contributions), in subsection (2) (which applies, in relation to orders under that section, the provisions of subsections (2) to (9) of section 115 of that Act) for the words '(2) to (9)' there shall be substituted the words '(2) to (6)'.

(4) For section 222 (Crown application) there shall be substituted—

'222. Crown application

(1) Subject to the provisions of this section, this Act binds the Crown.

(2) No contravention by the Crown of any provision made by or under this Act shall make the Crown criminally liable; but the High Court may, on the application of the Agency, declare unlawful any act or omission of the Crown which constitutes such a contravention.

(3) Notwithstanding anything in subsection (2) above, the provisions of this Act shall apply to persons in the public service of the Crown as they apply to other persons.

(4) If the Secretary of State certifies that it appears to him, as respects any Crown premises and any powers of entry exercisable in relation to them specified in the certificate, that it is requisite or expedient that, in the interests of national security, the powers should not be exercisable in relation to those premises, those powers shall not be exercisable in relation to those premises.

(5) Subject to subsection (4) above, the powers conferred by sections 154, 156, 160, 162(3) and 168 above shall be exercisable in relation to land in which there is a Crown or Duchy interest only with the consent of the appropriate authority.

(6) Nothing in this section shall be taken as in any way affecting Her Majesty in her private capacity; and this subsection shall be construed as if section 38(3) of the Crown Proceedings Act 1947 (interpretation of references to Her Majesty in her private capacity) were contained in this Act.

(7) Nothing in this Act, as read with the other provisions of this section, shall be construed as conferring any power of levying drainage charges in respect of lands below the high-water mark of ordinary spring tides.

(8) Section 74 of the Land Drainage Act 1991 (Crown application), so far as it relates to land in which there is a Crown or Duchy interest, shall apply in relation to the flood defence provisions of this Act as it applies in relation to that Act; but nothing in this subsection shall affect any power conferred by this Act for the purposes both of the Agency's functions under those provisions and of other functions of the Agency.

(9) In this section—

"the appropriate authority" has the same meaning as it has in Part XIII of the Town and Country Planning Act 1990 by virtue of section 293(2) of that Act;

"Crown or Duchy interest" means an interest which belongs to Her Majesty in right of the Crown or of the Duchy of Lancaster, or to the Duchy of Cornwall, or belonging to a government department or held in trust for Her Majesty for the purposes of a government department;

"Crown premises" means premises held by or on behalf of the Crown.

(10) The provisions of subsection (3) of section 293 of the Town and Country Planning Act 1990 (questions relating to Crown application) as to the determination of questions shall apply for the purposes of this section.'

PART II
ENACTMENTS RELATING TO SCOTLAND

The Sewerage (Scotland) Act 1968

3. For section 55 of the Sewerage (Scotland) Act 1968 (Crown application) there shall be substituted—

'55. Application of Act to Crown

(1) Subject to the provisions of this section, this Act shall bind the Crown.

(2) No contravention by the Crown of any provision made by or under this Act shall make the Crown criminally liable; but the Court of Session may, on the application of a sewerage authority, declare unlawful any act or omission of the Crown which constitutes such a contravention.

(3) Notwithstanding anything in subsection (2) above, any provision made by or under this Act shall apply to persons in the public service of the Crown as it applies to other persons.

(4) If the Secretary of State certifies that it appears to him, as respects any Crown premises and any powers of entry exercisable in relation to them specified in the certificate, that it is requisite or expedient that, in the interests of national security, the powers should not be exercisable in relation to those premises, those powers shall not be exercisable in relation to those premises.

(5) Nothing in this section shall be taken as in any way affecting Her Majesty in her private capacity.

(6) In this section "Crown premises" means premises held by or on behalf of the Crown.'.

The Control of Pollution Act 1974

4.—For subsection (3) of section 105 of the Control of Pollution Act 1974 (application to Crown) as it has effect in relation to Scotland, there shall be substituted the following subsections—

'(3)   Subject to subsections (3A) to (3D) below, this Act shall bind the Crown.

(3A)   No contravention by the Crown of any provision made by or under this Act shall make the Crown criminally liable; but the Court of Session may, on the application of—

(a)   the Scottish Environment Protection Agency; or

(b)   any other public or local authority charged with enforcing that provision,

declare unlawful any act or omission of the Crown which constitutes such a contravention.

(3B)   Notwithstanding anything in subsection (3A) above, any provision made by or under this Act shall apply to persons in the public service of the Crown as it applies to other persons.

(3C)   If the Secretary of State certifies that it appears to him, as respects any Crown premises and any powers of entry exercisable in relation to them specified in the certificate, that it is requisite or expedient that, in the interests of national security, the powers should not be exercisable in relation to those premises, those powers shall not be exercisable in relation to those premises; and in this subsection ''Crown premises'' means premises held or used by or on behalf of the Crown.

(3D)   Nothing in this section shall be taken as in any way affecting Her Majesty in her private capacity.'

The Water (Scotland) Act 1974

5.   After section 110 of the Water (Scotland) Act 1980 there shall be inserted—

'110A.   Application of Act to Crown

(1)   Subject to the provisions of this section, this Act shall bind the Crown.

(2)   No contravention by the Crown of any provision made by or under this Act shall make the Crown criminally liable; but the Court of Session may, on the application of a water authority, declare unlawful any act or omission of the Crown which constitutes such a contravention.

(3)   Notwithstanding anything in subsection (2) above, any provision made by or under this Act shall apply to persons in the public service of the Crown as it applies to other persons.

(4)   If the Secretary of State certifies that it appears to him, as respects any Crown premises and any powers of entry exercisable in relation to them specified in the certificate, that it is requisite or expedient that, in the interests of national security, the powers should not be exercisable in relation to those premises, those powers shall not be exercisable in relation to those premises.

(5)   Nothing in this section shall be taken as in any way affecting Her Majesty in her private capacity.

(6)   Subject to subsections (4) and (5) above, the powers conferred by sections 16 to 18 above shall be exercisable in relation to land in which there is a Crown interest only with the consent of the appropriate authority.

(7)   In this section—

''the appropriate authority'' has the same meaning as it has in section 253(7) of the Town and Country Planning (Scotland) Act 1972;

''Crown interest'' means an interest belonging to Her Majesty in right of the Crown, or belonging to a government department or held in trust for Her Majesty for the purposes of a government department;

''Crown premises'' means premises held by or on behalf of the Crown.

(8) The provisions of subsection (7) of section 253 of the Town and Country Planning (Scotland) Act 1972 (questions relating to Crown application) as to the determination of questions shall apply for the purposes of this section.'.

The Local Government etc. (Scotland) Act 1994

6. After section 125 of the Local Government etc. (Scotland) Act 1994 there shall be inserted—

'125A. Application of Part II to Crown

(1) Subject to the provisions of this section, this Part of this Act shall bind the Crown.

(2) No contravention by the Crown of any provision made by or under this Part of this Act shall make the Crown criminally liable; but the Court of Session may, on the application of a new water and sewerage authority, declare unlawful any act or omission of the Crown which constitutes such a contravention.

(3) Notwithstanding anything in subsection (2) above, any provision made by or under this Part of this Act shall apply to persons in the public service of the Crown as it applies to other persons.

(4) Nothing in this section shall be taken as in any way affecting Her Majesty in her private capacity.

(5) Subject to subsection (4) above, the powers conferred by section 99 above shall be exercisable in relation to land in which there is a Crown interest only with the consent of the appropriate authority.

(6) In this section—

"the appropriate authority" has the same meaning as it has in section 253(7) of the Town and Country Planning (Scotland) Act 1972;

"Crown interest" means an interest belonging to Her Majesty in right of the Crown, or belonging to a government department or held in trust for Her Majesty for the purposes of a government department;

"Crown premises" means premises held by or on behalf of the Crown.

(7) The provisions of subsection (7) of section 253 of the Town and Country Planning (Scotland) Act 1972 (questions relating to Crown application) as to the determination of questions shall apply for the purposes of this section.'.

SCHEDULE 22

MINOR AND CONSEQUENTIAL AMENDMENTS

The Alkali, &c., Works Regulation Act 1906

1.—(1) The Alkali, &c, Works Regulation Act 1906 shall be amended in accordance with the following provisions of this paragraph.

(2) In section 1(1) (alkali work to be carried on so as to secure that the condensation of hydrochloric acid gas, to the satisfaction of the chief inspector, falls below certain levels) for the words 'the chief inspector' there shall be substituted the words 'the appropriate Agency'.

(3) In section 2(1) (no objection to be taken by an inspector to certain discharges) for the words 'an inspector' there shall be substituted the words 'the appropriate Agency'.

(4) In section 9—

(a) in subsection (5) (condition of issue of certificate on first registration that the work is furnished with such appliances as appear to the chief inspector or, on appeal, the Secretary of State to be necessary for certain purposes) for the words 'the chief inspector' there shall be substituted the words 'the appropriate Agency';

(b) the proviso to that subsection (power of Secretary of State to dispense with certain requirements) shall cease to have effect; and

(c)   in subsection (7) (notice of certain changes to be sent to the Secretary of State) for the words which are to be construed as a reference to the Secretary of State, there shall be substituted the words 'the appropriate Agency'.

(5)   In section 22(1) (power of Secretary of State, after inquiring into a complaint, to direct proceedings to be taken by an inspector) for the words 'an inspector' there shall be substituted the words 'the appropriate Agency'.

(6)   In section 23(2) (damages not recoverable under the section from a person with a certificate of compliance from the chief inspector) for the words 'the chief inspector' there shall be substituted the words 'the appropriate Agency'.

(7)   Section 25 (basis on which the chief inspector may determine questions) shall cease to have effect.

(8)   In section 27(1) (interpretation of terms)—

(a)   after the definition of the expression 'alkali works' there shall be inserted—

'The expression "the appropriate Agency" means—

(a)   in relation to England and Wales, the Environment Agency; and

(b)   in relation to Scotland, the Scottish Environment Protection Agency:'; and

(b)   the definitions of the expressions 'chief inspector' and 'inspector' shall be omitted.

(9)   In paragraph (b) of section 28 (application to Scotland)—

(a)   the words 'other than offences under subsection four of section twelve of this Act',

(b)   in sub-paragraph (ii) (prosecution not to be instituted without consent) the words from 'without the consent' to 'direct, nor', and

(c)   sub-paragraph (iii) (person taking proceedings presumed to be inspector), shall cease to have effect.

The Statistics of Trade Act 1947

2.   In the Statistics of Trade Act 1947, after section 9 (restrictions on disclosure of information, there shall be inserted—

'9A.   Exceptions from section 9

(1)   Nothing in section nine of this Act shall prevent or penalise the disclosure by the Secretary of State of information obtained under this Act—

(a)   to the Environment Agency or the Scottish Environment Protection Agency; or

(b)   to an officer of either of those Agencies authorised by that Agency to receive the information.

(2)   A person to whom information is disclosed in pursuance of the last foregoing subsection shall not use the information for any purpose other than the purposes of any functions of the Agency in question.'

The Rivers (Prevention of Pollution) (Scotland) Act 1951

3.—(1)   The Rivers (Prevention of Pollution) (Scotland) Act 1951 shall be amended in accordance with the following provisions of this paragraph.

(2)   Part II (river purification boards) (so far as unrepealed) and section 17 (duties of river purification authorities) shall cease to have effect.

(3)   In section 18 (provision and obtaining of information)—

(a)   in subsection (1) (power to obtain information)—

(i)   for the word 'them' in each place where it occurs there shall be substituted the word 'it';

(ii)   for the words 'a river purification authority' there shall be substituted the words 'SEPA'; and

(iii)   the words 'of their area', 'in their area' (where first occurring) and 'in their area or any part thereof' shall cease to have effect;

(b)   in subsection (2) (Secretary of State's power to give directions) for the words 'any river purification authority' and 'the authority' there shall be substituted the words 'SEPA', and for the word 'them' there shall be substituted the word 'it'; and

(c)   in subsection (3) (duty to provide reasonable facilities for inspection of records)—

(i)   for the words 'Every river purification authority' and 'the river purification authority' there shall be substituted the words 'SEPA';

(ii)   for the word 'them' there shall be substituted the word 'it'; and

(iii)   the words 'in their area' and the words from 'whose' to 'authority' where it next occurs shall cease to have effect; and

(d)   in subsection (6) (interpretation of 'stream') for the words 'river purification authority's' there shall be substituted the words 'SEPA's'.

(4)   In section 19 (power to take samples of effluents)—

(a)   in subsection (1) (power to obtain and take away samples of water from any stream or effluent)—

(i)   for the words 'A river purification authority' there shall be substituted the words 'SEPA'; and

(ii)   the words 'in the area of the authority' shall cease to have effect; and

(b)   in subsection (3) (interpretation of 'stream') for the words 'the river purification authority's' there shall be substituted the words 'SEPA's'.

(5)   In section 35 (interpretation)—

(a)   the definitions of 'river purification authority', 'river purification board' and 'river purification board area' shall cease to have effect; and

(b)   there shall be inserted at the appropriate place—

'"SEPA" means the Scottish Environment Protection Agency;'.

The Public Records Act 1958

4.   In the First Schedule to the Public Records Act 1958 (definition of public records) in Part II of the Table at the end of paragraph 3 (organisations whose records are public records) there shall be inserted at the appropriate place the entry—

'The Environment Agency.'.

The Opencast Coal Act 1958

5.—(1)   In section 7(8) of the Opencast Coal Act 1958 (definitions etc. for the purposes of section 7) in paragraph (i) of the definition of 'statutory water undertakers' for the words 'National Rivers Authority' there shall be substituted the words 'Environment Agency'.

(2)   In section 52(3) of that Act (general application to Scotland) for the words 'a river purification authority within the meaning of the Rivers (Prevention of Pollution) (Scotland) Act 1951' there shall be substituted the words 'the Scottish Environment Protection Agency'.

The Rivers (Prevention of Pollution) (Scotland) Act 1965

6.   In section 10 of the Rivers (Prevention of Pollution) (Scotland) Act 1965 (samples of effluent)—

(a)   in subsection (2)—

(i)   for the words 'A river purification authority' there shall be substituted the words 'the Scottish Environment Protection Agency (in this section referred to as "SEPA")'; and

(ii)   for the words 'the river purification authority's' there shall be substituted the words 'SEPA's'; and

(b)   in subsections (3) to (5), for the words 'the river purification authority', in each place where they occur, and 'Every river purification authority' there shall be substituted the words 'SEPA'.

The Nuclear Installations Act 1965

7.—(1)   In section 3 of the Nuclear Installations Act 1965, after subsection (1) (grant of nuclear site licences) there shall be inserted—

'(1A)   The Health and Safety Executive shall consult the appropriate Agency before granting a nuclear site licence in respect of a site in Great Britain.'

(2)   In subsection (3) of that section (consultation with certain bodies), in paragraph (b), the words 'the National Rivers Authority,' shall cease to have effect.

(3)   After subsection (6) of that section (variation of nuclear site licences) there shall be inserted—

'(6A)   The Health and Safety Executive shall consult the appropriate Agency before varying a nuclear site licence in respect of a site in Great Britain, if the variation relates to or affects the creation, accumulation or disposal of radioactive waste, within the meaning of the Radioactive Substances Act 1993.'

8.   In section 4 of that Act (attachment of conditions to licences) after subsection (3) there shall be inserted—

'(3A)   The Health and Safety Executive shall consult the appropriate Agency—

(a)   before attaching any condition to a nuclear site licence in respect of a site in Great Britain, or

(b)   before varying or revoking any condition attached to such a nuclear site licence, if the condition relates to or affects the creation, accumulation or disposal of radioactive waste, within the meaning of the Radioactive Substances Act 1993.'

9.   In section 5 of that Act (revocation and surrender of licences) after subsection (1) there shall be inserted—

'(1A)   The Health and Safety Executive shall consult the appropriate Agency before revoking a nuclear site licence in respect of a site in Great Britain.'

10.   In section 26 (interpretation) in subsection (1), there shall be inserted at the appropriate place—

' "the appropriate Agency" means—

(a)   in the case of a site in England or Wales, the Environment Agency;

(b)   in the case of a site in Scotland, the Scottish Environment Protection Agency;'.

The Parliamentary Commissioner Act 1967

11.   In Schedule 2 to the Parliamentary Commissioner Act 1967 (departments and authorities subject to investigation)—

(a)   there shall be inserted at the appropriate places the entries—

(i)   'Environment Agency'; and

(ii)   'Scottish Environment Protection Agency';

(b)   after note 1, there shall be inserted—

'1A.   The reference to the Environment Agency is a reference to that Agency in relation to all its functions other than its flood defence functions, within the meaning of the Water Resources Act 1991.'; and

(c)   there shall be omitted—

(i)   the entry relating to the National Rivers Authority; and

(ii)   the note 9 inserted by paragraph 11 of Schedule 1 to the Water Act 1989 (which relates to that Authority).

The Sewerage (Scotland) Act 1968

12.—(1)   In section 38(3) of the Sewerage (Scotland) Act 1968 (duty of Secretary of State to consult on proposed extension of Part II to non-trade effluents)—

(a)   after the word 'consult' where it first occurs there shall be inserted the words 'the Scottish Environment Protection Agency and'; and

(b)   the words 'river purification authorities,' shall cease to have effect.

(2)   In section 59(1) of that Act (interpretation) the definition of 'river purification authority' shall cease to have effect.

The Local Authorities (Goods and Services) Act 1970

13.   The Local Authorities (Goods and Services) Act 1970 (supply of goods and services by local authorities to public bodies) shall have effect as if the Agency and SEPA were each both a local authority and a public body for the purposes of that Act other than section 2(2) (accounting requirements in relation to local authority agreements entered into in pursuance of section 1).

The Agriculture Act 1970

14.—(1)   The Agriculture Act 1970 shall be amended in accordance with the following provisions of this paragraph.
(2)   In section 92(1) (provision of flood warning systems)—
(a)   for the words from the beginning to 'may' where it first occurs there shall be substituted the words 'The Scottish Environment Protection Agency may';
(b)   the words 'for their area and 'both within (and in the case of a river purification board) outwith, that area,' shall cease to have effect;
(c)   in sub-paragraph (i) of the proviso—
   (i)   for the words 'a river purification board' there shall be substituted the words 'the Scottish Environment Protection Agency';
   (ii)   for the word 'them' there shall be substituted the word 'it'; and
   (iii)   for the words 'that board' there shall be substituted the words 'the Agency';
and
(d)   in sub-paragraph (ia) of the proviso for the words following 'exercise' to 'shall' there shall be substituted the words ', the Agency shall'.
(3)   In section 92(2)—
(a)   in paragraph (a)(iii) for the words 'the authority providing the system' there shall be substituted the words 'the Scottish Environment Protection Agency';
(b)   paragraph (c) (definition of 'river purification board') shall cease to have effect.
(4)   In section 94 (cooperation with other persons as regards flood warning systems)—
(a)   in subsection (1) for the words following 'warning system' to 'may' where it first occurs there shall be substituted the words 'the Scottish Environment Protection Agency may' and for the words following 'belonging to the' to 'for' there shall be substituted the words 'Agency for';
(b)   in subsection (2) for the words from the beginning to 'may' and for the words following 'apparatus of' there shall be substituted the words 'The Agency may' and ' the Agency' respectively.
(5)   In section 98 (extent of Part VI)—
(a)   for the words from the beginning to 'England' there shall be substituted the words 'The Scottish Environment Protection Agency';
(b)   for the words 'section 92(1)(b)' there shall be substituted the words 'section 92(1)'; and
(c)   for the words 'the National Rivers Authority' there shall be substituted the words 'the Environment Agency'.

The Prevention of Oil Pollution Act 1971

15.—(1)   The Prevention of Oil Pollution Act 1971 shall be amended in accordance with the following provisions of this paragraph.
(2)   After section 11 (duty to report discharge of oil into waters of harbours) there shall be inserted—

'**11A. Certain provisions not to apply where a discharge or escape is authorised under Part I of the Environmental Protection Act 1990**

(1) The provisions of sections 2(1) and (2A), 3(1) and 11(1) of this Act shall not apply to any discharge which is made under, and the provisions of section 11(1) of this Act shall not apply to any escape which is authorised by, an authorisation granted under Part I of the Environmental Protection Act 1990.

(2) This section does not extend to Northern Ireland.'

(3) In section 25(1) (power to extend certain provisions of the Act to the Isle of Man etc.), after the words 'other than section 3' there shall be inserted the word ', 11A'.

The Town and Country Planning (Scotland) Act 1972

16. In Schedule 7 to the Town and Country Planning (Scotland) Act 1972 (determination of certain appeals by persons appointed by the Secretary of State), in paragraph 2, after sub-paragraph (f) there shall be inserted—

'(g) in relation to appeals under paragraphs 6(11) and (12) and 11(1) of Schedule 13 and paragraph 9(1) of Schedule 14 to the Environment Act 1995, paragraph 6 of Schedule 10A to this Act.'.

The Local Government Act 1972

17. In section 223 of the Local Government Act 1972 (which includes provision for authorised members or officers of the National Rivers Authority to conduct certain magistrates' court proceedings on its behalf) in subsection (2)—

(a) after the words 'joint authority' there shall be inserted the word 'and'; and

(b) the words 'and the National Rivers Authority' shall cease to have effect.

The Local Government Act 1974

18. In section 25(1) of the Local Government Act 1974 (authorities subject to investigation by Local Commissioners), for paragraph (d) there shall be substituted—

'(d) in relation to the flood defence functions of the Environment Agency, within the meaning of the Water Resources Act 1991, the Environment Agency and any regional flood defence committee.'

The Control of Pollution Act 1974

19.—(1) Section 5 of the Control of Pollution Act 1974 (licences to dispose of waste) shall be amended in accordance with the following provisions of this paragraph.

(2) In subsection (3) (duty of recipient of application for licence where planning permission is in force)—

(a) for the words 'Where a disposal authority receives an application' there shall be substituted the words 'Where an application has been received'; and

(b) for the words 'the authority', where first occurring, there shall be substituted the words 'the appropriate Agency' and, where secondly occurring, there shall be substituted the words 'that Agency'.

(3) In subsection (4) (duty of disposal authority to refer to National Rivers Authority etc proposals to issue licences)—

(a) for the words 'a disposal authority' there shall be substituted the words 'the appropriate Agency';

(b) for the words 'the authority' there shall be substituted the words 'that Agency';

(c) for paragraph (a), there shall be substituted—

'(a) to refer the proposal to any collection authority whose area includes any part of the relevant land; and';

(d) in paragraph (b), for the words 'the disposal authority', in both places where they occur, there shall be substituted the words 'that Agency'; and (e)　the words following paragraph (b) (reference of proposal to Secretary of State in certain cases) shall cease to have effect.

(4) Subsection (5) (separate provision for Scotland) shall cease to have effect.

20.—(1)　Section 6 of that Act (provisions supplementary to section 5) shall be amended in accordance with the following provisions of this paragraph.

(2)　In subsection (2) (conditions which may be included in disposal licences)—

(a)　for the words 'the disposal authority which issues it' there shall be substituted the words 'the appropriate Agency'; and

(b)　for the words 'the authority' there shall be substituted the words 'that Agency'.

(3)　In subsection (3) (offence of contravening a licence condition without reasonable excuse) for the words 'the disposal authority which issued the licence' there shall be substituted the words 'the Environment Agency'.

(4)　In subsection (4) (duty of each disposal authority to maintain registers etc)—

(a)　for the words 'each disposal authority' there shall be substituted the words 'the Environment Agency and of SEPA';

(b)　for paragraph (a) there shall be substituted—

'(a)　to maintain a register containing copies of all disposal licences which are for the time being in force in respect of land in England and Wales or, as the case may be, Scotland;' and

(c)　in paragraph (c), for the words 'the authority' there shall be substituted the words 'that Agency'.

(5)　In subsection (5) (applications deemed to be refused if not granted within two months of receipt)—

(a)　for the words 'a disposal authority receives an application duly made to it for a disposal licence' there shall be substituted the words 'a duly made application for a disposal licence was received';

(b)　for the words 'the authority', in the first two places where they occur, there shall be substituted the words 'the appropriate Agency'; and

(c)　for the words 'the authority', wherever else occurring, there shall be substituted the words 'that Agency'.

21.—(1)　Section 7 of that Act (variation of conditions and revocation of licences) shall be amended in accordance with the following provisions of this paragraph.

(2)　In subsection (1) (modification of conditions of disposal licences issued by disposal authorities)—

(a)　the words 'issued by a disposal authority' shall be omitted; and

(b)　for the words 'the authority', where first occurring, there shall be substituted the words 'the appropriate Agency' and, wherever else occurring, there shall be substituted the words 'that Agency'.

(3)　In subsection (2) (application of section 5(4))—

(a)　the words 'or, in relation to Scotland, subsection (5)' shall cease to have effect; and

(b)　for paragraphs (a) and (b) there shall be substituted—

'(a)　the Environment Agency or SEPA, as the case may be, may postpone the reference in pursuance of the said subsection (4) so far as it considers that by reason of an emergency it is appropriate to do so; and

(b)　the Environment Agency or SEPA, as the case may be, may disregard any collection authority for the purposes of the preceding provisions of this subsection in relation to a modification which, in the opinion of that Agency, will not affect that authority.'

(4)　In subsection (4) (revocation of disposal licences issued by disposal authorities)—

(a)　the words 'issued by a disposal authority' shall be omitted;

(b)　for the words 'the authority', where first occurring, there shall be substituted the words 'the appropriate Agency' and, in the other place where they occur, there shall be substituted the words 'that Agency'.

22.—(1)　Section 8 of that Act (transfer and relinquishment of licences) shall be amended in accordance with the following provisions of this paragraph.

(2)　In subsection (1) (transfer of licences)—

(a)　for the words 'the authority which issued the licence' there shall be substituted the words 'the appropriate Agency'; and

(b)　for the words 'the authority', in both places where they occur, there shall be substituted the words 'that Agency'.

(3)　In subsection (4) (cancellation of licences)—

(a)　for the words 'the authority which issued it' there shall be substituted the words 'the appropriate Agency'; and

(b)　for the words 'the authority', in the other place where they occur, there shall be substituted the words 'that Agency'.

23.—(1)　Section 9 of that Act (supervision of licensed activities) shall be amended in accordance with the following provisions of this paragraph.

(2)　In subsection (1) (duties of the authority which issued the licence) for the words 'the authority which issued the licence' there shall be substituted the words 'the appropriate Agency'.

(3)　In subsection (2) (powers of entry of authorised officers to carry out works in an emergency)—

(a)　for the words 'a disposal authority' there shall be substituted the words 'the Environment Agency or SEPA, as the case may be,'; and

(b)　for the words 'the authority', wherever occurring, there shall be substituted the words 'that Agency'.

(4)　In subsection (3) (recovery of certain expenditure from licence holders)—

(a)　for the words 'a disposal authority' there shall be substituted the words 'the Environment Agency or SEPA'; and

(b)　for the words 'the authority' there shall be substituted the word 'it'.

(5)　In subsection (4) (breach of conditions of licences)—

(a)　for the words 'a disposal authority' there shall be substituted the words 'the appropriate Agency';

(b)　the words 'issued by the authority' shall be omitted; and

(c)　for the words 'the authority', wherever else occurring, there shall be substituted the words 'that Agency'.

24.—(1)　Section 10 of that Act (appeals to Secretary of State from decisions with respect to licences) shall be amended in accordance with the following provisions of this paragraph.

(2)　In subsection (1) (duty of disposal authority concerned to implement Secretary of State's determination) for the words 'the disposal authority concerned' there shall be substituted the words 'the appropriate Agency'.

(3)　In subsection (3) (cases where the decision under appeal is effective pending the determination of the appeal)—

(a)　for the words 'to a decision of a disposal authority' there shall be substituted the words 'if the decision in question is a decision';

(b)　for the words 'in the opinion of the authority' there shall be substituted the words 'in the opinion of the body making the decision in question';

(c)　for the words 'the authority acted' there shall be substituted the words 'that body acted'; and

(d)　in paragraph (b), for the words 'the authority' there shall be substituted the words 'the appropriate Agency'.

25. In section 11 of that Act (special provision for land occupied by disposal authorities: resolutions etc) subsections (1) to (11) shall cease to have effect.

26.—(1) Section 16 of that Act (removal of waste deposited in breach of licensing provisions) shall be amended in accordance with the following provisions of this paragraph.

(2) In subsection (1) (power of disposal or collection authority to serve notice on occupier of land in its area) for the words from 'in the area' to 'the authority may' there shall be substituted the words 'in contravention of section 3(1) of this Act, any authority to which this section applies may'.

(3) After subsection (7) there shall be added—

'(8) The authorities to which this section applies are—

(a) the appropriate Agency;

(b) any collection authority in whose area the land mentioned in subsection (1) above is situated.'

27. In section 30 of that Act (interpretation of Part 1) in subsection (1)—

(a) the following definition shall be inserted at the appropriate place—

'"the appropriate Agency" means—

(a) in relation to England and Wales, the Environment Agency;

(b) in relation to Scotland, SEPA;';

(b) for the definition of 'waste' there shall be substituted—

'"waste" has the same meaning as it has in Part II of the Environmental Protection Act 1990 by virtue of section 75(2) of that Act;'; and

(c) the words from 'and for the purposes' to the end (which provide a presumption that anything discarded is waste unless the contrary is proved) shall cease to have effect.

28. In section 62(2)(a) of that Act (exceptions to restrictions on the operation of loudspeakers in streets), as it has effect in relation to England and Wales, for the words 'National Rivers Authority' there shall be substituted the words 'Environment Agency'.

29.—(1) The Control of Pollution Act 1974, as it has effect in relation to Scotland, shall be amended in accordance with the following provisions of this paragraph.

(2) Subject to the amendments made by the following provisions of this paragraph, for the words 'a river purification authority', 'the river purification authority', 'river purification authority', 'river purification authorities', 'the river purification authorities', 'each river purification authority' and 'any river purification authority', in each place where they occur in the undernoted provisions, there shall be substituted the words 'SEPA'—

section 30A(2)(a) and (3);

section 30C(1);

section 30D;

section 31(4)(d) and (6);

section 31A(2);

section 33(1);

sections 34 to 39;

section 41;

sections 46 to 51;

section 96(3); and

Schedule 1A.

(3) In section 30A(2)(a) (Secretary of State to deposit maps showing fresh-water limits of every relevant river or watercourse) the words 'in the area of that authority' shall cease to have effect.

(4) In section 30C (water quality objectives)—

(a) in subsection (1) (Secretary of State to establish water quality objectives), the words 'within the area of that authority' shall cease to have effect;

(b)   in subsection (3)(b) (Secretary of State to review water quality objectives) for the words 'the river purification authority on which that notice has been served' there shall be substituted the words 'SEPA';

(c)   in subsection (4) (Secretary of State to give notice and consider representations when reviewing water quality objectives)—

(i)   the words 'in the area of a river purification authority' shall cease to have effect; and

(ii)   in paragraph (a) for the words 'that authority' there shall be substituted the words 'SEPA';

(d)   in subsection (5)(b) (form of notice to be given by the Secretary of State when varying water quality objectives) for the words 'the authority' there shall be substituted the words 'SEPA'; and

(e)   in subsection (6) (Secretary of State to serve further notice where water quality objectives remain unchanged)—

(i)   the words 'in the area of a river purification authority' shall cease to have effect; and

(ii)   for the words 'that authority' there shall be substituted the words 'SEPA'.

(5)   In section 30E (consultation and collaboration)—

(a)   for the word 'their' there shall be substituted the word 'its';

(b)   for the words 'river purification authorities' there shall be substituted the words 'SEPA'; and

(c)   for the words 'National Rivers Authority' there shall be substituted the words 'Environment Agency'.

(6)   In section 31 (control of pollution of rivers and coastal waters etc.)—

(a)   in subsection (4)(b) (Secretary of State power to restrict or prohibit prescribed activities in designated areas) for the words 'the river purification authority in whose area the place is situated' there shall be substituted the words 'SEPA'; and

(b)   in subsection (6) (power to make byelaws to prohibit or regulate prescribed activities)—

(i)   for the words 'the authority' there shall be substituted the word 'it'; and

(ii)   the words 'in its area' shall cease to have effect.

(7)   Section 31D (powers of entry in relation to agreements under section 31B) shall cease to have effect.

(8)   In section 33(1) (power to make byelaws regulating or prohibiting sanitary appliances on vessels)—

(a)   for the words 'the authority' where they first occur there shall be substituted the word 'it'; and

(b)   the words 'in the area of the authority' shall cease to have effect.

(9)   In section 34 (consents for discharges of trade and sewage effluent etc.)—

(a)   for the words 'the authority' and 'the authority's' in each place where they occur (other than the last reference in subsection (2)) there shall be substituted the words 'SEPA' and 'SEPA's' respectively;

(b)   in subsection (2) (disposal of application)—

(i)   for the words 'a river purification authority to which an application for consent is' there shall be substituted the words 'SEPA, in relation to an application for consent';

(ii)   for the word 'three' there shall be substituted the word 'four'; and

(iii)   for the words 'the authority shall be deemed to have refused the consent' there shall be substituted the words 'the applicant may treat the consent applied for as having been refused'; and

(c)   in subsection (3) (consent not to relate to discharges which occurred prior to consent) the words 'in its area' shall cease to have effect.

(10)   In the following provisions, for the words 'an authority', 'any authority', 'the authority', 'the authorities' and 'the relevant river purification authority' in each place where they occur there shall be substituted the words 'SEPA'—

sections 35 to 39;
section 41;
sections 46 to 49; and
Schedule 1A, paragraph 2.

(11) In section 36 (provisions supplementary to sections 34 and 35)—

(a) in subsection (1), after the word 'shall' there shall be inserted the words ', subject to subsections (2A) and (2B) below,'; and

(b) after subsection (2) there shall be inserted the following subsections—

'(2A) A person who proposes to make, or has made, an application to SEPA for consent in pursuance of section 34 of this Act may apply to the Secretary of State within a prescribed period for a certificate providing that subsection (1) above shall not apply to that application.

(2B) If the Secretary of State is satisfied that—

(a) it would be contrary to the interests of national security; or

(b) it would prejudice to an unreasonable degree the commercial interests of any person,

not to issue a certificate applied for under subsection (2A) above, he may issue the certificate and, if he does so, subsection (1) above shall not apply to the application specified in the certificate.'; and

(c) in subsection (6), for the word 'three' there shall be substituted the word 'four'.

(12) In section 37(1) (revocation of consents and alteration and imposition of conditions), for the words from the beginning to 'consent' in the second place where it occurs there shall be substituted the words 'SEPA may from time to time review any consent given in pursuance of section 34 of this Act'.

(13) In section 38 (restriction as to variation and revocation of consent and of previous variation), in each of subsections (1) and (2), for the word 'two' there shall be substituted the word 'four'.

(14) After section 38 there shall be inserted—

'38A. General review of consents

(1) If it appears appropriate to the Secretary of State to do so he may at any time direct SEPA to review—

(a) the consents given under section 34 of this Act; or

(b) any description of such consents,

and the conditions (if any) to which those consents are subject.

(2) A direction given by virtue of subsection (1) above—

(a) shall specify the purpose for which; and

(b) may specify the manner in which,

the review is to be conducted.

(3) After carrying out the review, SEPA shall submit to the Secretary of State its proposals (if any) for—

(a) the modification of the conditions of any consent reviewed pursuant to the direction; or

(b) in the case of any such consent which is unconditional, subjecting the consent to conditions.

(4) Where the Secretary of State has received any proposals under subsection (3) above in relation to any consent he may, if it appears appropriate to him to do so, direct SEPA, in relation to that consent—

(a) to make modifications of the conditions of the consent; or

(b) in the case of an unconditional consent, to subject the consent to conditions.

(5) A direction given by virtue of subsection (4) above may direct SEPA to do, in relation to any such consent, only—

(a) any such thing as SEPA has proposed should be done in relation to that consent; or

(b)   any such thing with such modifications as appear to the Secretary of State to be appropriate.'.

(15)   In section 39 (appeals to Secretary of State)—

(a)   in subsection (1), in each of paragraphs (b) and (c), for the words 'the preceding section' there shall be substituted the words 'section 38 of this Act';

(b)   in subsection (5), for the words 'terms and period as are' there shall be substituted the words 'period as is';

(c)   after that subsection there shall be inserted the following subsections—

'(5A)   Subject to subsection (5B) below, where a question is referred to the Secretary of State in pursuance of subsection (1)(b) above, the revocation of the consent or, as the case may be, the modification of the conditions of the consent or the provision that the consent (having been unconditional) shall be subject to conditions, shall not take effect while the reference is pending.

(5B)   Subsection (5A) above shall not apply to a reference where the notice effecting the revocation, modification or provision in question includes a statement that in the opinion of SEPA it is necessary for the purpose of preventing or, where that is not practicable, minimising—

(a)   the entry into controlled waters of any poisonous, noxious or polluting matter or any solid waste matter, or

(b)   harm to human health,

that that subsection should not apply.

(5C)   Where the reference falls within subsection (5B) above, if, on the application of the holder or former holder of the consent, the Secretary of State (or other person determining the question referred) determines that SEPA acted unreasonably in excluding the application of subsection (5A) above, then—

(a)   if the reference is still pending at the end of the day on which that determination is made, subsection (5A) above shall apply to the reference from the end of that day; and

(b)   the holder or former holder of the consent shall be entitled to recover compensation from SEPA in respect of any loss suffered by him in consequence of the exclusion of the application of that subsection;

and any dispute as to a person's entitlement to such compensation or as to the amount of it shall be determined by a single arbiter appointed, in default of agreement between the parties concerned, by the Secretary of State on the application of any of the parties.'; and

(d)   at the end there shall be added—

'(7)   This section is subject to section 114 of the Environment Act 1995 (delegation or reference of appeals).

(8)   In this section "the holder", in relation to a consent, is the person who has the consent.'

(16)   Section 40(4) (transitional provisions relating to consents) shall cease to have effect.

(17)   In section 41(1) (maintenance of registers)—

(a)   after the words 'prescribed particulars of' there shall be inserted the words 'or relating to';

(b)   the following provisions shall cease to have effect—

(i)   in paragraph (c) (information contained in registers) the words '(except section 40(4))';

(ii)   in paragraph (d) (duty to maintain registers of samples of effluent), sub-paragraph (ii); and

(iii)   paragraph (e) (duty to register certain notices);

(c)   there shall be added at the end the following paragraphs—

'(f)   enforcement notices served under section 49A of this Act;

(g)   directions given by the Secretary of State in relation to SEPA's functions under this Part of this Act;

(h)   convictions, for offences under this Part of this Act, of persons
who have the benefit of consents under section 34 of this Act;

(j)   information obtained or furnished in pursuance of conditions of such consents;

(k)   works notices under section 46A of this Act;

(l)   appeals under section 46C of this Act;

(m)   convictions for offences under section 46D of this Act; and

(n)   such other matters relating to the quality of water as may be prescribed.'

(18)   In section 41(2) (registers to be available for inspection by, and facilities for obtaining copies of entries to be afforded to, the public), after paragraph (b) there shall be added the words—

'and, for the purposes of this subsection, places may be prescribed at which any such registers or facilities as are mentioned in paragraph (a) or (b) above are to be available or afforded to the public in pursuance of the paragraph in question.'

(19)   At the end of section 41 there shall be added the following subsection—

'(3)   The Secretary of State may give SEPA directions requiring the removal from any register maintained by it under this section of any specified information which is not prescribed for inclusion under subsection (1) of this section or which, by virtue of section 42A or 42B of this Act, ought to have been excluded from the registers.'

(20)   For section 42, there shall be substituted the following sections—

'42A.   Exclusion from registers of information affecting national security

(1)   No information shall be included in a register kept or maintained by SEPA under section 41 of this Act if and so long as, in the opinion of the Secretary of State, the inclusion in such a register of that information, or information of that description, would be contrary to the interests of national security.

(2)   The Secretary of State may, for the purposes of securing the exclusion from registers of information to which subsection (1) of this section applies, give SEPA directions—

(a)   specifying information, or descriptions of information, to be excluded from their registers; or

(b)   specifying descriptions of information to be referred to the Secretary of State for his determination;

and no information to be referred to the Secretary of State in pursuance of paragraph (b) of this subsection shall be included in any such register until the Secretary of State determines that it should be so included.

(3)   SEPA shall notify the Secretary of State of any information it excludes from a register in pursuance of directions under subsection (2) of this section.

(4)   A person may, as respects any information which appears to him to be information to which subsection (1) of this section may apply, give a notice to the Secretary of State specifying the information and indicating its apparent nature; and, if he does so—

(a)   he shall notify SEPA that he has done so; and

(b)   no information so notified to the Secretary of State shall be included in any such register until the Secretary of State has determined that it should be so included.

42B.   Exclusion from registers of certain confidential information

(1)   No information relating to the affairs of any individual or business shall, without the consent of that individual or the person for the time being carrying on that business, be included in a register kept or maintained by SEPA under section 41 of this Act, if and so long as the information—

(a)   is, in relation to him, commercially confidential; and

(b)   is not required to be included in the register in pursuance of directions under subsection (7) of this section;

but information is not commercially confidential for the purposes of this section unless it is determined under this section to be so by SEPA, or, on appeal, by the Secretary of State.

(2)   Where information is furnished to SEPA for the purpose of—

(a)   an application for a consent under section 34 of this Act;

(b)   complying with any condition of such a consent; or

(c) complying with a notice under section 93 of this Act,

then, if the person furnishing it applies to SEPA to have the information excluded from any register kept or maintained by SEPA under section 41 of this Act, on the ground that it is commercially confidential (as regards himself or another person), SEPA shall determine whether the information is or is not commercially confidential.

(3)   A determination under subsection (2) of this section must be made within the period of fourteen days beginning with the date of the application and if SEPA fails to make a determination within that period it shall be treated as having determined that the information is commercially confidential.

(4)   Where it appears to SEPA that any information (other than information furnished in circumstances within subsection (2) of this section) which has been obtained by SEPA under or by virtue of any provision of any enactment might be commercially confidential, SEPA shall—

(a)   give to the person to whom or whose business it relates notice that that information is required to be included in a register kept or maintained by SEPA under section 41 of this Act, unless excluded under this section; and

(b)   give him a reasonable opportunity—

(i)   of objecting to the inclusion of the information on the ground that it is commercially confidential; and

(ii)   of making representations to SEPA for the purpose of justifying any such objection;

and, if any representations are made, SEPA shall, having taken the representations into account, determine whether the information is or is not commercially confidential.

(5)   Where, under subsection (2) or (4) of this section, SEPA determines that information is not commercially confidential—

(a)   the information shall not be entered on the register until the end of the period of twenty-one days beginning with the date on which the determination is notified to the person concerned; and

(b)   that person may appeal to the Secretary of State against the decision;

and, where an appeal is brought in respect of any information, the information shall not be entered on the register pending the final determination or withdrawal of the appeal.

(6)   Subsections (2), (4) and (7) of section 49B of this Act shall apply in relation to appeals under subsection (5) of this section; but

(a)   subsection (4) of that section shall have effect for the purposes of this subsection with the substitution for the words from ('which may' onwards of the words '(which must be held in private)'; and

(b)   subsection (5) of this section is subject to section 114 of the Environment Act 1995 (delegation or reference of appeals etc).

(7)   The Secretary of State may give SEPA directions as to specified information, or descriptions of information, which the public interest requires to be included in registers kept or maintained by SEPA under section 41 of this Act notwithstanding that the information may be commercially confidential.

(8)   Information excluded from a register shall be treated as ceasing to be commercially confidential for the purposes of this section at the expiry of the period of four years beginning with the date of the determination by virtue of which it was excluded; but the person who furnished it may apply to SEPA for the information to remain excluded from

the register on the ground that it is still commercially confidential and SEPA shall determine whether or not that is the case.

(9)   Subsections (5) and (6) of this section shall apply in relation to a determination under subsection (8) of this section as they apply in relation to a determination under subsection (2) or (4) of this section.

(10)   The Secretary of State may prescribe the substitution (whether in all cases or in such classes or descriptions of case as may be prescribed) for the period for the time being specified in subsection (3) above of such other period as he considers appropriate.

(11)   Information is, for the purposes of any determination under this section, commercially confidential, in relation to any individual or person, if its being contained in a register would prejudice to an unreasonable degree the commercial interests of that individual or person.'

(21)   In section 46 (operations to remedy or forestall pollution of water)—

(a)   in subsection (1)—

(i)   at the beginning there shall be inserted the words 'Subject to subsection 1B) below,'; and

(ii)   the words 'in its area' where they first occur and 'in its area or elsewhere' shall cease to have effect;

(b)   after subsection (1) there shall be inserted—

'(1A)   In either case mentioned in subsection (1) of this section, SEPA shall be entitled to carry out investigations for the purpose of establishing the source of the matter and the identity of the person who has caused or knowingly permitted it to be present in controlled waters or at a place from which it was likely, in the opinion of SEPA, to enter controlled waters.

(1B)   Without prejudice to the power of SEPA to carry out investigations under subsection (1A) above, the power conferred by subsection (1) above to carry out operations shall be exercisable only in a case where—

(a)   SEPA considers it necessary to carry out forthwith any operations falling within paragraph (a) or (b) of subsection (1) above; or

(b)   it appears to SEPA, after reasonable inquiry, that no person can be found on whom to serve a works notice under section 46A of this Act.';

(c)   in subsection (2) after the words 'any operations' there shall be inserted the words 'or investigations';

(d)   in subsection (3)(b)—

(i)   after the words 'any operations' there shall be inserted the words 'or investigations'; and

(ii)   after the words 'an abandoned mine' there shall be inserted the words 'or an abandoned part of a mine'; and

(e)   after subsection (3) there shall be inserted—

'(3A)   Subsection (3)(b) of this section shall not apply to the owner or former operator of any mine or part of a mine if the mine or part in question became abandoned after 31st December 1999.

(3B)   Subsections (5) and (6) of section 30J above shall apply in relation to subsections (3) and (3A) above as they apply in relation to subsections (3) and (4) of that section.'.

(22)   After section 46 there shall be inserted the following sections—

'**46A   Notices requiring persons to carry out anti-pollution operations**

(1)   Subject to the following provisions of this section where it appears to SEPA that any poisonous, noxious or polluting matter or any solid waste matter is likely to enter, or to be or to have been present in, any controlled waters, SEPA shall be entitled to serve a works notice on any person who, as the case may be,—

(a)   caused or knowingly permitted the matter in question to be present at the place from which it is likely, in the opinion of SEPA, to enter any controlled waters; or

(b)   caused or knowingly permitted the matter in question to be present in any controlled waters.

(2)   For the purposes of this section, a "works notice" is a notice requiring the person on whom it is served to carry out such of the following operations as may be specified in the notice, that is to say—

(a)   in a case where the matter in question appears likely to enter any controlled waters, operations for the purpose of preventing it from doing so; or

(b)   in a case where the matter appears to be or to have been present in any controlled waters, operations for the purpose—

(i)   of removing or disposing of the matter;

(ii)   of remedying or mitigating any pollution caused by its presence in the waters; or

(iii)   so far as it is reasonably practicable to do so, of restoring the waters, including any flora and fauna dependent on the aquatic environment of the waters, to their state immediately before the matter became present in the waters.

(3)   A works notice—

(a)   must specify the periods within which the person on whom it is served is required to do each of the things specified in the notice; and

(b)   is without prejudice to the powers of SEPA by virtue of section 46(1B)(a) of this Act.

(4)   Before serving a works notice on any person, SEPA shall reasonably endeavour to consult that person concerning the operations which are to be specified in the notice.

(5)   The Secretary of State may by regulations make provision for or in connection with—

(a)   the form or content of works notices;

(b)   requirements for consultation, before the service of a works notice, with persons other than the person on whom that notice is to be served;

(c)   steps to be taken for the purposes of any consultation required under subsection (4) above or regulations made by virtue of paragraph (b) above; and

(d)   any other steps of a procedural nature which are to be taken in connection with, or in consequence of, the service of a works notice.

(6)   A works notice shall not be regarded as invalid, or as invalidly served, by reason only of any failure to comply with the requirements of subsection (4) above or of regulations made by virtue of paragraph (b) of subsection (5) above.

(7)   Nothing in subsection (1) above shall entitle SEPA to require the carrying out of any operations which would impede or prevent the making of any discharge in pursuance of a consent given by SEPA by virtue of section 34 of this Act.

(8)   No works notice shall be served on any person requiring him to carry out any operations in respect of water from an abandoned mine or an abandoned part of a mine which that person permitted to reach such a place as is mentioned in subsection (1)(a) above or to enter any controlled waters.

(9)   Subsection (8) above shall not apply to the owner or former operator of any mine or part of a mine if the mine or part in question became abandoned after 31st December 1999.

(10)   Subsections (5) and (6) of section 30J of this Act shall apply in relation to subsections (8) and (9) above as they apply in relation to subsections (3) and (4) of that section.

(11)   Where SEPA—

(a)   carries out any such investigations as are mentioned in section 46(1A) of this Act, and

(b)   serves a works notice on a person in connection with the matter to which the investigations relate, it shall (unless the notice is quashed or withdrawn) be entitled to recover the costs or expenses reasonably incurred in carrying out those investigations from that person.

(12) The Secretary of State may, if he thinks fit in relation to any person, give directions to SEPA as to whether or how it should exercise its powers under this section.

46B. Grant of, and compensation for, rights of entry etc.

(1) A works notice may require a person to carry out operations in relation to any land or waters notwithstanding that he is not entitled to carry out those operations.

(2) Any person whose consent is required before any operations required by a works notice may be carried out shall grant, or join in granting, such rights in relation to any land or waters as will enable the person on whom the works notice is served to comply with any requirements imposed by the works notice.

(3) Before serving a works notice, SEPA shall reasonably endeavour to consult every person who appears to it—

(a) to be the owner or occupier of any relevant land, and

(b) to be a person who might be required by subsection (2) above to grant, or join in granting, any rights,

concerning the rights which that person may be so required to grant.

(4) A works notice shall not be regarded as invalid, or as invalidly served, by reason only of any failure to comply with the requirements of subsection (3) above.

(5) A person who grants, or joins in granting, any rights pursuant to subsection (2) above shall be entitled, on making an application within such period as may be prescribed and in such manner as may be prescribed to such person as may be prescribed, to be paid by the person on whom the works notice in question is served compensation of such amount as may be determined in such manner as may be prescribed.

(6) Without prejudice to the generality of the regulations that may be made by virtue of subsection (5) above, regulations by virtue of that subsection may make such provision in relation to compensation under this section as may be made by regulations by virtue of subsection (4) of section 35A of the Environmental Protection Act 1990 in relation to compensation under that section.

(7) In this section

"relevant land" means—

(a) any land or waters in relation to which the works notice in question requires, or may require, operations to be carried out; or

(b) any land adjoining or adjacent to that land or those waters;

"works notice" means a works notice under section 46A of this Act.

46C. Appeals against works notices

(1) A person on whom a works notice is served may, within the period of twenty-one days beginning with the day on which the notice is served, appeal against the notice to the Secretary of State.

(2) On any appeal under this section the Secretary of State—

(a) shall quash the notice, if he is satisfied that there is a material defect in the notice; but

(b) subject to that, may confirm the notice, with or without modification, or quash it.

(3) The Secretary of State may by regulations make provision with respect to—

(a) the grounds on which appeals under this section may be made; or

(b) the procedure on any such appeal.

(4) Regulations under subsection (3) above may (among other things)—

(a) include provisions comparable to those in section 290 of the Public Health Act 1936 (appeals against notices requiring the execution of works);

(b) prescribe the cases in which a works notice is, or is not, to be suspended until the appeal is decided, or until some other stage in the proceedings;

(c)   prescribe the cases in which the decision on an appeal may in some respects be less favourable to the appellant than the works notice against which he is appealing;

(d)   prescribe the cases in which the appellant may claim that a works notice should have been served on some other person and prescribe the procedure to be followed in those cases;

(e)   make provision as respects—

(i)   the particulars to be included in the notice of appeal;

(ii)   the persons on whom notice of appeal is to be served and the particulars, if any, which are to accompany the notice; or

(iii)   the abandonment of an appeal.

(5)   In this section "works notice" means a works notice under section 46A of this Act.

(6)   This section is subject to section 114 of the Environment Act 1995 (delegation or reference of appeals).

46D.   Consequences of not complying with a works notice

(1)   If a person on whom SEPA serves a works notice fails to comply with any of the requirements of the notice, he shall be guilty of an offence.

(2)   A person who commits an offence under subsection (1) above shall be liable—

(a)   on summary conviction, to imprisonment for a term not exceeding three months or to a fine not exceeding £20,000 or to both;

(b)   on conviction on indictment, to imprisonment for a term not exceeding two years or to a fine or to both.

(3)   If a person on whom a works notice has been served fails to comply with any of the requirements of the notice, SEPA may do what that person was required to do and may recover from him any costs or expenses reasonably incurred by SEPA in doing it.

(4)   If SEPA is of the opinion that proceedings for an offence under subsection (1) above would afford an ineffectual remedy against a person who has failed to comply with the requirements of a works notice, SEPA may take proceedings in any court of competent jurisdiction for the purpose of securing compliance with the notice.

(5)   In this section 'works notice' means a works notice under section 46A of this Act.'.

(23)   In section 47 (duty to deal with waste from vessels etc.)—

(a)   in subsection (1) (duty), the words 'in its area' shall cease to have effect; and

(b)   in subsection (2) (provision of facilities), the words 'in the authority's area' shall cease to have effect.

(24)   In section 48(1) (power to exclude unregistered vessels from rivers etc.) the words 'in its area' shall cease to have effect.

(25)   In section 49 (deposit and vegetation in rivers etc) at the end there shall be added—

'(5)   This section is subject to section 114 of the Environment Act 1995 (delegation or reference of appeals).'

(26)   After that section there shall be inserted—

'49A.   Enforcement notices as respects discharge consents

(1)   If SEPA is of the opinion that the holder of a relevant consent is contravening any condition of the consent, or is likely to contravene any such condition, it may serve on him a notice (an "enforcement notice").

(2)   An enforcement notice shall—

(a)   state that SEPA is of the said opinion;

(b)   specify the matters constituting the contravention or the matters making it likely that the contravention will arise;

(c)   specify the steps that must be taken to remedy the contravention or, as the case may be, to remedy the matters making it likely that the contravention will arise; and

(d)   specify the period within which those steps must be taken.

(3) Any person who fails to comply with any requirement imposed by an enforcement notice shall be guilty of an offence and liable—

(a) on summary conviction, to imprisonment for a term not exceeding three months or to a fine not exceeding £20,000 or to both;

(b) on conviction on indictment, to imprisonment for a term not exceeding two years or to a fine or to both.

(4) If SEPA is the opinion that proceedings for an offence under subsection (3) above would afford an ineffectual remedy against a person who has failed to comply with the requirements of an enforcement notice, SEPA may take proceedings in any court of competent jurisdiction for the purpose of securing compliance with the notice.

(5) The Secretary of State may, if he thinks fit in relation to any person, give to SEPA directions as to whether it should exercise its powers under this section and as to the steps which must be taken.

(6) In this section—

"relevant consent" means a consent for the purposes of section 30J(7)(a), 34 or 49(1) of this Act; and

"the holder", in relation to a relevant consent, is the person who has the consent in question.

49B. Appeals against enforcement notices

(1) A person upon whom an enforcement notice has been served under section 49A of this Act may appeal to the Secretary of State.

(2) This section is subject to section 114 of the Environment Act 1995 (delegation or reference of appeals etc.).

(3) An appeal under this section shall, if and to the extent a requirement to do so is prescribed, be advertised in the manner prescribed.

(4) If either party to the appeal so requests or the Secretary of State so decides, an appeal shall be or continue in the form of a hearing (which may, if the person hearing the appeal so decides, be held, or held to any extent, in private).

(5) On the determination of an appeal under this section, the Secretary of State may either quash or affirm the enforcement notice and, if he affirms it, may do so either in its original form or with such modifications as he may in the circumstances think fit.

(6) The bringing of an appeal under this section shall not have the effect of suspending the operation of the notice appealed against.

(7) The period within which and the manner in which appeals under this section are to be brought and the manner in which they are to be considered shall be as prescribed.'

(27) In section 50 (investigation of water pollution problems arising from closures of mines) the words 'in its area' shall cease to have effect.

(28) Sections 53 (charges in respect of consents to certain discharges in Scotland), 54 (directions to the river purification authority), 55 (discharges by islands councils) and 56(4) (meaning of the area of a river purification authority) shall cease to have effect.

(29) In section 56(1) (interpretation of Part II), the following definition shall be inserted in the appropriate place in alphabetical order—

'"operations" includes works;'.

(30) In section 90(3) (establishment charges etc. in relation to Scotland), for the words from 'a river' to the end there shall be substituted the words 'SEPA'.

(31) Section 91(5)(a) (application of that section to Scotland) shall cease to have effect.

(32) In section 96(3) (local inquiries) the words from 'but as if' to the end shall cease to have effect.

(33) In section 98 (interpretation of Part V), for paragraph (b) of the definition of 'relevant authority' there shall be substituted —

'(b) in Scotland—

(i) as respects sections 91 and 92, a council constituted under section 2 of the Local Government etc. (Scotland) Act 1994; and

(ii)   as respects this Part other than those sections, the Secretary of State, SEPA or a council constituted under section 2 of the Local Government etc. (Scotland) Act 1994.'.

(34)   In section 104(1) (orders and regulations) the words '59' shall cease to have effect.

(35)   In section 105 (interpretation etc. — general) there shall be inserted in the appropriate place—

'"SEPA" means the Scottish Environment Protection Agency;'.

The Health and Safety at Work etc. Act 1974

30.—(1)   The Health and Safety at Work etc. Act 1974 (in this paragraph referred to as 'the 1974 Act') shall have effect in accordance with the following provisions of this paragraph.

(2)   The appropriate new Agency shall, in consequence of the transfer effected by virtue of section 2(2)(c) or, as the case may be, 21(2)(a) of this Act, be regarded for the purposes of Part I of the 1974 Act as the authority which is, by any of the relevant statutory provisions, made responsible in relation to England and Wales or, as the case may be, Scotland for the enforcement of the relevant enactments (and, accordingly, as the enforcing authority in relation to those enactments).

(3)   Neither the Agency nor SEPA shall have power to appoint inspectors under section 19 of the 1974 Act.

(4)   Sections 21 to 23 (improvement notices and prohibition notices) shall have effect in any case where the relevant statutory provision in question is any of the relevant enactments as if references in those sections to an inspector were references to the appropriate new Agency.

(5)   Section 27 (obtaining of information by the Commission etc) shall have effect in relation to the appropriate new Agency, in its relevant capacity, as it has effect in relation to the Health and Safety Commission (and not as it has effect in relation to an enforcing authority), except that the consent of the Secretary of State shall not be required to the service by the appropriate new Agency of a notice under subsection (1) of that section; and, accordingly, where that section has effect by virtue of this sub-paragraph—

(a)   any reference in that section to the Commission shall be construed as a reference to the appropriate new Agency;

(b)   any reference to an enforcing authority shall be disregarded; and

(c)   in subsection (3) of that section, the words from 'and also' onwards shall be disregarded.

(6)   In section 28 (restrictions on disclosure of information)—

(a)   in paragraph (a) of subsection (3) (exception for disclosure of information to certain bodies) after the words 'the Executive,' there shall be inserted the words 'the Environment Agency, the Scottish Environment Protection Agency,';

(b)   in paragraph (c)(ii) of that subsection (exception for disclosure to officers of certain bodies) as it applies to England and Wales—

(i)   the words 'of the National Rivers Authority or', and

(ii)   the word 'Authority,' (where next occurring), shall be omitted;

(c)   for paragraph (c)(ii) of that subsection as it applies to Scotland there shall be substituted—

'(ii)   an officer of a water undertaker, sewerage undertaker, sewerage authority or water authority who is authorised by that authority to receive it;';

(d)   paragraph (c)(iii) of that subsection (exception for disclosure to officers of river purification boards) shall cease to have effect;

(e)   in subsection (4) (references to certain bodies to include references to officers or inspectors), after the words 'the Executive' (in the first place where they occur) there shall be inserted the words 'the Environment Agency, the Scottish Environment Protection Agency,';

(f) in subsection (5) (information disclosed in pursuance of subsection (3) not to be used by recipient except for specified purposes)—

(i) in paragraph (a) (use for a purpose of the Executive etc) after the words 'of the Executive or' there shall be inserted the words 'of the Environment Agency or of the Scottish Environment Protection Agency or';

(ii) in paragraph (b) as it applies to England and Wales (use for the purposes of certain bodies of information given to officers of those bodies), the words 'the National Rivers Authority' shall be omitted;

(iii) in the said paragraph (b) as it applies to Scotland, for the words from the beginning to 'in connection' there shall be substituted the words 'in the case of information given to an officer of a body which is a local authority, a water undertaker, a sewerage undertaker, a sewerage authority or a water authority the purposes of the body in connection'.

(7) In section 38 (restriction on institution of proceedings in England and Wales) after the words 'except by an inspector or' there shall be inserted the words 'the Environment Agency or'.

(8) In this paragraph—

'the appropriate new Agency' means—

(a) in relation to England and Wales, the Agency; and

(b) in relation to Scotland, SEPA;

'relevant capacity', in relation to the appropriate new Agency, means its capacity as the enforcing authority, for the purposes of Part I of the 1974 Act, which is responsible in relation to England and Wales or, as the case may be, Scotland for the enforcement of the relevant enactments;

'the relevant enactments' means the Alkali, &c, Works Regulation Act 1906 and section 5 of the 1974 Act;

'the relevant statutory provisions' has the same meaning as in Part I of the 1974 Act.

The House of Commons Disqualification Act 1975 and the Northern Ireland Assembly Disqualification Act 1975

31. In Part II of Schedule 1 to the House of Commons Disqualification Act 1975 (bodies of which all members are disqualified for membership of the House of Commons) the following entries shall be inserted at the appropriate places—

(a) 'The Environment Agency.';

(b) 'The Scottish Environment Protection Agency.';

and the like insertions shall be made in Part II of Schedule 1 to the Northern Ireland Assembly Disqualification Act 1975 (bodies of which all members are disqualified for membership of the Northern Ireland Assembly).

The Local Government (Scotland) Act 1975

32.—(1) The Local Government (Scotland) Act 1975 shall be amended in accordance with the following provisions.

(2) In section 16 (borrowing and lending by local authorities and certain other bodies)—

(a) after the words 'local authorities' there shall be inserted the word 'and';

(b) the words 'and river purification boards' shall cease to have effect.

(3) In Schedule 3 (further provision relating to borrowing and lending by local authorities and certain other bodies) in paragraph 28—

(a) in sub-paragraph (1)—

(i) after the word 'money' there shall be inserted the word 'and';

(ii) the words 'or a river purification board,' shall cease to have effect;

(b) in sub-paragraph (2) for sub-paragraph (a) there shall be substituted—

'(a) a joint board; and'.

The Local Government (Miscellaneous Provisions) Act 1976

33.　In section 44 of the Local Government (Miscellaneous Provisions) Act 1976 (interpretation of Part I of that Act) after subsection (1A) (certain provisions of that Act, including section 16 (obtaining information about land), to have effect as if the Broads Authority were a local authority) there shall be inserted—

'(1B)　Section 16 of this Act shall have effect as if the Environment Agency were a local authority.'.

The Water (Scotland) Act 1980

34.—(1)　The Water (Scotland) Act 1980 shall be amended in accordance with the following provisions of this paragraph.

(2)　In section 31(1) (consultation where limits of water supply adjoin any part of England) for paragraph (b) there shall be substituted—

'(b)　the Scottish Environment Protection Agency.'

(3)　In section 33(3)(a) (notice of temporary discharge of water into watercourses)—

(a)　sub-paragraph (ii) and the preceding 'and' shall cease to have effect; and

(b)　at the end of the paragraph there shall be inserted—

'and

(ii)　to the Scottish Environment Protection Agency.'

(4)　In section 109(1) (interpretation) the definitions of 'river purification authority' and 'river purification board' shall cease to have effect.

(5)　In Schedule 1—

(a)　in paragraph 2(ii) for the words following 'section 17(2)' to the end there shall be substituted the words 'on the Scottish Environment Protection Agency';

(b)　in paragraph 11(ii) the words 'and any river purification authority' shall cease to have effect and at the end there shall be added the words 'and on the Scottish Environment Protection Agency';

(c)　in paragraph 19 for the words following 'any fishery district' to the words 'any public undertakers' there shall be substituted the words 'any navigation authority exercising jurisdiction in relation to any watercourse from which water is proposed to be taken under the rights to be acquired, the Scottish Environment Protection Agency and any public undertakers'.

The Criminal Justice (Scotland) Act 1980

35.　In Schedule 1 to the Criminal Justice (Scotland) Act 1980 (sufficiency of evidence by certificate in certain routine matters) in the entry relating to the Control of Pollution Act 1974—

(a)　for the words from 'Section 31(1)' to 'such waters etc)' there shall be substituted the words 'Section 30F (pollution offences)'; and

(b)　for the words 'a river purification authority (within the meaning of that Act)' there shall be substituted the words 'the Scottish Environment Protection Agency'.

The Road Traffic Regulation Act 1984

36.—(1)　In section 1 of the Road Traffic Regulation Act 1984 (traffic regulation orders outside Greater London) in subsection (1), after paragraph (f) (which allows a traffic regulation order to be made for preserving or improving the amenities of the area through which the road runs) there shall be added 'or

(g)　for any of the purposes specified in paragraphs (a) to (c) of subsection (1) of section 87 of the Environment Act 1995 (air quality).'

(2)　In section 6 of that Act (orders similar to traffic regulation orders in Greater London) in subsection (1)(b) (which allows orders in Greater London to be made for equivalent purposes to those in section 1(1)(a) to (f) of that Act) for the words '(a) to (f)' there shall be substituted the words '(a) to (g)'.

(3) In section 122(2) of that Act (matters to which, so far as practicable, regard is to be had by local authorities in exercising their functions under the Act) after paragraph (b) there shall be inserted—

'(bb) the strategy prepared under section 80 of the Environment Act 1995 (national air quality strategy);'.

The Control of Pollution (Amendment) Act 1989

37.—(1) The Control of Pollution (Amendment) Act 1989 shall be amended in accordance with the following provisions of this paragraph.

(2) In section 2 (registration of carriers)—

(a) in subsection (3), without prejudice to the power of regulation authorities to impose a charge in respect of their consideration of any such application, paragraph (e) (power to require them to impose such charges) shall cease to have effect; and

(b) after that subsection there shall be added—

'(3A) Without prejudice to the generality of paragraphs (b) and (d) of subsection (3) above—

(a) the power to prescribe a form under paragraph (b) of that subsection includes power to require an application to be made on any form of any description supplied for the purpose by the regulation authority to which the application is to be made; and

(b) the power to impose requirements with respect to information under paragraph (d) of that subsection includes power to make provision requiring an application to be accompanied by such information as may reasonably be required by the regulation authority to which it is to be made.'

(3) In section 4 (appeals to the Secretary of State against refusal of registration etc) after subsection (8) there shall be added—

'(9) This section is subject to section 114 of the Environment Act 1995 (delegation or reference of appeals etc).

(4) In section 6 (seizure and disposal of vehicles used for illegal waste disposal) for subsection (6) there shall be substituted—

'(6) Regulations under this section shall not authorise a regulation authority to sell or destroy any property or to deposit any property at any place unless—

(a) the following conditions are satisfied, that is to say—

(i) the authority have published such notice, and taken such other steps (if any), as may be prescribed for informing persons who may be entitled to the property that it has been seized and is available to be claimed; and

(ii) the prescribed period has expired without any obligation arising under the regulations for the regulation authority to return the property to any person; or

(b) the condition of the property requires it to be disposed of without delay.'

(5) In section 7 (further enforcement provisions) in subsection (1) (which applies certain provisions of the Environmental Protection Act 1990) for the words 'sections 68(3), (4) and (5), 69, 70 and 71' there shall be substituted the words 'section 71'.

(6) Subsection (2) of that section (disclosure of information between certain authorities) shall cease to have effect.

(7) Subsection (8) of that section (which applies section 72 of the 1990 Act) shall cease to have effect.

(8) In section 9, for the definition of 'regulation authority' there shall be substituted—

''"regulation authority" means—

(a) in relation to England and Wales, the Environment Agency; and

(b) in relation to Scotland, the Scottish Environment Protection Agency;

and any reference to the area of a regulation authority shall accordingly be construed as a reference to any area in England and Wales or, as the case may be, in Scotland;'.

The Electricity Act 1989

38.—(1)   Section 3 of the Electricity Act 1989 (general duties of the Secretary of State and the Director General of Electricity Supply when exercising certain functions) shall be amended in accordance with the following provisions of this paragraph.

(2)   In subsection (1)(c) (duty, subject to subsection (2), to promote competition), for the words 'subsection (2)' there shall be substituted the words 'subsections (2) and (2A)'.

(3)   After subsection (2) (duties as regards the supply of electricity in Scotland in certain cases) there shall be inserted—

'(2A)   If an order under section 32(1) below requires a public electricity supplier to make, or produce evidence showing that he has made, arrangements or additional arrangements which will secure the result mentioned in subsection (2B) below, the order, so far as relating to any such requirement, may be made for the purpose of, or for purposes which include, promoting the supply to any premises of—

   (a)   heat produced in association with electricity, or

   (b)   steam produced from, or air or water heated by, such heat.

(2B)   The result referred to in subsection (2A) above is that, for a period specified in the order, there will be available to the public electricity supplier—

   (a)   from combined heat and power stations; or

   (b)   from combined heat and power stations of any particular description,

an aggregate amount of generating capacity which is not less than that specified in relation to him in the order.

(2C)   In subsection (2B) above, "combined heat and power station" has the meaning given by section 32(8) below.'.

(4)   In subsection (3) (further duties), for the words 'and (2)' there shall be substituted the words ', (2) and (2A)'.

39.—(1)   Section 32 of that Act (electricity from non-fossil fuel sources) shall be amended in accordance with the following provisions of this paragraph.

(2)   After subsection (2) (result to be secured by arrangements made pursuant to an order under subsection (1)) there shall be inserted—

'(2A)   For the purposes of this section—

   (a)   combined heat and power stations generally; and

   (b)   combined heat and power stations of any particular description,

are to be taken as being particular descriptions of non-fossil fuel generating stations.

(2B)   A particular description of combined heat and power stations may be described by reference to, or by reference to matters which include—

   (a)   the heat or, as the case may be, the steam or heated air or water to be supplied from the station to any premises;

   (b)   any premises to which any such heat, steam or heated air or water is to be supplied (including, without prejudice to the generality of the foregoing, the use to which any such premises are put);

   (c)   the means or method by which any such heat, steam or heated air or water is to be supplied to any premises (including, without prejudice to the generality of the foregoing, any system or network of supply or distribution); or

   (d)   the arrangements (including financial or contractual arrangements) under which any such heat, steam or heated air or water is to be supplied to any premises.

(2C)   Subsections (2A) and (2B) above are without prejudice to—

   (a)   the generality of subsection (2)(b) above, or

   (b)   section 111(2) below;

and subsection (2B) above is without prejudice to the generality of subsection (2A)(b) above.'.

(3)   In subsection (8) (interpretation), after the definition of 'coal products' there shall be inserted—

'combined heat and power station' means a non-fossil fuel generating station which is (or may be) operated for purposes including the supply to any premises of—

    (a)   heat produced in association with electricity, or

    (b)   steam produced from, or air or water heated by, such heat;'.

40.   In Schedule 4 to that Act (other powers etc. of licence holders) in paragraph 4(1)(b) (power for certain bodies to execute works involving alterations of electric lines or plant) for the words 'National Rivers Authority' there shall be substituted the words 'Environment Agency'.

41.   In Schedule 5 to that Act (water rights) in paragraph 8(b) for the words 'river purification authority within whose area the watercourse or loch affected is situated' there shall be substituted the words 'Scottish Environment Protection Agency'.

The Town and Country Planning Act 1990

42.   In section 2 of the Town and Country Planning Act 1990 (joint planning boards for National Parks and other areas) after subsection (6) there shall be inserted—

'(6A)   Section 241 of the Local Government Act 1972 shall be taken to authorise the application to a joint planning board, subject to any necessary modifications, of any provisions of Part III (accounts and audit) of the Local Government Finance Act 1982 (as well as of any provisions of the Local Government Act 1972) by such an order as is mentioned in subsection (6) above.'

43.   In Schedule 5 to that Act (conditions relating to mineral working) in paragraph 4 (consultations) after sub-paragraph (4) there shall be inserted—

'(4A)   Without prejudice to the application of this paragraph in relation to consultation with the Forestry Commission, where the Minister is consulted pursuant to any provision of this paragraph—

    (a)   he is not required to inspect any land or to express a view on any matter or question; and

    (b)   he is not precluded from responding in general terms or otherwise in terms which are not specific to the land in question.'.

44.   In Schedule 6 to that Act (determination of certain appeals by person appointed by the Secretary of State) in paragraph 1(1) (power, in respect of appeals under certain provisions, to prescribe classes of appeals to be determined by an appointed person instead of by the Secretary of State), after '208,' there shall be inserted 'and paragraphs 6(11) and (12) and 11(1) of Schedule 13 and paragraph 9(1) of Schedule 14 to the Environment Act 1995,'.

The Environmental Protection Act 1990

45.—(1)   Section 1 of the Environmental Protection Act 1990 (interpretation of Part I) shall be amended in accordance with the following provisions of this paragraph.

(2)   In subsection (7) (definition of 'enforcing authority' in relation to England and Wales), for the words 'the chief inspector or the local authority by whom' there shall be substituted the words 'the Environment Agency or the local authority by which'.

(3)   For subsection (8) (definition of 'enforcing authority' in relation to Scotland) there shall be substituted—

'(8)   In relation to Scotland, references to the ''enforcing authority'' and a ''local enforcing authority'' are references to the Scottish Environment Protection Agency (in this Part referred to as ''SEPA'').'

(4)   After subsection (13) there shall be added—

'(14)   In this Part "the appropriate Agency" means—

(a)   in relation to England and Wales, the Environment Agency; and

(b)   in relation to Scotland, SEPA.'

46.—(1)   Section 4 of that Act (determination of authority by whom functions are exercisable) shall be amended in accordance with the following provisions of this paragraph.

(2)   In subsection (2) (functions of the chief inspector etc in relation to prescribed processes designated for central control) for the words 'the chief inspector appointed for England and Wales by the Secretary of State under section 16 below and, in relation to Scotland, of the chief inspector so appointed for Scotland or of the river purification authority, as determined under regulations made under section 5(1) below' there shall be substituted the words 'the appropriate Agency'.

(3)   In subsection (3) (discharge of functions designated for local control) for paragraphs (a) and (b) there shall be substituted—

'(a)   in the case of a prescribed process carried on (or to be carried on) by means of a mobile plant, where the person carrying on the process has his principal place of business—

(i)   in England and Wales, the local authority in whose area that place of business is;

(ii)   in Scotland, SEPA;

(b)   in any other cases, where the prescribed processes are (or are to be) carried on—

(i)   in England and Wales, the local authority in whose area they are (or are to be) carried on;

(ii)   in Scotland, SEPA;'.

(4)   In subsection (4) (directions transferring functions to the chief inspector) for the words 'the chief inspector' there shall be substituted the words 'the Environment Agency'.

(5)   After that subsection there shall be inserted—

'(4A)   In England and Wales, a local authority, in exercising the functions conferred or imposed on it under this Part by virtue of subsection (3) above, shall have regard to the strategy for the time being published pursuant to section 80 of the Environment Act 1995.'

(6)   In subsection (5) (effect of such a transfer)—

(a)   for the words 'the chief inspector' there shall be substituted the words 'the Environment Agency'; and

(b)   for the word 'him' there shall be substituted the words 'that Agency'.

(7)   In subsection (8) (giving or withdrawal of directions)—

(a)   for the words 'the chief inspector' in each place where they occur there shall be substituted the words 'the Environment Agency'; and

(b)   the words 'or, as the case may be, in the Edinburgh Gazette', in each place where they occur, shall be omitted.

(8)   After subsection (8) there shall be inserted—

'(8A)   The requirements of sub-paragraph (ii) of paragraph (a) or, as the case may be, of paragraph (b) of subsection (8) above shall not apply in any case where, in the opinion of the Secretary of State, the publication of notice in accordance with that sub-paragraph would be contrary to the interests of national security.

(8B)   Subsections (4) to (8A) shall not apply to Scotland.'

(9)   For subsection (9) (which, among other things, imposed a duty on the chief inspector etc to follow developments in technology etc and which is partly superseded by this Act) there shall be substituted—

'(9)   It shall be the duty of local authorities to follow such developments in technology and techniques for preventing or reducing pollution of the environment due to releases of substances from prescribed processes as concern releases into the air of substances from prescribed processes designated for local control.'

(10)   In subsection (10) (duty of chief inspector etc to give effect to directions) for the words 'the chief inspector, river purification authorities' there shall be substituted the words 'the Environment Agency, SEPA'.

(11)   In subsection (11) (meaning of 'local authority')—

(a)   at the beginning of paragraph (b) there shall be inserted the words 'in England and Wales,' and

(b)   paragraph (c) and the word 'and' immediately preceding it shall cease to have effect.

47.   Section 5 of that Act (further provision for Scotland as to discharge and scope of functions) shall cease to have effect.

48.   In section 6 of that Act, in subsection (2) (fee payable on application for authorisation) after the words 'shall be accompanied by' there shall be inserted—

'(a)   in a case where, by virtue of section 41 of the Environment Act 1995, a charge prescribed by a charging scheme under that section is required to be paid to the appropriate Agency in respect of the application, the charge so prescribed; or

(b)   in any other case,'.

49.—(1)   In section 7 of that Act (conditions of authorisations) in subsection (9) the words from 'and, in relation to Scotland,' to the end of the subsection shall be omitted.

(2)   At the end of subsection (12) of that section (defintion of 'relevant enactments' for the purposes of subsection (2)) there shall be added '; and

(g)   section 87 of the Environment Act 1995.'.

50.—(1)   Section 8 of that Act (fees and charges for authorisations) shall be amended in accordance with the following provisions of this paragraph.

(2)   In subsection (1) (payments to be charged by, or paid to, the enforcing authority in accordance with schemes), for the words 'enforcing authority' there shall be substituted the words 'local enforcing authority'.

(3)   Subsection (4) (separate schemes for different descriptions of enforcing authority) shall cease to have effect.

(4)   In subsection (7) (meaning of 'relevant expenditure attributable to authorisations')—

(a)   for the words 'enforcing authorities' there shall be substituted the words 'local enforcing authorities'; and

(b)   the words from 'together with the expenditure incurred by the National Rivers Authority' onwards shall be omitted.

(5)   In subsection (8) (power to revoke authorisation for non-payment of charge), for the words 'enforcing authority' there shall be substituted the words 'local enforcing authority'.

(6)   Subsection (9) (payments by the Secretary of State to the National Rivers Authority) shall cease to have effect.

(7)   For subsections (10) and (11) (special provision as respects Scotland) there shall be substituted—

'(10)   The foregoing provisions of this section shall not apply to Scotland.'

51.—(1)   Section 10 of that Act (variation of authorisations by enforcing authority) shall be amended in accordance with the following provisions of this paragraph.

(2)   In subsection (3) (which provides for the variation specified in a variation notice to take effect on the date so specified unless the notice is withdrawn) after the words 'unless the notice is withdrawn' there shall be inserted the words 'or is varied under subsection (3A) below'.

(3)   After that subsection there shall be inserted—

'(3A)   An enforcing authority which has served a variation notice may vary that notice by serving on the holder of the authorisation in question a further notice—

(a) specifying the variations which the enforcing authority has decided to make to the variation notice; and

(b) specifying the date or dates on which the variations specified in the variation notice, as varied by the further notice, are to take effect;

and any reference in this Part to a variation notice, or to a variation notice served under subsection (2) above, includes a reference to such a notice as varied by a further notice served under this subsection.'

(4) In subsection (4) of that section, for paragraph (b) (requirement to pay the fee prescribed under section 8 of that Act) there shall be substituted—

'(b) require the holder to pay, within such period as may be specified in the notice,—

(i) in a case where the enforcing authority is the Environment Agency or SEPA, the charge (if any) prescribed for the purpose by a charging scheme under section 41 of the Environment Act 1995; or

(ii) in any other case, the fee (if any) prescribed by a scheme under section 8 above.'

(5) In subsection (8) of that section, in the definition of 'vary', after the word '"vary"' there shall be inserted '(a)' and after the words 'any of them;' there shall be added the words 'and

(b) in relation to a variation notice, means adding to, or varying or rescinding the notice or any of its contents;'.

52. In section 11 of that Act (application by holders of authorisations for variation of conditions etc) for subsection (9) (fees) there shall be substituted—

'(9) Any application to the enforcing authority under this section shall be accompanied—

(a) in a case where the enforcing authority is the Environment Agency or SEPA, by the charge (if any) prescribed for the purpose by a charging scheme under section 41 of the Environment Act 1995; or

(b) in any other case, by the fee (if any) prescribed by a scheme under section 8 above.'

53. At the end of section 13 of that Act (enforcement notices) there shall be added—

'(4) The enforcing authority may, as respects any enforcement notice it has issued to any person, by notice in writing served on that person, withdraw the notice.'

54.—(1) Section 15 of that Act (appeals against certain authorisations and notices) shall be amended in accordance with the following provisions of this paragraph.

(2) In subsection (2) (appeals against variation notices, enforcement notices or prohibition notices to the Secretary of State) after the words 'to the Secretary of State' there shall be added the words '(except where the notice implements a direction of his).'

(3) For subsection (3) (reference of matters involved in appeals under that section to, and determination of such appeals by, persons appointed by the Secretary of State) there shall be substituted—

'(3) This section is subject to section 114 of the Environment Act 1995 (delegation or reference of appeals etc).'

(4) For subsection (5) (hearings) there shall be substituted—

'(5) Before determining an appeal under this section, the Secretary of State may, if he thinks fit—

(a) cause the appeal to take or continue in the form of a hearing (which may, if the person hearing the appeal so decides, be held, or held to any extent, in private); or

(b) cause a local inquiry to be held;

and the Secretary of State shall act as mentioned in paragraph (a) or (b) above if a request is made by either party to the appeal to be heard with respect to the appeal.'

(5)   In subsection (10) (regulations about appeals) after paragraph (b) there shall be added—

'and any such regulations may make different provision for different cases or different circumstances.'

55.   Sections 16 to 18 of that Act (appointment of inspectors, powers of inspectors and others and power to deal with cause of imminent danger of serious harm) shall cease to have effect.

56.   In section 19 of that Act (obtaining of information from persons and authorities) in subsection (2) (power of specified authorities by notice in writing to require provision of information)—

(a)   for paragraphs (c) and (d) (the chief inspector and river purification authorities) there shall be substituted—

'(c)   the Environment Agency, and

(d)   SEPA,'; and

(b)   after the words 'service of the notice' there shall be inserted the words ', or at such time,'.

57.—(1)   Section 20 of that Act (public registers of information) shall be amended in accordance with the following provisions of this paragraph.

(2)   In subsection (2) (local registers also to contain prescribed particulars of relevance to the area which are contained in central registers) after the word 'authority', where it first occurs, there shall be inserted the words 'in England and Wales' and for the words 'the chief inspector or river purification authority', in each place where they occur, there shall be substituted the words 'the Environment Agency'.

(3)   Subsection (3) (registers in Scotland) shall cease to have effect.

(4)   In subsection (4) (port health authorities) after the word 'authority' where it first occurs there shall be inserted the words 'in England and Wales' and for the words 'the chief inspector' there shall be substituted the words 'the Environment Agency'.

(5)   In subsection (7) (registers to be available for inspection by, and facilities for obtaining copies of entries to be afforded to, the public) after paragraph (b) there shall be added the words—

'and, for the purposes of this subsection, places may be prescribed by the Secretary of State at which any such registers or facilities as are mentioned in paragraph (a) or (b) above are to be available or afforded to the public in pursuance of the paragraph in question.'

(6)   Subsection (9) (duty to furnish the National Rivers Authority with information for purposes of its register) shall cease to have effect.

58.—(1)   Section 22 of that Act (exclusion from registers of certain confidential information) shall be amended in accordance with the following provisions of this paragraph.

(2)   In subsection (5) (information not to be entered on the register until expiration of certain time limits)—

(a)   in paragraph (a), for the words 'on the register' there shall be substituted the words 'in the register'; and

(b)   in the words following paragraph (b), for the words from 'on the register' onwards there shall be substituted the words 'in the register until the end of the period of seven days following the day on which the appeal is finally determined or withdrawn'.

(3)   For subsection (6) (which applies subsections (3), (5) and (10) of section 15 in relation to appeals to the Secretary of State against decisions that information is not commercially confidential) there shall be substituted—

'(6) Subsections (5) and (10) of section 15 above shall apply in relation to an appeal under subsection (5) above as they apply in relation to an appeal under that section, but—

(a) subsection (5) of that section shall have effect for the purposes of this subsection with the substitution for the words from "(which may" onwards of the words "(which must be held in private)"; and

(b) subsection (5) above is subject to section 114 of the Environment Act 1995 (delegation or reference of appeals etc).'

59.—(1) Section 23 of that Act (offences) shall be amended in accordance with the following provisions of this paragraph.

(2) In subsection (1) (offences) paragraphs (d) to (f) and (k) shall cease to have effect.

(3) In subsection (2)(a) (which provides for a fine not exceeding £20,000 on summary conviction of any offence under section 23(i)(a), (c) or (l)) after the words '£20,000' there shall be inserted the words 'or to imprisonment for a term not exceeding three months, or to both'.

(4) Subsection (4) (punishment for offences under paragraph (d), (e), (f) or (k) of subsection (l)) shall cease to have effect.

(5) Subsection (5) (right of inspector to prosecute before a magistrates' court if authorised to do so by the Secretary of State) shall cease to have effect.

60.—(1) In section 27 of that Act (power of chief inspector etc to remedy harm) in subsection (1), for the words 'the chief inspector or, in Scotland, a river purification authority' there shall be substituted the words 'the appropriate Agency'.

(2) In subsection (2) of that section (powers not to be exercised without the Secretary of State's written approval) for the words from 'The chief inspector' to 'their' there shall be substituted the words 'The Environment Agency or SEPA, as the case may be, shall not exercise its'.

61.—(1) In section 28 of that Act, in subsection (1) (which includes provision that the enforcing authority shall notify the waste regulation authority if a process involves final disposal of controlled waste by deposit in or on land) the words from 'but the enforcing authority shall notify' onwards shall cease to have effect.

(2) Subsections (3) and (4) of that section (which involve liaison between the enforcing authority and the National Rivers Authority) shall cease to have effect.

62.—(1) Section 30 of that Act (authorities for purposes of Part II) shall be amended in accordance with the following provisions of this paragraph.

(2) For subsection (1) (waste regulation authorities) there shall be substituted—

'(1) Any reference in this Part to a waste regulation authority—

(a) in relation to England and Wales, is a reference to the Environment Agency; and

(b) in relation to Scotland, is a reference to the Scottish Environment Protection Agency;

and any reference in this Part to the area of a waste regulation authority shall accordingly be taken as a reference to the area over which the Environment Agency or the Scottish Environment Protection Agency, as the case may be, exercises its functions or, in the case of any particular function, the function in question.'

(3) In subsection (4) of that section (construction of references to authorities constituted as particular descriptions of authority and provision for the section to be subject to orders under section 10 of the Local Government Act 1985 establishing authorities for certain purposes)—

(a) the words 'or regulation', and

(b) the words from 'establishing authorities' onwards,

shall cease to have effect.

(4) Subsections (6) (definition of 'river purification authority'), (7) and (8) (which relate to authorities which are both waste disposal and waste regulation authorities) shall cease to have effect.

63. Section 31 of that Act (power to create regional authorities for purposes of waste regulation) shall cease to have effect.

64. In section 33 of that Act (prohibition on unauthorised or harmful deposit, treatment or disposal etc of waste) in subsection (7) (defences) for paragraph (c) there shall be substituted—

'(c) that the acts alleged to constitute the contravention were done in an emergency in order to avoid danger to human health in a case where—

    (i) he took all such steps as were reasonably practicable in the circumstances for minimising pollution of the environment and harm to human health; and

    (ii) particulars of the acts were furnished to the waste regulation authority as soon as reasonably practicable after they were done.'

65. In section 34 of that Act (duty of care etc as respects waste), after subsection (3) (which specifies the persons who are authorised persons for the purposes of subsection (1)(c)) there shall be inserted—

'(3A) The Secretary of State may by regulations amend subsection (3) above so as to add, whether generally or in such circumstances as may be prescribed in the regulations, any person specified in the regulations, or any description of person so specified, to the persons who are authorised persons for the purposes of subsection (1)(c) above.'

66.—(1) Section 35 of that Act (waste management licences: general) shall be amended in accordance with the following provisions of this paragraph.

(2) After subsection (7) there shall be inserted—

'(7A) In any case where—

    (a) an entry is required under this section to be made in any record as to the observance of any condition of a licence, and

    (b) the entry has not been made,

that fact shall be admissible as evidence that that condition has not been observed.

(7B) Any person who—

    (a) intentionally makes a false entry in any record required to be kept under any condition of a licence, or

    (b) with intent to deceive, forges or uses a licence or makes or has in his possession a document so closely resembling a licence as to be likely to deceive,

shall be guilty of an offence.

(7C) A person guilty of an offence under subsection (7B) above shall be liable—

    (a) on summary conviction, to a fine not exceeding the statutory maximum;

    (b) on conviction on indictment, to a fine or to imprisonment for a term not exceeding two years, or to both.'

67. After section 35 of that Act there shall be inserted—

'**67. Compensation where rights granted pursuant to section 35(4) or 38(9A).**

(1) This section applies in any case where—

    (a) the holder of a licence is required—

        (i) by the conditions of the licence; or

        (ii) by a requirement imposed under section 38(9) below,

to carry out any works or do any other thing which he is not entitled to carry out or do;

    (b) a person whose consent would be required has, pursuant to the requirements of section 35(4) above or 38(9A) below, granted, or joined in granting, to the holder of the licence any rights in relation to any land; and (c)	those rights, or those rights together with other rights, are such as will enable the holder of the licence to comply with any requirements imposed on him by the licence or, as the case may be, under section 38(9) below.

(2)	In a case where this section applies, any person who has granted, or joined in granting, the rights in question shall be entitled to be paid compensation under this section by the holder of the licence.

(3)	The Secretary of State shall by regulations provide for the descriptions of loss and damage for which compensation is payable under this section.

(4)	The Secretary of State may by regulations—

(a)	provide for the basis on which any amount to be paid by way of compensation under this section is to be assessed;

(b)	without prejudice to the generality of subsection (3) and paragraph (a) above, provide for compensation under this section to be payable in respect of—

(i)	any effect of any rights being granted, or

(ii)	any consequence of the exercise of any rights which have been granted;

(c)	provide for the times at which any entitlement to compensation under this section is to arise or at which any such compensation is to become payable;

(d)	provide for the persons or bodies by whom, and the manner in which, any dispute—

(i)	as to whether any, and (if so) how much and when, compensation under this section is payable; or

(ii)	as to the person to or by whom it shall be paid,
is to be determined;

(e)	provide for when or how applications may be made for compensation under this section;

(f)	without prejudice to the generality of paragraph (d) above, provide for when or how applications may be made for the determination of any such disputes as are mentioned in that paragraph;

(g)	without prejudice to the generality of paragraphs (e) and (f) above, prescribe the form in which any such applications as are mentioned in those paragraphs are to be made;

(h)	make provision similar to any provision made by paragraph 8 of Schedule 19 to the Water Resources Act 1991;

(j)	make different provision for different cases, including different provision in relation to different persons or circumstances;

(k)	include such incidental, supplemental, consequential or transitional provision as the Secretary of State considers appropriate.'.

68.—(1)	Section 36 of that Act (grant of licences) shall be amended in accordance with the following provisions of this paragraph.

(2)	In subsection (1) (making of applications) for the words following paragraph (b) there shall be substituted—

'and shall be made on a form provided for the purpose by the waste regulation authority and accompanied by such information as that authority reasonably requires and the charge prescribed for the purpose by a charging scheme under section 41 of the Environment Act 1995.

(1A)	Where an applicant for a licence fails to provide the waste regulation authority with any information required under subsection (1) above, the authority may refuse to proceed with the application, or refuse to proceed with it until the information is provided.'

(3)	In subsection (4) (reference of proposals to, and consideration of representations made by, other bodies)—

(a)	in paragraph (a), for the words 'the National Rivers Authority' there shall be substituted the words 'the appropriate planning authority', and

(b) in paragraph (b), for the word 'Authority' there shall be substituted the word 'authority'.

(4) Subsections (5) (reference by National Rivers Authority to the Secretary of State) and (6) (which makes provision for Scotland in place of subsection (4)) shall cease to have effect.

(5) After subsection (9) (application deemed to be rejected if not granted or refused within four months from being received) there shall be inserted—

'(9A) Subsection (9) above—

(a) shall not have effect in any case where, by virtue of subsection (1A) above, the waste regulation authority refuses to proceed with the application in question, and

(b) shall have effect in any case where, by virtue of subsection (1A) above, the waste regulation authority refuses to proceed with it until the required information is provided, with the substitution for the period of four months there mentioned of the period of four months beginning with the date on which the authority received the information.'

(6) For subsection (10) (period of 21 days allowed for bodies to make representations) there shall be substituted—

'(10) The period allowed to the appropriate planning authority, the Health and Safety Executive or the appropriate nature conservancy body for the making of representations under subsection (4) or (7) above about a proposal is the period of twenty-eight days beginning with the day on which the proposal is received by the waste regulation authority or such longer period as the waste regulation authority, the appropriate planning authority, the Executive or the body, as the case may be, agree in writing.

(11) In this section—

"the appropriate planning authority" means—

(a) where the relevant land is situated in the area of a London borough council, that London borough council;

(b) where the relevant land is situated in the City of London, the Common Council of the City of London;

(c) where the relevant land is situated in a non-metropolitan county in England, the council of that county;

(d) where the relevant land is situated in a National Park or the Broads, the National Park authority for that National Park or, as the case may be, the Broads Authority;

(e) where the relevant land is situated elsewhere in England or Wales, the council of the district or, in Wales, the county or county borough, in which the land is situated;

(f) where the relevant land is situated in Scotland, the council constituted under section 2 of the Local Government etc. (Scotland) Act 1994 for the area in which the land is situated;

"the Broads" has the same meaning as in the Norfolk and Suffolk Broads Act 1988;

"National Park authority", subject to subsection (12) below, means a National Park authority established under section 63 of the Environment Act 1995 which has become the local planning authority for the National Park in question;

"the relevant land" means—

(a) in relation to a site licence, the land to which the licence relates; and

(b) in relation to a mobile plant licence, the principal place of business of the operator of the plant to which the licence relates.

(12) As respects any period before a National Park authority established under section 63 of the Environment Act 1995 in relation to a National Park becomes the local planning authority for that National Park, any reference in this section to a National Park authority shall be taken as a reference to the National Park Committee or joint or special planning board for that National Park.

(13) The Secretary of State may by regulations amend the definition of "appropriate planning authority" in subsection (11) above.'

(14) This section shall have effect subject to section 36A below.'

69. After section 36 of that Act there shall be inserted—

'36A. Consultation before the grant of certain licences

(1) This section applies where an application for a licence has been duly made to a waste regulation authority, and the authority proposes to issue a licence subject (by virtue of section 35(4) above) to any condition which might require the holder of the licence to—

(a) carry out any works, or

(b) do any other thing,

which he might not be entitled to carry out or do.

(2) Before issuing the licence, the waste regulation authority shall serve on every person appearing to the authority to be a person falling within subsection (3) below a notice which complies with the requirements set out in subsection (4) below.

(3) A person falls within this subsection if—

(a) he is the owner, lessee or occupier of any land; and

(b) that land is land in relation to which it is likely that, as a consequence of the licence being issued subject to the condition in question, rights will have to be granted by virtue of section 35(4) above to the holder of the licence.

(4) A notice served under subsection (2) above shall—

(a) set out the condition in question;

(b) indicate the nature of the works or other things which that condition might require the holder of the licence to carry out or do; and

(c) specify the date by which, and the manner in which, any representations relating to the condition or its possible effects are to be made to the waste regulation authority by the person on whom the notice is served.

(5) The date which, pursuant to subsection (4)(c) above, is specified in a notice shall be a date not earlier than the date on which expires the period—

(a) beginning with the date on which the notice is served, and

(b) of such length as may be prescribed in regulations made by the Secretary of State.

(6) Before the waste regulation authority issues the licence it must, subject to subsection (7) below, consider any representations made in relation to the condition in question, or its possible effects, by any person on whom a notice has been served under subsection (2) above.

(7) Subsection (6) above does not require the waste regulation authority to consider any representations made by a person after the date specified in the notice served on him under subsection (2) above as the date by which his representations in relation to the condition or its possible effects are to be made.

(8) In subsection (3) above—

"owner", in relation to any land in England and Wales, means the person who—

(a) is for the time being receiving the rack-rent of the land, whether on his own account or as agent or trustee for another person; or

(b) would receive the rack-rent if the land were let at a rack-rent,

but does not include a mortgagee not in possession; and

"owner", in relation to any land in Scotland, means a person (other than a creditor in a heritable security not in possession of the security subjects) for the time being entitled to receive or who would, if the land were let, be entitled to receive, the rents of the land in connection with which the word is used and includes a trustee, factor, guardian or curator and in the case of public or municipal land includes the persons to whom the management of the land is entrusted.'.

70.—(1) In section 37 of that Act (variation of licences) in subsection (1)(b) (which requires an application to be accompanied by the prescribed fee) for the words 'the prescribed fee payable under section 41 below,' there shall be substituted the words 'the charge prescribed for the purpose by a charging scheme under section 41 of the Environment Act 1995,'.

(2) In subsection (5) of that section (which applies certain provisions of section 36) the words '(5), (6),' and '(8)' shall be omitted.

(3) After subsection (6) of that section (cases where an application for modification is deemed to have been rejected) there shall be added—

'(7) This section shall have effect subject to section 37A below.'

71. After section 37 of that Act there shall be inserted—

'37A. Consultation before certain variations

(1) This section applies where—

(a) a waste regulation authority proposes to modify a licence under section 37(1) or (2)(a) above; and

(b) the licence, if modified as proposed, would be subject to a relevant new condition.

(2) For the purposes of this section, a 'relevant new condition' is any condition by virtue of which the holder of the licence might be required to carry out any works or do any other thing—

(a) which he might not be entitled to carry out or do, and

(b) which he could not be required to carry out or do by virtue of the conditions to which, prior to the modification, the licence is subject.

(3) Before modifying the licence, the waste regulation authority shall serve on every person appearing to the authority to be a person failing within subsection (4) below a notice which complies with the requirements set out in subsection (5) below.

(4) A person falls within this subsection if—

(a) he is the owner, lessee or occupier of any land; and

(b) that land is land in relation to which it is likely that, as a consequence of the licence being modified so as to be subject to the relevant new condition in question, rights will have to be granted by virtue of section 35(4) above to the holder of the licence.

(5) A notice served under subsection (3) above shall—

(a) set out the relevant new condition in question;

(b) indicate the nature of the works or other things which that condition might require the holder of the licence to carry out or do but which he could not be required to carry out or do by virtue of the conditions (if any) to which, prior to the modification, the licence is subject; and

(c) specify the date by which, and the manner in which, any representations relating to the condition or its possible effects are to be made to the waste regulation authority by the person on whom the notice is served.

(6) The date which, pursuant to subsection (5)(c) above, is specified in a notice shall be a date not earlier than the date on which expires the period—

(a) beginning with the date on which the notice is served, and

(b) of such length as may be prescribed in regulations made by the Secretary of State.

(7) Before the waste regulation authority issues the licence it must, subject to subsection (8) below, consider any representations made in relation to the condition in question, or its possible effects, by any person on whom a notice has been served under subsection (3) above.

(8) Subsection (7) above does not require the waste regulation authority to consider any representations made by a person after the date specified in the notice served on him under subsection (3) above as the date by which his representations in relation to the condition or its possible effects are to be made.

(9) A waste regulation authority may postpone the service of any notice or the consideration of any representations required under the foregoing provisions of this section so far as the authority considers that by reason of an emergency it is appropriate to do so.

(10) In subsection (3) above, 'owner' has the same meaning as it has in subsection (3) of section 36A above by virtue of subsection (8) of that section.'.

72.—(1) In section 38 of that Act (revocation and suspension of licences) after subsection (9) (power to require certain measures to be taken where licence suspended) there shall be inserted—

'(9A) A requirement imposed under subsection (9) above may require the holder of a licence to carry out works or do other things notwithstanding that he is not entitled to carry out the works or do the thing and any person whose consent would be required shall grant, or join in granting, the holder of the licence such rights in relation to the land as will enable the holder of the licence to comply with any requirements imposed on him under that subsection.

(9B) Subsections (2) to (8) of section 36A above shall, with the necessary modifications, apply where the authority proposes to impose a requirement under subsection (9) above which may require the holder of a licence to carry out any such works or do any such thing as is mentioned in subsection (9A) above as they apply where the authority proposes to issue a licence subject to any such condition as is mentioned in subsection (1) of that section, but as if—

(a) the reference in subsection (3) of that section to section 35(4) above were a reference to subsection (9A) above; and

(b) any reference in those subsections—

(i) to the condition, or the condition in question, were a reference to the requirement; and

(ii) to issuing a licence were a reference to serving a notice, under subsection (12) below, effecting the requirement.

(9C) The authority may postpone the service of any notice or the consideration of any representations required under section 36A above, as applied by subsection (9B) above, so far as the authority considers that by reason of an emergency it is appropriate to do so.'

(2) After subsection (12) of that section (revocations and suspensions etc. to be effected by service of notice) there shall be added—

'(13) If a waste regulation authority is of the opinion that proceedings for an offence under subsection (10) or (11) above would afford an ineffectual remedy against a person who has failed to comply with any requirement imposed under subsection (9) above, the authority may take proceedings in the High Court or, in Scotland, in any court of competent jurisdiction for the purpose of securing compliance with the requirement.'

73.—(1) Section 39 of that Act (surrender of licences) shall be amended in accordance with the following provisions of this paragraph.

(2) In subsection (3) (application for surrender of a site licence) for the words from 'in such form' onwards there shall be substituted the words 'on a form provided by the authority for the purpose, giving such information and accompanied by such evidence as the authority reasonably requires and accompanied by the charge prescribed for the purpose by a charging scheme under section 41 of the Environment Act 1995.'

(3) In subsection (7) (consideration of representations before accepting surrender of a licence)—

(a) for the words 'the National Rivers Authority' and 'the Authority' there shall be substituted the words 'the appropriate planning authority'; and

(b) the words following paragraph (b) shall cease to have effect.

(4)   Subsection (8) (which makes provision for Scotland in place of subsection (7)) shall cease to have effect.

(5)   In subsection (11) (meaning of 'the allowed period') for the words 'subsections (7) and (8) above' there shall be substituted the words 'subsection (7) above'.

(6)   After subsection (11) there shall be added—

'(12)   In this section—

"the appropriate planning authority'' means—

(a)   where the relevant land is situated in the area of a London borough council, that London borough council;

(b)   where the relevant land is situated in the City of London, the Common Council of the City of London;

(c)   where the relevant land is situated in a non-metropolitan county in England, the council of that county;

(d)   where the relevant land is situated in a National Park or the Broads, the National Park authority for that National Park or, as the case may be, the Broads Authority;

(e)   where the relevant land is situated elsewhere in England or Wales, the council of the district or, in Wales, the county or county borough, in which the land is situated;

(f)   where the relevant land is situated in Scotland, the council constituted under section 2 of the Local Government etc. (Scotland) Act 1994 for the area in which the land is situated;

"the Broads'' has the same meaning as in the Norfolk and Suffolk Broads Act 1988;

"National Park authority'', subject to subsection (13) below, means a National Park authority established under section 63 of the Environment Act 1995 which has become the local planning authority for the National Park in question;

"the relevant land'', in the case of any site licence, means the land to which the licence relates.

(13)   As respects any period before a National Park authority established under section 63 of the Environment Act 1995 in relation to a National Park becomes the local planning authority for that National Park, any reference in this section to a National Park authority shall be taken as a reference to the National Park Committee or joint or special planning board for that National Park.

(14)   The Secretary of State may by regulations amend the definition of "appropriate planning authority'' in subsection (12) above.'

74.   In section 40 of that Act (transfer of licences) in subsection (3) (mode of making application for transfer of licence) for the words from 'in such form' to section 41 below' there shall be substituted the words 'on a form provided by the authority for the purpose, accompanied by such information as the authority may reasonably require, the charge prescribed for the purpose by a charging scheme under section 41 of the Environment Act 1995'.

75.   Section 41 of that Act (fees and charges for licences) shall cease to have effect.

76.—(1)   Section 42 of that Act (supervision of licensed activities) shall be amended in accordance with the following provisions of this paragraph.

(2)   Subsection (2) (consultation with the National Rivers Authority etc) shall cease to have effect.

(3)   In subsection (4) (recovery of expenditure from the holder or, if it has been surrendered, the former holder of a licence) for the words 'the holder of the licence or, if the licence has been surrendered, from the former holder of it' there shall be substituted the words 'the holder, or (as the case may be) the former holder, of the licence'.

(4)   In subsection (5) (powers where it appears that a condition of a licence is not being complied with) after the words 'is not being complied with' there shall be inserted the words 'or is likely not to be complied with,'.

(5)   For paragraph (a) of that subsection there shall be substituted—

'(a)   serve on the holder of the licence a notice—

(i)   stating that the authority is of the opinion that a condition of the licence is not being complied with or, as the case may be, is likely not to be complied with;

(ii)   specifying the matters which constitute the non-compliance or, as the case may be, which make the anticipated non-compliance likely;

(iii)   specifying the steps which must be taken to remedy the non-compliance or, as the case may be, to prevent the anticipated non-compliance from occurring; and

(iv)   specifying the period within which those steps must be taken; and'

(6)   In paragraph (b) of that subsection (powers which become exercisable on non-compliance) for the words 'has not complied with the condition within that time,' there shall be substituted the words 'has not taken the steps specified in the notice within the period so specified,'

(7)   After subsection (6) (power to revoke or suspend a licence) there shall be inserted—

'(6A)   If a waste regulation authority is of the opinion that revocation or suspension of the licence, whether entirely or to any extent, under subsection (6) above would afford an ineffectual remedy against a person who has failed to comply with any requirement imposed under subsection (5)(a) above, the authority may take proceedings in the High Court or, in Scotland, in any court of competent jurisdiction for the purpose of securing compliance with the requirement.'

(8)   In subsection (7) (application of certain provisions of section 38 to revocation or suspension of a licence)—

(a)   for the words from 'subsections (5)' to '38' there shall be substituted the words 'subsections (5) and (12) or, as the case may be, subsections (8) to (12) of section 38'; and

(b)   the words from 'and the power' onwards shall cease to have effect.

77.   In section 43 of that Act, in subsection (2), paragraphs (a) and (b) (reference of matters involved in appeals under that section to, and determination of such appeals by, persons appointed by the Secretary of State) shall cease to have effect and after that section there shall be inserted—

'(2A) This section is subject to section 114 of the Environment Act 1995 (delegation or reference of appeals etc).'

78.   Section 50 of that Act (waste disposal plans of waste regulation authorities) shall cease to have effect.

79.   Section 61 of that Act (duty of waste regulation authorities as respects closed landfills) shall cease to have effect.

80.—(1)   Section 62 of that Act (special provision with respect to certain dangerous and intractable waste) shall be amended in accordance with the following provisions of this paragraph.

(2)   In subsection (3), for paragraph (a) (regulations providing for the supervision of certain activities and the recovery of the costs from persons carrying on the activities) there shall be substituted—

'(a)   for the supervision by waste regulation authorities—

(i)   of activities authorised by virtue of the regulations or of activities by virtue of carrying on which persons are subject to provisions of the regulations, or

(ii)   of persons who carry on activities authorised by virtue of the regulations or who are subject to provisions of the regulations,

and for the recovery from persons falling within sub-paragraph (ii) above of the costs incurred by waste regulation authorities in performing functions conferred upon those authorities by the regulations;'.

(3)   After that subsection (which also includes provision for regulations to provide for appeals to the Secretary of State) there shall be added—

'(3A) This section is subject to section 114 of the Environment Act 1995 (delegation or reference of appeals etc).'

81. In section 63 of that Act (waste other than controlled waste) for subsection (2) (offences relating to the deposit of waste which is not controlled waste but which, if it were such waste, would be special waste) there shall be substituted—

'(2) A person who deposits, or knowingly causes or knowingly permits the deposit of, any waste—
    (a) which is not controlled waste, but
    (b) which, if it were controlled waste, would be special waste,
in a case where he would be guilty of an offence under section 33 above if the waste were special waste and any waste management licence were not in force, shall, subject to subsection (3) below, be guilty of that offence and punishable as if the waste were special waste.'

82.—(1) Section 64 of that Act (public registers) shall be amended in accordance with the following provisions of this paragraph.

(2) After subsection (2) there shall be inserted—

'(2A) The Secretary of State may give to a waste regulation authority directions requiring the removal from any register of its of any specified information not prescribed for inclusion under subsection (1) above or which, by virtue of section 65 or 66 below, ought to be excluded from the register.'

(3) In subsection (4) (duty of waste collection authorities in England to maintain registers)—
    (a) after the word 'England' there shall be inserted the words 'or Wales'; and
    (b) the words 'which is not a waste regulation authority' shall be omitted.

(4) For subsection (5) (waste regulation authorities in England to furnish information to waste collection authorities) there shall be substituted—

'(5) The waste regulation authority in relation to England and Wales shall furnish any waste collection authorities in its area with the particulars necessary to enable them to discharge their duty under subsection (4) above.'

(5) In subsection (6) (registers to be available for inspection by, and facilities for obtaining copies of entries to be afforded to, the public)—
    (a) after the words 'waste collection authority' there shall be inserted '(a)';
    (b) after the words 'hours and' there shall be inserted '(b)'; and
    (c) after the paragraph (b) so formed, there shall be added the words—
'and, for the purposes of this subsection, places may be prescribed by the Secretary of State at which any such registers or facilities as are mentioned in paragraph (a) or (b) above are to be available or afforded to the public in pursuance of the paragraph in question.'

83.—(1) In section 66 of that Act (exclusion from registers of certain confidential information) in subsection (5) (information not to be entered on the register until expiration of certain time limits) in the words following paragraph (b), for the words from 'pending' onwards there shall be substituted the words 'until the end of the period of seven days following the day on which the appeal is finally determined or withdrawn'.

(2) For subsection (6) (which applies section 43(2) and (8) to appeals to the Secretary of State against decisions that information is not commercially confidential) there shall be substituted—

'(6) Subsections (2) and (8) of section 43 above shall apply in relation to appeals under subsection (5) above as they apply in relation to appeals under that section; but
    (a) subsection (2)(c) of that section shall have effect for the purposes of this subsection with the substitution for the words from '(which may' onwards of the words '(which must be held in private)'; and
    (b) subsection (5) above is subject to section 114 of the Environment Act 1995 (delegation or reference of appeals etc).'

84. Section 67 of that Act (annual reports of waste regulation authorities) shall cease to have effect.

85. Sections 68 to 70 of that Act (functions of the Secretary of State and appointment etc of inspectors, powers of entry and power to deal with cause of imminent danger of serious pollution) shall cease to have effect.

86.—(1) In section 71 of that Act (obtaining of information from persons and authorities) subsection (1) (which is superseded by this Act) shall cease to have effect.

(2) In subsection (2) of that section (power by notice to require a person to furnish information within such period as may be specified in the notice) after the words 'service of the notice' there shall be inserted the words ', or at such time,'.

87. Section 72 of that Act (default powers of the Secretary of State) shall cease to have effect.

88.—(1) Section 75 of that Act (meaning of 'waste' etc.) shall be amended in accordance with the following provisions of this paragraph.

(2) For subsection (2) (definition of 'waste') there shall be substituted—

'(2) "Waste" means any substance or object in the categories set out in Schedule 2B to this Act which the holder discards or intends or is required to discard; and for the purposes of this definition—

"holder" means the producer of the waste or the person who is in possession of it; and

"producer" means any person whose activities produce waste or any person who carries out preprocessing, mixing or other operations resulting in a change in the nature or composition of this waste.'

(3) Subsection (3) (presumption that anything discarded is waste unless the contrary is proved) shall cease to have effect.

(4) After subsection (9) there shall be added—

'(10) Schedule 2B to this Act (which reproduces Annex I to the Waste Directive) shall have effect.

(11) Subsection (2) above is substituted, and Schedule 2B to this Act is inserted, for the purpose of assigning to "waste" in this Part the meaning which it has in the Waste Directive by virtue of paragraphs (a) to (c) of Article 1 of, and Annex I to, that Directive, and those provisions shall be construed accordingly.

(12) In this section "the Waste Directive" means the directive of the Council of the European Communities, dated 15th July 1975, on waste, as amended by—

(a) the directive of that Council, dated 18th March 1991, amending directive 75/442/EEC on waste; and

(b) the directive of that Council, dated 23rd December 1991, standardising and rationalising reports on the implementation of certain Directives relating to the environment.'

89.—(1) Section 79 of that Act (statutory nuisances) shall be amended in accordance with the following provisions of this paragraph.

(2) In subsection (1) (the paragraphs of which specify, subject to subsections (2) to (6A), the matters which constitute statutory nuisances) for the words 'Subject to subsections (2) to (6A) below' there shall be substituted the words 'Subject to subsections (1A) to (6A) below'.

(3) After that subsection there shall be inserted—

'(1A) No matter shall constitute a statutory nuisance to the extent that it consists of, or is caused by, any land being in a contaminated state.

(1B) Land is in a "contaminated state" for the purposes of subsection (1A) above if, and only if, it is in such a condition, by reason of substances in, on or under the land, that—

(a) harm is being caused or there is a possibility of harm being caused; or

(b) pollution of controlled waters is being, or is likely to be, caused;

and in this subsection "harm", "pollution of controlled waters" and "substance" have the same meaning as in Part IIA of this Act.'.

90. In section 141 of that Act (power to prohibit or restrict the importation or exportation of waste) subsection (5)(a)(ii) (power of Secretary of State by direction to make functions of certain authorities exercisable instead by him) shall cease to have effect.

91. Section 143 of that Act (public registers of land which may be contaminated) shall cease to have effect.

92. In section 161 of that Act (regulations and orders) in subsection (4) (which specifies the orders under that Act which are not subject to negative resolution procedure under subsection (3)) after the words 'does not apply to' there shall be inserted the words 'a statutory instrument—

(a) which contains an order under section 78M(4) above, or

(b) by reason only that it contains'.

93.—(1) Schedule 1 to that Act (authorisations for processes: supplementary provisions) shall be amended in accordance with the following provisions of this paragraph.

(2) In Part I (grant of authorisations) in paragraph 3(3) (local inquiry or hearing to be held where request to be heard made by the applicant or the local enforcing authority) for the words 'the local enforcing authority' there shall be substituted the words 'the enforcing authority'.

(3) In Part II (variation of authorisations) in paragraph 6, at the beginning of sub-paragraph (1) there shall be inserted the words 'Except as provided by sub-paragraph (1A) below,'.

(4) After that sub-paragraph there shall be inserted—

'(1A) The requirements of this paragraph shall not apply in relation to any variations of an authorisation which an enforcing authority has decided to make in consequence of representations made in accordance with this paragraph and which are specified by way of variation of a variation notice by a further notice under section 10(3A) of this Act.'

(5) After paragraph 7 (applications for variation) there shall be inserted—

'Call in of applications for variation

8.—(1) The Secretary of State may give directions to the enforcing authority requiring that any particular application or any class of applications for the variation of an authorisation shall be transmitted to him for determination pending a further direction under sub-paragraph (5) below.

(2) The enforcing authority shall inform the applicant of the fact that his application is being transmitted to the Secretary of State.

(3) Where an application for the variation of an authorisation is referred to him under sub-paragraph (1) above the Secretary of State may—

(a) cause a local inquiry to be held in relation to the application; or

(b) afford the applicant and the authority concerned an opportunity of appearing before and being heard by a person appointed by the Secretary of State;

and he shall exercise one of the powers under this sub-paragraph in any case where, in the manner prescribed by regulations made by the Secretary of State, a request is made to be heard with respect to the application by the applicant or the enforcing authority concerned.

(4) Subsections (2) to (5) of section 250 of the Local Government Act 1972 (supplementary provisions about local inquiries under that section) or, in relation to Scotland, subsections (2) to (8) of section 210 of the Local Government (Scotland) Act

1973 (which make similar provision) shall, without prejudice to the generality of subsection (1) of either of those sections, apply to local inquiries or other hearings in pursuance of sub-paragraph (3) above as they apply to inquiries in pursuance of either of those sections and, in relation to England and Wales, as if the reference to a local authority in subsection (4) of the said section 250 included a reference to the enforcing authority.

(5)   The Secretary of State shall, on determining any application transferred to him under this paragraph, give to the enforcing authority such a direction as he thinks fit as to whether it is to grant the application and, if so, as to the conditions that are to be attached to the authorisation by means of the variation notice.

9.   The Secretary of State may give the enforcing authority a direction with respect to any particular application or any class of applications for the variation of an authorisation requiring the authority not to determine or not to proceed with the application or applications of that class until the expiry of any such period as may be specified in the direction, or until directed by the Secretary of State that they may do so, as the case may be.

10.—(1)   Except in a case where an application for the variation of an authorisation has been referred to the Secretary of State under paragraph 8 above and subject to sub-paragraph (3) below, the enforcing authority shall determine an application for the variation of an authorisation within the period of four months beginning with the day on which it received the application or within such longer period as may be agreed with the applicant.

(2)   If the enforcing authority fails to determine an application for the variation of an authorisation within the period allowed by or under this paragraph the application shall, if the applicant notifies the authority in writing that he treats the failure as such, be deemed to have been refused at the end of that period.

(3)   The Secretary of State may, by order, substitute for the period for the time being specified in sub-paragraph (1) above such other period as he considers appropriate and different periods may be substituted for different classes of application.'

94.   In Schedule 2 to that Act (waste disposal authorities and companies) in paragraph 17(2) (which requires a waste regulation authority or waste disposal authority to furnish information on request to the Secretary of State) the words 'a waste regulation authority or' shall cease to have effect.

95.   After Schedule 2A to that Act there shall be inserted—

'SCHEDULE 2B

CATEGORIES OF WASTE

1.   Production or consumption residues not otherwise specified below.

2.   Off-specification products.

3.   Products whose date for appropriate use has expired.

4.   Materials spilled, lost or having undergone other mishap, including any materials, equipment, etc, contaminated as a result of the mishap.

5. Materials contaminated or soiled as a result of planned actions (e.g. residues from cleaning operations, packing materials, containers, etc.).

6.   Unusable parts (e.g. reject batteries, exhausted catalysts, etc.).

7.   Substances which no longer perform satisfactorily (e.g. contaminated acids, contaminated solvents, exhausted tempering salts, etc.).

8. Residues of industrial processes (e.g. slags, still bottoms, etc.).

9. Residues from pollution abatement processes (e.g. scrubber sludges, baghouse dusts, spent filters, etc.).

10. Machining or finishing residues (e.g. lathe turnings, mill scales, etc.).

11. Residues from raw materials extraction and processing (e.g. mining residues, oil field slops, etc.).

12. Adulterated materials (e.g. oils contaminated with PCBs, etc.).

13. Any materials, substances or products whose use has been banned by law.

14. Products for which the holder has no further use (e.g. agricultural, household, office, commercial and shop discards, etc.).

15. Contaminated materials, substances or products resulting from remedial action with respect to land.

16. Any materials, substances or products which are not contained in the above categories.'

The Natural Heritage (Scotland) Act 1991

96.—(1) The Natural Heritage (Scotland) Act 1991 shall be amended in accordance with the following provisions of this paragraph.

(2) In section 15—

(a) in subsection (2) for the words 'a river purification authority, acting in pursuance of their duties under section 17(1) of the Rivers (Prevention of Pollution) (Scotland) Act 1951' there shall be substituted the words 'SEPA acting in pursuance of its duties under section 34(1) of the Environment Act 1995';

(b) in subsection (3) for the words 'said Act of' and 'a river purification authority' where they first occur there shall be substituted the words 'Rivers (Prevention of Pollution (Scotland) Act' and 'SEPA' respectively and the words 'and a river purification authority of whom such a requirement is made shall make such an application' shall cease to have effect;

(c) for subsection (5) there shall be substituted—

'(5) A control area shall comprise an area or areas shown in a map or plan contained in the order.'

(3) In section 17—

(a) in subsection (1) for the words 'A river purification authority' there shall be substituted the words 'SEPA';

(b) in subsection (3) for the words 'A river purification authority', 'their' in both places where it occurs, 'they' and 'the authority' there shall be substituted the words 'SEPA', 'its', 'it' and 'SEPA' respectively.

(4) In section 18—

(a) in subsection (1) for the words 'a river purification authority' and 'they' there shall be substituted the words 'SEPA' and 'it', respectively;

(b) in subsection (2) for the words 'the river purification authority decide' there shall be substituted the words 'SEPA decides';

(c) in subsection (3) for the words 'a river purification authority' and 'the authority' there shall be substituted the words 'SEPA' and 'it' respectively;

(d) in subsection (4) for the words 'the river purification authority declare' there shall be substituted the words 'SEPA declares';

(e) in subsection (5) for the words 'A river purification authority' and 'them' there shall be substituted the words 'SEPA' and 'it' respectively.

(5) In section 24—

(a) in subsection (1)—

(i) for the words 'a river purification authority' there shall be substituted the words 'SEPA'; and

(ii) in paragraph (a), after the word 'on' there shall be inserted the words 'SEPA or'; and

(b) in subsection (9)—

(i) for the words 'a river purification authority or' there shall be substituted the words 'SEPA or a'; and

(ii) in paragraph (a), after the word 'by' where it second occurs there shall be inserted the words 'SEPA or'.

(6) After section 26 there shall be inserted—

'26A. Meaning of SEPA

In this Act "SEPA" means the Scottish Environment Protection Agency.'

(7) In Schedule 5—

(a) in paragraph 1 for the words 'the river purification authority concerned consider' there shall be substituted the words 'SEPA considers';

(b) in paragraph 2 for the words 'the river purification authority concerned' there shall be substituted the words 'SEPA' and the words 'in their area and' shall cease to have effect;

(c) in paragraph 3 for the words 'the river purification authority' and 'their' wherever they occur there shall be substituted the words 'SEPA' and 'its' respectively;

(d) in paragraphs 4 and 9 for the words 'the river purification authority' wherever they occur there shall be substituted the words 'SEPA'.

(8) In Schedule 6—

(a) in paragraph 1—

(i) in sub-paragraph (1) for the words 'the river purification authority' there shall be substituted the words 'SEPA';

(ii) in sub-paragraph (2) for the words 'A river purification authority', 'them', 'the authority' and 'their' there shall be substituted respectively the words 'SEPA', 'it', 'it' and 'its' respectively;

(iii) in sub-paragraph (3) for the words 'the river purification authority' there shall be substituted the words 'SEPA';

(iv) in sub-paragraph (4) for the words 'the river purification authority', 'the authority fail' and 'their' there shall be substituted the words 'SEPA', 'it fails' and 'its' respectively;

(v) sub-paragraph (5) shall cease to have effect;

(vi) in sub-paragraph (6) for the words 'the river purification authority to whom the application has been made' there shall be substituted the words 'SEPA';

(b) in paragraph 2—

(i) in sub-paragraph (1) for the words 'the river purification authority' wherever they occur there shall be substituted the words 'SEPA';

(ii) in sub-paragraphs (3) and (4) for the words 'the river purification authority' wherever they occur there shall be substituted the words 'SEPA';

(iii) at the end there shall be added—

'(6) This paragraph is subject to section 114 of the Environment Act 1995 (delegation or reference of appeals etc).'

(c) in paragraph 3—

(i) in sub-paragraph (1) for the words 'A river purification authority' there shall be substituted the words 'SEPA';

(ii) in sub-paragraph (2) for the words 'A river purification authority' and 'they are' there shall be substituted the words 'SEPA' and 'it is' respectively;

(iii)   in sub-paragraph (4) for the words 'the river purification authority' there shall be substituted the words 'SEPA';

(iv)   in sub-paragraph (5) for the words 'the river purification authority' and 'them' there shall be substituted the words 'SEPA' and 'it' respectively;

(v)   in sub-paragraph (6) for the words 'the authority fail to intimate their' and 'the river purification authority' there shall be substituted the words 'SEPA fails to intimate its' and 'SEPA' respectively;

(d)   in paragraph 4 for the words 'A river purification authority' and 'them' there shall be substituted the words 'SEPA' and 'it' respectively;

(e)   in paragraph 5(2) for the words 'the river purification authority' there shall be substituted the words 'SEPA'.

(9)   In Schedule 8, in paragraph 1—

(a)   for sub-paragraph (1) there shall be substituted—

'(1)   Before making an application for a drought order, the applicant shall consult—

(a)   SEPA, in a case where notice of the application is required to be served on it under this paragraph; and

(b)   any district salmon fishery board on whom notice of the application is required to be served under this paragraph.';

(b)   in sub-paragraph (3), in the second column of the Table, in the fourth entry (relating to orders concerning the taking of water from a source or the discharge of water to a place), in paragraph (a) the words ', river purification authority' shall cease to have effect and at the end there shall be added—

'(c)   SEPA.';

(c)   in sub-paragraph (3), in the second column of the Table, in the fifth entry (relating to orders which authorise the execution of any works) for the words 'every river purification authority and' there shall be substituted the words 'SEPA and every'.

The Water Industry Act 1991

97.   In section 3 of the Water Industry Act 1991 (general environmental and recreational duties) in subsection (4) (which imposes duties on the Director and relevant undertakers in relation to proposals relating to functions of the National Rivers Authority etc) for the words 'the NRA', in each place where they occur, there shall be substituted the words 'the Environment Agency'.

98.   In section 5 of that Act (codes of practice with respect to environmental duties) in subsection (4), in paragraph (a) (which requires consultation with the National Rivers Authority) for the words 'the NRA' there shall be substituted the words 'the Environment Agency'.

99.   In section 40 of that Act (bulk supplies of water) in subsection (5) (which requires the Director to consult the National Rivers Authority before making an order) for the words 'the NRA' there shall be substituted the words 'the Environment Agency'.

100.   In section 40A of that Act (variation and termination of bulk supply agreements) in subsection (3) (which requires the Director to consult the National Rivers authority before making an order) for the words 'the NRA' there shall be substituted the words 'the Environment Agency'.

101.—(1)   In section 71 of that Act (waste from water resources) in subsection (6) (power of court to authorise the National Rivers Authority to take steps to execute an order) for the words 'the NRA' there shall be substituted—

(a)   where it first occurs, the words 'the Environment Agency'; and

(b)   where it next occurs, the words 'the Agency'.

(2)   In subsection (7) (powers of entry etc of persons designated by the National Rivers Authority) for the words 'the NRA' in each place where it occurs there shall be substituted the words 'the Environment Agency'.

102.   After section 93 of that Act (interpretation of Part III) there shall be inserted—

'PART IIIA
PROMOTION OF THE EFFICIENT USE OF WATER

93A.   Duty to promote the efficient use of water

(1)   It shall be the duty of every water undertaker to promote the efficient use of water by its customers.

(2)   The duty of a water undertaker under this section shall be enforceable under section 18 above—

(a)   by the Secretary of State; or

(b)   with the consent of or in accordance with a general authorisation given by the Secretary of State, by the Director.

(3)   Nothing in this Part shall have effect to authorise or require a water undertaker to impose any requirement on any of its customers or potential customers.

93B.   Power of Director to impose requirements on water undertakers

(1)   The Director may require a water undertaker, in its performance of its duty under section 93A above, to—

(a)   take any such action; or

(b)   achieve any such overall standards of performance,

as he may specify in the document imposing the requirement.

(2)   Where the Director, in the document imposing a requirement on a water undertaker under subsection (1) above, stipulates that any contravention of the requirement by the undertaker will be a breach of its duty under section 93A above, any contravention of that requirement by the undertaker shall be a breach of that duty.

(3)   Without prejudice to the generality of subsection (1) above, a requirement under that subsection may—

(a)   require a water undertaker to make available to its customers or potential customers such facilities as may be specified in the document imposing the requirement;

(b)   require a water undertaker to provide or make available to its customers or potential customers such information as may be specified in the document imposing the requirement, and may specify the form in which, the times at which or the frequency with which any such information is to be provided or made available.

(4)   In exercising his powers under this section in relation to any water undertaker the Director shall have regard to the extent to which water resources are available to that undertaker.

(5)   Before imposing any requirement on a water undertaker under subsection (1) above the Director shall consult that undertaker.

(6)   Nothing in this section authorises the Director to impose any requirement on a water undertaker which has or may have the effect of authorising or requiring that undertaker to impose any requirement on any of its customers or potential customers.

93C.   Publicity of requirements imposed under section 93B

(1)   Where, under section 93B(1) above, the Director imposes any requirement on a water undertaker, the Director may arrange for that requirement to be publicised in any such manner as he may consider appropriate for the purpose of bringing it to the attention of that undertaker's customers.

(2)   Without prejudice to the generality of subsection (1) above, the Director may arrange for such publicising of the requirement as is mentioned in that subsection by—

(a)   himself publicising the requirement or causing it to be publicised; or

(b)   directing the undertaker to inform or arrange to inform its customers of the requirement.

93D.   Information as to compliance with requirements under section 93B

(1)   Where a water undertaker is subject to any requirement imposed under section 93B(1) above, the Director may arrange for there to be given to the customers of that undertaker at any such times or with such frequency, and in any such manner, as he may consider appropriate, such information about the level of performance achieved by the undertaker in relation to that requirement as appears to the Director to be expedient to be given to those customers.

(2)   Without prejudice to the generality of subsection (1) above, the Director may arrange for such giving of information as is mentioned in that subsection by—

(a)   himself disseminating the information or causing it to be disseminated; or

(b)   directing the undertaker to give or arrange to give the information to its customers.

(3)   At such times and in such form or manner as the Director may direct, a water undertaker shall provide the Director with such information as may be specified in the direction in connection with the undertaker's performance in relation to any requirement imposed upon the undertaker under section 93B(1) above.

(4)   A water undertaker who fails without reasonable excuse to do anything required of him by virtue of subsection (3) above shall be guilty of an offence and liable on summary conviction to a fine not exceeding level 5 on the standard scale.'.

103.   After section 101 of that Act (which provides for the determination of certain details in relation to requisitioned sewers) there shall be inserted—

'Provision of public sewers otherwise than by requisition

101A.   Further duty to provide sewers

(1)   Without prejudice to section 98 above, it shall be the duty of a sewerage undertaker to provide a public sewer to be used for the drainage for domestic sewerage purposes of premises in a particular locality in its area if the conditions specified in subsection (2) below are satisfied.

(2)   The conditions mentioned in subsection (1) above are—

(a)   that the premises in question, or any of those premises, are premises on which there are buildings each of which, with the exception of any shed, glasshouse or other outbuilding appurtenant to a dwelling and not designed or occupied as living accommodation, is a building erected before, or whose erection was substantially completed by, 20th June 1995;

(b)   that the drains or sewers used for the drainage for domestic sewerage purposes of the premises in question do not, either directly or through an intermediate drain or sewer, connect with a public sewer; and

(c)   that the drainage of any of the premises in question in respect of which the condition specified in paragraph (a) above is satisfied is giving, or is likely to give, rise to such adverse effects to the environment or amenity that it is appropriate, having regard to any guidance issued under this section by the Secretary of State and all other relevant considerations, to provide a public sewer for the drainage for domestic sewerage purposes of the premises in question.

(3)   Without prejudice to the generality of subsection (2)(c) above, regard shall be had to the following considerations, so far as relevant, in determining whether it is appropriate for any sewer to be provided by virtue of this section—

(a)   the geology of the locality in question or of any other locality;

(b)   the number of premises, being premises on which there are buildings, which might reasonably be expected to be drained by means of that sewer;

(c)   the costs of providing that sewer;

(d)   the nature and extent of any adverse effects to the environment or amenity arising, or likely to arise, as a result of the premises or, as the case may be, the locality in question not being drained by means of a public sewer; and

(e)   the extent to which it is practicable for those effects to be overcome otherwise than by the provision (whether by virtue of this section or otherwise) of public sewers, and the costs of so overcoming those effects.

(4)   Guidance issued by the Secretary of State under this section may—

(a)   relate to how regard is to be had to the considerations mentioned in paragraphs (a) to (e) of subsection (3) above;

(b)   relate to any other matter which the Secretary of State considers may be a relevant consideration in any case and to how regard is to be had to any such matter;

(c)   set out considerations, other than those mentioned in paragraphs (a) to (e) of subsection (3) above, to which (so far as relevant) regard shall be had in determining whether it is appropriate for any sewer to be provided by virtue of this section;

(d)   relate to how regard is to be had to any such consideration as is mentioned in paragraph (c) above;

(e)   without prejudice to paragraphs (a) to (d) above, relate to how a sewerage undertaker is to discharge its functions under this section.

(5)   Before issuing guidance under this section the Secretary of State shall consult—

(a)   the Environment Agency;

(b)   the Director; and

(c)   such other bodies or persons as he considers appropriate;

and the Secretary of State shall arrange for any guidance issued by him under this section to be published in such manner as he considers appropriate.

(6)   Subject to the following provisions of this section, the duty of a sewerage undertaker by virtue of subsection (1) above shall be enforceable under section 18 above—

(a)   by the Secretary of State; or

(b)   with the consent of or in accordance with a general authorisation given by the Secretary of State, by the Director.

(7)   Any dispute between a sewerage undertaker and an owner or occupier of any premises in its area as to—

(a)   whether the undertaker is under a duty by virtue of subsection (1) above to provide a public sewer to be used for any such drainage of those premises as is mentioned in that subsection;

(b)   the domestic sewerage purposes for which any such sewer should be provided; or

(c)   the time by which any such duty of the undertaker should be performed,

shall be determined by the Environment Agency, and may be referred to the Environment Agency for determination by either of the parties to the dispute.

(8)   The Environment Agency—

(a)   shall notify the parties of the reasons for its decision on any dispute referred to it under subsection (7) above; and

(b)   may make any such recommendations, or give any such guidance, relating to or in connection with the drainage of the premises or locality in question as it considers appropriate.

(9)   The decision of the Environment Agency on any dispute referred to it under subsection (7) above shall be final.

(10)   A sewerage undertaker shall only be taken to be in breach of its duty under subsection (1) above where, and to the extent that, it has accepted, or the Environment Agency has determined under this section, that it is under such a duty and where any time

accepted by it, or determined by the Environment Agency under this section, as the time by which the duty is to that extent to be performed has passed.'.

104. In section 110A of that Act (new connections with public sewers) in subsection (6) (which requires the Director to consult the National Rivers Authority before making an order) for the words 'the NRA' there shall be substituted the words 'the Environment Agency'.

105.—(1) Section 120 of that Act (application for the discharge of special category effluent) shall be amended in accordance with the following provisions of this paragraph.

(2) In subsection (1) (sewerage undertakers to refer certain questions to the Secretary of State) for the words 'the Secretary of State' there shall be substituted the words 'the Environment Agency'.

(3) In subsection (4) (undertaker not to give consent etc until Secretary of State gives notice of his determination of the questions) for the words 'the Secretary of State' there shall be substituted the words 'the Environment Agency'.

(4) For subsections (7) and (8) (enforcement by Secretary of State) there shall be substituted—

'(9) If a sewerage undertaker fails, within the period provided by subsection (2) above, to refer to the Environment Agency any question which he is required by subsection (1) above to refer to the Agency, the undertaker shall be guilty of an offence and liable—

(a) on summary conviction, to a fine not exceeding the statutory maximum;

(b) on conviction on indictment, to a fine.

(10) If the Environment Agency becomes aware of any such failure as is mentioned in subsection (9) above, the Agency may—

(a) if a consent under this Chapter to make discharges of any special category effluent has been granted on the application in question, exercise its powers of review under section 127 or 131 below, notwithstanding anything in subsection (2) of the section in question; or

(b) in any other case, proceed as if the reference required by this section had been made.'

106. In section 123 of that Act (appeals with respect to the discharge of special category effluent) for the words 'the Secretary of State' or 'the Secretary of State's', wherever occurring, there shall be substituted respectively the words 'the Environment Agency' or 'the Environment Agency's'.

107. In section 127 of that Act (review by the Secretary of State of consents relating to special category effluent) for the words 'the Secretary of State' or 'the Secretary of State's', wherever occurring, there shall be substituted respectively the words 'the Environment Agency' or 'the Environment Agency's'.

108.—(1) Section 130 of that Act (reference to the Secretary of State of agreements relating to special category effluent) shall be amended in accordance with the following provisions of this paragraph.

(2) For the words 'the Secretary of State', wherever occurring, there shall be substituted the words 'the Environment Agency'.

(3) For subsections (5) and (6) (enforcement by Secretary of State) there shall be substituted—

'(7) If a sewerage undertaker fails, before giving any consent or entering into any agreement with respect to any such operations as are mentioned in paragraph (a) of subsection (1) above, to refer to the Environment Agency any question which he is required by that subsection to refer to the Agency, the undertaker shall be guilty of an offence and liable—

    (a)   on summary conviction, to a fine not exceeding the statutory maximum;

    (b)   on conviction on indictment, to a fine.

    (8)   If the Environment Agency becomes aware—

    (a)   that a sewerage undertaker and the owner or occupier of any trade premises are proposing to enter into any such agreement as is mentioned in subsection (1) above, and

    (b)   that the sewerage undertaker has not referred to the Agency any question which it is required to refer to the Agency by that subsection,

the Agency may proceed as if the reference required by that subsection had been made.

    (9)   If the Environment Agency becomes aware that any consent has been given or agreement entered into with respect to any such operations as are mentioned in paragraph (a) of subsection (1) above without the sewerage undertaker in question having referred to the Environment Agency any question which he is required by that subsection to refer to the Agency, the Agency may exercise its powers of review under section 127 above or, as the case may be, section 131 below, notwithstanding anything in subsection (2) of the section in question.'

109.   In section 131 of that Act (review by the Secretary of State of agreements relating to special category effluent) for the words 'the Secretary of State' or 'the Secretary of State's', wherever occurring, there shall be substituted respectively the words 'the Environment Agency' or 'the Environment Agency's'.

110.—(1)   Section 132 of that Act (powers and procedure on references and reviews) shall be amended in accordance with the following provisions of this paragraph.

    (2)   For the words 'the Secretary of State', wherever occurring, there shall be substituted the words 'the Environment Agency'.

    (3)   In subsection (2)(b) of that section (duty of the Secretary of State to consider representations or objections duly made to him) for the words 'him' and 'he' there shall be substituted the word 'the Agency'.

    (4)   In subsection (6) of that section (section 121(1) and (2) not to restrict power to impose conditions under subsection (4)(b)) for the word 'he' there shall be substituted the words 'the Agency'.

    (5)   Subsection (7) (powers of entry) shall cease to have effect.

111.   In section 133 of that Act (effect of determination on reference or review)
for subsection (4) (duties of sewerage undertaker to be enforceable under section 18 by the Secretary of State) there shall be substituted—

    '(5)   A sewerage undertaker which fails to perform its duty under subsection (1) above shall be guilty of an offence and liable—

    (a)   on summary conviction, to a fine not exceeding the statutory maximum;

    (b)   on conviction on indictment, to a fine.

    (6)   The Environment Agency may, for the purpose of securing compliance with the provisions of a notice under section 132 above, by serving notice on the sewerage undertaker in question and on the person specified in section 132(2)(a)(ii) above, vary or revoke—

    (a)   any consent given under this Chapter to make discharges of any special category effluent, or

    (b)   any agreement under section 129 above.'

112.   In section 134 of that Act (compensation in respect of determinations made for the protection of public health etc)—

    (a)   for the words 'the Secretary of State' or 'the Secretary of State's', wherever occurring, there shall be substituted respectively the words 'the Environment Agency' or 'the Environment Agency's'; and

    (b)   in subsection (2)(b) for the word 'him' there shall be substituted the words 'the Agency'.

113.   After section 135 there shall be inserted—

'135A   Power of the Environment Agency to acquire information for the purpose of its functions in relation to special category effluent

(1)   For the purpose of the discharge of its functions under this Chapter, the Environment Agency may, by notice in writing served on any person, require that person to furnish such information specified in the notice as that Agency reasonably considers it needs, in such form and within such period following service of the notice, or at such time, as is so specified.

(2)   A person who—

(a)   fails, without reasonable excuse, to comply with a requirement imposed under subsection (1) above, or

(b)   in furnishing any information in compliance with such a requirement, makes any statement which he knows to be false or misleading in a material particular, or recklessly makes a statement which is false or misleading in a material particular,

shall be guilty of an offence.

(3)   A person guilty of an offence under subsection (2) above shall be liable—

(a)   on summary conviction, to a fine not exceeding the statutory maximum;

(b)   on conviction on indictment, to a fine or to imprisonment for a term not exceeding two years, or to both.'

114.—(1)   Section 142 of that Act (powers of undertakers to charge) shall be amended in accordance with the following provisions of this paragraph.

(2)   In subsection (2) (manner in which charging powers to be exercised) for the words 'subsection (3)' there shall be substituted the words 'subsections (3) and (3A)'.

(3)   After subsection (3) (restriction on charging by agreement for trade effluent functions) there shall be inserted—

'(3A)   The power of a sewerage undertaker to charge, by virtue of subsection (1) above, for any services provided in the course of carrying out its duty under section 101A(1) above shall be exercisable only by or in accordance with a charges scheme under section 143 below.'

115.   In section 143 of that Act (charges schemes) after subsection (3) (charges which may be imposed in certain cases) there shall be inserted—

'(3A)   A sewerage undertaker is under a duty to ensure that any charges scheme made by the undertaker, so far as having effect to recover the undertaker's costs of providing a sewer by virtue of its duty under section 101A(1) above, causes those costs to be borne by the undertaker's customers generally; and a sewerage undertaker's duty under this subsection shall be enforceable under section 18 above—

(a)   by the Secretary of State; or

(b)   with the consent of or in accordance with a general authorisation

given by the Secretary of State, by the Director.'

116.   Section 151 of that Act shall cease to have effect.

117.   In section 161 of that Act (power to deal with foul water and pollution) in subsections (3) and (4) for the words 'the NRA', wherever occurring, there shall be substituted the words 'the Environment Agency'.

118.   In section 166 of that Act (consents for certain discharges under section 165) in subsection (1) (which requires the consent of the National Rivers Authority to certain discharges) for the words 'the NRA' there shall be substituted the words 'the Environment Agency'.

119. In section 184 of that Act (power of certain undertakers to alter public sewers etc) in subsection (1) for the words 'NRA', in each place where it occurs, there shall be substituted the words 'Environment Agency'.

120. In section 202 of that Act (duties of undertakers to furnish the Secretary of State with information) in subsection (6) (which defines the expression 'the other consolidation Acts') for the words 'the NRA' there shall be substituted the words 'the Environment Agency'.

121.—(1) In section 206 of that Act (restriction on disclosure of information) in subsection (2) (information furnished under section 196 or 204) the words '196 or' shall cease to have effect.

(2) In subsection (3)(a) of that section (exception for disclosure of information for purposes of functions under certain enactments)—

(a) for the words 'the NRA' there shall be substituted the words 'the Environment Agency, the Scottish Environment Protection Agency'; and

(b) for the words 'or the Water Act 1989' there shall be substituted the words ', the Water Act 1989, Part I or IIA of the Environmental Protection Act 1990 or the Environment Act 1995'.

(3) In subsection (4), in paragraph (a) (which provides that nothing in subsection (1) shall limit the matters which may be included in reports made by specified bodies under specified enactments)—

(a) for the words 'the NRA' there shall be substituted the words 'the Environment Agency, the Scottish Environment Protection Agency'; and

(b) for the words 'or of the Water Resources Act 1991' there shall be substituted the words ', Part I or IIA of the Environmental Protection Act 1990, the Water Resources Act 1991 or the Environment Act 1995'.

122. In section 209 of that Act (civil liability of undertakers for escapes of water etc) in subsection (3) (exceptions for loss sustained by other public undertakers) for the words 'the NRA' there shall be substituted the words 'the Environment Agency'.

123. In section 215 of that Act (local inquiries) in subsection (3) (application of section 250(4) of the Local Government Act 1972 in relation to the National Rivers Authority) for the words 'the NRA', in each place where they occur, there shall be substituted the words 'the Environment Agency'.

124. In section 217 of that Act (construction of provisions conferring powers by reference to undertakers' functions) for the words 'NRA', wherever occurring, there shall be substituted the words 'Environment Agency'.

125. In section 219 of that Act (general interpretation) in subsection (1)—

(a) the definition of 'the NRA' shall be omitted; and

(b) subject to that, for the words 'the NRA', wherever occurring, there shall be substituted the words 'the Environment Agency'.

126. In Schedule 11 to that Act (orders conferring compulsory works powers) in paragraph 1(3) (persons on whom copy notices are to be served) in paragraph (a), for the words 'the NRA' there shall be substituted the words 'the Environment Agency'.

127. In Schedule 13 to that Act (protective provisions in respect of certain undertakers) in paragraph 1, in sub-paragraphs (2) and (5)(a), for the words 'the NRA', wherever occurring, there shall be substituted the words 'the Environment Agency'.

The Water Resources Act 1991

128. Subject to the other provisions of this Act, in the Water Resources Act 1991, for the word 'Authority' or 'Authority's', wherever occurring, other than in section 119(1), there shall be substituted respectively the word 'Agency' or 'Agency's'.

129. Sections 1 to 14 of that Act (the National Rivers Authority and committees with functions in relation to that Authority) shall cease to have effect.

130. In section 15 of that Act (general duties with respect to the water industry), in subsection (2)(a) (provisions conferring powers in the exercise of which the Ministers are to take into account the duties imposed on the Agency by subsection (1)) after the words 'by virtue of' there shall be inserted the words 'the 1995 Act,'.

131. Sections 16 to 19 of that Act (which relate to the environmental and recreational duties of the National Rivers Authority and the general management of resources by that Authority) shall cease to have effect.

132. In section 20 of that Act (water resources management schemes) in subsection (1) of that section (duty to enter into arrangements with water undertakers for the management or operation of certain waters etc) for the words ', section 19(1) above' there shall be substituted the words 'section 6(2) of the 1995 Act'.

133.—(1) In section 21 of that Act (minimum acceptable flows) in subsection (3), at the end of paragraph (f) (consultation with person authorised by a licence under Part I of the Electricity Act 1989 to generate electricity) there shall be added the words 'who has a right to abstract water from those waters'.

(2) In subsection (4)(b) of that section (which refers to certain enactments which are repealed, but whose effect is reproduced, by this Act) for the words 'sections 2(2), 16 and 17 above' there shall be substituted the words 'sections 6(1), 7 and 8 of the 1995 Act'.

134. In section 43 of that Act (appeals to the Secretary of State from decisions with respect to licences) after subsection (1) there shall be inserted—

'(1A) This section is subject to section 114 of the 1995 Act (delegation or reference of appeals etc).'

135.—(1) In section 50 of that Act, in subsection (1) (power to make regulations, in relation to cases to which section 49 applies, for conferring succession rights to abstraction licences where a person becomes the occupier of part of the relevant land) for the words 'cases to which section 49 above applies' there shall be substituted the words 'cases in which the holder of a licence under this Chapter to abstract water ('the prior holder') is the occupier of the whole or part of the land specified in the licence as the land on which water abstracted in pursuance of the licence is to be used ('the relevant land')'.

(2) That section shall have effect, and be taken always to have had effect, as if it had originally been enacted with the amendment made by sub-paragraph (1) above.

136. Section 58 (revocation of licence for non-payment of charges) shall cease to have effect.

137. Section 68 of that Act (power by order to establish a tribunal to which certain appeals and references shall lie) shall cease to have effect.

138. Section 69(5) of that Act (which refers to the tribunal established under section 68) shall cease to have effect.

139.—(1) Section 73 of that Act (power to make ordinary and emergency drought orders) shall be amended in accordance with the following provisions of this paragraph.

(2) In subsection (1) (power to make ordinary drought orders) for the words from the beginning to 'then' there shall be substituted the words—

'(1) If the Secretary of State is satisfied that, by reason of an exceptional shortage of rain, there exists or is threatened—

(a) a serious deficiency of supplies of water in any area, or

(b)   such a deficiency in the flow or level of water in any inland waters as to pose a serious threat to any of the flora or fauna which are dependent on those waters, then,'.

(3)   In subsection (3) (power to make drought order not to be exercisable except where an application is made by the National Rivers Authority or a water undertaker)—

(a)   for the words 'except where' there shall be substituted the word 'unless'; and

(b)   at the beginning of paragraph (b) (water undertakers) there shall be inserted the words 'except in the case of an ordinary drought order under subsection (1)(b) above,'.

140.   After section 79 of that Act (compensation and charges where drought order made) there shall be inserted—

'79A   Drought permits

(1)   If the Agency is satisfied that, by reason of an exceptional shortage of rain, a serious deficiency of supplies of water in any area exists or is threatened then, subject to the following provisions of this section, it may, upon the application of a water undertaker which supplies water to premises in that area, issue to that undertaker a drought permit making such provision authorised by this section as appears to the Agency to be expedient with a view to meeting the deficiency.

(2)   A drought permit may contain any of the following provisions, that is to say—

(a)   provision authorising the water undertaker to which it is issued to take water from any source specified in the permit subject to any conditions or restrictions so specified;

(b)   provision suspending or modifying, subject to any conditions specified in the permit, any restriction or obligation to which that undertaker is subject as respects the taking of water from any source.

(3)   A drought permit shall specify—

(a)   the day on which it comes into force; and

(b)   the period for which, subject to subsections (4) and (5) below, any authorisation given, or suspension or modification effected, by the permit is to have effect.

(4)   Subject to subsection (5) below, the period for which—

(a)   an authorisation given by a drought permit, or

(b)   a suspension or modification effected by such a permit,

has effect shall expire before the end of the period of six months beginning with the day on which the permit comes into force.

(5)   At any time before the expiration of the period for which such an authorisation, suspension or modification has effect, the Agency may, by giving notice to the water undertaker to which the permit in question was issued, extend that period, but not so as to extend it beyond the end of the period of one year beginning with the day on which the permit came into force.

(6)   A drought permit which—

(a)   authorises the taking of water from a source from which water is supplied to an inland navigation; or

(b)   suspends or modifies—

(i)   a restriction as respects the taking of water from a source from which water is supplied to an inland navigation; or

(ii)   an obligation to discharge compensation water into a canal or into any river or stream which forms part of, or from which water is supplied to, an inland navigation,

shall not be issued without the consent of every navigation authority exercising functions over any or all of the parts of the canal or inland navigation in question which are affected by the permit.

(7)   Schedule 8 to this Act shall have effect with respect to the procedure on an application for a drought permit as it has effect with respect to the procedure on an application for a drought order, but with the following modifications, that is to say—

(a)   with the substitution for any reference to a drought order of a reference to a drought permit;

(b)   with the substitution for any reference to the Secretary of State of a reference to the Agency;

(c)   with the omission of the reference to the Agency in the Table in paragraph 1;

(d)   with the insertion, in paragraph 1(3)(c), of a requirement that the notice in question shall specify the address at which any objections are to be made to the Agency; and

(e)   with the omission—

(i)   of paragraph 2(1)(a) and the word "either" immediately preceding it, and

(ii)   of paragraph 2(6).

(8)   For the purposes of sections 125 to 129 below any water authorised by a drought permit to be abstracted from a source of supply shall be treated as if it had been authorised to be so abstracted by a licence granted under Chapter II of this Part, whether the water undertaker to which the permit is issued is the holder of such a licence or not.

(9)   Section 79 above and Schedule 9 to this Act shall apply in relation to drought permits and their issue as they apply in relation to ordinary drought orders and their making.

(10)   A drought permit may—

(a)   make different provision for different cases, including different provision in relation to different persons, circumstances or localities; and

(b)   contain such supplemental, consequential and transitional provisions as the Agency considers appropriate.

(11)   In this section—

"compensation water" has the same meaning as in section 77 above;

"drought permit" means a drought permit under this section;

"inland navigation" has the same meaning as in section 77 above.'

141.   In section 80 of that Act (offences against drought orders)—

(a)   in subsection (1)(a) (taking or using water otherwise than in accordance with any condition or restriction imposed by or under a drought order) for the words 'so imposed' there shall be substituted the words 'imposed by or under any drought order or by any drought permit';

(b)   in subsection (2)(a) (failure to construct or maintain measuring apparatus required by any drought order) after the words 'by any drought order' there shall be inserted the words 'or drought permit'; and

(c)   in subsection (2)(b) (failure to allow person authorised by or under any such order to inspect etc apparatus or records) after the words 'by or under any such order' there shall be inserted the words 'or by virtue of any such permit'.

142.   After section 90 of that Act (offences in connection with deposits and vegetation in rivers) there shall be inserted—

'Consents for the purposes of sections 88 to 90

90A.   Applications for consent under section 89 or 90

(1)   Any application for a consent for the purposes of section 89(4)(a) or 90(1) or (2) above—

(a)   must be made on a form provided for the purpose by the Agency, and

(b)   must be advertised in such manner as may be required by regulations made by the Secretary of State,

except that paragraph (b) above shall not have effect in the case of an application of any class or description specified in the regulations as being exempt from the requirements of that paragraph.

(2)   The applicant for such a consent must, at the time when he makes his application, provide the Agency—

(a)   with all such information as it reasonably requires; and

(b)   with all such information as may be prescribed for the purpose by the Secretary of State.

(3)   The information required by subsection (2) above must be provided either on, or together with, the form mentioned in subsection (1) above.

(4)   The Agency may give the applicant notice requiring him to provide it with all such further information of any description specified in the notice as it may require for the purpose of determining the application.

(5)   If the applicant fails to provide the Agency with any information required under subsection (4) above, the Agency may refuse to proceed with the application or refuse to proceed with it until the information is provided.

90B.   Enforcement notices

(1)   If the Agency is of the opinion that the holder of a relevant consent is contravening any condition of the consent, or is likely to contravene any such condition, the Agency may serve on him a notice (an ''enforcement notice'').

(2)   An enforcement notice shall—

(a)   state that the Agency is of the said opinion;

(b)   specify the matters constituting the contravention or the matters making it likely that the contravention will arise;

(c)   specify the steps that must be taken to remedy the contravention or, as the case may be, to remedy the matters making it likely that the contravention will arise; and

(d)   specify the period within which those steps must be taken.

(3)   Any person who fails to comply with any requirement imposed by an enforcement notice shall be guilty of an offence and liable—

(a)   on summary conviction, to imprisonment for a term not exceeding three months or to a fine not exceeding £20,000 or to both;

(b)   on conviction on indictment, to imprisonment for a term not exceeding two years or to a fine or to both.

(4)   If the Agency is of the opinion that proceedings for an offence under subsection (3) above would afford an ineffectual remedy against a person who has failed to comply with the requirements of an enforcement notice, the Agency may take proceedings in the High Court for the purpose of securing compliance with the notice.

(5)   The Secretary of State may, if he thinks fit in relation to any person, give to the Agency directions as to whether the Agency should exercise its powers under this section and as to the steps which must be taken.

(6)   In this section—

''relevant consent'' means—

(a)   a consent for the purposes of section 89(4)(a) or 90(1) or (2) above; or

(b)   a discharge consent, within the meaning of section 91 below; and

''the holder'', in relation to a relevant consent, is the person who has the consent in question.'

143.—(1)   In section 91 of that Act (appeals in respect of consents under Chapter II of Part III of that Act), in subsection (1) (which specifies the decisions which are subject to appeal)—

(a)   in paragraph (d) (which refers to paragraph 7(1) or (2) of Schedule 10) for the words '7(1)' there shall be substituted the words '8(1)'; and

(b)   at the end there shall be added—

'(g)   has refused a person a variation of any such consent as is mentioned in paragraphs (a) to (f) above or, in allowing any such variation, has made the consent subject to conditions; or

(h)   has served an enforcement notice on any person.'

(2)   In subsection (2) of that section (persons who may appeal)—

(a)   after the words 'who applied for the consent' there shall be inserted the words 'or variation'; and

(b)   after the words 'would be authorised by the consent' there shall be inserted the words ', or the person on whom the enforcement notice was served,'.

(3)   For subsections (3) to (7) of that section there shall be substituted—

'(2A)   This section is subject to section 114 of the 1995 Act (delegation or reference of appeals etc).

(2B)   An appeal under this section shall, if and to the extent required by regulations under subsection (2K) below, be advertised in such manner as may be prescribed by regulations under that subsection.

(2C)   If either party to the appeal so requests or the Secretary of State so decides, an appeal shall be or continue in the form of a hearing (which may, if the person hearing the appeal so decides, be held, or held to any extent, in private).

(2D)   On determining an appeal brought by virtue of any of paragraphs (a) to (g) of subsection (1) above against a decision of the Agency, the Secretary of State—

(a)   may affirm the decision;

(b)   where the decision was a refusal to grant a consent or a variation of a consent, may direct the Agency to grant the consent or to vary the consent, as the case may be;

(c)   where the decision was as to the conditions of a consent, may quash all or any of those conditions;

(d)   where the decision was to revoke a consent, may quash the decision;

(e)   where the decision relates to a period specified for the purposes of paragraph 8(1) or (2) of Schedule 10 to this Act, may modify any provisions specifying that period; and where he exercises any of the powers in paragraphs (b), (c) or (d) above, he may give directions as to the conditions to which the consent is to be subject.

(2E)   On the determination of an appeal brought by virtue of paragraph (h) of subsection (1) above, the Secretary of State may either quash or affirm the enforcement notice and, if he affirms it, may do so either in its original form or with such modifications as he may in the circumstances think fit.

(2F)   Subject to subsection (2G) below, where an appeal is brought by virtue of subsection (1)(c) above against a decision—

(a)   to revoke a discharge consent,

(b)   to modify the conditions of any such consent, or

(c)   to provide that any such consent which was unconditional shall be subject to conditions,

the revocation, modification or provision shall not take effect pending the final determination or the withdrawal of the appeal.

(2G)   Subsection (2F) above shall not apply to a decision in the case of which the notice affecting the revocation, modification or provision in question includes a statement that in the opinion of the Agency it is necessary for the purpose of preventing or, where that is not practicable, minimising—

(a)   the entry into controlled waters of any poisonous, noxious or polluting matter or any solid waste matter, or

(b)   harm to human health,

that that subsection should not apply.

(2H)   Where the decision under appeal is one falling within subsection (2G) above, if, on the application of the holder or former holder of the consent, the Secretary of State or other person determining the appeal determines that the Agency acted unreasonably in excluding the application of subsection (2F) above, then—

(a)   if the appeal is still pending at the end of the day on which the determination is made, subsection (2F) above shall apply to the decision from the end of that day; and

(b) the holder or former holder of the consent shall be entitled to recover compensation from the Agency in respect of any loss suffered by him in consequence of the exclusion of the application of that subsection;

and any dispute as to a person's entitlement to such compensation or as to the amount of it shall be determined by arbitration.

(2J) Where an appeal is brought under this section against an enforcement notice, the bringing of the appeal shall not have the effect of suspending the operation of the notice.

(2K) Provision may be made by the Secretary of State by regulations with respect to appeals under this section and in particular—

(a) as to the period within which and the manner in which appeals are to be brought; and

(b) as to the manner in which appeals are to be considered.'

(4) In subsection (8) of that section (which refers to paragraph 5 of Schedule 10) for the word '5' there shall be substituted the word '6'.

144. In section 92 of that Act (requirements to take precautions against pollution) after subsection (2) (which includes provision for regulations to provide for appeals to the Secretary of State) there shall be added—

'(3) This section is subject to section 114 of the 1995 Act (delegation or reference of appeals etc).'

145. In section 96 of that Act (regulations with respect to consents required by virtue of section 93 etc, including provision with respect to appeals) after subsection (3) there shall be added—

'(4) This section is subject to section 114 of the 1995 Act (delegation or reference of appeals etc).'

146. Section 105(1) of that Act (National Rivers Authority to exercise general supervision over matters relating to flood defence) shall cease to have effect.

147.—(1) In section 110 of that Act (applications for consents and approvals under section 109) in subsection (1) (which confers power to charge an application fee of £50 or such other sum as may be specified by order made by the Ministers) for the words 'specified by order made by the Ministers' there shall be substituted the word 'prescribed'.

(2) In subsection (4)(b) of that section (which provides for questions as to unreasonable withholding of any consent or approval to be referred to the Ministers or the Secretary of State if the parties cannot agree on an arbitrator) for the words 'the Ministers' there shall be substituted the words 'the Minister'.

(3) After subsection (5) of that section there shall be inserted—

'(6) In subsection (1) above "prescribed" means specified in, or determined in accordance with, an order made by the Ministers; and any such order may make different provision for different cases, including different provision in relation to different persons, circumstances or localities.'

148. Section 114 (general fisheries duty of the National Rivers Authority) shall cease to have effect.

149. Section 117 (general financial duties of the National Rivers Authority) shall cease to have effect.

150.—(1) Section 118 of that Act (special duties with respect to flood defence revenue) shall be amended in accordance with the following provisions of this paragraph.

(2) In subsection (1)(b) (such revenue to be disregarded in determining the amount of any surplus for the purposes of section 117(3)) for the words 'section 117(3) above' there shall be substituted the words 'section 44(4) of the 1995 Act'.

(3)   In subsection (2)(b) (flood defence revenue to include revenue raised by general drainage charges under sections 134 to 136) for the words 'to 136' there shall be substituted the words 'and 135'.

151.—(1)   In section 119 of that Act (duties with respect to certain funds raised under local enactments) for subsection (1) (duty of the National Rivers Authority, in respect of funds created for fishery purposes under local enactments, not to use those funds except for the purposes for which they could have been used if the Water Resources Act 1963 had not been passed) there shall be substituted—

'(1)   Where the Agency holds any funds, or any interest in any funds, which immediately before the transfer date the National Rivers Authority, by virtue of this subsection as originally enacted, was not permitted to use except for particular purposes, those funds or that interest shall not be used except for the purposes for which they could be used by virtue of this subsection as originally enacted.

(1A)   For the purposes of subsection (1) above, "the transfer date" has the same meaning as in Part I of the 1995 Act.'

(2)   In subsection (2) of that section (certain funds raised under local enactments to be disregarded in determining the amount of any surplus for the purposes of section 117(3)) for the words 'section 117(3) above' there shall be substituted the words 'section 44(3) of the 1995 Act'.

152.   Sections 121 to 124 of that Act (accounts of the Authority, audit and schemes imposing water resources charges) shall cease to have effect.

153.   Sections 126(6) and 129(4) of that Act (each of which applies section 68) shall cease to have effect.

154.   Sections 131 and 132 of that Act (schemes of charges in connection with control of pollution) shall cease to have effect.

155.   Section 146 of that Act (revenue grants by the Secretary of State to the National Rivers Authority) shall cease to have effect.

156.   Sections 150 to 153 of that Act (grants for national security purposes, borrowing powers of the National Rivers Authority, loans to the Authority, and Treasury guarantees of the Authority's borrowing) shall cease to have effect.

157.   In section 154 of that Act (compulsory purchase etc) in subsection (6), for the words '(including section 4 above) or otherwise' there shall be substituted the words 'or otherwise (including section 37 of the 1995 Act (incidental general powers of the Agency))'.

158.   In section 156 of that Act (acquisition of land etc for fisheries purposes) for the words 'Without prejudice to section 4 above', in each place where they occur, there shall be substituted the words 'Without prejudice to section 37 of the 1995 Act (incidental general powers of the Agency)'.

159.   In section 157 of that Act (restriction on disposals of compulsorily acquired land) for subsection (6) (meaning of 'compulsorily acquired land') there shall be substituted—

'(6)   In this section "compulsorily acquired land", in relation to the Agency, means any land of the Agency which—

(a)   was acquired by the Agency compulsorily under the provisions of section 154 above or of an order under section 168 below;

(b)   was acquired by the Agency at a time when it was authorised under those provisions to acquire the land compulsorily;

(c)   being land which has been transferred to the Agency from the Authority by section 3 of the 1995 Act, was acquired by the Authority—

(i)   compulsorily, under the provisions of section 154 above or of an order under section 168 below or under the provisions of section 151 of the Water Act 1989 or of an order under section 155 of that Act; or

(ii)   at a time when it was authorised under those provisions to acquire the land compulsorily;

(d)   being land—

(i)   which has been so transferred, and

(ii)   which was transferred to the Authority in accordance with a scheme under Schedule 2 to the Water Act 1989,

was acquired by a predecessor of the Authority compulsorily under so much of any enactment in force at any time before 1st September 1989 as conferred powers of compulsory acquisition; or

(e)   being land transferred as mentioned in sub-paragraphs (i) and (ii) of paragraph (d) above, was acquired by such a predecessor at a time when it was authorised to acquire the land by virtue of any such powers as are mentioned in that paragraph.'

160.   In section 158 of that Act (works agreements for water resources purposes) in subsection (1) (which is expressed to be without prejudice to the generality of the powers conferred by section 4) for the words 'section 4 above' there shall be substituted the words 'section 37 of the 1995 Act (incidental general powers of the Agency)'.

161.—(1)   Section 161 of that Act (anti-pollution works and operations) shall be amended in accordance with the following provisions of this paragraph.

(2)   In subsection (1) (power, subject to subsection (2), to carry out works and operations etc) for the words 'Subject to subsection (2) below,' there shall be substituted the words 'Subject to subsections (1A) and (2) below,'.

(3)   After that subsection there shall be inserted—

'(1A)   Without prejudice to the power of the Agency to carry out investigations under subsection (1) above, the power conferred by that subsection to carry out works and operations shall only be exercisable in a case where—

(a)   the Agency considers it necessary to carry out forthwith any works or operations failing within paragraph (a) or (b) of that subsection; or

(b)   it appears to the Agency, after reasonable inquiry, that no person can be found on whom to serve a works notice under section 161A below.'

162.   After that section there shall be inserted—

'**161A.   Notices requiring persons to carry out anti-pollution works and operations**

(1)   Subject to the following provisions of this section, where it appears to the Agency that any poisonous, noxious or polluting matter or any solid waste matter is likely to enter, or to be or to have been present in, any controlled waters, the Agency shall be entitled to serve a works notice on any person who, as the case may be,—

(a)   caused or knowingly permitted the matter in question to be present at the place from which it is likely, in the opinion of the Agency, to enter any controlled waters; or

(b)   caused or knowingly permitted the matter in question to be present in any controlled waters.

(2)   For the purposes of this section, a "works notice" is a notice requiring the person on whom it is served to carry out such of the following works or operations as may be specified in the notice, that is to say—

(a)   in a case where the matter in question appears likely to enter any controlled waters, works or operations for the purpose of preventing it from doing so; or

(b)   in a case where the matter appears to be or to have been present in any controlled waters, works or operations for the purpose—

(i)   of removing or disposing of the matter;

(ii)   of remedying or mitigating any pollution caused by its presence in the waters; or

(iii) so far as it is reasonably practicable to do so, of restoring the waters, including any flora and fauna dependent on the aquatic environment of the waters, to their state immediately before the matter became present in the waters.

(3) A works notice—

(a) must specify the periods within which the person on whom it is served is required to do each of the things specified in the notice; and

(b) is without prejudice to the powers of the Agency by virtue of section 161(1A)(a) above.

(4) Before serving a works notice on any person, the Agency shall reasonably endeavour to consult that person concerning the works or operations which are to be specified in the notice.

(5) The Secretary of State may by regulations make provision for or in connection with—

(a) the form or content of works notices;

(b) requirements for consultation, before the service of a works notice, with persons other than the person on whom that notice is to be served;

(c) steps to be taken for the purposes of any consultation required under subsection (4) above or regulations made by virtue of paragraph (b) above; or

(d) any other steps of a procedural nature which are to be taken in connection with, or in consequence of, the service of a works notice.

(6) A works notice shall not be regarded as invalid, or as invalidly served, by reason only of any failure to comply with the requirements of subsection (4) above or of regulations made by virtue of paragraph (b) of subsection (5) above.

(7) Nothing in subsection (1) above shall entitle the Agency to require the carrying out of any works or operations which would impede or prevent the making of any discharge in pursuance of a consent given under Chapter II of Part III of this Act.

(8) No works notice shall be served on any person requiring him to carry out any works or operations in respect of water from an abandoned mine or an abandoned part of a mine which that person permitted to reach such a place as is mentioned in subsection (1)(a) above or to enter any controlled waters.

(9) Subsection (8) above shall not apply to the owner or former operator of any mine or part of a mine if the mine or part in question became abandoned after 31st December 1999.

(10) Subsections (3B) and (3C) of section 89 above shall apply in relation to subsections (8) and (9) above as they apply in relation to subsections (3) and (3A) of that section.

(11) Where the Agency—

(a) carries out any such investigations as are mentioned in section 161 (1) above, and

(b) serves a works notice on a person in connection with the matter to which the investigations relate,

it shall (unless the notice is quashed or withdrawn) be entitled to recover the costs or expenses reasonably incurred in carrying out those investigations from that person.

(12) The Secretary of State may, if he thinks fit in relation to any person, give directions to the Agency as to whether or how it should exercise its powers under this section.

(13) In this section—

"controlled waters" has the same meaning as in Part III of this Act;

"mine" has the same meaning as in the Mines and Quarries Act 1954.

161B. Grant of, and compensation for, rights of entry etc.

(1) A works notice may require a person to carry out works or operations in relation to any land or waters notwithstanding that he is not entitled to carry out those works or operations.

(2) Any person whose consent is required before any works or operations required by a works notice may be carried out shall grant, or join in granting, such rights in relation to any land or waters as will enable the person on whom the works notice is served to comply with any requirements imposed by the works notice.

(3) Before serving a works notice, the Agency shall reasonably endeavour to consult every person who appears to it—

(a) to be the owner or occupier of any relevant land, and

(b) to be a person who might be required by subsection (2) above to grant, or join in granting, any rights,

concerning the rights which that person may be so required to grant.

(4) A works notice shall not be regarded as invalid, or as invalidly served, by reason only of any failure to comply with the requirements of subsection (3) above.

(5) A person who grants, or joins in granting, any rights pursuant to subsection (2) above shall be entitled, on making an application within such period as may be prescribed and in such manner as may be prescribed to such person as may be prescribed, to be paid by the person on whom the works notice in question is served compensation of such amount as may be determined in such manner as may be prescribed.

(6) Without prejudice to the generality of the regulations that may be made by virtue of subsection (5) above, regulations by virtue of that subsection may make such provision in relation to compensation under this section as may be made by regulations by virtue of subsection (4) of section 35A of the Environmental Protection Act 1990 in relation to compensation under that section.

(7) In this section—

"prescribed" means prescribed in regulations made by the Secretary of State;

"relevant land" means—

(a) any land or waters in relation to which the works notice in question requires, or may require, works or operations to be carried out; or

(b) any land adjoining or adjacent to that land or those waters;

"works notice" means a works notice under section 161A above.

161C. Appeals against works notices

(1) A person on whom a works notice is served may, within the period of twenty-one days beginning with the day on which the notice is served, appeal against the notice to the Secretary of State.

(2) On any appeal under this section the Secretary of State—

(a) shall quash the notice, if he is satisfied that there is a material defect in the notice; but

(b) subject to that, may confirm the notice, with or without modification, or quash it.

(3) The Secretary of State may by regulations make provision with respect to—

(a) the grounds on which appeals under this section may be made; or

(b) the procedure on any such appeal.

(4) Regulations under subsection (3) above may (among other things)—

(a) include provisions comparable to those in section 290 of the Public Health Act 1936 (appeals against notices requiring the execution of works);

(b) prescribe the cases in which a works notice is, or is not, to be suspended until the appeal is decided, or until some other stage in the proceedings;

(c) prescribe the cases in which the decision on an appeal may in some respects be less favourable to the appellant than the works notice against which he is appealing;

(d) prescribe the cases in which the appellant may claim that a works notice should have been served on some other person and prescribe the procedure to be followed in those cases;

(e) make provision as respects—

(i)   the particulars to be included in the notice of appeal;

(ii)   the persons on whom notice of appeal is to be served and the particulars, if any, which are to accompany the notice; or

(iii)   the abandonment of an appeal.

(5)   In this section "works notice" means a works notice under section 161A above.

(6)   This section is subject to section 114 of the 1995 Act (delegation or reference of appeals).

161D.   Consequences of not complying with a works notice

(1)   If a person on whom the Agency serves a works notice falls to comply with any of the requirements of the notice, he shall be guilty of an offence.

(2)   A person who commits an offence under subsection (1) above shall be liable—

(a)   on summary conviction, to imprisonment for a term not exceeding three months or to a fine not exceeding £20,000 or to both;

(b)   on conviction on indictment to imprisonment for a term not exceeding two years or to a fine or to both.

(3)   If a person on whom a works notice has been served fails to comply with any of the requirements of the notice, the Agency may do what that person was required to do and may recover from him any costs or expenses reasonably incurred by the Agency in doing it.

(4)   If the Agency is of the opinion that proceedings for an offence under subsection (1) above would afford an ineffectual remedy against a person who has failed to comply with the requirements of a works notice, the Agency may take proceedings in the High Court for the purpose of securing compliance with the notice.

(5)   In this section "works notice" means a works notice under section 161A above.'

163.   In section 162 of that Act (other powers to deal with foul water or pollution) in subsection (1) (which refers to section 161 of that Act) for the words 'section 161' there shall be substituted the words 'sections 161 to 161D'.

164.   In section 166 of that Act (power to carry out works for purposes of flood warning system) in subsection (1) (which is expressed to be without prejudice to the Agency's other powers by virtue of section 4) for the words 'section 4 above' there shall be substituted the words 'section 37 of the 1995 Act (incidental general powers of the Agency)'.

165.   In section 169 of that Act (powers of entry for enforcement purposes) at the beginning of subsection (3) there shall be inserted the words 'Subject to subsection (4) below,' and after that subsection there shall be added—

'(4)   The powers conferred by this section shall not have effect for the purposes of any of the Agency's pollution control functions, within the meaning of section 108 of the 1995 Act.'

166.   In section 172 of that Act (powers of entry for other purposes) at the beginning of subsection (3) there shall be inserted the words 'Subject to subsection (3A) below,' and after that subsection there shall be added—

'(3A)   The powers conferred by this section shall not have effect for the purposes of any of the Agency's pollution control functions, within the meaning of section 108 of the 1995 Act.'

167.   In section 174 of that Act (impersonation of persons exercising powers of entry) in subsection (1) (which creates a summary offence punishable by a fine not exceeding level 4) for the words from 'liable, on summary conviction,' onwards there shall be substituted the words 'liable—

(a)   on summary conviction, to a fine not exceeding the statutory maximum;

(b)   on conviction on indictment, to a fine or to imprisonment for a term not exceeding two years, or to both.'

168.   Section 187 of that Act (annual report of the Authority) shall cease to have effect.

169.—(1)   Section 190 of that Act (pollution control register) shall be amended in accordance with the following provisions of this paragraph.

(2)   In subsection (1) (which requires a register to be kept containing prescribed particulars of the items there specified) after the words 'prescribed particulars of' there shall be inserted the words 'or relating to'.

(3)   Paragraph (d) of that subsection (which relates to certificates under paragraph 1(7) of Schedule 10) shall be omitted.

(4)   Paragraph (f) of that subsection, and the word 'and' immediately preceding it, shall be omitted and at the end of that subsection there shall be added—

'(g)   applications made to the Agency for the variation of discharge consents;

(h)   enforcement notices served under section 90B above;

(j)   revocations, under paragraph 7 of Schedule 10 to this Act, of discharge consents;

(k)   appeals under section 91 above;

(l)   directions given by the Secretary of State in relation to the Agency's functions under the water pollution provisions of this Act;

(m)   convictions, for offences under Part III of this Act, of persons who have the benefit of discharge consents;

(n)   information obtained or furnished in pursuance of conditions of discharge consents;

(o)   works notices under section 161A above;

(p)   appeals under section 161C above;

(q)   convictions for offences under section 161D above;

(r)   such other matters relating to the quality of water or the pollution of water as may be prescribed by the Secretary of State.

(1A)   Where information of any description is excluded from any register by virtue of section 191B below, a statement shall be entered in the register indicating the existence of information of that description.'

(5)   In subsection (2) (registers to be available for inspection by, and facilities for obtaining copies of entries to be afforded to, the public) after paragraph (b) there shall be added the words—

'and, for the purposes of this subsection, places may be prescribed by the Secretary of State at which any such registers or facilities as are mentioned in paragraph (a) or (b) above are to be available or afforded to the public in pursuance of the paragraph in question.'

(6)   After subsection (3) there shall be added—

'(4)   The Secretary of State may give to the Agency directions requiring the removal from any register maintained by it under this section of any specified information which is not prescribed for inclusion under subsection (1) above or which, by virtue of section 191A or 191B below, ought to have been excluded from the register.

(5)   In this section "discharge consent" has the same meaning as in section 91 above.'

170.   After section 191 of that Act (register for the purposes of works discharges) there shall be inserted—

'**191A.   Exclusion from registers of information affecting national security**

(1)   No information shall be included in a register kept or maintained by the Agency under any provision of this Act if and so long as, in the opinion of the Secretary of State, the inclusion in such a register of that information, or information of that description, would be contrary to the interests of national security.

(2)   The Secretary of State may, for the purpose of securing the exclusion from registers of information to which subsection (1) above applies, give to the Agency directions—

(a) specifying information, or descriptions of information, to be excluded from their registers; or

(b) specifying descriptions of information to be referred to the Secretary of State for his determination;
and no information referred to the Secretary of State in pursuance of paragraph (b) above shall be included in any such register until the Secretary of State determines that it should be so included.

(3) The Agency shall notify the Secretary of State of any information it excludes from a register in pursuance of directions under subsection (2) above.

(4) A person may, as respects any information which appears to him to be information to which subsection (1) above may apply, give a notice to the Secretary of State specifying the information and indicating its apparent nature; and, if he does so—

(a) he shall notify the Agency that he has done so; and

(b) no information so notified to the Secretary of State shall be included in any such register until the Secretary of State has determined that it should be so included.

191B. Exclusion from registers of certain confidential information

(1) No information relating to the affairs of any individual or business shall, without the consent of that individual or the person for the time being carrying on that business, be included in a register kept or maintained by the Agency under any provision of this Act, if and so long as the information—

(a) is, in relation to him, commercially confidential; and

(b) is not required to be included in the register in pursuance of directions under subsection (7) below;
but information is not commercially confidential for the purposes of this section unless it is determined under this section to be so by the Agency or, on appeal, by the Secretary of State.

(2) Where information is furnished to the Agency for the purpose of—

(a) an application for a discharge consent or for the variation of a discharge consent,

(b) complying with any condition of a discharge consent, or

(c) complying with a notice under section 202 below,
then, if the person furnishing it applies to the Agency to have the information excluded from any register kept or maintained by the Agency under any provision of this Act, on the ground that it is commercially confidential (as regards himself or another person), the Agency shall determine whether the information is or is not commercially confidential.

(3) A determination under subsection (2) above must be made within the period of fourteen days beginning with the date of the application and if the Agency fails to make a determination within that period it shall be treated as having determined that the information is commercially confidential.

(4) Where it appears to the Agency that any information (other than information furnished in circumstances within subsection (2) above) which has been obtained by the Agency under or by virtue of any provision of any enactment might be commercially confidential, the Agency shall—

(a) give to the person to whom or whose business it relates notice that that information is required to be included in a register kept or maintained by the Agency under any provision of this Act, unless excluded under this section; and

(b) give him a reasonable opportunity—

(i) of objecting to the inclusion of the information on the ground that it is commercially confidential; and

(ii) of making representations to the Agency for the purpose of justifying any such objection;
and, if any representations are made, the Agency shall, having taken the representations into account, determine whether the information is or is not commercially confidential.

(5) Where, under subsection (2) or (4) above, the Agency determines that information is not commercially confidential—

(a) the information shall not be entered on the register until the end of the period of twenty-one days beginning with the date on which the determination is notified to the person concerned; and

(b) that person may appeal to the Secretary of State against the decision; and, where an appeal is brought in respect of any information, the information shall not be entered on the register until the end of the period of seven days following the day on which the appeal is finally determined or withdrawn.

(6) Subsections (2A), (2C) and (2K) of section 91 above shall apply in relation to appeals under subsection (5) above; but—

(a) subsection (2C) of that section shall have effect for the purposes of this subsection with the substitution for the words from ''(which may'' onwards of the words ''(which must be held in private)''; and

(b) subsection (5) above is subject to section 114 of the 1995 Act (delegation or reference of appeals etc).

(7) The Secretary of State may give to the Agency directions as to specified information, or descriptions of information, which the public interest requires to be included in registers kept or maintained by the Agency under any provision of this Act notwithstanding that the information may be commercially confidential.

(8) Information excluded from a register shall be treated as ceasing to be commercially confidential for the purposes of this section at the expiry of the period of four years beginning with the date of the determination by virtue of which it was excluded; but the person who furnished it may apply to the Agency for the information to remain excluded from the register on the ground that it is still commercially confidential and the Agency shall determine whether or not that is the case.

(9) Subsections (5) and (6) above shall apply in relation to a determination under subsection (8) above as they apply in relation to a determination under subsection (2) or (4) above.

(10) The Secretary of State may by regulations substitute (whether in all cases or in such classes or descriptions of case as may be specified in the regulations) for the period for the time being specified in subsection (3) above such other period as he considers appropriate.

(11) Information is, for the purposes of any determination under this section, commercially confidential, in relation to any individual or person, if its being contained in the register would prejudice to an unreasonable degree the commercial interests of that individual or person.

(12) In this section ''discharge consent'' has the same meaning as in section 91 above.'

171. Section 196 of that Act (provision of information by the Authority to Ministers) shall cease to have effect.

172.—(1) In section 202 of that Act (information and assistance required in connection with the control of pollution) in subsection (4) (which creates a summary offence punishable by a fine not exceeding level 5 on the standard scale) for the words from 'liable, on summary conviction,' onwards there shall be substituted the words 'liable—

(a) on summary conviction, to a fine not exceeding the statutory maximum;

(b) on conviction on indictment, to a fine or to imprisonment for a term not exceeding two years, or to both.'

(2) Subsection (5) of that section (which is superseded in consequence of the amendment made by sub-paragraph (1) above) shall cease to have effect.

173.—(1) Section 204 of that Act (restriction on disclosure of information with respect to any particular business) shall be amended in accordance with the following provisions of this paragraph.

(2) In subsection (2)(a) (exception for disclosure of information for purposes of functions under certain enactments)—

(a) for the words 'the Authority' there shall be substituted the words 'the Agency, the Scottish Environment Protection Agency'; and

(b) for the words 'or the Water Act 1989' there shall be substituted the words ', the Water Act 1989, Part I or IIA of the Environmental Protection Act 1990 or the 1995 Act'.

(3) In subsection (3), in paragraph (a) (which provides that nothing in subsection (1) shall limit the matters which may be included in reports made by specified bodies under specified enactments)—

(a) after sub-paragraph (i), there shall be inserted—

'(ia)   the Scottish Environment Protection Agency;'; and

(b) for the words 'or that Act of 1991' there shall be substituted the words ', Part I or IIA of the Environmental Protection Act 1990, that Act of 1991 or the 1995 Act'.

(4) In paragraph (b) of that subsection, after the words 'that Act' there shall be inserted the words 'of 1991'.

174.   Sections 213 to 215 of that Act (local inquiries) shall cease to have effect.

175.   Section 218 of that Act (no judicial disqualification by virtue of liability to pay charges to the Authority) shall cease to have effect.

176.   In section 219 of that Act (powers to make regulations)—

(a) in subsection (2), the words 'Subject to subsection (3) below,', and

(b) subsection (3) (which restricts certain powers to make regulations), shall cease to have effect.

177.—(1)   Section 221(1) of that Act (general interpretation) shall be amended in accordance with the following provisions of this paragraph.

(2) Before the definition of 'abstraction' there shall be inserted—
'the 1995 Act' means the Environment Act 1995;'.

(3) After the definition of 'accessories' there shall be inserted—
'"the Agency" means the Environment Agency;'.

(4) The definition of 'the Authority' shall be omitted.

(5) The definition of 'constituent council' shall be omitted.

(6) After the definition of 'enactment' there shall be inserted—
'"enforcement notice" has the meaning given by section 90B above;'.

(7) For the definition of 'flood defence functions' there shall be substituted—
'"flood defence functions", in relation to the Agency, means—

(a) its functions with respect to flood defence and land drainage by virtue of Part IV of this Act, the Land Drainage Act 1991 and section 6 of the 1995 Act;

(b) those functions transferred to the Agency by section 2(1)(a)(iii) of the 1995 Act which were previously transferred to the Authority by virtue of section 136(8) of the Water Act 1989 and paragraph 1(3) of Schedule 15 to that Act (transfer of land drainage functions under local statutory provisions and subordinate legislation); and

(c) any other functions of the Agency under any of the flood defence provisions of this Act;'.

(8) For the definition of 'flood defence provisions' there shall be substituted—
'"flood defence provisions", in relation to this Act, means—

(a) any of the following provisions of this Act, that is to say—

(i) Part IV;

(ii) sections 133 to 141 (including Schedule 15), 143, 147 to 149, 155, 165 to 167, 180, 193, 194 and paragraph 5 of Schedule 25;

(b) any of the following provisions of the 1995 Act, that is to say—

(i) section 6(4) (general supervision of flood defence);

  (ii) section 53 (inquiries and other hearings); and

  (iii) Schedule 5 (membership and proceedings of regional and local flood defence committees); and

 (c) any other provision of this Act or the 1995 Act so far as it relates to a provision falling within paragraph (a) or (b) above;'.

(9) For the definition of 'the related water resources provisions' there shall be substituted—

'"the related water resources provisions", in relation to Chapter II of Part II of this Act, means—

 (a) the following provisions of this Act, that is to say, the provisions—

  (i) of sections 21 to 23 (including Schedule 5);

  (ii) of sections 120, 125 to 130, 158, 189, 199 to 201, 206(3), 209(3), 211(1) and 216; and

  (iii) of paragraph 1 of Schedule 25; and

 (b) the following provisions of the 1995 Act, that is to say, the provisions—

  (i) of sections 41 and 42 (charging schemes) as they have effect by virtue of subsection (1)(a) of section 41 (licences under Chapter II of Part II of this Act); and

  (ii) of subsections (1) to (3) of section 53 (inquiries and other hearings);'.

(10) In the definition of 'water pollution provisions'—

 (a) in paragraph (b)—

  (i) after the words '161' there shall be inserted the words 'to 161D'; and

  (ii) for the words '203 and 213(2) above' there shall be substituted the words 'and 203'; and

 (b) after paragraph (c), there shall be added the words—

'and the following provisions of the 1995 Act, that is to say, the provisions of subsections (1) and (2) of section 53.'

178. Schedule 1 to that Act (the National Rivers Authority) shall cease to have effect.

179. Schedules 3 and 4 to that Act (boundaries of regional flood defence areas and membership and proceedings of regional and local flood defence committees) shall cease to have effect.

180. In Schedule 5 to that Act (procedure relating to statements on minimum acceptable flow) in paragraph 2(3)(g) (copy of notice to be served on person authorised by a licence under Part I of the Electricity Act 1989 to generate electricity) after the words 'to generate electricity' there shall be added the words 'who has a right to abstract water from any such waters or related inland waters'.

181. In Schedule 6 to that Act (orders providing for exemption from restrictions on abstraction) in paragraph 1(4)(h) (copy of notice to be served on person authorised by a licence under Part I of the Electricity Act 1989 to generate electricity) after the words 'to generate electricity' there shall be added the words 'who has a right to abstract water from any such source of supply or related inland waters'.

182. In Schedule 10 to that Act (discharge consents) after paragraph 7 (restriction on variation and revocation of consent and previous variation) there shall be added—

'General review of consents

 8.—(1) If it appears appropriate to the Secretary of State to do so he may at any time direct the Authority to review—

 (a) the consents given under paragraphs 2 and 5 above, or

 (b) any description of such consents,

and the conditions (if any) to which those consents are subject.

(2)   A direction given by virtue of sub-paragraph (1) above—

(a)   shall specify the purpose for which, and

(b)   may specify the manner in which,

the review is to be conducted.

(3)   After carrying out a review pursuant to a direction given by virtue of sub-paragraph (1) above, the Authority shall submit to the Secretary of State its proposals (if any) for—

(a)   the modification of the conditions of any consent reviewed pursuant to the direction, or

(b)   in the case of any unconditional consent reviewed pursuant to the direction, subjecting the consent to conditions.

(4)   Where the Secretary of State has received any proposals from the Authority under sub-paragraph (3) above in relation to any consent he may, if it appears appropriate to him to do so, direct the Authority to do, in relation to that consent, anything mentioned in paragraph 6(2)(b) or (c) above.

(5)   A direction given by virtue of sub-paragraph (4) above may only direct the Authority to do, in relation to any consent,—

(a)   any such thing as the Authority has proposed should be done in relation to that consent, or

(b)   any such thing with such modifications as appear to the Secretary of State to be appropriate.'

183.   For that Schedule there shall be substituted—

'SCHEDULE 10

DISCHARGE CONSENTS

Application for consent

1.—(1)   An application for a consent, for the purposes of section 88(1)(a) of this Act, for any discharges—

(a)   shall be made to the Agency on a form provided for the purpose by the Agency; and

(b)   must be advertised by or on behalf of the applicant in such manner as may be required by regulations made by the Secretary of State.

(2)   Regulations made by the Secretary of State may make provision for enabling the Agency to direct or determine that any such advertising of an application as is required under sub-paragraph (1)(b) above may, in any case, be dispensed with if, in that case, it appears to the Agency to be appropriate for that advertising to be dispensed with.

(3)   The applicant for such a consent must provide to the Agency, either on, or together with, the form mentioned in sub-paragraph (1) above—

(a)   such information as the Agency may reasonably require; and

(b)   such information as may be prescribed for the purpose by the Secretary of State;

but, subject to paragraph 3(3) below and without prejudice to the effect (if any) of any other contravention of the requirements of this Schedule in relation to an application under this paragraph, a failure to provide information in pursuance of this sub-paragraph shall not invalidate an application.

(4)   The Agency may give the applicant notice requiring him to provide it with such further information of any description specified in the notice as it may require for the purpose of determining the application.

(5)   An application made in accordance with this paragraph which relates to proposed discharges at two or more places may be treated by the Agency as separate applications for consents for discharges at each of those places.

Consultation in connection with applications

2.—(1) Subject to sub-paragraph (2) below, the Agency shall give notice of any application under paragraph 1 above, together with a copy of the application, to the persons who are prescribed or directed to be consulted under this paragraph and shall do so within the specified period for notification.

(2) The Secretary of State may, by regulations, exempt any class of application from the requirements of this paragraph or exclude any class of information contained in applications from those requirements, in all cases or as respects specified classes only of persons to be consulted.

(3) Any representations made by the persons so consulted within the period allowed shall be considered by the Agency in determining the application.

(4) For the purposes of sub-paragraph (1) above—

(a) persons are prescribed to be consulted on any description of application if they are persons specified for the purposes of applications of that description in regulations made by the Secretary of State;

(b) persons are directed to be consulted on any particular application if the Secretary of State specifies them in a direction given to the Agency;
and the 'specified period for notification' is the period specified in the regulations or in the direction.

(5) Any representations made by any other persons within the period allowed shall also be considered by the Agency in determining the application.

(6) Subject to sub-paragraph (7) below, the period allowed for making representations is—

(a) in the case of persons prescribed or directed to be consulted, the period of six weeks beginning with the date on which notice of the application was given under sub-paragraph (1) above, and

(b) in the case of other persons, the period of six weeks beginning with the date on which the making of the application was advertised in pursuance of paragraph 1(1)(b) above.

(7) The Secretary of State may, by regulations, substitute for any period for the time being specified in sub-paragraph (6)(a) or (b) above, such other period as he considers appropriate.

Consideration and determination of applications

3.—(1) On an application under paragraph 1 above the Agency shall be under a duty, if the requirements—

(a) of that paragraph, and

(b) of any regulations made under paragraph 1 or 2 above or of any directions under paragraph 2 above,
are complied with, to consider whether to give the consent applied for, either unconditionally or subject to conditions, or to refuse it.

(2) Subject to the following provisions of this Schedule, on an application made in accordance with paragraph 1 above, the applicant may treat the consent applied for as having been refused if it is not given within the period of four months beginning with the day on which the application is received or within such longer period as may be agreed in writing between the Agency and the applicant.

(3) Where any person, having made an application to the Agency for a consent, has failed to comply with his obligation under paragraph 1(3) or (4) above to provide information to the Agency, the Agency may refuse to proceed with the application, or refuse to proceed with it until the information is provided.

(4) The conditions subject to which a consent may be given under this paragraph shall be such conditions as the Agency may think fit and, in particular, may include conditions—

(a)   as to the places at which the discharges to which the consent relates may be made and as to the design and construction of any outlets for the discharges;

(b)   as to the nature, origin, composition, temperature, volume and rate of the discharges and as to the periods during which the discharges may be made;

(c)   as to the steps to be taken, in relation to the discharges or by way of subjecting any substance likely to affect the description of matter discharged to treatment or any other process, for minimising the polluting effects of the discharges on any controlled waters;

(d)   as to the provision of facilities for taking samples of the matter discharged and, in particular, as to the provision, maintenance and use of manholes, inspection chambers, observation wells and boreholes in connection with the discharges;

(e)   as to the provision, maintenance and testing of meters for measuring or recording the volume and rate of the discharges and apparatus for determining the nature, composition and temperature of the discharges;

(f)   as to the keeping of records of the nature, origin, composition, temperature, volume and rate of the discharges and, in particular, of records of readings of meters and other recording apparatus provided in accordance with any other condition attached to the consent; and

(g)   as to the making of returns and the giving of other information to the Authority about the nature, origin, composition, temperature, volume and rate of the discharges; and it is hereby declared that a consent may be given under this paragraph subject to different conditions in respect of different periods.

(5)   The Secretary of State may, by regulations, substitute for any period for the time being specified in sub-paragraph (2) above, such other period as he considers appropriate.

4.   The Secretary of State may give the Agency a direction with respect to any particular application, or any description of applications, for consent under paragraph 1 above requiring the Agency not to determine or not to proceed with the application or applications of that description until the expiry of any such period as may be specified in the direction, or until directed by the Secretary of State that it may do so, as the case may be.

Reference to Secretary of State of certain applications for consent

5.—(1)   The Secretary of State may, either in consequence of representations or objections made to him or otherwise, direct the Agency to transmit to him for determination such applications for consent under paragraph 1 above as are specified in the direction or are of a description so specified.

(2)   Where a direction is given to the Agency under this paragraph, the Agency shall comply with the direction and inform every applicant to whose application the direction relates of the transmission of his application to the Secretary of State.

(3)   Paragraphs 1(1) and 2 above shall have effect in relation to an application transmitted to the Secretary of State under this paragraph with such modifications as may be prescribed.

(4)   Where an application is transmitted to the Secretary of State under this paragraph, the Secretary of State may at any time after the application is transmitted and before it is granted or refused—

(a)   cause a local inquiry to be held with respect to the application; or

(b)   afford the applicant and the Agency an opportunity of appearing before, and being heard by, a person appointed by the Secretary of State for the purpose.

(5)   The Secretary of State shall exercise his power under sub-paragraph (4) above in any case where a request to be heard with respect to the application is made to him in the prescribed manner by the applicant or by the Agency.

(6)   It shall be the duty of the Secretary of State, if the requirements of this paragraph and of any regulations made under it are complied with, to determine an application for

consent transmitted to him by the Agency under this paragraph by directing the Agency to refuse its consent or to give its consent under paragraph 3 above (either unconditionally or subject to such conditions as are specified in the direction).

(7) Without prejudice to any of the preceding provisions of this paragraph, the Secretary of State may by regulations make provision for the purposes of, and in connection with, the consideration and disposal by him of applications transmitted to him under this paragraph.

Consents without applications

6.—(1) If it appears to the Agency—

    (a) that a person has caused or permitted effluent or other matter to be discharged in contravention—

        (i) of the obligation imposed by virtue of section 85(3) of this Act; or

        (ii) of any prohibition imposed under section 86 of this Act; and

    (b) that a similar contravention by that person is likely,

the Agency may, if it thinks fit, serve on him an instrument in writing giving its consent, subject to any conditions specified in the instrument, for discharges of a description so specified.

(2) A consent given under this paragraph shall not relate to any discharge which occurred before the instrument containing the consent was served on the recipient of the instrument.

(3) Sub-paragraph (4) of paragraph 3 above shall have effect in relation to a consent given under this paragraph as it has effect in relation to a consent given under that paragraph.

(4) Where a consent has been given under this paragraph, the Agency shall publish notice of the consent in such manner as may be prescribed by the Secretary of State and send copies of the instrument containing the consent to such bodies or persons as may be so prescribed.

(5) It shall be the duty of the Agency to consider any representations or objections with respect to a consent under this paragraph as are made to it in such manner, and within such period, as may be prescribed by the Secretary of State and have not been withdrawn.

(6) Where notice of a consent is published by the Agency under sub-paragraph (4) above, the Agency shall be entitled to recover the expenses of publication from the person on whom the instrument containing the consent was served.

Revocation of consents and alteration and imposition of conditions

7.—(1) The Agency may from time to time review any consent given under paragraph 3 or 6 above and the conditions (if any) to which the consent is subject.

(2) Subject to such restrictions on the exercise of the power conferred by this sub-paragraph as are imposed under paragraph 8 below, where the Agency has reviewed a consent under this paragraph, it may by a notice served on the person making a discharge in pursuance of the consent—

    (a) revoke the consent;

    (b) make modifications of the conditions of the consent; or

    (c) in the case of an unconditional consent, provide that it shall be subject to such conditions as may be specified in the notice.

(3) If on a review under sub-paragraph (1) above it appears to the Agency that no discharge has been made in pursuance of the consent to which the review relates at any time during the preceding twelve months, the Agency may revoke the consent by a notice served on the holder of the consent.

(4) If it appears to the Secretary of State appropriate to do so—

(a)   for the purpose of enabling Her Majesty's Government in the United Kingdom
to give effect to any Community obligation or to any international agreement to which
the United Kingdom is for the time being a party;

(b)   for the protection of public health or of flora and fauna dependent on an aquatic
environment; or

(c)   in consequence of any representations or objections made to him or otherwise,
he may, subject to such restrictions on the exercise of the power conferred by virtue of
paragraph (c) above as are imposed under paragraph 8 below, at any time direct the
Agency, in relation to a consent given under paragraph 3 or 6 above, to do anything
mentioned in sub-paragraph (2)(a) to (c) above.

(5)   The Agency shall be liable to pay compensation to any person in respect of any
loss or damage sustained by that person as a result of the Agency's compliance with a
direction given in relation to any consent by virtue of sub-paragraph (4)(b) above if—

(a)   in complying with that direction the Agency does anything which, apart from
that direction, it would be precluded from doing by a restriction imposed under paragraph
8 below; and

(b)   the direction is not shown to have been given in consequence of—

(i)   a change of circumstances which could not reasonably have been foreseen
at the beginning of the period to which the restriction relates; or

(ii)   consideration by the Secretary of State of material information which was
not reasonably available to the Agency at the beginning of that period.

(6)   For the purposes of sub-paragraph (5) above information is material, in relation
to a consent, if it relates to any discharge made or to be made by virtue of the consent,
to the interaction of any such discharge with any other discharge or to the combined effect
of the matter discharged and any other matter.

Restriction on variation and revocation of consent and previous variation

8.—(1)   Each instrument signifying the consent of the Agency under paragraph 3 or 6
above shall specify a period during which no notice by virtue of paragraph 7(2) or (4)(c)
above shall be served in respect of the consent except, in the case of a notice doing anything
mentioned in paragraph 7(2)(b) or (c), with the agreement of the holder of the consent.

(2)   Each notice served by the Agency by virtue of paragraph 7(2) or (4)(c) above
(except a notice which only revokes a consent) shall specify a period during which a
subsequent such notice which alters the effect of the first-mentioned notice shall not be
served except, in the case of a notice doing anything mentioned in paragraph 7(2)(b) or
(c) above, with the agreement of the holder of the consent.

(3)   The period specified under sub-paragraph (1) or (2) above in relation to any consent
shall not, unless the person who proposes to make or makes discharges in pursuance of the
consent otherwise agrees, be less than the period of four years beginning—

(a)   in the case of a period specified under sub-paragraph (1) above, with the day
on which the consent takes effect; and

(b)   in the case of a period specified under sub-paragraph (2) above, with the day
on which the notice specifying that period is served.

(4)   A restriction imposed under sub-paragraph (1) or (2) above shall not prevent the
service by the Agency of a notice by virtue of paragraph 7(2) or (4)(c) above in respect
of a consent given under paragraph 6 above if—

(a)   the notice is served not more than three months after the beginning of the period
prescribed under paragraph 6(5) above for the making of representations and objections
with respect to the consent; and

(b)   the Agency or, as the case may be, the Secretary of State considers, in
consequence of any representations or objections received by it or him within that period,
that it is appropriate for the notice to be served.

(5)   A restriction imposed under sub-paragraph (1) or (2) above shall not prevent the service by the Agency of a notice by virtue of paragraph 7(2)(b) or (c) or (4)(c) above in respect of a consent given under paragraph 6 above if the holder has applied for a variation under paragraph 10 below.

General review of consents

9.—(1)   If it appears appropriate to the Secretary of State to do so he may at any time direct the Agency to review—
(a)   the consents given under paragraph 3 or 6 above, or
(b)   any description of such consents,
and the conditions (if any) to which those consents are subject.
(2)   A direction given by virtue of sub-paragraph (1) above—
(a)   shall specify the purpose for which, and
(b)   may specify the manner in which,
the review is to be conducted.
(3)   After carrying out a review pursuant to a direction given by virtue of sub-paragraph (1) above, the Agency shall submit to the Secretary of State its proposals (if any) for—
(a)   the modification of the conditions of any consent reviewed pursuant to the direction, or
(b)   in the case of any unconditional consent reviewed pursuant to the direction, subjecting the consent to conditions.
(4)   Where the Secretary of State has received any proposals from the Agency under sub-paragraph (3) above in relation to any consent he may, if it appears appropriate to him to do so, direct the Agency to do, in relation to that consent, anything mentioned in paragraph 7(2)(b) or (c) above.
(5)   A direction given by virtue of sub-paragraph (4) above may only direct the Agency to do, in relation to any consent,—
(a)   any such thing as the Agency has proposed should be done in relation to that consent, or
(b)   any such thing with such modifications as appear to the Secretary of State to be appropriate.

Applications for variation

10.—(1)   The holder of a consent under paragraph 3 or 6 above may apply to the Agency, on a form provided for the purpose by the Agency, for the variation of the consent.
(2)   The provisions of paragraphs 1 to 5 above shall apply (with the necessary modifications) to applications under sub-paragraph (1) above, and to the variation of consents in pursuance of such applications, as they apply to applications for, and the grant of, consents.

Transfer of consents

11.—(1)   A consent under paragraph 3 or 6 above may be transferred by the holder to a person who proposes to carry on the discharges in place of the holder.
(2)   On the death of the holder of a consent under paragraph 3 or 6 above, the consent shall, subject to sub-paragraph (4) below, be regarded as property forming part of the deceased's personal estate, whether or not it would be so regarded apart from this sub-paragraph, and shall accordingly vest in his personal representatives.
(3)   If a bankruptcy order is made against the holder of a consent under paragraph 3 or 6 above, the consent shall, subject to sub-paragraph (4) below, be regarded for the purposes of any of the Second Group of Parts of the Insolvency Act 1986 (insolvency of

individuals; bankruptcy), as property forming part of the bankrupt's estate, whether or not it would be so regarded apart from this sub-paragraph, and shall accordingly vest as such in the trustee in bankruptcy.

(4)   Notwithstanding anything in the foregoing provisions of this paragraph, a consent under paragraph 3 or 6 above (and the obligations arising out of, or incidental to, such a consent) shall not be capable of being disclaimed.

(5)   A consent under paragraph 3 or 6 above which is transferred to, or which vests in, a person under this section shall have effect on and after the date of the transfer or vesting as if it had been granted to that person under paragraph 3 or 6 above, subject to the same conditions as were attached to it immediately before that date.

(6)   Where a consent under paragraph 3 or 6 above is transferred under sub-paragraph (1) above, the person from whom it is transferred shall give notice of that fact to the Agency not later than the end of the period of twenty-one days beginning with the date of the transfer.

(7)   Where a consent under paragraph 3 or 6 above vests in any person as mentioned in sub-paragraph (2) or (3) above, that person shall give notice of that fact to the Agency not later than the end of the period of fifteen months beginning with the date of the vesting.

(8)   If—

(a)   a consent under paragraph 3 or 6 above vests in any person as mentioned in sub-paragraph (2) or (3) above, but

(b)   that person fails to give the notice required by sub-paragraph (7) above within the period there mentioned,

the consent, to the extent that it permits the making of any discharges, shall cease to have effect.

(9)   A person who fails to give a notice which he is required by sub-paragraph (6) or (7) above to give shall be guilty of an offence and liable—

(a)   on summary conviction, to a fine not exceeding the statutory maximum;

(b)   on conviction on indictment, to a fine or to imprisonment for a term not exceeding two years, or to both.'

184.   In Schedule 11 to that Act (water protection zone orders) in paragraph 4 (which is expressed to be without prejudice to section 213 of that Act) for the words 'section 213 of this Act' there shall be substituted the words 'section 53 of the 1995 Act (inquiries and other hearings)'.

185.   In Schedule 12 to that Act (nitrate sensitive area orders) in paragraph 6 (which is expressed to be without prejudice to section 213 of that Act) for the words 'section 213 of this Act' there shall be substituted the words 'section 53 of the 1995 Act (inquiries and other hearings)'.

186.   In Schedule 13 to that Act (transitional water pollution provisions) in paragraph 4 (discharge consents on application of undertakers etc)—

(a)   in sub-paragraph (2), in paragraphs (a) and (b) (which contain references to paragraph 4 of Schedule 10) for the word '4', in each place where it occurs, there shall be substituted the word '5';

(b)   in sub-paragraph (3) (which contains references to various provisions of Schedule 10) for the words 'paragraphs 1(4) to (6) and 2(1) or, as the case may be, paragraph 4(3)' there shall be substituted the words 'paragraph 1(1), apart from paragraph (a), paragraph 2 or, as the case may be, paragraph 5(3)'; and

(c)   in sub-paragraph (4)(a) (which contains a reference to paragraph 2(5) of Schedule 10) for the words '2(5)' there shall be substituted the words '3(4)'.

187.—(1)   In Schedule 15 to that Act (supplemental provisions with respect to drainage charges) in paragraphs 4(3) and 9(4) (which specify the penalty for certain offences of failing, and after conviction continuing, without reasonable excuse, to comply with notices) after the words 'he continues without reasonable excuse' there shall be inserted the words 'to fail'.

(2)   In paragraph 12(2) of that Schedule (which is expressed to be without prejudice to powers by virtue of section 4 or paragraph 5 of Schedule 1) for the words 'section 4 of this Act and paragraph 5 of Schedule 1 to this Act' there shall be substituted the words 'section 37 of, and paragraph 6 of Schedule 1 to, the 1995 Act'.

188.   In Schedule 20 to that Act (supplemental provisions with respect to powers of entry) in paragraph 7 (which creates an offence of obstruction, punishable on summary conviction by a fine not exceeding level 3) for the words from 'liable, on summary conviction,' onwards there shall be substituted the words 'liable—
   (a)   on summary conviction, to a fine not exceeding the statutory maximum;
   (b)   on conviction on indictment, to a fine or to imprisonment for a term not exceeding two years, or to both.'

189.   In Schedule 22 to that Act (protection for particular undertakings) in paragraph 5 (protection for telecommunication systems) for the words 'section 4(1) of this Act)' there shall be substituted the words 'section 37 of the 1995 Act)'.

190.   In Schedule 25 to that Act (byelaw-making powers) in paragraph l(l), for the words 'paragraphs (a), (c) and (d) of section 2(1) of this Act' there shall be substituted the words 'sub-paragraphs (i), (iii) and (v) of section 2(1)(a) of the 1995 Act'.

The Land Drainage Act 1991

191.—(1)   In the Land Drainage Act 1991, for the words 'NRA', wherever occurring, there shall be substituted the word 'Agency'.

192.—(1)   In section 23 of that Act (prohibition on obstructions etc in watercourses) in subsection (2) (which confers power to charge an application fee of £50 or such other sum as may be specified by order made by the Ministers) for the words 'specified by order made by the Ministers' there shall be substituted the word 'prescribed'.

(2)   After subsection (7) of that section there shall be inserted—
   '(7A)   In subsection (2) above "prescribed" means specified in, or determined in accordance with, an order made by the Ministers; and any such order may make different provision for different cases, including different provision in relation to different persons, circumstances or localities.'

193.   At the beginning of Part V of that Act (miscellaneous and supplemental provisions) there shall be inserted—

'Spray irrigation

61F.   Powers of internal drainage boards and local authorities to facilitate spray irrigation
   (1)   Any internal drainage board or local authority may, with the consent of the Agency, operate any drainage works under the control of the board or authority so as to manage the level of water in a watercourse for the purpose of facilitating spray irrigation.
   (2)   Subsection (1) above is without prejudice to—
      (a)   the powers of an internal drainage board or local authority in relation to drainage; or
      (b)   any requirement—
         (i)   for any other consent of the Agency or any other person; or
         (ii)   for any licence, approval, authorisation or other permission or registration.'

194.—(1)   In section 72 of that Act, in subsection (1) (general definitions) there shall be inserted at the appropriate place—

'"the Agency" means the Environment Agency;'.

(2) In that subsection, the definition of 'the NRA' shall be omitted.

The Clean Air Act 1993

195. In section 2 of the Clean Air Act 1993 (emission of dark smoke from industrial or trade premises) in subsection (5) (which creates a summary offence punishable with a fine not exceeding level 5 on the standard scale) for the words 'level 5 on the standard scale' there shall be substituted the words '£20,000'.

196.—(1) Section 19 of that Act (power to require creation of smoke control areas by local authorities) as it applies to Scotland shall be amended in accordance with the following provisions of this paragraph.

(2) In subsection (1)—

(a) for the words 'Secretary of State' there shall be substituted the words 'Scottish Environment Protection Agency (in this section referred to as "the Agency")'; and

(b) for the words 'he', 'him' and 'his' there shall be substituted respectively 'the Agency', 'it' and 'its'.

(3) In subsections (2), (3), (4)(a) and (6), for the words 'Secretary of State' there shall be substituted the words 'Agency'.

(4) In subsection (3), for the word 'him' there shall be substituted the word 'it'.

(5) In subsection (4), before the words 'the Secretary of State' in the second place where they occur there shall be inserted the words 'the Agency, with the consent of'.

197. In section 59 of that Act (local inquiries) in subsection (1)—

(a) for the words 'a local inquiry' there shall be substituted the words 'an inquiry'; and

(b) for the words 'such an inquiry' there shall be substituted the words 'an inquiry'; and for the side-note to that section there shall accordingly be substituted 'Inquiries.'.

198. In section 60(7)(b) of that Act as it applies to Scotland for the words 'the Secretary of State' and 'Secretary of State's' there shall be substituted the words 'SEPA' and 'SEPA's' respectively.

199. In section 63(1)(c) of that Act as it applies to Scotland for the words 'sections 19(4) and' there shall be substituted the word 'section'.

The Radioactive Substances Act 1993

200. Subject to the other provisions of this Act, in the Radioactive Substances Act 1993, for the words 'chief inspector' or 'chief inspector's', wherever occurring, there shall be substituted respectively the words 'appropriate Agency' or 'appropriate Agency's'.

201. Sections 4 and 5 of that Act (appointment of inspectors and chief inspectors) shall cease to have effect.

202.—(1) In section 7 of that Act (registration of users of radioactive material) in subsection (1)(c) (application to be accompanied by prescribed fee), for the words 'prescribed fee' there shall be substituted the words 'charge prescribed for the purpose by a charging scheme under section 41 of the Environment Act 1995'.

(2) In subsection (7) of that section (chief inspector to have regard exclusively to amount and character of radioactive waste), for the word 'him' there shall be substituted the word 'it'.

203. In section 8 of that Act (exemptions from registration under section 7), in subsection (2) (power of chief inspector to impose conditions) for the word 'he' there shall be substituted the word 'it'.

204.—(1) In section 10 of that Act (registration of mobile radioactive apparatus) in subsection (1)(c) (application to be accompanied by prescribed fee), for the words 'prescribed fee' there shall be substituted the words 'charge prescribed for the purpose by a charging scheme under section 41 of the Environment Act 1995'.

(2) In each of subsections (3) and (5)(b) of that section (duty to supply copy of aplication, and to send copy of certificate, to local authority) for the word 'him' there shall be substituted the words 'the appropriate Agency'.

205.—(1) Section 16 of that Act (authorisations) shall be amended in accordance with the following provisions of this paragraph.

(2) In subsection (2) (power to grant authorisations to be exercisable by the chief   inspector) the words 'Subject to subsection (3)' shall be omitted.

(3) Subsection (3) (power to grant authorisations in England, Wales and Northern Ireland) shall be omitted.

(4) In subsection (4) (application to be accompanied by prescribed fee), for the words 'prescribed fee' there shall be substituted the words 'charge prescribed for the purpose by a charging scheme under section 41 of the Environment Act 1995'.

(5) After subsection (4) there shall be inserted—

'(4A) Without prejudice to subsection (5), on any application for an authorisation under section 13(1) in respect of the disposal of radioactive waste on or from any premises situated on a nuclear site in any part of Great Britain, the appropriate Agency—

(a) shall consult the relevant Minister and the Health and Safety Executive before deciding whether to grant an authorisation on that application and, if so, subject to what limitations or conditions, and

(b) shall consult the relevant Minister concerning the terms of the authorisation, for which purpose that Agency shall, before granting any authorisation on that application, send that Minister a copy of any authorisation which it proposes so to grant.'

(6) In subsection (5) (consultation by chief inspector and, where the premises are in England, Wales or Northern Ireland, the appropriate Minister with local authorities etc)—

(a) for the words from 'and, where' to 'shall each' there shall be substituted the word 'shall'; and

(b) for the word 'him', in each place where it occurs, there shall be substituted the words 'that Agency'.

(7) In subsection (7) (applications, other than those to which subsection (3) applies, deemed to be refused if not determined within prescribed period) for the words '(other than an application to which subsection (3) applies)' there shall be substituted the words '(other than an application for an authorisation under section 13(1) in respect of the disposal of radioactive waste on or from any premises situated on a nuclear site in any part of Great Britain)'.

(8) In subsection 8(b) (conditions or limitations subject to which authorisations may be granted) for the words from 'or, as' to 'think' there shall be substituted the word 'thinks'.

(9) In subsection (10) of that section (fixing of date from which authorisation is to have effect)—

(a) the words from 'or, as' to 'appropriate Minister' shall cease to have effect; and

(b) for the words 'him or them' and 'his or their' there shall be substituted respectively the words 'it' and 'its'.

(10) After that subsection there shall be inserted—

'(11) In this section, ''the relevant Minister'' means—

(a) in relation to premises in England, the Minister of Agriculture, Fisheries and Food, and

(b) in relation to premises in Wales or Scotland, the Secretary of State.'

206.—(1)　In section 17 of that Act, after subsection (2) (variation of authorisations) there shall be inserted—

'(2A)　On any proposal to vary an authorisation granted under section 13(1) in respect of the disposal of radioactive waste on or from any premises situated on a nuclear site in any part of Great Britain, the appropriate Agency—

(a)　shall consult the relevant Minister and the Health and Safety Executive before deciding whether to vary the authorisation and, if so, whether by attaching, revoking or varying any limitations or conditions or by attaching further limitations or conditions, and

(b)　shall consult the relevant Minister concerning the terms of any variation, for which purpose that Agency shall, before varying the authorisation, send that Minister a copy of any variations which it proposes to make.'

(2)　Subsection (4) of that section (adaptations for authorisations granted by the chief inspector and the appropriate Minister) shall cease to have effect.

(3)　At the end of that section there shall be added—

'(5)　In this section, "the relevant Minister" has the same meaning as in section 16 above.'

207.—(1)　In section 18 of that Act (functions of public and local authorities in relation to authorisations under section 13) in subsection (1)—

(a)　the words from '(or, in a case' to 'that Minister)', and

(b)　the words 'or the appropriate Minister, as the case may be,',

shall cease to have effect.

(2)　In subsection (2)(b) of that section (special precautions taken with the approval of the chief inspector etc) the words from '(or, where' to 'that Minister)' shall cease to have effect.

208.　In section 20 of that Act (retention and production of site or disposal records) subsection (3) (adaptation where powers exercisable by chief inspector and appropriate Minister) shall cease to have effect.

209.—(1)　In section 21 of that Act (enforcement notices) in subsection (1) (power of chief inspector to serve such a notice) for the word 'he' there shall be substituted the word 'it'.

(2)　Subsection (3) (adaptation in case of authorisations granted by the chief inspector and the appropriate Minister) shall cease to have effect.

(3)　In subsection (4) of that section (copies of notices to be sent to certain public or local authorities) the words from 'or, where' to 'that Minister' shall cease to have effect.

210.—(1)　In section 22 of that Act (prohibition notices) in subsection (1) (power of chief inspector to serve such a notice) for the word 'he' there shall be substituted the word 'it'.

(2)　Subsection (5) of that section (adaptation in case of authorisations granted by the chief inspector and the appropriate Minister) shall cease to have effect.

(3)　In subsection (6) of that section (copies of notices to be sent to certain public or local authorities) the words from 'or, where' to 'that Minister' shall cease to have effect.

(4)　In subsection (7) of that section (withdrawal of notices)—

(a)　the words from 'or, where' to 'that Minister' shall cease to have effect; and

(b)　for the word 'he', in each place where it occurs, there shall be substituted the words 'that Agency'.

211.—(1)　In section 23 of that Act (powers of Secretary of State to give directions to the chief inspector)—

(a)　in subsections (1) and (3) for the word 'him' there shall be substituted the word 'it'; and

(b)　in subsection (2) for the word 'his' there shall be substituted the word 'its'.

(2)　After subsection (4) of that section there shall be inserted—

'(4A)　In the application of this section in relation to authorisations, and applications for authorisations, under section 13 in respect of premises situated on a nuclear site in

England, references to the Secretary of State shall have effect as references to the Secretary of State and the Minister of Agriculture, Fisheries and Food.'

212.—(1)   In section 24 of that Act (power of Secretary of State, to require certain applications to be determined by him) in subsections (1) and (4), for the word 'him', in each place where it occurs, there shall be substituted the word 'it'.

(2)   After subsection (4) of that section there shall be inserted—

'(4A)   In the application of this section in relation to authorisations, and applications for authorisations, under section 13 in respect of premises situated on a nuclear site in England, references to the Secretary of State shall have effect as references to the Secretary of State and the Minister of Agriculture, Fisheries and Food.'

213.—(1)   In section 25 of that Act (power of Secretary of State to restrict knowledge of applications etc) in subsection (1) (applications under section 7 to 10 etc), after the words 'knowledge of' there shall be inserted the words 'such information as may be specified or described in the directions, being information contained in or relating to—'.

(2)   In subsection (2) of that section (applications under section 13 or 14 etc)—

(a)   the words from 'or, in a case' to 'Food,' and 'or their' shall cease to have effect; and

(b)   after the words 'knowledge of' there shall be inserted the words 'such information as may be specified or described in the directions, being information contained in or relating to—'.

(3)   In subsection (3) of that section (copies of certain applications etc which are the subject
of a direction not to be sent to local or public authorities)—

(a)   after the words 'send a copy of' there shall be inserted the words 'so much of'; and

(b)   after the words 'as the case may be' there shall be inserted the words 'as contains the information specified or described in the directions—'.

(4)   After that subsection there shall be inserted—

'(3A)   No direction under this section shall affect—

(a)   any power or duty of the Agency to which it is given to consult the relevant Minister; or

(b)   the information which is to be sent by that Agency to that Minister.'

(5)   At the end of that section there shall be added—

'(5)   In this section ''the relevant Minister'' has the same meaning as in section 16 above.'

214.—(1)   Section 26 of that Act (appeals) shall be amended in accordance with the following provisions of this paragraph.

(2)   Subsection (3)(a) (appeal not to lie in relation to authorisations subject to section 16(3)) shall cease to have effect.

(3)   In subsection (4) (appeals in respect of enforcement or prohibition notices) the words 'England, Wales or' shall be omitted.

(4)   After subsection (5) there shall be inserted—

'(5A)   In the application of this section in relation to authorisations, and applications for authorisations, under section 13 in respect of premises situated on a nuclear site in England, references in subsection (1) to (3) to the Secretary of State shall have effect as references to the Secretary of State and the Minister of Agriculture, Fisheries and Food.

215.—(1)   Section 27 of that Act (procedure on appeals under section 26) shall be amended in accordance with the following provisions of this paragraph.

(2)   In subsection (1) (power of Secretary of State to refer appeal to appointed person) after the word '26' there shall be inserted the words ', other than an appeal against any decision of, or notice served by, SEPA,'.

(3)   After that subsection there shall be inserted—

'(1A)   As respects an appeal against any decision of, or notice served by, SEPA, this section is subject to section 114 of the Environment Act 1995 (delegation or reference of appeals).'

(4)   After subsection (7) there shall be inserted—

'(7A)   In the application of this section in relation to authorisations, and applications for authorisations, under section 13 in respect of premises situated on a nuclear site in England, references in subsections (1) to (6) to the Secretary of State shall have effect as references to the Secretary of State and the Minister of Agriculture, Fisheries and Food.'

216.   Section 28 of that Act (representations in relation to authorisations and notices where appropriate Minister is concerned) shall cease to have effect.

217.—(1)   Section 30 of that Act (power of Secretary of State to dispose of radioactive waste) shall be amended in accordance with the following provisions of this paragraph.

(2)   In subsection (1) (which confers the power)—

(a)   for the words 'the Secretary of State', in the first place where they occur, there shall be substituted the words 'the appropriate Agency';

(b)   for those words, wherever else occurring, there shall be substituted the words 'that Agency'; and

(c)   for the word 'his' there shall be substituted the word 'its'.

(3)   In subsection (3) of that section (application of certain definitions of 'owner') for the words 'Secretary of State' there shall be substituted the words 'Environment Agency'.

(4)   In subsection (4) of that section (adaptations for Scotland) for the words 'the Secretary of State' there shall be substituted the words 'SEPA'.

218.   Section 31 of that Act (rights of entry and inspection) shall cease to have effect.

219.   In section 32 of that Act (offences relating to registration or authorisation, including the offence of failure to comply with the requirements of an enforcement or prohibition notice under section 21 or 22 of the Act) after subsection (2) there shall be added—

'(3)   If the appropriate Agency is of the opinion that proceedings for an offence under subsection (1)(d) would afford an ineffectual remedy against a person who has failed to comply with the requirements of a notice served on him under section 21 or 22, that Agency may take proceedings in the High Court or, in Scotland, in any court of competent jurisdiction, for the purpose of securing compliance with the notice.'

220.   In section 34(1) of that Act (which, with certain exceptions, makes it an offence to disclose certain trade secrets) after paragraph (b) (no offence where disclosure made in accordance with directions) there shall be inserted—

'(bb)   under or by virtue of section 113 of the Environment Act 1995, or'.

221.   Section 35 of that Act (obstruction of inspectors or other persons) shall cease to have effect.

222.   In section 38 of that Act (restriction on prosecution) in subsection (1) (provision for England and Wales) for paragraph (b) there shall be substituted

'(b)   by the Environment Agency, or'.

223.—(1)   In section 39 of that Act (public access to documents and records) in subsection (1) (duties of chief inspector)—

(a)   for the word 'him', in each place where it occurs, there shall be substituted the word 'it';

(b) for the word 'he' there shall be substituted the words 'the appropriate Agency'; and

(c) for the words 'applications or certificates' there shall be substituted the word 'information'.

(2) In subsection (2), the words 'or, as the case may be, the appropriate Minister and the chief inspector,' shall cease to have effect.

224. In section 40 of that Act (radioactivity to be disregarded for purposes of certain statutory provisions) in subsection (2)(b)(ii), after the words 'imposed by the statutory provision on' there shall be inserted the words 'the Environment Agency or SEPA or on'.

225. Section 42(5) of that Act (which precludes, in the interests of national security, the exercise of certain powers of entry in relation to Crown premises and which is superseded by provisions of this Act) shall cease to have effect.

226. Section 43 of that Act (which relates to fees and charges and which is superseded by provisions of this Act) shall cease to have effect.

227.—(1) Subsection (1) of section 47 of that Act (general definitions) shall be amended in accordance with the following provisions of this paragraph.

(2) There shall be inserted at the appropriate place—
'"the appropriate Agency" means—
(a) in relation to England and Wales, the Environment Agency; and
(b) in relation to Scotland, SEPA;'.

(3) In the definition of 'the appropriate Minister', paragraphs (a) and (b) shall cease to have effect.

(4) In the definition of 'the chief inspector', paragraphs (a) and (b) shall cease to have effect.

(5) In the definition of 'prescribed', the words from 'or, in relation to fees' onwards shall cease to have effect.

(6) In the definition of 'relevant water body'—
(a) in paragraph (a), the words 'the National Rivers Authority', and
(b) in paragraph (b), the words 'a river purification authority within the meaning of the Rivers (Prevention of Pollution) (Scotland) Act 1951',
shall be omitted.

(7) There shall be inserted at the appropriate place—
'"SEPA" means the Scottish Environment Protection Agency;'.

228. In section 48 of that Act (index of defined expressions) in the Table—
(a) the following entries shall be inserted at the appropriate place—
(i) 'the appropriate Agency   section 47(1)';
(ii) 'SEPA   section 47(1)';
(b) the entry relating to the chief inspector shall be omitted.

229. Schedule 2 to that Act (exercise of rights of entry and inspection) shall cease to have effect.

230.—(1) In Schedule 3 to that Act (enactments, other than local enactments, to which s. 40 applies) in paragraph 9 (which specifies certain provisions in the Water Resources Act 1991) for the words '203 and 213' there shall be substituted the words 'and 203'.

(2) For paragraph 16 of that Schedule there shall be substituted—
'16. Sections 30A, 30B, 30D, 30F, 30G, 30H(1), 31(4), (5), (8) and (9), 31A, 34 to 42B, 46 to 46D and 56(1) to (3) of the Control of Pollution Act 1974.

The Local Government (Wales) Act 1994

231 In Schedule 9 to the Local Government (Wales) Act 1994 (which makes provision for the transfer to the new principal councils in Wales of functions in relation to public health and related matters), in paragraph 17(2) (which amends the definitions of waste regulation and disposal authorities for the purposes of Part II of the Environmental Protection Act 1990) for the words 'each of subsections (1)(f) and (2)(f)' there shall be substituted the words 'subsection (2)(f)'.

The Local Government etc. (Scotland) Act 1994

232.—(1) In section 2(2) of the Local Government etc. (Scotland) Act 1994 (constitution of councils) after the words 'this Act' there shall be inserted the words 'and of the Environment Act 1995'.

(2) In Schedule 13 to that Act (minor and consequential amendments) in paragraph 75(27) (which amends certain provisions of the Sewerage (Scotland) Act 1968) for the words from the beginning to 'premises)' there shall be substituted the words 'In section 53 (notices to be in writing)'.

Subordinate legislation and local statutory provisions

233.—(1) In any subordinate legislation or local statutory provisions, for any reference (however framed) to the National Rivers Authority, and for any reference which falls to be construed as such a reference, there shall be substituted a reference to the Agency.

(2) In any subordinate legislation, for any reference (however framed) to a relevant inspector, and for any reference which falls to be construed as such a reference, there shall be substituted a reference to the appropriate Agency.

(3) The provisions of this paragraph are subject to the other provisions of this Act and to any provision made under or by virtue of this Act.

(4) In this paragraph—

'the appropriate Agency' means—

    (a) in relation to England and Wales, the Agency;

    (b) in relation to Scotland, SEPA;

'local statutory provision' means—

    (a) a provision of a local Act (including an Act confirming a provisional order);

    (b) a provision of so much of any public general Act as has effect with respect to particular persons or works or with respect to particular provisions falling within any paragraph of this definition;

    (c) a provision of an instrument made under any provision falling within paragraph (a) or (b) above;

    (d) a provision of any other instrument which is in the nature of a local enactment;

'relevant inspector' means—

    (i) the chief inspector for England and Wales constituted under section 16(3) of the Environmental Protection Act 1990;

    (ii) the chief inspector for Scotland constituted under section 16(3) of that Act;

    (iii) the chief inspector for England and Wales appointed under section 4(2)(a) of the Radioactive Substances Act 1993;

    (iv) the chief inspector for Scotland appointed under section 4(2)(b) of that Act;

    (v) the chief, or any other, inspector, within the meaning of the Alkali, &c, Works Regulation Act 1906;

    (vi) an inspector appointed under section 19 of the Health and Safety at Work etc. Act 1974 by the Secretary of State in his capacity as the enforcing authority responsible for the enforcement of the Alkali, &c, Works Regulation Act 1906 or section 5 of the said Act of 1974;

'subordinate legislation' has the same meaning as in the Interpretation Act 1978.

SCHEDULE 23

TRANSITIONAL AND TRANSITORY PROVISIONS AND SAVINGS

PART I

GENERAL TRANSITIONAL PROVISIONS AND SAVINGS

Interpretation of Part I

1. In this Part of this Schedule, the 'transfer date' has the same meaning as in Part I of this Act.

Directions

2. Any directions given to the National Rivers Authority for the purposes of section 19 of the 1991 Act shall have effect on and after the transfer date as directions given to the Agency for the purposes of section 6(2) of this Act.

Regional and local fisheries advisory committees

3. If and so long as the Agency requires, on and after the transfer date any advisory committee established and maintained before the transfer date by the National Rivers Authority under section 8(1) of the Water Resources Act 1991 shall be treated as if—

  (a) it had been established by the Agency,

  (b) the area by reference to which that committee was established had been determined by the Agency, and

  (c) in the case of a regional advisory committee, the chairman of that committee had been appointed,

in accordance with section 13 of this Act.

Charging schemes

4.—(1) Without prejudice to section 55 of this Act, any charging scheme—

  (a) which relates to any transferred functions,

  (b) which was made before the transfer date, and

  (c) which is in force immediately before that date or would (apart from this Act) have come into force at any time after that date,

shall, subject to the provisions of section 41 of this Act, have effect on and after the transfer date, with any necessary modifications, and for the remainder of the period for which the charging scheme would have been in force apart from any repeal made by this Act, as a scheme made under that section by the transferee in accordance with section 42 of this Act.

  (2) Any costs or expenses incurred before the transfer date by any person in carrying out functions transferred to a new Agency by or under this Act may be treated for the purposes of subsections (3) and (4) of section 42 of this Act as costs or expenses incurred by that new Agency in carrying out those functions.

  (3) In this paragraph—

'charging scheme' means a scheme specifying, or providing for the determination of, any fees or charges;

'new Agency' means the Agency or SEPA;

'transferred functions' means any functions which, by virtue of any provision made by or under this Act, become functions of a new Agency and 'the transferee' means the new Agency whose functions they so become.

Preparation of reports

5.—(1) The first report prepared by the Agency under section 52 of this Act may, to the extent that it relates to functions transferred to the Agency from any other body or person include a report on the exercise and performance of those functions by the transferor during the period between the end of the last year in respect of which the transferor prepared a report and the transfer date.

(2) SEPA shall, as soon as reasonably practicable after the transfer date, prepare a report on—

(a) the exercise and performance of the functions of each river purification board during the period between the end of the last year in respect of which the board sent a report to the Secretary of State under section 16 of the Rivers (Prevention of Pollution) (Scotland) Act 1951 and the transfer date; and

(b) the exercise and performance of the functions of each waste regulation authority during the period between the end of the last financial year in respect of which the authority prepared and published a report under section 67 of the Environmental Protection Act 1990 and the transfer date.

(3) Subsections (3) and (4) of section 52 of this Act shall apply to a report prepared under sub-paragraph (2) above as they apply to a report prepared under that section.

Preparation of accounts

6. Notwithstanding the repeal by this Act of subsection (9) of section 135 of the Local Government (Scotland) Act 1973 (application to river purification board of certain provisions of that Act), the provisions applied to a river purification board by virtue of that section shall, as respects the period between the end of the last financial year in respect of which accounts have been made up by the board and the transfer date, continue to apply in relation to the board; but anything which shall or may be done or enjoyed, or any access, inspection or copying which shall or may be allowed, under or by virtue of any of those provisions or of section 118 of that Act (financial returns) by, or by an officer of, the board shall, or as the case may be may, after the transfer date, be done, enjoyed or allowed by, or by an officer of, SEPA in place of the board or of an officer of the board.

Membership of Welsh National Park authorities

7.—(1) Where a body corporate constituted as a Welsh National Park planning board becomes, or has become, the National Park authority in relation to the National Park in question by virtue of an order under section 63 of this Act made by virtue of section 64(1) of this Act, paragraph 2 of Schedule 7 to this Act shall, in its application in relation to that National Park authority at any time before 31st March 1997, have effect with the following modifications.

(2) In sub-paragraph (5)—

(a) in paragraph (a), after the word 'council' there shall be inserted the words 'or, if earlier, until the council which appointed him as a local authority member of that authority is excluded from the councils by whom such members of that authority are to be appointed'; and

(b) in paragraph (b), after the word 'cessation' there shall be inserted the words 'or exclusion'.

(3) In sub-paragraph (6), after the words 'Sub-paragraph (5)(a) above' there shall be inserted the words ', so far as relating to cessation of membership of a council,'.

(4) In this paragraph, 'Welsh National Park planning board' means a National Park planning board, as defined in section 64 of this Act, for the area of a National Park in Wales.

The Alkali, &c., Works Regulation Act 1906

8. Any dispensation which was granted under the proviso to subsection (5) of section 9 of the Alkali, &c, Works Regulation Act 1906 before the transfer date and which would, apart from this Act, have been in force on that date shall have effect on and after that date notwithstanding the repeal of that proviso by this Act.

The Public Records Act 1958

9.—(1)   Such of the administrative and departmental records (in whatever form or medium) of a transferor as are transferred to and vested in the Agency by or under section 3 of this Act shall be treated for the purposes of the Public Records Act 1958 as administrative or departmental records of the Agency.

(2)   In this paragraph, 'transferor' means any body or person any or all of whose administrative and departmental records are transferred to and vested in the Agency by or under section 3 of this Act.

The Parliamentary Commissioner Act 1967

10.—(1)   Nothing in this Act shall prevent the completion on or after the transfer date of any investigation begun before that date under the Parliamentary Commissioner Act 1967 in pursuance of a complaint made in relation to the National Rivers Authority.

(2)   Nothing in this Act shall prevent the making on or after the transfer date of a complaint under that Act in respect of any action which was taken by or on behalf of the National Rivers Authority before that date.

(3)   Notwithstanding the amendment of that Act by paragraph 11 of Schedule 22 to this Act, the provisions of that Act shall have effect on and after the transfer date in relation to any complaint to which sub-paragraph (1) or (2) above applies and to its investigation as they would have had effect before that date; but, in relation to any such complaint, the Agency shall on and after that date stand in the place of the National Rivers Authority for the purposes of this paragraph.

The Local Government Act 1974

11.—(1)   Where for any year, a Rate Support Grant Report under section 60 of the Local Government, Planning and Land Act 1980, or a supplementary report under section 61 of that Act, has effect to determine the amount of supplementary grants to be paid under section 7 of the Local Government Act 1974 to the council of a county or county borough in Wales, and at any time—

(a)   after that report or, as the case may be, that supplementary report is approved by a resolution of the House of Commons, but

(b)   not later than the end of that year,

a body corporate constituted as a National Park planning board for a National Park the whole or any part of which is included in that county or county borough becomes the National Park authority for that National Park by virtue of section 64 of this Act, those supplementary grants shall, subject to the provisions of any, or any further, such supplementary report, continue to be paid for that year notwithstanding that that body corporate has ceased to be a National Park planning board.

(2)   In this paragraph—

'National Park planning board' has the meaning given by section 64(9) of this Act; and 'year' means a period of 12 months beginning with 1st April.

12.—(1)   Nothing in this Act shall prevent the completion on or after the transfer date by a Local Commissioner of any investigation which he began to conduct before that date and which is an investigation under Part III of the Local Government Act 1974 in pursuance of a complaint made in relation to the National Rivers Authority.

(2)   Nothing in this Act shall prevent the making on or after the transfer date of a complaint under Part III of that Act in respect of any action which was taken by or on behalf of the National Rivers Authority before that date.

(3)   Notwithstanding the amendment of Part III of that Act by paragraph 18 of Schedule 22 to this Act, the provisions of that Part shall have effect on and after the transfer date in relation to any complaint to which sub-paragraph (1) or (2) above applies and to its

investigation as they would have had effect before that date; but, in relation to any such complaint, the Agency shall on and after that date stand in the place of the National Rivers Authority for the purposes of this paragraph.

The Control of Pollution Act 1974

13. As respects England and Wales, any resolution passed in pursuance of section 11 of the Control of Pollution Act 1974 (special provision for land occupied by disposal authorities: resolutions etc) which is in force immediately before the day on which the repeals in that section made by this Act come into force shall have effect on and after that day as if it were a waste management licence granted by the Environment Agency under Part II of the Environmental Protection Act 1990 subject to the conditions specified in the resolution pursuant to subsection (3)(e) of that section.

The Salmon and Freshwater Fisheries Act 1975

14.—(1) Any approval or certificate given under or by virtue of section 8(2), 9(1) or 11(4) of the Salmon and Freshwater Fisheries Act 1975 by a Minister of the Crown before the transfer date shall, so far as is required for continuing its effect on and after that date, have effect as if given by the Agency.

(2) Any application for the grant of an approval or certificate by a Minister of the Crown under or by virtue of any of the provisions specified in sub-paragraph (1) above which, at the transfer date, is in the process of being determined shall on and after that date be treated as having been made to the Agency.

(3) Any notice given by a Minister of the Crown under section 11(2) of that Act before the transfer date shall, so far as is required for continuing its effect on and after that date, have effect as if given by the Agency.

(4) Any extension of a period granted by a Minister of the Crown under section 11(3) of that Act before the transfer date shall, so far as is required for continuing its effect on and after that date, have effect as if granted by the Agency.

(5) Without prejudice to section 16 or 17 of the Interpretation Act 1978, any exemption granted under subsection (1) or (2) of section 14 of the Salmon and Freshwater Fisheries Act 1975 which is in force immediately before the substitution date shall have effect on and after that date as an exemption granted by the Agency under subsection (2) or, as the case may be, subsection (3) of section 14 of that Act as substituted by paragraph 13 of Schedule 15 to this Act.

(6) Any grating constructed and placed in a manner and position approved under section 14(3) of that Act as it had effect before the substitution date (including a grating so constructed and placed at any time as a replacement for a grating so constructed and placed) shall, if—

(a) the approval was in force immediately before the substitution date, and

(b) the grating is maintained in accordance with the approval,

be taken for the purposes of section 14 of that Act, as substituted by paragraph 13 of Schedule 15 to this Act, to be a screen which complies with the requirements of subsection (2)(a) or (3)(a) of that section, according to the location of the grating, and with the requirements of subsections (4) to (6) of that section.

(7) Any notice given, or objection made, under subsection (2) of section 18 of that Act before the transfer date shall, so far as is required for continuing its effect on and after that date, have effect as a notice given under that subsection as it has effect on and after that date.

(8) In this paragraph—

'approval' includes a provisional approval;

'grating' means a device in respect of which there is in force, immediately before the substitution date, an approval given for the purposes of the definition of 'grating' in section 41(1) of the Salmon and Freshwater Fisheries Act 1975 as it had effect before that date;

'the substitution date' means the date on which paragraph 13 of Schedule 15 to this Act comes into force;

'the transfer date' means the date which, by virtue of section 56(1) of this Act, is the transfer date for the purposes of Part I of this Act as it applies in relation to the Agency.

The Local Government Finance Act 1988

15.—(1) Without prejudice to the generality of subsection (4) of section 64 of this Act, where an order has been made under section 63 of this Act by virtue of section 64(1) of this Act designating a date in relation to a Welsh National Park planning board, the body corporate constituted as that board may at any time before the designated date issue a levy by virtue of section 71 of this Act for a year at or before the beginning of which that body becomes the National Park authority for the National Park in question by virtue of section 64 of this Act as if it were the National Park authority for that National Park, notwithstanding that it has not in fact become a National Park authority at the date when it issues the levy.

(2) Without prejudice to the generality of section 74 of the Local Government Finance Act 1988, where—

(a) an order is made under section 63 of this Act by virtue of section 64(1) of this Act designating a date in relation to a Welsh National Park planning board; and

(b) the designated date is a date falling after the beginning, but before the end, of a year in respect of which, at the time the order is made, that board has not issued any levy under that section 74,

that board may nonetheless issue such a levy in respect of that year as if the body corporate constituted as that board was not in fact going to become the National Park authority for the National Park in question by virtue of that order before the end of that year.

(3) Sub-paragraph (5) below applies in a case where a levy is issued in respect of any year by a Welsh National Park planning board under section 74 of the Local Government Finance Act 1988 and—

(a) that levy is issued by that board at a time when no order has been made under section 63 of this Act by virtue of section 64(1) of this Act designating a date in relation to that board; and

(b) after the levy is issued, but no later than the end of the year in respect of which it is issued, such an order is so made designating in relation to that board a date falling not later than the end of that year.

(4) Sub-paragraph (5) below also applies in a case where a levy is issued in respect of any year by a Welsh National Park planning board under section 74 of the Local Government Finance Act 1988 and—

(a) that levy is issued by that board at a time after an order has been made under section 63 of this Act by virtue of section 64(1) of this Act designating a date in relation to that board; and

(b) the designated date is a date failing after the beginning, but before the end, of that year.

(5) In a case where this sub-paragraph applies, the levy in question or any levy substituted for that levy—

(a) shall have effect or, as the case may be, continue to have effect; and

(b) in particular, but without prejudice to the generality of paragraph (a) above, shall be paid or, as the case may be, continue to be paid,

as if the body corporate constituted as that board was not to, or had not, so become the National Park authority for the National Park in question (but was to continue, or had continued, to be the National Park planning board for that Park for the whole of that year).

(6) Where a body corporate constituted as a Welsh National Park planning board has or is to become the National Park authority for the National Park in question by virtue of an

order made under section 63 of this Act by virtue of section 64(1) of this Act, nothing in this paragraph authorises that body corporate to issue for any year both a levy under section 74 of the Local Government Finance Act 1988 and a levy by virtue of section 71 of this Act.

(7) In this paragraph—

'the designated date' has the same meaning as in section 64 of this Act;

'National Park planning board' has the meaning given by section 64(9) of this Act;

'Welsh National Park planning board' means a National Park planning board for the area of a National Park in Wales;

'year' means a period of 12 months beginning with 1st April;

and any reference to the issue of a levy under section 74 of the Local Government Finance Act 1988 by a Welsh National Park planning board is a reference to the issue of a levy under that section by such a board by virtue of subsection (7) of that section.

The Environmental Protection Act 1990

16.—(1) Subject to sub-paragraph (2) below, if, at the transfer date, the content of the strategy required by section 44A of the Environmental Protection Act 1990 has not been finally determined, any plan or modification under section 50 of that Act, in its application to England and Wales, whose content has been finally determined before that date shall continue in force until the contents of the strategy are finally determined, notwithstanding the repeal by this Act of that section.

(2) If the strategy required by section 44A of that Act consists, or is to consist, of more than one statement, sub-paragraph (1) above shall apply as if—

(a) references to the strategy were references to any such statement; and

(b) references to a plan or modification under section 50 of that Act were references to such plans or modifications as relate to the area covered, or to be covered, by that statement.

17. If, at the transfer date, the content of the strategy required by section 44B of that Act has not been finally determined, any plan or modification under section 50 of that Act, in its application to Scotland, whose content has been finally determined before that date shall continue in force until the contents of the strategy are finally determined, notwithstanding the repeal by this Act of that section.

18.—(1) This paragraph applies to—

(a) any resolution of a waste regulation authority under section 54 of that Act (special provision for land occupied by disposal authorities in Scotland);

(b) any resolution of a waste disposal authority having effect by virtue of subsection (16) of that section as if it were a resolution of a waste regulation authority under that section,

which is in force on the transfer date.

(2) A resolution to which this paragraph applies shall continue in force,—

(a) where no application is made under section 36(1) of that Act for a waste management licence in respect of the site or mobile plant covered by the resolution, until the end of the period of 6 months commencing with the transfer date;

(b) where an application as mentioned in sub-paragraph (a) above is made, until—

(i) the application is withdrawn;

(ii) the application is rejected and no appeal against the rejection is timeously lodged under section 43 of that Act;

(iii) any appeal against a rejection of the application is withdrawn or rejected; or

(iv) the application is granted.

(3) In relation to a resolution continued in force by sub-paragraph (2) above, the said section 54 shall have effect subject to the amendments set out in the following provisions of this paragraph.

(4)   In subsection (2), for paragraph (b) there shall be substituted—

'(b)   specified in a resolution passed by a waste regulation authority, or by a waste disposal authority under Part I of the Control of Pollution Act 1974, before the transfer date within the meaning of section 56(1) of the Environment Act 1995'.

(5)   In subsection (3) for paragraph (b) there shall be substituted—

'(b)   by another person, that it is on land which is the subject of a resolution, that it is with the consent of the waste disposal authority and that any conditions to which such consent is subject are within the terms of the resolution.'

(6)   Subsections (4) to (7) shall cease to have effect.

(7)   For subsections (8) and (9) there shall be substituted—

'(8)   Subject to subsection (9) below, a resolution continued in force by paragraph 18 of Schedule 23 to the Environment Act 1995 may be varied or rescinded by SEPA by a resolution passed by it.

(9)   Before passing a resolution under subsection (8) above varying a resolution, SEPA shall—

(a)   prepare a statement of the variation which it proposes to make;

(b)   refer that statement to the Health and Safety Executive and to the waste disposal authority in whose area the site is situated or, as the case may be, which is operating the plant; and

(c)   consider any representations about the variation which the Health and Safety Executive or the waste disposal authority makes to it during the allowed period.

(9A)   The period allowed to the Health and Safety Executive and the waste disposal authority for the making of representations under subsection (9)(c) above is the period of 28 days beginning with that on which the statement is received by that body, or such longer period as SEPA and that body agree in writing.

(9B)   SEPA may—

(a)   postpone the reference under subsection (9)(b) above so far as it considers that by reason of an emergency it is appropriate to do so;

(b)   disregard the Health and Safety Executive in relation to a resolution which in SEPA's opinion will not affect the Health and Safety Executive.'

(8)   In subsection (10)—

(a)   for the words 'the authority which passed the resolution' and 'the waste regulation authority' there shall be substituted the words 'SEPA';

(b)   the words 'the waste disposal authority to discontinue the activities and of' shall cease to have effect.

(9)   Subsections (11) to (15) shall cease to have effect.

The Water Industry Act 1991

19.—(1)   Where, before the coming into force of the repeal by this Act of section 151 of the Water Industry Act 1991 (financial contributions to rural services), the Secretary of State has received an application from a relevant undertaker for a contribution under that section, he may, notwithstanding the coming into force of that repeal—

(a)   give any such undertaking for any contribution sought by that application as he could have given under that section prior to the coming into force of that repeal;

(b)   make any payments provided for in an undertaking given by virtue of this sub-paragraph.

(2)   Notwithstanding the coming into force of the repeal by this Act of that section—

(a)   the Secretary of State may make any payments provided for in an undertaking given by him under that section prior to the coming into force of that repeal;

(b)   subsection (4) of that section (withholding and reduction of contributions) shall—

(i)   continue to have effect in relation to contributions which the Secretary of State, before that repeal of that section, gave an undertaking under that section to make; and

(ii)   have effect in relation to contributions which the Secretary of State has, by virtue of sub-paragraph (1) above, undertaken to make.

The Water Resources Act 1991

20.   Notwithstanding any provision restricting the power of the Agency to grant a licence under Chapter II of Part II of the Water Resources Act 1991 (abstracting or impounding of water), or the power of the Secretary of State to direct the Agency to grant such a licence, the Agency may grant, and the Secretary of State may direct it to grant, such licences as are necessary to ensure that water may continue to be abstracted or impounded by or on behalf of the Crown in the manner in which, and to the extent to which,—

(a)   it may be so abstracted or impounded immediately before the coming into force of sub-paragraph (4) of paragraph 2 of Schedule 21 to this Act in relation to that Chapter, or

(b)   it has been so abstracted or impounded at any time in the period of five years immediately preceding the coming into force of that sub-paragraph in relation to that Chapter.

21.—(1)   This paragraph applies to any consent—

(a)   which was given under paragraph 2 of Schedule 10 to the Water Resources Act 1991 (discharge consents), as in force before the transfer date; and

(b)   which is in force immediately before that date.

(2)   On and after the transfer date, a consent to which this paragraph applies—

(a)   shall, for so long as it would have continued in force apart from this Act, have effect as a consent given under paragraph 3 of Schedule 10 to that Act, as substituted by this Act, subject to the same conditions as were attached to the consent immediately before the transfer date; and

(b)   shall—

(i)   during the period of six months beginning with the transfer date, not be limited to discharges by any particular person but extend to discharges made by any person; and

(ii)   after that period, extend, but be limited, to discharges made by any person who before the end of that period gives notice to the Agency that he proposes to rely on the consent after that period.

PART II

TRANSITORY PROVISIONS IN RESPECT OF FLOOD DEFENCE

Disqualification for membership of regional flood defence committee

22.   Where a person is disqualified for membership of a regional flood defence committee by virtue of having been adjudged bankrupt before the coming into force of the Insolvency Act 1986, the rules applicable apart from the repeals made by the Consequential Provisions Act or this Act, rather than paragraph 3(2) of Schedule 5 to this Act, shall apply for determining when that disqualification shall cease.

Savings in relation to local flood defence schemes

23.—(1)   In any case where—

(a)   immediately before the coming into force of section 17 of this Act, any scheme or committee continues, by virtue of paragraph 14 of Schedule 2 to the Consequential Provisions Act, to be treated as a local flood defence scheme or a local flood defence committee, or

(b)   immediately before the coming into force of section 18 of this Act, any person continues, by virtue of that paragraph, to hold office, the scheme or committee shall continue to be so treated or, as the case may be, the person shall continue so to hold office, notwithstanding the provisions of section 18 of, or Schedule 5 to, this Act or the repeal of any enactment by this Act.

(2)   Where a person is disqualified for membership of a local flood defence committee by virtue of having been adjudged bankrupt before the coming into force of the Insolvency Act 1986, the rules applicable apart from the repeals made by the Consequential Provisions Act or this Act, rather than paragraph 3(2) of Schedule 5 to this Act, shall apply for determining when that disqualification shall cease.

Interpretation

24.   In this Part of this Schedule, 'the Consequential Provisions Act' means the Water Consolidation (Consequential Provisions) Act 1991.

SCHEDULE 24

REPEALS AND REVOCATIONS

Reference	Short title or title	Extent of repeal or revocation
60 & 61 Vict. c. 38.	The Public Health (Scotland) Act 1897.	Sections 16 to 26. Sections 36 and 37.
6 Edw. 7. c. 14.	The Alkali, &c, Works Regulation Act 1906.	In section 9, the proviso to subsection (5). Section 25. In section 27(1), the definitions of the expressions 'chief inspector' and 'inspector'. In section 28(b), the words 'other than offences under subsection four of section twelve of this Act'; in sub-paragraph (ii), the words from 'without the consent' to 'direct, nor'; and sub-paragraph (iii).
12, 13 & 14 Geo. 6. c. 97.	The National Parks and Access to the Countryside Act 1949.	In section 6(6), the words from 'or a local planning authority' to 'part of a National Park'. Section 11. In section 11A(6)(b), the words 'district council'. Section 12(2). In section 13(1), the words 'and within the area of the authority'. In section 111A(3)(b), the words 'for the purposes of sections 64, 65 and 77'.
14 & 15 Geo. 6. c. 66.	The Rivers (Prevention of Pollution) (Scotland) Act 1951.	Part II Section 17. In section 18, in subsection (1), the words 'of their area', 'in their area' (where first occurring) and 'in their area or any part thereof'; and in subsection (3), the words 'in their area' and the words from 'whose' to 'authority' where next occurring;

Reference	Short title or title	Extent of repeal or revocation
		In section 19, in subsection (1), the words 'in the area of the authority', subsections (2) to (2B) and, in subsection (4), the words from 'any', where first occurring, to 'and', where last occurring. In section 35, the definitions of 'river purification authority', 'river purification board' and 'river purification board area'.
2 & 3 Eliz. 2. c. 70.	The Mines and Quarries Act 1954.	Section 151(5).
8 & 9 Eliz. 2. c. 62.	The Caravan Sites and Control of Development Act 1960.	In section 24(8), the words from 'and a joint planning board' to 'such a National Park'.
1965 c. 13.	The Rivers (Prevention of Pollution) (Scotland) Act 1965.	Section 10(6)(a).
1965 c. 57.	The Nuclear Installations Act 1965.	In section 3(3)(b), the words 'the National Rivers Authority,'.
1967 c. 13.	The Parliamentary Commissioner Act 1967.	In Schedule 2, the entry relating to the National Rivers Authority and the note 9 inserted by paragraph 11 of Schedule 1 to the Water Act 1989.
1967 c. 22.	The Agriculture Act 1967.	In section 50(3), paragraph (e) and the words from 'and "National Parks planning authority" means' onwards.
1968 c. 41.	The Countryside Act 1968.	In section 6(2), paragraph (c) and the word 'or' immediately preceding it. Section 13(11). Section 40. In section 42(1), the words 'whether or not within the area of the local planning authority'. In section 47A— (a) in subsection (2), the word '18'; and (b) subsection (4).
1968 c. 47.	The Sewerage (Scotland) Act 1968.	In section 38(3), the words 'river purification authorities'. Section 49. In section 59(1), the definition of 'river purification authority'.
1968 c. 59.	The Hovercraft Act 1968.	In section 1(1)(g), the words 'Part III of the Control of Pollution Act 1974 or'.

Reference	Short title or title	Extent of repeal or revocation
1970 c. 40.	The Agriculture Act 1970.	In section 92(1), the words 'for their area' and 'both within (and in the case of a river purification board) outwith, that area'. Section 92(2)(c).
1972 c. 52.	The Town and Country Planning (Scotland) Act 1972.	Section 251A.
1972 c. 70.	The Local Government Act 1972.	Section 101(9)(h). In section 140A(2), in the definition of 'local authority', the words 'or reconstituted in pursuance of Schedule 17 to this Act'. In section 184— (a) in subsection (2), the words 'and Schedule 17 to this Act'; (b) in subsection (4), the words 'subject to Schedule 17 to this Act'; and (c) subsection (6). In section 223(2), the words 'and the National Rivers Authority'. In Schedule 16, paragraph 55(2). Part I of Schedule 17.
1972 c. v.	The Clyde River Purification Act 1972.	The whole Act.
1973 c. 65.	The Local Government (Scotland) Act 1973.	Sections 135 and 135A. Section 200. In Schedule 16, paragraphs 1 to 5 and 7 to 10. In Schedule 27, in Part II, paragraphs 30 to 32, 37 and 38.
1974 c. 7.	The Local Government Act 1974.	Section 7.
1974 c. 37.	The Health and Safety at Work etc. Act 1974.	In section 28, in subsection (3)(c)(ii), so far as extending to England and Wales, the words 'of the National Rivers Authority or' and the word 'Authority' (where next occurring), subsection (3)(c)(iii) and, in subsection (5)(b), so far as extending to England and Wales, the words 'the National Rivers Authority'.
1974 c. 40.	The Control of Pollution Act 1974.	In section 5, in subsection (4), the words following paragraph (b), and subsection (5). In section 7, in subsections (1) and (4), the words 'issued by a disposal authority' and, in subsection (2), the words 'or, in relation to Scotland, subsection (5)'.

Reference	Short title or title	Extent of repeal or revocation
		In section 9(4), the words 'issued by the authority'.
		In section 11, subsections (1) to (11).
		In section 30(1), the words from 'and for the purposes' to the end.
		In section 30A(2)(a), the words 'in the area of that authority'.
		In section 30C, in subsection (1), the words 'within the area of that authority'; and in each of subsections (4) and (6), the words 'in the area of a river purification authority'.
		In section 31, subsections (1) to (3), in subsection (6), the words 'in its area' and subsections (7), and (10).
		Section 31 D.
		Section 32.
		In section 33(1), the words 'in the area of the authority'.
		In section 34(3), the words 'in its area'.
		Section 40(4).
		In section 41(1), in paragraph (c), the words '(except section 40(4))' and paragraphs (d)(ii) and (e).
		In section 46(1), the words 'in its area' where they first occur and 'in its area or elsewhere'.
		In section 47, in subsection (1), the words 'in its area' and in subsection (2), the words 'in the authority's area'.
		In section 48(1), the words 'in its area'.
		In section 50, the words 'in its area'.
		Sections 53, 54, 55 and 56(4).
		In section 57, paragraph (a).
		Section 58.
		Section 58A.
		Section 58B.
		Section 59.
		Section 59A.
		In sections 61(9) and 65(8) the words 'section 59 of this Act (in relation to Scotland) or' and the words '(in relation to England and Wales)'.
		In section 69, in subsection (1), paragraph (a) and, in paragraph (c) the words 'section 59(2) or', and in subsection (3) the words 'section 59(6) or' and paragraph (i).

Reference	Short title or title	Extent of repeal or revocation
		In section 73, in subsection (1), the definition of 'equipment', in the definition of 'person responsible' paragraphs (b) and (c), and the definition of 'road noise', and in subsection (3) the words from ';but a requirement' to the end of the subsection. In section 74, the words 'Subject to sections 58A(8) and 59A(9) of this Act'. In section 87(3), the words from the beginning to 'offence; and' and the words 'in its application to Scotland'. Section 91(5)(a). In section 96(3), the words from 'but as if' to the end. In section 104(1), the word '59'. Section 106(2). In Schedule 2, paragraphs 1 to 3. In Schedule 3, paragraphs 12 and 13.
S.I. 1974/2170.	The Clean Air Enactments (Repeals and Modifications) Regulations 1974.	In Schedule 2, paragraph 1.
1975 c. 24.	The House of Commons Disqualification Act 1975.	In Schedule 1, in Part II, the entry relating to the National Rivers Authority.
1975 c. 25.	The Northern Ireland Assembly Disqualification Act 1975.	In Schedule 1, in Part II, the entry relating to the National Rivers Authority.
1975 c. 30.	The Local Government (Scotland) Act 1975.	In section 16, the words 'and river purification boards'. Section 23(1)(e). In Schedule 3, in paragraph 28(1), the words 'or a river purification board'.
1975 c. 51.	The Salmon and Freshwater Fisheries Act 1975.	In section 5(2), the words following paragraph (b). In section 10, in subsections (1) and (2), the words 'with the written consent of the Minister' in each place where they occur. In section 15, in subsections (1) and (3), the words 'with the written consent of the Minister' in each place where they occur. In section 30, the paragraph defining 'fish farm'. In section 41(1), the definition of 'grating'.

Reference	Short title or title	Extent of repeal or revocation
1975 c. 70.	The Welsh Development Agency Act 1975.	In section 16(9), in the definition of 'local authority', paragraph (b) and the word 'or' immediately preceding it.
1976 c. 74.	The Race Relations Act 1976.	In section 19A(2)(a), the words 'a special planning board or a National Park Committee'.
1980 c. 45.	The Water (Scotland) Act 1980.	In section 33(3)(a), sub-paragraph (ii) and the preceding 'and'. In section 109(1), the definitions of 'river purification authority' and 'river purification board'. In Schedule 1, in paragraph 11(ii) the words 'and any river purification authority'.
1980 c. 65.	The Local Government, Planning and Land Act 1980.	In section 52(1), paragraph (b) and the word 'and' immediately preceding it. In section 103(2)(c), the word 'and' immediately preceding sub-paragraph (ii). In Schedule 2, paragraph 9(2) and (3).
1980 c. 66.	The Highways Act 1980.	In section 25(2)(a) the words from 'or a joint planning board' to 'National Park'. In section 27(6), the words from 'or any such joint planning board' onwards. In section 29, the words 'and joint planning boards'. In section 72(2), the words 'or joint planning board'. Section 118(7).
1981 c. 67.	The Acquisition of Land Act 1981.	In section 17, in subsection (3), the words 'the Peak Park Joint or Lake District Special Planning Board' and, in subsection (4), in the definition of 'a Welsh planning board', paragraph (b) and the word 'or' immediately preceding it. In paragraph 4 of Schedule 3, in sub-paragraph (3), the words 'the Peak Park Joint or Lake District Special Planning Board' and, in sub-paragraph (4), in the definition of 'a Welsh planning board', paragraph (b) and the word 'or' immediately preceding it.
1981 c. 69.	The Wildlife and Countryside Act 1981.	Section 39(5)(a). In section 44, subsection (1) and in subsection (1A), the words from the beginning to 'but'. Section 46.

Reference	Short title or title	Extent of repeal or revocation
		In section 52(2), paragraph (a) and, in paragraph (b), the words 'in any other provision'. Section 72(10).
1982 c. 30.	The Local Government (Miscellaneous Provisions) Act 1982.	In section 33(9), in paragraph (a), the words from 'or reconstituted' to '1972' and, in paragraph (b), the words 'or reconstituted'. In section 41(13), in paragraph (b) of the definition of 'local authority' the words from 'or reconstituted' to '1972'. In section 45(2)(b), the words from 'or reconstituted' to '1972'.
1982 c. 42.	The Derelict Land Act 1982.	In section 1(11), in the definition of 'local authority', paragraph (b) and the word 'or' immediately preceding it.
1982 c. 48.	The Criminal Justice Act 1982.	In Schedule 15, paragraphs 6 and 7.
1983 c. 35.	The Litter Act 1983.	In section 4(1)— (a) paragraph (b) and the word 'and' immediately preceding it; and (b) the words 'the National Park Committee (if any)' in each place where they occur. In section 6(8), the words 'or a Park board'. In section 10, paragraph (h) of the definition of 'litter authority' and the definitions of 'National Park Committee' and 'Park board'.
1984 c. 54.	The Roads (Scotland) Act 1984.	In Schedule 9, paragraph 17(3).
1985 c. 51.	The Local Government Act 1985.	In Schedule 3— (a) paragraph 4; (b) in paragraph 5, sub-paragraphs (2) to (8); (c) paragraph 6; and (d) in paragraph 7, sub-paragraph (3) and in sub-paragraph (4), the words '42' and '44'.
1985 c. 68.	The Housing Act 1985.	In section 573, in subsection (1), the entries relating to the Peak Park Joint Planning Board and the Lake District Special Planning Board and, in subsection (1A), paragraph (b) and the word 'or' immediately preceding it.

Reference	Short title or title	Extent of repeal or revocation
S.I. 1987/180.	The Control of Industrial Air Pollution (Transfer of Powers of Enforcement) Regulations 1987.	Regulations 2 and 4.
1988 c. 4.	The Norfolk and Suffolk Broads Act 1988.	In Schedule 6, paragraphs 2 and 13.
1988 c. 9.	The Local Government Act 1988.	In Schedule 2, the entries relating to the Lake District Special Planning Board, the Peak Park Joint Planning Board and a special planning board constituted under paragraph 3A of Schedule 17 to the Local Government Act 1972.
1988 c. 41.	The Local Government Finance Act 1988.	In section 74(7), paragraph (b) and the word 'and' immediately preceding it.
1989 c. 14.	The Control of Pollution (Amendment) Act 1989.	Section 2(3)(e). Section 7(2) and (8). Section 11(3).
1989 c. 15.	The Water Act 1989.	In Schedule 1, paragraphs 11, 12 and 13. In Schedule 17, paragraphs 3(2) and (3), 5(2), 7(9)(d) and 9(1). In Schedule 25, paragraphs 43(1) and paragraph 48(3) and (4).
1989 c. 29.	The Electricity Act 1989.	In Schedule 8, paragraph 2(6)(a)(i).
1989 c. 42.	The Local Government and Housing Act 1989.	Section 5(4)(c). Section 13(4)(d). In section 21(1), paragraph (m) and the word 'and' immediately preceding it. Section 39(1)(h). Section 67(3)(o). Section 152(2)(k). In Schedule 1, in paragraph 2(1)(b), the word '(m)' and paragraph 2(1)(f).
1990 c. 8.	The Town and Country Planning Act 1990.	In section 1, in subsection (5)— (a) in paragraph (a), the words from 'and Part I' to 'National Parks)'; and (b) in paragraph (c), the words 'section 4 and'; and, in subsection (6), the words 'section 4(3) and'. In section 2(7), the words from 'and Part I' to 'National Parks)'. Section 4. In section 4A(1), the words 'instead of section 4(1) to (4)'.

Reference	Short title or title	Extent of repeal or revocation
		Section 105. In section 244(1), the words from 'or a board' to '1972'. In Schedule 1— (a) in paragraph 4(2), the words 'or county planning authority' and the words 'or, as the case may be, which is'; (b) in paragraph 6, the words from '(including' to 'National Park'; (c) in paragraph 13(1), paragraph (d) and the word 'or' immediately preceding it (d) in paragraph 19, sub-paragraph (2); and (e) in paragraph 20(4), paragraph (a) and, in paragraph (b), the word 'other'.
1990 c. 9.	The Planning (Listed Buildings and Conservation Areas) Act 1990.	In section 66(3), the words from 'and a board' onwards. In Schedule 4— (a) in paragraph 2, the word '4'; (b) in paragraph 3, the words 'or county planning authority' and the words 'or, as the case may be, which is'; and (c) in paragraph 4(1), the words '4(3) and (4)'.
1990 c. 10.	The Planning (Hazardous Substances) Act 1990.	In section 3— (a) in subsection (1), paragraph (a) and the words after paragraph (c); (b) subsection (2); and (c) in subsections (3) to (5A), the words 'or (2)', wherever occurring.
1990 c. 11.	The Planning (Consequential Provisions) Act 1990.	In Schedule 2— (a) paragraph 20; (b) paragraph 28(6); and (c) in paragraph 45, sub-paragraph (2) and in sub-paragraph (7), the words '118(7)'.
1990 c. 43.	The Environmental Protection Act 1990.	In section 4, in subsection (8), the words 'or, as the case may be, in the Edinburgh Gazette', in each place where they occur, and, in subsection (11), the words 'and Wales' in paragraph (b) and paragraph (c) and the word 'and' immediately preceding it. Section 5. In section 7(9), the words from 'and, in relation to Scotland,' to the end. In section 8, subsection (4) and, in subsection (7) the words from 'together with' onwards and subsection (9). Sections 16 to 18.

Reference	Short title or title	Extent of repeal or revocation
		Section 20(3) and (9).
		In section 23, in subsection (1), paragraphs (d) to (f) and (k), and subsections (4) and (5).
		In section 28, in subsection (1), the words from 'but' onwards and subsections (3) and (4).
		In section 30, in subsection (4), the words 'or regulation authorities' and the words from 'establishing authorities' onwards and subsections (6) to (8).
		Section 31.
		In section 33(1), the words 'and, in relation to Scotland, section 54 below,'.
		In section 36, subsections (5) and (6), in subsection (11), in the definition of 'National Park authority', the words 'subject to subsection (12) below' and subsection (12).
		In section 37(5), the words '(5), (6),' and '(8)'.
		In section 39, in subsection (7), the words following paragraph (b), subsection (8), in subsection (12), in the definition of 'National Park authority', the words 'subject to subsection (13) below', and subsection (13).
		Section 41.
		In section 42, subsection (2) and, in subsection (7), the words from 'and the power' onwards.
		Section 43(2)(a) and (b).
		Section 50.
		Section 54.
		Section 61.
		In section 64, subsection (1)(1) and, in subsection (4), the words 'which is not a waste regulation authority'.
		Sections 67 to 70.
		In section 71, subsection (1) and, in subsection (3), paragraph (b) and the word 'or' immediately preceding it.
		Section 72.
		Section 75(3).
		In the heading immediately preceding section 79, the words ':England and Wales'.
		In section 79, in subsection (7), in the definition of 'local authority', the word 'and' following paragraph (b).

Reference	Short title or title	Extent of repeal or revocation
		Section 83. In section 88, in subsection (9), paragraphs (c) and (d), and, in subsection (10), in the definition of 'authorised officer', the words from 'or in the case' to 'on behalf of' and the definitions of 'National Park Committee' and 'Park board'. In section 141, in subsection (5)(a), sub-paragraph (ii) and the word 'and' immediately preceding it. Section 143. In Schedule 2, in paragraph 17(2), the words 'a waste regulation authority or'. In Schedule 8— (a) paragraph 1(13); (b) paragraph 3; and (c) in paragraph 4, the words from the beginning to 'in Wales)' and'. In Schedule 15, paragraphs 5(4) and 16 and, in paragraph 31, in sub-paragraph (2), the word '(6),' where secondly occurring, the word '(2)', where thirdly occurring, and sub-paragraphs (4)(c) and (5)(c).
1991 c. 28.	The Natural Heritage (Scotland) Act 1991.	In section 15(3) the words 'and a river purification authority of whom such a requirement is made shall make such an application'. In Schedule 2, paragraph 10(3). In Schedule 5, in paragraph 2 the words 'in their area and'. In Schedule 6, paragraph 1(5). In Schedule 8, in sub-paragraph (3) of paragraph 1, in the second column of the Table, in the fourth entry, the words ', river purification authority'. In Schedule 10, paragraphs 1, 6, 7(2) and 9(3)(b) and (6)
1991 c. 34.	The Planning and Compensation Act 1991.	In Schedule 4, paragraph 39.
1991 c. 56.	The Water Industry Act 1991.	In section 4(6), the definition of 'National Park authority' and the word 'and' immediately preceding it. Section 132(7). Section 151. Section 171(4) and (5). In section 206(2), the words '196 or'. In section 219(1), the definition of 'the NRA'.

Reference	Short title or title	Extent of repeal or revocation
1991 c. 57.	The Water Resources Act 1991.	Sections 1 to 14. Sections 16 to 19. In section 34, the word 'planning', wherever it occurs, and subsection (5). In section 45,— (a) in subsection (2), the word 'planning', wherever it occurs; and (b) in subsection (3), the words 'and (5)'. Section 58. Section 68. Section 69(5). In section 91, in subsection (1), the word 'or' immediately preceding paragraph (f). Section 105(1). In section 113(1), in the definition of 'drainage', the word 'and' immediately preceding paragraph (c). Section 114. Section 117. Sections 121 to 124. Section 126(6). Section 129(4). Sections 131 and 132. Section 144. Section 146. Sections 150 to 153. Section 187. In section 190(1), paragraph (d), paragraph (f) and the word 'and' immediately preceding it. Section 196. Section 202(5). Section 206(2). Section 209(1), (2) and (4). Sections 213 to 215. Section 218. In section 219, in subsection (2), the words 'Subject to subsection (3) below,' and subsection (3). In section 221(1), the definitions of 'the Authority' and 'constituent council'. Schedule 1. Schedules 3 and 4.
1991 c. 59.	The Land Drainage Act 1991.	In section 61C(5), the definition of 'National Park authority' and the word 'and' immediately preceding it. In section 72(1), the definition of 'the NRA'.

Reference	Short title or title	Extent of repeal or revocation
1991 c. 60.	The Water Consolidation (Consequential Provisions) Act 1991.	In Schedule 1, paragraphs 17, 18(a), 25, 27(2) and 56(3) and (4).
1992 c. 14.	The Local Government Finance Act 1992.	Section 35(5)(a) and (b). In Schedule 13, paragraph 95.
1993 c. 11.	The Clean Air Act 1993.	Section 3(2)(b) and the word 'or' which immediately precedes it. Section 17. Section 42(5). Section 51(1)(b) and the word 'or' which immediately precedes it. In Schedule 3, paragraph 4(b).
1993 c. 12.	The Radioactive Substances Act 1993.	Section 4. Section 5. In section 16, in subsection (2), the words 'Subject to subsection (3),' subsection (3) and, in subsection (10), the words from 'or, as' to 'appropriate Minister'. Section 17(4). In section 18, in subsection (1), the words '(or, in a case' to 'or that Minister)' and 'or the appropriate Minister, as the case may be,' and, in subsection (2)(b), the words from '(or, where' to 'that Minister)'. Section 20(3). In section 21, subsection (3) and, in subsection (4), the words from 'or, where' to 'that Minister'. In section 22, subsection (5), in subsection (6), the words from 'or, where' to 'that Minister' and in subsection (7), the words from 'or, where' to 'that Minister'. In section 25, in subsection (2), the words from 'or, in a case' to 'Food,' and 'or their'. In section 26, subsection (3)(a) and, in subsection (4), the words 'England, Wales or'. Section 28. Section 31. Section 35. In section 39, in subsection (2), the words from 'or, as' to 'and the chief inspector,'. Section 42(5)

Reference	Short title or title	Extent of repeal or revocation
		Section 43.
		In section 47, in subsection (1), in the definition of 'the appropriate Minister', paragraphs (a) and (b), in the definition of 'the chief inspector', paragraphs (a) and (b), in the definition of 'prescribed' the words from 'or, in relation to fees' onwards and in the definition of 'relevant water body', in paragraph (a), the words 'the National Rivers Authority' and, in paragraph (b), the words 'a river purification authority within the meaning of the Rivers (Prevention of Pollution) (Scotland) Act 1951'.
		In section 48, in the Table, the entry relating to the chief inspector.
		Schedule 2.
		In Schedule 3, in Part II, in paragraph 11 the words '16, 17'.
1993 c. 25.	The Local Government (Overseas Assistance) Act 1993.	Section 1(10)(g).
1993 c. 40.	The Noise and Statutory Nuisance Act 1993.	Section 6. Section 13(2). Schedule 1.
1994 c. 19.	The Local Government (Wales) Act 1994.	Section 19(2) and (3). Section 59(15). In Schedule 5, in Part III, paragraph 10. In Schedule 6, paragraphs 3 to 12, 18, 23, 24(1), 28 and 29. In Schedule 9, paragraph 17(4) and (12). In Schedule 11, paragraph 3(1) and (2). In Schedule 15, paragraph 64(b). In Schedule 16, paragraph 65(5) and (9). In Schedule 17, paragraph 13.
1994 c. 39.	The Local Government etc. (Scotland) Act 1994.	Section 37. Section 54(5). In section 165(6), the words 'a river purification board'. In Schedule 13, paragraphs 38(2) to (7), 85(3)(a) and (b)(i) and (4), 92(34) and (35), 93(2), 95(2), (4), (8) and (9), and 119(54)(a)(ii) and (h)(iii) and, in paragraph 167, sub-paragraph (2), in sub-paragraph (3) the words '(1)(g),', and sub-paragraphs (4), (5), (7) and (9).

Reference	Short title or title	Extent of repeal or revocation
1995 c. 25.	The Environment Act 1995.	In section 8, in the definition of 'National Park authority' in subsection (5), the words 'subject to subsection (6) below' and subsection (6). In Schedule 10, paragraph 22(1) and (7) and, in paragraph 34(1), so much of paragraph (b) as precedes the word 'and'. In Schedule 11, in paragraph 1, in the definition of 'National Park authority' in sub-paragraph (3), the words 'subject to sub-paragraph (4) below' and sub-paragraph (4). In Schedule 22, paragraphs 19 to 27, 46(11)(a), 182 and 231.

Index